W9-BBZ-617

THE RUBY WAY, SECOND EDITION

THE RUBY WAY, SECOND EDITION

Hal Fulton

♠ Addison-Wesley

Upper Saddle River, NJ • Boston • Indianapolis • San Francisco
New York • Toronto • Montreal • London • Munich • Paris • Madrid
Capetown • Sydney • Tokyo • Singapore • Mexico City

Many of the designations used by manufacturers and sellers to distinguish their products are claimed as trademarks. Where those designations appear in this book, and the publisher was aware of a trademark claim, the designations have been printed with initial capital letters or in all capitals.

The author and publisher have taken care in the preparation of this book, but make no expressed or implied warranty of any kind and assume no responsibility for errors or omissions. No liability is assumed for incidental or consequential damages in connection with or arising out of the use of the information or programs contained herein.

The publisher offers excellent discounts on this book when ordered in quantity for bulk purchases or special sales, which may include electronic versions and/or custom covers and content particular to your business, training goals, marketing focus, and branding interests. For more information, please contact:

U.S. Corporate and Government Sales
(800) 382-3419
corpsales@pearsontechgroup.com

For sales outside the United States please contact:

International Sales
international@pearsoned.com

This Book Is Safari Enabled

The Safari® Enabled icon on the cover of your favorite technology book means the book is available through Safari Bookshelf. When you buy this book, you get free access to the online edition for 45 days.

Safari Bookshelf is an electronic reference library that lets you easily search thousands of technical books, find code samples, download chapters, and access technical information whenever and wherever you need it.

To gain 45-day Safari Enabled access to this book:

- Go to http://www.awprofessional.com/safarienabled
- Complete the brief registration form
- Enter the coupon code B6KN-PQVJ-62UT-HEJ6-LDGE

If you have difficulty registering on Safari Bookshelf or accessing the online edition, please e-mail customer-service@safaribooksonline.com.

Visit us on the Web: www.awprofessional.com

Library of Congress Cataloging-in-Publication Data:

Fulton, Hal Edwin, 1961-
  The Ruby way : solutions and techniques in Ruby programming / Hal Fulton. -- 2nd ed.
    p. cm.
  Includes index.
  ISBN 0-672-32884-4 (pbk. : alk. paper) 1. Object-oriented programming (Computer science) 2. Ruby (Computer program language) I. Title.

QA76.64.F85 2006
005.1'17—dc22

2006028547

ISBN 0-672-32884-4
This product is printed digitally on demand.
First printing, October 2006

To my parents, without whom I would not be possible

Contents

Foreword

Foreword to the Second Edition

In ancient China, people, especially philosophers, thought that something was hidden behind the world and every existence. It can never be told, nor explained, nor described in concrete words. They called it *Tao* in Chinese and *Do* in Japanese. If you translate it into English, it is the word for *Way*. It is the *Do* in Judo, Kendo, Karatedo, and Aikido. They are not only martial arts, but they also include a philosophy and a way of life.

Likewise, Ruby the programming language has its philosophy and way of thinking. It enlightens people to think differently. It helps programmers have more fun in their work. It is not because Ruby is from Japan but because programming is an important part of the human being (well, at least *some* human beings), and Ruby is designed to help people have a better life.

As always, "Tao" is difficult to describe. I feel it but have never tried to explain it in words. It's just too difficult for me, even in Japanese, my native tongue. But a guy named Hal Fulton tried, and his first try (the first edition of this book) was pretty good. This second version of his trial to describe the Tao of Ruby becomes even better with help from many people in the Ruby community. As Ruby becomes more popular (partly due to Ruby on Rails), it becomes more important to understand the secret of programmers' productivity. I hope this book helps you to become an efficient programmer.

Happy Hacking.

Yukihiro "Matz" Matsumoto
August 2006, Japan
まつもと ゆきひろ

Foreword to First Edition

Shortly after I first met with computers in the early 80s I became interested in programming languages. Since then I have been a "language geek." I think the reason for this interest is that programming languages are ways to express human thought. They are fundamentally human-oriented.

Despite this fact, programming languages have tended to be machine-oriented. Many languages were designed for the convenience of the computer.

But as computers became more powerful and less expensive, this situation gradually changed. For example, look at structured programming. Machines do not care whether programs are structured well; they just execute them bit by bit. Structured programming is not for machines, but for humans. This is true of object-oriented programming as well.

The time for language design focusing on humans has been coming.

In 1993, I was talking with a colleague about scripting languages, about their power and future. I felt scripting to be the way future programming should be—human-oriented.

But I was not satisfied with existing languages such as Perl and Python. I wanted a language that was more powerful than Perl and more object-oriented than Python. I couldn't find the ideal language, so I decided to make my own.

Ruby is not the simplest language, but the human soul is not simple in its natural state. It loves simplicity and complexity at the same time. It can't handle too many complex things, nor too many simple things. It's a matter of balance.

So to design a human-oriented language, Ruby, I followed the Principle of Least Surprise. I consider that everything that surprises me less is good. As a result I feel a natural feeling, even a kind of joy, when programming in Ruby. And since the first release of Ruby in 1995, many programmers worldwide have agreed with me about the joy of Ruby programming.

As always I'd like to express my greatest appreciation to the people in the Ruby community. They are the heart of Ruby's success.

I am also thankful to the author of this book, Hal E. Fulton, for declaring the Ruby Way to help people.

This book explains the philosophy behind Ruby, distilled from my brain and the Ruby community. I wonder how it can be possible for Hal to read my mind to know and reveal this secret of the Ruby Way. I have never met him face to face; I hope to meet him soon.

I hope this book and Ruby both serve to make your programming fun and happy.

Yukihiro "Matz" Matsumoto
September 2001, Japan
まつもと ゆきひろ

Acknowledgments

Acknowledgments for the Second Edition

Common sense says that a second edition will only require half as much work as the first edition required. Common sense is wrong.

Even though a large part of this book came directly from the first edition, even that part had to be tweaked and tuned. Every single sentence in this book had to pass through (at the very least) a filter that asked: Is what was true in 2001 still true in 2006? And that, of course, was only the beginning.

In short, I put in many hundreds of hours of work on this second edition—nearly as much time as on the first. And yet I am "only the author."

A book is possible only through the teamwork of many people. On the publisher's side, I owe thanks to Debra Williams Cauley, Songlin Qiu, and Mandie Frank for their hard work and infinite patience. Thanks go to Geneil Breeze for her tireless copy-editing and picking bits of lint from my English. There are also others I can't name because their work was completely behind the scenes, and I never talked with them.

Technical editing was done primarily by Shashank Date and Francis Hwang. They did a great job, and I appreciate it. Errors that slipped through are my responsibility, of course.

Thanks go to the people who supplied explanations, wrote sample code, and answered numerous questions for me. These include Matz himself (Yukihiro Matsumoto), Dave Thomas, Christian Neukirchen, Chad Fowler, Curt Hibbs, Daniel Berger, Armin Roehrl, Stefan Schmiedl, Jim Weirich, Ryan Davis, Jenny W., Jim

Freeze, Lyle Johnson, Martin DeMello, Matt Lawrence, the infamous *why the lucky stiff*, Ron Jeffries, Tim Hunter, Chet Hendrickson, Nathaniel Talbott, and Bil Kleb.

Special thanks goes to the heavier contributors. Andrew Johnson greatly enhanced my regular expression knowledge. Paul Battley made great contributions to the internationalization chapter. Masao Mutoh added to that same chapter and also contributed material on GTK. Austin Ziegler taught me the secrets of writing PDF files. Caleb Tennis added to the Qt material. Eric Hodel added to the Rinda and Ring material, and James Britt contributed heavily to the web development chapter.

Thanks and appreciation again must go to Matz, not only for his assistance but for creating Ruby in the first place. *Domo arigato gozaimasu!*

Again I have to thank my parents. They have encouraged me without ceasing and are looking forward to seeing this book. I will make programmers of them both yet.

And once again, I have to thank all of the Ruby community for their tireless energy, productivity, and community spirit. I particularly thank the readers of this book (in both editions). I hope you find it informative, useful, and perhaps even entertaining.

Acknowledgments for the First Edition

Writing a book is truly a team effort; this is a fact I could not fully appreciate until I wrote one myself. I recommend the experience, although it is a humbling one. It is a simple truth that without the assistance of many other people, this book would not have existed.

Thanks and appreciation must first go to Matz (Yukihiro Matsumoto), who created the Ruby language in the first place. Domo arigato gozaimasu!

Thanks goes to Conrad Schneiker for conceiving the overall idea for the book and helping to create its overall structure. He also did me the service of introducing me to the Ruby language in 1999.

Several individuals have contributed material to the body of the book. The foremost of these was Guy Hurst, who wrote substantial parts of the earlier chapters as well as two of the appendices. His assistance was absolutely invaluable.

Thanks also goes to the other contributors, whom I'll name in no particular order. Kevin Smith did a great job on the GTK section of Chapter 6, saving me from a potentially steep learning curve on a tight schedule. Patrick Logan, in the same chapter, shed light on the mysteries of the FOX GUI. Chad Fowler, in Chapter 9, plumbed the depths of XML and also contributed to the CGI section.

Thanks to those who assisted in proofreading or reviewing or in other miscellaneous ways: Don Muchow, Mike Stok, Miho Ogishima, and others already mentioned. Thanks to David Eppstein, the mathematics professor, for answering questions about graph theory.

One of the great things about Ruby is the support of the community. There were many on the mailing list and the newsgroup who answered questions and gave me ideas and assistance. Again in no particular order, these are Dave Thomas, Andy Hunt, Hee-Sob Park, Mike Wilson, Avi Bryant, Yasushi Shoji ("Yashi"), Shugo Maeda, Jim Weirich, "arton," and Masaki Suketa. I'm sorry to say I have probably overlooked someone.

To state the obvious, a book would never be published without a publisher. Many people behind the scenes worked hard to produce this book; primarily I have to thank William Brown, who worked closely with me and was a constant source of encouragement; and Scott Meyer, who delved deeply into the details of putting the material together. Others I cannot even name because I have never heard of them. You know who you are.

I have to thank my parents, who watched this project from a distance, encouraged me along the way, and even bothered to learn a little bit of computer science for my sake.

A writer friend of mine once told me, "If you write a book and nobody reads it, you haven't really written a book." So, finally, I want to thank the reader. This book is for you. I hope it is of some value.

About the Author

Hal Fulton has two degrees in computer science from the University of Mississippi. He taught computer science for four years at the community college level before moving to Austin, Texas, for a series of contracts (mainly at IBM Austin). He has worked for more than 15 years with various forms of UNIX, including AIX, Solaris, and Linux. He was first exposed to Ruby in 1999, and in 2001 he began work on the first edition of this book, which was the second Ruby book in the English language. He has attended six Ruby conferences and has given presentations at four of those, including the first European Ruby Conference in Karlsruhe, Germany. He currently works at Broadwing Communications in Austin, Texas, working on a large data warehouse and related telecom applications. He works daily with C++, Oracle, and of course, Ruby.

Hal is still active daily on the Ruby mailing list and IRC channel, and has several Ruby projects in progress. He is a member of the ACM and the IEEE Computer Society. In his personal life, he enjoys music, reading, writing, art, and photography. He is a member of the Mars Society and is a space enthusiast who would love to go into space before he dies. He lives in Austin, Texas.

Introduction

The way that can be named is not the true Way.

— *Lao Tse,* Tao Te Ching

The title of this book is *The Ruby Way*. This is a title that begs for a disclaimer.

It has been my aim to align this book with the philosophy of Ruby as well as I could. That has also been the aim of the other contributors. Credit for success must be shared with these others, but the blame for any mistakes must rest solely with me.

Of course, I can't presume to tell you with exactness what the spirit of Ruby is all about. That is primarily for Matz to say, and I think even he would have difficulty communicating all of it in words.

In short, *The Ruby Way* is only a book; but the Ruby Way is the province of the language creator and the community as a whole. This is something difficult to capture in a book.

Still I have tried in this introduction to pin down a little of the ineffable spirit of Ruby. The wise student of Ruby will not take it as totally authoritative.

Be aware that this is a second edition. Many things have stayed the same, but many things have changed. Most of this introduction has been preserved, but you will want to visit the upcoming section, "About the Second Edition," where I summarize the changes and the new material.

About the Second Edition

Everything changes, and Ruby is no exception. As I write this introduction in August 2006, the first edition of this book is nearly five years old. It is certainly time for an update.

There are many changes and much new material in this edition. The old Chapter 4 ("Simple Data Tasks") is now split into *six* chapters, two of which ("Ranges and Symbols" and "Internationalization in Ruby") are totally new; the other four also have new examples and commentary added to them. The coverage of regualr expressions is particularly expanded, covering not only "classic" regexes but the newer Oniguruma regex engine.

Chapters 8 and 9 were originally one chapter. This was split as material was added and the chapter grew too big.

In the same way, the current chapters 18, 19, and 20 grew out of the old chapter 9 as material was added. The appendices were deleted to make room for more material.

Other new chapters are:

- Chapter 15, "Ruby and Data Formats." This covers XML, RSS, image files, writing PDF files, and more.

- Chapter 16, "Testing and Debugging." This deals with unit testing, profiling, debugging, code coverage, and similar topics.

- Chapter 17, "Packaging and Distributing Code." This chapter covers the use of setup.rb, the creation of RubyGems, and more.

- Chapter 21, "Ruby Development Tools." This offers a look at Ruby editor support and IDEs, the ri utility, and RubyGems from a user's perspective.

- Chapter 22, "The Ruby Community." This chapter summarizes all the major websites, mailing lists, newsgroups, conferences, IRC channels, and more.

In a larger sense, every single chapter in this book is "new." I have revised and updated every one of them, making hundreds of minor changes and dozens of major changes. I deleted items that were obsolete or of lesser importance; I changed material to fit changes in Ruby itself; and I added new examples and commentary to every chapter.

You may wonder what has been added to the old chapters. Some of the highlights are the Oniguruma coverage, which I already mentioned; coverage of math libraries and classes such as `BigDecimal`, `mathn`, and `matrix`; and new classes such as `Set` and `DateTime`.

In Chapter 10, "I/O and Data Storage," I added material on `readpartial`, on nonblocking I/O, and on the `StringIO` class. I also added material on CSV, YAML, and KirbyBase. In the database portion of that same chapter I added Oracle, SQLite, DBI, and a discussion of Object-Relational Mappers (ORMs).

Chapter 11, "OOP and Dynamic Features in Ruby," now includes more recent additions to Ruby such as `initialize_copy`, `const_get`, `const_missing`, and `define_method`. I also added coverage of delegation and forwarding techniques.

All of Chapter 12, "Graphical Interfaces for Ruby," had to be revised (especially the GTK and Fox sections). The QtRuby section is totally new.

Chapter 14, "Scripting and System Administration," now discusses the Windows one-click installer and a few similar packages. It also has several improvements in the example code.

Chapter 18, "Network Programming," now has a section on email attachments and another new section on interacting with an IMAP server. It also has coverage of the OpenURI library.

Chapter 19, "Ruby and Web Applications," now covers Ruby on Rails, Nitro, Wee, IOWA, and other web tools. It also has coverage of WEBrick and some coverage of Mongrel.

Chapter 20, "Distributed Ruby," has new material explaining Rinda, the Ruby tuplespace implementation. It also covers Ring, which is closely related.

Were all these additions necessary? I assure you they were.

For the record, *The Ruby Way* was the second Ruby book in the English language (following the famous "Pickaxe," or *Programming Ruby*, by Dave Thomas and Andy Hunt). It was carefully designed to be complementary to that book rather than overlapping it; this is a large part of the reason for its popularity.

When I began writing the first edition, there was no international Ruby conference. There was no RubyForge, no ruby-doc.org, and no rubygarden.org wiki. In essence there was little on the Web besides the main Ruby site. The Ruby Application Archive had a few hundred entries in it.

At that time, few publications (online or off) seemed to know of Ruby's existence. Any time an article was published about Ruby, it was cause for us to take notice; it was announced on the mailing list and discussed there.

Many common Ruby tools and libraries also did not exist. There was no RDoc; there was no REXML to parse XML; the math library was considerably less rich than it is now. Database support was spotty, and there was no ODBC. Tk was by far the most used GUI toolkit. The most common way of doing web development was the low-level CGI library.

There was no "one-click" Windows installer. Windows users typically used Cygwin or a mingw-based compile.

The RubyGems system did not exist even in primitive form. Finding and installing libraries and applications was typically a completely manual process involving tar and make commands.

No one had heard of Ruby on Rails. No one (so far as I recall) had yet used the term "duck typing." There was no YAML for Ruby, and there was no Rake.

We used Ruby 1.6.4 at that time, and we thought it was pretty cool. But Ruby 1.8.5 (the version I typically use now) is even cooler.

There have been a few changes in syntax but nothing to write home about. Mostly these were "edge cases" that now make a little more sense than before. Ruby has always been slightly quirky about when it considered parentheses to be optional; 98% of the time you won't notice the difference, and when you do, hopefully it is smoother and more consistent now than it was.

The semantics of some of the core methods have changed. Again, these are mostly minor changes. For example, Dir#chdir formerly did not take a block, but in recent years it can.

Some core methods have been obsoleted or renamed. The class method has lost its alias type (because we don't usually talk about the *types* of objects in Ruby). The intern method is now the friendlier to_sym method; Array#indices is now Array#values_at. I could go on, but you get the idea.

There are also new core methods such as Enumerable#inject, Enumerable#zip, and IO#readpartial. The old futils library is now fileutils, and it has its own module namespace FileUtils instead of adding methods into the File class.

There have been numerous other changes as well. It's important to realize, however, that these were made with great care and caution. Ruby is still Ruby. Much of the beauty of Ruby is derived from the fact that it changes slowly and deliberately, crafted by the wisdom of Matz and the other developers.

Today we have a proliferation of books on Ruby and more articles published than we can bother to notice. Web-based tutorials and documentation resources abound.

New tools and libraries have appeared. For whatever reasons, the most common of these seem to be web frameworks and tools, blogging tools, markup tools, and object-relational mappers (ORMs). But there are many others, of course—tools and libs for databases, GUIs, number-crunching, web services, image manipulation, source control, and more.

Ruby editor support is widespread and sophisticated. IDEs are available that are useful and mature (which partly overlap with the GUI builders).

It's also undeniable that the community has grown and changed. Ruby is by no means a niche language today; it is used at NASA, NOAA, Motorola, and many other large companies and institutions. It is used for graphics work, database work, numerical analysis, web development, and more. In short—and I mean this in the positive sense—Ruby has gone mainstream.

Updating this book has been a labor of love. I hope it is useful to you.

How This Book Works

You probably won't learn Ruby from this book. There is relatively little in the way of introductory or tutorial information. If you are totally new to Ruby, you might want start with another book.

Having said that, programmers are a tenacious bunch, and I grant that it might be possible to learn Ruby from this book. Chapter 1, "Ruby in Review," does contain a brief introduction and some tutorial information.

Chapter 1 also contains a comprehensive "gotcha" list (which has been difficult to keep up-to-date). The usefulness of this list in Chapter 1 will vary widely from one reader to another because we cannot all agree on what is intuitive.

This book is largely intended to answer questions of the form "How do I...?" As such, you can expect to do a lot of skipping around. I'd be honored if everyone read every page from front to back, but I don't expect that. It's more my expectation that you will browse the table of contents in search of techniques you need or things you find interesting.

As it turns out, I have talked to many people since the first edition, and they *did* in fact read it cover to cover. What's more, I have had more than one person report to me that they did learn Ruby here. So anything is possible.

Some things this book covers may seem elementary. That is because people vary in background and experience; what is obvious to one person may not be to another. I have tried to err on the side of completeness. On the other hand, I have tried to keep the book at a reasonable size (obviously a competing goal).

This book can be viewed as a sort of "inverted reference." Rather than looking up the name of a method or a class, you will look things up by function or purpose. For example, the `String` class has several methods for manipulating case: `capitalize`, `upcase`, `casecmp`, `downcase`, and `swapcase`. In a reference work, these would quite properly be listed alphabetically, but in this book they are all listed together.

Of course, in striving for completeness, I have sometimes wandered onto the turf of the reference books. In many cases, I have tried to compensate for this by offering more unusual or diverse examples than you might find in a reference.

I have tried for a high code-to-commentary ratio. Overlooking the initial chapter, I think I've achieved this. Writers may grow chatty, but programmers always want to see the code. (If not, they *should* want to.)

The examples here are sometimes contrived, for which I must apologize. To illustrate a technique or principle *in isolation from a real-world problem* can be difficult. However, the more complex or high-level the task was, the more I attempted a real-world solution. Thus if the topic is concatenating strings, you may find an unimaginative code fragment involving `"foo"` and `"bar"`, but when the topic is something like parsing XML, you will usually find a much more meaningful and realistic piece of code.

This book has two or three small quirks to which I'll confess up front. One is the avoidance of the "ugly" Perl-like global variables such as `$_` and the others. These are present in Ruby, and they work fine; they are used daily by most or all Ruby programmers. But in nearly all cases their use can be avoided, and I have taken the liberty of omitting them in most of the examples.

Another quirk is that I avoid using standalone expressions when they don't have side effects. Ruby is expression-oriented, and that is a good thing; I have tried to take advantage of that feature. But in a code fragment, I prefer to not write expressions that merely return a value that is not usable. For example, the expression `"abc" + "def"` can illustrate string concatenation, but I would write something like `str = "abc" + "def"` instead. This may seem wordy to some, but it may seem more natural to you if you are a C programmer who really notices when functions are void or nonvoid (or an old-time Pascal programmer who thinks in procedures and functions).

My third quirk is that I don't like the "pound" notation to denote instance methods. Many Rubyists will think I am being verbose in saying "instance method `crypt` of class `String`" rather than saying `String#crypt`, but I think no one will be confused. (Actually, I am slowly being converted to this usage, as it is obvious the pound notation is not going away.)

I have tried to include "pointers" to outside resources whenever appropriate. Time and space did not allow putting everything into this book that I wanted, but I hope I have partially made up for that by telling you where to find related materials. The Ruby Application Archive on the Web is probably the foremost of these sources; you will see it referenced many times in this book.

Here at the front of the book there is usually a gratuitous reference to the typefaces used for code, and how to tell code fragments from ordinary text. But I won't insult your intelligence; you've read computer books before.

I want to point out that roughly 10 percent of this book was written by other people. That does not even include tech editing and copyediting. You should read the acknowledgements in this (and every) book. Most readers skip them. Go read them now. They're good for you, like vegetables.

About The Book's Source Code

Every significant code fragment has been collected into an archive for the reader to download. Look for this archive on the www.awprofessional.com site or at my own site (www.rubyhacker.com).

It is offered both as a .tgz file and as a .zip file. For the files in this archive, the general naming convention is that the actual code listings are named according to the listing number (for example, `listing14-1.rb`). The shorter code fragments are named according to page number and an optional letter (for example, `p260a.rb` and `p260b.rb`). Code fragments that are very short or can't be run "out of context" will usually not appear in the archive.

What Is the "Ruby Way"?

Let us prepare to grapple with the ineffable itself, and see if we may not eff it after all.

—*Douglas Adams,* Dirk Gently's Holistic Detective Agency

What do we mean by the Ruby Way? My belief is that there are two related aspects: One is the philosophy of the *design* of Ruby; the other is the philosophy of its *usage*. It is natural that design and use should be interrelated, whether in software or hardware; why else should there be such a field as ergonomics? If I build a device and put a handle on it, it is because I expect someone to grab that handle.

Ruby has a nameless quality that makes it what it is. We see that quality present in the design of the syntax and semantics of the language, but it is also present in the programs written for that interpreter. Yet as soon as we make this distinction, we blur it.

Clearly Ruby is not just a tool for creating software, but it is a piece of software in its own right. Why should the workings of Ruby *programs* follow laws different from those that guide the workings of the *interpreter*? After all, Ruby is highly dynamic and extensible. There might be reasons that the two levels should differ here and there, probably for accommodating to the inconvenience of the real world. But in general, the thought processes can and should be the same. Ruby could be implemented in Ruby, in true Hofstadter-like fashion, though it is not at the time of this writing.

We don't often think of the etymology of the word *way*; but there are two important senses in which it is used. On the one hand, it means *a method or technique*, but it can also mean *a road or path*. Obviously these two meanings are interrelated, and I think when I say "the Ruby Way," I mean both of them.

So what we are talking about is a thought process, but it is also a path that we follow. Even the greatest software guru cannot claim to have reached perfection but only to follow the path. And there may be more than one path, but here I can only talk about one.

The conventional wisdom says that *form follows function*. And the conventional wisdom is, of course, conventionally correct. But Frank Lloyd Wright (speaking in his own field) once said: "Form follows function—that has been misunderstood. Form and function should be one, joined in a spiritual union."

What did Wright mean? I would say that this truth is not something you learn from a book, but from experience.

However, I would argue that Wright expressed this truth elsewhere in pieces easier to digest. He was a great proponent of simplicity, saying once, "An architect's most useful tools are an eraser at the drafting board and a wrecking bar at the site."

So one of Ruby's virtues is simplicity. Shall I quote other thinkers on the subject? According to Antoine de St. Exupery, "Perfection is achieved, not when there is nothing left to add, but when there is nothing left to take away."

But Ruby is a complex language. How can I say that it is simple?

If we understood the universe better, we might find a "law of conservation of complexity"—a fact of reality that disturbs our lives like entropy so that we cannot avoid it but can only redistribute it.

And that is the key. We can't avoid complexity, but we can push it around. We can bury it out of sight. This is the old "black box" principle at work; a black box performs a complex task, but it possesses simplicity *on the outside*.

If you haven't already lost patience with my quotations, a word from Albert Einstein is appropriate here: "Everything should be as simple as possible, but no simpler."

So in Ruby we see simplicity embodied from the programmer's view (if not from the view of those maintaining the interpreter). Yet we also see the capacity for compromise. In the real world, we must bend a little. For example, every entity in a Ruby program should be a true object, but certain values such as integers are stored as immediate values. In a trade-off familiar to computer science students for decades, we have traded elegance of design for practicality of implementation. In effect, we have traded one kind of simplicity for another.

What Larry Wall said about Perl holds true: "When you say something in a small language, it comes out big. When you say something in a big language, it comes out small." The same is true for English. The reason that biologist Ernst Haeckel could say "Ontogeny recapitulates phylogeny" in only three words was that he had these powerful words with highly specific meanings at his disposal. We allow inner complexity of the language because it enables us to shift the complexity away from the individual utterance.

I would state this guideline this way: Don't write 200 lines of code when 10 will do.

I'm taking it for granted that brevity is generally a good thing. A short program fragment will take up less space in the programmer's brain; it will be easier to grasp as a single entity. As a happy side effect, fewer bugs will be injected while the code is being written.

Of course, we must remember Einstein's warning about simplicity. If we put brevity too high on our list of priorities, we will end up with code that is hopelessly obfuscated. Information theory teaches us that compressed data is statistically similar to random noise; if you have looked at C or APL or regular expression notation—especially badly written—you have experienced this truth firsthand. "Simple, but not too simple"; that is the key. Embrace brevity, but do not sacrifice readability.

It is a truism that both brevity and readability are good. But there is an underlying reason for this, one so fundamental that we sometimes forget it. The reason is that computers exist for humans, not humans for computers.

In the old days, it was almost the opposite. Computers cost millions of dollars and ate electricity at the rate of many kilowatts. People acted as though the computer were a minor deity and the programmers were humble supplicants. An hour of the computer's time was more expensive than an hour of a person's time.

When computers became smaller and cheaper, high-level languages also became more popular. These were inefficient from the computer's point of view but efficient from the human perspective. Ruby is simply a later development in this line of thought. Some, in fact, have called it a *VHLL* (Very High-Level Language); though this term is not well-defined, I think its use is justified here.

The computer is supposed to be the servant, not the master, and, as Matz has said, a smart servant should do a complex task with a few short commands. This has been true through all the history of computer science. We started with machine languages and progressed to assembly language and then to high-level languages.

What we are talking about here is a shift from a *machine-centered* paradigm to a *human-centered* one. In my opinion, Ruby is an excellent example of human-centric programming.

I'll shift gears a little. There was a wonderful little book from the 1980s called *The Tao of Programming* (by Geoffrey James). Nearly every line is quotable, but I'll repeat only this: "A program should follow the 'Law of Least Astonishment.' What is this law? It is simply that the program should always respond to the user in the way that astonishes him least." (Of course, in the case of a language interpreter, the *user* is the programmer.)

I don't know whether James coined this term, but his book was my first introduction to the phrase. This is a principle that is well known and often cited in the Ruby community, though it is usually called the *Principle of Least Surprise* or *POLS*. (I myself stubbornly prefer the acronym *LOLA*.)

Whatever you call it, this rule is a valid one, and it has been a guideline throughout the ongoing development of the Ruby language. It is also a useful guideline for those who develop libraries or user interfaces.

The only problem, of course, is that different people are surprised by different things; there is no universal agreement on how an object or method "ought" to behave. We can strive for consistency and strive to justify our design decisions, and each person can train his own intuition.

For the record, Matz has said that "least surprise" should refer to *him* as the designer. The more you think like him, the less Ruby will surprise you. And I assure you, imitating Matz is not a bad idea for most of us.

No matter how logically constructed a system may be, your intuition needs to be trained. Each programming language is a world unto itself, with its own set of assumptions, and human languages are the same. When I took German, I learned that all nouns were capitalized, but the word *deutsch* was not. I complained to my professor; after all, this was the *name* of the language, wasn't it? He smiled and said, "Don't fight it."

What he taught me was to *let German be German.* By extension, that is good advice for anyone coming to Ruby from some other language. Let Ruby be Ruby. Don't expect it to be Perl, because it isn't; don't expect it to be LISP or Smalltalk, either. On the other hand, Ruby has common elements with all three of these. Start by following your expectations, but when they are violated, don't fight it. (Unless Matz agrees it's a needed change.)

Every programmer today knows the orthogonality principle (which would better be termed the *orthogonal completeness* principle). Suppose we have an imaginary pair of axes with a set of comparable language entities on one and a set of attributes or capabilities on the other. When we talk of "orthogonality," we usually mean that the space defined by these axes is as "full" as we can logically make it.

Part of the Ruby Way is to strive for this orthogonality. An array is in some ways similar to a hash; so the operations on each of them should be similar. The limit is reached when we enter the areas where they are different.

Matz has said that "naturalness" is to be valued over orthogonality. But to fully understand what is natural and what is not may take some thinking and some coding.

Ruby strives to be friendly to the programmer. For example, there are aliases or synonyms for many method names; `size` and `length` will both return the number of entries in an array. The variant spellings `indexes` and `indices` both refer to the same method. Some consider this sort of thing to be an annoyance or anti-feature, but I consider it a good design.

Ruby strives for consistency and regularity. There is nothing mysterious about this; in every aspect of life, we yearn for things to be regular and parallel. What makes it a little more tricky is learning when to violate this principle.

For instance, Ruby has the habit of appending a question mark (?) to the name of a predicatelike method. This is well and good; it clarifies the code and makes the namespace a little more manageable. But what is more controversial is the similar use of the exclamation point in marking methods that are "destructive" or "dangerous" in the sense that they modify their receivers. The controversy arises because *not all* of the destructive methods are marked in this way. Shouldn't we be consistent?

No, in fact we should not. Some of the methods by their very nature change their receiver (such as the `Array` methods `replace` and `concat`). Some of them are "writer" methods allowing assignment to a class attribute; we should *not* append an exclamation point to the attribute name or the equal sign. Some methods arguably change the state of the receiver, such as `read`; this occurs too frequently to be marked in this way. If every destructive method name ended in a `!`, our programs soon would look like sales brochures for a multilevel marketing firm.

Do you notice a kind of tension between opposing forces, a tendency for all rules to be violated? Let me state this as Fulton's Second Law: *Every rule has an exception, except Fulton's Second Law.* (Yes, there is a joke there, a very small one.)

What we see in Ruby is not a "foolish consistency" nor a rigid adherence to a set of simple rules. In fact, perhaps part of the Ruby Way is that it is *not* a rigid and inflexible approach. In language design, as Matz once said, you should "follow your heart."

Yet another aspect of the Ruby philosophy is: *Do not fear change at runtime; do not fear what is dynamic.* The world is dynamic; why should a programming language be static? Ruby is one of the most dynamic languages in existence.

I would also argue that another aspect is: Do not be a slave to performance issues. When performance is unacceptable, the issue must be addressed, but it should normally not be the first thing you think about. Prefer elegance over efficiency where efficiency is less than critical. Then again, if you are writing a library that may be used in unforeseen ways, performance may be critical from the start.

When I look at Ruby, I perceive a balance between different design goals, a complex interaction reminiscent of the *n*-body problem in physics. I can imagine it might be modeled as an Alexander Calder mobile. It is perhaps this interaction itself, the harmony, that embodies Ruby's philosophy rather than just the individual parts. Programmers know that their craft is not just science and technology but art. I hesitate to say that there is a spiritual aspect to computer science, but just between you and me, there certainly is. (If you have not read Robert Pirsig's *Zen and the Art of Motorcycle Maintenance*, I recommend that you do so.)

Ruby arose from the human urge to create things that are useful and beautiful. Programs written in Ruby should spring from that same God-given source. That, to me, is the essence of the Ruby Way.

CHAPTER 1

Ruby in Review

Language shapes the way we think and determines what we can think about.

—*Benjamin Lee Whorf*

It is worth remembering that a new programming language is sometimes viewed as a panacea, especially by its adherents. But no one language will supplant all the others; no one tool is unarguably the best for every possible task. There are many different problem domains in the world and many possible constraints on problems within those domains.

Above all, there are different ways of *thinking* about these problems, stemming from the diverse backgrounds and personalities of the programmers themselves. For these reasons, there is no foreseeable end to the proliferation of languages. And as long as there is a multiplicity of languages, there will be a multiplicity of personalities defending and attacking them. In short, there will always be "language wars"; in this book, however, we do not intend to participate in them.

Yet in the constant quest for newer and better program notations, we have stumbled across ideas that endure, that transcend the context in which they were created. Just as Pascal borrowed from Algol, just as Java borrowed from C, so will every language borrow from its predecessors.

1

A language is both a toolbox and a playground; it has a practical side, but it also serves as a test bed for new ideas that may or may not be widely accepted by the computing community.

One of the most far-reaching of these ideas is the concept of object-oriented programming (OOP). Although many would argue that the overall significance of OOP is evolutionary rather than revolutionary, no one can say that it has not had an impact on the industry. Twenty-five years ago, object orientation was for the most part an academic curiosity; today it is a universally accepted paradigm.

In fact, the ubiquitous nature of OOP has led to a significant amount of "hype" in the industry. In a classic paper of the late 1980s, Roger King observed, "If you want to sell a cat to a computer scientist, you have to tell him it's object-oriented." Additionally, there are differences of opinion about what OOP really is, and even among those who are essentially in agreement, there are differences in terminology.

It is not our purpose here to contribute to the hype. We do find OOP to be a useful tool and a meaningful way of thinking about problems; we do not claim that it cures cancer.

As for the exact nature of OOP, we have our pet definitions and favorite terminology; but we make these known only to communicate effectively, not to quibble over semantics.

We mention all this because it is necessary to have a basic understanding of OOP to proceed to the bulk of this book and understand the examples and techniques. Whatever else might be said about Ruby, it is definitely an object-oriented language.

1.1 An Introduction to Object Orientation

Before talking about Ruby specifically, it is a good idea to talk about object-oriented programming in the abstract. These first few pages review those concepts with only cursory references to Ruby before we proceed to a review of the Ruby language itself.

1.1.1 What Is an Object?

In object-oriented programming, the fundamental unit is the *object*. An object is an entity that serves as a container for data and also controls access to the data. Associated with an object is a set of *attributes*, which are essentially no more than variables belonging to the object. (In this book, we will loosely use the ordinary term *variable* for an attribute.) Also associated with an object is a set of functions that provide an interface to the functionality of the object, called *methods*.

It is essential that any OOP language provide *encapsulation*. As the term is commonly used, it means first that the attributes and methods of an object are associated specifically with that object, or bundled with it; second, it means that the scope of those attributes and methods is by default the object itself (an application of the principle of *data hiding*).

An object is considered to be an instance or manifestation of an *object class* (usually simply called a *class*). The class may be thought of as the blueprint or pattern; the object itself is the thing created from that blueprint or pattern. A class is often thought of as an *abstract type*—a more complex type than, for example, integer or character string.

When an object (an instance of a class) is created, it is said to be *instantiated*. Some languages have the notion of an explicit *constructor* and *destructor* for an object—functions that perform whatever tasks are needed to initialize an object and (respectively) to "destroy" it. We may as well mention prematurely that Ruby has what might be considered a constructor but certainly does not have any concept of a destructor (because of its well-behaved garbage collection mechanism).

Occasionally a situation arises in which a piece of data is more "global" in scope than a single object, and it is inappropriate to put a copy of the attribute into each instance of the class. For example, consider a class called `MyDogs`, from which three objects are created: `fido`, `rover`, and `spot`. For each dog, there might be such attributes as age and date of vaccination. But suppose that we want to store the owner's name (the owner of *all* the dogs). We could certainly put it in each object, but that is wasteful of memory and at the very least a misleading design. Clearly the *owner_name* attribute belongs not to any individual object but to the class itself. When it is defined that way (and the syntax varies from one language to another), it is called a *class attribute* (or *class variable*).

Of course, there are many situations in which a class variable might be needed. For example, suppose that we wanted to keep a count of how many objects of a certain class had been created. We could use a class variable that was initialized to zero and incremented with every instantiation; the class variable would be associated with the class and not with any particular object. In scope, this variable would be just like any other attribute, but there would only be one copy of it for the entire class and the entire set of objects created from that class.

To distinguish between class attributes and ordinary attributes, the latter are sometimes explicitly called *object attributes* (or *instance attributes*). We use the convention that any attribute is assumed to be an instance attribute unless we explicitly call it a class attribute.

Just as an object's methods are used to control access to its attributes and provide a clean interface to them, so is it sometimes appropriate or necessary to define a method associated with a class. A *class method*, not surprisingly, controls access to the class variables and also performs any tasks that might have classwide effects rather than merely objectwide. As with data attributes, methods are assumed to belong to the object rather than the class unless stated otherwise.

It is worth mentioning that there is a sense in which all methods are class methods. We should not suppose that when 100 objects are created we actually copy the code for the methods 100 times! But the rules of scope assure us that each object method operates only on the object whose method is being called, providing us with the necessary illusion that object methods are associated strictly with their objects.

1.1.2   Inheritance

We come now to one of the real strengths of OOP, which is *inheritance*. Inheritance is a mechanism that allows us to extend a previously existing entity by adding features to create a new entity. In short, inheritance is a way of reusing code. (Easy, effective code reuse has long been the Holy Grail of computer science, resulting in the invention decades ago of parameterized subroutines and code libraries. OOP is only one of the later efforts in realizing this goal.)

Typically we think of inheritance at the class level. If we have a specific class in mind, and there is a more general case already in existence, we can define our new class to inherit the features of the old one. For example, suppose that we have a class `Polygon` that describes convex polygons. If we then find ourselves dealing with a `Rectangle` class, we can inherit from `Polygon` so that `Rectangle` has all the attributes and methods that `Polygon` has. For example, there might be a method that calculates perimeter by iterating over all the sides and adding their lengths. Assuming that everything was implemented properly, this method would automatically work for the new class; the code would not have to be rewritten.

When a class B inherits from a class A, we say that B is a *subclass* of A, or conversely, A is the *superclass* of B. In slightly different terminology, we may say that A is a *base class* or *parent class*, and B is a *derived class* or *child class*.

A derived class, as we have seen, may treat a method inherited from its base class as if it were its own. On the other hand, it may redefine that method entirely if it is necessary to provide a different implementation; this is referred to as *overriding* a method. In addition, most languages provide a way for an overridden method to call its namesake in the parent class; that is, the method `foo` in B knows how to call method `foo` in `A` if it wants to. (Any language that does not provide this feature is under suspicion of not being truly object-oriented.) Essentially the same is true for data attributes.

The relationship between a class and its superclass is interesting and important; it is usually described as the *is-a* relationship, because a `Square` "is a" `Rectangle`, and a `Rectangle` "is a" `Polygon`, and so on. Thus if we create an inheritance hierarchy (which tends to exist in one form or another in any OOP language), we see that the more specific entity "is a" subclass of the more general entity at any given point in the hierarchy. Note that this relationship is transitive—in the previous example, we easily see that a `Square` "is a" `Polygon`. Note also that the relationship is not commutative—we know that every `Rectangle` is a `Polygon`, but not every `Polygon` is a `Rectangle`.

This brings us to the topic of *multiple inheritance (MI)*. It is conceivable that a new class could inherit from more than one class. For example, the classes `Dog` and `Cat` can both inherit from the class `Mammal`, and `Sparrow` and `Raven` can inherit from `WingedCreature`. But what if we want to define a `Bat`? It can reasonably inherit from both the classes `Mammal` and `WingedCreature`. This corresponds well with our real-life experience in which things are not members of just one category but of many non-nested categories.

MI is probably the most controversial area in OOP. One camp will point out the potential for ambiguity that must be resolved. For example, if `Mammal` and `WingedCreature` both have an attribute called `size` (or a method called `eat`), which one will be referenced when we refer to it from a `Bat` object? Another related difficulty is the *diamond inheritance problem*—so called because of the shape of its inheritance diagram with both superclasses inheriting from a single common superclass. For example, imagine that `Mammal` and `WingedCreature` both inherit from `Organism`; the hierarchy from `Organism` to `Bat` forms a diamond. But what about the attributes that the two intermediate classes both inherit from their parent? Does `Bat` get two copies of each of them? Or are they merged back into single attributes because they come from a common ancestor in the first place?

These are both issues for the language designer rather than the programmer. Different OOP languages deal with the issues differently. Some provide rules allowing one definition of an attribute to "win out," or a way to distinguish between attributes of the same name, or even a way of aliasing or renaming the identifiers. This in itself is considered by many to be an argument against MI—the mechanisms for dealing with name clashes and the like are not universally agreed upon but are language dependent. C++ offers a minimal set of features for dealing with ambiguities; those of Eiffel are probably better; and those of Perl are different from both.

The alternative, of course, is to disallow MI altogether. This is the approach taken by such languages as Java and Ruby. This sounds like a drastic compromise; however, as we shall see later, it is not so bad as it sounds. We will look at a viable alternative to traditional MI, but we must first discuss *polymortphism*, yet another OOP buzzword.

1.1.3   Polymorphism

Polymorphism is the term that perhaps inspires the most semantic disagreement in the field. Everyone seems to know what it is, but everyone has a different definition. (In recent years, "What is polymorphism?" has become a popular interview question. If it is asked of you, I recommend quoting an expert such as Bertrand Meyer or Bjarne Stroustrup; that way, if the interviewer disagrees, his beef is with the expert and not with you.)

The literal meaning of polymorphism is "the ability to take on multiple forms or shapes." In its broadest sense, this refers to the ability of different objects to respond in different ways to the same message (or method invocation).

Damian Conway, in his book *Object-Oriented Perl*, distinguishes meaningfully between two kinds of polymorphism. The first, *inheritance polymorphism*, is what most programmers are referring to when they talk about polymorphism.

When a class inherits from its superclass, we know (by definition) that any method present in the superclass is also present in the subclass. Thus a chain of inheritance represents a linear hierarchy of classes that can respond to the same set of methods. Of course, we must remember that any subclass can redefine a method; that is what gives inheritance its power. If I call a method on an object, typically it will be either the one it inherited from its superclass, or a more appropriate (more specialized) method tailored for the subclass.

In statically typed languages such as C++, inheritance polymorphism establishes type compatibility down the chain of inheritance (but not in the reverse direction). For example, if B inherits from A, a pointer to an A object can also point to a B object; but the reverse is not true. This type compatibility is an essential OOP feature in such languages—indeed it almost sums up polymorphism—but polymorphism certainly exists in the absence of static typing (as in Ruby).

The second kind of polymorphism Conway identifies is *interface polymorphism*. This does not require any inheritance relationship between classes; it only requires that the interfaces of the objects have methods of a certain name. The treatment of such objects as being the same "kind" of thing is thus a kind of polymorphism (though in most writings it is not explicitly referred to as such).

Readers familiar with Java will recognize that it implements both kinds of polymorphism. A Java class can extend another class, inheriting from it via the `extends` keyword; or it may implement an interface, acquiring a known set of methods (which must then be overridden) via the `implements` keyword. Because of syntax requirements, the Java interpreter can determine at compile time whether a method can be invoked on a particular object.

Ruby supports interface polymorphism but in a different way, providing *modules* whose methods may be *mixed in* to existing classes (interfacing to user-defined methods that are expected to exist). This, however, is not the way modules are usually used. A module consists of methods and constants that may be used as though they were actual parts of that class or object; when a module is mixed in via the `include` statement, this is considered to be a restricted form of multiple inheritance. (According to the language designer, Yukihiro Matsumoto, it can be viewed as *single inheritance with implementation sharing*.) This is a way of preserving the benefits of MI without suffering all the consequences.

1.1.4   A Few More Terms

In languages such as C++, there is the concept of *abstract classes*—classes that must be inherited from and cannot be instantiated on their own. This concept does not exist in the more dynamic Ruby language, although if the programmer really wants, it is possible to fake this kind of behavior by forcing the methods to be overridden. Whether this is useful is left as an exercise for the reader.

The creator of C++, Bjarne Stroustrup, also identifies the concept of a *concrete type*. This is a class that exists only for convenience; it is not designed to be inherited from, nor is it expected that there will ever be another class derived from it. In other words, the benefits of OOP are basically limited to encapsulation. Ruby does not specifically support this concept through any special syntax (nor does C++), but it is naturally well-suited for the creation of such classes.

Some languages are considered to be more "pure" OO than others. (We also use the term *radically object-oriented*.) This refers to the concept that *every* entity in the language is an object; every primitive type is represented as a full-fledged class, and variables and constants alike are recognized as object instances. This is in contrast to such languages as Java, C++, and Eiffel. In these, the more primitive data types (especially constants) are not first-class objects, though they may sometimes be treated that way with "wrapper" classes. Arguably there are languages that are *more* radically object-oriented than Ruby, but they are relatively few.

Most OO languages are static; the methods and attributes belonging to a class, the global variables, and the inheritance hierarchy are all defined at compile time. Perhaps the largest conceptual leap for a Ruby programmer is that these are all handled *dynamically* in Ruby. Definitions and even inheritance can happen at runtime—in fact, we can truly say that every declaration or definition is actually *executed* during the running of the program. Among many other benefits, this obviates the need for conditional compilation and can produce more efficient code in many circumstances.

This sums up the whirlwind tour of OOP. Throughout the rest of the book, we have tried to make consistent use of the terms introduced here. Let's proceed now to a brief review of the Ruby language itself.

1.2   Basic Ruby Syntax and Semantics

In the previous pages, we have already seen that Ruby is a *pure, dynamic, OOP* language.

Let's look briefly at some other attributes before summarizing the syntax and semantics.

Ruby is an *agile* language. It is "malleable" and encourages frequent, easy refactoring.

Ruby is an *interpreted* language. Of course, there may be later implementations of a Ruby compiler for performance reasons, but we maintain that an interpreter yields great benefits not only in rapid prototyping but also in the shortening of the development cycle overall.

Ruby is an *expression-oriented* language. Why use a statement when an expression will do? This means, for instance, that code becomes more compact as the common parts are factored out and repetition is removed.

Ruby is a *very high-level language* (*VHLL*). One principle behind the language design is that the computer should work for the programmer rather than vice versa. The "density" of Ruby means that sophisticated and complex operations can be carried out with relative ease as compared to lower-level languages.

Let's start by examining the overall look and feel of the language and some of its terminology. We'll briefly examine the nature of a Ruby program before looking at examples.

To begin with, Ruby is essentially a line-oriented language—more so than languages such as C but not so much as antique languages such as FORTRAN. Tokens can be crowded onto a single line as long as they are separated by whitespace as needed. Statements may occur more than one to a line if they are separated by semicolons; this is the only time the terminating semicolon is really needed. A line may be continued to the next line by ending with a backslash or by letting the parser know that the statement is not complete—for example, by ending a line with a comma.

There is no main program as such; execution proceeds in general from top to bottom. In more complex programs, there may be numerous definitions at the top followed by the (conceptual) main program at the bottom; but even in that case, execution proceeds from the top down because definitions in Ruby are executed.

1.2.1 Keywords and Identifiers

The keywords (or reserved words) in Ruby typically cannot be used for other purposes. These are as follows:

BEGIN	END	alias	and	begin
break	case	class	def	defined?
do	else	elsif	end	ensure
false	for	if	in	module
next	nil	not	or	redo
rescue	retry	return	self	super
then	true	undef	unless	until
when	while	yield		

Variables and other identifiers normally start with an alphabetic letter or a special modifier. The basic rules are as follows:

- Local variables (and pseudovariables such as `self` and `nil`) begin with a lowercase letter or an underscore.
- Global variables begin with a `$` (dollar sign).
- Instance variables (within an object) begin with an `@` (at sign).
- Class variables (within a class) begin with two `@` signs.
- Constants begin with capital letters.
- For purposes of forming identifiers, the underscore (`_`) may be used as a lowercase letter.
- Special variables starting with a dollar sign (such as `$1` and `$/`) are not dealt with here.

Here are some examples of each of these:

- Local variables—`alpha, _ident, some_var`

- Pseudovariables—`self, nil, __FILE__`

- Constants—`K6chip, Length, LENGTH`

- Instance variables—`@foobar, @thx1138, @NOT_CONST`

- Class variable—`@@phydeaux, @@my_var, @@NOT_CONST`

- Global variables—`$beta, $B12vitamin, $NOT_CONST`

1.2.2   Comments and Embedded Documentation

Comments in Ruby begin with a pound sign (#) outside a string or character constant and proceed to the end of the line:

```
x = y + 5 # This is a comment.
# This is another comment.
print "# But this isn't."
```

Embedded documentation is intended to be retrieved from the program text by an external tool. From the point of view of the interpreter, it is like a comment and can be used as such. Given two lines starting with =begin and =end, everything between those lines (inclusive) is ignored by the interpreter.(These can't be preceded by whitespace.)

```
=begin
The purpose of this program
is to cure cancer
and instigate world peace.
=end
```

1.2.3   Constants, Variables, and Types

In Ruby, variables do not have types, but the objects they refer to still have types. The simplest data types are character, numeric, and string.

Numeric constants are mostly intuitive, as are strings. Generally, a double-quoted string is subject to additional interpretation, and a single-quoted string is more "as is," allowing only an escaped backslash.

In double-quoted strings, we can do "interpolation" of variables and expressions as shown here:

```
a = 3
b = 79
puts "#{a} times #{b} = #{a*b}"   #  3 times 79 = 237
```

For more information on literals (numbers, strings, regular expressions, and so on), refer to later chapters.

There is a special kind of string worth mentioning, primarily useful in small scripts used to glue together larger programs. The command output string is sent to the operating system as a command to be executed, whereupon the output of the command is substituted back into the string. The simple form of this string uses the *grave accent* (sometimes called a *back-tick* or *back-quote*) as a beginning and ending delimiter; the more complex form uses the %x notation:

```
`whoami`
`ls -l`
%x[grep -i meta *.html | wc -l]
```

Regular expressions in Ruby look similar to character strings, but they are used differently. The usual delimiter is a slash character.

For those familiar with Perl, regular expression handling is similar in Ruby. Incidentally, we'll use the abbreviation *regex* throughout the remainder of the book; many people abbreviate it as *regexp*, but that is not as pronounceable. For details on regular expressions, see Chapter 3, "Working with Regular Expressions."

Arrays in Ruby are a powerful construct; they may contain data of any type or may even mix types. As we shall see in Chapter 8 ("Arrays, Hashes, and Other Enumerables"), all arrays are instances of the class Array and thus have a rich set of methods that can operate on them. An array constant is delimited by brackets; the following are all valid array expressions:

```
[1, 2, 3]
[1, 2, "buckle my shoe"]
[1, 2, [3,4], 5]
["alpha", "beta", "gamma", "delta"]
```

The second example shows an array containing both integers and strings; the third example in the preceding code shows a nested array, and the fourth example shows an array of strings. As in most languages, arrays are zero-based; for instance, in the last array in the preceding code, "gamma" is element number 2. Arrays are dynamic and do not need to have a size specified when they are created.

Since the array of strings is so common (and so inconvenient to type), a special syntax has been set aside for it, similar to what we have seen before:

```
%w[alpha beta gamma delta]
%w(Jan Feb Mar Apr May Jun Jul Aug Sep Oct Nov Dec)
%w/am is are was were be being been/
```

In these, the quotes and commas are not needed; only whitespace separates the individual elements. In the case of an element that contained whitespace, of course, this would not work.

An array variable can use brackets to index into the array. The resulting expression can be both examined and assigned to:

```
val = myarray[0]
print stats[j]
x[i] = x[i+1]
```

Another powerful construct in Ruby is the *hash*, also known in other circles as an *associative array* or *dictionary*. A hash is a set of associations between paired pieces of data; it is typically used as a lookup table or a kind of generalized array in which the index need not be an integer. Each hash is an instance of the class Hash.

A hash constant is typically represented between delimiting braces, with the symbol => separating the individual keys and values. The key can be thought of as an index where the corresponding value is stored. There is no restriction on types of the keys or the corresponding values. Here are some hashes:

```
{1=>1, 2=>4, 3=>9, 4=>16, 5=>25, 6=>36}
{"cat"=>"cats", "ox"=>"oxen", "bacterium"=>"bacteria"}
{"hydrogen"=>1, "helium"=>2, "carbon"=>12}
{"odds"=>[1,3,5,7], "evens"=>[2,4,6,8]}
{"foo"=>123, [4,5,6]=>"my array", "867-5309"=>"Jenny"}
```

A hash variable can have its contents accessed by essentially the same bracket notation that arrays use:

```
print phone_numbers["Jenny"]
plurals["octopus"] = "octopi"
```

It should be stressed, however, that both arrays and hashes have many methods associated with them; these methods give them their real usefulness. The section "OOP in Ruby" later in the chapter will expand on this a little more.

1.2.4 Operators and Precedence

Now that we have established our most common data types, let's look at Ruby's operators. They are arranged here in order from highest to lowest precedence:

::	Scope
[]	Indexing
**	Exponentiation
+ - ! ~	Unary pos/neg, not, ...
* / %	Multiplication, division, ...
+ -	Addition/subtraction
<< >>	Logical shifts, ...
&	Bitwise and
| ^	Bitwise or, xor
> >= < <=	Comparison
== === <=> != =~ !~	Equality, inequality, ...
&&	Boolean and
||	Boolean or
.. ...	Range operators
= (also +=, -=, ...)	Assignment
?:	Ternary decision
not	Boolean negation
and or	Boolean and, or

Some of the preceding symbols serve more than one purpose; for example, the operator << is a bitwise left shift but is also an append operator (for arrays, strings, and so on) and a marker for a here-document. Likewise the + is for numeric addition as well as for string concatenation. As we shall see later, many of these operators are just shortcuts for method names.

Now we have defined most of our data types and many of the possible operations on them. Before going any further, let's look at a sample program.

1.2.5   A Sample Program

In a tutorial, the first program is always Hello, world! But in a whirlwind tour like this one, let's start with something slightly more advanced. Here is a small interactive console-based program to convert between Fahrenheit and Celsius temperatures:

```
print "Please enter a temperature and scale (C or F): "
str = gets
exit if str.nil? or str.empty?
str.chomp!
temp, scale = str.split(" ")

abort "#{temp} is not a valid number." if temp !~ /-?\d+/

temp = temp.to_f
case scale
  when "C", "c"
    f = 1.8*temp + 32
  when "F", "f"
    c = (5.0/9.0)*(temp-32)
else
  abort "Must specify C or F."
end

if f.nil?
  print "#{c} degrees C\n"
else
  print "#{f} degrees F\n"
end
```

Here are some examples of running this program. These show that the program can convert from Fahrenheit to Celsius, convert from Celsius to Fahrenheit, and handle an invalid scale or an invalid number:

```
Please enter a temperature and scale (C or F): 98.6 F
37.0 degrees C

Please enter a temperature and scale (C or F): 100 C
212.0 degrees F

Please enter a temperature and scale (C or F): 92 G
Must specify C or F.

Please enter a temperature and scale (C or F): junk F
junk is not a valid number.
```

Now, as for the mechanics of the program: We begin with a print statement, which is actually a call to the Kernel method print, to write to standard output. This is an easy way of leaving the cursor "hanging" at the end of the line.

Following this, we call gets (get string from standard input), assigning the value to str. We then do a chomp! to remove the trailing newline.

Note that any apparently "free-standing" function calls such as print and gets are actually methods of Object (probably originating in Kernel). In the same way, chop is a method called with str as a receiver. Method calls in Ruby usually can omit the parentheses; print "foo" is the same as print("foo").

The variable str holds a character string, but there is no reason it could not hold some other type instead. In Ruby, data have types, but variables do not. A variable springs into existence as soon as the interpreter sees an assignment to that variable; there are no "variable declarations" as such.

The exit is a call to a method that terminates the program. On this same line there is a control structure called an *if-modifier*. This is like the if statement that exists in most languages, but backwards; it comes after the action, does not permit an else, and does not require closing. As for the condition, we are checking two things: Does str have a value (is it non-nil), and is it a non-null string? In the case of an immediate end-of-file, our first condition will hold; in the case of a newline with no preceding data, the second condition will hold.

The same statement could be written this way:

```
exit if not str or not str[0]
```

The reason these tests work is that a variable can have a nil value, and nil evaluates to false in Ruby. In fact, nil and false evaluate as false, and everything else evaluates as true. Specifically, the null string "" and the number 0 do *not* evaluate as false.

The next statement performs a chomp! operation on the string (to remove the trailing newline). The exclamation point as a prefix serves as a warning that the operation actually changes the value of its receiver rather than just returning a value. The exclamation point is used in many such instances to remind the programmer that a method has a side effect or is more "dangerous" than its unmarked counterpart. The method chomp, for example, returns the same result but does not modify its receiver.

The next statement is an example of multiple assignment. The split method splits the string into an array of values, using the space as a delimiter. The two assignable entities on the left-hand side will be assigned the respective values resulting on the right-hand side.

The if statement that follows uses a simple regex to determine whether the number is valid; if the string fails to match a pattern consisting of an optional minus sign followed by one or more digits, it is an invalid number (for our purposes), and the program exits. Note that the if statement is terminated by the keyword end; though it was not needed here, we could have had an else clause before the end. The keyword then is optional; we tend not to use it in this book.

The to_f method is used to convert the string to a floating point number. We are actually assigning this floating point value back to temp, which originally held a string.

The case statement chooses between three alternatives—the cases in which the user specified a C, specified an F, or used an invalid scale. In the first two instances, a calculation is done; in the third, we print an error and exit.

Ruby's case statement, by the way, is far more general than the example shown here. There is no limitation on the data types, and the expressions used are all arbitrary and may even be ranges or regular expressions.

There is nothing mysterious about the computation. But consider the fact that the variables c and f are referenced first inside the branches of the case. There are no declarations as such in Ruby; since a variable only comes into existence when it is assigned, this means that when we fall through the case statement, only one of these variables actually has a valid value.

We use this fact to determine after the fact which branch was followed, so that we can do a slightly different output in each instance. Testing f for a nil is effectively a test of whether the variable has a meaningful value. We do this here only to show that it can be done; obviously two different print statements could be used inside the case statement if we wanted.

The perceptive reader will notice that we used only "local" variables here. This might be confusing since their scope certainly appears to cover the entire program. What is happening here is that the variables are all local to the *top level* of the program (written *toplevel* by some). The variables appear global because there are no lower-level contexts in a program this simple; but if we declared classes and methods, these top-level variables would not be accessible within those.

1.2.6 Looping and Branching

Let's spend some time looking at control structures. We have already seen the simple if statement and the if-modifier; there are also corresponding structures based on the keyword unless (which also has an optional else), as well as expression-oriented forms of if and unless. We summarize all of these in Table 1.1.

Table 1.1 Conditional Statements

"if" Form	"unless" Form
```if x < 5 then``` ``` statement1``` ```end```	```unless x >= 5 then``` ``` statement1``` ```end```
```if x < 5 then``` ``` statement1``` ```else``` ``` statement2``` ```end```	```unless x < 5 then``` ``` statement2``` ```else``` ``` statement1``` ```end```
```statement1 if y == 3```	```statement1 unless y != 3```
```x = if a>0 then b else c end```	```x = unless a<=0 then c else b end```

In Table 1.1, the if and unless forms that are on the same table row have exactly the same function. Note that the keyword then may always be omitted except in the final (expression-oriented) cases. Note also that the modifier forms (in the third row) cannot have an else clause.

The case statement in Ruby is more powerful than in most languages. This multi-way branch can even test for conditions other than equality—for example, a matched pattern. The test done by the case statement corresponds to the *case equality operator* (===), which has a behavior that varies from one object to another. Let's look at this example:

```
case "This is a character string."
  when "some value"
    puts "Branch 1"
  when "some other value"
    puts "Branch 2"
  when /char/
    puts "Branch 3"
  else
    puts "Branch 4"
end
```

The preceding code prints Branch 3. Why? It first tries to check for equality between the tested expression and one of the strings "some value" or "some other value"; this fails, so it proceeds. The third test is for the presence of a pattern within the tested expression; that pattern is there, so the test succeeds, and the third print statement is performed. The else clause always handles the default case in which none of the preceding tests succeeds.

If the tested expression is an integer, the compared value can be an integer range (for example, 3..8). In this case, the expression is tested for membership in that range. In all instances, the first successful branch will be taken.

As for looping mechanisms, Ruby has a rich set. The while and until control structures are both pretest loops, and both work as expected: One specifies a continuation condition for the loop, and the other specifies a termination condition. They also occur in "modifier" form such as if and unless. There is also the loop method of the Kernel module (by default an infinite loop), and there are iterators associated with various classes.

The examples in Table 1.2 assume an array called list, defined something like this: list = %w[alpha bravo charlie delta echo]; they all step through the array and write out each element.

Table 1.2   Looping Constructs

```
# Loop 1 (while)
i=0
while i < list.size do
  print "#{list[i]} "
  i += 1
end
```

```
# Loop 2 (until)
i=0
until i == list.size do
  print "#{list[i]} "
  i += 1
end
```

```
# Loop 3 (for)
for x in list do
  print "#{x} "
end
```

```
# Loop 4 ('each' iterator)
list.each do |x|
  print "#{x} "
end
```

```
# Loop 5 ('loop' method)
i=0
n=list.size-1
loop do
  print "#{list[i]} "
  i += 1
  break if i > n
end
```

```
# Loop 6 ('loop' method)
i=0
n=list.size-1
loop do
  print "#{list[i]} "
  i += 1
  break unless i <= n
end
```

```
# Loop 7 ('times' iterator)
n=list.size
n.times do |i|
  print "#{list[i]} "
end
```

```
# Loop 8 ('upto' iterator)
n=list.size-1
0.upto(n) do |i|
  print "#{list[i]} "
end
```

```
# Loop 9 (for)
n=list.size-1
for
  i in 0..n do
  print "#{list[i]} "
end
```

```
# Loop 10 ('each_index')
list.each_index do |x|
  print "#{list[x]} "
end
```

Let's examine these in detail. Loops 1 and 2 are the "standard" forms of the while and until loops; they behave essentially the same, but their conditions are negations of each other. Loops 3 and 4 are the same thing in "post-test" versions; the test is performed at the end of the loop rather than at the beginning. Note that the use of begin and end in this context is strictly a kludge or hack; what is really happening is that a begin/end block (used for exception handling) is followed by a while or until modifier. For someone really wanting a post-test loop, however, this is effectively the same.

Loops 3 and 4 are arguably the "proper" way to write this loop. Note the simplicity of these two compared with the others; there is no explicit initialization and no explicit test or increment. This is because an array "knows" its own size, and the standard iterator each (loop 6) handles such details automatically. Indeed, loop 3 is merely an indirect reference to this same iterator because the for loop works for any object having the iterator each defined. The for loop is only a shorthand for a call to each; such a shorthand is frequently called "syntax sugar" because it offers a more convenient alternative to another syntactic form.

Loops 5 and 6 both use the loop construct; as we said previously, loop looks like a keyword introducing a control structure, but it is really a method of the module Kernel, not a control structure at all.

Loops 7 and 8 take advantage of the fact that the array has a numeric index; the times iterator executes a specified number of times, and the upto iterator carries its parameter up to the specified value. Neither of these is truly suitable for this instance.

Loop 9 is a for loop that operates specifically on the index values, using a range, and loop 10 likewise uses the each_index iterator to run through the list of array indices.

In the preceding examples, we have not laid enough emphasis on the "modifier" form of the while and until loops. These are frequently useful, and they have the virtue of being concise. The following are additional examples, both of which mean the same thing:

```
perform_task() until finished

perform_task() while not finished
```

Another fact is largely ignored in Table 1.2: Loops do not always run smoothly from beginning to end, in a predictable number of iterations, or ending in a single predictable way. We need ways to control these loops further.

The first way is the `break` keyword, shown in loops 5 and 6 above. This is used to "break out" of a loop; in the case of nested loops, only the innermost one is halted. This will be intuitive for C programmers.

The keyword `retry` is used in two situations—in the context of an iterator and in the context of a begin/end block (exception handling). Within the body of any iterator (or `for` loop), it forces the iterator to restart, re-evaluating any arguments passed to the iterator. Note that it does not work for loops in general (`while` and `until`).

The `redo` keyword is the generalized form of `retry` for loops. It works for `while` and `until` loops just as `retry` works for iterators.

The `next` keyword effectively jumps to the end of the innermost loop and resumes execution from that point. It works for any loop or iterator.

The iterator is an important concept in Ruby, as we have already seen. What we have not seen is that the language allows user-defined iterators in addition to the predefined ones.

The default iterator for any object is called `each`. This is significant partly because it allows the `for` loop to be used. But iterators may be given different names and used for varying purposes.

As a crude example, consider this multipurpose iterator, which mimics a post-test loop (like C's do-while or Pascal's repeat-until):

```
def repeat(condition)
  yield
  retry if not condition
end
```

In this example, the keyword `yield` is used to call the block that is specified when the iterator is called in this way:

```
j=0
repeat (j >= 10) do
  j+=1
  puts j
end
```

It is also possible to pass parameters via `yield`, which will be substituted into the block's parameter list (between vertical bars). As a somewhat contrived example, the

following iterator does nothing but generate the integers from 1 to 10, and the call of
the iterator generates the first ten cubes:

```
def my_sequence
  for i in 1..10 do
    yield i
  end
end


my_sequence { |x| puts x**3 }
```

Note that do and end may be substituted for the braces that delimit a block. There
are differences, but they are fairly subtle.

1.2.7   Exceptions

Like many other modern programming languages, Ruby supports *exceptions*.

Exceptions are a means of handling errors that has significant advantages over
older methods. Return codes are avoidable, as is the "spaghetti logic" that results from
checking them, and the code that detects the error can be distinguished from the code
that knows how to handle the error (since these are often separate anyway).

The raise statement raises an exception. Note that raise is not a reserved word
but a method of the module Kernel. (There is an alias named fail.)

```
raise                                      # Example 1
raise "Some error message"                 # Example 2
raise ArgumentError                        # Example 3
raise ArgumentError, "Bad data"            # Example 4
raise ArgumentError.new("Bad data")        # Example 5
raise ArgumentError, "Bad data", caller[0] # Example 6
```

In the first example in the preceding code, the last exception encountered is re-
raised. In example 2, a RuntimeError (the default error) is created using the message
Some error message.

In example 3, an ArgumentError is raised; in example 4, this same error is raised
with the message Bad data associated with it. Example 5 behaves exactly the same as

example 4. Finally, example 6 adds traceback information of the form `"filename:line"` or `"filename:line:in `method'"` (as stored in the `caller` array).

Now, how do we handle exceptions in Ruby? The `begin-end` block is used for this purpose. The simplest form is a `begin-end` block with nothing but our code inside:

```ruby
begin
  # No real purpose.
  # ...
end
```

This is of no value in catching errors. The block, however, may have one or more rescue clauses in it. If an error occurs at any point in the code, between `begin` and `rescue`, control will be passed immediately to the appropriate `rescue` clause.

```ruby
begin
  x = Math.sqrt(y/z)
  # ...
rescue ArgumentError
  puts "Error taking square root."
rescue ZeroDivisionError
  puts "Attempted division by zero."
end
```

Essentially the same thing can be accomplished by this fragment:

```ruby
begin
  x = Math.sqrt(y/z)
  # ...
rescue => err
  puts err
end
```

Here the variable `err` is used to store the value of the exception; printing it causes it to be translated to some meaningful character string. Note that since the error type is not specified, the `rescue` clause will catch any descendant of `StandardError`. The notation `rescue => variable` can be used with or without an error type before the `=>` symbol.

In the event that error types are specified, it may be that an exception does not match any of these types. For that situation, we are allowed to use an else clause after all the rescue clauses.

```
begin
  # Error-prone code...
rescue Type1
  # ...
rescue Type2
  # ...
else
  # Other exceptions...
end
```

In many cases, we want to do some kind of recovery. In that event, the keyword retry (within the body of a rescue clause) restarts the begin block and tries those operations again:

```
begin
  # Error-prone code...
rescue
  # Attempt recovery...
  retry  # Now try again
end
```

Finally, it is sometimes necessary to write code that "cleans up" after a begin-end block. In the event this is necessary, an ensure clause can be specified:

```
begin
  # Error-prone code...
rescue
  # Handle exceptions
ensure
  # This code is always executed
end
```

The code in an ensure clause is always executed before the begin-end block exits. This happens regardless of whether an exception occurred.

Exceptions may be caught in two other ways. First, there is a modifier form of the rescue clause:

```
x = a/b rescue puts("Division by zero!")
```

In addition, the body of a method definition is an implicit begin-end block; the begin is omitted, and the entire body of the method is subject to exception handling, ending with the end of the method:

```
def some_method
  # Code...
rescue
  # Recovery...
end
```

This sums up the discussion of exception handling as well as the discussion of fundamental syntax and semantics.

There are numerous aspects of Ruby we have not discussed here. The rest of this chapter is devoted to the more advanced features of the language, including a collection of Ruby lore that will help the intermediate programmer learn to "think in Ruby."

1.3 OOP in Ruby

Ruby has all the elements more generally associated with OOP languages, such as objects with encapsulation and data hiding, methods with polymorphism and over-riding, and classes with hierarchy and inheritance. It goes further and adds limited metaclass features, singleton methods, modules, and mixins.

Similar concepts are known by other names in other OOP languages, but concepts of the same name may have subtle differences from one language to another. This section elaborates on the Ruby understanding and usage of these elements of OOP.

1.3.1 Objects

In Ruby, all numbers, strings, arrays, regular expressions, and many other entities are actually objects. Work is done by executing the methods belonging to the object:

```
3.succ                # 4
"abc".upcase          # "ABC"
[2,1,5,3,4].sort      # [1,2,3,4,5]
someObject.someMethod # some result
```

In Ruby, *every* object is an instance of some class; the class contains the implementation of the methods:

```
"abc".class        # String
"abc".class.class  # Class
```

In addition to encapsulating its own attributes and operations, an object in Ruby has an identity:

```
"abc".object_id    # 53744407
```

This object ID is usually of limited usefulness to the programmer.

1.3.2   Built-in Classes

More than 30 built-in classes are predefined in the Ruby class hierarchy. Like many other OOP languages, Ruby does not allow multiple inheritance, but that does not necessarily make it any less powerful. Modern OO languages frequently follow the single inheritance model. Ruby does support modules and mixins, which are discussed in the next section. It also implements object IDs, as we just saw, which support the implementation of persistent, distributed, and relocatable objects.

To create an object from an existing class, the new method is typically used:

```
myFile = File.new("textfile.txt","w")
myString = String.new("This is a string object")
```

This is not always explicitly required, however. In particular, you would not normally bother to call new for a String object as in the previous example:

```
yourString = "This is also a string object"
aNumber = 5  # new not needed here, either
```

Variables are used to hold references to objects. As previously mentioned, variables themselves have no type, nor are they objects themselves; they are simply references to objects.

```
x = "abc"
```

An exception to this is that small immutable objects of some built-in classes, such as Fixnum, are copied directly into the variables that refer to them. (These objects are no bigger than pointers, and it is more efficient to deal with them in this way.) In this case assignment makes a copy of the object, and the heap is not used.

Variable assignment causes object references to be shared.

```
y = "abc"
x = y
x            # "abc"
```

After executing x = y, variables x and y both refer to the same object:

```
x.object_id      # 53732208
y.object_id      # 53732208
```

If the object is mutable, a modification done to one variable will be reflected in the other:

```
x.gsub!(/a/,"x")
y                # "xbc"
```

Reassigning one of these variables has no effect on the other, however:

```
# Continuing previous example...
x = "abc"

y                     # still has value "xbc"
```

A mutable object can be made immutable using the freeze method:

```
x.freeze
x.gsub!(/b/,"y")   # Error!
```

A symbol in Ruby refers to a variable by name rather than by reference. In many cases, it may not refer to an identifier at all but rather acts like a kind of immutable string. A symbol can be converted to a string with the to_s method.

```
Hearts   = :Hearts    # This is one way of assigning
Clubs    = :Clubs     # unique values to constants,
Diamonds = :Diamonds  # somewhat like an enumeration
Spades   = :Spades    # in Pascal or C.

puts Hearts.to_s      # Prints "Hearts"
```

The "enumeration" trick we reference here probably made more sense in the earlier days of Ruby, when there was no Symbol class, and applying the colon to an identifier yielded a simple integer. If you do use this trick, don't rely on the actual symbol values being regular or predictable; just use them as constants whose value is irrelevant.

1.3.3   Modules and Mixins

Many built-in methods are available from class ancestors. Of special note are the Kernel methods mixed-in to the Object superclass; because Object is universally available, the methods added to it from Kernel are also universally available. These methods form an important part of Ruby.

The terms *module* and *mixin* are nearly synonymous. A module is a collection of methods and constants that is external to the Ruby program. It can be used simply for namespace management, but the most common use of a module is to have its features "mixed" into a class (by using include). In this case, it is used as a mixin.

This term was apparently borrowed most directly from Python. (It is sometimes written as *mix-in*; but we write it as a single word.) It is worth noting that some LISP variants have had this feature for more than two decades.

Do not confuse this usage of the term *module* with another usage common in computing. A Ruby module is not an external source or binary file (though it may be stored in one of these). A Ruby module instead is an OOP abstraction similar to a class.

An example of using a module for namespace management is the frequent use of the Math module. To use the definition of *pi*, for example, it is not necessary to include the Math module; you can simply use Math::PI as the constant.

A mixin is a way of getting some of the benefits of multiple inheritance without dealing with all the difficulties. It can be considered a restricted form of multiple inheritance, but the language creator Matz has called it *single inheritance with implementation sharing*.

Note that include appends features of a namespace (a module) to the current space; the extend method appends functions of a module to an object. With include, the module's methods become available as instance methods; with extend, they become available as class methods.

We should mention that load and require do not really relate to modules but rather to nonmodule Ruby sources and binaries (statically or dynamically loadable). A load operation essentially reads a file and inserts it at the current point in the source file so that its definitions become available at that point. A require operation is similar to a load, but it will not load a file if it has already been loaded.

The Ruby novice, especially from a C background, may be tripped up by `require` and `include`, which are basically unrelated to each other. You may easily find yourself doing a `require` followed by an `include` to use some externally stored module.

1.3.4   Creating Classes

Ruby has numerous built-in classes, and additional classes may be defined in a Ruby program. To define a new class, the following construct is used:

```
class ClassName
# ...
end
```

The name of the class is itself a global constant and thus must begin with an uppercase letter. The class definition can contain class constants, class variables, class methods, instance variables, and instance methods. Class data are available to all objects of the class, whereas instance data are available only to the one object.

By the way: Classes in Ruby do not *strictly speaking* have names. The "name" of a class is only a constant that is a reference to an object of type `Class` (since in Ruby, `Class` is a class). There can certainly be more than one constant referring to a class, and these can be assigned to variables just as we can with any other object (since in Ruby, `Class` is an object). If all this confuses you, don't worry about it. For the sake of convenience, the novice can think of a Ruby class name as being like a C++ class name.

Here we define a simple class.

```
class Friend
  @@myname = "Fred" # a class variable

  def initialize(name, sex, phone)
    @name, @sex, @phone = name, sex, phone
    # These are instance variables
  end

  def hello    # an instance method
    puts "Hi, I'm #{@name}."
  end

  def Friend.our_common_friend   # a class method
    puts "We are all friends of #{@@myname}."
  end

end
```

```
f1 = Friend.new("Susan","F","555-0123")
f2 = Friend.new("Tom","M","555-4567")

f1.hello                   # Hi, I'm Susan.
f2.hello                   # Hi, I'm Tom.
Friend.our_common_friend   # We are all friends of Fred.
```

Since class-level data is accessible throughout the class, it can be initialized at the time the class is defined. If a method named initialize is defined, it is guaranteed to be executed right after an instance is allocated. The initialize is similar to the traditional concept of a constructor, but it does not have to handle memory allocation. Allocation is handled internally by new, and deallocation is handled transparently by the garbage collector.

Now consider this fragment, and pay attention to the getmyvar, setmyvar, and myvar= methods:

```
class MyClass

  NAME = "Class Name" # class constant
  @@count = 0 #  Initialize a class variable
  def initialize # called when object is allocated
    @@count += 1
    @myvar = 10
  end

  def MyClass.getcount # class method
    @@count # class variable
  end

  def getcount # instance returns class variable!
    @@count # class variable
  end

  def getmyvar # instance method
    @myvar # instance variable
  end

  def setmyvar(val) # instance method sets @myvar
    @myvar = val
  end
```

```
  def myvar=(val) # Another way to set @myvar
    @myvar = val
  end
end

foo = MyClass.new # @myvar is 10
foo.setmyvar 20 # @myvar is 20
foo.myvar = 30 # @myvar is 30
```

Here we see that `getmyvar` returns the value of `@myvar`, and `setmyvar` sets it. (In the terminology of many programmers, these would be referred to as a *getter* and a *setter*.) These work fine, but they do not exemplify the Ruby way of doing things. The method `myvar=` looks like assignment overloading (though strictly speaking, it isn't); it is a better replacement for `setmyvar`, but there is a better way yet.

The class called `Module` contains methods called `attr`, `attr_accessor`, `attr_reader`, and `attr_writer`. These can be used (with symbols as parameters) to automatically handle controlled access to the instance data. For example, the three methods `getmyvar`, `setmyvar`, and `myvar=` can be replaced by a single line in the class definition:

```
attr_accessor :myvar
```

This creates a method `myvar` that returns the value of `@myvar` and a method `myvar=` that enables the setting of the same variable. Methods `attr_reader` and `attr_writer` create read-only and write-only versions of an attribute, respectively.

Within the instance methods of a class, the pseudovariable `self` can be used as needed. This is only a reference to the current receiver, the object on which the instance method is invoked.

The modifying methods `private`, `protected`, and `public` can be used to control the visibility of methods in a class. (Instance variables are always private and inaccessible from outside the class except by means of accessors.) Each of these modifiers takes a symbol like `:foo` as a parameter; if this is omitted, the modifier applies to all subsequent definitions in the class. For example:

```
class MyClass

  def method1
  # ...
  end
```

```
      def method2
      # ...
      end

      def method3
      # ...
      end


      private :method1
      public

      :method2
      protected :method3

      private

      def my_method
      # ...
      end

      def another_method
      # ...
      end

    end
```

In the preceding class, method1 will be private, method2 will be public, and method3 will be protected. Because of the private method with no parameters, both my_method and another_method will be private.

The public access level is self-explanatory; there are no restrictions on access or visibility. The private level means that the method is accessible only within the class or its subclasses, and it is callable only in "function form"—with self, implicit or explicit, as a receiver. The protected level means that a method is callable only from within its class, but unlike a private method, it can be called with a receiver other than self.

The default visibility for the methods defined in a class is public. The exception is the instance initializing method initialize. Methods defined at the top level are also public by default; if they are private, they can be called only in function form (as, for example, the methods defined in Object).

Ruby classes are themselves objects, being instances of the metaclass `Class`. Ruby classes are always concrete; there are no abstract classes. However, it is theoretically possible to implement abstract classes in Ruby if you really want to do so.

The class `Object` is at the root of the hierarchy. It provides all the methods defined in the built-in `Kernel` module.

To create a class that inherits from another class, define it in this way:

```
class MyClass < OtherClass
  # ...
end
```

In addition to using built-in methods, it is only natural to define your own and also to redefine and override existing ones. When you define a method with the same name as an existing one, the previous method is overridden. If a method needs to call the "parent" method that it overrides (a frequent occurrence), the keyword `super` can be used for this purpose.

Operator overloading is not strictly an OOP feature, but it is familiar to C++ programmers and certain others. Because most operators in Ruby are simply methods anyway, it should come as no surprise that these operators can be overridden or defined for user-defined classes. Overriding the meaning of an operator for an existing class may be rare, but it is common to want to define operators for new classes.

It is possible to create aliases or synonyms for methods. The syntax (used inside a class definition) is as follows:

```
alias newname oldname
```

The number of parameters will be the same as for the old name, and it will be called in the same way. Note that there is no comma here; `alias` is not a method name, but a keyword. There is a method called `alias_method`, which behaves similarly; like all other methods, its parameters *do* require separation by commas.

1.3.5   Methods and Attributes

As we've seen, methods are typically used with simple class instances and variables by separating the receiver from the method with a period (`receiver.method`). In the case of method names that are punctuation, the period is omitted. Methods can take arguments:

```
Time.mktime(2000, "Aug", 24, 16, 0)
```

Because every expression returns a value, method calls may typically be chained or stacked:

```
3.succ.to_s
/(x.z).*?(x.z).*?/.match("x1z_1a3_x2z_1b3_").to_a[1..3]
3+2.succ
```

Note that there can be problems if the cumulative expression is of a type that does not support that particular method. Specifically, some methods return `nil` under certain conditions, and this usually causes any methods tacked onto that result to fail. (Of course, `nil` is an object in its own right, but it will not have all the same methods that, for example, an array would have.)

Certain methods may have blocks passed to them. This is true of all iterators, whether built-in or user-defined. A block is usually passed as a `do-end` block or a brace-delimited block; it is not treated like the other parameters preceding it, if any. See especially the `File.open` example:

```
my_array.each do |x|
   some_action
end

File.open(filename) { |f| some_action }
```

Named parameters will be supported in a later Ruby version but are not supported at the time of this writing. These are called *keyword arguments* in the Python realm; the concept dates back at least as far as the Ada language.

Methods may take a variable number of arguments:

```
receiver.method(arg1, *more_args)
```

In this case, the method called treats `more_args` as an array that it deals with as it would any other array. In fact, an asterisk in the list of formal parameters (on the last or only parameter) can likewise "collapse" a sequence of actual parameters into an array:

```
def mymethod(a, b, *c)
   print a, b
```

```
    c.each do |x| print x end
  end

  mymethod(1,2,3,4,5,6,7)

  # a=1, b=2, c=[3,4,5,6,7]
```

Ruby has the capability to define methods on a per-object basis (rather than per-class). Such methods are called *singletons*; they belong solely to that object and have no effect on its class or superclasses. As an example, this might be useful in programming a GUI; you can define a button action for a widget by defining a singleton method for the button object.

Here is an example of defining a singleton method on a string object:

```
str = "Hello, world!"
str2 = "Goodbye!"

def str.spell
  self.split(/./).join("-")
end

str.spell      # "H-e-l-l-o-,- -w-o-r-l-d-!"
str2.spell     # error!
```

Be aware that the method is defined on the object, not the variable.

It is theoretically possible to create a prototype-based object system using singleton methods. This is a less traditional form of OOP without classes. The basic structuring mechanism is to construct a new object using an existing object as a delegate; the new object is exactly like the old object except for things that are overridden. This enables you to build prototype/delegation-based systems rather than inheritance based, and, although we do not have experience in this area, we do feel that this demonstrates the power of Ruby.

1.4   Dynamic Aspects of Ruby

Ruby is a dynamic language in the sense that objects and classes may be altered at runtime. Ruby has the capability to construct and evaluate pieces of code in the course of executing the existing statically coded program. It has a sophisticated reflection API that makes it more "self-aware"; this enables the easy creation of debuggers, profilers, and similar tools and also makes certain advanced coding techniques possible.

This is perhaps the most difficult area a programmer will encounter in learning Ruby. In this section we briefly examine some of the implications of Ruby's dynamic nature.

1.4.1 Coding at Runtime

We have already mentioned load and require. But it is important to realize that these are not built-in statements or control structures or anything of that nature; they are actual methods. Therefore it is possible to call them with variables or expressions as parameters or to call them conditionally. Contrast with this the #include directive in C or C++, which is evaluated and acted on at compile time.

Code can be constructed piecemeal and evaluated. As another contrived example, consider this calculate method and the code calling it:

```
def calculate(op1, operator, op2)
  string = op1.to_s + operator + op2.to_s
    # operator is assumed to be a string; make one big
    # string of it and the two operands
  eval(string)    # Evaluate and return a value
end

@alpha = 25
@beta = 12

puts calculate(2, "+", 2)          # Prints 4
puts calculate(5, "*", "@alpha")   # Prints 125
puts calculate("@beta", "**", 3)   # Prints 1728
```

As an even more extreme example, the following code prompts the user for a method name and a single line of code; then it actually defines the method and calls it:

```
puts "Method name: "
meth_name = gets
puts "Line of code: "
code = gets

string = %[def #{meth_name}\n #{code}\n end]    # Build a string
eval(string)                                    # Define the method
eval(meth_name)                                 # Call the method
```

Frequently programmers want to code for different platforms or circumstances and still maintain only a single code base. In such a case, a C programmer would use `#ifdef` directives, but in Ruby, definitions are executed. There is no "compile time," and everything is dynamic rather than static. So if we want to make some kind of decision like this, we can simply evaluate a flag at runtime:

```
if platform == Windows
  action1
elsif platform == Linux
  action2
else
  default_action
end
```

Of course, there is a small runtime penalty for coding in this way since the flag may be tested many times in the course of execution. But this example does essentially the same thing, enclosing the platform-dependent code in a method whose name is the same across all platforms:

```
if platform == Windows
  def my_action
    action1
  end
elsif platform == Linux
  def my_action
    action2
  end
else
  def my_action
    default_action
  end
end
```

In this way, the same result is achieved, but the flag is only evaluated *once*; when the user's code calls `my_action`, it will already have been defined appropriately.

1.4.2   Reflection

Languages such as Smalltalk, LISP, and Java implement (to varying degrees) the notion of a *reflective* programming language—one in which the active environment can query the objects that define itself and extend or modify them at runtime.

Ruby allows reflection quite extensively but does not go as far as Smalltalk, which even represents control structures as objects. Ruby control structures and blocks are *not* objects (A `Proc` object can be used to "objectify" a block, but control structures are never objects.)

The keyword `defined?` (with an appended question mark) may be used to determine whether an identifier name is in use:

```
if defined? some_var
  puts "some_var = #{some_var}"
else
  puts "The variable some_var is not known."
end
```

Similarly, the method `respond_to?` determines whether an object can respond to the specified method call (that is, whether that method is defined for that object). The `respond_to?` method is defined in class `Object`.

Ruby supports runtime type information in a radical way. The type (or class) of an object can be determined at runtime using the method `type` (defined in `Object`). Similarly, `is_a?` tells whether an object is of a certain class (including the superclasses); `kind_of?` is an alias. For example:

```
puts "abc".class ""# Prints String
puts 345.class # Prints Fixnum
rover = Dog.new

print rover.class # Prints Dog

if rover.is_a? Dog
  puts "Of course he is."
end

if rover.kind_of? Dog
  puts "Yes, still a dog."
end

if rover.is_a? Animal
  puts "Yes, he's an animal, too."
end
```

It is possible to retrieve an exhaustive list of all the methods that can be invoked for a given object; this is done by using the methods method, defined in Object. There are also variations such as private_instance_methods, public_instance_methods, and so on.

Similarly, you can determine the class variables and instance variables associated with an object. By the nature of OOP, the lists of methods and variables include the entities defined not only in the object's class but also in its superclasses. The Module class has a method constants used to list the constants defined within a module.

The class Module has a method ancestors that returns a list of modules included in the given module. This list is self-inclusive; Mod.ancestors will always have at least Mod in the list. This list comprises not only parent classes (through inheritance) but "parent" modules (through module inclusion).

The class Object has a method superclass that returns the superclass of the object or returns nil. Because Object itself is the only object without a superclass, it is the only case in which nil will be returned.

The ObjectSpace module is used to access any and all "living" objects. The method _idtoref can be used to convert an object ID to an object reference; it can be considered the inverse of the colon notation. ObjectSpace also has an iterator called each_object that iterates over all the objects currently in existence, including many that you will not otherwise explicitly know about. (Remember that certain small immutable objects, such as objects of class Fixnum, NilClass, TrueClass, and FalseClass are not kept on the stack for optimization reasons.)

1.4.3   Missing Methods

When a method is invoked (myobject.mymethod), Ruby first searches for the named method according to this search order:

1. Singleton methods in the receiver myobject

2. Methods defined in myobject's class

3. Methods defined among myobject's ancestors

If the method mymethod is not found, Ruby searches for a default method called method_missing. If this method is defined, it is passed the name of the missing method (as a symbol) and all the parameters that were passed to the nonexistent mymethod. This facility can be used for the dynamic handling of unknown messages sent at runtime.

1.4.4   Garbage Collection (GC)

Managing memory on a low level is hard and error prone, especially in a dynamic environment such as Ruby; having a garbage collection facility is a significant advantage. In languages such as C++, memory allocation and deallocation are handled by the programmer; in more recent languages such as Java, memory is reclaimed (when objects go out of scope) by a garbage collector.

Memory management done by the programmer is the source of two of the most common kinds of bugs. If an object is freed while still being referenced, a later access may find the memory in an inconsistent state. These so-called *dangling pointers* are difficult to track down because they often cause errors in code that is far removed from the offending statement. *Memory leaks* are caused when an object is not freed even though there are no references to it. Programs with this bug typically use up more and more memory until they crash; this kind of error is also difficult to find. Ruby uses a GC facility that tracks down unused objects and reclaims the storage that was allocated to them. For those who care about such things, Ruby's GC is done using a *mark and sweep* algorithm rather than reference counting (which frequently has difficulties with recursive structures).

Certain performance penalties may be associated with garbage collection. There are some limited controls in the GC module so that the programmer can tailor garbage collection to the needs of the individual program. We can also define an object *finalizer*, but this is an advanced topic (see section 11.3.14, "Defining Finalizers for Objects").

1.5   Training Your Intuition: Things to Remember

It may truly be said that "everything is intuitive once you understand it." This verity is the heart of this section because Ruby has many features and personality quirks that may be different from what the traditional programmer is used to.

Some readers may feel their time is wasted by a reiteration of some of these points; if that is the case for you, you are free to skip the paragraphs that seem obvious to you. Programmers' backgrounds vary widely; an old-time C hacker and a Smalltalk guru will each approach Ruby from different viewpoints. We hope, however, that a perusal of these following paragraphs will assist many readers in following what some call *the Ruby Way*.

1.5.1 Syntax Issues

The Ruby parser is complex and relatively forgiving. It tries to make sense out of what it finds instead of forcing the programmer into slavishly following a set of rules. However, this behavior may take some getting used to. Here is a list of things to know about Ruby syntax:

- Parentheses are usually optional with a method call. These calls are all valid:

```
foobar
foobar()
foobar(a,b,c)
foobar a, b, c
```

- Given that parentheses are optional, what does x y z mean, if anything? As it turns out, this means, "Invoke method y, passing z as a parameter, and pass the result as a parameter to method x." In short, the statement x(y(z)) means the same thing.
  This behavior will change in the future. Refer to the discussion of poetry mode in section 1.6 "Ruby Jargon and Slang" later in the chapter.

- Let's try to pass a hash to a method:

```
my_method {a=>1, b=>2}
```

This results in a syntax error, because the left brace is seen as the start of a block. In this instance, parentheses are necessary:

```
my_method({a=>1, b=>2})
```

- Now let's suppose that the hash is the *only* parameter (or the last parameter) to a method. Ruby forgivingly lets us omit the braces:

```
my_method(a=>1, b=>2)
```

Some people might think that this looks like a method invocation with named parameters. Really it isn't, though it could be used as such.

- There are other cases in which blank spaces are semi-significant. For example, these four expressions may all seem to mean the same:

```
x = y + z
x = y+z
x = y+ z
x = y +z
```

  And in fact, the first three do mean the same. However, in the fourth case, the parser thinks that y is a method call and +z is a parameter passed to it! It will then give an error message for that line if there is no method named y. The moral is to use blank spaces in a reasonable way.

- Similarly, x = y*z is a multiplication of y and z, whereas x = y *z is an invocation of method y, passing an expansion of array z as a parameter.

- In constructing identifiers, the underscore is considered to be lowercase. Thus an identifier may start with an underscore, but it will *not* be a constant even if the next letter is uppercase.

- In linear nested-if statements, the keyword elsif is used rather than else if or elif as in some languages.

- Keywords in Ruby are not really reserved words. When a method is called with a receiver (or in other cases where there is no ambiguity), a keyword may be used as a method name. Do this with caution, remembering that programs should be readable by humans.

- The keyword then is optional (in if and case statements). Those who want to use it for readability may do so. The same is true for do in while and until loops.

- The question mark and exclamation point are not really part of the identifier that they modify but should be considered suffixes. Thus we see that although, for example, chop and chop! are considered different identifiers, it is not permissible to use these characters in any other position in the word. Likewise, we use defined? in Ruby, but defined is the keyword.

- Inside a string, the pound sign (#) is used to signal expressions to be evaluated. That means that in some circumstances, when a pound sign occurs in a string, it has to be escaped with a backslash, but this is *only* when the next character is a { (left brace), $ (dollar sign), or @ (at sign).

- Because of the fact that the question mark may be appended to an identifier, care should be taken with spacing around the ternary operator. For example, suppose we have a variable my_flag, which stores either true or false. Then the first line of code shown here will be correct, but the second will give a syntax error:

```
x = my_flag ? 23 : 45    # OK
x = my_flag? 23 : 45     # Syntax error
```

- The ending marker =end for embedded documentation should not be considered a token. It marks the entire line and thus any characters on the rest of that line are not considered part of the program text but belong to the embedded document.

- There are no arbitrary blocks in Ruby; that is, you can't start a block whenever you feel like it as in C. Blocks are allowed only where they are needed—for example, attached to an iterator. The exception is the begin-end block, which can be used basically anywhere.

- Remember that the keywords BEGIN and END are completely different from the begin and end keywords.

- When strings bump together (static concatenation), the concatenation is of a lower precedence than a method call. For example:

```
str = "First " 'second'.center(20)      # Examples 1 and 2
str = "First " + 'second'.center(20)     # are the same.
str = "First second".center(20)          # Examples 3 and 4
str = ("First " + 'second').center(20)   # are the same.
```

- Ruby has several pseudovariables, which look like local variables but really serve specialized purposes. These are self, nil, true, false, __FILE__, and __LINE__.

1.5.2   Perspectives in Programming

Presumably everyone who knows Ruby (at this point in time) has been a student or user of other languages in the past. This of course makes learning Ruby easy in the sense that numerous features in Ruby are just like the corresponding features in other languages. On the other hand, the programmer may be lulled into a false sense of security by some of the familiar constructs in Ruby and may draw unwarranted conclusions based on past experience—which we might term "geek baggage."

Many people are coming to Ruby from Smalltalk, Perl, C/C++, and various other languages. Their presuppositions and expectations may all vary somewhat, but they will always be present. For this reason, we discuss here a few of the things that some programmers may "trip over" in using Ruby:

- A character in Ruby truly is an integer. It is not a type of its own, as in Pascal, and is not the same as a string of length 1. *This is slated to change in the near future so that a character constant will be much the same as a string. As of the time of this writing, this has not happened yet.* Consider the following code fragment:

```
x = "Hello"
y = ?A
puts "x[0] = #{x[0]}"    # Prints: x[0] = 72
puts "y = #{y}"          # Prints: y = 65
if y == "A"              # Prints: no
  puts "yes"
else
  puts "no"
end
```

- There is no Boolean type such as many languages have. `TrueClass` and `FalseClass` are distinct classes, and their only instantiations are `true` and `false`.

- Many of Ruby's operators are similar or identical to those in C. Two notable exceptions are the increment and decrement operators (++ and --). These are not available in Ruby, neither in "pre" nor "post" forms.

- The modulus operator is known to work somewhat differently in different languages with respect to negative numbers. The two sides of this argument are beyond the scope of this book; Ruby's behavior is as follows:

```
puts (5 % 3)      # Prints 2
puts (-5 % 3)     # Prints 1
puts (5 % -3)     # Prints -1
puts (-5 % -3)    # Prints -2
```

- Some may be used to thinking that a false value may be represented as a zero, a null string, a null character, or various other things. But in Ruby, all of these are true; in fact, *everything is true* except `false` and `nil`.

- In Ruby, variables don't have classes; only values have classes.

- There are no declarations of variables in Ruby. It is good practice, however, to assign `nil` to a variable initially. This certainly does not assign a type to the variable and does not truly initialize it, but it does inform the parser that this is a variable name rather than a method name.

- `ARGV[0]` is truly the first of the command-line parameters, numbering naturally from zero; it is not the file or script name preceding the parameters, like `argv[0]` in C.

- Most of Ruby's operators are really methods; the "punctuation" form of these methods is provided for familiarity and convenience. The first exception is the set of reflexive assignment operators (`+=`, `-=`, `*=`, and so on); the second exception is the following set: `= .. ... ! not && and || or != !~`.

- Like most (though not all) modern languages, Boolean operations are always short-circuited; that is, the evaluation of a Boolean expression stops as soon as its truth value is known. In a sequence of `or` operations, the first `true` will stop evaluation; in a string of `and` operations, the first `false` will stop evaluation.

- The prefix `@@` is used for class variables (which are associated with the class rather than the instance).

- `loop` is not a keyword; it is a `Kernel` method, not a control structure.

- Some may find the syntax of `unless-else` to be slightly unintuitive. Because `unless` is the opposite of `if`, the `else` clause will be executed if the condition is *true*.

- The simpler `Fixnum` type is passed as an immediate value and thus may not be changed from within methods. The same is true for `true`, `false`, and `nil`.

- Do not confuse the `&&` and `||` operators with the `&` and `|` operators. These are used as in C; the former are for Boolean operations, and the latter are for arithmetic or bitwise operations.

- The `and-or` operators have lower precedence than the `&&`-`||` operators. See the following code fragment:

```
a = true
b = false
c = true
d = true
a1 = a && b or c && d   # &&'s are done first
a2 = a && (b or c) && d # or is done first
puts a1                 # Prints false
puts a2                 # Prints true
```

- Additionally, be aware that the assignment "operator" has a *higher* precedence than the and and or operators! (This is also true for the reflexive assignment operators +=, -=, and the others.) For example, in the following code x = y or z looks like a normal assignment statement, but it is really a freestanding expression (equivalent to (x=y) or z, in fact). The third section shows a real assignment statement x = (y or z), which may be what the programmer really intended.

```
y = false
z = true

x = y or z     # = is done BEFORE or!
puts x         # Prints false

(x = y) or z   # Line 5: Same as previous
puts x         # Prints false

x = (y or z)   # or is done first
puts x         # Prints true
```

- Don't confuse object attributes and local variables. If you are accustomed to C++ or Java, you might forget this. The variable @my_var is an instance variable (or attribute) in the context of whatever class you are coding, but my_var, used in the same circumstance, is only a local variable within that context.

- Many languages have some kind of for loop, as does Ruby. The question sooner or later arises as to whether the index variable can be modified. Some languages do not allow the control variable to be modified at all (printing a warning or error either at compile time or runtime), and some will cheerfully allow the loop behavior to be altered in midstream by such a change. Ruby takes yet a third approach. When a variable is used as a for loop control variable, it is an ordinary variable and can be modified at will; however, such a modification does not affect the loop behavior! The for loop sequentially assigns the values to the variable on each iteration without regard for what may have happened to that variable inside the loop. For example, this loop will execute exactly 10 times and print the values 1 through 10:

```
for var in 1..10
  puts "var = #{var}"
  if var > 5
    var = var + 2
  end
end
```

- Variable names and method names are not always distinguishable "by eye" in the immediate context. How does the parser decide whether an identifier is a variable or a method? The rule is that if the parser sees the identifier being assigned a value prior to its being used, it will be considered a variable; otherwise, it is considered to be a method name. (Note also that the assignment does not have to be *executed* but only *seen* by the interpreter.)

1.5.3 Ruby's **case** Statement

Every modern language has some kind of multiway branch, such as the switch statement in C/C++ and Java or the case statement in Pascal. These serve basically the same purpose and function much the same in most languages.

Ruby's case statement is similar to these others, but on closer examination it is so unique that it makes C and Pascal look like close friends. The case statement in Ruby has no precise analogue in any other language that I am familiar with, and this makes it worth additional attention here.

We have already seen the syntax of this statement. We will concentrate here on its actual semantics:

- To begin with, consider the trivial case statement shown here. The expression shown is compared with the value, not surprisingly, and if they correspond, some_action is performed.

```
case expression
  when value
    some_action
end
```

  Ruby uses the special operator === (called the *relationship operator*) for this. This operator is also referred to (somewhat inappropriately) as the *case equality* operator. We say "inappropriately" because it does not always denote equality.

- Thus the preceding simple statement is equivalent to this statement:

```
if value === expression
  some_action
end
```

- However, do not confuse the relationship operator with the equality operator (==). They are utterly different, although their behavior may be the same in many circumstances. The relationship operator is defined differently for different classes and, for a given class, may behave differently for different operand types passed to it.

- Do not fall into the trap of thinking that the tested expression is the receiver and the value is passed as a parameter to it. The opposite is true (as we saw previously).

- This points up the fact that x === y is *not* typically the same as y === x! There will be situations in which this is true, but overall the relationship operator is not commutative. (That is why we do not favor the term *case equality operator*— because equality is always commutative.) In other words, reversing our original example, the following code does not behave the same way:

```
case value
  when expression
    some_action
end
```

- As an example, consider a string str and a pattern (regular expression) pat, which matches that string. The expression str =~ pat is true, just as in Perl. Because Ruby defines the opposite meaning for =~ in Regexp, you can also say that pat =~ str is true. Following this logic further, we find that (because of how Regexp defines ===) pat === str is also true. However, note that str === pat is *not* true. This means that this code fragment:

```
case "Hello"
  when /Hell/
    puts "We matched."
else
  puts "We didn't match."
end
```

does not do the same thing as this fragment:

```
case /Hell/
  when "Hello"
    puts "We matched."
else
  puts "We didn't match."
end
```

If this confuses you, just memorize the behavior. If it does not confuse you, so much the better.

- Programmers accustomed to C may be puzzled by the absence of `break` statements in the `case` statement; such a usage of `break` in Ruby is unnecessary (and illegal). This is due to the fact that "falling through" is rarely the desired behavior in a multiway branch. There is an implicit jump from each when-clause (or *case limb*, as it is sometimes called) to the end of the `case` statement. In this respect, Ruby's `case` statement resembles the one in Pascal.

- The values in each case limb are essentially arbitrary. They are not limited to any certain type. They need not be constants but can be variables or complex expressions. Ranges or multiple values can be associated with each case limb.

- Case limbs may have empty actions (null statements) associated with them. The values in the limbs need not be unique, but may overlap. Look at this example:

```ruby
case x
  when 0
  when 1..5
    puts "Second branch"
  when 5..10
    puts "Third branch"
else
  puts "Fourth branch"
end
```

Here a value of 0 for x will do nothing; a value of 5 will print Second branch, even though 5 is also included in the next limb.

- The fact that case limbs may overlap is a consequence of the fact that they are evaluated in sequence *and* that short-circuiting is done. In other words, if evaluation of the expressions in one limb results in success, the limbs that follow are never evaluated. Thus it is a bad idea for case limb expressions to have method calls that have side effects. (Of course, such calls are questionable in most circumstances anyhow.) Also, be aware that this behavior may mask runtime errors that would occur if expressions were evaluated. For example:

```ruby
case x
  when 1..10
    puts "First branch"
  when foobar()        # Possible side effects?
    puts "Second branch"
  when 5/0             # Dividing by zero!
    puts "Third branch"
```

```
else
  puts "Fourth branch"
end
```

As long as x is between 1 and 10, foobar() will not be called, and the expression 5/0 (which would naturally result in a runtime error) will not be evaluated.

1.5.4   Rubyisms and Idioms

Much of this material overlaps conceptually with the preceding pages. Don't worry too much about why we divided it as we did; many of these tidbits were difficult to classify or organize. Our most important motivation was simply to break the information into digestible chunks.

Ruby was designed to be consistent and orthogonal. But it is also complex, and so, like every language, it has its own set of idioms and quirks. We discuss some of these in the following list:

- alias can be used to give alternate names for global variables and methods.

- The numbered global variables $1, $2, $3, and so on, cannot be aliased.

- We do not recommend the use of the "special variables" such as $=, $_, $/, and the rest. Though they can sometimes make code more compact, they rarely make it any clearer; we use them sparingly in this book and recommend the same practice.

- Do not confuse the .. and ... range operators. The former is *inclusive* of the upper bound, and the latter is *exclusive*. For example, 5..10 includes the number 10, but 5...10 does not.

- There is a small detail relating to ranges that may cause confusion. Given a range m..n, the method end will return the endpoint of the range; its alias last will do the same thing. However, these methods will return the same value n for the range m...n, even though n is not included in the latter range. The method end_excluded? is provided to distinguish between these two situations.

- Do not confuse ranges with arrays. These two assignments are entirely different:

```
x = 1..5
x = [1, 2, 3, 4, 5]
```

However, there is a convenient method to_a for converting ranges to arrays. (Many other types also have such a method.)

- Often we want to assign a variable a value only if it does not already have a value. Because an unassigned variable has the value `nil`, we can do for example, `x = x || 5` shortened to `x ||= 5`. Beware that the value `false` will be overwritten just as `nil` will.

- In most languages, swapping two variables takes an additional temporary variable. In Ruby, multiple assignment makes this unnecessary: `x, y = y, x` will interchange the values of `x` and `y`.

- Keep a clear distinction in your mind between *class* and *instance*. For example, a class variable such as `@@foobar` has a classwide scope, but an instance variable such as `@foobar` has a separate existence in each object of the class.

- Similarly, a class method is associated with the class in which it is defined; it does not belong to any specific object and cannot be invoked as though it did. A class method is invoked with the name of a class, and an instance method is invoked with the name of an object.

- In writing about Ruby, the *pound notation* is sometimes used to indicate an instance method—for example, we say `File.chmod` to denote the class method `chmod` of class `File`, and `File#chmod` to denote the instance method that has the same name. This notation is not part of Ruby syntax but only Ruby folklore. We have tried to avoid it in this book.

- In Ruby, constants are not truly constant. They cannot be changed from within instance methods, but otherwise their values *can* be changed.

- In writing about Ruby, the word *toplevel* is common as both an adjective and a noun. We prefer to use *top level* as a noun and *top-level* as an adjective, but our meaning is the same as everyone else's.

- The keyword `yield` comes from CLU and may be misleading to some programmers. It is used within an iterator to invoke the block with which the iterator is called. It does not mean "yield" as in producing a result or returning a value but is more like the concept of "yielding a timeslice."

- The reflexive assignment operators `+=`, `-=`, and the rest, are not methods (nor are they really operators); they are only "syntax sugar" or "shorthand" for their longer forms. Thus, to say `x += y` is really identical to saying `x = x + y`, and if the `+` operator is overloaded, the `+=` operator is defined "automagically" as a result of this predefined shorthand.

- Because of way the reflexive assignment operators are defined, they cannot be used to initialize variables. If the first reference to x is x += 1, an error will result. This will be intuitive to most programmers unless they are accustomed to a language where variables are initialized to some sort of zero or null value.

- It is actually possible in some sense to get around this behavior. One can define operators for nil such that the initial nil value of the variable produces the result we want. Here is a nil.+ method that will allow += to initialize a String or a Fixnum value, basically just returning other and thus ensuring that nil + other is equal to other:

```
def nil.+(other)
   other
end
```

This illustrates the power of Ruby; but whether it is useful or appropriate to code this way is left as an exercise for the reader.

- It is wise to recall that Class *is an object,* and Object *is a class.* We will try to make this clear in a later chapter; for now, simply recite it every day as a mantra.

- Some operators can't be overloaded because they are built into the language rather than implemented as methods. These are: = ... and or not && || ! != !~. Additionally, the reflexive assignment operators (+=, -=, and so on) cannot be overloaded. These are not methods, and it can be argued they are not true operators either.

- Be aware that although assignment is not overloadable, it is still possible to write an instance method with a name such as foo= (allowing statements such as x.foo = 5). Consider the equal sign to be like a suffix.

- Recall that a "bare" scope operator has an implied Object before it, so that ::Foo means Object::Foo.

- Recall that fail is an alias for raise.

- Recall that definitions in Ruby are executed. Because of the dynamic nature of the language, it possible (for example) to define two methods completely differently based on a flag that is tested at runtime.

- Remember that the `for` construct (`for x in a`) is really calling the default iterator `each`. Any class having this iterator can be walked through with a `for` loop.

- Be aware that a method defined at the top level is added to `Kernel` and is thus a member of `Object`.

- A "*setter*" method (such as `foo=`) must be called with a receiver; otherwise, it will look like a simple assignment to a local variable of that name.

- Recall that `retry` can be used in iterators but not in general loops. In iterators, it causes the reassignment of all the parameters and the restarting of the current iteration.

- The keyword `retry` is also used in exception handling. Don't confuse the two usages.

- An object's `initialize` method is always private.

- Where an iterator ends in a left brace (or in `end`) and results in a value, that value can be used as the receiver for further method calls. For example:

```
squares = [1,2,3,4,5].collect do |x| x**2 end.reverse
# squares is now [25,16,9,4,1]
```

- The idiom `if $0 == __FILE__` is sometimes seen near the bottom of a Ruby program. This is a check to see whether the file is being run as a standalone piece of code (`true`) or is being used as some kind of auxiliary piece of code such as a library (`false`). A common use of this is to put a sort of "main program" (usually with test code in it) at the end of a library.

- Normal subclassing or inheritance is done with the < symbol:

```
class Dog < Animal
  # ...
end
```

But creation of a singleton class (an anonymous class that extends a single instance) is done with the << symbol:

```
class << platypus
  # ...
end
```

- When passing a block to an iterator, there is a slight difference between braces ({}) and a do-end pair. This is a precedence issue:

```
mymethod param1, foobar do ... end
# Here, do-end binds with mymethod

mymethod param1, foobar { ... }
# Here, {} binds with foobar, assumed to be a method
```

- It is somewhat traditional in Ruby to put single-line blocks in braces and multi-line blocks in do-end pairs. Examples:

```
my_array.each { |x| puts x }

my_array.each do |x|
  print x
  if x % 2 == 0
    puts " is even."
  else
    puts " is odd."
  end
end
```

This habit is not required, and there may be occasions where it is inappropriate to follow this rule.

- Bear in mind that strings are in a sense two-dimensional; they can be viewed as sequences of characters or sequences of lines. Some may find it surprising that the default iterator each operates on lines (where a "line" is a group of characters terminated by a record separator that defaults to newline); an alias for each is each_line. If you want to iterate by characters, you can use each_byte. The iterator sort also works on a line-by-line basis. There is no iterator each_index for strings because of the ambiguity involved. Do we want to handle the string by character or by line? This all becomes habitual with repeated use.

- A closure remembers the context in which it was created. One way to create a closure is by using a Proc object. As a crude example, consider the following:

```
def power(exponent)
  proc {|base| base**exponent}
end
```

```
square = power(2)
cube = power(3)

a = square.call(11)     # Result is 121
b = square.call(5)      # Result is 25
c = cube.call(6)        # Result is 216
d = cube.call(8)        # Result is 512
```

Observe that the closure "knows" the value of exponent that it was given at the time it was created.

- However, let's assume that a closure uses a variable defined in an outer scope (which is perfectly legal). This property can be useful, but here we show a misuse of it:

```
$exponent = 0

def power
  proc {|base| base**$exponent}
end

$exponent = 2
square = power

$exponent = 3
cube = power

a = square.call(11)     # Wrong!  Result is 1331

b = square.call(5)      # Wrong!  Result is 125

# The above two results are wrong because the CURRENT value
# of $exponent is being used. This would be true even if it
# had been a local variable that had gone out of scope (e.g.,
# using define_method).

c = cube.call(6) # Result is 216
d = cube.call(8) # Result is 512
```

- Finally, consider this somewhat contrived example. Inside the block of the `times` iterator, a new context is started, so that x is a local variable. The variable `closure` is already defined at the top level, so it will not be defined as local to the block.

```
closure = nil        # Define closure so the name will be known
1.times do           # Start a new context
  x = 5              # x is local to this block
  closure = Proc.new { puts "In closure, x = #{x}" }
end


x = 1


# Define x at top level


closure.call         # Prints: In closure, x = 5
```

Now note that the variable x that is set to 1 is a new variable, defined at the top level. It is not the same as the other variable of the same name. The closure therefore prints 5 because it remembers its creation context with the previous variable x and its previous value.

- Variables starting with a single @, defined inside a class, are generally instance variables. However, if they are defined outside any method, they are really *class instance* variables. (This usage is somewhat contrary to most OOP terminology in which a class instance is regarded to be the same as an instance or an object.) Example:

```
class Myclass

  @x = 1        # A class instance variable
  @y = 2        # Another one

  def mymethod
    @x = 3       # An instance variable
    # Note that @y is not accessible here.
  end

end
```

The class instance variable `@y` in the preceding code example is really an attribute of the class object `Myclass`, which is an instance of the class `Class`. (Remember, `Class` is an object, and `Object` is a class.) Class instance variables cannot be referenced from within instance methods and, in general, are not very useful.

- `attr`, `attr_reader`, `attr_writer`, and `attr_accessor` are shorthand for the actions of defining "setters" and "getters"; they take symbols as arguments (that is, instances of class `Symbol`).

- There is never any assignment with the scope operator; for example, the assignment `Math::PI = 3.2` is illegal.

1.5.5   Expression Orientation and Other Miscellaneous Issues

In Ruby, expressions are nearly as significant as statements. If you are a C programmer, this will be somewhat familiar to you; if your background is in Pascal, it may seem utterly foreign. But Ruby carries expression orientation even further than C.

In addition, we use this section to remind you of a couple of minor issues regarding regular expressions. Consider them to be a small bonus:

- In Ruby, any kind of assignment returns the same value that was assigned. Thus we can sometimes take little shortcuts like the ones shown here, but be careful when you are dealing with objects! Remember that these are nearly always *references* to objects.

```
x = y = z = 0       # All are now zero.

a = b = c = []      # Danger! a, b, and c now all refer
                    # to the SAME empty array.
x = 5
y = x += 2          # Now x and y are both 7
```

Remember, however, that values such as `Fixnums` are actually stored as immediate values, not as object references.

- Many control structures return values—if, unless, and case. The following code is all valid; it demonstrates that the branches of a decision need not be statements but can simply be expressions:

```
a = 5
x = if a < 8 then 6 else 7 end     # x is now 6

y = if a < 8        # y is 6 also; the
  6                 # if-statement can be
else                # on a single line
  7                 # or on multiple lines.
end


# unless also works; z will be assigned 4
z = unless x == y then 3 else 4 end

t = case a          # t gets assigned
  when 0..3         # the value
    "low"           # "medium"
  when 4..6
    "medium"
else
  "high"
end
```

Here we indent as though the case started with the assignment. This looks proper to our eyes, but you may disagree.

- Note by way of contrast that the while and until loops do not return useful values but typically return nil:

```
i = 0
x = while (i < 5)     # x is nil
  puts i+=1
end
```

- The ternary decision operator can be used with statements or expressions. For syntactic reasons (or parser limitations) the parentheses here are necessary:

```
x = 6
y = x == 5 ? 0 : 1                      # y is now 1
x == 5 ? puts("Hi") : puts("Bye")  # Prints Bye
```

- The `return` at the end of a method can be omitted. A method always returns the last expression evaluated in its body, regardless of where that happens.

- When an iterator is called with a block, the last expression evaluated in the block is returned as the value of the block. Thus if the body of an iterator has a statement like `x = yield`, that value can be captured.

- *Regular expressions*: Recall that the multiline modifier /m can be appended to a regex, in which case . (dot) will match a newline character.

- *Regular expressions*: Beware of zero-length matches. If all elements of a regex are optional, then "nothingness" will match that pattern, and a match will always be found at the beginning of a string. This is a common error for regex users, particularly novices.

1.6   Ruby Jargon and Slang

You don't have to re-learn English when you learn Ruby. But certain pieces of jargon and slang are commonly used in the community. Some of these may be used in slightly different ways from the rest of the computer science world. Most of these are discussed in this section.

In Ruby, the term *attribute* is used somewhat unofficially. We can think of an attribute as being an instance variable that is exposed to the outside world via one of the `attr` family of methods. This is a gray area because we could have methods such as `foo` and `foo=` that don't correspond to `@foo` as we would expect. And certainly not all instance variables are considered attributes. As always, common sense should guide your usage.

Attributes in Ruby can be broken down into `readers` and `writers` (called *getters* and *setters* in some languages—terms we don't commonly use). An *accessor* is both a reader and a writer; this is consistent with the name of the `attr_accessor` method but disagrees with common usage in other communities where an accessor is read-only.

The operator === is unique to Ruby (as far as I am aware). The common name for it is the *case equality operator* because it is used implicitly by case statements. But this is slightly misleading, as I said earlier, because it is not really "equality" at all. In this book, I often use the term *relationship operator*. I did not invent this term, but I can't find its origin, and it is not in common use today. The "hip and trendy" name for this is the *threequal operator* ("three equals").

The <=> operator is probably best called the *comparison operator*. Common slang is *spaceship operator* because it looks like a side view of a flying saucer in an old-fashioned video game or text-based computer game.

The term *poetry mode* is used by some to indicate the omission of needless punctuation and tokens (a tongue-in-cheek reference to the punctuation habits of poets in the last six decades or so). Poetry mode is often taken to mean "omission of parentheses around method calls":

```
some_method(1, 2, 3)    # unneeded parentheses
some_method 1, 2, 3     # "poetry mode"
```

But I think the principle is more general than that. For example, when a hash is passed as the last or lone parameter, the braces may be omitted. At the end of a line, the semicolon may be omitted (and really always is). In most cases, the keyword then may be omitted, whether in if statements or case statements.

Some coders even go so far as to omit parentheses in a method definition, though most do not:

```
def my_method(a, b, c)  # Also legal:  def my_method a, b, c
  # ...
end
```

It is worth noting that in some cases, the complexity of the Ruby grammar causes the parser to be confused easily. When method calls are nested, it is better to use parentheses for clarity. In some cases, warnings are printed in current versions of Ruby:

```
def alpha(x)
  x*2
end

def beta(y)
  y*3
end

gamma = 5
delta = alpha beta gamma  # 30 -- same as alpha(beta(gamma))
# Produces warning:
# warning: parenthesize argument(s) for future version
```

The term *duck typing*, as far as I can tell, originated with Dave Thomas. It refers to the old saying that if something looks like a duck, walks like a duck, and quacks like a duck, it might as well be a duck. Exactly what this term means may be open to discussion; I would say that it refers to the tendency of Ruby to be less concerned with the *class* of an object and more concerned with what methods can be called on it and what operations can be performed on it. Thus in Ruby we rarely use is_a? or kind_of, but we might more often use respond_to?. Most often of all, we might simply pass an object to a method and know that an exception will be raised if it is used inappropriately. This usually happens sooner rather than later.

The unary asterisk that is used to expand an array could be called an *array expansion* operator, but I don't think I have ever heard that. Terms such as *star* and *splat* are inevitable in hacker circles along with derivatives such as *splatted* and *unsplatted*. David Alan Black cleverly calls this the *unary unarray* operator.

The term *singleton* is sometimes regarded as overused. It is useful to remember that this is a perfectly good English word in its own right—referring to a thing that is solitary or unique. As long as we use it as a modifier, there should be no confusion.

The *Singleton Pattern* is a well-known design pattern in which a class allows itself to be instantiated only once; the singleton library in Ruby facilitates the use of this pattern.

A *singleton class* in Ruby is the classlike entity where methods are stored that are per-object rather than per-class. It is arguably not a "true class" because it cannot be instantiated. The following is an example of opening up the singleton class for a string object and adding a method:

```
str = "hello"
class << str                      # Alternatively:
  def hyphenated                  # def str.hyphenated
    self.split("").join("-")
  end
end


str.hyphenated                    # "h-e-l-l-o"
```

Some have started to use the term *eigenclass* for this, derived from the German *eigen* ("its own"), and corresponding to terms from math and physics such as *eigenvalue*. This is clever, but this usage is not communitywide, and some people hate it.

Let's go back to our previous example. Because the method hyphenate exists in no other object or class, it is a *singleton method* on that object. This also is unambiguous. Sometimes the object itself will be called a singleton because it is one of a kind— it is the only object that has that method.

But remember that in Ruby, a class is itself an object. Thus we can add a method to the singleton class *of a class*, and that method will be unique to that object, which happens to be a class. Here is an example:

```
class MyClass
  class << self                    # Alternatively: def self.hello
    def hello                      # or: def MyClass.hello
      puts "Hello from #{self}!"
    end
  end
end
```

So we don't have to instantiate MyClass to call this method.

```
MyClass.hello                      # Hello from MyClass!
```

But you will notice that this is simply what we call a *class method* in Ruby. In other words, a class method is a singleton method on a class. We could also say it's a singleton method on an object that *happens to be* a class.

There are a couple more terms to cover. A *class variable* is one that starts with a double-@, of course; it is perhaps a slight misnomer because of its nontrivial behavior with regard to inheritance. A *class instance variable* is a somewhat different animal. It is an ordinary instance variable where the object it belongs to happens to be a class. For more information, see Chapter 11, "OOP and Dynamic Features in Ruby."

1.7 Conclusion

That ends our review of object-oriented programming and our whirlwind tour of the Ruby language. Later chapters will expand on this material greatly.

Although it was not my intention to "teach Ruby" to the beginner in this chapter, it is possible that the beginner might pick it up here anyhow. However, the later material in the book should be useful to the beginning and intermediate Rubyist alike. It is my hope that even the advanced Ruby programmer may still gain some new knowledge here and there.

CHAPTER 2

Working with Strings

Atoms were once thought to be fundamental, elementary building blocks of nature; protons were then thought to be fundamental, then quarks. Now we say the string is fundamental.

—*David Gross, professor of theoretical physics, Princeton University*

A computer science professor in the early 1980s started out his data structures class with a single question. He didn't introduce himself or state the name of the course; he didn't hand out a syllabus or give the name of the textbook. He walked to the front of the class and asked, "What is the most important data type?"

There were one or two guesses. Someone guessed "pointers," and he brightened but said no, that wasn't it. Then he offered his opinion: The most important data type was *character* data.

He had a valid point. Computers are supposed to be our servants, not our masters, and character data has the distinction of being human readable. (Some humans can read binary data easily, but we will ignore them.) The existence of characters (and thus strings) enables communication between humans and computers. Every kind of information we can imagine, including natural language text, can be encoded in character strings.

A *string*, as in other languages, is simply a sequence of characters. Like most entities in Ruby, strings are first-class objects. In everyday programming, we need to manipulate strings in many ways. We want to concatenate strings, tokenize them, analyze them, perform searches and substitutions, and more. Ruby makes most of these tasks easy.

Most of this chapter assumes that a byte is a character. When we get into an internationalized environment, this is not really true. For issues involved with internationalization, refer to Chapter 4, "Internationalization in Ruby."

2.1   Representing Ordinary Strings

A string in Ruby is simply a sequence of 8-bit bytes. It is not null-terminated as in C, so it can contain null characters. It may contain bytes above 0xFF, but such strings are meaningful only if some certain character set (encoding) is assumed. (For more information on encodings, refer to Chapter 4.

The simplest string in Ruby is single-quoted. Such a string is taken absolutely literally; the only escape sequences recognized are the single quote (\') and the escaped backslash itself (\\):

```
s1 = 'This is a string'    # This is a string
s2 = 'Mrs. O\'Leary'       # Mrs. O'Leary
s3 = 'Look in C:\\TEMP'    # Look in C:\TEMP
```

A double-quoted string is more versatile. It allows many more escape sequences, such as backspace, tab, carriage return, and linefeed. It also allows control characters to be embedded as octal numbers:

```
s1 = "This is a tab: (\t)"
s2 = "Some backspaces: xyz\b\b\b"
s3 = "This is also a tab: \011"
s4 = "And these are both bells: \a \007"
```

Double-quoted strings also allow expressions to be embedded inside them. See section 2.21, "Embedding Expressions Within Strings."

2.2   Representing Strings with Alternate Notations

Sometimes we want to represent strings that are rich in metacharacters such as single quotes, double quotes, and more. For these situations, we have the %q and %Q notations. Following either of these is a string within a pair of delimiters; I personally favor square brackets ([]).

The difference between the %q and %Q variants is that the former acts like a single-quoted string, and the latter like a double-quoted string.

```
S1 = %q[As Magritte said, "Ceci n'est pas une pipe."]
s2 = %q[This is not a tab: (\t)]   # same as: 'This is not a tab: \t'
s3 = %Q[This IS a tab: (\t)]       # same as: "This IS a tab: \t"
```

Both kinds of notation can be used with different delimiters. Besides brackets, there are other paired delimiters (parentheses, braces, angle brackets):

```
s1 = %q(Bill said, "Bob said, 'This is a string.'")
s2 = %q{Another string.}
s3 = %q<Special characters '"[](){} in this string.>
```

There are also "nonpaired" delimiters. Basically any character may be used that is not alphanumeric, not whitespace, printable, and not a paired character.

```
s1 = %q:"I think Mrs. O'Leary's cow did it," he said.:
s2 = %q*\r is a control-M and \n is a control-J.*
```

2.3   Using Here-Documents

If you want to represent a long string spanning multiple lines, you can certainly use a regular quoted string:

```
str = "Once upon a midnight dreary,
       While I pondered, weak and weary..."
```

However, the indentation will be part of the string.

Another way is the *here-document*, a string that is inherently multiline. (This concept and term are borrowed from older languages and contexts.) The syntax is the

<< symbol, followed by an end marker, then zero or more lines of text, and finally the same end marker on a line by itself:

```
str = <<EOF
Once upon a midnight dreary,
While I pondered weak and weary,...
EOF
```

Be careful about things such as trailing spaces on the final end marker line. Current versions of Ruby will fail to recognize the end marker in those situations.

Note that here-documents may be "stacked"; for example, here is a method call with three such strings passed to it:

```
some_method(<<str1, <<str2, <<str3)
first piece
of text...
str1
second piece...
str2
third piece
of text.
str3
```

By default, a here-document is like a double-quoted string—that is, its contents are subject to interpretation of escape sequences and interpolation of embedded expressions. But if the end marker is single-quoted, the here-document behaves like a single-quoted string:

```
str = <<'EOF'
This isn't a tab: \t
and this isn't a newline: \n
EOF
```

If a here-document's end marker is preceded by a hyphen, the end marker may be indented. *Only* the spaces before the end marker are deleted from the string, not those on previous lines.

```
str = <<-EOF
  Each of these lines
  starts with a pair
```

```
    of blank spaces.
EOF
```

Here is a style I personally like. Let's assume the existence of the margin method defined here:

```
class String
  def margin
    arr = self.split("\n")              # Split into lines
    arr.map! {|x| x.sub!(/\s*\|/,"")}   # Remove leading characters
    str = arr.join("\n")                # Rejoin into a single line
    self.replace(str)                   # Replace contents of string
  end
end
```

I've commented this fairly heavily for clarity. Parts of it involve features explained elsewhere in this chapter or later chapters.

It's used in this way:

```
str = <<end.margin
  |This here-document has a "left margin"
  |at the vertical bar on each line.
  |
  |  We can do inset quotations,
  |  hanging indentions, and so on.
end
```

The word end is used naturally enough as an end marker. (This, of course, is a matter of taste. It "looks" like the reserved word end but is really just an arbitrary marker.) Each line starts with a vertical bar, which is then stripped off each line (along with the leading whitespace).

2.4 Finding the Length of a String

The method length can be used to find a string's length. A synonym is size.

```
str1 = "Carl"
x = str1.length      # 4
str2 = "Doyle"
x = str2.size        # 5
```

2.5   Processing a Line at a Time

A Ruby string can contain newlines. For example, a file can be read into memory and stored in a single string. The default iterator each processes such a string one line at a time:

```
str = "Once upon\na time...\nThe End\n"
num = 0
str.each do |line|
  num += 1
  print "Line #{num}: #{line}"
end
```

The preceding code produces three lines of output:

```
Line 1: Once upon
Line 2: a time...
Line 3: The End
```

The method each_with_index could also be used in this case.

2.6   Processing a Byte at a Time

Because Ruby is not fully internationalized at the time of this writing, a character is essentially the same as a byte. To process these in sequence, use the each_byte iterator:

```
str = "ABC"
str.each_byte {|char| print char, " " }
# Produces output: 65 66 67
```

In current versions of Ruby, you can break a string into an array of one-character strings by using scan with a simple wildcard regular expression matching a single character:

```
str = "ABC"
chars = str.scan(/./)
chars.each {|char| print char, " " }
# Produces output: A B C
```

2.7   Performing Specialized String Comparisons

Ruby has built-in ideas about comparing strings; comparisons are done lexicographically as we have come to expect (that is, based on character set order). But if we want, we can introduce rules of our own for string comparisons, and these can be of arbitrary complexity.

For example, suppose that we want to ignore the English articles *a*, *an*, and *the* at the front of a string, and we also want to ignore most common punctuation marks. We can do this by overriding the built-in method <=> (which is called for <, <=, >, and >=). Listing 2.1 shows how we do this.

Listing 2.1   Specialized String Comparisons

```
class String

  alias old_compare <=>

  def <=>(other)
    a = self.dup
    b = other.dup
    # Remove punctuation
    a.gsub!(/[\,\.\?\!\:\;]/, "")
    b.gsub!(/[\,\.\?\!\:\;]/, "")
    # Remove initial articles
    a.gsub!(/^(a |an |the )/i, "")
    b.gsub!(/^(a |an |the )/i, "")
    # Remove leading/trailing whitespace
    a.strip!
    b.strip!
    # Use the old <=>
    a.old_compare(b)
  end

end


title1 = "Calling All Cars"
title2 = "The Call of the Wild"

# Ordinarily this would print "yes"

if title1 < title2
  puts "yes"
else
  puts "no"         # But now it prints "no"
end
```

Note that we "save" the old <=> with an alias and then call it at the end. This is because if we tried to use the < method, it would call the new <=> rather than the old one, resulting in infinite recursion and a program crash.

Note also that the == operator does not call the <=> method (mixed in from Comparable). This means that if we need to check equality in some specialized way, we will have to override the == method separately. But in this case, == works as we want it to anyhow.

Suppose that we wanted to do case-insensitive string comparisons. The built-in method casecmp will do this; we just have to make sure that it is used instead of the usual comparison.

Here is one way:

```
class String
  def <=>(other)
    casecmp(other)
  end
end
```

But there is a slightly easier way:

```
class String
  alias <=> casecmp
end
```

However, we haven't finished. We need to redefine == so that it will behave in the same way:

```
class String
  def ==(other)
    casecmp(other) == 0
  end
end
```

Now all string comparisons will be strictly case-insensitive. Any sorting operation that depends on <=> will likewise be case-insensitive.

2.8 Tokenizing a String

The split method parses a string and returns an array of tokens. It accepts two parameters, a delimiter and a field limit (which is an integer).

The delimiter defaults to whitespace. Actually, it uses $; or the English equivalent $FIELD_SEPARATOR. If the delimiter is a string, the explicit value of that string is used as a token separator.

```
s1 = "It was a dark and stormy night."
words = s1.split         # ["It", "was", "a", "dark", "and",
                         #  "stormy", "night"]
s2 = "apples, pears, and peaches"
list = s2.split(", ")    # ["apples", "pears", "and peaches"]

s3 = "lions and tigers and bears"
zoo = s3.split(/ and /)  # ["lions", "tigers", "bears"]
```

The limit parameter places an upper limit on the number of fields returned, according to these rules:

1. If it is omitted, trailing null entries are suppressed.

2. If it is a positive number, the number of entries will be limited to that number (stuffing the rest of the string into the last field as needed). Trailing null entries are retained.

3. If it is a negative number, there is no limit to the number of fields, and trailing null entries are retained.

These three rules are illustrated here:

```
str = "alpha,beta,gamma,,"
list1 = str.split(",")    # ["alpha","beta","gamma"]
list2 = str.split(",",2)  # ["alpha", "beta,gamma,,"]
list3 = str.split(",",4)  # ["alpha", "beta", "gamma", ",,"]
list4 = str.split(",",8)  # ["alpha", "beta", "gamma", "", ""]
list5 = str.split(",",-1) # ["alpha", "beta", "gamma", "", ""]
```

The scan method can be used to match regular expressions or strings against a target string:

```
str = "I am a leaf on the wind..."

# A string is interpreted literally, not as a regex
arr = str.scan("a")       # ["a","a","a"]
```

```
# A regex will return all matches
arr = str.scan(/\w+/)         # ["I", "am", "a", "leaf", "on", "the",
"wind"]

# A block can be specified
str.scan(/\w+/) {|x| puts x }
```

The StringScanner class, from the standard library, is different in that it maintains state for the scan rather than doing it all at once:

```
require 'strscan'
str = "Watch how I soar!"
ss = StringScanner.new(str)
loop do
  word = ss.scan(/\w+/)      # Grab a word at a time
  break if word.nil?
  puts word
  sep = ss.scan(/\W+/)       # Grab next non-word piece
  break if sep.nil?
end
```

2.9 Formatting a String

This is done in Ruby as it is in C, with the sprintf method. It takes a string and a list of expressions as parameters and returns a string. The format string contains essentially the same set of specifiers available with C's sprintf (or printf).

```
name = "Bob"
age = 28
str = sprintf("Hi, %s... I see you're %d years old.", name, age)
```

You might ask why we would use this instead of simply interpolating values into a string using the #{expr} notation. The answer is that sprintf makes it possible to do extra formatting such as specifying a maximum width, specifying a maximum number of decimal places, adding or suppressing leading zeroes, left-justifying, right-justifying, and more.

```
str = sprintf("%-20s  %3d", name, age)
```

The `String` class has a method `%` that does much the same thing. It takes a single value or an array of values of any type:

```
str = "%-20s  %3d" % [name, age]   # Same as previous example
```

We also have the methods `ljust`, `rjust`, and `center`; these take a length for the destination string and pad with spaces as needed:

```
str = "Moby-Dick"
s1 = str.ljust(13)          # "Moby-Dick"
s2 = str.center(13)         # "  Moby-Dick  "
s3 = str.rjust(13)          # "    Moby-Dick"
```

If a second parameter is specified, it is used as the pad string (which may possibly be truncated as needed):

```
str = "Captain Ahab"
s1 = str.ljust(20,"+")      # "Captain Ahab++++++++"
s2 = str.center(20,"-")     # "—Captain Ahab—"
s3 = str.rjust(20,"123")    # "12312312Captain Ahab"
```

2.10   Using Strings As IO Objects

Besides `sprintf` and `scanf`, there is another way to fake input/output to a string—the `StringIO` class.

Because this is a very `IO`-like object, we cover it in a later chapter. See section 10.1.24, "Treating a String As a File."

2.11   Controlling Uppercase and Lowercase

Ruby's `String` class offers a rich set of methods for controlling case. This section offers an overview of these.

The `downcase` method converts a string to all lowercase. Likewise `upcase` converts it to all uppercase:

```
s1 = "Boston Tea Party"
s2 = s1.downcase            # "boston tea party"
s3 = s2.upcase              # "BOSTON TEA PARTY"
```

The `capitalize` method capitalizes the first character of a string while forcing all the remaining characters to lowercase:

```
s4 = s1.capitalize          # "Boston tea party"
s5 = s2.capitalize          # "Boston tea party"
s6 = s3.capitalize          # "Boston tea party"
```

The `swapcase` method exchanges the case of each letter in a string:

```
s7 = "THIS IS AN ex-parrot."
s8 = s7.swapcase            # "this is an EX-PARROT."
```

As of Ruby 1.8, there is a `casecmp` method which acts like the default `<=>` method but ignores case:

```
n1 = "abc".casecmp("xyz")   # -1
n2 = "abc".casecmp("XYZ")   # -1
n3 = "ABC".casecmp("xyz")   # -1
n4 = "ABC".casecmp("abc")   # 0
n5 = "xyz".casecmp("abc")   # 1
```

Each of these has its in-place equivalent (`upcase!`, `downcase!`, `capitalize!`, `swapcase!`).

There are no built-in methods for detecting case, but this is easy to do with regular expressions, as shown in the following example:

```
if string =~ /[a-z]/
  puts "string contains lowercase characters"
end

if string =~ /[A-Z]/
  puts "string contains uppercase characters"
end

if string =~ /[A-Z]/ and string =~ /a-z/
  puts "string contains mixed case"
end
```

```
if string[0..0] =~ /[A-Z]/
  puts "string starts with a capital letter"
end
```

Note that all these methods ignore locale.

2.12 Accessing and Assigning Substrings

In Ruby, substrings may be accessed in several different ways. Normally the bracket notation is used, as for an array, but the brackets may contain a pair of Fixnums, a range, a regex, or a string. Each case is discussed in turn.

If a pair of Fixnum values is specified, they are treated as an offset and a length, and the corresponding substring is returned:

```
str = "Humpty Dumpty"
sub1 = str[7,4]        # "Dump"
sub2 = str[7,99]       # "Dumpty" (overrunning is OK)
sub3 = str[10,-4]      # nil (length is negative)
```

It is important to remember that these are an offset and a length (number of characters), not beginning and ending offsets.

A negative index counts backward from the end of the string. In this case, the index is one-based, not zero-based. The length is still added in the forward direction:

```
str1 = "Alice"
sub1 = str1[-3,3]    # "ice"
str2 = "Through the Looking-Glass"
sub3 = str2[-13,4]   # "Look"
```

A range may be specified. In this case, the range is taken as a range of indices into the string. Ranges may have negative numbers, but the numerically lower number must still be first in the range. If the range is "backward" or if the initial value is outside the string, nil is returned:

```
str = "Winston Churchill"
sub1 = str[8..13]    # "Church"
sub2 = str[-4..-1]   # "hill"
sub3 = str[-1..-4]   # nil
sub4 = str[25..30]   # nil
```

If a regular expression is specified, the string matching that pattern will be returned. If there is no match, nil will be returned:

```
str = "Alistair Cooke"
sub1 = str[/l..t/]    # "list"
sub2 = str[/s.*r/]    # "stair"
sub3 = str[/foo/]     # nil
```

If a string is specified, that string will be returned if it appears as a substring (or nil if it does not):

```
str = "theater"
sub1 = str["heat"]   # "heat"
sub2 = str["eat"]    # "eat"
sub3 = str["ate"]    # "ate"
sub4 = str["beat"]   # nil
sub5 = str["cheat"]  # nil
```

Finally, in the trivial case, a single Fixnum as index will yield an ASCII code (or nil if out of range):

```
str = "Aaron Burr"
ch1 = str[0]     # 65
ch1 = str[1]     # 97
ch3 = str[99]    # nil
```

It is important to realize that the notations described here will serve for assigning values as well as for accessing them:

```
str1 = "Humpty Dumpty"
str1[7,4] = "Moriar"      # "Humpty Moriarty"

str2 = "Alice"
str2[-3,3] = "exandra"    # "Alexandra"

str3 = "Through the Looking-Glass"
str3[-13,13]  = "Mirror"  # "Through the Mirror"
```

```
str4 = "Winston Churchill"
str4[8..13] = "H"          # "Winston Hill"


str5 = "Alistair Cooke"
str5[/e$/] ="ie Monster"   # "Alistair Cookie Monster"


str6 = "theater"
str6["er"] = "re"          # "theatre"


str7 = "Aaron Burr"
str7[0] = 66               # "Baron Burr"
```

Assigning to an expression evaluating to `nil` will have no effect.

2.13 Substituting in Strings

We've already seen how to perform simple substitutions in strings. The `sub` and `gsub` methods provide more advanced pattern-based capabilities. There are also `sub!` and `gsub!`, their in-place counterparts.

The `sub` method substitutes the first occurrence of a pattern with the given substitute-string or the given block:

```
s1 = "spam, spam, and eggs"
s2 = s1.sub(/spam/,"bacon")              # "bacon, spam, and eggs"

s3 = s2.sub(/(\w+), (\w+),/,'\2, \1,')   # "spam, bacon, and eggs"

s4 = "Don't forget the spam."
s5 = s4.sub(/spam/) { |m| m.reverse }    # "Don't forget the maps."

s4.sub!(/spam/) { |m| m.reverse }
# s4 is now "Don't forget the maps."
```

As this example shows, the special symbols \1, \2, and so on may be used in a substitute string. However, special variables such as $& (or the English version $MATCH) may not.

If the block form is used, the special variables may be used. However, if all you need is the matched string, it will be passed into the block as a parameter. If it is not needed at all, the parameter can of course be omitted.

The gsub method (global substitution) is essentially the same except that all matches are substituted rather than just the first:

```
s5 = "alfalfa abracadabra"
s6 = s5.gsub(/a[bl]/,"xx")        # "xxfxxfa xxracadxxra"
s5.gsub!(/[lfdbr]/) { |m| m.upcase + "-" }
# s5 is now "aL-F-aL-F-a aB-R-acaD-aB-R-a"
```

The method Regexp.last_match is essentially identical to $& or $MATCH.

2.14   Searching a String

Besides the techniques for accessing substrings, there are other ways of searching within strings. The index method returns the starting location of the specified substring, character, or regex. If the item is not found, the result is nil:

```
str = "Albert Einstein"
pos1 = str.index(?E)          # 7
pos2 = str.index("bert")      # 2
pos3 = str.index(/in/)        # 8
pos4 = str.index(?W)          # nil
pos5 = str.index("bart")      # nil
pos6 = str.index(/wein/)      # nil
```

The method rindex (right index) starts from the righthand side of the string (that is, from the end). The numbering, however, proceeds from the beginning as usual:

```
str = "Albert Einstein"
pos1 = str.rindex(?E)         # 7
pos2 = str.rindex("bert")     # 2
pos3 = str.rindex(/in/)       # 13 (finds rightmost match)
pos4 = str.rindex(?W)         # nil
pos5 = str.rindex("bart")     # nil
pos6 = str.rindex(/wein/)     # nil
```

The include? method simply tells whether the specified substring or character occurs within the string:

```
str1 = "mathematics"
flag1 = str1.include? ?e       # true
flag2 = str1.include? "math"   # true
```

```
str2 = "Daylight Saving Time"
flag3 = str2.include? ?s          # false
flag4 = str2.include? "Savings"  # false
```

The scan method repeatedly scans for occurrences of a pattern. If called without a block, it returns an array. If the pattern has more than one (parenthesized) group, the array will be nested:

```
str1 = "abracadabra"
sub1 = str1.scan(/a./)
# sub1 now is ["ab","ac","ad","ab"]

str2 = "Acapulco, Mexico"
sub2 = str2.scan(/(.)(c.)/)
# sub2 now is [ ["A","ca"], ["l","co"], ["i","co"] ]
```

If a block is specified, the method passes the successive values to the block:

```
str3 = "Kobayashi"
str3.scan(/[^aeiou]+[aeiou]/) do |x|
  print "Syllable: #{x}\n"
end
```

This code produces the following output:

```
Syllable: Ko
Syllable: ba
Syllable: ya
Syllable: shi
```

2.15 Converting Between Characters and ASCII Codes

In Ruby, a character is already an integer. *This behavior is slated to change in 2.0 or perhaps sooner.* In future versions of Ruby, the current plan is to store a character as a one-character string.

```
str = "Martin"
print str[0]         # 77
```

If a `Fixnum` is appended directly onto a string, it is converted to a character:

```
str2 = str << 111   # "Martino"
```

2.16   Implicit and Explicit Conversion

At first glance, the `to_s` and `to_str` methods seem confusing. They both convert an object into a string representation, don't they?

There are several differences. First, *any* object can in principle be converted to some kind of string representation; that is why nearly every core class has a `to_s` method. But the `to_str` method is never implemented in the core.

As a rule, `to_str` is for objects that are really very much like strings—that can "masquerade" as strings. Better yet, think of the short name `to_s` as being *explicit conversion* and the longer name `to_str` as being *implicit conversion*.

You see, the core does not *define* any `to_str` methods (that I am aware of). But core methods do *call* `to_str` sometimes (if it exists for a given class).

The first case we might think of is a *subclass* of `String`; but in reality, any object of a subclass of `String` already "is-a" `String`, so `to_str` is unnecessary there.

Here is a real-life example. The `Pathname` class is defined for convenience in manipulating filesystem pathnames (for example, concatenating them). However, a pathname maps naturally to a string (even though it does *not* inherit from `String`).

```
require 'pathname'
path = Pathname.new("/tmp/myfile")

name = path.to_s   # "/tmp/myfile"
name = path.to_str # "/tmp/myfile" (So what?)

# Here's why it matters...

heading = "File name is " + path
puts heading        # "File name is /tmp/myfile"
```

Notice that in the preceding code fragment, we take a string `"File name is"` and directly append a path onto it. Normally this would give us a runtime error, since the + operator expects the second operand to be another string. But because `Pathname` has a `to_str` method, that method is called. A `Pathname` can "masquerade" as a `String`; it is implicitly converted to a `String` in this case.

In real life, `to_s` and `to_str` usually return the same value; but they don't *have* to do so. The implicit conversion should result in the "real string value" of the object; the explicit conversion can be thought of as a "forced" conversion.

The `puts` method calls an object's `to_s` method in order to find a string representation. This behavior might be thought of as an implicit call of an explicit conversion. The same is true for string interpolation. Here's a crude example:

```
class Helium
  def to_s
    "He"
  end
  def to_str
    "helium"
  end
end


e = Helium.new
print "Element is "
puts e                      # Element is He
puts "Element is " + e      # Element is helium
puts "Element is #{e}"      # Element is He
```

So you can see how defining these appropriately in your own classes can give you a little extra flexibility. But what about honoring the definitions of the objects passed into your methods?

For example, suppose that you have a method that is "supposed" to take a `String` as a parameter. Despite our "duck typing" philosophy, this is frequently done and is often completely appropriate. For example, the first parameter of `File.new` is "expected" to be a string.

The way to handle this is simple. When you expect a string, check for the existence of `to_str` and call it as needed.

```
def set_title(title)
  if title.respond_to? :to_str
    title = title.to_str
  end
  # ...
end
```

Now, what if an object *doesn't* respond to to_str? We could do several things. We could force a call to to_s; we could check the class to see whether it is a String or a subclass thereof; or we could simply keep going, knowing that if we apply some meaningless operation to this object, we will eventually get an ArgumentError anyway.

A shorter way to do this is

```
title = title.to_str rescue title
```

which depends on an unimplemented to_str raising an exception. The rescue modifiers can of course be nested:

```
title = title.to_str rescue title.to_s rescue title
# Handle the unlikely case that even to_s isn't there
```

Implicit conversion *would* allow you to make strings and numbers essentially equivalent. You could do this:

```
class Fixnum
  def to_str
    self.to_s
  end
end

str = "The number is " + 345     # The number is 345
```

However, I don't recommend this sort of thing. There is such a thing as "too much magic"; Ruby, like most languages, considers strings and numbers to be different, and I believe that most conversions should be explicit for the sake of clarity.

Another thing to remember: There is nothing *magical* about the to_str method. It is intended to return a string, but if you code your own, it is your responsibility to see that it does.

2.17 Appending an Item Onto a String

The append operator << can be used to append a string onto another string. It is "stackable" in that multiple operations can be performed in sequence on a given receiver.

```
str = "A"
str << [1,2,3].to_s << " " << (3.14).to_s
# str is now "A123 3.14"
```

If a Fixnum in the range 0..255 is specified, it will be converted to a character:

```
str = "Marlow"
str << 101 << ", Christopher"
# str is now "Marlowe, Christopher"
```

2.18   Removing Trailing Newlines and Other Characters

Often we want to remove extraneous characters from the end of a string. The prime example is a newline on a string read from input.

The chop method removes the last character of the string (typically a trailing newline character). If the character before the newline is a carriage return (\r), it will be removed also. The reason for this behavior is the discrepancy between different systems' conceptions of what a newline is. On some systems such as UNIX, the newline character is represented internally as a linefeed (\n). On others such as DOS and Windows, it is stored as a carriage return followed by a linefeed (\r\n).

```
str = gets.chop          # Read string, remove newline
s2 = "Some string\n"     # "Some string" (no newline)
s3 = s2.chop!            # s2 is now "Some string" also
s4 = "Other string\r\n"
s4.chop!                 # "Other string" (again no newline)
```

Note that the "in-place" version of the method (chop!) will modify its receiver.

It is also important to note that in the absence of a trailing newline, the last character will be removed anyway:

```
str = "abcxyz"
s1 = str.chop            # "abcxy"
```

Because a newline may not always be present, the chomp method may be a better alternative:

```
str = "abcxyz"
str2 = "123\n"
str3 = "123\r"
str4 = "123\r\n"
s1 = str.chomp          # "abcxyz"
s2 = str2.chomp         # "123"
# With the default record separator, \r and \r\n are removed
# as well as \n
s3 = str3.chomp         # "123"
s4 = str4.chomp         # "123"
```

There is also a chomp! method as we would expect.

If a parameter is specified for chomp, it will remove the set of characters specified from the end of the string rather than the default record separator. Note that if the record separator appears in the middle of the string, it is ignored:

```
str1 = "abcxyz"
str2 = "abcxyz"
s1 = str1.chomp("yz")   # "abcx"
s2 = str2.chomp("x")    # "abcxyz"
```

2.19   Trimming Whitespace from a String

The strip method removes whitespace from the beginning and end of a string. Its counterpart strip! modifies the receiver in place.

```
str1 = "\t  \nabc  \t\n"
str2 = str1.strip       # "abc"
str3 = str1.strip!      # "abc"
# str1 is now "abc" also
```

Whitespace, of course, consists mostly of blanks, tabs, and end-of-line characters.

If we want to remove whitespace only from the beginning or end of a string, we can use the lstrip and rstrip methods:

```
str = "   abc   "
s2 = str.lstrip         # "abc   "
s3 = str.rstrip         # "   abc"
```

There are in-place variants `rstrip!` and `lstrip!` also.

2.20   Repeating Strings

In Ruby, the multiplication operator (or method) is overloaded to enable repetition of strings. If a string is multiplied by n, the result is n copies of the original string concatenated together:

```
etc = "Etc. "*3                              # "Etc. Etc. Etc. "
ruler = "+" + ("."*4+"5"+"."*4+"+")*3
# "+....5....+....5....+....5....+"
```

2.21   Embedding Expressions Within Strings

The `#{}` notation makes this easy. We need not worry about converting, appending, and concatenating; we can interpolate a variable value or other expression at any point in a string:

```
puts "#{temp_f} Fahrenheit is #{temp_c} Celsius"
puts "The discriminant has the value #{b*b - 4*a*c}."
puts "#{word} is #{word.reverse} spelled backward."
```

Bear in mind that full statements can also be used inside the braces. The last evaluated expression will be the one returned.

```
str = "The answer is #{ def factorial(n)
                          n==0 ? 1 : n*factorial(n-1)
                        end

                        answer = factorial(3) * 7}, of course."
# The answer is 42, of course.
```

There are some shortcuts for global, class, and instance variables, in which case the braces can be dispensed with:

```
print "$gvar = #$gvar and ivar = #@ivar."
```

Note that this technique is not applicable for single-quoted strings (because their contents are not expanded), but it does work for double-quoted here-documents and regular expressions.

2.22   Delayed Interpolation of Strings

Sometimes we might want to delay the interpolation of values into a string. There is no perfect way to do this. One way is to use a block:

```
str = proc {|x,y,z| "The numbers are #{x}, #{y}, and #{z}" }

s1 = str.call(3,4,5)    # The numbers are 3, 4, and 5
s2 = str.call(7,8,9)    # The numbers are 7, 8, and 9
```

A more heavyweight solution is to store a single-quoted string, wrap it in double quotes, and evaluate it:

```
str = '#{name} is my name, and #{nation} is my nation'
name, nation = "Stephen Dedalus", "Ireland"
s1  = eval('"' + str + '"')
# Stephen Dedalus is my name, and Ireland is my nation.
```

It's also possible to pass in a different binding to eval:

```
bind = proc do
  name,nation = "Gulliver Foyle", "Terra"
  binding
end.call    # Contrived example; returns binding of block's context
s2 = eval('"' + str + '"',bind)
# Gulliver Foyle is my name, and Terra is my nation.
```

The eval technique may naturally have some "gotchas" associated with it. For example, be careful with escape sequences such as \n for newline.

2.23   Parsing Comma-Separated Data

Comma-delimited data are common in computing. It is a kind of "lowest common denominator" of data interchange used (for example) to transfer information between incompatible databases or applications that know no other common format.

We assume here that we have a mixture of strings and numbers and that all strings are enclosed in quotes. We further assume that all characters are escaped as necessary (commas and quotes inside strings, for example).

The problem becomes simple because this data format looks suspiciously like a Ruby array of mixed types. In fact, we can simply add brackets to enclose the whole expression, and we have an array of items.

```
string = gets.chop!
# Suppose we read in a string like this one:
# "Doe, John", 35, 225, "5'10\"", "555-0123"
data = eval("[" + string + "]")   # Convert to array
data.each {|x| puts "Value = #{x}"}
```

This fragment produces the following output:

```
Value = Doe, John
Value = 35
Value = 225
Value = 5' 10"
Value = 555-0123
```

For a more heavy-duty solution, refer to the CSV library (which is a standard library). There is also a somewhat improved tool called FasterCSV. Search for it online; it is not part of the standard Ruby distribution.

2.24   Converting Strings to Numbers (Decimal and Otherwise)

Basically there are two ways to convert strings to numbers: the Kernel method Integer and Float and the to_i and to_f methods of String. (Capitalized method names such as Integer are usually reserved for special data conversion functions like this.)

The simple case is trivial, and these are equivalent:

```
x = "123".to_i        # 123
y = Integer("123")    # 123
```

When a string is not a valid number, however, their behaviors differ:

```
x = "junk".to_i       # silently returns 0
y = Integer("junk")   # error
```

to_i stops converting when it reaches a non-numeric character, but Integer raises an error:

```
x = "123junk".to_i       # 123
y = Integer("123junk")   # error
```

Both allow leading and trailing whitespace:

```
x = " 123 ".to_i         # 123
y = Integer(" 123 ")     # 123
```

Floating point conversion works much the same way:

```
x = "3.1416".to_f        # 3.1416
y = Float("2.718")       # 2.718
```

Both conversion methods honor scientific notation:

```
x = Float("6.02e23")     # 6.02e23
y = "2.9979246e5".to_f   # 299792.46
```

to_i and Integer also differ in how they handle different bases. The default, of course, is decimal or base ten; but we can work in other bases also. (The same is not true for floating point.)

When talking about converting between numeric bases, strings always are involved. After all, an integer is an integer, and they are all stored in binary.

Base conversion, therefore, always means converting to or from some kind of string. Here we're looking at converting *from* a string. (For the reverse, see section 5.18 "Performing Base Conversions" and section 5.5 "Formatting Numbers for Output.")

When a number appears in program text as a literal numeric constant, it may have a "tag" in front of it to indicate base. These tags are 0b for binary, a simple 0 for octal, and 0x for hexadecimal.

These tags are honored by the Integer method but *not* by the to_i method:

```
x = Integer("0b111")     # binary      - returns 7
y = Integer("0111")      # octal       - returns 73
z = Integer("0x111")     # hexadecimal - returns 291
```

```
x = "0b111".to_i          # 0
y = "0111".to_i           # 0
z = "0x111".to_i          # 0
```

to_i, however, allows an optional second parameter to indicate base. Typically, the only meaningful values are 2, 8, 10 (the default), and 16. However, tags are not recognized even with the base parameter.

```
x = "111".to_i(2)         # 7
y = "111".to_i(8)         # octal        - returns 73
z = "111".to_i(16)        # hexadecimal - returns 291

x = "0b111".to_i          # 0
y = "0111".to_i           # 0
z = "0x111".to_i          # 0
```

Because of the "standard" behavior of these methods, a digit that is inappropriate for the given base will be treated differently:

```
x = "12389".to_i(8)       # 123    (8 is ignored)
y = Integer("012389")     # error  (8 is illegal)
```

Although it might be of limited usefulness, to_i handles bases up to 36, using all letters of the alphabet. (This may remind you of the base64 encoding; for information on that, see section 2.37, "Encoding and Decoding base64 Strings.")

```
x = "123".to_i(5)         # 66
y = "ruby".to_i(36)       # 1299022
```

It's also possible to use the scanf standard library to convert character strings to numbers. This library adds a scanf method to Kernel, to IO, and to String:

```
str = "234 234 234"
x, y, z = str.scanf("%d %o %x")    # 234, 156, 564
```

The scanf methods implement all the meaningful functionality of their C counterparts scanf, sscanf, and fscanf. It does not handle binary.

2.25   Encoding and Decoding `rot13` Text

The `rot13` method is perhaps the weakest form of encryption known to humankind. Its historical use is simply to prevent people from "accidentally" reading a piece of text. It is commonly seen in Usenet; for example, a joke that might be considered offensive might be encoded in `rot13`, or you could post the entire plot of *Star Wars: Episode 12* on the day before the premiere.

The encoding method consists simply of "rotating" a string through the alphabet, so that A becomes N, B becomes O, and so on. Lowercase letters are rotated in the same way; digits, punctuation, and other characters are ignored. Because 13 is half of 26 (the size of our alphabet), the function is its own inverse; applying it a second time will "decrypt" it.

The following example is an implementation as a method added to the `String` class. We present it without further comment:

```
class String

  def rot13
    self.tr("A-Ma-mN-Zn-z","N-Zn-zA-Ma-m")
  end

end

joke = "Y2K bug"
joke13 = joke.rot13      # "L2X oht"

episode2 = "Fcbvyre: Naanxva qbrfa'g trg xvyyrq."
puts episode2.rot13
```

2.26   Encrypting Strings

There are times when we don't want strings to be immediately legible. For example, passwords should not be stored in plaintext, no matter how tight the file permissions are.

The standard method `crypt` uses the standard function of the same name to DES-encrypt a string. It takes a "salt" value as a parameter (similar to the seed value for a random number generator). On non-UNIX platforms, this parameter may be different.

A trivial application for this follows, where we ask for a password that Tolkien fans should know:

```
coded = "hfCghHIE5LAM."

puts "Speak, friend, and enter!"

print "Password: "
password = gets.chop

if password.crypt("hf") == coded
  puts "Welcome!"
else
  puts "What are you, an orc?"
end
```

It is worth noting that you should never rely on encryption of this nature for a server-side web application because a password entered on a web form is still transmitted over the Internet in plaintext. In a case like this, the easiest security measure is the Secure Sockets Layer (SSL). Of course, you could still use encryption on the server side, but for a different reason—to protect the password as it is stored rather than during transmission.

2.27 Compressing Strings

The `zlib` library provides a way of compressing and decompressing strings and files.

Why might we want to compress strings in this way? Possibly to make database I/O faster, to optimize network usage, or even to obscure stored strings so that they are not easily read.

The `Deflate` and `Inflate` classes have class methods named `deflate` and `inflate`, respectively. The `deflate` method (which obviously compresses) has an extra parameter to specify the style of compression. The styles show a typical trade-off between compression quality and speed; `BEST_COMPRESSION` results in a smaller compressed string, but compression is relatively slow; `BEST_SPEED` compresses faster but does not compress as much. The default (`DEFAULT_COMPRESSION`) is typically somewhere in between in both size and speed.

```
require 'zlib'
include Zlib

long_string = ("abcde"*71 + "defghi"*79 + "ghijkl"*113)*371
# long_string has 559097 characters

s1 = Deflate.deflate(long_string,BEST_SPEED)          # 4188 chars
s3 = Deflate.deflate(long_string)                     # 3568 chars
s2 = Deflate.deflate(long_string,BEST_COMPRESSION)    # 2120 chars
```

Informal experiments suggest that the speeds vary by a factor of two, and the compression amounts vary inversely by the same amount. Speed and compression are greatly dependent on the contents of the string. Speed of course also is affected by hardware.

Be aware that there is a "break-even" point below which it is essentially useless to compress a string (unless you are trying to make the string unreadable). Below this point, the overhead of compression may actually result in a *longer* string.

2.28   Counting Characters in Strings

The count method counts the number of occurrences of any of a set of specified characters:

```
s1 = "abracadabra"
a  = s1.count("c")      # 1
b  = s1.count("bdr")    # 5
```

The string parameter is like a simple regular expression. If it starts with a caret, the list is negated:

```
c = s1.count("^a")      # 6
d = s1.count("^bdr")    # 6
```

A hyphen indicates a range of characters:

```
e = s1.count("a-d")     # 9
f = s1.count("^a-d")    # 2
```

2.29   Reversing a String

A string may be reversed simply by using the reverse method (or its in-place counterpart reverse!):

```
s1 = "Star Trek"
s2 = s1.reverse          # "kerT ratS"
s1.reverse!              # s1 is now "kerT ratS"
```

Suppose that you want to reverse the word order (rather than character order). You can use String#split, which gives you an array of words. The Array class also has a reverse method; so you can then reverse the array and join to make a new string:

```
phrase = "Now here's a sentence"
phrase.split(" ").reverse.join(" ")
# "sentence a here's Now"
```

2.30   Removing Duplicate Characters

Runs of duplicate characters may be removed using the squeeze method:

```
s1 = "bookkeeper"
s2 = s1.squeeze          # "bokeper"
s3 = "Hello..."
s4 = s3.squeeze          # "Helo."
If a parameter is specified, only those characters will be squeezed.
s5 = s3.squeeze(".")     # "Hello."
```

This parameter follows the same rules as the one for the count method (see the section 2.28, "Counting Characters in Strings" earlier in this chapter); that is, it understands the hyphen and the caret.

There is also a squeeze! method.

2.31   Removing Specific Characters

The `delete` method removes characters from a string if they appear in the list of characters passed as a parameter:

```
s1 = "To be, or not to be"
s2 = s1.delete("b")              # "To e, or not to e"
s3 = "Veni, vidi, vici!"
s4 = s3.delete(",!")            # "Veni vidi vici"
```

This parameter follows the same rules as the one for the `count` method (see section 2.28, "Counting Characters in Strings" earlier in this chapter); that is, it understands the hyphen and the caret.

There is also a `delete!` method.

2.32   Printing Special Characters

The `dump` method provides explicit printable representations of characters that may ordinarily be invisible or print differently:

```
s1 = "Listen" << 7 << 7 << 7    # Add three ASCII BEL characters
puts s1.dump                    # Prints: Listen\007\007\007
s2 = "abc\t\tdef\tghi\n\n"
puts s2.dump                    # Prints: abc\t\tdef\tghi\n\n
s3 = "Double quote: \""
puts s3.dump                    # Prints: Double quote: \"
```

For the default setting of $KCODE, `dump` behaves the same as calling `inspect` on a string. The $KCODE variable is discussed in Chapter 4.

2.33   Generating Successive Strings

On rare occasions we may want to find the "successor" value for a string; for example, the successor for "aaa" is "aab" (then "aad", "aae", and so on).

Ruby provides the method `succ` for this purpose:

```
droid = "R2D2"
improved  = droid.succ          # "R2D3"
pill  = "Vitamin B"
pill2 = pill.succ               # "Vitamin C"
```

We don't recommend the use of this feature unless the values are predictable and reasonable. If you start with a string that is esoteric enough, you will eventually get strange and surprising results.

There is also an `upto` method that applies `succ` repeatedly in a loop until the desired final value is reached:

```
"Files, A".upto "Files, X" do |letter|
  puts "Opening: #{letter}"
end

# Produces 24 lines of output
```

Again, we stress that this is not used frequently, and you use it at your own risk. Also we want to point out that there is no corresponding "predecessor" function at the time of this writing.

2.34   Calculating a 32-Bit CRC

The Cyclic Redundancy Checksum (CRC) is a well-known way of obtaining a "signature" for a file or other collection of bytes. The CRC has the property that the chance of data being changed and keeping the same CRC is 1 in $2**N$, where N is the number of bits in the result (most often 32 bits).

The `zlib` library, created by Ueno Katsuhiro, enables you to do this.

The method `crc32` computes a CRC given a string as a parameter:

```
require 'zlib'
include Zlib
crc = crc32("Hello")            # 4157704578
crc = crc32(" world!",crc)      # 461707669
crc = crc32("Hello world!")     # 461707669 (same as above)
```

A previous CRC can be specified as an optional second parameter; the result will be as if the strings were concatenated and a single CRC was computed. This can be used, for example, to compute the checksum of a file so large that we can only read it in chunks.

2.35   Calculating the MD5 Hash of a String

The MD5 message-digest algorithm produces a 128-bit *fingerprint* or *message digest* of a message of arbitrary length. This is in the form of a hash, so the encryption is one-way and does not allow for the discovery of the original message from the digest. Ruby has an extension for a class to implement MD5; for those interested in the source code, it's in the ext/md5 directory of the standard Ruby distribution.

There are two class methods, new and md5, to create a new MD5 object. There is really no difference in them:

```
require 'md5'
hash = MD5.md5
hash = MD5.new
```

There are four instance methods: clone, digest, hexdigest, and update. The clone method simply copies the object; update is used to add content to the object as follows:

```
hash.update("More information...")
```

You can also create the object and add to the message at the same time:

```
secret = MD5.new("Sensitive data")
```

If a string argument is given, it is added to the object using update. Repeated calls are equivalent to a single call with concatenated arguments:

```
# These two statements...
cryptic.update("Data...")
cryptic.update(" and more data.")

# ...are equivalent to this one.
cryptic.update("Data... and more data.")
```

The digest method provides a 16-byte binary string containing the 128-bit digest.

The hexdigest method is actually the most useful. It provides the digest as an ASCII string of 32 hex characters representing the 16 bytes. This method is equivalent to the following:

```
def hexdigest
  ret = ''
  digest.each_byte {|i| ret << sprintf('%02x', i) }
  ret
end

secret.hexdigest  #  "b30e77a94604b78bd7a7e64ad500f3c2"
```

In short, you can get an MD5 hash as follows:

```
require 'md5'
m = MD5.new("Sensitive data").hexdigest
```

2.36 Calculating the Levenshtein Distance Between Two Strings

The concept of distance between strings is important in inductive learning (AI), cryptography, proteins research, and in other areas.

The Levenshtein distance is the minimum number of modifications needed to change one string into another, using three basic modification operations: del(-etion), ins(-ertion), and sub(-stitution). A substitution is also considered to be a combination of a deletion and insertion (indel).

There are various approaches to this, but we will avoid getting too technical. Suffice it to say that this Ruby implementation (in Listing 2.2) allows you to provide optional parameters to set the cost for the three types of modification operations and defaults to a single indel cost basis (cost of insertion = cost of deletion).

Listing 2.2 The Levenshtein Distance

```
class String

  def levenshtein(other, ins=2, del=2, sub=1)
    # ins, del, sub are weighted costs
    return nil if self.nil?
    return nil if other.nil?
    dm = []         # distance matrix

    # Initialize first row values
    dm[0] = (0..self.length).collect { |i| i * ins }
    fill = [0] * (self.length - 1)
```

Continues

```
    # Initialize first column values
    for i in 1..other.length
      dm[i] = [i * del, fill.flatten]
    end

    # populate matrix
    for i in 1..other.length
      for j in 1..self.length
    # critical comparison
        dm[i][j] = [
             dm[i-1][j-1] +
               (self[j-1] == other[i-1] ? 0 : sub),
                 dm[i][j-1] + ins,
             dm[i-1][j] + del
       ].min
      end
    end

    # The last value in matrix is the
    # Levenshtein distance between the strings
    dm[other.length][self.length]
  end

end


s1 = "ACUGAUGUGA"
s2 = "AUGGAA"
d1 = s1.levenshtein(s2)     # 9


s3 = "pennsylvania"
s4 = "pencilvaneya"
d2 = s3.levenshtein(s4)     # 7


s5 = "abcd"
s6 = "abcd"
d3 = s5.levenshtein(s6)     # 0
```

Now that we have the Levenshtein distance defined, it's conceivable that we could define a similar? method, giving it a threshold for similarity. For example:

```
class String

  def similar?(other, thresh=2)
    if self.levenshtein(other) < thresh
      true
```

```
      else
         false
      end
   end

   end


   if "polarity".similar?("hilarity")
     puts "Electricity is funny!"
   end
```

Of course, it would also be possible to pass in the three weighted costs to the `similar?` method so that they could in turn be passed into the `levenshtein` method. We have omitted these for simplicity.

2.37   Encoding and Decoding base64 Strings

base64 is frequently used to convert machine-readable data into a text form with no special characters in it. For example, newsgroups that handle binary files such as program executables frequently will use base64.

The easiest way to do a base64 encode/decode is to use the built-in features of Ruby. The `Array` class has a `pack` method that returns a base64 string (given the parameter "m"). The `String` class has a method `unpack` that likewise unpacks the string (decoding the base64):

```
str = "\007\007\002\abdce"

new_string = [str].pack("m")         # "BwcCB2JkY2U="
original   = new_string.unpack("m")  # ["\a\a\002\abdce"]
```

Note that an array is returned by `unpack`.

2.38   Encoding and Decoding Strings (uuencode/uudecode)

The *uu* in these names means *UNIX-to-UNIX*. The uuencode and uudecode utilities are a time-honored way of exchanging data in text form (similar to the way base64 is used).

```
str = "\007\007\002\abdce"

new_string = [str].pack("u")        # '(!P<"!V)D8V4`'
original   = new_string.unpack("u") # ["\a\a\002\abdce"]
```

Note that an array is returned by unpack.

2.39   Expanding and Compressing Tab Characters

Occasionally we have a string with tabs in it and we want to convert them to spaces
(or vice versa). The two methods shown here do these operations.

```
class String

  def detab(ts=8)
    str = self.dup
    while (leftmost = str.index("\t")) != nil
      space = " "*(ts-(leftmost%ts))
      str[leftmost]=space
    end
    str
  end

  def entab(ts=8)
    str = self.detab
    areas = str.length/ts
    newstr = ""
    for a in 0..areas
      temp = str[a*ts..a*ts+ts-1]
      if temp.size==ts
        if temp =~ / +/
          match=Regexp.last_match[0]
          endmatch = Regexp.new(match+"$")
          if match.length>1
            temp.sub!(endmatch,"\t")
          end
        end
      end
      newstr += temp
    end
    newstr
  end
```

```
end

foo = "This        is        only    a       test.          "

puts foo
puts foo.entab(4)
puts foo.entab(4).dump
```

Note that this code is not smart enough to handle backspaces.

2.40   Wrapping Lines of Text

Occasionally we may want to take long text lines and print them within margins of
our own choosing. The code fragment shown here accomplishes this, splitting only on
word boundaries and honoring tabs (but not honoring backspaces or preserving tabs):

```
str = <<-EOF
    When in the Course of human events it becomes necessary
    for one people to dissolve the political bands which have
    connected them with another, and to assume among the powers
    of the earth the separate and equal station to which the Laws
    of Nature and of Nature's God entitle them, a decent respect
    for the opinions of mankind requires that they should declare
    the causes which impel them to the separation.
EOF

max = 20

line = 0
out = [""]

input = str.gsub(/\n/," ")
words = input.split(" ")

while input != ""
  word = words.shift
  break if not word
  if out[line].length + word.length > max
    out[line].squeeze!(" ")
    line += 1
    out[line] = ""
  end
```

```
    out[line] << word + " "
  end

  out.each {|line| puts line}  # Prints 24 very short lines
```

The `Format` library also handles this and similar operations. Search for it online.

2.41 Conclusion

Here we have seen the basics of representing strings (both single-quoted and double-quoted). We've seen how to interpolate expressions into double-quoted strings, and how the double quotes also allow certain special characters to be inserted with escape sequences. We've seen the `%q` and `%Q` forms, which permit us to choose our own delimiters for convenience. Finally, we've seen the here-document syntax, carried over from older contexts such as Unix shells.

This chapter has demonstrated all the important operations a programmer wants to perform on a string. These include concatenation, searching, extracting substrings, tokenizing, and much more. We have seen how to iterate over a string by line or by byte. We have seen how to transform a string to and from a coded form such as base64 or compressed form.

It's time now to move on to a related topic—regular expressions. Regular expressions are a powerful tool for detecting patterns in strings. We'll cover this in the next chapter.

CHAPTER 3

Working with Regular Expressions

I would choose
To lead him in a maze along the patterned paths...

—*Amy Lowell, "Patterns"*

The power of regular expressions as a computing tool has often been underestimated. From their earliest theoretical beginnings in the 1940s, they found their way onto computer systems in the 1960s and from there into various tools in the UNIX operating system. In the 1990s, the popularity of Perl helped make regular expressions a household item rather than the esoteric domain of bearded gurus.

The beauty of regular expressions is that almost everything in our experience can be understood in terms of patterns. Where there are patterns that we can describe, we can detect matches; we can find the pieces of reality that correspond to those matches; and we can replace those pieces with others of our own choosing.

As this is being written, Ruby is in flux. The regular expression engine is slated to be replaced with the new one named *Oniguruma*. A later section of the chapter (section 3.13, "Ruby and Oniguruma") is devoted to this newer engine. As for internationalization, most specific issues related to that are dealt with in Chapter 4, "Internationalization in Ruby."

3.1   Regular Expression Syntax

The typical regular expression is delimited by a pair of slashes; the %r form can also be used. Table 3.1, "Basic Regular Expressions," gives some simple examples:

Table 3.1   Basic Regular Expressions

Regex	Explanation
/Ruby/	Match the single word Ruby
/[Rr]uby/	Match *Ruby* or *ruby*
/^abc/	Match an *abc* at beginning of line
%r(xyz$)	Match an *xyz* at end of line
%r|[0-9]*|	Match any sequence of (zero or more) digits

It is also possible to place a modifier, consisting of a single letter, immediately after a regex. Table 3.2 shows the most common modifiers:

Table 3.2   Regular Expression Modifiers

Modifier	Meaning
i	Ignore case in regex
o	Perform expression substitution only once
m	Multiline mode (dot matches newline)
x	Extended regex (allow whitespace, comments)

Others will be covered in Chapter 4.

To complete our introduction to regular expressions, Table 3.3 lists the most common symbols and notations available:

Table 3.3 Common Notations Used in Regular Expressions

Notation	Meaning
^	Beginning of a line or string
$	End of a line or string
.	Any character except newline (unless multiline)
\w	Word character (digit, letter, or underscore)
\W	Non-word character
\s	Whitespace character (space, tab, newline, and so on)
\S	Non-whitespace character
\d	Digit (same as [0-9])
\D	Non-digit
\A	Beginning of a string
\Z	End of a string or before newline at the end
\z	End of a string
\b	Word boundary (outside [] only)
\B	Non-word boundary
\b	Backspace (inside [] only)
[]	Any single character of set
*	0 or more of previous subexpression
*?	0 or more of previous subexpression (non-greedy)
+	1 or more of previous subexpression
+?	1 or more of previous subexpression (non-greedy)
{m,n}	m to n instances of previous subexpression
{m,n}?	m to n instances of previous subexpression (non-greedy)
?	0 or 1 of previous regular expression
|	Alternatives
(?=)	Positive lookahead
(?!)	Negative lookahead
()	Grouping of subexpressions
(?>)	Embedded subexpression
(?:)	Non-capturing group
(?imx-imx)	Turn options on/off henceforth
(?imx-imx:expr)	Turn options on/off for this expression
(?#)	Comment

An understanding of regex handling greatly benefits the modern programmer. A complete discussion of this topic is far beyond the scope of this book, but if you're interested see the definitive work *Mastering Regular Expressions* by Jeffrey Friedl.

For additions and extensions to the material in this section, refer to section 3.13, "Ruby and Oniguruma."

3.2   Compiling Regular Expressions

Regular expressions can be compiled using the class method `Regexp.compile` (which is really only a synonym for `Regexp.new`). The first parameter is required and may be a string or a regex. (Note that if the parameter is a regex with options, the options will not carry over into the newly compiled regex.)

```
pat1 = Regexp.compile("^foo.*")   # /^foo.*/
pat2 = Regexp.compile(/bar$/i)    # /bar/ (i not propagated)
```

The second parameter, if present, is normally a bitwise OR of any of the following constants `Regexp::EXTENDED`, `Regexp::IGNORECASE`, and `Regexp::MULTILINE`. Additionally, any non-`nil` value will have the result of making the regex case-insensitive; we do not recommend this practice.

```
options = Regexp::MULTILINE || Regexp::IGNORECASE
pat3 = Regexp.compile("^foo", options)
pat4 = Regexp.compile(/bar/, Regexp::IGNORECASE)
```

The third parameter, if it is specified, is the language parameter, which enables multibyte character support. It can take any of four string values:

```
"N" or "n" means None
"E" or "e" means EUC
"S" or "s" means Shift-JIS
"U" or "u" means UTF-8
```

Of course, regular expression literals may be specified without calling new or compile, simply by enclosing them in slash delimiters.

```
pat1 = /^foo.*/
pat2 = /bar$/i
```

For more information, see Chapter 4.

3.3   Escaping Special Characters

The class method `Regexp.escape` escapes any characters that are special characters used in regular expressions. Such characters include the asterisk, question mark, and brackets.

```
str1 = "[*?]"
str2 = Regexp.escape(str1)  # "\[\*\?\]"
```

The method `Regexp.quote` is an alias.

3.4   Using Anchors

An *anchor* is a special expression that matches a *position* in a string rather than a character or sequence of characters. As we'll see later, this is a simple case of a *zero-width assertion*, a match that doesn't consume any of the string when it matches.

The most common anchors were already listed at the beginning of this chapter. The simplest are ^ and $, which match the beginning and end of the string.

```
string  = "abcXdefXghi"
/def/   =~ string    # 4
/abc/   =~ string    # 0
/ghi/   =~ string    # 8
/^def/  =~ string    # nil
/def$/  =~ string    # nil
/^abc/  =~ string    # 0
/ghi$/  =~ string    # 8
```

However, I've told a small lie. These anchors don't actually match the beginning and end of the string but of the *line*. Consider the same patterns applied to a similar string with embedded newlines:

```
string  = "abc\ndef\nghi"
/def/   =~ string    # 4
/abc/   =~ string    # 0
/ghi/   =~ string    # 8
/^def/  =~ string    # 4
/def$/  =~ string    # 4
```

```
/^abc/ =~ string     # 0
/ghi$/ =~ string     # 8
```

However, we also have the special anchors \A and \z, which match the real beginning and end of the string itself.

```
string  = "abc\ndef\nghi"
/\Adef/ =~ string    # nil
/def\Z/ =~ string    # nil
/\Aabc/ =~ string    # 0
/ghi\Z/ =~ string    # 8
```

The \z is the same as \Z except that the latter matches *before* a terminating newline, whereas the former must match explicitly.

```
string  = "abc\ndef\nghi"
str2 << "\n"
/ghi\Z/ =~ string    # 8
/\Aabc/ =~ str2      # 8
/ghi\z/ =~ string    # 8
/ghi\z/ =~ str2      # nil
```

It's also possible to match a *word boundary* with \b, or a position that is *not* a word boundary with \B. These gsub examples make it clear how this works:

```
str = "this is a test"
str.gsub(/\b/,"|")     # "|this| |is| |a| |test|"
str.gsub(/\B/,"-")     # "t-h-i-s i-s a t-e-s-t"
```

There is no way to distinguish between beginning and ending word boundaries.

3.5   Using Quantifiers

A big part of regular expressions is handling optional items and repetition. An item followed by a question mark is optional; it may be present or absent, and the match depends on the rest of the regex. (It doesn't make sense to apply this to an anchor but only to a subpattern of non-zero width.)

```
pattern = /ax?b/
pat2    = /a[xy]?b/
```

```
pattern =~ "ab"      # 0
pattern =~ "acb"     # nil
pattern =~ "axb"     # 0
pat2    =~ "ayb"     # 0
pat2    =~ "acb"     # nil
```

It is common for entities to be repeated an indefinite number of times (which we can specify with the + quantifier). For example, this pattern matches any positive integer:

```
pattern = /[0-9]+/
pattern =~ "1"          # 0
pattern =~ "2345678"    # 0
```

Another common occurrence is a pattern that occurs *zero or more* times. We could do this with + and ?, of course; here we match the string Huzzah followed by zero or more exclamation points:

```
pattern = /Huzzah(!+)?/   # Parentheses are necessary here
pattern =~ "Huzzah"       # 0
pattern =~ "Huzzah!!!!"   # 0
```

However, there's a better way. The * quantifier describes this behavior.

```
pattern = /Huzzah!*/      # * applies only to !
pattern =~ "Huzzah"       # 0
pattern =~ "Huzzah!!!!"   # 0
```

What if we want to match a U.S. Social Security Number? Here's a pattern for that:

```
ssn = "987-65-4320"
pattern = /\d\d\d-\d\d-\d\d\d\d/
pattern =~ ssn       # 0
```

But that's a little unclear. Let's explicitly say how many digits are in each group. A number in braces is the quantifier to use here:

```
pattern = /\d{3}-\d{2}-\d{4}/
```

This is not necessarily a shorter pattern, but it is more explicit and arguably more readable.

Comma-separated ranges can also be used. Imagine that an Elbonian phone number consists of a part with three to five digits and a part with three to seven digits. Here's a pattern for that:

```
elbonian_phone = /\d{3,5}-\d{3,7}/
```

The beginning and ending numbers are optional (though we must have one or the other):

```
/x{5}/        # Match 5 xs
/x{5,7}/      # Match 5-7 xs
/x{,8}/       # Match up to 8 xs
/x{3,}/       # Match at least 3 xs
```

Obviously, the quantifiers ?, +, and * *could* be rewritten in this way:

```
/x?/          # same as /x{0,1}/
/x*/          # same as /x{0,}
/x+/          # same as /x{1,}
```

The terminology of regular expressions is full of colorful personifying terms such as *greedy, reluctant, lazy,* and *possessive.* The greedy/non-greedy distinction is one of the most important.

Consider this piece of code. You might expect that this regex would match "Where the", but it matches the larger substring "Where the sea meets the" instead:

```
str = "Where the sea meets the moon-blanch'd land,"
match = /.*the/.match(str)
p match[0]  # Display the entire match:
            # "Where the sea meets the"
```

The reason is that the * operator is greedy—in matching, it consumes as much of the string as it can for the longest match possible. We can make it non-greedy by appending a question mark:

```
str = "Where the sea meets the moon-blanch'd land,"
match = /.*?the/.match(str)
p match[0]  # Display the entire match:
            # "Where the"
```

This shows us that the * operator is greedy by default unless a ? is appended. The same is true for the + and {m,n} quantifiers, and even for the ? quantifier itself.

I haven't been able to find good examples for the {m,n}? and ?? cases. If you know of any, please share them.

For more information on quantifiers, see section 3.13, "Ruby and Oniguruma."

3.6   Positive and Negative Lookahead

Naturally, a regular expression is matched against a string in a linear fashion (with backtracking as necessary). Therefore there is the concept of the "current location" in the string—rather like a file pointer or a cursor.

The term *lookahead* refers to a construct that matches a part of the string *ahead* of the current location. It is a zero-width assertion because even when a match succeeds, no part of the string is consumed (that is, the current location does not change).

In this next example, the string "New World" will be matched *if* it is followed by "Symphony" or "Dictionary"; however, the third word is not part of the match:

```
s1 = "New World Dictionary"
s2 = "New World Symphony"
s3 = "New World Order"

reg = /New World(?= Dictionary| Symphony)/
m1 = reg.match(s1)
m.to_a[0]                # "New World"
m2 = reg.match(s2)
m.to_a[0]                # "New World"
m3 = reg.match(s3)       # nil
```

Here is an example of negative lookahead:

```
reg2 = /New World(?! Symphony)/
m1 = reg.match(s1)
m.to_a[0]                # "New World"
m2 = reg.match(s2)
m.to_a[0]                # nil
m3 = reg.match(s3)       # "New World"
```

In this example, "New World" is matched only if it is *not* followed by "Symphony."

3.7   Accessing Backreferences

Each parenthesized piece of a regular expression will be a submatch of its own. These are numbered and can be referenced by these numbers in more than one way. Let's examine the more traditional "ugly" ways first.

The special global variables $1, $2, and so on, can be used to reference matches:

```
str = "a123b45c678"
if /(a\d+)(b\d+)(c\d+)/ =~ str
  puts "Matches are: '#$1', '#$2', '#$3'"
  # Prints: Matches are: 'a123', 'b45', 'c768'
end
```

Within a substitution such as sub or gsub, these variables *cannot* be used:

```
str = "a123b45c678"
str.sub(/(a\d+)(b\d+)(c\d+)/, "1st=#$1, 2nd=#$2, 3rd=#$3")
# "1st=, 2nd=, 3rd="
```

Why didn't this work? Because the arguments to sub are evaluated before sub is called. This code is equivalent:

```
str = "a123b45c678"
s2 = "1st=#$1, 2nd=#$2, 3rd=#$3"
reg = /(a\d+)(b\d+)(c\d+)/
str.sub(reg,s2)
# "1st=, 2nd=, 3rd="
```

This code, of course, makes it much clearer that the values $1 through $3 are *unrelated* to the match done inside the sub call.

In this kind of case, the special codes \1, \2, and so on, can be used:

```
str = "a123b45c678"
str.sub(/(a\d+)(b\d+)(c\d+)/, '1st=\1, 2nd=\2, 3rd=\3')
# "1st=a123, 2nd=b45, 3rd=c768"
```

Notice that we used single quotes (hard quotes) in the preceding example. If we used double quotes (soft quotes) in a straightforward way, the backslashed items would be interpreted as octal escape sequences:

```
str = "a123b45c678"
str.sub(/(a\d+)(b\d+)(c\d+)/, "1st=\1, 2nd=\2, 3rd=\3")
# "1st=\001, 2nd=\002, 3rd=\003"
```

The way around this is to double-escape:

```
str = "a123b45c678"
str.sub(/(a\d+)(b\d+)(c\d+)/, "1st=\\1, 2nd=\\2, 3rd=\\3")
# "1st=a123, 2nd=b45, 3rd=c678"
```

It's also possible to use the block form of a substitution, in which case the global variables may be used:

```
str = "a123b45c678"
str.sub(/(a\d+)(b\d+)(c\d+)/)  { "1st=#$1, 2nd=#$2, 3rd=#$3" }
# "1st=a123, 2nd=b45, 3rd=c678"
```

When using a block in this way, it is *not* possible to use the special backslashed numbers inside a double-quoted string (or even a single-quoted one). This is reasonable if you think about it.

As an aside here, I will mention the possibility of *noncapturing groups*. Sometimes you may want to regard characters as a group for purposes of crafting a regular expression; but you may not need to capture the matched value for later use. In such a case, you can use a noncapturing group, denoted by the (?:...) syntax:

```
str = "a123b45c678"
str.sub(/(a\d+)(?:b\d+)(c\d+)/, "1st=\\1, 2nd=\\2, 3rd=\\3")
# "1st=a123, 2nd=c678, 3rd="
```

In the preceding example, the second grouping was thrown away, and what was the third submatch became the *second*.

I personally don't like either the \1 or the $1 notations. They are convenient sometimes, but it isn't ever necessary to use them. We can do it in a "prettier," more object-oriented way.

The class method Regexp.last_match returns an object of class MatchData (as does the instance method match). This object has instance methods that enable the programmer to access backreferences.

The MatchData object is manipulated with a bracket notation as though it were an array of matches. The special element 0 contains the text of the entire matched string. Thereafter, element n refers to the nth match:

```
pat = /(.+[aiu])(.+[aiu])(.+[aiu])(.+[aiu])/i
# Four identical groups in this pattern
refs = pat.match("Fujiyama")
# refs is now: ["Fujiyama","Fu","ji","ya","ma"]
x = refs[1]
y = refs[2..3]
refs.to_a.each {|x| print "#{x}\n"}
```

Note that the object refs is not a true array. Thus when we want to treat it as one by using the iterator each, we must use to_a (as shown) to convert it to an array.

We may use more than one technique to locate a matched substring within the original string. The methods begin and end return the beginning and ending offsets of a match. (It is important to realize that the ending offset is really the index of the next character after the match.)

```
str = "alpha beta gamma delta epsilon"
#       0....5....0....5....0....5....
#       (for  your counting convenience)

pat = /(b[^ ]+ )(g[^ ]+ )(d[^ ]+ )/
# Three words, each one a single match
refs = pat.match(str)

# "beta "
p1 = refs.begin(1)          # 6
p2 = refs.end(1)            # 11
# "gamma "
p3 = refs.begin(2)          # 11
p4 = refs.end(2)            # 17
# "delta "
p5 = refs.begin(3)          # 17
p6 = refs.end(3)            # 23
# "beta gamma delta"
p7 = refs.begin(0)          # 6
p8 = refs.end(0)            # 23
```

Similarly, the `offset` method returns an array of two numbers, which are the beginning and ending offsets of that match. To continue the previous example:

```
range0 = refs.offset(0)     # [6,23]
range1 = refs.offset(1)     # [6,11]
range2 = refs.offset(2)     # [11,17]
range3 = refs.offset(3)     # [17,23]
```

The portions of the string before and after the matched substring can be retrieved by the instance methods `pre_match` and `post_match`, respectively. To continue the previous example:

```
before = refs.pre_match     # "alpha "
after  = refs.post_match    # "epsilon"
```

3.8 Using Character Classes

Character classes are simply a form of alternation (specification of alternative possibilities) where each submatch is a single character. In the simplest case, we list a set of characters inside square brackets:

```
/[aeiou]/     # Match any single letter a, e, i, o, u; equivalent
              # to /(a|e|i|o|u)/ except for group-capture
```

Inside a character class, escape sequences such as \n are still meaningful, but metacharacters such as . and ? do not have any special meanings:

```
/[.\n?]/      # Match any of: period, newline, question mark
```

The caret (^) has special meaning inside a character class if used at the beginning; it negates the list of characters (or refers to their complement):

```
[^aeiou]      # Any character EXCEPT a, e, i, o, u
```

The hyphen, used within a character class, indicates a range of characters (a lexicographic range, that is):

```
/[a-mA-M]/    # Any letter in the first half of the alphabet
/[^a-mA-M]/   # Any OTHER letter, or number, or non-alphanumeric
              # character
```

When a hyphen is used at the beginning or end of a character class, or a caret is used in the middle of a character class, these characters lose their special meaning and only represent themselves literally. The same is true of a left bracket, but a right bracket must obviously be escaped:

```
/[-^[\]]/      # Match a hyphen, caret, or right bracket
```

Ruby regular expressions may contain references to named character classes, which are basically named patterns (of the form [[:name:]]). For example, [[:digit:]] means the same as [0-9] in a pattern. In many cases, this turns out to be shorthand or is at least more readable.

Some others are [[:print:]] (printable characters) and [[:alpha:]] (alphabetic characters):

```
s1 = "abc\007def"
/[[:print:]]*/.match(s1)
m1 = Regexp::last_match[0]               # "abc"

s2 = "1234def"
/[[:digit:]]*/.match(s2)
m2 = Regexp::last_match[0]               # "1234"

/[[:digit:]]+[[:alpha:]]/.match(s2)
m3 = Regexp::last_match[0]               # "1234d"
```

A caret before the character class name negates the class:

```
/[[:^alpha:]]/   # Any non-alpha character
```

There are also shorthand notations for many classes. The most common ones are \d (to match a digit), \w (to match any "word" character), and \s (to match any whitespace character such as a space, tab, or newline):

```
str1 = "Wolf 359"
/\w+/.match(str1)        # matches "Wolf" (same as /[a-zA-Z_0-9]+/)
/\w+ \d+/.match(str1)    # matches "Wolf 359"
/\w+ \w+/.match(str1)    # matches "Wolf 359"
/\s+/.match(str1)        # matches " "
```

The "negated" forms are typically capitalized:

```
/\W/                       # Any non-word character
/\D/                       # Any non-digit character
/\S/                       # Any non-whitespace character
```

For additional information specific to Oniguruma, refer to section 3.13, "Ruby and Oniguruma."

3.9 Extended Regular Expressions

Regular expressions are frequently cryptic, especially as they get longer. The x directive enables you to stretch out a regex across multiple lines; spaces and newlines are ignored, so that you can use these for indentation and readability. This also encourages the use of comments, although comments are possible even in simple regexes.

For a contrived example of a moderately complex regular expression, let's suppose that we had a list of addresses like this:

```
addresses =
  [ "409 W Jackson Ave",          "No. 27 Grande Place",
    "16000 Pennsylvania Avenue",  "2367 St. George St.",
    "22 Rue Morgue",              "33 Rue St. Denis",
    "44 Rue Zeeday",              "55 Santa Monica Blvd.",
    "123 Main St., Apt. 234",     "123 Main St., #234",
    "345 Euneva Avenue, Suite 23", "678 Euneva Ave, Suite A"]
```

In these examples, each address consists of three parts—a number, a street name, and an optional suite or apartment number. I'm making the arbitrary rules that there can be an optional No. on the front of the number, and the period may be omitted. Likewise let's arbitrarily say that the street name may consist of ordinary word characters but also allows the apostrophe, hyphen, and period. Finally, if the optional suite number is used, it must be preceded by a comma and one of the tokens Apt., Suite, or # (number sign).

Here is the regular expression I created for this. Notice that I've commented it heavily (maybe even too heavily):

```
regex = / ^                      # Beginning of string
           ((No\.?)\s+)?          # Optional: No[.]
           \d+ \s+               # Digits and spacing
           ((\w|[.'-])+          # Street name... may be
            \s*                  #   multiple words.
           )+
           (,\s*                 # Optional: Comma etc.
            (Apt\.?|Suite|\#)    # Apt[.], Suite, #
            \s+                  # Spacing
            (\d+|[A-Z])          # Numbers or single letter
           )?
           $                     # End of string
         /x
```

The point here is clear. When your regex reaches a certain threshold (which is a matter of opinion), make it an extended regex so that you can format it and add comments.

You may have noticed that I used ordinary Ruby comments here (# ...) instead of regex comments ((?#...)). Why did I do that? Simply because I could. The regex comments are needed only when the comment needs to be *closed* other than at the end of the line (for example, when more "meat" of the regex follows the comment on the same line).

3.10   Matching a Newline with a Dot

Ordinarily a dot matches any character except a newline. When the m (multiline) modifier is used, a newline will be matched by a dot. The same is true when the Regexp::MULTILINE option is used in creating a regex:

```
str = "Rubies are red\nAnd violets are blue.\n"
pat1 = /red./
pat2 = /red./m

str =~ pat1     # nil
str =~ pat2     # 11
```

This multiline mode has no effect on where anchors match (such as ^, $, \A, and \z); they match in the same places. All that is affected is whether a dot matches a newline.

3.11   Using Embedded Options

The common way to specify options for a regex is to use a trailing option (such as i or m). But what if we want an option to apply only to part of a regular expression?

We can turn options on and off with a special notation. Within parentheses, a question mark followed by one or more options "turns on" those options for the remainder of the regular expression. A minus sign preceding one or more options "turns off" those options:

```
/abc(?i)def/          # Will match abcdef, abcDEF, abcDef, ...
                      #   but not ABCdef
/ab(?i)cd(?-i)ef/     # Will match abcdef, abCDef, abcDef, ...
                      #   but not ABcdef or abcdEF
/(?imx).*/            # Same as /.*/imx
/abc(?i-m).*/m        # For last part of regex, turn on case
                      #   sensitivity, turn off multiline
```

If we want, we can use a colon followed by a subexpression, and those options specified will be in effect only for that subexpression:

```
/ab(?i:cd)ef/         # Same as /ab(?i)cd(?-i)ef/
```

For technical reasons, it is not possible to treat the o option this way. The x option *can* be treated this way, but I don't know why anyone ever would.

3.12   Using Embedded Subexpressions

We can use the ?> notation to specify subexpressions in a regex:

```
re = /(?>abc)(?>def)/        # Same as /abcdef/
re.match("abcdef").to_a      # ["abcdef"]
```

Notice that the subexpressions themselves don't imply grouping. We *can* turn them into capturing groups with additional parentheses, of course.

Note that this notation is *possessive*—that is, it is greedy, and it does *not* allow backtracking into the subexpression.

```
str = "abccccdef"
re1 = /(abc*)cdef/
re2 = /(?>abc*)cdef/
```

```
re1 =~ str              # 0
re2 =~ str              # nil
re1.match(str).to_a     # ["abccccdef", "abccc"]
re2.match(str).to_a     # []
```

In the preceding example, re2's subexpression abc* consumes all the instances of the letter *c*, and it (possessively) won't give them back to allow backtracking.

3.13   Ruby and Oniguruma

Ruby's new regular expression engine is code-named *Oniguruma*, a Japanese name meaning roughly *ghost wheel* or *demon wheel*. (It is commonly misspelled by non-Japanese; remember you can't spell Oniguruma without "guru.")

The new engine offers several benefits over the old one. Notably, it handles internationalized strings better, and it adds some powerful features to Ruby's regular expressions. Additionally, it is offered under a less restrictive license, comparable to the rest of Ruby. As this book is being written, Oniguruma is not yet fully integrated into the standard distribution.

The next section deals with detecting the presence of the Oniguruma engine. The section after that outlines how to build it if you don't have it built in.

3.13.1   Testing the Presence of Oniguruma

If you're concerned with Oniguruma, the first step is to find out whether you are already using it. If you are running Ruby 1.8.4 or earlier, you probably don't have the new engine. It is standard in 1.9.

Here is a simple method that uses a three-pronged approach to determine whether the new engine is in place. First, as I said, it's standard in 1.9 and later. In recent versions of *both* engines, a Regexp::ENGINE is defined; if this string contains the substring Oniguruma, this is the new engine. Finally, we use a trick. If we still haven't determined which engine we have, we will try to evaluate a regex with "new" syntax. If it raises a SyntaxError, we have the old engine; otherwise, the new one.

```
def oniguruma?
  return true if RUBY_VERSION >= "1.9.0"

  if defined?(Regexp::ENGINE)  # Is ENGINE defined?
    if Regexp::ENGINE.include?('Oniguruma')
      return true               # Some version of Oniguruma
    else
      return false              # Pre-Oniguruma engine
    end
  end

  eval("/(?<!a)b/")             # Newer syntax
  return true                   # It worked: New engine.
rescue SyntaxError              # It failed: We're using the
  return false                  #   old engine.
end

puts oniguruma?
```

3.13.2   Building Oniguruma

If you don't have Oniguruma, you *can* compile Ruby yourself and link it in. The current instructions are shown below. These should work with versions as far back as 1.6.8 (though these are fairly old).

You should be able to obtain the Oniguruma archive from the RAA (http://raa.ruby-lang.org/) or other sources. The Ruby source itself, of course, is always available from the main Ruby site.

If you are on a UNIX-like platform (including a Cygwin environment on Windows or Mac OS/X), you can follow the procedure shown here:

1. gunzip oniguruma.tar.gz

2. tar xvf oniguruma.tar

3. cd oniguruma

4. ./configure —with-rubydir=<ruby-source-dir>

5. One of:

    make 16 # for Ruby 1.6.8

    make 18 # for Ruby 1.8.0/1.8.1

6. cd ruby-source-dir

7. `./configure`

8. `make clean`

9. `make`

10. `make test # Simple test of Ruby interpreter`

11. `cd ../oniguruma # adjust path as needed`

12. `make rtest`

    Or:

    `make rtest RUBYDIR=ruby-install-dir`

If you are on a pure Win32 such as Windows XP, you will need both Visual C++ and a copy of the `patch.exe` executable. Then perform the following steps:

1. Unzip the archive with whatever software you use.

2. `copy win32\Makefile Makefile`

3. One of:

   ```
   nmake 16 RUBYDIR=ruby-source-dir # for Ruby 1.6.8
   nmake 18 RUBYDIR=ruby-source-dir # for Ruby 1.8.0/1.8.1
   ```

4. Follow the directions in `ruby-source-dir\win32\README.win32`.

If there are problems, use the mailing list or newsgroup as a resource.

3.13.3   A Few New Features of Oniguruma

Oniguruma adds many new features to regular expressions in Ruby. Among the simplest of these is an additional character class escape sequence. Just as `\d` and `\D` match digits and nondigits, respectively (for decimal numbers), `\h` and `\H` do the same for hexadecimal digits:

```
"abc" =~ /\h+/   # 0
"DEF" =~ /\h+/   # 0
"abc" =~ /\H+/   # nil
```

Character classes in brackets get a little more power. The && operator can be used to nest character classes. Here is a regex that matches any letter *except* the vowels a, e, i, o, and u:

```
reg1 = /[a-z&&[^aeiou]]/      # Set intersection
```

Here is an example matching the entire alphabet but "masking off" m through p:

```
reg2 = /[a-z&&[^m-p]]/
```

Because this can be confusing, I recommend using this feature sparingly.

Other Oniguruma features such as lookbehind and named matches are covered in the rest of section 3.13. Features related to internationalization are deferred until Chapter 4.

3.13.4   Positive and Negative Lookbehind

If lookahead isn't enough for you, Oniguruma offers *lookbehind*—detecting whether the current location is preceded by a given pattern.

Like many areas of regular expressions, this can be difficult to understand and motivate. Thanks goes to Andrew Johnson for the following example.

Imagine that we are analyzing some genetic sequence. (The DNA molecule consists of four "base" molecules, abbreviated A, C, G, and T.) Suppose that we are scanning for all nonoverlapping nucleotide sequences (of length 4) that follow a T. We couldn't just try to match a T and four characters because the T may have been the last character of the previous match.

```
gene = 'GATTACAAACTGCCTGACATACGAA'
seqs = gene.scan(/T(\w{4})/)
# seqs is: [["TACA"], ["GCCT"], ["ACGA"]]
```

But in this preceding code, we miss the GACA sequence that follows GCCT. Using a positive lookbehind (as follows), we catch them all:

```
gene = 'GATTACAAACTGCCTGACATACGAA'
seqs = gene.scan(/(?<=T)(\w{4})/)
# seqs is: [["TACA"], ["GCCT"], ["GACA"], ["ACGA"]]
```

This next example is adapted from one by K. Kosako. Suppose that we want to take a bunch of text in XML (or HTML) and shift to uppercase all the text *outside* the tags (that is, the cdata). Here is a way to do that using lookbehind:

```
text = <<-EOF
<body> <h1>This is a heading</h1>
<p> This is a paragraph with some
<i>italics</i> and some <b>boldface</b>
in it...</p>
</body>
EOF


pattern = /(?:^|              # Beginning or...
            (?<=>)     #  following a '>'
          )
          ([^<]*)       # Then all non-'<' chars (captured).
          /x


puts text.gsub(pattern) {|s| s.upcase }


# Output:
# <body> <h1>THIS IS A HEADING</h1>
# <p>THIS IS A PARAGRAPH WITH SOME
# <i>ITALICS</i> AND SOME <b>BOLDFACE</b>
# IN IT...</p>
# </body>
```

3.13.5   More on Quantifiers

We've already seen the atomic subexpression in Ruby's "regex classic" engine. This uses the notation (?>...), and it is "possessive" in the sense that it is *greedy* and *does not allow backtracking* into the subexpression.

Oniguruma allows another way of expressing possessiveness, with the postfix + quantifier. This is distinct from the + meaning "one or more" and can in fact be combined with it. (In fact, it is a "secondary" quantifier, like the ? which gives us ??, +?, and *?).

In essence, + applied to a repeated pattern is the same as enclosing that repeated pattern in an independent subexpression. For example:

```
r1 = /x*+/    # Same as:  /(?>x*)/
r2 = /x++/    # Same as:  /(?>x+)/
r3 = /x?+/    # Same as:  /(?>x?)/
```

For technical reasons, Ruby does not honor the {n,m}+ notation as possessive.

Obviously, this new quantifier is largely a notational convenience. It doesn't really offer any new functionality.

3.13.6   Named Matches

A special form of subexpression is the *named* expression. This in effect gives a name to a pattern (rather than just a number).

The syntax is simple: (?<name>expr) where *name* is some name starting with a letter (like a Ruby identifier). Notice how similar this is to the non-named atomic subexpression.

What can we do with a named expression? One thing is to use it as a backreference. The following example is a simple regex that matches a doubled word (see also section 3.14.6, "Detecting Doubled Words in Text"):

```
re1 = /\s+(\w+)\s+\1\s+/
str = "Now is the the time for all..."
re1.match(str).to_a          # ["the the","the"]
```

Note how we capture the word and then use \1 to reference it. We can use named references in much the same way. We give the name to the subexpression when we first use it, and we access the backreference by \k followed by that same name (always in angle brackets).

```
re2 = /\s+(?<anyword>\w+)\s+\k<anyword>\s+/
```

The second variant is longer but arguably more readable. (Be aware that if you use named backreferences, you *cannot* use numbered backreferences in the same regex.) Use this feature at your discretion.

Ruby has long had the capability to use backreferences in strings passed to sub and gsub; in the past, this has been limited to numbered backreferences, but in very recent versions, named matches can be used:

```
str = "I breathe when I sleep"

# Numbered matches...
r1  = /I (\w+) when I (\w+)/
s1  = str.sub(r1,'I \2 when I \1')

# Named matches...
r1  = /I (?<verb1>\w+) when I (?<verb2>\w+)/
s2  = str.sub(r2,'I \k<verb2> when I \k<verb1>')

puts s1      # I sleep when I breathe
puts s2      # I sleep when I breathe
```

Another use for named expressions is to *re-invoke* that expression. In this case, we use \g (rather than \k) preceding the name.

For example, let's defines a spaces subpattern so that we can use it again. The last regex then becomes

```
re3 = /(?<spaces>\s+)(?<anyword>\w+)\g<spaces>\k<anyword>\g<spaces>/
```

Note how we invoke the pattern repeatedly by means of the \g marker. This feature makes more sense if the regular expression is recursive; that is the topic of the next section.

A notation such as \g<1> may also be used *if* there are no named subexpressions. This re-invokes a captured subexpression by referring to it by number rather than name.

One final note on the use of named matches. In the most recent versions of Ruby, the name can be used (as a symbol or a string) as a MatchData index. For example:

```
str = "My hovercraft is full of eels"
reg = /My (?<noun>\w+) is (?<predicate>.*)/
m = reg.match(str)
puts m[:noun]              # hovercraft
puts m["predicate"]        # full of eels
puts m[1]                  # same as m[:noun] or m["noun"]
```

As shown, ordinary indices may still be used. There is also some discussion of adding singleton methods to the `MatchData` object.

```
puts m.noun
puts m.predicate
```

At the time of this writing, this has not been implemented.

3.13.7 Recursion in Regular Expressions

The ability to re-invoke a subexpression makes it possible to craft recursive regular expressions. For example, here is one that matches any properly nested parenthesized expression. (Thanks again to Andrew Johnson.)

```
str = "a * ((b-c)/(d-e) - f) * g"

reg = /(?             # begin named expression
        \(            # match open paren
        (?:           # non-capturing group
          (?>         # possessive subexpr to match:
            \\[()]    #   either an escaped paren
          |           # OR
            [^()]     #   a non-paren character
          )           # end possessive
        |             # OR
          \g          # a nested parens group (recursive call)
        )*            # repeat non-captured group zero or more
        \)            # match closing paren
      )               # end named expression
    /x
m = reg.match(str).to_a    # ["((b-c)/(d-e) - f)", "((b-c)/(d-e) - f)"]
```

Note that *left-recursion* is not allowed. This is legal:

```
str = "bbbaccc"
re1 = /(?<foo>a|b\g<foo>c)/
re1.match(str).to_a        # ["bbbaccc","bbbaccc"]
```

But this is *illegal*:

```
re2 = /(?<foo>a|\g<foo>c)/ # Syntax error!
```

This example is illegal because of the recursion at the head of each alternative. This leads, if you think about it, to an infinite regress.

3.14   A Few Sample Regular Expressions

This section presents a small list of regular expressions that might be useful either in actual use or as samples to study. For simplicity, none of these patterns depends on Oniguruma.

3.14.1   Matching an IP Address

Suppose that we want to determine whether a string is a valid IPv4 address. The standard form of such an address is a *dotted quad* or *dotted decimal* string. This is, in other words, four decimal numbers separated by periods, each number ranging from 0 to 255.

The pattern given here will do the trick (with a few exceptions such as "127.1"). We break up the pattern a little just for readability. Note that the \d symbol is double-escaped so that the slash in the string gets passed on to the regex. (We'll improve on this in a minute.)

```
num = "(\\d|[01]?\\d\\d|2[0-4]\\d|25[0-5])"
pat = "^(#{num}\.){3}#{num}$"
ip_pat = Regexp.new(pat)

ip1 = "9.53.97.102"

if ip1 =~ ip_pat                    # Prints "yes"
  puts "yes"
else
  puts "no"
end
```

Note how we have an excess of backslashes when we define num in the preceding example. Let's define it as a regex instead of a string:

```
num = /(\d|[01]?\d\d|2[0-4]\d|25[0-5])/
```

When a regex is interpolated into another, to_s is called, which preserves all the information in the original regex.

```
num.to_s    # "(?-mix:(\\d|[01]?\\d\\d|2[0-4]\\d|25[0-5]))"
```

In some cases, it is more important to use a regex instead of a string for embedding. A good rule of thumb is to interpolate regexes unless there is some reason you must interpolate a string.

IPv6 addresses are not in widespread use yet, but we include them for completeness. These consist of eight colon-separated 16-bit hex numbers with zeroes suppressed.

```
num = /[0-9A-Fa-f]{0,4}/
pat = /^(#{num}:){7}#{num}$/
ipv6_pat = Regexp.new(pat)

v6ip = "abcd::1324:ea54::dead::beef"

if v6ip =~ ipv6_pat      # Prints "yes"
  puts "yes"
else
  puts "no"
end
```

3.14.2 Matching a Keyword-Value Pair

Occasionally we want to work with strings of the form "attribute=value" (as, for example, when we parse some kind of configuration file for an application).

The following code fragment extracts the keyword and the value. The assumptions are that the keyword or attribute is a single word, the value extends to the end of the line, and the equal sign may be surrounded by whitespace:

```
pat = /(\w+)\s*=\s*(.*?)$/
str = "color = blue"

matches = pat.match(str)

puts matches[1]        # "color"
puts matches[2]        # "blue"
```

3.14.3   Matching Roman Numerals

In the following example we match against a complex pattern to determine whether a string is a valid Roman number (up to decimal 3999). As before, the pattern is broken up into parts for readability:

```
rom1 = /m{0,3}/i
rom2 = /(d?c{0,3}|c[dm])/i
rom3 = /(l?x{0,3}|x[lc])/i
rom4 = /(v?i{0,3}|i[vx])/i
roman = /^#{rom1}#{rom2}#{rom3}#{rom4}$/

year1985 = "MCMLXXXV"

if year1985 =~ roman        # Prints "yes"
  puts "yes"
else
  puts "no"
end
```

You might be tempted to put the i on the end of the whole expression and leave it off the smaller ones:

```
# This doesn't work!

rom1 = /m{0,3}/
rom2 = /(d?c{0,3}|c[dm])/
rom3 = /(l?x{0,3}|x[lc])/
rom4 = /(v?i{0,3}|i[vx])/
roman = /^#{rom1}#{rom2}#{rom3}#{rom4}$/i
```

Why doesn't this work? Look at this for the answer:

```
rom1.to_s   # "(?-mix:m{0,3})"
```

Notice how the to_s captures the flags for each subexpression, and these then override the flag on the big expression.

3.14.4   Matching Numeric Constants

A simple decimal integer is the easiest number to match. It has an optional sign and consists thereafter of digits (except that Ruby allows an underscore as a digit separator). Note that the first digit should not be a zero; then it would be interpreted as an octal constant:

```
int_pat = /^[+-]?[1-9][\d_]*$/
```

Integer constants in other bases are similar. Note that the hex and binary patterns have been made case-insensitive because they contain at least one letter:

```
hex_pat = /^[+-]?0x[\da-f_]+$/i
oct_pat = /^[+-]?0[0-7_]+$/
bin_pat = /^[+-]?0b[01_]+$/i
```

A normal floating point constant is a little tricky; the number sequences on each side of the decimal point are optional, but one or the other must be included:

```
float_pat = /^(\d[\d_]*)*\.[\d_]*$/
```

Finally, scientific notation builds on the ordinary floating-point pattern:

```
sci_pat = /^(\d[\d_]*)?\.[\d_]*(e[+-]?)?(_*\d[\d_]*)$/i
```

These patterns can be useful if, for instance, you have a string and you want to verify its validity as a number before trying to convert it.

3.14.5   Matching a Date/Time String

Suppose that we want to match a date/time in the form mm/dd/yy hh:mm:ss. This pattern is a good first attempt: datetime = /(\d\d)\/(\d\d)\/(\d\d) (\d\d):(\d\d):(\d\d)/.

However, that will also match invalid date/times and miss valid ones. The following example is pickier. Note how we build it up by interpolating smaller regexes into larger ones:

```
mo = /(0?[1-9]|1[0-2])/      # 01 to 09 or 1 to 9 or 10-12
dd = /([0-2]?[1-9]|[1-3][01])/  # 1-9 or 01-09 or 11-19 etc.
yy = /(\d\d)/                # 00-99
hh = /([01]?[1-9]|[12][0-4])/   # 1-9 or 00-09 or...
```

```
mi = /([0-5]\d)/              # 00-59, both digits required
ss = /([0-6]\d)?/             # allows leap seconds ;-)

date = /(#{mo}\/#{dd}\/#{yy})/
time = /(#{hh}:#{mi}:#{ss})/

datetime = /(#{date} #{time})/
```

Here's how we might call it using `String#scan` to return an array of matches:

```
str="Recorded on 11/18/07 20:31:00"
str.scan(datetime)
# [["11/18/07 20:31:00", "11/18/07", "11", "18", "00",
#   "20:31:00", "20", "31", ":00"]]
```

Of course, this could all have been done as a large extended regex:

```
datetime = %r{(
  (0?[1-9]|1[0-2])/              # mo: 01 to 09 or 1 to 9 or 10-12
  ([0-2]?[1-9]|[1-3][01])/       # dd: 1-9 or 01-09 or 11-19 etc.
  (\d\d) [ ]                     # yy: 00-99
  ([01]?[1-9]|[12][0-4]):        # hh: 1-9 or 00-09 or...
  ([0-5]\d):                     # mm: 00-59, both digits required
  (([0-6]\d))?                   # ss: allows leap seconds ;-)
)}x
```

Note the use of the `%r{}` notation so that we don't have to escape the slashes.

3.14.6   Detecting Doubled Words in Text

In this section we implement the famous double-word detector. Typing the same word twice in succession is a common typing error. The following code detects instances of that occurrence:

```
double_re = /\b(['A-Z]+) +\1\b/i

str="There's there's the the pattern."
str.scan(double_re)   #  [["There's"],["the"]]
```

Note that the trailing `i` in the regex is for case-insensitive matching. There is an array for each grouping, hence the resulting array of arrays.

3.14.7 Matching All-Caps Words

This example is simple if we assume no numerics, underscores, and so on:

```
allcaps = /\b[A-Z]+\b/

string = "This is ALL CAPS"
string[allcaps]                    #   "ALL"
Suppose you want to extract every word in all-caps:
string.scan(allcaps)               #   ["ALL", "CAPS"]
```

If we wanted, we could extend this concept to include Ruby identifiers and similar items.

3.14.8 Matching Version Numbers

A common convention is to express a library or application version number by three dot-separated numbers. This regex matches that kind of string, with the package name and the individual numbers as submatches

```
package = "mylib-1.8.12"
matches = package.match(/(.*)-(\d+)\.(\d+)\.(\d+)/)
name, major, minor, tiny = matches[1..-1]
```

3.14.9 A Few Other Patterns

Let's end this list with a few more "odds and ends." As usual, most of these could be done in more than one way.

Suppose that we wanted to match a two-character USA state postal code. The simple way is just /[A-Z]{2}/, of course. But this matches names such as XY and ZZ that look legal but are meaningless. The following regex matches all the 51 usual codes (50 states and the District of Columbia):

```
state =   /^A[LKZR] | C[AOT] | D[EC] | FL | GA | HI | I[DLNA] |
          K[SY] | LA | M[EDAINSOT] | N[EVHJMYCD] | O[HKR] |
          PA | RI | S[CD] | T[NX] | UT | V[TA] | W[AVIY]$/x
```

For clarity, I've made this an extended regex (by using the x modifier). The spaces and newlines are ignored.

In a similar vein, here is a regex to match a U.S. ZIP Code (which may be five or nine digits):

```
zip = /^\d{5}(-\d{4})?$/
```

The anchors (in this regex and others) are only to ensure that there are no extraneous characters before or after the matched string. Note that this regex will *not* catch all invalid codes. In that sense, it is less useful than the preceding one.

The following regex matches a phone number in the NANP format (North American Numbering Plan). It allows three common ways of writing such a phone number:

```
phone = /^((\(\d{3}\) |\d{3}-)\d{3}-\d{4}|\d{3}\.\d{3}\.\d{4})$/
"(512) 555-1234" =~ phone       # true
"512.555.1234"   =~ phone       # true
"512-555-1234"   =~ phone       # true
"(512)-555-1234" =~ phone       # false
"512-555.1234"   =~ phone       # false
```

Matching a dollar amount with optional cents is also trivial:

```
dollar = /^\$\d+(\.\d\d)?$/
```

This one obviously requires at least one digit to the left of the decimal and disallows spaces after the dollar sign. Also note that if you only wanted to *detect* a dollar amount rather than *validate* it, the anchors would be removed and the optional cents would be unnecessary.

3.15 Conclusion

That ends our discussion of regular expressions in Ruby. Now that we have looked at both strings and regexes, let's take a look at some issues with internationalization in Ruby. This topic builds on both the string and regex material we have already seen.

CHAPTER 4

Internationalization
in Ruby

*Therefore, [the place] was called Babel, because there the Lord confused the
language of all the earth; and from there the Lord scattered them abroad over
the face of all the earth.*

—*Genesis 11:9*

Earlier we said that character data was arguably the most important data type. But
what do we mean by character data? Whose characters, whose alphabet, whose language and culture?

In the past computing has had an Anglocentric bias, perhaps going back as far as
Charles Babbage. This is not necessarily a bad thing. We had to start somewhere, and
it might as well be with an alphabet of 26 letters and no diacritic marks (accents and
other marks added to a base character).

But computing is a global phenomenon now. Probably every country in the world
has at least some computers and some Net access. Naturally everyone would prefer to
work with web pages, email, and other data not just in English but in that person's
own language.

Human written languages are amazingly diverse. Some are nearly phonetic; others are hardly phonetic at all. Some have true alphabets, whereas others are mostly

large collections of thousands of symbols evolved from pictograms. Some languages have more than one alphabet. Some are intended to be written vertically; some are written horizontally, as most of us are used to—but from right to left, as most of us are not used to. Some alphabets are fairly plain; some have letters adorned with a bewildering array of dots, accents, circles, lines, and ticks. Some languages have letters that can be combined with their neighboring letters in certain circumstances; sometimes this is mandatory, sometimes optional. Some languages have the concept of upper- and lowercase letters; most do not.

We've come a long way in 25 years or so. We've managed to create a little order out of the chaos of characters and languages.

If you deal much with programming applications that are meant to be used in linguistically diverse environments, you know the term *internationalization*. This could be defined as the enabling of software to handle more than one written language.

Related terms are *multilingualization* and *localization*. All of these are traditionally abbreviated by the curious practice of deleting the middle letters and replacing them with the number of letters deleted:

```
def shorten(str)
  (str[0..0] + str[1..-2].length.to_s + str[-1..-1]).upcase
end

shorten("internationalization")      # I18N
shorten("multilingualization")       # M17N
shorten("localization")              # L10N
```

The terms *I18N* and *M17N* are largely synonymous; *globalization* has also been used, but this has other meanings in other contexts. The term *L10N* refers to something a little broader—the complete support for local conventions and culture, such as currency symbols, ways of formatting dates and times, using a comma as a decimal separator, and much more.

Let's start by examining a little terminology, since this area of computing is fairly prone to jargon. This will also include a little history, since the current state of affairs makes sense only as we view its slow evolution. The history lessons will be kept to a minimum.

4.1 Background and Terminology

In the "bad old days" of computing, roughly contemporaneous with the use of punched cards, there was a proliferation of character sets. Fortunately, those days are largely forgotten after the emergence of ASCII in the 1970s.

ASCII stands for *American Standard Code for Information Interchange*. It was a big step forward, but the operant word here is *American*. It was never designed to handle even European languages much less Asian ones.

But there were loopholes. This character set had 128 characters (being a 7-bit code). But an 8-bit byte was standard; how could we waste that extra bit? The natural idea is to make a superset of ASCII, using the codes 128 through 255 for other purposes. The trouble is, this was done many times in many different ways by IBM and others. There was no widespread agreement on what, for example, character 221 was.

The shortcomings of such an approach are obvious. Not only do the sender and receiver have to agree on the exact character set, but they are limited in what languages they can use all at once. If you wanted to write in German but quote a couple of sources in Greek and Hebrew, you probably couldn't do it at all. And this scheme didn't begin to address the problems of Asian languages such as Chinese, Japanese, and Korean.

There were two basic kinds of solutions to this problem. One was to use a much larger character set—one with 16 bits, for example (so-called *wide characters*). The other was to use variable-length multibyte encodings. In such a scheme, some characters might be represented in a single byte, some in two bytes, and some in three or even more. Obviously this raised many issues: For one, a string had to be uniquely decodable. The first byte of a multibyte character could be in a special class so that we could know to expect another byte, but what about the second and later bytes? Are they allowed to overlap with the set of single-byte characters? Are certain characters allowed as second or third bytes, or are they disallowed? Will we be able to jump into the middle of a string and still make sense of it? Will we be able to iterate backwards over a string if we want? Different encodings made different design decisions.

Eventually the idea for Unicode was born. Think of it as a "world character set." Unfortunately, nothing is ever that simple.

You may have heard it said that Unicode was (or is) limited to 65,536 characters (the number that can be stored in 16 bits). This is a common misconception. Unicode was never designed with that kind of constraint; it was understood from the beginning that in many usages, it would be a multibyte scheme. The number of characters that can be represented is essentially limitless—a good thing, because 65,000 would never suffice to handle all the languages of the world.

One of the first things to understand about I18N is that *the interpretation of a string is not intrinsic to the string itself.* That kind of old-fashioned thinking comes from the notion that there is only one way of storing strings.

I can't stress this enough. Internally, a string is just a series of bytes. To emphasize this, let's imagine a single ASCII character stored in a byte of memory. If we store the letter that we call "capital A," we really are storing the number 65.

Why do we view a 65 as an A? It's because of how the data item is used (or how it is interpreted). If we take that item and add it to another number, we are using it (interpreting it) as a number; if we send it to an ASCII terminal over a serial line, we are interpreting it as an ASCII character.

Just as a single byte can be interpreted in more than one way, so obviously can a whole sequence of bytes. In fact, the intended interpretation scheme (or *encoding*) has to be *known in advance* for a string to make any real sense. An encoding is simply a mapping between binary numbers and characters. And yet it still isn't *quite* this simple.

Because Ruby originated in Japan, it handles two different Japanese encodings (as well as ASCII) very well. I won't spend much time on Japanese; if you are a Japanese reader, you have access to a wide variety of Ruby books in that language. For the rest of us, Unicode is the most widely usable encoding. This chapter focuses on Unicode.

But before we get too deeply into these issues, let's look at some terminology. Calling things by useful names is one of the foundations of wisdom.

- A *byte* is simply eight bits (though in the old days, even this was not true). Traditionally many of us think of a byte as corresponding to a single character. Obviously we can't think that way in an I18N context.

- A *codepoint* is simply a single entry in the imaginary table that represents the character set. As a half-truth, you may think of a codepoint as mapping one-to-one to a character. Nearer to the truth, it sometimes takes more than a single codepoint to uniquely specify a character.

- A *glyph* is the visual representation of a codepoint. It may seem a little unintuitive, but a character's identity is distinct from its visual representation. (I may open my word processor and type a capital A in a dozen different fonts, but I still name each of them *A*.)

- A *grapheme* is similar in concept to a glyph, but when we talk about graphemes, we are coming from the context of the language, not the context of our software. A grapheme may be the combination (naive or otherwise) of two or more glyphs. It is the way a user thinks about a character in his own native language context. The distinction is subtle enough that many programmers will simply never worry about it.

What then is a *character?* Even in the Unicode world, there is some fuzziness associated with this concept because different languages behave a little differently and programmers think differently from other people. Let's say that a character is *an abstraction of a writing symbol that can be visually represented in one or more ways.*

Let's get a little more concrete. First, let me introduce a notation to you. We habitually represent Unicode codepoints with the notation U+ followed by four or more uppercase hexadecimal digits. So what we call the letter "A" can be specified as U+0041.

Now take the letter "é" for example (lowercase e with an acute accent). This can actually be represented in two ways in Unicode. The first way is the single codepoint U+00E9 (*LATIN SMALL LETTER E WITH ACUTE*). The second way is two codepoints—a small e followed by an acute accent: U+0065 and U+0301 (or *LATIN SMALL LETTER E* followed by *COMBINING ACUTE ACCENT*).

Both forms are equally valid. The shorter one is referred to as the *precomposed* form. Bear in mind, though, that not every language has precomposed variants, so it isn't always possible to reduce such a character to a single codepoint.

I've referred to Unicode as an *encoding*, but that isn't strictly correct. Unicode maps characters to codepoints; there are different ways to map codepoints to binary storage. In effect, Unicode is a *family* of encodings.

Let's take the string "Matz" as an example. This consists of four Unicode codepoints:

```
"Matz"    # U+004d U+0061 U+0074 U+007a
```

The straightforward way to store this would be as a simple sequence of bytes.

```
00 4d 00 61 00 74 00 7a
```

This is called UCS-2 (as in *two bytes*) or UTF-16 (as in *16 bits*). Note that this encoding itself actually comes in two "flavors," a big-endian and a little-endian form.

However notice that every other byte is zero. This isn't mere coincidence; it is typical for English text, which rarely goes beyond codepoint U+00FF. It's somewhat wasteful of memory.

This brings us to the idea of UTF-8. This is a Unicode encoding where the "traditional" characters are represented as single bytes, but others may be multiple bytes. Here is a UTF-8 encoding of this same string:

```
4d 61 74 7a
```

Notice that all we have done is strip off the zeroes; more importantly, note that this is the same as ordinary ASCII. This is obviously by design; "plain ASCII" can be thought as a proper subset of UTF-8.

One implication of this is that when UTF-8 text is interpreted as ASCII, it sometimes appears "normal" (especially if the text is mostly English). Sometimes you may find that in a browser or other application English text is displayed correctly, but there are additional "garbage" characters. In such a case, it's likely that the application is making the wrong assumption about what encoding is being used.

So we can argue that UTF-8 saves memory. Of course, I'm speaking from an Anglocentric point of view again (or at least ASCII-centric). When the text is primarily ASCII, memory will be conserved, but for other writing systems such as Greek or Cyrillic, the strings will actually *grow* in size.

Another obvious benefit is that UTF-8 is "backward compatible" with ASCII, still arguably the most common single-byte encoding in the world. Finally, UTF-8 also has some special features to make it convenient for programmers.

For one thing, the bytes used in multibyte characters are assigned carefully. The null character (ASCII 0) is never used as the nth byte in a sequence (where n > 1), nor are such common characters as the slash (commonly used as a pathname delimiter). As a matter of fact, no byte in the full ASCII range (0x00–0x7F) can be used as part of any other character.

The second byte in a multibyte character uniquely determines how many bytes will follow. The second byte is always in the range 0xC0 to 0xFD, and any following bytes are always in the range 0x80 to 0xBF. This ensures that the encoding scheme is stateless and allows recovery after missing or garbled bytes.

UTF-8 is one of the most flexible and common encodings in the world. It has been in use since the early 1990s and is the default encoding for XML. Most of our attention in this chapter will be focused on UTF-8.

4.2 Coding in a Post-ASCII World

The "age of ASCII" is gone, though some have not realized it yet. Many assumptions commonly made by programmers in the past are no longer true. We need a new way of thinking.

There are two concepts that I consider to be fundamental, almost axiomatic. First, *a string has no intrinsic interpretation*. It must be interpreted according to some external standard. Second, *a byte does not correspond to a character*; a character may be one or more bytes. There are other lessons to be learned, but these two come first.

These facts may sometimes affect our programming in subtle ways. Let's examine in detail how to handle character strings in a modern fashion.

4.2.1 The `jcode` Library and `$KCODE`

To use different character sets in Ruby, you must first be aware of the global variable $KCODE, which determines the behavior of many core methods that manipulate strings. (The *K*, by the way, comes from *kanji*, which are the Japanese nonalphabetic writing symbols.) There are five usual settings for this variable; each is a single case-insensitive letter ("ASCII" and "NONE" are the same).

```
a    ASCII
n    NONE (ASCII)
e    EUC
s    SJIS
u    UTF-8
```

Actually, you can use a full description for clarity if you want (for example, $KCODE = "UTF-8"). Only the first character of the string is significant.

ASCII we already know about. EUC and Shift-JIS (SJIS) are of minimal interest to us here. We'll concentrate on the "utf-8" setting.

After you set $KCODE, you get a lot of functionality for free. For example, the inspect method (called automatically when you invoke the p method to print an object in readable form) will typically honor the $KCODE setting.

```
$KCODE = "n"

# In case you didn't know, the French word "épée"
# refers to a kind of sword.
```

```
eacute = ""
eacute << 0303 << 0251                    # U+00E9
sword = eacute + "p" + eacute + "e"
p eacute                                  # "\303\251"

p sword                                   # "\303\251p\303\251e"

$KCODE = "u"
p eacute                         # "é"
p sword                          # "épée"
```

Regular expressions also become a little smarter in UTF-8 mode.

```
$KCODE = "n"
letters = sword.scan(/(.)/)
# [["\303"], ["\251"], ["p"], ["\303"], ["\251"], ["e"]]
puts letters.size               # 6

$KCODE = "u"

letters = sword.scan(/(.)/)
# [["é"], ["p"], ["é"], ["e"]]
puts letters.size               # 4
```

The jcode library also provides some useful methods such as jlength and each_char. It's not a bad idea to require this library anytime you use UTF-8.

In the next section, we'll revisit common operations with strings and regular expressions. We'll learn more about jcode there.

4.2.2   Revisiting Common String and Regex Operations

When using UTF-8, some operations work exactly as before. Concatenation of strings is unchanged:

```
"ép" + "ée"     # "épée"
"ép" << "ée"    # "épée"
```

Because UTF-8 is stateless, checking for the presence of a substring requires no special considerations either:

```
"épée".include?("é")    # true
```

However, some common assumptions require rethinking when we internationalize. Obviously a character is no longer always a byte. When we count characters or bytes, we have to consider what we really want to count and why. The same is true for iteration.

There is a convention that a codepoint is sometimes thought of as a "programmer's character." This is another half-truth, but one that is sometimes useful.

The `jlength` method will return the actual number of codepoints in a string rather than bytes. If you actually want bytes, you can still call the `length` method.

```
$KCODE = "u"
require 'jcode'

sword = "épée"
sword.jlength       # 4
sword.length        # 6
```

Methods such as `upcase` and `capitalize` will typically fail with special characters. This is a limitation in current Ruby. (It is not really appropriate to view this as a bug because capitalization in general is a complex issue and simply isn't handled in internationalized Ruby. Consider it a set of missing features.)

```
$KCODE = "u"
sword.upcase        # "éPéE"
sword.capitalize    # "épée"
```

If you are using a decomposed form, this might *appear* to work in some cases, as the Latin letters are separated from the diacritics. But in the general case it won't work; it will fail for Turkish, German, Dutch, and any other language where the capitalization rules are nontrivial.

You might think that unaccented characters would be treated as equivalent in some sense to their unaccented counterparts. In general, this is never true. They're simply different characters. Here's an example with count:

```
$KCODE = "u"
sword.count("e")    # 1 (not 3)
```

Again, the opposite is true for decomposed characters. The Latin letter *is* detected in that case.

Similarly, count will return a misleading result when passed a multibyte character. The jcount method will handle the latter case, however.

```
$KCODE = "u"
sword.count("eé")    # 5 (not 3)
sword.jcount("eé")   # 3
```

There is a convenience method mbchar?, which detects whether a string has any multibyte characters in it.

```
$KCODE = "u"
sword.mbchar?    # 0  (offset of first multibyte char)
"foo".mbchar?    # nil
```

The jcode library also redefines such methods as chop, delete, squeeze, succ, tr, and tr_s. Anytime you use these in UTF-8 mode, be aware you are using the "multibyte-aware" version. If you handle multibyte strings without the jcode library, you may get surprising or erroneous results.

We can iterate over a string by bytes as usual; or we can iterate by characters using each_char. The latter method deals with single-character strings; the former (in current versions of Ruby) deals with single-byte integers.

Of course, we're once again equating a codepoint with a character. Despite the name, each_char actually iterates over codepoints, strictly speaking, not characters.

```
$KCODE = "u"
sword.each_byte {|x| puts x }    # Six lines of integers
sword.each_char {|x| puts x }    # Four lines of strings
```

If you're confused, don't feel bad. Most of us are. I've attempted to summarize the situation in Table 4.1.

Table 4.1   Precomposed and Decomposed Forms

Precomposed Form of "é"

Character name	Glyph	Codepoint	UTF-8 Bytes	Comments
LATIN SMALL LETTER E WITH ACUTE	é	U+00E9	0xC3 0xA9	One character, one codepoint, two UTF-8 bytes

Decomposed Form of "é"

Character name	Glyph	Codepoint	UTF-8 Bytes	Comments
LATIN SMALL LETTER E	e	U+0065	0x65	One character, two codepoints (two "programmer's characters"), three UTF-8 bytes
COMBINING ACUTE ACCENT	´	U+0301	0xCC 0x81	

What else do we need to consider with internationalized strings? Obviously the "bracket" notation still refers to bytes, not characters. But you could change this if you wanted. Here is one implementation (not especially efficient, but easy to understand):

```
class String

  def [](index)
    self.scan(/./)[index]
  end

  def []=(index,value)
    arr = self.scan(/./)
    arr[index] = value
    self.replace(arr.join)
    value
  end

end
```

Of course, this omits much of the functionality of the real [] method, which can understand ranges, regular expressions, and so on. If you really want this functionality, you will have to do some more coding.

The unpack method has options that help us manipulate Unicode strings. By using U* as a directive in the template string, we can convert UTF-8 strings into arrays of codepoints (U on its own will convert only the first codepoint):

```
codepoints = sword.unpack('U*') # [233, 112, 233, 101]
```

Here is a slightly more useful example, which converts all non-ASCII codepoints (everything from U+0080 up) in a string into the U+XXXX notation we used earlier:

```
def reveal_non_ascii(str)
  str.unpack('U*').map do |cp|
    if cp < 0x80
      cp.chr
    else
      '(U+%04X)'% cp
    end
  end.join
end
```

The String#unpack method has a cousin, Array#pack, which performs the inverse operation:

```
[233, 112, 233, 101].pack('U*') # "épée"
```

We can use this to allow us to insert Unicode characters that we can't easily type:

```
eacute = [0xE9].pack('U')
cafe = "caf#{eacute}"        # "café"
```

Regular expressions also are multibyte-aware, especially if you are using Oniguruma (which we looked at in Chapter 3, "Working with Regular Expressions"). For example, /./ will match a single multibyte character.

The u modifier will make a regex UTF-8-aware. If $KCODE is set to "u", this isn't necessary; but the redundancy doesn't hurt anything. (And such redundancy can be useful when the code is part of a larger context where we don't necessarily know how $KCODE is set.)

Even without Oniguruma, regexes are smart enough to recognize multibyte characters as being "word" characters or not.

```
$KCODE = "u"
sword =~ /\w/    # 0
sword =~ /\W/    # nil
```

With Oniguruma, the backslash sequences (such as \w, \s) recognize a wider range of codepoints as being words, spaces, and so on.

Regular expressions let us perform some simple string actions in a safe manner. We can already truncate an ASCII string easily. The following code will return at most 20 characters from ascii_string:

```
ascii_string[0,20]
```

However, because a Unicode codepoint can span more than one byte, we can't safely use the same technique in a UTF-8 string. There's a risk that invalid byte sequences will be left on the end of the string. In addition, it's less useful because we can't tell in advance how many codepoints are going to result. Regular expressions come to our rescue:

```
def truncate(str, max_length)
  str[/.{0,#{max_length}}/m]
end
```

4.2.3 Detecting Character Encodings

Detecting which encoding is used by a given string is a complex problem. Multibyte encodings often have distinctive patterns that can be used to recognize them, but single-byte encodings—like most of the ones used in Western languages—are much more difficult. Statistical solutions can be used for detection, but they are outside the scope of this book (and they are not especially reliable solutions in general).

Fortunately, however, we usually want to do something more simple—to determine whether a string is UTF-8. This can be determined with good reliability. Here's a simple method (depending on the fact that unpack raises an exception on an invalid string):

```
class String
  def utf8?
    unpack('U*') rescue return false
    true
  end
end
```

We can detect pure ASCII just by verifying that every byte is less than 128:

```ruby
class String
  def ascii?
    self.split(/./).all? {|ch| ch < 128 }
  end
end
```

4.2.4   Normalizing Unicode Strings

Up until now, we've been using *precomposed* characters—ones in which the base character and diacritic are combined into a single entity and a single Unicode codepoint. In general, though, Unicode separates the encoding of characters and their diacritics. Instead of storing "é" as a single *LATIN SMALL LETTER E WITH ACUTE ACCENT* codepoint, we can store it in a *decomposed* form, as *LATIN SMALL LETTER E* plus *COMBINING ACUTE ACCENT*.

Why would we want to do this? It provides flexibility and allows us to apply diacritic marks to any character, not just the combinations considered by the encoding designer. In fact, fonts will include glyphs for common combinations of character and diacritic, but the *display* of an entity is separate from its encoding.

Unicode has numerous design considerations such as efficiency and *round-trip compatibility* with existing national encodings. Sometimes these constraints may introduce some redundancy; for example, not only does Unicode include codepoints for decomposed forms but also for many of the *precomposed* forms already in use. This means that there is also a codepoint for *LATIN SMALL LETTER E WITH ACUTE ACCENT*, as well as for things such as the double-*f* ligature.

For example, let's consider the German word "öffnen" (to open). Without even considering case, there are four ways to encode it:

1. o + COMBINING DIAERESIS (U+0308) + f + f + n + e + n
2. LATIN SMALL LETTER O WITH DIAERESIS (U+00F6) + f + f + n + e + n
3. o + COMBINING DIAERESIS + DOUBLE-F LIGATURE (U+FB00) + n + e + n
4. LATIN SMALL LETTER O WITH DIAERESIS + DOUBLE-F LIGATURE + n + e + n

The *diaeresis* (also spelled *dieresis*) is simply a pair of dots over a character. In German it is called an *umlaut*.

Normalizing is the process of standardizing the character representations used. After normalizing, we can be sure that a given character is encoded in a particular way.

Exactly what those forms are depends on what we are trying to achieve. Annex 15 of the Unicode Standard lists four normalization forms:

```
1. D  (Canonical Decomposition)
2. C  (Canonical Decomposition followed by Canonical Composition)
3. KD (Compatibility Decomposition)
4. KC (Compatibility Decomposition followed by Canonical Composition)
```

You'll also see these written as *NFKC* (*Normalization Form KC*) and so on.

The precise rules set out in the standard are complex and cover the difference between "canonical equivalence" and "compatibility equivalence." (Korean and Japanese require particular attention, but we won't address these here.) Table 4.2 summarizes the effects of each normalization form on the strings we started with previously.

Table 4.2 Normalized Unicode Forms

Original	NFD	NFC	NFKD	NFKC
o+¨+f+f+n+e+n	o+¨+f+f+n+e+n	ö+f+f+n+e+n	o+¨+f+f+n+e+n	ö+f+f+n+e+n
ö+f+f+n+e+n	o+¨+f+f+n+e+n	ö+f+f+n+e+n	o+¨+f+f+n+e+n	ö+f+f+n+e+n
o+¨+ff+n+e+n	o+¨+ff+n+e+n	ö+ff+n+e+n	o+¨+f+f+n+e+n	ö+f+f+n+e+n
ö+ff+n+e+n	o+¨+ff+n+e+n	ö+ff+n+e+n	o+¨+f+f+n+e+n	ö+f+f+n+e+n

Forms C and D are reversible, whereas KC and KD are not. On the other hand, the data lost in KC and KD means that all four strings are binary-identical. Which form is most appropriate depends on the application at hand. We'll talk about this a bit more in the next section.

Although Ruby doesn't include it as standard, a library is available that performs these normalizations. Refer to http://www.yoshidam.net/Ruby.html (installed via `gem install unicode`).

With the `unicode` library installed, it's easy to perform normalization for each of the previous forms with the `Unicode.normalize_X` family of methods:

```ruby
require 'unicode'
sword_kd = Unicode.normalize_KD(sword)
sword_kd.scan(/./)                       # ["e", "´", "p", "e", "´", "e"]
sword_kc = Unicode.normalize_KC(sword)
sword_kc.scan(/./)                       # ["é", "p", "é", "e"]
```

4.2.5   Issues in String Collation

In computing, *collation* refers to the process of arranging text according to a particular order. Generally, but not always, this implies some kind of alphabetical or similar order. Collation is closely connected to normalization and uses some of the same concepts and code.

For example, let's consider an array of strings that we want to collate:

```
eacute = [0x00E9].pack('U')
acute = [0x0301].pack('U')
array = ["epicurian", "#{eacute}p#{eacute}e", "e#{acute}lan"]
# ["epicurian", "épée", "élan"]
```

What happens when we use Ruby's `Array#sort` method?

```
array.sort   # ["epicurian", "élan", "épée"]
```

That's not what we want. But let's try to understand why it happens. Ruby's string sort is done by a simple byte-by-byte comparison. We can see this by looking at the first few bytes of each string:

```
array.map {|item| "#{item}: #{item.unpack('C*')[0,3].join(',')}" }
# ["epicurian: 101,112,105", "épée: 195,169,112",
# "e´lan: 101,204,129"]
```

There are two complications. First, the fact that non-ASCII UTF-8 characters start with a large byte value means that they will inevitably be sorted *after* their ASCII counterparts. Second, decomposed Latin characters are sorted *before* precomposed characters because of their leading ASCII byte.

Operating systems typically include *collation* functions that allow two strings to be compared according to the locale's encoding and language specifications. In the case of the C locale, this is handled by the `strxfrm` and `strcoll` functions in the standard library.

Bear in mind that this is something of an issue even with ASCII. When we sort ASCII strings in Ruby, we're doing a straight lexicographic sort; in a complex real-life situation (for example, sorting the titles in the Library of Congress) there are many special rules that aren't followed by such a simplistic sorting technique.

To collate strings, we can generate an intermediate value that is used to sort them. Exactly how we construct this value depends on our own requirements and those of the language that we are processing; there is no single universal collation algorithm.

Let's assume that we are processing our list according to English rules and that we are going to ignore accents. The first step is to define our transformation method. We'll normalize our strings to decomposed forms and then elide the diacritics, leaving just the base characters. The Unicode range for combining diacritical marks runs from U+0300 to U+036F:

```
def transform(str)
  Unicode.normalize_KD(str).unpack('U*').select{ |cp|
    cp < 0x0300 || cp > 0x036F
  }.pack('U*')
end


array.map{|x| transform(x) }      # ["epicurian", "epee", "elan"]
```

Next, we create a hash table to map strings to their transformed versions and use that to sort the original strings. The hash table means that we only need to calculate the transformed form once per original string.

```
def collate(array)
  transformations = array.inject({}) do |hash, item|
    hash[item] = yield item
    hash
  end
  array.sort_by {|x| transformations[x] }
end


collate(array) {|a| transform(a) }    # ["élan", "épée", "epicurian"]
```

That's better, but we haven't addressed capitalization or character equivalents yet. Let's look at German as an example.

In fact, there is more than one collation for German; we'll use the DIN-2 collation (or *phone book collation*) for this exercise, in which the German character "ß" is equivalent to "ss", and the umlaut is equivalent to a letter "e", so "ö" is equivalent to "oe" and so on.

Our transformation method should address this. Once again, we will start by normalizing our string to a decomposed form. For reference, the combining diaeresis (or umlaut) is U+0308. We'll also use Ruby's case conversion, but we need to augment it a little. Here, then, is a basic transformation method:

```ruby
def transform_de(str)
  decomposed = Unicode.normalize_KD(str).downcase
  decomposed.gsub!('ß', 'ss')
  decomposed.gsub([0x0308].pack('U'), 'e')
end


array = ["Straße", "öffnen"]
array.map {|x| transform_de(x) }     # ["strasse", "oeffnen"]
```

Not all languages are so straightforward. Spanish, for example, adds an additional letter, "ñ", between "n" and "o". However, as long as we shift the remaining letters along somehow, we can cope with this. Notice how Listing 4.1 uses the precomposed normalized form to simplify our processing. We are also going to make things easier by ignoring the distinction between accented and nonaccented letters.

Listing 4.1   Collation in Spanish

```ruby
def map_table(list)
  table = {}
  list.each_with_index do |item, i|
    item.split(',').each do |subitem|
      table[Unicode.normalize_KC(subitem)] = (?a + i).chr
    end
  end
  table
end

ES_SORT = map_table(%w(
  a,A,á,Á b,B c,C d,D e,E,é,É f,F g,G h,H i,I,í,Í j,J k,K l,L m,M
  n,N ñ,Ñ o,O,ó,Ó p,P q,Q r,R s,S t,T u,U,ú,Ú v,V w,W x,X y,Y z,Z
))

def transform_es(str)
  array = Unicode.normalize_KC(str).scan(/./u)
  array.map {|c| ES_SORT[c] || c}.join
end

array = %w[éste estoy año apogeo amor]
array.map {|a| transform_es(a) }
# ["etue", "etupz", "aop", "aqpgep", "amps"]

collate(array) {|a| transform_es(a) }
# ["amor", "año", "apogeo", "éste", "estoy"]
```

Real-world collation is slightly more complex than the preceding examples and typically employs up to three levels. Usually, the first level tests the character identity only, ignoring accents and case, the second level differentiates accents, while the third level also takes case into consideration. The second and third levels are used only if two strings have equal collation at preceding levels. Furthermore, some languages sort multiple-character sequences as a single semantic unit (for example, "lj" in Croatian is placed between "l" and "m"). The development of a language-specific or generalized collation algorithm is therefore not a trivial task; it demands knowledge of the language in question. It's also not possible to devise a truly generic collation algorithm that works for all languages, although there are algorithms that attempt to achieve something close.

4.2.6   Converting Between Encodings

Ruby's standard library includes an interface to the iconv library for converting between character encodings. This should work on all platforms, including Windows with the one-click installer.

If we want to convert a UTF-8 string to ISO-8859-15, we can use iconv as follows:

```
require 'iconv'
converter = Iconv.new('ISO-8859-15', 'UTF-8')
sword_iso = converter.iconv(sword)
```

It's important to remember that the encodings are listed in the order *destination, source* (rather like an assignment). The number and names of the encodings available depend on the platform, but the more common and popular encodings tend to be well standardized and available everywhere. If the iconv command-line program is available, we can get a list of the recognized encodings by issuing the iconv -l command.

In addition to the name of the encoding, iconv accepts a couple of switches to control its behavior. These are appended to the destination encoding string.

Usually, iconv raises an error if it encounters invalid input or if it otherwise cannot represent the input in the output encoding. The //IGNORE switch tells it to skip these errors silently:

```
broken_utf8_string = "hello\xfe"
converter = Iconv.new('ISO-8859-15', 'UTF-8')
converter.iconv(broken_utf8_string)      # raises
Iconv::IllegalSequence
```

```
converter = Iconv.new('ISO-8859-15//IGNORE', 'UTF-8')
converter.iconv(broken_utf8_string)      # "hello"
```

The same switch also lets us clean up a string:

```
broken_sword = "épée\xfe"
converter = Iconv.new('UTF-8//IGNORE', 'UTF-8')
converter.iconv(broken_sword) # "épée"
```

Sometimes characters can't be represented in the target encoding. Usually these will raise an exception. The //TRANSLIT switch tells iconv to approximate characters (where possible) instead of raising an error:

```
converter = Iconv.new('ASCII', 'UTF-8')
converter.iconv(sword)         # raises Iconv::IllegalSequence
converter = Iconv.new('ASCII//IGNORE', 'UTF-8')
converter.iconv(sword)         # "pe"
converter = Iconv.new('ASCII//TRANSLIT', 'UTF-8')
converter.iconv(sword)         # "'ep'ee"
```

We could use this to make an ASCII-clean URL, for example:

```
str = "Straße épée"
converter = Iconv.new('ASCII//TRANSLIT', 'UTF-8')
converter.iconv(sword).gsub(/ /, '-').gsub(/[^a-z\-]/in).downcase
# "strasse-epee"
```

However, this will only work for the Latin alphabet.

Listing 4.2 illustrates a real-life example of iconv being used with open-uri to retrieve a web page and transcode its content into UTF-8.

Listing 4.2   Transcoding a Web Page into UTF-8

```
require 'open-uri'
require 'iconv'

def get_web_page_as_utf8(url)
  open(url) do |io|
    source = io.read
    type, *parameters = io.content_type_parse
```

```
    # Don't transcode anything that isn't (X)HTML
    unless type =~ %r!^(?:text/html|application/xhtml+xml)$!
      return source
    end
    # Check server headers first:
    if pair = parameters.assoc('charset')
      encoding = pair.last
    # Next, look in the HTML:
    elsif source =~ /\]*?charset=([^\s'"]+)/i
      encoding = $1
    # Finally, use the HTTP default
    else
      encoding = 'ISO-8859-1'
    end
    converter = Iconv.new('UTF-8//IGNORE', encoding)
    return converter.iconv(source)
  end
end
```

There are other OS issues relating to character conversion. Suppose that the operating system on which Ruby is running is set to a non-UTF-8 locale, or Ruby doesn't use UTF-8 to communicate with the OS (as is the case with the Win32 package). Then there are additional complications.

For example, Windows supports Unicode filenames and uses Unicode internally. But Ruby at the present time communicates with Windows through the *legacy code page*. In the case of English and most other western European editions, this is code page 1252 (or WINDOWS-1252).

You can still use UTF-8 inside your application, but you'll need to convert to the legacy code page to specify filenames. This can be done using iconv, but it's important to remember that the legacy code page can describe only a small subset of the characters available in Unicode.

In addition, this means that Ruby on Windows cannot, at present, open existing files whose names cannot be described in the legacy code page. This restriction does not apply to Mac OS X, Linux, or other systems using UTF-8 locales.

4.3   Using Message Catalogs

Lojban is culturally fully neutral. Its vocabulary was built algorithmically using today's six most widely spoken languages: Chinese, Hindi, English, Russian, Spanish, and Arabic.

— What is Lojban?, *Nick Nicholas and John Cowan*

A *message catalog* is a collection of messages in a specific language. This is integral to the idea of localization (L10N). The idea is to "isolate" the language-specific strings from the rest of the application so that we can simply "plug in" a different catalog to get messages and strings in a different language.

The "best" way to do this in Ruby is to use the library formally called Ruby-GetText-Package. I'll simply refer to this as gettext, after the filename of the library; this is not to be confused with the gettext utility. This excellent library is the work of Masao Mutoh, who helped extensively with this section.

This library is a Ruby implementation (not a wrapper) modeled after the GNU gettext utilities (the most famous set of utilities in this area). The official site is at http://gettext.rubyforge.org/, and the official GNU gettext utilities site is at http://www.gnu.org/software/gettext/.

4.3.1   Background and Terminology

The gettext library is really more than one library, as we'll see. The basic functionality is accessed with a require 'gettext', and certain useful utilities are accessed through require 'gettext/utils' (for maintaining message catalogs).

The primary reason to use message catalogs, of course, is to translate messages between languages. We also handle cases where singular and plural forms need to be distinguished (one *file*, two *files*); these rules vary widely from one language to another, of course.

Typically each library or application will have its own message catalog. This means that sets of translated catalogs can be included as part of a distributed package.

Environment variables such as LANG and GETTEXT_PATH are honored. We'll explain these later.

There are two basic maintenance operations you might perform on a message catalog (outside your Ruby code). One is to extract messages from your Ruby source to create an initial catalog; the other is to update (merge) new messages from Ruby source into an existing catalog. We'll look at the extract and merge operations in section 4.3.3, "Localizing a Simple Application."

4.3.2 Getting Started with Message Catalogs

You may already have this library installed. If not, `gem install gettext` is the easiest way to get it.

For development purposes, you will need the related GNU utilities. If you're on a UNIX-like system, you probably already have them. If you're on Win32, one way to get them is to install Glade/GTK+ for Windows. Either way, the utilities are needed only for development, not at runtime.

If you don't have `rake`, install the gem. It's convenient to have in these situations.

Assuming that your environment is all set up and everything is installed, you can begin to work with catalogs. Let's look at some terminology:

- A *po-file* is a *portable object file*. These are the text forms (or human-readable forms) of the message catalogs; each of these files has a counterpart under each different locale supported. A *pot-file* is a template file.

- A *mo-file* is a portable binary message catalog file. It is created from a po-file. Our Ruby library reads mo-files, not po-files.

- A *text domain* is, in effect, just the basename of a mo-file. This text domain is associated with an application (or *bound* to it).

4.3.3 Localizing a Simple Application

The following example defines a `Person` class and manipulates it. The `show` method shows the localized messages.

```
require 'gettext'

class Person
  include GetText

  def initialize(name, age, children_num)
    @name, @age, @children_num = name, age, children_num
    bindtextdomain("myapp")
  end

  def show
    puts _("Information")
    puts _("Name: %{name}, Age: %{age}") % {:name => @name, :age => @age}
    puts n_("%{name} has a child.", "%{name} has %{num} children.",
            @children_num) % {:name => @name, :num => @children_num}
  end
end
```

```
john = Person.new("John", 25, 1)
john.show
linda = Person.new("Linda", 30, 3)
linda.show
```

Assume that we save this code to `myapp/person.rb`. The directory hierarchy is significant, as we'll see later. The call to `bindtextdomain` binds the text domain `"myapp"` to the `Person` object at runtime.

In the `show` method, there are three `gettext` calls. The method is named `_` (a single underscore) to be unobtrusive.

The first call just displays the localized message corresponding to the `"Information"` string. The second demonstrates a localized message with two arguments. The hash specifies a list of values to be substituted into the string; we can't interpolate directly into the string because that would interfere with our whole purpose of storing a small number of messages in a catalog.

Also remember that the parameters are separated so that they can appear in different orders if necessary. Sometimes the data will get rearranged during translation because languages may have differing word order.

You can do the same method call in this shorter way:

```
puts _("Name: %s, Age: %d") % [@name, @age]
```

However, the longer style is recommended. It is more descriptive and gives more information to the translator.

The `n_` method handles singular and plural cases. The `@children` value is used to compute an index telling us which of the specified strings to use. (The `Plural-Forms` entry, which I will explain soon, specifies how to calculate the index.)

Note that these default messages need to be in English (even if you as a programmer are not a native English speaker). Like it or not, English is the nearest thing to a universal language from the viewpoint of most translators.

I said we would find `rake` to be useful. Let's create a `Rakefile` (under `myapp`) to maintain message catalogs. We'll give it the two common operations update po-files and make mo-files.

```
require 'gettext/utils'

desc "Update pot/po files."
task :updatepo do
```

```
    GetText.update_pofiles("myapp", ["person.rb"], "myapp 1.0.0")
end
desc "Create mo-files"
task :makemo do
  GetText.create_mofiles
end
```

This code uses the `gettext/utils` library, which contains various functions to help in maintaining message catalogs. The `update_pofiles` method creates the initial `myapp/po/myapp.pot` file from the `person.rb` source. When it is invoked the second time (or more), this function performs an update or merge of the `myapp/po/myapp.pot` file and all of the `myapp/po/#{lang}/myapp.po` files.

The second parameter is an array of target files. Usually you will specify something like the following:

```
GetText.update_pofiles("myapp",
Dir.glob("{lib,bin}/**/*.{rb,rhtml}"),
                    "myapp 1.0.0")
```

The `GetText.create_mofiles` call creates `data/locale/` subdirectories as needed and generates mo-files from po-files.

So if we issue the command `rake updatepo`, we create the `myapp/po` directory and create `myapp.pot` under it.

Now edit the header part of the `po/myapp.pot`. This is basically a description of your application (name, author, email, license, and so on).

```
# My sample application.              (Some descriptive title)
# Copyright (C) 2006  Foo Bar         (Author of this app)
# This file is distributed under XXX license. (License info)
#
# FIRST AUTHOR <EMAIL@ADDRESS>, YEAR.     (Translator's info)
#
#, fuzzy
msgid ""
msgstr ""
"Project-Id-Version: myapp 1.0.0\n"        (Project ID and version)
#...
```

You may wonder what the `fuzzy` marker is. This is simply marking something that has not been translated or has a doubtful translation. When messages are generated automatically, they will be marked `fuzzy` so that a human can check them and change them.

You will then send the `myapp.pot` file to the translators. (Of course, you may be translating it yourself.)

Now suppose that you're a Japanese translator. The locale is `ja_JP.UTF-8`, meaning "Japanese (ja) as spoken in Japan (JP), with encoding UTF-8."

Start by copying `myapp.pot` to `myapp.po`. If you have the GNU `gettext` utilities, it is better to use `msginit` instead of a simple `cp` command; this utility will honor the environment variables and set certain header variables correctly. Invoke it this way (on UNIX):

```
LANG=ja_JP.UTF-8 msginit -i myapp.pot -o myapp.po
```

Then edit `myapp.po` as shown in Listing 4.3. Note that you need to edit this file in the same charset of the definition in the `Content-Type` line.

Listing 4.3   The Completed `myapp.pot` File

```
# My sample application.
# Copyright (C) 2006  Foo Bar
# This file is distributed under XXX license.
#
# Your name <yourname@foo.com>, 2006.         (All translator's info)
#                                             (Remove the 'fuzzy' line)
msgid ""
msgstr ""
"Project-Id-Version: myapp 1.0.0\n"
"POT-Creation-Date: 2006-05-22 23:27+0900\n"
"PO-Revision-Date: 2006-05-23 14:39+0900\n"
"Last-Translator: Your Name <foo@bar.com>\n" (Current translator's info)
"Language-Team: Japanese\n"                   (Your language)
"MIME-Version: 1.0\n"
"Content-Type: text/plain; charset=UTF-8\n"  (Encoding of this file)
"Content-Transfer-Encoding: 8bit\n"
"Plural-Forms: nplurals=2; plural=(n != 1);\n" (Pluralization form)

#: person.rb:12
msgid "Information"
msgstr "Jouhou"
```

```
#: person.rb:13
msgid "Name: %{name}, Age: %{age}"
msgstr "Namae: %{name}, Nenrei: %{age}"

#: person.rb:14
msgid "%{name} has a child."
msgid_plural "%{name} has %{num} children."
msgstr[0] "%{name} ha hitori kodomo ga imasu."
msgstr[1] "%{name} ha %{num} nin no kodomo ga imasu."
```

The `msgid` tag marks the original message, and `msgstr` marks the translated message. If you find `msgid_plural`, you need to separate the `msgstr[i]` values to follow the `Plural-Forms` rule. The index i is the number calculated from the `Plural-Forms` expression. In this case, when n `!= 1`, we will use `msgstr[1]` (plural messages).

The behavior of `Plural-Forms` betrays its origins in the C language. The usage we see here depends on the fact that Boolean expressions in C return 0 or 1.

Be aware that singular and plural forms vary widely from one language to another. In fact, many languages have more than one plural form. In Polish, the word *plik* (file) is singular; for numbers greater than one, there are two plural forms. The form *pliki* is for numbers ending in 2, 3, or 4, and *plików* is for all other numbers.

So in Polish, our `Plural-Forms` would look something like this:

```
Plural-Forms: nplurals=3; \
              plural=n==1 ? 0 : \
              n%10>=2 && n%10<=4 && (n%100=20) ? 1 : 2;
```

Obviously the header is important. In particular, `Content-Type` and `Plural-Forms` are indispensable. If you can use `msginit`, they are inserted automatically; otherwise, you need to add them manually.

At this point, the translator sends back the localized files to the developer. (So you can put on your "developer's hat" again.)

The `myapp.po` files from the translators go under their respective language directories (under `myapp/po`). So, for example, the French version would be stored in `myapp/po/fr/myapp.po`, the German version in `myapp/po/de/myapp.po`, and so on.

Then issue the commend `rake makemo`. This will convert the po-files to mo-files. These generated mo-files go under `myapp/data/locale/` (which has a subdirectory for each language).

So our entire directory structure looks like this:

```
myapp/
    Rakefile
    person.rb
    po/
        myapp.pot
        de/myapp.po
        fr/myapp.po
        ja/myapp.po
        :
    data/
        locale/
            de/LC_MESSAGES/myapp.mo
            fr/LC_MESSAGES/myapp.mo
            ja/LC_MESSAGES/myapp.mo
            :
```

All our translation tasks are finished. Now let's test this example. But before we do, you need to specify where the mo-files are located and which locale you are testing. Set the GETTEXT_PATH and LANG environment variables, run the program, and observe the output.

```
export GETTEXT_PATH="data/locale"
export LANG="ja_JP.UTF-8"
ruby person.rb
```

The application will output localized messages depending on the value of the LANG variable.

4.3.4   Other Notes

If you include message catalogs along with your application, it's best to package everything using RubyGems or the setup.rb library. Refer to section 17.2, "Installation and Packaging," for more information.

With RubyGems, the message catalogs are installed to a directory of this form:

```
(gem-packages-installed-dir)/myapp-x.x.x/data/locale/
```

This is included as the search path of the gettext library. Your application will be localized without using GETTEXT_PATH.

Using setup.rb, they are installed to the (system-dir)/share/locale/ directory. Again the application will be localized without GETTEXT_PATH.

Remember that this library is *not* a wrapper of the GNU gettext utilities. However, the message files are compatible, so you can use the GNU maintenance tools if you want. Of course, these utilities are not required at runtime (that is, the end user does not need them).

4.4   Conclusion

In this chapter, we discussed one of the most complex and challenging aspects of programming—the problem of internationalizing code. This topic builds on the previous two chapters because I18N is largely concerned with strings and regular expressions.

We saw how Ruby makes some aspects of this fairly easy with the jcode library and related tools. We also got an overview of character sets in general and Unicode in particular.

We looked at how regular expressions are generally more "Unicode-aware" than strings and examined pack and unpack in terms of their usefulness in manipulating Unicode strings.

Finally, we looked at message catalogs in some detail. We know why they exist and how to create and maintain them.

Now that we have seen strings and regular expressions in detail, let's go back to the main path of our discussion. Chapter 5, "Performing Numerical Calculations," will deal with numbers and numeric processing in Ruby.

CHAPTER 5

Performing Numerical Calculations

On two occasions I have been asked [by members of Parliament], 'Pray, Mr. Babbage, if you put into the machine wrong figures, will the right answers come out?' I am not able rightly to apprehend the kind of confusion of ideas that could provoke such a question.

—*Charles Babbage*

Numeric data is the original data type, the native language of the computer. We would be hard-pressed to find areas of our experience where numbers are not applicable. It doesn't matter whether you're an accountant or an aeronautical engineer; you can't survive without numbers. We present in this chapter a few ways to process, manipulate, convert, and analyze numeric data.

Like all modern languages, Ruby works well with both integers and floating point numbers. It has the full range of standard mathematical operators and functions that you would expect, but it also has a few pleasant surprises such as the `Bignum`, `BigDecimal`, and `Rational` classes.

Besides covering all of the numeric features in the core and standard libraries, a little domain-specific material has been added (in such areas as trigonometry, calculus, and statistics). These examples serve not only as informative examples in math, but as examples of Ruby code that illustrates principles from the rest of this book.

5.1   Representing Numbers in Ruby

If you know any other language, the representation of numbers in Ruby is mostly intuitive. A `Fixnum` may be signed or unsigned:

```
237      # unsigned (positive) number
+237     # same as above
-237     # negative number
```

When numbers are long, we can insert underscores at will (between any two digits). This is purely cosmetic and does not affect the value of the constant. Typically, we would insert them at the same places where accountants might insert commas:

```
1048576      # a simple number
1_048_576    # the same value
```

It's also possible to represent integers in the most common alternative bases (bases 2, 8, and 16). These are "tagged" with the prefixes 0b, 0, and 0x, respectively.

```
0b10010110     # binary
0b1211         # error!
01234          # octal (base 8)
01823          # error!
0xdeadbeef     # hexadecimal (base 16)
0xDEADBEEF     # same
0xdeadpork     # error!
```

Floating point numbers have to have a decimal point and may optionally have a signed exponent.

```
3.14           # pi to two digits
-0.628         # -2*pi over 10, to two digits
6.02e23        # Avogadro's number
6.626068e-34   # Planck's constant
```

Certain constants in the `Float` class help define limits for floating point numbers. These are machine-dependent. Some of the more important ones are as follows:

```
Float::MIN        # 2.2250738585072e-308 (on this machine)
Float::MAX        # 1.79769313486232e+308
Float::EPSILON    # 2.22044604925031e-16
```

5.2 Basic Operations on Numbers

The normal operations of addition, subtraction, multiplication, and division are implemented in Ruby much as in the typical programming language with the operators +, -, *, and /. Most of the operators are actually methods (and therefore can be overridden).

Exponentiation (raising to a power) is done with the ** operator as in older languages such as BASIC and FORTRAN. It obeys the "normal" mathematical laws of exponentiation.

```
a = 64**2    # 4096
b = 64**0.5  # 8.0
c = 64**0    # 1
d = 64**-1   # 0.015625
```

Division of one integer by another results in a truncated integer. This is a feature, not a bug. If you need a floating point number, make sure that at least one operand is a floating point.

```
3 / 3        # 3
5 / 3        # 1
3 / 4        # 0
3.0 / 4      # 0.75
3 / 4.0      # 0.75
3.0 / 4.0    # 0.75
```

If you are using variables and are in doubt about the division, `Float` or `to_f` will ensure that an operand is a floating point number.

```
z = x.to_f / y
z = Float(x) / y
```

See also section 5.17 "Performing Bit-level Operations on Numbers."

5.3   Rounding Floating Point Values

Kirk: What would you say the odds are on our getting out of here?
Spock: It is difficult to be precise, Captain. I should say approximately 7824.7
to one.

— Star Trek, *"Errand of Mercy"*

If you want to round a floating point value to an integer, the method `round` will do
the trick:

```
pi = 3.14159
new_pi = pi.round    # 3
temp = -47.6
temp2 = temp.round   # -48
```

Sometimes we want to round not to an integer but to a specific number of decimal places. In this case, we could use `sprintf` (which knows how to round) and `eval`
to do this:

```
pi = 3.1415926535
pi6 = eval(sprintf("%8.6f",pi))   # 3.141593
pi5 = eval(sprintf("%8.5f",pi))   # 3.14159
pi4 = eval(sprintf("%8.4f",pi))   # 3.1416
```

Of course, this is somewhat ugly. Let's encapsulate this behavior in a method that
we'll add to `Float`:

```
class Float

  def roundf(places)
    temp = self.to_s.length
    sprintf("%#{temp}.#{places}f",self).to_f
  end

end
```

Occasionally we follow a different rule in rounding to integers. The tradition of
rounding n+0.5 upward results in slight inaccuracies at times; after all, n+0.5 is no

closer to n+1 than it is to n. So there is an alternative tradition that rounds to the nearest even number in the case of 0.5 as a fractional part. If we wanted to do this, we might extend the Float class with a method of our own called round2, as shown here:

```
class Float

  def round2
    whole = self.floor
    fraction = self - whole
    if fraction == 0.5
      if (whole % 2) == 0
        whole
      else
        whole+1
      end
    else
      self.round
    end
  end

end

a = (33.4).round2   # 33
b = (33.5).round2   # 34
c = (33.6).round2   # 34
d = (34.4).round2   # 34
e = (34.5).round2   # 34
f = (34.6).round2   # 35
```

Obviously round2 differs from round only when the fractional part is exactly 0.5; note that 0.5 can be represented perfectly in binary, by the way. What is less obvious is that this method works fine for negative numbers also. (Try it.) Also note that the parentheses used here are not actually necessary but are used for readability.

Now, what if we wanted to round to a number of decimal places, but we wanted to use the "even rounding" method? In this case, we could add a method called roundf2 to Float:

```
class Float

  # round2 definition as before
```

```
def roundf2(places)
  shift = 10**places
  (self * shift).round2 / shift.to_f
end

end


a = 6.125
b = 6.135
x = a.roundf2(a)    # 6.12
y = b.roundf2(b)    # 6.13
```

The preceding code (roundf and roundf2) has certain limitations, in that a large floating point number naturally causes problems when it is multiplied by a large power of ten. For these occurrences, error-checking should be added.

5.4 Comparing Floating Point Numbers

It is a sad fact of life that computers do not represent floating point values exactly. The following code fragment, in a perfect world, would print "yes"; on every architecture we have tried, it will print "no" instead:

```
x = 1000001.0/0.003
y = 0.003*x
if y == 1000001.0
  puts "yes"
else
  puts "no"
end
```

The reason, of course, is that a floating point number is stored in some finite number of bits; and no finite number of bits is adequate to store a repeating decimal with an infinite number of digits.

Because of this inherent inaccuracy in floating point comparisons, we may find ourselves in situations (like the one we just saw) in which the values we are comparing are the same for all practical purposes, but the hardware stubbornly thinks they are different.

The following code is a simple way to ensure that floating point comparisons are done "with a fudge factor"—that is, the comparisons will be done within any tolerance specified by the programmer:

```
class Float

  EPSILON = 1e-6    # 0.000001

  def ==(x)
    (self-x).abs < EPSILON
  end

end


x = 1000001.0/0.003
y = 0.003*x
if y == 1.0          # Using the new ==
  puts "yes"         # Now we output "yes"
else
  puts "no"
end
```

We may find that we want different tolerances for different situations. For this case, we define a new method equals? as a member of Float. (This name avoids confusion with the standard methods equal? and eql?; the latter in particular should not be overridden.)

```
class Float

  EPSILON = 1e-6

  def equals?(x, tolerance=EPSILON)
    (self-x).abs < tolerance
  end

end

flag1 = (3.1416).equals? Math::PI             # false
flag2 = (3.1416).equals?(Math::PI, 0.001)     # true
```

We could also use a different operator entirely to represent approximate equality; the =~ operator might be a good choice.

Bear in mind that this sort of thing is not a real solution. As successive computations are performed, error is compounded. If you must use floating point math, be prepared for the inaccuracies. If the inaccuracies are not acceptable, use BigDecimal or some other solution. (See section 5.8 "Using BigDecimal" and section 5.9 "Working with Rational Values.")

5.5 Formatting Numbers for Output

To output numbers in a specific format, you can use the printf method in the Kernel module. It is virtually identical to its C counterpart. For more information, see the documentation for the printf method.

```
x = 345.6789
i = 123
printf("x = %6.2f\n", x)     # x = 345.68
printf("x = %9.2e\n", x)     # x = 3.457e+02
printf("i = %5d\n", i)       # i =   123
printf("i = %05d\n", i)      # i = 00123
printf("i = %-5d\n", i)      # i = 123
```

To store a result in a string rather than printing it immediately, sprintf can be used in much the same way. The following method returns a string:

```
str = sprintf("%5.1f",x)     # "345.7"
```

Finally, the String class has a % method that performs this same task. The % method has a format string as a receiver; it takes a single argument (or an array of values) and returns a string.

```
# Usage is 'format % value'
str = "%5.1f" % x             # "345.7"
str = "%6.2f, %05d" % [x,i]  # "345.68, 00123"
```

5.6 Formatting Numbers with Commas

There may be better ways to do it, but this one works. We reverse the string to make it easier to do global substitution and then reverse it again at the end:

```
def commas(x)
  str = x.to_s.reverse
  str.gsub!(/([0-9]{3})/,"\\1,")
  str.gsub(/,$/,"").reverse
end

puts commas(123)       # "123"
puts commas(1234)      # "1,234"
puts commas(12345)     # "12,435"
puts commas(123456)    # "123,456"
puts commas(1234567)   # "1,234,567"
```

5.7 Working with Very Large Integers

The control of large numbers is possible, and like unto that of small numbers, if we subdivide them.

—*Sun Tze*

In the event it becomes necessary, Ruby programmers can work with integers of arbitrary size. The transition from a Fixnum to a Bignum is handled automatically and transparently. In this following piece of code, notice how a result that is large enough is promoted from Fixnum to Bignum:

```
num1 = 1000000        # One million (10**6)
num2 = num1*num1      # One trillion (10**12)
puts num1             # 1000000
puts num1.class       # Fixnum
puts num2             # 1000000000000
puts num2.class       # Bignum
```

The size of a `Fixnum` varies from one architecture to another. Calculations with `Bignums` are limited only by memory and processor speed. They take more memory and are obviously somewhat slower, but number-crunching with very large integers (hundreds of digits) is still reasonably practical.

5.8 Using `BigDecimal`

The `bigdecimal` standard library enables us to work with large numbers of significant digits in fractional numbers. In effect, it stores numbers as arrays of digits rather than converting to a binary floating point representation. This allows arbitrary precision, though of course at the cost of speed.

To motivate ourselves, look at the following simple piece of code using floating point numbers:

```
if (3.2 - 2.0) == 1.2
  puts "equal"
else
  puts "not equal"     # prints "not equal"!
end
```

This is the sort of situation that `BigDecimal` helps with. However, note that with infinitely repeating decimals, we *still* will have problems. For yet another approach, see the upcoming section 5.9 "Working with Rational Values."

A `BigDecimal` is initialized with a string. (A `Float` would not suffice because the error would creep in before we could construct the `BigDecimal` object.) The method `BigDecimal` is equivalent to `BigDecimal.new`; this is another special case where a method name starts with a capital letter. The usual mathematical operations such as + and * are supported. Note that the `to_s` method can take a parameter to specify its format. For more details, see the ruby-doc.org site.

```
require 'bigdecimal'

x = BigDecimal("3.2")
y = BigDecimal("2.0")
z = BigDecimal("1.2")

if (x - y) == z
  puts "equal"           # prints "equal"!
```

```
else
  puts "not equal"
end

a = x*y*z
a.to_s                      # "0.768E1"  (default: engineering notation)
a.to_s("F")                 # "7.68"     (ordinary floating point)
```

We can specify the number of significant digits if we want. The precs method retrieves this information as an array of two numbers: the number of bytes used and the *maximum* number of significant digits.

```
x = BigDecimal("1.234",10)
y = BigDecimal("1.234",15)
x.precs                     # [8, 16]
y.precs                     # [8, 20]
```

The bytes currently used may be less than the maximum. The maximum may also be greater than what you requested (because BigDecimal tries to optimize its internal storage).

The common operations (addition, subtraction, multiplication, and division) have counterparts that take a number of digits as an extra parameter. If the resulting significant digits are *more* than that parameter specifies, the result will be rounded to that number of digits.

```
a = BigDecimal("1.23456")
b = BigDecimal("2.45678")

# In these comments, "BigDecimal:objectid" is omitted
c  = a+b          # <'0.369134E1',12(20)>
c2 = a.add(b,4)   # <'0.3691E1',8(20)>

d  = a-b          # <'-0.122222E1',12(20)>
d2 = a.sub(b,4)   # <'-0.1222E1',8(20)>

e  = a*b          # <'0.3033042316 8E1',16(36)>
e2 = a.mult(b,4)  # <'0.3033E1',8(36)>

f  = a/b          # <'0.5025114173 8372992290 7221E0',24(32)>
f2 = a.div(b,4)   # <'0.5025E0',4(16)>
```

The `BigDecimal` class defines many other functions such as `floor`, `abs`, and others. There are operators such as `%` and `**` as you would expect, along with relational operators such as `<`). The `==` is *not* intelligent enough to round off its operands; that is still the programmer's responsibility.

The `BigMath` module defines constants `E` and `PI` to arbitrary precision. (They are really methods, not constants.) It also defines functions such as `sin`, `cos`, `exp`, and others, all taking a digits parameter.

The following sublibraries are all made to work with `BigDecimal`.

bigdecimal/math   The `BigMath` module

bigdecimal/jacobian   Methods for finding a Jacobian matrix

bigdecimal/ludcmp   The `LUSolve` module, for LU decomposition

bigdecimal/newton   Provides `nlsolve` and `norm`

These sublibraries are not documented in this chapter. For more information, consult the ruby-doc.org site or any detailed reference.

5.9   Working with Rational Values

The `Rational` class enables us (in many cases) to work with fractional values with "infinite" precision. It helps us only when the values involved are true rational numbers (the quotient of two integers). It won't help with irrational numbers such as `pi`, `e`, or the square root of 2.

To create a rational number, we use the special method `Rational` (which is one of our rare capitalized method names, usually used for data conversion or initialization).

```
r = Rational(1,2)    # 1/2 or 0.5
s = Rational(1,3)    # 1/3 or 0.3333...
t = Rational(1,7)    # 1/7 or 0.14...
u = Rational(6,2)    # "same as" 3.0
z = Rational(1,0)    # error!
```

An operation on two rationals will typically be another rational:

```
r+t         #  Rational(9, 14)
r-t         #  Rational(5, 14)
r*s         #  Rational(1, 6)
r/s         #  Rational(3, 2)
```

Let's look once again at our floating point inaccuracy example (see section 5.4, "Comparing Floating Point Numbers"). In the following example, we do the same thing with rationals rather than reals, and we get the "mathematically expected" results instead:

```
x = Rational(1000001,1)/Rational(3,1000)
y = Rational(3,1000)*x
if y == 1000001.0
  puts "yes"          # Now we get "yes"!
else
  puts "no"
end
```

Some operations, of course, don't always give us rationals back.

```
x = Rational(9,16)     #  Rational(9, 16)
Math.sqrt(x)           #  0.75
x**0.5                 #  0.75
x**Rational(1,2)       #  0.75
```

However, the mathn library changes some of this behavior. See section 5.12 "Using mathn."

5.10 Matrix Manipulation

If you want to deal with numerical matrices, the standard library matrix is for you. This actually defines two separate classes, Matrix and Vector.

You should also be aware of the excellent NArray library by Masahiro Tanaka (which can be found at www.rubyforge.org). This is not a standard library but is well-known and very useful. If you have speed requirements, if you have specific data representation needs, or if you need capabilities such as Fast Fourier Transform, you should definitely look into this package. For most general purposes, however, the standard matrix library should suffice, and that is what we cover here.

To create a matrix, we naturally use a class-level method. There are multiple ways to do this. One way is simply to call Matrix.[] and list the rows as arrays. In the following example we do this in multiple lines, though of course that isn't necessary:

```
m = Matrix[[1,2,3],
           [4,5,6],
           [7,8,9]]
```

A similar method is to call rows, passing in an array of arrays (so that the "extra" brackets are necessary). The optional copy parameter, which defaults to true, determines whether the individual arrays are copied or simply stored. Therefore, let this parameter be true to protect the original arrays, or false if you want to save a little memory, and you are not concerned about this issue.

```
row1 = [2,3]
row2 = [4,5]
m1 = Matrix.rows([row1,row2])          # copy=true
m2 = Matrix.rows([row1,row2],false)    # don't copy
row1[1] = 99                           # Now change row1
p m1                                   # Matrix[[2, 3], [4, 5]]
p m2                                   # Matrix[[2, 99], [4, 5]]
```

Matrices can similarly be specified in column order with the columns method. It does not accept the copy parameter because the arrays are split up anyway to be stored internally in row-major order.

```
m1 = Matrix.rows([[1,2],[3,4]])
m2 = Matrix.columns([[1,3],[2,4]])   # m1 == m2
```

Matrices are assumed to be rectangular, but the code does not enforce this. If you assign a matrix with rows or columns that are shorter or longer than the others, you may naturally get errors or unusual results later.

Certain special matrices, especially square ones, are easily constructed. The "identity" matrix can be constructed with the identity method (or its aliases I and unit):

```
im1 = Matrix.identity(3)   # Matrix[[1,0,0],[0,1,0],[0,0,1]]
im2 = Matrix.I(3)          # same
im3 = Matrix.unit(3)       # same
```

A more general form is scalar, which assigns some value other than 1 to the diagonal:

```
sm = Matrix.scalar(3,8)   # Matrix[[8,0,0],[0,8,0],[0,0,8]]
```

Still more general is the diagonal, which assigns an arbitrary sequence of values to the diagonal. (Obviously, it does not need the dimension parameter.)

```
dm = Matrix.diagonal(2,3,7)   # Matrix[[2,0,0],[0,3,0],[0,0,7]]
```

The `zero` method creates a special matrix of the specified dimension, full of zero values:

```
zm = Matrix.zero(3)   # Matrix[[0,0,0],[0,0,0],[0,0,0]]
```

Obviously, the `identity`, `scalar`, `diagonal`, and `zero` methods all construct square matrices.

To create a *1xN* or an *Nx1* matrix, you can use the `row_vector` or `column_vector` shortcut methods, respectively:

```
a = Matrix.row_vector(2,4,6,8)      # Matrix[[2,4,6,8]]
b = Matrix.column_vector(6,7,8,9)   # Matrix[[6],[7],[8],[9]]
```

Individual matrix elements can naturally be accessed with the bracket notation (with both indices specified in a single pair of brackets). Note that there is no `[]=` method. This is for much the same reason that `Fixnum` lacks that method: Matrices are immutable objects (evidently a design decision by the library author).

```
m = Matrix[[1,2,3],[4,5,6]]
puts m[1,2]     # 6
```

Be aware that indexing is from 0 as with Ruby arrays; this may contradict your mathematical expectation, but there is no option for 1-based rows and columns unless you implement it yourself.

```
# Naive approach... don't do this!

class Matrix
  alias bracket []

  def [](i,j)
    bracket(i-1,j-1)
  end
end

m = Matrix[[1,2,3],[4,5,6],[7,8,9]]
p m[2,2]        # 5
```

The preceding code does seem to work. Many or most matrix operations still behave as expected with the alternate indexing. Why might it fail? Because we don't know all the internal implementation details of the Matrix class. If it always uses its own [] method to access the matrix values, it should always be consistent. But if it ever accesses some internal array directly or uses some kind of shortcut, it might fail. Therefore if you use this kind of trick at all, it should be with caution and testing.

In reality, you would have to change the row and vector methods as well. These methods use indices that number from zero without going through the [] method. I haven't checked to see what else might be required.

Sometimes we need to discover the dimensions or shape of a matrix. There are various methods for this purpose, such as row_size and column_size. Let's look at these.

The row_size method returns the number of rows in the matrix. The column_size method comes with a caveat, however: It checks the size of the first row only. If your matrix is for some reason not rectangular, this may not be meaningful. Furthermore, because the square? method calls these other two, it may not be reliable.

```
m1 = Matrix[[1,2,3],[4,5,6],[7,8,9]]
m2 = Matrix[[1,2,3],[4,5,6],[7,8]]
m1.row_size         # 3
m1.column_size      # 3
m2.row_size         # 3
m2.column_size      # 3     (misleading)
m1.square?          # true
m2.square?          # true  (incorrect)
```

One answer to this minor problem would be to define a rectangular? method.

```
class Matrix
  def rectangular?
    arr = to_a
    first = arr[0].size
    arr[1..-1].all? {|x| x.size == first }
  end
end
```

You could, of course, modify square? to check first for a rectangular matrix. In that case, you might want to modify column_size to return nil for a nonrectangular matrix.

To retrieve a section or piece of a matrix, several methods are available. The row_vectors method returns an array of Vector objects representing the rows of the matrix. (See the following discussion of the Vector class.) The column_vectors method works similarly. Finally, the minor method returns a smaller matrix from the larger one; its parameters are either four numbers (lower and upper bounds for the rows and columns) or two ranges.

```
m = Matrix[[1,2,3,4],[5,6,7,8],[6,7,8,9]]

rows = m.row_vectors       # three Vector objects
cols = m.column_vectors    # four Vector objects
m2 = m.minor(1,2,1,2)      # Matrix[[6,7,],[7,8]]
m3 = m.minor(0..1,1..3)    # Matrix[[2,3,4],[6,7,8]]
```

The usual matrix operations can be applied: addition, subtraction, multiplication, and division. Some of these make certain assumptions about the dimensions of the matrices and may raise exceptions if the operands are incompatible (for example, trying to multiply a 3x3 matrix with a 4x4 matrix).

Ordinary transformations such as inverse, transpose, and determinant are supported. For matrices of integers, the determinant will usually be better behaved if the mathn library is used (see the section 5.12 "Using mathn").

A Vector is in effect a special one-dimensional matrix. It can be created with the [] or elements methods; the first takes an expanded array, and the latter takes an unexpanded array and an optional copy parameter (which defaults to true).

```
arr = [2,3,4,5]
v1 = Vector[*arr]                 # Vector[2,3,4,5]
v2 = Vector.elements(arr)         # Vector[2,3,4,5]
v3 = Vector.elements(arr,false)   # Vector[2,3,4,5]
arr[2] = 7                        # v3 is now Vector[2,3,7,5]
```

The covector method converts a vector of length N to an $Nx1$ (effectively transposed) matrix.

```
v = Vector[2,3,4]
m = v.covector    # Matrix[[2,3,4]]
```

Addition and subtraction of similar vectors is supported. A vector may be multiplied by a matrix or by a scalar. All these operations are subject to normal mathematical rules.

```
v1 = Vector[2,3,4]
v2 = Vector[4,5,6]
v3 = v1 + v2          # Vector[6,8,10]
v4 = v1*v2.covector   # Matrix[[8,10,12],[12,15,18],[16,20,24]]
v5 = v1*5             # Vector[10,15,20]
```

There is an `inner_product` method:

```
v1 = Vector[2,3,4]
v2 = Vector[4,5,6]
x  = v1.inner_product(v2)   # 47
```

For additional information on the `Matrix` and `Vector` classes, go to any reference such as the `ri` command-line tool or the ruby-doc.org website.

5.11   Working with Complex Numbers

The standard library `complex` enables us to handle imaginary and complex numbers in Ruby. Much of it is self-explanatory.

Complex values can be created with this slightly unusual notation:

```
z = Complex(3,5)      # 3+5i
```

What is unusual about this is that we have a method name that is the same as the class name. In this case, the presence of the parentheses indicates a method call rather than a reference to a constant. In general, method names do not look like constants, and I don't recommend the practice of capitalizing method names *except* in special cases like this. (Note that there are also methods called `Integer` and `Float`; in general, the capitalized method names are for data conversion or something similar.)

The `im` method converts a number to its imaginary counterpart (effectively multiplying it by i). So we can represent imaginary and complex numbers with a more convenient notation:

```
a = 3.im       # 3i
b = 5 - 2.im   # 5-2i
```

If we're more concerned with polar coordinates, we can also call the `polar` class method:

```
z = Complex.polar(5,Math::PI/2.0)   # radius, angle
```

The `Complex` class also gives us the constant `I`, which of course represents *i*, the square root of negative one:

```
z1 = Complex(3,5)
z2 = 3 + 5*Complex::I    # z2 == z1
```

When `complex` is loaded, certain common math functions have their behavior changed. Trig functions such as `sin`, `sinh`, `tan`, and `tanh` (along with others such as `exp` and `log`) accept complex arguments in addition to their normal behavior. In some cases, such as `sqrt`, they are "smart" enough to return complex results also.

```
x = Math.sqrt(Complex(3,5))   # roughly: Complex(2.1013, 1.1897)
y = Math.sqrt(-1)             # Complex(0,1)
```

For more information, refer to any comprehensive source of documentation such as the ruby-doc.org site.

5.12   Using `mathn`

For math-intensive programs, you will want to know about the excellent `mathn` library created by Keiju Ishitsuka. It provides a few convenience methods and classes, and in general helps to unify all of Ruby's numeric classes so that they "play well" together.

The easiest way to "use" this library is simply to require it and forget it. Because it requires the `complex`, `rational`, and `matrix` libraries (in that order), there is no need to do separate requires of those if you are using them.

In general, the `mathn` library tries to produce "sensible" results from computations— for example, the square root of a `Rational` will be returned when possible as another `Rational` rather than a `Float`. Table 5.1 shows some typical effects of loading this library.

Table 5.1   Computation With and Without the mathn Library

Expression	Without mathn	With mathn
`Math.sqrt(Rational(9,16))`	`0.75`	`Rational(3,4)`
`1/2`	`0`	`Rational(1,2)`
`Matrix.identity(3)/3`	`Matrix[[0,0,0],` `[0,0,0],[0,0,0]]`	`Matrix[[1/3,0,0],` `[0,1/3,0],[0,0,1/3]]`
`Math.sqrt(64/25)`	`1.4142...`	`Rational(8,5)`
`Rational(1,10).inspect`	`Rational(1,10)`	`1/10`

The `mathn` library adds `**` and `power2` methods to `Rational`. It changes the behavior of `Math.sqrt` and adds the rational-aware function `Math.rsqrt`.

See also sections 5.13 "Finding Prime Factorization, GCD, and LCM" and 5.14, "Working with Prime Numbers."

5.13   Finding Prime Factorization, GCD, and LCM

The `mathn` library also defines some new methods on the `Integer` class. One is `gcd2`, which finds the greatest common divisor of the receiver and the other specified number:

```
n = 36.gcd2(120)    # 12
k = 237.gcd2(79)    # 79
```

The `prime_division` method performs a prime factorization of its receiver. The result returned is an array of arrays where each smaller array consists of a prime number and its exponent:

```
factors = 126.prime_division  # [[2,1], [3,2], [7,1]]
                              # i.e. 2**1 * 3**2 * 7**1
```

There is also a class method `Integer.from_prime_division`, which reverses that factorization. It is a class method because it is like a "constructor" for an integer.

```
factors = [[2,1],[3,1],[7,1]]
num = Integer.from_prime_division(factors)    # 42
```

The following code is an example of using prime factorization to find the Least Common Multiple (LCM) of a pair of numbers:

```
require 'mathn'

class Integer
  def lcm(other)
    pf1 = self.prime_division.flatten
    pf2 = other.prime_division.flatten
    h1 = Hash[*pf1]
    h2 = Hash[*pf2]
    hash = h2.merge(h1) {|key,old,new| [old,new].max }
    Integer.from_prime_division(hash.to_a)
  end
end

p 15.lcm(150)     # 150
p 2.lcm(3)        # 6
p 4.lcm(12)       # 12
p 200.lcm(30)     # 600
```

5.14 Working with Prime Numbers

The mathn library defines a class for generating prime numbers. The iterator each generates these in succession in an infinite loop. The succ method naturally generates the next prime number.

For example, here are two ways to list the first 100 primes:

```
require 'mathn'

list = []
gen = Prime.new
gen.each do |prime|
  list << prime
  break if list.size == 100
end

# or alternatively:

list = []
gen = Prime.new
100.times { list << gen.succ }
```

The following code tests the primality of a number. Note that for large numbers and slow machines, this may take a while:

```ruby
require 'mathn'

class Integer
  def prime?
    max = Math.sqrt(self).ceil
    max -= 1 if max % 2 == 0
    pgen = Prime.new
    pgen.each do |factor|
      return false if self % factor == 0
      return true if factor > max
    end
  end
end


31.prime?            # true
237.prime?           # false
1500450271.prime?    # true
```

5.15   Implicit and Explicit Numeric Conversion

The new Rubyist is often confused that there are methods named to_i and to_int (and by analogy, to_f and to_flt, as well as others). In general, explicit conversion is done using the "short name" and implicit conversion using the "long name."

What does this mean? First, most classes define explicit convertors but not implicit; to_int and to_flt are not defined anywhere in the core that I am aware of.

Second, your own classes will tend to *define* implicit convertors, but you will not usually call them manually (unless you are writing "client" code or library-oriented code that tries to play well with the outside world).

The following code is a contrived example. The class MyClass as defined in this example returns constants from to_i and to_int. This is nonsensical behavior, but it illustrates a point:

```ruby
class MyClass

  def to_i
    3
  end
```

```
def to_int
  5
end

end
```

If we want to convert a `MyClass` object explicitly to an integer, we can call `to_i`:

```
m = MyClass.new
x = m.to_i        # 3
```

But the `to_int` method gets called implicitly ("behind our backs") when we pass in a `MyClass` object to something that expects an integer. For example, suppose that we want to create an array with an initial number of values; `Array.new` can take an integer, but what happens if we give it a `MyClass` object instead?

```
m = MyClass.new
a = Array.new(m)   # [nil,nil,nil,nil,nil]
```

As we see, the `new` method was smart enough to call `to_int` and thus create an array with five entries.

For more explanation in a different context (strings), see the section 2.16, "Implicit and Explicit Conversion." See also the following section 5.16 "Coercing Numeric Values."

5.16   Coercing Numeric Values

Coercion can be thought of as another form of implicit conversion. When a method (+ for example) is passed an argument it doesn't understand, it tries to coerce the receiver and the argument to compatible types and then do the addition based on those types. The pattern for using `coerce` in a class you write is straightforward:

```
class MyNumberSystem

def +(other)
  if other.kind_of?(MyNumberSystem)
    result = some_calculation_between_self_and_other
    MyNumberSystem.new(result)
  else
    n1, n2 = other.coerce(self)
```

```
      n1 + n2
    end
  end

end
```

The value returned by coerce is a two-element array containing its argument and its receiver converted to compatible types.

In this example, we're relying on the type of our argument to perform some kind of coercion for us. If we want to be good citizens, we also need to implement coercion in our class, allowing other types of numbers to work with us. To do this, we need to know the specific types that we can work with directly and convert to those types when appropriate. When we can't do that, we fall back on asking our parent class.

```
def coerce(other)
  if other.kind_of?(Float)
    return other, self.to_f
  elsif other.kind_of?(Integer)
    return other, self.to_i
  else
    super
  end
end
```

Of course, for this to work, our object must implement to_i and to_f.

You can use coerce as part of the solution for implementing a Perl-like autoconversion of strings to numbers:

```
class String

  def coerce(n)
    if self['.']
      [n, Float(self)]
    else
      [n, Integer(self)]
    end
  end

end

x = 1 + "23"       # 24
y = 23 * "1.23"    # 28.29
```

We don't necessarily recommend this. But we do recommend that you implement a coerce method whenever you are creating some kind of numeric class.

5.17 Performing Bit-level Operations on Numbers

Occasionally we may need to operate on a Fixnum as a binary entity. This is less common in application level programming, but the need still arises.

Ruby has a relatively full set of capabilities in this area. For convenience, numeric constants may be expressed in binary, octal, or hexadecimal. The usual operators AND, OR, XOR, and NOT are expressed by the Ruby operators &, |, ^, and ~, respectively.

```
x = 0377          # Octal   (decimal 255)
y = 0b00100110    # Binary  (decimal  38)
z = 0xBEEF        # Hex     (decimal 48879)

a = x | z         # 48895 (bitwise OR)
b = x & z         #   239 (bitwise AND)
c = x ^ z         # 48656 (bitwise XOR)
d = ~ y           #   -39 (negation or 1's complement)
```

The instance method size can be used to determine the word size of the specific architecture on which the program is running.

```
bytes = 1.size    # Returns 4 for one particular machine
```

There are left-shift and right-shift operators (<< and >>, respectively). These are logical shift operations; they do not disturb the sign bit (though >> does propagate it).

```
x = 8
y = -8

a = x >> 2        # 2
b = y >> 2        # -2
c = x << 2        # 32
d = y << 2        # -32
```

Of course, anything shifted far enough to result in a zero value will lose the sign bit because -0 is merely 0.

Brackets can be used to treat numbers as arrays of bits. The 0th bit is the least significant bit regardless of the bit order (endianness) of the architecture.

```
x = 5              # Same as 0b0101
a = x[0]           # 1
b = x[1]           # 0
c = x[2]           # 1
d = x[3]           # 0
# Etc.             # 0
```

It is not possible to assign bits using this notation (because a Fixnum is stored as an immediate value rather than an object reference). However, you can always fake it by left-shifting a 1 to the specified bit position and then doing an OR or AND operation.

```
# We can't do x[3] = 1
# but we can do:
x |= (1<<3)
# We can't do x[4] = 0
# but we can do:
x &= ~(1<<4)
```

5.18   Performing Base Conversions

Obviously all integers are representable in any base, because they are all stored internally in binary. Further, we know that Ruby can deal with integer constants in any of the four commonly used bases. This means that if we are concerned about base conversions, we must be concerned with strings in some fashion.

If you are concerned with converting a string to an integer, that is covered in section 2.24, "Converting Strings to Numbers (Decimal and Otherwise)."

If you are concerned with converting numbers to strings, the simplest way is to use the to_s method with the optional base parameter. This naturally defaults to 10, but it does handle bases up to 36 (using all letters of the alphabet).

```
237.to_s(2)        # "11101101"
237.to_s(5)        # "1422"
237.to_s(8)        # "355"
237.to_s           # "237"
237.to_s(16)       # "ed"
237.to_s(30)       # "7r"
```

Another way is to use the `%` method of the `String` class:

```ruby
hex = "%x" % 1234     # "4d2"
oct = "%o" % 1234     # "2322"
bin = "%b" % 1234     # "10011010010"
```

The `sprintf` method also works:

```ruby
str = sprintf(str,"Nietzsche is %x\n",57005)
# str is now: "Nietzsche is dead\n"
```

Obviously, `printf` will also suffice if you want to print out the value as you convert it.

5.19 Finding Cube Roots, Fourth Roots, and so on

Ruby has a built-in square root function (`Math.sqrt`) because that function is so commonly used. But what if you need higher level roots? If you remember your math, this is easy.

One way is to use logarithms. Recall that e to the x is the inverse of the natural log of x, and that when we multiply numbers, that is equivalent to adding their logarithms.

```ruby
x = 531441
cuberoot = Math.exp(Math.log(x)/3.0)     # 81.0
fourthroot = Math.exp(Math.log(x)/4.0)   # 27.0
```

However, it is just as easy and perhaps clearer simply to use fractions with an exponentiation operator (which can take any integer or floating point value).

```ruby
include Math
y = 4096
cuberoot = y**(1.0/3.0)      # 16.0
fourthroot = y**(1.0/4.0)    # 8.0
fourthroot = sqrt(sqrt(y))   # 8.0 (same thing)
twelfthroot = y**(1.0/12.0)  # 2.0
```

Note that in all these examples, we have used floating point numbers when dividing (to avoid truncation to an integer).

5.20   Determining the Architecture's Byte Order

It is an interesting fact of the computing world that we cannot all agree on the order in which binary data ought to be stored. Is the most significant bit stored at the higher-numbered address or the lower? When we shove a message over a wire, do we send the most significant bit first, or the least significant?

Believe it or not, it's not entirely arbitrary. There are good arguments on both sides (which we will not delve into here).

For more than twenty years, the terms *little-endian* and *big-endian* have been applied to the two extreme opposites. These apparently were first used by Danny Cohen; refer to his classic article "On Holy Wars and a Plea for Peace" (*IEEE Computer*, October 1981). The actual terms are derived from the novel *Gulliver's Travels* by Jonathan Swift.

Most of the time we don't care what byte order our architecture uses. But what if we do need to know?

The following method determines this for us. It returns a string that is LITTLE, BIG, or OTHER. It depends on the fact that the l directive packs in native mode, and the N directive unpacks in network order (or big-endian).

```
def endianness
  num=0x12345678
  little = "78563412"
  big    = "12345678"
  native = [num].pack('l')
  netunpack = native.unpack('N')[0]
  str = "%8x" % netunpack
  case str
    when little
      "LITTLE"
    when big
      "BIG"
    else
      "OTHER"
  end
end

puts endianness   # In this case, prints "LITTLE"
```

This technique might come in handy if, for example, you are working with binary data (such as scanned image data) imported from another system.

5.21   Numerical Computation of a Definite Integral

I'm very good at integral and differential calculus...

—*W. S. Gilbert,* The Pirates of Penzance, *Act 1*

If you want to estimate the value of a definite integral, there is a time-tested technique for doing so. This is what the calculus student will remember as a Riemann sum.

The `integrate` method shown here takes beginning and ending values for the dependent variable as well as an increment. The fourth parameter (which is not really a parameter) is a block. This block should evaluate a function based on the value of the dependent variable passed into that block. (Here we are using "variable" in the mathematical sense, not in the computing sense.) It is not necessary to define a function to call in this block, but we do so here for clarity:

```
def integrate(x0, x1, dx=(x1-x0)/1000.0)
  x = x0
  sum = 0
  loop do
    y = yield(x)
    sum += dx * y
    x += dx
    break if x > x1
  end
  sum
end

def f(x)
  x**2
end

z = integrate(0.0,5.0) {|x| f(x) }

puts z, "\n"          # 41.7291875
```

Note that in the preceding example, we are relying on the fact that a block returns a value that `yield` can retrieve. We also make certain assumptions here. First, we assume that x0 is less than x1 (otherwise, an infinite loop results); the reader can easily improve the code in details such as this one. Second, we assume that the function can be evaluated at arbitrary points in the specified domain. If at any time we try to evaluate the function at such a point, chaos will ensue. (Such functions are generally not integrable anyway, at least over that set of x values. Consider the function `f(x)=x/(x-3)` when x is 3.)

Drawing on our faded memories of calculus, we might compute the result here to be `41.666` or thereabout (5 cubed divided by 3). Why is the answer not as exact as we might like? It is because of the size of the "slice" in the Riemann sum; a smaller value for `dx` will result in greater accuracy (at the expense of an increase in runtime).

Finally, we will point out that a function like this is more useful when we have a variety of functions of arbitrary complexity, not just a simple function like `f(x) = x**2`.

5.22   Trigonometry in Degrees, Radians, and Grads

When it comes to measuring arc, the mathematical or "natural" unit is the radian, defined in such a way that an angle of one radian corresponds to an arclength equal to the radius of the circle. A little thought will show that there are 2π radians in a circle.

The *degree of arc*, which we use in everyday life is a holdover from ancient Babylonian base-60 units; this system divides the circle into 360 degrees. The less-familiar *grad* is a pseudometric unit defined in such a way that there are 100 grads in a right angle (or 400 in a circle).

Programming languages often default to the radian when calculating trigonometric functions, and Ruby is no exception. But we show here how to do these calculations in degrees or grads, in the event that any of our readers are engineers or ancient Babylonians.

Because the number of units in a circle is a simple constant, it follows that there are simple conversion factors between all these units. We define these here and simply use the constant names in subsequent code. As a matter of convenience, we'll stick them in the `Math` module:

```
module Math

  RAD2DEG  = 360.0/(2.0*PI)   # Radians to degrees
  RAD2GRAD = 400.0/(2.0*PI)   # Radians to grads

end
```

Now we can define new trig functions if we want. Because we are converting to radians in each case, we will divide by the conversion factor we calculated previously. We could place these in the Math module if we wanted, though we don't show it here.

```
def sin_d(theta)
  Math.sin (theta/Math::RAD2DEG)
end

def sin_g(theta)
  Math.sin (theta/Math::RAD2GRAD)
end
```

Of course, the corresponding cos and tan functions may be similarly defined.

The atan2 function is a little different. It takes two arguments (the opposite and adjacent legs of a right triangle) and returns an angle. Thus we convert the result, not the argument, handling it this way:

```
def atan2_d(y,x)
  Math.atan2(y,x)/Math::RAD2DEG
end

def atan2_g(y,x)
  Math.atan2(y,x)/Math::RAD2GRAD
end
```

5.23 More Advanced Trigonometry

Earlier versions of Ruby did not have the functions arcsin and arccos. Hyperbolic functions such as sinh, cosh, and tanh were also not defined. These were defined in the first edition of this book, but they are now a standard part of the Math module.

5.24 Finding Logarithms with Arbitrary Bases

When working with logarithms, we frequently use the *natural* logarithms (or base *e*, sometimes written *ln*); we may also use the *common* or base 10 logarithms. These are defined in Ruby as Math.log and Math.log10, respectively.

In computer science, specifically in such areas as coding and information theory, a base 2 log is not unusual. For example, this will tell the minimum number of bits needed to store a number. We define this function here as `log2`:

```
def log2(x)
  Math.log(x)/Math.log(2)
end
```

The inverse is obviously `2**x` just as the inverse of `log x` is `Math::E**x` or `Math.exp(x)`.

Furthermore, this same technique can be extended to any base. In the unlikely event that you ever need a base 7 logarithm, this will do the trick.

```
def log7(x)
  Math.log(x)/Math.log(7)
end
```

In practice, the denominator should be calculated once and kept around as a constant.

5.25 Finding the Mean, Median, and Mode of a Data Set

Given an array x, let's find the mean of all the values in that array. Actually, there are three common kinds of mean. The ordinary or *arithmetic mean* is what we call the *average* in everyday life. The *harmonic mean* is the number of terms divided by the sum of all their reciprocals. And finally, the *geometric mean* is the nth root of the product of the n values. We show each of these in the following example:

```
def mean(x)
  sum=0
  x.each {|v| sum += v}
  sum/x.size
end

def hmean(x)
  sum=0
  x.each {|v| sum += (1.0/v)}
  x.size/sum
end
```

```
def gmean(x)
  prod=1.0
  x.each {|v| prod *= v}
  prod**(1.0/x.size)
end

data = [1.1, 2.3, 3.3, 1.2, 4.5, 2.1, 6.6]

am = mean(data)    # 3.014285714
hm = hmean(data)   # 2.101997946
gm = gmean(data)   # 2.508411474
```

The median value of a data set is the value that occurs approximately in the middle of the (sorted) set. (The following code fragment computes a median.) For this value, half the numbers in the set should be less, and half should be greater. Obviously, this statistic will be more appropriate and meaningful for some data sets than others. See the following code:

```
def median(x)
  sorted = x.sort
  mid = x.size/2
  sorted[mid]
end

data = [7,7,7,4,4,5,4,5,7,2,2,3,3,7,3,4]
puts median(data)          # 4
```

The mode of a data set is the value that occurs most frequently. If there is only one such value, the set is *unimodal*; otherwise, it is *multimodal*. A multimodal data set is a more complex case that we do not consider here. The interested reader can extend and improve the code we show here:

```
def mode(x)
  f = {}       # frequency table
  fmax = 0     # maximum frequency
  m = nil      # mode
  x.each do |v|
    f[v] ||= 0
    f[v] += 1
    fmax,m = f[v], v if f[v] > fmax
  end
```

```
    return m
end

data = [7,7,7,4,4,5,4,5,7,2,2,3,3,7,3,4]
puts mode(data)              # 7
```

5.26   Variance and Standard Deviation

The *variance* of a set of data is a measure of how "spread out" the values are. (Here we do not distinguish between biased and unbiased estimates.) The standard deviation, usually represented by a sigma (σ) is simply the square root of the variance.

```
data = [2, 3, 2, 2, 3, 4, 5, 5, 4, 3, 4, 1, 2]

def variance(x)
  m = mean(x)
  sum = 0.0
  x.each {|v| sum += (v-m)**2 }
  sum/x.size
end

def sigma(x)
  Math.sqrt(variance(x))
end

puts variance(data)    # 1.461538462
puts sigma(data)       # 1.20894105
```

Note that the variance function in the preceding code uses the mean function defined earlier.

5.27   Finding a Correlation Coefficient

The *correlation coefficient* is one of the simplest and most universally useful statistical measures. It is a measure of the "linearity" of a set of x-y pairs, ranging from −1.0 (complete negative correlation) to +1.0 (complete positive correlation).

We compute this using the mean and sigma (standard deviation) functions defined previously in sections 5.25 and 5.26. For an explanation of this tool, consult any statistics text.

The following version assumes two arrays of numbers (of the same size):

```ruby
def correlate(x,y)
  sum = 0.0
  x.each_index do |i|
    sum += x[i]*y[i]
  end
  xymean = sum/x.size.to_f
  xmean  = mean(x)
  ymean  = mean(y)
  sx = sigma(x)
  sy = sigma(y)
  (xymean-(xmean*ymean))/(sx*sy)
end

a = [3, 6, 9, 12, 15, 18, 21]
b = [1.1, 2.1, 3.4, 4.8, 5.6]
c = [1.9, 1.0, 3.9, 3.1, 6.9]

c1 = correlate(a,a)           # 1.0
c2 = correlate(a,a.reverse)   # -1.0
c3 = correlate(b,c)           # 0.8221970228
```

The following version is similar, but it operates on a single array, each element of which is an array containing an x-y pair:

```ruby
def correlate2(v)
  sum = 0.0
  v.each do |a|
    sum += a[0]*a[1]
  end
  xymean = sum/v.size.to_f
  x = v.collect {|a| a[0]}
  y = v.collect {|a| a[1]}
  xmean  = mean(x)
  ymean  = mean(y)
  sx = sigma(x)
  sy = sigma(y)
  (xymean-(xmean*ymean))/(sx*sy)
end
```

```
d = [[1,6.1], [2.1,3.1], [3.9,5.0], [4.8,6.2]]

c4 = correlate2(d)          # 0.2277822492
```

Finally, the following version assumes that the x-y pairs are stored in a hash. It simply builds on the previous example:

```
def correlate_h(h)
  correlate2(h.to_a)
end

e = { 1 => 6.1, 2.1 => 3.1, 3.9 => 5.0, 4.8 => 6.2}

c5 = correlate_h(e)          # 0.2277822492
```

5.28   Generating Random Numbers

If a pseudorandom number is good enough for you, you're in luck. This is what most language implementations supply you with, and Ruby is no exception.

The Kernel method rand returns a pseudorandom floating point number x such that x>=0.0 and x<1.0. For example (note yours will vary)

```
a = rand      # 0.6279091137
```

If it is called with an integer parameter max, it returns an integer in the range 0...max (noninclusive of the upper bound). For example (note yours will vary)

```
n = rand(10)  # 7
```

If we want to seed the random number generator, we can do so with the Kernel method srand, which takes a single numeric parameter. If we pass no value to it, it will construct its own using (among other things) the time of day. If we pass a number to it, it will use that number as the seed. This can be useful in testing, when we want a repeatable sequence of pseudorandom numbers from one script invocation to the next.

```
srand(5)
i, j, k = rand(100), rand(100), rand(100)
# 26, 45, 56
```

```
srand(5)
l, m, n = rand(100), rand(100), rand(100)
# 26, 45, 56
```

5.29   Caching Functions with `memoize`

Suppose you have a computationally expensive mathematical function that will be called repeatedly in the course of execution. If speed is critical and you can afford to sacrifice a little memory, it may be effective to store the function results in a table and look them up. This makes the implicit assumption that the function will likely be called more than once with the same parameters; we are simply avoiding "throwing away" an expensive calculation only to redo it later on. This technique is sometimes called *memoizing*, hence the name of the memoize library.

This is not part of the standard library, so you'll have to install it.

The following example defines a complex function called zeta. (This solves a simple problem in population genetics, but we won't explain it here.)

```
require 'memoize'
include Memoize

def zeta(x,y,z)
  lim = 0.0001
  gen = 0
  loop do
    gen += 1
    p,q = x + y/2.0, z + y/2.0
    x1, y1, z1 =  p*p*1.0, 2*p*q*1.0, q*q*0.9
    sum = x1 + y1 + z1
    x1 /= sum
    y1 /= sum
    z1 /= sum
    delta = [[x1,x],[y1,y],[z1,z]]
    break if delta.all? {|a,b|  (a-b).abs < lim }
    x,y,z = x1,y1,z1
  end
      gen
end

g1 = zeta(0.8,0.1,0.1)
```

```
memoize(:zeta)                  # store table in memory
g2 = zeta(0.8,0.1,0.1)

memoize(:zeta,"z.cache")  # store table on disk
g3 = zeta(0.8,0.1,0.1)
```

Notice that we can specify a filename if we want. This may slow us down a little, but it saves memory and allows us to persist the memoization over subsequent program executions.

In our informal tests, we ran each of these 50,000 times in a tight loop. We found that g2 was calculated about 1,100 times faster than g1, and g3 about 700 times faster. Your results will vary.

One more thing should be noted here. The memoize library is not just for mathematical functions. It can be used for any computationally expensive method.

5.30   Conclusion

In this chapter, we have looked at various representations for numbers, including integers (in different bases) and floats. We've seen problems with floating-point math, and how working with rational values can help avoid these problems. We've looked at implicit and explicit numeric conversion and coercion.

We've seen numerous ways to manipulate numbers, vectors, and matrices. We've had a good overview of most of the number-related standard libraries, in particular the mathn library.

Let's move on. In the next chapter, we discuss two very Rubyish data types: symbols and ranges.

CHAPTER 6

Symbols and Ranges

I hear, and I forget. I see, and I remember. I do, and I understand.

—Confucius

Two fairly Rubyesque objects are symbols and ranges. They are covered together in this chapter not because they are related but because there is not so much to say about them.

The Ruby concept of a symbol is sometimes difficult to grasp. If you are familiar with the concept of "atoms" in Lisp, you can think of Ruby symbols as being similar. But rather than give a lengthy and abstruse definition, I will concentrate on what can be done with a symbol and how it can be used. After all, the question "What is a number?" could have a complex answer, but we all understand how to use and manipulate numbers.

Ranges are simpler. A range is simply a representation of a group or collection delimited by its endpoints. Similar constructs exist in Pascal, PHP, and even SQL.

Let's look at symbols and ranges in greater detail, and see how we can use them in everyday Ruby code.

6.1   Symbols

A *symbol* in Ruby is an instance of the class `Symbol`. The syntax is simple in the typical case: a colon followed by an identifier.

A symbol is like a string in that it corresponds to a sequence of characters. It is *unlike* a string in that each symbol has only one instance (just as a `Fixnum` works). Therefore, there is a memory or performance issue to be aware of. For example, in the following code, the string `"foo"` is stored as three separate objects in memory, but the symbol `:foo` is stored as a single object (referenced more than once):

```
array = ["foo", "foo", "foo", :foo, :foo, :foo]
```

Some people are confused by the leading colon on a symbol name. There is no need for confusion; it's a simple matter of syntax. Strings, arrays, and hashes have both beginning and ending delimiters; a symbol has only a beginning delimiter. Think of it as a *unary* delimiter rather than a *binary* one. You may consider the syntax strange at first, but there is no mystery.

It's worth mentioning that in older versions of Ruby (prior to 1.6), a symbol constant was not a first-class object as such but was translated into a `Fixnum` and stored. This is still true internally; a symbol corresponds to a number and is stored as an immediate value. The number can be retrieved with `to_i`, but there is little need for it.

According to Jim Weirich, a symbol is "an object that has a name." Austin Ziegler prefers to say "an object that *is* a name." In any case, there is a one-to-one correspondence between symbols and names. What kinds of things do we need to apply names to? Such things as variables, methods, and arbitrary constants.

One common use of symbols is to represent the name of a variable or method. For example, we know that if we want to add a read/write attribute to a class, we can do it this way:

```
class SomeClass
  attr_accessor :whatever
end
```

This is equivalent to saying:

```
class SomeClass
  def whatever
    @whatever
  end
```

```
  def whatever=(val)
    @whatever = val
  end
end
```

In other words, the symbol :whatever tells the attr_accessor method that the "getter" and "setter" (as well as the instance variable) will all be given names corresponding to that symbol.

You might well ask why we couldn't use a string instead. As it happens, we could. Many or most core methods that expect symbols are content to get strings instead.

```
attr_reader :alpha
attr_reader "beta"    # This is also legal
```

In fact, a symbol is "like" a string in that it corresponds to a sequence of characters. This leads some people to say that "a symbol is just an immutable string." However, the Symbol class does *not* inherit from String, and the typical operations we might apply to a string are not necessarily applicable to symbols.

Another misunderstanding is to think that symbols necessarily correspond directly to identifiers. This leads some people to talk of "the symbol table" (as they would in referring to an assembled object program). But this is not really a useful concept; although symbols are certainly stored in a kind of table internally, Ruby does not expose the table as an entity we can access, and we as programmers don't care that it is there.

What is more, symbols need not even look like identifiers. Typically they do, whatever that means; but they can also contain punctuation if they are enclosed in quotes. These are also valid Ruby symbols:

```
sym1 = :"This is a symbol"
sym2 = :"This is, too!"
sym3 = :")(*&^%$"          # and even this
```

You could even use such symbols to define instance variables and methods, but then you would need such techniques as send and instance_variable_get to reference them. In general, such a thing is not recommended.

6.1.1   Symbols As Enumerations

Languages such as Pascal and later versions of C have the concept of an enumerated type. Ruby can't really have such a thing; there is no type checking anyhow. But symbols are frequently useful for their mnemonic value; we might represent directions as :north, :south, :east, and :west.

It might be a little clearer to store these as constants.

```
North, South, East, West = :north, :south, :east, :west
```

If these were strings rather than symbols, defining them as constants would save memory, but each symbol exists only once in object space anyhow. (Symbols, like Fixnums, are stored as immediate values.)

6.1.2   Symbols As Metavalues

Frequently we use exceptions as a way of avoiding return codes. But if you prefer to use return codes, you can. The fact that Ruby's methods are not limited to a single return type makes it possible to pass back "out of band" values.

We frequently have need for such values. At one time, the ASCII NUL character was considered to be not a character at all. C has the idea of the NULL pointer, Pascal has the nil pointer, SQL has NULL, and so on. Ruby, of course, has nil.

The trouble with such metavalues is that they keep getting absorbed into the set of valid values. Everyone today considers NUL a true ASCII character. And in Ruby, nil isn't really a non-object; it can be stored and manipulated. Thus we have minor annoyances such as hash[key] returning nil; did it return nil because the key was not found, or because the key is really associated with a nil?

The point here is that symbols can sometimes be used as good metavalues. Imagine a method that somehow grabs a string from the network (perhaps via http or something similar). If we want, we can return nonstring values to indicate exceptional occurrences.

```
str = get_string
case str
  when String
    # Proceed normally
  when :eof
    # end of file, socket closed, whatever
  when :error
```

```
      # I/O or network error
  when :timeout
      # didn't get a reply
end
```

Is this really "better" or clearer than using exceptions? Not necessarily. But it is a technique to keep in mind, especially when you want to deal with conditions that may be "edge cases" but not necessarily errors.

6.1.3   Symbols, Variables, and Methods

Probably the best known use of symbols is in defining attributes on a class:

```
class MyClass
  attr_reader :alpha, :beta
  attr_writer :gamma, :delta
  attr_accessor :epsilon
  # ...
end
```

Bear in mind that there is some code at work here. For example, `attr_accessor` uses the symbol name to determine the name of the instance variable and the reader and writer methods. That does *not* mean that there is always an exact correspondence between that symbol and that instance variable name. For example, if we use `instance_variable_set`, we have to specify the exact name of the variable, including the at-sign:

```
sym1 = :@foo
sym2 = :foo
instance_variable_set(sym1,"str")   # Works
instance_variable_set(sym2,"str")   # error
```

In short, a symbol passed into the `attr` family of methods is just an argument, and these methods create instance variables and methods as needed, *based on* the value of that symbol. (The writer has an equal sign appended to the end, and the instance variable name has an at-sign added to the front.) In other cases, the symbol must exactly correspond to the identifier it is referencing.

In most, if not all cases, methods that expect symbols can also take strings. The reverse is not necessarily true.

6.1.4   Converting to/from Symbols

Strings and symbols can be freely interconverted with the to_str and to_sym methods:

```
a = "foobar"
b = :foobar
a == b.to_str      # true
b == a.to_sym      # true
```

If you're doing metaprogramming, the following method might prove useful sometimes.

```
class Symbol
  def +(other)
    (self.to_s + other.to_s).to_sym
  end
end
```

The preceding method allows us to concatenate symbols (or append a string onto a symbol). The following is an example that uses it; this trivial piece of code accepts a symbol and tries to tell us whether it represents an accessor (that is, a reader and writer both exist):

```
class Object
  def accessor?(sym)
    return (self.respond_to?(sym) and self.respond_to?(sym+"="))
  end
end
```

There is a clever usage of symbols that I'll mention here. When we do a map operation, sometimes a complex block may be attached. But in many cases, we are simply calling a method on each element of the array or collection:

```
list = words.map {|x| x.capitalize }
```

In such a case, it may seem we are doing a little too much punctuation for the benefit we're getting. Let's open the Symbol class and define a to_proc method. This ensures that any symbol can be coerced into a proc object. But what proc should we return? Obviously, one corresponding to the symbol itself *in the context* of the object—in other words, one that will send the symbol itself as a message to the object.

```
def to_proc
  proc {|obj, *args| obj.send(self, *args) }
end
```

This code, by the way, came from Gavin Sinclair's "Ruby Extensions" project. With this method in place, we can rewrite our original code fragment:

```
list = words.map(&:capitalize)
```

It's worth spending a minute understanding how this works. The `map` method ordinarily takes only a block (no other parameters). The ampersand notation allows us to pass a `proc` instead of an explicit attached block if we want. Because we use the ampersand on an object that isn't a `proc`, the interpreter tries to call `to_proc` on that object. The resulting `proc` takes the place of an explicit block so that `map` will call it repeatedly, once for each element in the array. Now, why does `self` make sense as the thing passed as a message to the array element? It's because a `proc` is a *closure* and therefore remembers the context in which it was created. At the time it was created, `self` referred to the symbol on which the `to_proc` was called.

6.2 Ranges

Ranges are fairly intuitive, but they do have a few confusing uses and qualities. A numeric range is one of the simplest:

```
digits = 0..9
scale1 = 0..10
scale2 = 0...10
```

The `..` operator is *inclusive* of its endpoint, and the `...` is *exclusive* of its endpoint. (This may seem unintuitive to you; if so, just memorize this fact.) So `digits` and `scale2` shown in the preceding example are effectively the same.

But ranges are not limited to integers or numbers. The beginning and end of a range may be any Ruby object. However, not all ranges are meaningful or useful, as we shall see.

The primary operations you might want to do on a range are to iterate over it, convert it to an array, or determine whether it includes a given object. Let's look at all the ramifications of these and other operations.

6.2.1   Open and Closed Ranges

We call a range *closed* if it includes its end, and *open* if it does not:

```
r1 = 3..6       # closed
r2 = 3...6      # open
a1 = r1.to_a    # [3,4,5,6]
a2 = r2.to_a    # [3,4,5]
```

There is no way to construct a range that excludes its beginning point. This is arguably a limitation of the language.

6.2.2   Finding Endpoints

The `first` and `last` methods return the left and right endpoints of a range. Synonyms are `begin` and `end` (which are normally keywords but may be called as methods when there is an explicit receiver).

```
r1 = 3..6
r2 = 3...6
r1a, r1b = r1.first, r1.last    # 3, 6
r1c, r1d = r1.begin, r1.end     # 3, 6
r2a, r2b = r1.begin, r1.end     # 3, 6
```

The `exclude_end?` method tells us whether the endpoint is excluded:

```
r1.exclude_end?    # false
r2.exclude_end?    # true
```

6.2.3   Iterating Over Ranges

Typically it's possible to iterate over a range. For this to work, the class of the endpoints must define a meaningful `succ` method.

```
(3..6).each {|x| puts x }   # prints four lines
                            # (parens are necessary)
```

So far, so good. But be *very cautious* when dealing with string ranges! That class does define a succ operator, but it is of limited usefulness. You should use this kind of feature only in well-defined, isolated circumstances because the succ method for strings is not defined with exceptional rigor. (It is "intuitive" rather than lexicographic, and thus there are strings that have a successor that is surprising or meaningless.)

```
r1 = "7".."9"
r2 = "7".."10"
r1.each {|x| puts x }   # Prints three lines
r2.each {|x| puts x }   # Prints no output!
```

The preceding examples look similar but work differently. The reason lies partly in the fact that in the second range, the endpoints are strings of different length. To our eyes, we expect this range to cover the strings "7", "8", "9", and "10", but what really happens?

When we try to iterate over r2, we start with a value of "7" and enter a loop that terminates when the current value is greater than the right-hand endpoint. But because "7" and "10" are strings, not numbers, they are compared as such. In other words, they are compared lexicographically, and we find that the left endpoint is *greater* than the right endpoint. So we don't loop at all.

What about floating point ranges? We can construct them, and we can certainly test membership in them, which makes them useful. But we can't iterate over them because there is no succ method.

```
fr = 2.0..2.2
fr.each {|x| puts x }   # error!
```

Why isn't there a floating point succ method? It would be theoretically possible to increment the floating point number by *epsilon* each time. But this would be highly architecture-dependent, it would result in a frighteningly high number of iterations for even "small" ranges, and it would be of limited usefulness.

6.2.4   Testing Range Membership

Ranges are not much good if we can't determine whether an item lies within a given range. As it turns out, the include? method makes this easy:

```
r1 = 23456..34567
x = 14142
y = 31416
r1.include?(x)      # false
r1.include?(y)      # true
```

The method member? is an alias.

But how does this work internally? How does the interpreter determine whether an item is in a given range? Actually, it makes this determination simply by comparing the item with the endpoints (so that range membership is dependent on the existence of a meaningful <=> operator).

Therefore to say (a..b).include?(x) is equivalent to saying x >= a and x <= b. Once again, beware of string ranges.

```
s1 = "2".."5"
str = "28"
s1.include?(str)    # true (misleading!)
```

6.2.5   Converting to Arrays

When we convert a range to an array, the interpreter simply applies succ repeatedly until the end is reached, appending each item onto an array that is returned:

```
r = 3..12
arr = r.to_a    # [3,4,5,6,7,8,9,10,11,12]
```

This naturally won't work with Float ranges. It may sometimes work with String ranges, but this should be avoided because the results will not always be obvious or meaningful.

6.2.6 Backward Ranges

Does a *backward* range make any sense? Yes and no. This is a perfectly valid range:

```
r = 6..3
x = r.begin            # 6
y = r.end              # 3
flag = r.end_excluded? # false
```

As you see, we can determine its starting and ending points and whether the end is included in the range. However, that is nearly *all* we can do with such a range.

```
arr = r.to_a         # []
r.each {|x| p x}     # No iterations
y = 5
r.include?(y)        # false (for any value of y)
```

Does that mean that backward ranges are necessarily "evil" or useless? Not at all. It is still useful, in some cases, to have the endpoints encapsulated in a single object.

In fact, arrays and strings frequently take "backward ranges" because these are zero-indexed from the left but "minus one"-indexed from the right. Therefore we can use expressions like these:

```
string = "flowery"
str1    = string[0..-2]    # "flower"
str2    = string[1..-2]    # "lower"
str3    = string[-5..-3]   # "owe" (actually a forward range)
```

6.2.7 The Flip-Flop Operator

When a range is used in a condition, it is treated specially. This usage of .. is called the *flip-flop operator* because it is essentially a toggle that keeps its own state.

This trick, apparently originating with Perl, is useful. But understanding how it works takes a little effort.

Imagine we had a Ruby source file with embedded docs between =begin and =end tags. How would we extract and output only those sections? (Our state toggles between "inside" a section and "outside" a section, hence the flip-flop concept.) The following piece of code, while perhaps unintuitive, will work:

```
loop do
  break if eof?
  line = gets
  puts line if (line=~/=begin/)..(line=~/=end/)
end
```

How can this work? The magic all happens in the flip-flop operator.

First, realize that this "range" is preserving a state internally, but this fact is hidden. When the left endpoint becomes true, the range itself returns true; it then remains true until the right endpoint becomes true, and the range toggles to false.

This kind of feature might be needed in many cases. Some examples are parsing HTML, parsing section-oriented config files, selecting ranges of items from lists, and so on.

However, I personally don't like the syntax. Others are also dissatisfied with it, perhaps even Matz himself. This behavior may be removed from Ruby in the future. But I'll show a convenient way to get the same functionality.

What's wrong with the flip-flop? This is my own opinion.

First, in the preceding example, take a line with the value =begin. A reminder: The =~ operator does not return true or false as we might expect; it returns the position of the match (a Fixnum) or nil if there was no match. So then the expressions in the range evaluate to 0 and nil, respectively.

However, if we try to construct a range from 0 to nil, it gives us an error because it is nonsensical:

```
range = 0..nil     # error!
```

Furthermore, bear in mind that in Ruby, only false and nil evaluate to false; everything else evaluates as true. Then a *range* ordinarily would not evaluate as false.

```
puts "hello" if x..y
# Prints "hello" for any valid range x..y
```

And again, suppose we stored these values in variables and then used the variables to construct the range. This doesn't work; the test is always true.

```
loop do
  break if eof?
  line = gets
  start = line=~/=begin/
  stop = line=~/=end/
  puts line if start..stop
end
```

What if we put the range itself in a variable? This doesn't work either. Once again, the test is always true.

```
loop do
  break if eof?
  line = gets
  range = (line=~/=begin/)..(line=~/=end/)
  puts line if range
end
```

To understand this, we have to understand that the entire range (with both end-points) is re-evaluated each time the loop is run, but the internal state is also factored in. The flip-flop operator is therefore not a true range at all. The fact that it looks like a range but is not is considered a bad thing by some.

Finally, think of the endpoints of the flip-flop. They are re-evaluated every time, but this re-evaluation cannot be captured in a variable that can be substituted. In effect, the flip-flop's endpoints are like procs. They are not values; they are code. The fact that something that looks like an ordinary expression is really a proc is also undesirable.

Having said all that, the functionality is still useful. Can we write a class that encapsulates this function without being so cryptic and magical? As it turns out, this is not difficult. In Listing 6.1, we introduce a simple class called Transition, which mimics the behavior of the flip-flop.

Listing 6.1   The Transition Class

```
class Transition
  A, B = :A, :B
  T, F = true, false

          # state,p1,p2  => newstate, result
  Table = {[A,F,F]=>[A,F], [B,F,F]=>[B,T],
           [A,T,F]=>[B,T], [B,T,F]=>[B,T],
```

Continues

```
                  [A,F,T]=>[A,F],  [B,F,T]=>[A,T],
                  [A,T,T]=>[A,T],  [B,T,T]=>[A,T]}
      def initialize(proc1, proc2)
        @state = A
        @proc1, @proc2 = proc1, proc2
        check?
      end
      def check?
        p1 = @proc1.call ? T : F
        p2 = @proc2.call ? T : F
        @state, result = *Table[[@state,p1,p2]]
        return result
      end
    end
```

In the `Transition` class, we use a simple state machine to manage transitions. We initialize it with a pair of `procs` (the same ones used in the flip-flop). We do lose a little convenience in that any variables (such as `line`) used in the `procs` must already be in scope. But we now have a solution with no "magic" in it, where all expressions behave as they do any other place in Ruby.

Here's a slight variant on the same solution. Let's change the `initialize` method to take a proc and two arbitrary expressions:

```
def initialize(var,flag1,flag2)
  @state = A
  @proc1 = proc { flag1 === var.call }
  @proc2 = proc { flag2 === var.call }
  check?
end
```

The case equality operator is used to check the relationship of the starting and ending flags with the variable. The variable is wrapped in a `proc` because we pass this value in only once; we need to be able to re-evaluate it. Because a `proc` is a closure, this is not a problem.

Here is how we use the new code version:

```
line = nil
trans = Transition.new(proc {line}, /=begin/, /=end/)
loop do        break if eof?        line = gets
  puts line if trans.check?
end
```

I do recommend an approach like this, which is more explicit and less magical.
This will be especially important when the flip-flop operator does in fact go away.

6.2.8 Custom Ranges

Let's look at an example of a range made up of some arbitrary object. Listing 6.2 shows
a simple class to handle Roman numerals.

Listing 6.2 A Roman Numeral Class

```
class Roman
  include Comparable

  I,IV,V,IX,X,XL,L,XC,C,CD,D,CM,M =
    1, 4, 5, 9, 10, 40, 50, 90, 100, 400, 500, 900, 1000

  Values = %w[M CM D CD C XC L XL X IX V IV I]

  def Roman.encode(value)
    return "" if self == 0
    str = ""
    Values.each do |letters|
      rnum = const_get(letters)
      if value >= rnum
        return(letters + str=encode(value-rnum))
      end
    end
    str
  end

  def Roman.decode(rvalue)
    sum = 0
    letters = rvalue.split('')
    letters.each_with_index do |letter,i|
      this = const_get(letter)
      that = const_get(letters[i+1]) rescue 0
      op = that > this ? :- : :+
      sum = sum.send(op,this)
    end
    sum
  end

  def initialize(value)
    case value
      when String
        @roman = value
        @decimal = Roman.decode(@roman)
      when Symbol
        @roman = value.to_s
```

Continues

```
        @decimal = Roman.decode(@roman)
      when Numeric
        @decimal = value
        @roman = Roman.encode(@decimal)
    end
  end

  def to_i
    @decimal
  end

  def to_s
    @roman
  end

  def succ
    Roman.new(@decimal+1)
  end

  def <=>(other)
    self.to_i <=> other.to_i
  end
end

def Roman(val)
  Roman.new(val)
end
```

I'll cover a few highlights of this class first. It can be constructed using a string or a symbol (representing a Roman numeral) or a Fixnum (representing an ordinary Hindu-Arabic decimal number). Internally, conversion is performed, and both forms are stored. There is a "convenience method" called Roman, which simply is a shortcut to calling the Roman.new method. The class-level methods encode and decode handle conversion to and from Roman form, respectively.

For simplicity, I haven't done any error checking. I also assume that the Roman letters are uppercase.

The to_i method naturally returns the decimal value, and the to_s method predictably returns the Roman form. We define succ to be the next Roman number—for example, Roman(:IV).succ would be Roman(:V).

We implement the comparison operator by comparing the decimal equivalents in a straightforward way. We do an include of the Comparable module so that we can get the less-than and greater-than operators (which depend on the existence of the comparison method <=>).

Notice the gratuitous use of symbols in this fragment:

```
op = that > this ? :- : :+
sum = sum.send(op,this)
```

In the preceding fragment, we're actually choosing which operation (denoted by a symbol) to perform—addition or subtraction. This code fragment is just a short way of saying:

```
if that > this
  sum -= this
else
  sum += this
end
```

The second fragment is longer but arguably clearer.

Because this class has both a succ method and a full set of relational operators, we can use it in a range. The following sample code demonstrates this:

```
require 'roman'

y1 = Roman(:MCMLXVI)
y2 = Roman(:MMIX)
range = y1..y2                  # 1966..2009
range.each {|x| puts x}         # 44 lines of output

epoch = Roman(:MCMLXX)
range.include?(epoch)           # true

doomsday = Roman(2038)
range.include?(doomsday)        # false

Roman(:V) == Roman(:IV).succ    # true
Roman(:MCM) < Roman(:MM)        # true
```

6.3 Conclusion

In this chapter we've seen what symbols are in Ruby and how they are used. We've seen both standard and user-defined uses of symbols.

We've also looked at ranges in depth. We've seen how to convert them to arrays, how to use them as array or string indices, how to iterate over them, and other such operations. We've looked in detail at the flip-flop operator (and an alternative to the old syntax). Finally we've seen in detail how to construct a class so that it works well with range operators.

That ends our discussion of symbols and ranges. But as they are commonly used in Ruby (and are extremely useful), you'll see more of them both in incidental code throughout the rest of the book.

## CHAPTER 7

Working with Times and Dates

Does anybody really know what time it is?

—*Chicago*, Chicago IV

One of the most complex and confusing areas of human life is that of measuring time. To come to a complete understanding of the subject, you would need to study physics, astronomy, history, law, business, and religion. Astronomers know (as most of us don't!) that solar time and sidereal time are not quite the same thing, and why a "leap second" is occasionally added to the end of the year. Historians know that the calendar skipped several days in October 1582, when Italy converted from the Julian calendar to the Gregorian. Few people know the difference between astronomical Easter and ecclesiastical Easter (which are almost always the same). Many people don't know that century years not divisible by 400 (such as the year 1900) are not leap years.

Performing calculations with times and dates is common in computing but has traditionally been somewhat tedious in most programming languages. It is tedious in Ruby, too, because of the nature of the data. However, Ruby has taken some incremental steps toward making these operations easier.

As a courtesy to the reader, we'll go over a few terms that may not be familiar to everyone. Most of these come from standard usage or from other programming languages.

Greenwich Mean Time (*GMT*) is an old term not really in official use anymore. The new global standard is *Coordinated Universal Time* (or *UTC*, from the French version of the name). GMT and UTC are virtually the same thing; over a period of years, the difference will be on the order of seconds. Much of the software in the industry does not distinguish between the two at all (nor does Ruby).

Daylight Saving Time is semiannual shift in the official time, amounting to a difference of one hour. Thus the U.S. time zones usually end in *ST* (Standard Time) or *DT* (Daylight Time). This annoying trick is used in most (though not all) of the United States and in many other countries.

The *epoch* is a term borrowed from UNIX lore. In this realm, a time is typically stored internally as a number of seconds from a specific point in time (called the epoch), which was midnight January 1, 1970, GMT. (Note that in U.S. time zones, this will actually be the preceding December 31.) The same term is used to denote not only the point of origin but also the distance in time from that point.

The `Time` class is used for most operations. The `Date` and `DateTime` classes provide some extra flexibility. Let's look at some common uses of these.

7.1 Determining the Current Time

The most fundamental problem in time/date manipulation is to answer the question: What is the time and date right now? In Ruby, when we create a `Time` object with no parameters, it is set to the current date and time.

```
t0 = Time.new
```

`Time.now` is a synonym:

```
t0 = Time.now
```

Note that the resolution of system clocks varies from one architecture to another. It may include microseconds in which case two `Time` objects created in succession may actually record different times.

7.2 Working with Specific Times (Post-epoch)

Most software only needs to work with dates in the future or in the recent past. For these circumstances, the `Time` class is adequate. The relevant class methods are `mktime`, `local`, `gm`, and `utc`.

The `mktime` method creates a new `Time` object based on the parameters passed to it. These time units are given in reverse from longest to shortest: year, month, day, hours, minutes, seconds, microseconds. All but the year are optional; they default to the lowest possible value. The microseconds may be ignored on many architectures. The hours must be between 0 and 23 (that is, a 24-hour clock).

```
t1 = Time.mktime(2001)              # January 1, 2001 at 0:00:00
t2 = Time.mktime(2001,3)
t3 = Time.mktime(2001,3,15)
t4 = Time.mktime(2001,3,15,21)
t5 = Time.mktime(2001,3,15,21,30)
t6 = Time.mktime(2001,3,15,21,30,15) # March 15, 2001 9:30:15 pm
```

Note that `mktime` assumes the local time zone. In fact, `Time.local` is a synonym for it.

```
t7 = Time.local(2001,3,15,21,30,15)  # March 15, 2001 9:30:15 pm
```

The `Time.gm` method is basically the same, except that it assumes GMT (or UTC). Because the authors are in the U.S. Central time zone, we would see an eight-hour difference here:

```
t8 = Time.gm(2001,3,15,21,30,15)     # March 15, 2001 9:30:15 pm
# This is only 1:30:15 pm in Central time!
```

The `Time.utc` method is a synonym:

```
t9 = Time.utc(2001,3,15,21,30,15)    # March 15, 2001 9:30:15 pm
# Again, 1:30:15 pm Central time.
```

There is one more important item to note. All these methods can take an alternate set of parameters. The instance method `to_a` (which converts a time to an array of relevant values) returns a set of values in this order: seconds, minutes, hours, day, month, year, day of week (0..6), day of year (1..366), daylight saving (true or false), and time zone (as a string).

Thus these are also valid calls:

```
t0 = Time.local(0,15,3,20,11,1979,2,324,false,"GMT-8:00")
t1 = Time.gm(*Time.now.to_a)
```

However, in the first example, do not fall into the trap of thinking that you can change the computable parameters such as the day of the week (in this case, 2 meaning Tuesday). A change like this simply contradicts the way our calendar works, and it will have no effect on the time object created. November 20, 1979, was a Tuesday regardless of how we might write our code.

Finally, note that there are obviously many ways to attempt coding incorrect times, such as a thirteenth month or a 35th day of the month. In cases like these an ArgumentError will be raised.

7.3   Determining the Day of the Week

There are several ways to determine the day of the week. First, the instance method to_a returns an array of time information. You can access the seventh element, which is a number from 0 to 6 (0 meaning Sunday and 6 meaning Saturday).

```
time = Time.now
day = time.to_a[6]            # 2 (meaning Tuesday)
```

It's better to use the instance method wday as shown here:

```
day = time.wday               # 2 (meaning Tuesday)
```

But both these techniques are a little cumbersome. Sometimes we want the value coded as a number, but more often we don't. To get the actual name of the weekday as a string, we can use the strftime method. This name will be familiar to C programmers. There are nearly two dozen different specifiers that it recognizes, enabling us to format dates and times more or less as we want. (See section 7.21, "Formatting and Printing Date/Time Values.")

```
day = time.strftime("%a")     # "Tuesday"
```

It's also possible to obtain an abbreviated name.

```
long = time.strftime("%A")    # "Tuesday"
```

7.4 Determining the Date of Easter

Traditionally this holiday is one of the most difficult to compute because it is tied to the lunar cycle. The lunar month does not go evenly into the solar year, and thus anything based on the moon can be expected to vary from year to year.

The algorithm we present here is a well-known one that has made the rounds. We have seen it coded in BASIC, Pascal, and C. We now present it to you in Ruby:

```
def easter(year)
  c = year/100
  n = year - 19*(year/19)
  k = (c-17)/25
  i = c - c/4 - (c-k)/3 + 19*n + 15
  i = i - 30*(i/30)
  i = i - (i/28)*(1 -(i/28)*(29/(i+1))*((21-n)/11))
  j = year + year/4 + i + 2 - c + c/4
  j = j - 7*(j/7)
  l = i - j
  month = 3 + (l+40)/44
  day = l + 28 - 31*(month/4)
  [month, day]
end
```

```
date = easter 2001      # Find month/day for 2001
date = [2001] + date    # Tack year on front
t = Time.local *date    # Pass parameters to Time.local
puts t                  # Sun Apr 15 01:00:00 GMT-8:00 2001
```

One reader on seeing this section on Easter, asked: "Ecclesiastical or astronomical?" Truthfully, I don't know. If you find out, let us all know.

I'd love to explain this algorithm to you, but I don't understand it myself. Some things must be taken on faith, and in the case of Easter, this may be especially appropriate.

7.5 Finding the Nth Weekday in a Month

Sometimes for a given month and year, we want to find the date of the third Monday in the month, or the second Tuesday, and so on. The code in Listing 7.1 makes that calculation simple.

If we are looking for the nth occurrence of a certain weekday, we pass n as the first parameter. The second parameter is the number of that weekday (0 meaning Sunday, 1 meaning Monday, and so on). The third and fourth parameters are the month and year, respectively.

Listing 7.1   Finding the Nth Weekday

```
def nth_wday(n, wday, month, year)
  if (!n.between? 1,5) or
     (!wday.between? 0,6) or
     (!month.between? 1,12)
    raise ArgumentError
  end
  t = Time.local year, month, 1
  first = t.wday
  if first == wday
    fwd = 1
  elsif first < wday
    fwd = wday - first + 1
  elsif first > wday
    fwd = (wday+7) - first + 1
  end
  target = fwd + (n-1)*7
  begin
    t2 = Time.local year, month, target
  rescue ArgumentError
    return nil
  end
  if t2.mday == target
    t2
  else
    nil
  end
end
```

The peculiar-looking code near the end of the method is put there to counteract a long-standing tradition in the underlying time-handling routines. You might expect that trying to create a date of November 31 would result in an error of some kind. You would be mistaken. Most systems would happily (and silently) convert this to December 1. If you are an old-time UNIX hacker, you may think this is a feature; otherwise, you may consider it a bug.

We will not venture an opinion here as to what the underlying library code ought to do or whether Ruby ought to change that behavior. But we don't want to have this routine perpetuate the tradition. If you are looking for the date of, say, the fifth Friday in November 2000, you will get a nil value back (rather than December 1, 2000).

7.6 Converting Between Seconds and Larger Units

Sometimes we want to take a number of seconds and convert to days, hours, minutes, and seconds. This following routine will do just that:

```ruby
def sec2dhms(secs)
  time = secs.round           # Get rid of microseconds
  sec = time % 60             # Extract seconds
  time /= 60                  # Get rid of seconds
  mins = time % 60            # Extract minutes
  time /= 60                  # Get rid of minutes
  hrs = time % 24             # Extract hours
  time /= 24                  # Get rid of hours
  days = time                 # Days (final remainder)
  [days, hrs, mins, sec]      # Return array [d,h,m,s]
end

t = sec2dhms(1000000)         # A million seconds is...

puts "#{t[0]} days,"          # 11 days,
puts "#{t[1]} hours,"         # 13 hours,
puts "#{t[2]} minutes,"       # 46 minutes,
puts " and #{t[3]} seconds."  # and 40 seconds.
```

We could, of course, go up to higher units. But a week is not an overly useful unit; a month is not a well-defined term; and a year is far from being an integral number of days.

We also present here the inverse of that function:

```ruby
def dhms2sec(days,hrs=0,min=0,sec=0)
  days*86400 + hrs*3600 + min*60 + sec
end
```

7.7   Converting To and From the Epoch

For various reasons we may want to convert back and forth between the internal (or traditional) measure and the standard date form. Internally, dates are stored as a number of seconds since the epoch.

The `Time.at` class method creates a new time given the number of seconds since the epoch:

```
epoch = Time.at(0)           # Find the epoch (1 Jan 1970 GMT)
newmil = Time.at(978307200)  # Happy New Millennium! (1 Jan 2001)
The inverse is the instance method to_i which converts to an integer.
now = Time.now               # 16 Nov 2000 17:24:28
sec = now.to_i               # 974424268
```

If you need microseconds, and your system supports that resolution, you can use `to_f` to convert to a floating point number.

7.8   Working with Leap Seconds: Don't!

Ah, but my calculations, people say,
Reduced the year to better reckoning? Nay,
'Twas only striking from the calendar
Unborn Tomorrow and dead Yesterday.

—*Omar Khayyam*, The Rubaiyat *(trans. Fitzgerald)*

You want to work with leap seconds? Our advice is: Don't.

Leap seconds are very real. One was added to the year 2005—its final minute had 61 seconds rather than the usual 60. Although the library routines have for years allowed for the possibility of a 61-second minute, our experience has been that most systems do not keep track of leap seconds. When we say "most," we mean all the ones we've ever checked.

For example, a leap second is known to have been inserted at the end of the last day of 1998. Immediately following 23:59:59 came that rare event 23:59:60. But the underlying C libraries on which Ruby is built are ignorant of this.

```
t0 = Time.gm(1998, 12, 31, 23, 59, 59)
t1 = t0 + 1
puts t1      # Fri Jan 01 00:00:00 GMT 1999
```

It is (barely) conceivable that Ruby could add a layer of intelligence to correct for this. At the time of this writing, however, there are no plans to add such functionality.

7.9 Finding the Day of the Year

The day number within the year is sometimes called the *Julian date*, which is not directly related to the Julian calendar, which has gone out of style. Other people insist that this usage is not correct, so we won't use it from here on.

No matter what you call it, there will be times you want to know what day of the year it is, from 1 to 366. This is easy in Ruby; we use the yday method:

```
t = Time.now
day = t.yday      # 315
```

7.10 Validating a Date/Time

As we saw in section 7.5 "Finding the Nth Weekday in a Month," the standard date/time functions do not check the validity of a date, but "roll it over" as needed. For example, November 31 is translated to December 1.

At times, this may be the behavior you want. If it is not, you will be happy to know that the standard library Date does not regard such a date as valid. We can use this fact to perform validation of a date as we instantiate it.

```
class Time

  def Time.validate(year, month=1, day=1,
                    hour=0, min=0, sec=0, usec=0)
    require "date"

    begin
      d = Date.new(year,month,day)
    rescue
      return nil
    end
```

```
    Time.local(year,month,day,hour,min,sec,usec)
  end

end

t1 = Time.validate(2000,11,30)   # Instantiates a valid object
t2 = Time.validate(2000,11,31)   # Returns nil
```

Here we have taken the lazy way out; we simply set the return value to nil if the parameters passed in do not form a valid date (as determined by the Date class). We have made this method a class method of Time by analogy with the other methods that instantiate objects.

Note that the Date class can work with dates prior to the epoch. This means that passing in a date such as 31 May 1961 will succeed as far as the Date class is concerned. But when these values are passed into the Time class, an ArgumentError will result. We don't attempt to catch that exception here because we think it's appropriate to let it be caught at the same level as (for example) Time.local, in the user code.

Speaking of Time.local, we used that method here; but if we wanted GMT instead, we could have called the gmt method. It would be a good idea to implement both flavors.

7.11   Finding the Week of the Year

The definition of "week number" is not absolute and fixed. Various businesses, coalitions, government agencies, and standards bodies have differing concepts of what it means. This stems, of course, from the fact that the year can start on any day of the week; we may or may not want to count partial weeks, and we may start on Sunday or Monday.

We offer only three alternatives in this section. The first two are made available by the Time method strftime. The %U specifier numbers the weeks starting from Sunday, and the %W specifier starts with Monday.

The third possibility comes from the Date class. It has an accessor called cweek, which returns the week number based on the ISO 8601 definition (which says that week 1 is the week containing the first Thursday of the year).

If none of these three suits you, you may have to "roll your own." We present these three in a single code fragment:

```
require "date"

# Let's look at May 1 in the years
# 2002 and 2005.

t1 = Time.local(2002,5,1)
d1 = Date.new(2002,5,1)

week1a = t1.strftime("%U").to_i   # 17
week1b = t1.strftime("%W").to_i   # 17
week1c = d1.cweek                 # 18

t2 = Time.local(2005,5,1)
d2 = Date.new(2005,5,1)

week2a = t2.strftime("%U").to_i   # 18
week2b = t2.strftime("%W").to_i   # 18
week2c = d2.cweek                 # 17
```

7.12   Detecting Leap Years

The Date class has two class methods julian_leap? and gregorian_leap?; only the latter is of use in recent years. It also has a method leap?, which is an alias for the gregorian_leap? method.

```
require "date"
flag1 = Date.julian_leap? 1700      # true
flag2 = Date.gregorian_leap? 1700   # false
flag3 = Date.leap? 1700             # false
```

Every child knows the first rule for leap years: The year number must be divisible by four. Fewer people know the second rule, that the year number must not be divisible by 100; and fewer still know the exception, that the year can be divisible by 400. In other words: A century year is a leap year only if it is divisible by 400, so 1900 was not a leap year, but 2000 was. (This adjustment is necessary because a year is not exactly 365.25 days, but a little less, approximately 365.2422 days.)

The `Time` class does not have a method like this, but if we needed one, it would be simple to create.

```ruby
class Time

  def Time.leap? year
    if year % 400 == 0
      true
    elsif year % 100 == 0
      false
    elsif year % 4 == 0
      true
    else
      false
  end

end
```

I've written this to make the algorithm explicit; an easier implementation, of course, would be simply to call the `Date.leap?` method from this one. I implement this as a class method by analogy with the `Date` class methods. It could also be implemented as an instance method.

7.13   Obtaining the Time Zone

The accessor `zone` in the `Time` class returns a `String` representation of the time zone name.

```ruby
z1 = Time.gm(2000,11,10,22,5,0).zone      # "GMT-6:00"
z2 = Time.local(2000,11,10,22,5,0).zone   # "GMT-6:00"
```

Unfortunately, times are stored relative to the current time zone, not the one with which the object was created. If necessary, you can do a little arithmetic here.

7.14   Working with Hours and Minutes Only

We may want to work with times of day as strings. Once again `strftime` comes to our aid.

We can print the time with hours, minutes, and seconds if we want:

```
t = Time.now
puts t.strftime("%H:%M:%S")     # Prints 22:07:45
```

We can print hours and minutes only (and, using the trick of adding 30 seconds to the time, we can even round to the nearest minute):

```
puts t.strftime("%H:%M")         # Prints 22:07
puts (t+30).strftime("%H:%M")    # Prints 22:08
```

Finally, if we don't like the standard 24-hour (or military) clock, we can switch to the 12-hour clock. It's appropriate to add a meridian indicator then (AM/PM):

```
puts t.strftime("%I:%M %p")      # Prints 10:07 PM
```

There are other possibilities, of course. Use your imagination.

7.15   Comparing Date/Time Values

The Time class conveniently mixes in the Comparable module, so that dates and times may be compared in a straightforward way.

```
t0 = Time.local(2000,11,10,22,15)    # 10 Nov 2000 22:15
t1 = Time.local(2000,11,9,23,45)     #  9 Nov 2000 23:45
t2 = Time.local(2000,11,12,8,10)     # 12 Nov 2000  8:10
t3 = Time.local(2000,11,11,10,25)    # 11 Nov 2000 10:25

if t0 < t1 then puts "t0 < t1" end
if t1 != t2 then puts "t1 != t2" end
if t1 <= t2 then puts "t1 <= t2" end
if t3.between?(t1,t2)
  puts "t3 is between t1 and t2"
end

# All four if statements test true
```

7.16   Adding Intervals to Date/Time Values

We can obtain a new time by adding an interval to a specified time. The number is interpreted as a number of seconds.

```
t0 = Time.now
t1 = t0 + 60          # Exactly one minute past t0
t2 = t0 + 3600        # Exactly one hour past t0
t3 = t0 + 86400       # Exactly one day past t0
```

The function dhms2sec (defined in section 7.6 "Converting Between Seconds and Larger Units" earlier in the chapter) might be helpful here. Recall that the hours, minutes, and seconds all default to 0.

```
t4 = t0 + dhms2sec(5,10)       # Ahead 5 days, 10 hours
t5 = t0 + dhms2sec(22,18,15)   # Ahead 22 days, 18 hrs, 15 min
t6 = t0 - dhms2sec(7)          # Exactly one week ago
```

Don't forget that we can move backward in time by subtracting. This is shown in the calculation of t6 in the preceding code example.

7.17   Computing the Difference in Two Date/Time Values

We can find the interval of time between two points in time. Subtracting one Time object from another gives us a number of seconds:

```
today = Time.local(2000,11,10)
yesterday = Time.local(2000,11,9)
diff = today - yesterday        # 86400 seconds
```

Once again, the function sec2dhms comes in handy. (This is defined in section 7.6 "Converting Between Seconds and Larger Units" earlier in the chapter.)

```
past = Time.local(1998,9,13,4,15)
now = Time.local(2000,11,10,22,42)
diff = now - past
unit = sec2dhms(diff)
puts "#{unit[0]} days,"          # 789 days,
puts "#{unit[1]} hours,"         # 18 hours,
puts "#{unit[2]} minutes,"       # 27 minutes,
puts "and #{unit[3]} seconds."   # and 0 seconds.
```

7.18   Working with Specific Dates (Pre-epoch)

The standard library Date provides a class of the same name for working with dates
that precede midnight GMT, January 1, 1970.

Although there is some overlap in functionality with the Time class, there are significant differences. Most notably, the Date class does not handle the time of day at
all. Its resolution is a single day. Also, the Date class performs more rigorous error-
checking than the Time class; if you attempt to refer to a date such as June 31 (or even
February 29 in a non-leap year) you will get an error. The code is smart enough to
know the different cutoff dates for Italy and England switching to the Gregorian calendar (in 1582 and 1752, respectively), and it can detect "nonexistent" dates that are
a result of this switchover. This standard library is a tangle of interesting and arcane
code. We do not have space to document it further here.

7.19   Interconverting Between Time, Date, and DateTime

Ruby has three basic classes dealing with dates and times: Time, Date, and DateTime.
The following is a description of each:

- The Time class is mostly a wrapper for the underlying time functions in the C
  library. These are typically based on the UNIX epoch and thus cannot represent
  times before 1970.

- The Date class was created to address this shortcoming of the Time class. It can
  easily deal with older dates such as Leonardo da Vinci's birthday (April 15, 1452),
  and it is intelligent about the dates of calendar reform. But it has its own shortcoming; it can't deal with the time of day that Leonardo was born. It deals strictly
  with dates.

- The DateTime class inherits from Date and tries to be the best of both worlds. It
  can represent dates as well as Date can, and times as well as Time can. This is often
  the "right" way to represent a date-time value.

  But don't be fooled into thinking that a DateTime is just a Date with an embedded Time. There are, in fact, several methods missing from DateTime, such as
  usec, dst?, and others.

So we have these three classes. Unfortunately there is no good standard way to convert between them. As Ruby continues to change, some of these details will be ironed out. For now, these methods in Listing 7.2 will suffice. Thanks to Kirk Haines for providing them.

Listing 7.2   Interconverting Between Date and Time Classes

```ruby
class Time
  def to_date
    Date.new(year, month, day)
  rescue NameError
    nil
  end

  def to_datetime
    DateTime.new(year, month, day, hour, min, sec)
  rescue NameError
    nil
  end
end

class DateTime
  def to_time
    Time.local(year,month,day,hour,min,sec)
  end
end

class Date
  def to_time
    Time.local(year,month,day)
  end
end
```

Any exceptions will be propagated except `NameError`. Why do we check for this one? Because it is conceivable that the program doesn't do a `require` of the `date` library (remember that `Date` and `DateTime` are part of this standard library, not part of the core). In such a case, `to_datetime` and `to_date` will both return `nil`.

7.20   Retrieving a Date/Time Value from a String

A date and time can be formatted as a string in many different ways because of abbreviations, varying punctuation, different orderings, and so on. Because of the various ways of formatting, writing code to decipher such a character string can be daunting. Consider these examples:

```
s1 = "9/13/98 2:15am"
s2 = "1961-05-31"
s3 = "11 July 1924"
s4 = "April 17, 1929"
s5 = "20 July 1969 16:17 EDT"   # That's one small step...
s6 = "Mon Nov 13 2000"
s7 = "August 24, 79"            # Destruction of Pompeii
s8 = "8/24/79"
```

Fortunately, much of the work has already been done for us. The `ParseDate` module has a single class of the same name, which has a single method called `parsedate`. This method returns an array of elements in this order: year, month, day, hour, minute, second, time zone, day of week. Any fields that cannot be determined are returned as `nil` values.

```
require "parsedate.rb"
include ParseDate

p parsedate(s1)        # [98, 9, 13, 2, 15, nil, nil, nil]
p parsedate(s2)        # [1961, 5, 31, nil, nil, nil, nil, nil]
p parsedate(s3)        # [1924, 7, 11, nil, nil, nil, nil, nil]
p parsedate(s4)        # [1929, 4, 17, nil, nil, nil, nil, nil]
p parsedate(s5)        # [1969, 7, 20, 16, 17, nil, "EDT", nil]
p parsedate(s6)        # [2000, 11, 13, nil, nil, nil, nil, 1]
p parsedate(s7)        # [79, 8, 24, nil, nil, nil, nil, nil]
p parsedate(s8,true)   # [1979, 8, 24, nil, nil, nil, nil, nil]
```

The last two strings illustrate the purpose of `parsedate`'s second parameter `guess_year`; because of our cultural habit of representing a year as two digits, ambiguity can result. Thus the last two strings are interpreted differently because we parse s8 with `guess_year` set to `true`, resulting in its conversion to a four-digit year. On the other hand, s7 refers to the eruption of Vesuvius in 79 AD, so we definitely want a two-digit year there.

The rule for `guess_year` is this: If the year is less than 100 and `guess_year` is `true`, convert to a four-digit year. The conversion will be done as follows: If the year is 70 or greater, add 1900 to it; otherwise, add 2000. Thus 75 will translate to 1975, but 65 will translate to 2065. This rule is not uncommon in the computing world.

What about s1, where we probably intended 1998 as the year? All is not lost, so long as we pass this number to some other piece of code that interprets it as 1998.

Note that parsedate does virtually no error checking. For example, if you feed it a date with a weekday and a date that does not correspond correctly, it will not detect this discrepancy. It is only a parser, and it does this job pretty well, but no other.

Also note an American bias in this code. An American writing 3/4/2001 usually means March 4, 2001; in Europe and most other places, this would mean April 3 instead. But if all the data are consistent, this is not a huge problem; because the return value is simply an array, you can mentally switch the meaning of elements 1 and 2. Be aware also that this bias happens even with a date such as 15/3/2000, where it is clear (to us) that 15 is the day. The parsedate method will happily return 15 as the month value.

7.21   Formatting and Printing Date/Time Values

You can obtain the canonical representation of the date and time by calling the asctime method ("ASCII time"); it has an alias called ctime, for those who already know it by that name.

You can obtain a similar result by calling the to_s method. This is the same as the result you would get if doing a simple puts of a date/time value.

The strftime method of class Time formats a date and time in almost any form you can think of. Other examples in this chapter have shown the use of the directives %a, %A, %U, %W, %H, %M, %S, %I, and %p; we list here all the remaining directives that strftime recognizes:

```
%b    Abbreviated month name ("Jan")
%B    Full month name ("January")
%c    Preferred local date/time representation
%d    Day of the month (1..31)
%j    Day of the year (1..366); so-called "Julian date"
%m    Month as a number (1..12)
%w    Day of the week as a number (0..6)
%x    Preferred representation for date (no time)
%y    Two-digit year (no century)
%Y    Four-digit year
%Z    Time zone name
%%    A literal "%" character
```

For more information, consult a Ruby reference.

7.22   Time Zone Conversions

It is only convenient to work with two time zones: GMT (or UTC) is one, and the other is whatever time zone you happen to be in.

The `gmtime` method converts a time to GMT (changing the receiver in place). There is an alias named `utc`.

You might expect that it would be possible to convert a time to an array, tweak the time zone, and convert it back. The trouble with this is that all the class methods such as `local` and `gm` (or their aliases `mktime` and `utc`) want to create a `Time` object using either your local time zone or GMT.

There is a workaround to get time zone conversions. This does require that you know the time difference in advance. See the following code fragment:

```
mississippi = Time.local(2000,11,13,9,35)  # 9:35 am CST
california  = mississippi - 2*3600          # Minus two hours

time1 = mississippi.strftime("%X CST")      # 09:35:00 CST
time2 = california.strftime("%X PST")       # 07:35:00 PST
```

The `%X` directive to `strftime` that we see here simply uses the hh:mm:ss format as shown.

7.23   Determining the Number of Days in a Month

At the time of this writing, there is no built-in function to do this. You can easily write a simple method for this:

```
require 'date'
def month_days(month,year=Date.today.year)
  mdays = [nil,31,28,31,30,31,30,31,31,30,31,30,31]
  mdays[2] = 29 if Date.leap?(year)
  mdays[month]
end

days = month_days(5)          # 31 (May)
days = month_days(2,2000)     # 29 (February 2000)
days = month_days(2,2100)     # 28 (February 2000)
```

7.24   Dividing a Month into Weeks

Imagine that you wanted to divide a month into weeks—for example, to print a calendar. The following code does that. The array returned is made up of subarrays, each of size seven (7); Sunday corresponds to the first element of each inner array. Leading entries for the first week and trailing entries for the last week may be `nil`.

```ruby
def calendar(month,year)
  days = month_days(month,year)
  t = Time.mktime(year,month,1)
  first = t.wday
  list = *1..days
  weeks = [[]]
  week1 = 7 - first
  week1.times { weeks[0] << list.shift }
  nweeks = list.size/7 + 1
  nweeks.times do |i|
    weeks[i+1] ||= []
    7.times do
      break if list.empty?
      weeks[i+1] << list.shift
    end
  end
  pad_first = 7-weeks[0].size
  pad_first.times { weeks[0].unshift(nil) }
  pad_last = 7-weeks[0].size
  pad_last.times { weeks[-1].unshift(nil) }
  weeks
end


arr = calendar(12,2008)    # [[nil, 1, 2, 3, 4, 5, 6],
                           #  [7, 8, 9, 10, 11, 12, 13],
                           #  [14, 15, 16, 17, 18, 19, 20],
                           #  [21, 22, 23, 24, 25, 26, 27],
                           #  [28, 29, 30, 31, nil, nil, nil]]
```

To illustrate it a little better, the following method prints out this array of arrays:

```ruby
def print_calendar(month,year)
  weeks = calendar(month,year)
  weeks.each do |wk|
    wk.each do |d|
```

```
      item = d.nil? ? " "*4 : " %2d " % d
      print item
   end
   puts
 end
 puts
end


# Output:
#          1    2    3    4    5    6
#     7    8    9   10   11   12   13
#    14   15   16   17   18   19   20
#    21   22   23   24   25   26   27
#    28   29   30   31
```

7.25 Conclusion

In this chapter, we have looked at how the `Time` class works as a wrapper for the under-lying C-based functions. We've seen its features and its limitations.

We've seen the motivation for the `Date` and `DateTime` classes and the functional-ity they provide. We've looked at how to convert between these three kinds of objects, and we've added a few useful methods of our own.

That ends our discussion of times and dates. Let's move on to look at arrays, hashes, and other enumerable data structures in Ruby.

CHAPTER 8

Arrays, Hashes, and Other Enumerables

All parts should go together without forcing. You must remember that the parts you are reassembling were disassembled by you. Therefore, if you can't get them together again, there must be a reason. By all means, do not use a hammer.

—*IBM maintenance manual (1925)*

Simple variables are not adequate for real-life programming. Every modern language supports more complex forms of structured data and also provides mechanisms for creating new abstract data types.

Historically, *arrays* are the earliest known and most widespread of the complex data structures. Long ago, in FORTRAN, they were called *subscripted variables*; today they have changed somewhat, but the basic idea is the same in all languages.

More recently, the *hash* has become an extremely popular programming tool. Like the array, it is an indexed collection of data items; unlike the array, it may be indexed by any arbitrary object. (In Ruby, as in most languages, array elements are accessed by a numerical index.)

Finally, we'll take a more general look at the Enumerable module itself and how it works. Arrays and hashes both mix in this module, as can any other class for which this functionality makes sense.

But let's not get ahead of ourselves. We will begin with arrays.

8.1   Working with Arrays

Arrays in Ruby are indexed by integers and are zero-based, just like C arrays. There the resemblance ends, however.

A Ruby array is dynamic. It is possible (but not necessary) to specify its size when you create it. After creation, it can grow as needed without any intervention by the programmer.

A Ruby array is *heterogeneous* in the sense that it can store multiple data types rather than just one type. Actually, it stores object references rather than the objects themselves, except in the case of immediate values such as Fixnums.

An array keeps up with its own length so that we don't have to waste our time calculating it or keeping an external variable in sync with the array. Iterators also are defined so that, in practice, we rarely need to know the array length anyway.

Finally, the Array class in Ruby provides arrays with many useful functions for accessing, searching, concatenating, and otherwise manipulating arrays. We'll spend the remainder of this section exploring the built-in functionality and expanding on it.

8.1.1   Creating and Initializing an Array

The special class method [] is used to create an array; the data items listed in the brackets are used to populate the array. The three ways of calling this method are shown in the following lines. (Arrays a, b, and c will all be populated identically.)

```
a = Array.[](1,2,3,4)
b = Array[1,2,3,4]
c = [1,2,3,4]
```

There is also a class method called new that can take 0, 1, or 2 parameters. The first parameter is the initial size of the array (number of elements). The second parameter is the initial value of each of the elements:

```
d = Array.new              # Create an empty array
e = Array.new(3)           # [nil, nil, nil]
f = Array.new(3, "blah")   # ["blah", "blah", "blah"]
```

Look carefully at the last line of this preceding example. A common "beginner's error" is to think that the objects in the array are distinct. Actually, they are three references to the same object. Therefore if you change that object (as opposed to

replacing it with another object), you will change all elements of the array. To avoid
this behavior, use a block. Then that block is evaluated once for each element, and all
elements are different objects:

```
f[0].capitalize!              # f is now: ["Blah", "Blah", "Blah"]
g = Array.new(3) { "blah" }   # ["blah", "blah", "blah"]
g[0].capitalize!              # g is now: ["Blah", "blah", "blah"]
```

8.1.2 Accessing and Assigning Array Elements

Element reference and assignment are done using the class methods [] and []=, respectively. Each can take an integer parameter, a pair of integers (start and length), or a
range. A negative index counts backward from the end of the array, starting at -1.

The special instance method at works like the simple case of element reference.
Because it can take only a single integer parameter, it is slightly faster.

```
a = [1, 2, 3, 4, 5, 6]
b = a[0]                   # 1
c = a.at(0)                # 1
d = a[-2]                  # 5
e = a.at(-2)               # 5
f = a[9]                   # nil
g = a.at(9)                # nil
h = a[3,3]                 # [4, 5, 6]
i = a[2..4]                # [3, 4, 5]
j = a[2...4]               # [3, 4]

a[1] = 8                   # [1, 8, 3, 4, 5, 6]
a[1,3] = [10, 20, 30]      # [1, 10, 20, 30, 5, 6]
a[0..3] = [2, 4, 6, 8]     # [2, 4, 6, 8, 5, 6]
a[-1] = 12                 # [2, 4, 6, 8, 5, 12]
```

Note in the following example how a reference beyond the end of the array causes
the array to grow. Note also that a subarray can be replaced with more elements than
were originally there, also causing the array to grow.

```
k = [2, 4, 6, 8, 10]
k[1..2] = [3, 3, 3]        # [2, 3, 3, 3, 8, 10]
k[7] = 99                  # [2, 3, 3, 3, 8, 10, nil, 99]
```

Finally, we should mention that an array assigned to a single element actually inserts that element as a nested array (unlike an assignment to a range):

```
m = [1, 3, 5, 7, 9]
m[2] = [20, 30]          # [1, 3, [20, 30], 7, 9]

# On the other hand...
m = [1, 3, 5, 7, 9]
m[2..2] = [20, 30]       # [1, 3, 20, 30, 7, 9]
```

The method slice is simply an alias for the [] method:

```
x = [0, 2, 4, 6, 8, 10, 12]
a = x.slice(2)               # 4
b = x.slice(2,4)             # [4, 6, 8, 10]
c = x.slice(2..4)            # [4, 6, 8]
```

The special methods first and last return the first and last elements of an array, respectively. They return nil if the array is empty:

```
x = %w[alpha beta gamma delta epsilon]
a = x.first     # "alpha"
b = x.last      # "epsilon"
```

We have seen that some of the element-referencing techniques actually can return an entire subarray. There are other ways to access multiple elements, which we'll look at now.

The method values_at takes a list of indices (or *indexes*, if you prefer) and returns an array consisting of only those elements. It can be used where a range cannot (when the elements are not all contiguous).

In previous versions of Ruby, values_at was called indices, with an alias called indexes. These are no longer to be used.

```
x = [10, 20, 30, 40, 50, 60]
y = x.values_at(0, 1, 4)       # [10, 20, 50]
z = x.values_at(0..2,5)        # [10, 20, 30, 60]
```

8.1.3   Finding an Array's Size

The method `length` or its alias `size` gives the number of elements in an array. (As always, this is one greater than the index of the last item.)

```
x = ["a", "b", "c", "d"]
a = x.length            # 4
b = x.size              # 4
```

The method `nitems` is the same except that it does not count `nil` elements:

```
y = [1, 2, nil, nil, 3, 4]
c = y.size              # 6
d = y.length            # 6
e = y.nitems            # 4
```

8.1.4   Comparing Arrays

Comparing arrays is tricky. If you do it at all, do it with caution.

The instance method `<=>` is used to compare arrays. It works the same as in the other contexts in which it is used, returning either -1 (meaning "less than"), 0 (meaning "equal"), or 1 (meaning "greater than"). The methods `==` and `!=` depend on this method.

Arrays are compared in an "elementwise" manner; the first two elements that are not equal determine the inequality for the whole comparison. (Thus preference is given to the leftmost elements, just as if we were comparing two long integers "by eye," looking at one digit at a time.)

```
a = [1, 2, 3, 9, 9]
b = [1, 2, 4, 1, 1]
c = a <=> b             # -1 (meaning a < b)
```

If all elements are equal, the arrays are equal. If one array is longer than another, and they are equal up to the length of the shorter array, the longer array is considered to be greater.

```
d = [1, 2, 3]
e = [1, 2, 3, 4]
```

```
f = [1, 2, 3]
if d < e                          # false
  puts "d is less than e"
end
if d == f
  puts "d equals f"              # Prints "d equals f"
end
```

Because the Array class does not mix in the Comparable module, the usual operators <, >, <=, and >= are not defined for arrays. But we can easily define them ourselves if we choose:

```
class Array

  def <(other)
    (self <=> other) == -1
  end

  def <=(other)
    (self < other) or (self == other)
  end

  def >(other)
    (self <=> other) == 1
  end

  def >=(other)
    (self > other) or (self == other)
  end

end
```

However, it would be easier simply to include Comparable ourselves:

```
class Array
  include Comparable
end
```

Having defined these new operators, we can use them as you would expect:

```
if a < b
  print "a < b"       # Prints "a < b"
else
  print "a >= b"
end
if d < e
  puts "d < e"        # Prints "d < e"
end
```

It is conceivable that comparing arrays will result in the comparison of two elements for which <=> is undefined or meaningless. The following code results in a run-time error (a `TypeError`) because the comparison 3 `<=>` "x" is problematic:

```
g = [1, 2, 3]
h = [1, 2, "x"]
if g < h            # Error!
  puts "g < h"      # No output
end
```

However, in case you are still not confused, equal and not-equal will still work in this case. This is because two objects of different types are naturally considered to be unequal even though we can't say which is greater or less than the other.

```
if g != h           # No problem here.
  puts "g != h"     # Prints "g != h"
end
```

Finally, it is conceivable that two arrays containing mismatched data types will still compare with < and > operators. In the case shown here, we get a result before we stumble across the incomparable elements:

```
i = [1, 2, 3]
j = [1, 2, 3, "x"]
if i < j            # No problem here.
  puts "i < j"      # Prints "i < j"
end
```

8.1.5 Sorting an Array

The easiest way to sort an array is to use the built-in sort method as follows:

```
words = %w(the quick brown fox)
list = words.sort  # ["brown", "fox", "quick", "the"]
# Or sort in place:
words.sort!        # ["brown", "fox", "quick", "the"]
```

This method assumes that all the elements in the array are comparable with each other. A mixed array such as [1, 2, "three", 4] normally gives a type error.

In a case like this one, you can use the block form of the same method call. The following example assumes that there is at least a to_s method for each element (to convert it to a string):

```
a = [1, 2, "three", "four", 5, 6]
b = a.sort {|x,y| x.to_s <=> y.to_s}
# b is now [1, 2, 5, 6, "four", "three"]
```

Of course, such an ordering (in this case, depending on ASCII) may not be meaningful. If you have such a heterogeneous array, you may want to ask yourself why you are sorting it in the first place or why you are storing different types of objects.

This technique works because the block returns an integer (-1, 0, or 1) on each invocation. When a -1 is returned, meaning that x is less than y, the two elements are swapped. Thus, to sort in descending order, we could simply swap the order of the comparison:

```
x = [1, 4, 3, 5, 2]
y = x.sort {|a,b| b <=> a}    # [5, 4, 3, 2, 1]
```

The block style can also be used for more complex sorting. Let's suppose that we want to sort a list of book and movie titles in a certain way: We ignore case, we ignore spaces entirely, and we want to ignore certain kinds of embedded punctuation. Here we present a simple example. (Both English teachers and computer programmers will be equally confused by this kind of alphabetizing.)

```
titles = ["Starship Troopers",
          "A Star is Born",
          "Star Wars",
```

```
            "Star 69",
            "The Starr Report"]
 sorted = titles.sort do |x,y|
   # Delete leading articles
   a = x.sub(/^(a |an |the )/i, "")
   b = y.sub(/^(a |an |the )/i, "")
   # Delete spaces and punctuation
   a.delete!(" .,-?!")
   b.delete!(" .,-?!")
   # Convert to uppercase
   a.upcase!
   b.upcase!
   # Compare a and b
   a <=> b
 end

 # sorted is now:
 # [ "Star 69", "A Star is Born", "The Starr Report"
 #   "Starship Troopers", "Star Wars"]
```

This example is not overly useful, and it could certainly be written more compactly. The point is that any arbitrarily complex set of operations can be performed on two operands to compare them in a specialized way. (Note, however, that we left the original operands untouched by manipulating copies of them.) This general technique can be useful in many situations—for example, sorting on multiple keys or sorting on keys that are computed at runtime.

In more recent versions of Ruby, the Enumerable module has a sort_by method (which of course is mixed into Array). This is important to understand.

The sort_by method employs what Perl people call a *Schwartzian transform* (after Randal Schwartz). Rather than sort based on the array elements themselves, we apply some kind of function or mapping and sort based on those.

For a contrived example, imagine that we had a list of files and wanted to sort them by size. A straightforward way would be as follows:

```
files = files.sort {|x,y| File.size(x) <=> File.size(y) }
```

However, there are two problems here. First, this seems slightly verbose. We should be able to condense it a little.

Second, this results in multiple disk accesses, each of which is a fairly expensive operation (compared to simple in-memory operations). To make it worse, we are doing many of these operations more than once.

Using sort_by addresses both these issues. Here is the "right" way to do it:

```
files = files.sort_by {|x| File.size(x) }
```

In the preceding example each key is computed only once and is then stored internally as part of a key/data tuple. For smaller arrays, this may actually *decrease* efficiency, but it may be worth the more readable code.

There is no sort_by! method. However, you could always write your own.

What about a multikey sort? Imagine that we had an array of objects and needed to sort them based on three of their attributes: name, age, and height. The fact that arrays are comparable means that this technique will work:

```
list = list.sort_by {|x| [x.name, x.age, x.height] }
```

Of course, you're not limited to simple array elements like these. Any arbitrary expression could be an array element.

8.1.6   Selecting from an Array by Criteria

Sometimes we want to locate an item or items in an array much as though we were querying a table in a database. There are several ways to do this; the ones we outline here are all mixed in from the Enumerable module.

The detect method will find at most a single element. It takes a block (into which the elements are passed sequentially) and returns the first element for which the block evaluates to a value that tests true.

```
x = [5, 8, 12, 9, 4, 30]
# Find the first multiple of 6
x.detect {|e| e % 6 == 0 }          # 12
# Find the first multiple of 7
x.detect {|e| e % 7 == 0 }          # nil
```

Of course, the objects in the array can be of arbitrary complexity, as can the test in the block.

The `find` method is a synonym for `detect`; the method `find_all` is a variant that returns multiple elements as opposed to a single element. Finally, the method `select` is a synonym for `find_all`:

```
# Continuing the above example...
x.find {|e| e % 2 == 0}          # 8
x.find_all {|e| e % 2 == 0}      # [8, 12, 4, 30]
x.select {|e| e % 2 == 0}        # [8, 12, 4, 30]
```

The `grep` method invokes the relationship operator (that is, the case equality operator) to match each element against the pattern specified. In its simplest form, it returns an array containing the matched elements. Because the relationship operator (`===`) is used, the so-called pattern need not be a regular expression. (The name *grep*, of course, comes from the UNIX world, historically related to the old editor command g/re/p.)

```
a = %w[January February March April May]
a.grep(/ary/)        # ["January, "February"]
b = [1, 20, 5, 7, 13, 33, 15, 28]
b.grep(12..24)       # [20, 13, 15]
```

There is a block form that effectively transforms each result before storing it in the array; the resulting array contains the return values of the block rather than the values passed into the block:

```
# Continuing above example...
# Let's store the string lengths
a.grep(/ary/) {|m| m.length}     # [7, 8]
# Let's square each value
b.grep(12..24) {|n| n*n}         # {400, 169, 225}
```

The `reject` method is complementary to `select`. It excludes each element for which the block evaluates to `true`. The in-place mutator `reject!` is also defined:

```
c = [5, 8, 12, 9, 4, 30]
d = c.reject {|e| e % 2 == 0}    # [5, 9]
c.reject! {|e| e % 3 == 0}
# c is now [5, 8, 4]
```

The min and max methods may be used to find the minimum and maximum values in an array. There are two forms of each of these; the first form uses the "default" comparison, whatever that may be in the current situation (as defined by the <=> method). The second form uses a block to do a customized comparison.

```
a = %w[Elrond Galadriel Aragorn Saruman Legolas]
b = a.min                                # "Aragorn"
c = a.max                                # "Saruman"
d = a.min {|x,y| x.reverse <=> y.reverse} # "Elrond"
e = a.max {|x,y| x.reverse <=> y.reverse} # "Legolas"
```

Suppose we wanted to find the *index* of the minimum or maximum element (assuming it is unique). We could use the index method for tasks such as this:

```
# Continuing above example...
i = a.index a.min    # 2
j = a.index a.max    # 3
```

This same technique can be used in other similar situations. However, if the element is not unique, the first one in the array will naturally be the one found.

8.1.7 Using Specialized Indexing Functions

The internals of a language handle the mapping of array indices to array elements through an *indexing function*. Because the methods that access array elements can be overridden, we can in effect index an array in any way we want.

For example, in the following code we implement an array that is one-based rather than zero-based:

```
class Array2 < Array

  def [](index)
    if index>0
      super(index-1)
    else
      raise IndexError
    end
  end

  def []=(index,obj)
```

```
    if index>0
      super(index-1,obj)
    else
      raise IndexError
    end
  end

end


x = Array2.new

x[1]=5
x[2]=3
x[0]=1  # Error
x[-1]=1 # Error
```

Note that the negative indexing (from the end of an array) is disallowed here. And be aware that if this were a real-life solution, there would be other changes to make, such as the `slice` method and others. But this gives the general idea.

A similar approach can be used to implement multidimensional arrays (as we will see in section 8.1.11 "Using Multidimensional Arrays").

It is also possible to implement something like a triangular matrix as shown here. This is like a special case of a two-dimensional array in which element x,y is always the same as element y,x (so that only one need be stored). This is sometimes useful, for example, in storing an undirected graph (as we will see toward the end of this chapter).

```
    class TriMatrix

      def initialize
        @store = []
      end

      def [](x,y)
        if x > y
          index = (x*x+x)/2 + y
          @store[index]
        else
          raise IndexError
        end
      end
```

```
    def []=(x,y,v)
      if x > y
        index = (x*x+x)/2 + y
        @store[index] = v
      else
        raise IndexError
      end
    end

end


t = TriMatrix.new

t[3,2] = 1
puts t[3,2]   # 1

puts t[2,3]   # IndexError
```

In the preceding example we chose to implement the matrix so that the row number must be greater than or equal to the column number; we also could have coded it so that the same pair of indices simply mapped to the same element. These design decisions will depend on your use of the matrix.

It would have been possible to inherit from Array, but we thought this solution was easier to understand. The indexing formula is a little complex, but 10 minutes with pencil and paper should convince anyone it is correct. Enhancements probably could be made to this class to make it truly useful, but we will leave that to you.

Also, it is possible to implement a triangular matrix as an array containing arrays that increase in size as the row number gets higher. This is similar to what we do in section 8.1.11 "Using Multidimensional Arrays." The only tricky part would be to make sure that a row does not accidentally grow past its proper size.

8.1.8   Implementing a Sparse Matrix

Sometimes we need an array that has very few elements defined; the rest of its elements can be undefined (or more often zero). This so-called *sparse matrix* has historically been a waster of memory that led people to seek indirect ways of implementing it.

Of course, in most cases, a Ruby array will suffice because modern architectures typically have large amounts of memory. An unassigned element will have the value nil, which takes only a few bytes to store.

But on the other hand, assigning an array element beyond the previous bounds of the array also creates all the `nil` elements in between. For example, if elements 0 through 9 are defined, and we suddenly assign to element 1000, we have in effect caused elements 10 through 999 to spring into being as `nil` values. If this is unacceptable, you might consider another alternative.

The alternative we have to suggest, however, does not involve arrays at all. If we really need a sparse matrix, a hash might be the best solution. See section 8.2.14 "Using a Hash As a Sparse Matrix."

8.1.9   Using Arrays As Mathematical Sets

Most languages do not directly implement sets (Pascal being one exception). But Ruby arrays have some features that make them usable as sets. We'll present these here and add a few of our own.

Recent versions of Ruby include a `Set` class in the standard library. If your needs are more than incidental, consider using `Set` objects rather than actual arrays. These are covered in Chapter 9, "More Advanced Data Structures."

An array isn't a perfect fit for representing a set because an array can have duplicate entries. If you specifically want to treat the array as a set, you can remove these (using `uniq` or `uniq!`).

The two most basic operations performed on sets are union and intersection. These are accomplished by the | ("or") and & ("and") operators, respectively. In accordance with the idea that a set does not contain duplicates, any duplicates will be removed. (This may be contrary to your expectations if you are used to array union and intersection operations in some other language.)

```
a = [1, 2, 3, 4, 5]
b = [3, 4, 5, 6, 7]
c = a | b              # [1, 2, 3, 4, 5, 6, 7]
d = a & b              # [3, 4, 5]

# Duplicates are removed...
e = [1, 2, 2, 3, 4]
f = [2, 2, 3, 4, 5]
g = e & f              # [2, 3, 4]
```

The concatenation operator + can be used for set union, but it does *not* remove duplicates.

The - method is a "set difference" operator that produces a set with all the members of the first set except the ones appearing in the second set. (See section 8.1.12, "Finding Elements in One Array But Not Another.")

```
a = [1, 2, 3, 4, 5]
b = [4, 5, 6, 7]
c = a - b              # [1, 2, 3]
# Note that the extra items 6 and 7 are irrelevant.
```

To "accumulate" sets it is possible to use the |= operator; as expected, a |= b simply means a = a | b. Likewise &= can progressively "narrow down" the elements of a set.

There is no exclusive-or defined for arrays, but we can make our own easily. In set terms, this corresponds to elements that are in the union of two sets but *not* in the intersection.

```
class Array

  def ^(other)
    (self | other) - (self & other)
  end

end

x = [1, 2, 3, 4, 5]
y = [3, 4, 5, 6, 7]
z = x ^ y              # [1, 2, 6, 7]
```

To check for the presence of an element in a set, we can use the method include? or member? (essentially an alias mixed in from Comparable):

```
x = [1, 2, 3]
if x.include? 2
  puts "yes"     # Prints "yes"
else
  puts "no"
end
```

Of course, this is a little backward from what we are used to in mathematics, where the operator resembling a Greek epsilon denotes set membership. It is backward in the sense that the set is on the left rather than on the right; we are not asking "Is this element in this set?" but rather "Does this set contain this element?"

Many people will not be bothered by this at all. But if you are used to Pascal or Python (or you have ingrained mathematical inclinations), you may want a different way. We present an option in the following code:

```
class Object

  def in(other)
    other.include? self
  end

end

x = [1, 2, 3]
if 2.in x
  puts "yes"      # Prints "yes"
else
  puts "no"
end
```

I personally have made a Ruby Change Request (RCR 241) proposing an in operator for Ruby. This would be similar to the operator in Pascal or Python or even SQL.

The idea has its advantages (and in is already a reserved word), but it has been received with mixed popularity. It may or may not ever be part of Ruby.

Now let's look at subsets and supersets. How do we tell whether a set is a subset or a superset of another? There are no built-in methods, but we can do it this way:

```
class Array

  def subset?(other)
    self.each  do |x|
      if !(other.include? x)
        return false
      end
    end
    true
  end
```

```
  def superset?(other)
    other.subset?(self)
  end

end

a = [1, 2, 3, 4]
b = [2, 3]
c = [2, 3, 4, 5]

flag1 = c.subset? a     # false
flag2 = b.subset? a     # true
flag3 = c.superset? b   # true
```

Note that we've chosen the "natural" ordering—that is, x.subset? y means "Is x a subset of y?" rather than vice versa.

To detect the null set (or empty set), we simply detect the empty array. The empty? method does this.

The concept of set negation (or complement) depends on the concept of a *universal set*. Because in practical terms this varies from one application or situation to another, the best way is the simplest: Define the universe; then do a set difference.

```
universe = [1, 2, 3, 4, 5, 6]
a = [2, 3]
b = universe - a    # complement of a = [1, 4, 5, 6]
```

Of course, if you really felt the need, you could define a unary operator (such as - or ~) to do this.

You can iterate through a set just by iterating through the array. The only difference is that the elements will come out in order, which you may not want. To iterate randomly, see section 8.1.18, "Iterating Over an Array."

Finally, we may sometimes want to compute the powerset of a set. This is simply the set of all possible subsets (including the null set and the original set itself). Those familiar with discrete math or especially combinatorics will see that there must be 2^n of these subsets. We can generate the powerset as follows:

```
class Array

  def powerset
    num = 2**size
```

```
    ps = Array.new(num, [])
    self.each_index do |i|
      a = 2**i
      b = 2**(i+1) - 1
      j = 0
      while j < num-1
        for j in j+a..j+b
          ps[j] += [self[i]]
        end
        j += 1
      end
    end
    ps
  end

end

x = [1, 2, 3]
y = x.powerset
# y is now:
#   [[], [1], [2], [1,2], [3], [1,3], [2,3], [1,2,3]]
```

8.1.10   Randomizing an Array

Sometimes we want to scramble an array into a random order. The first example that might come to mind is a card game, but there are other circumstances such as presenting a list of questions to a user in a random order.

To accomplish this task, we can use the rand in the Kernel module. The following is one way to do this:

```
class Array

  def randomize
    self.sort_by { rand }      # sort by a key which is a
  end                          #   random number

  def randomize!
    self.replace(self.randomize)
  end

end
```

```
x = [1, 2, 3, 4, 5]
y = x.randomize       # [3, 2, 4, 1 ,5]
x.randomize!          # x is now [3, 5, 4, 1, 2]
```

Because of the nature of the sorting, there is probably a slight bias introduced here. In most cases it won't matter.

If we wanted simply to pick an array element at random (without disallowing duplicates), we could do that as follows:

```
class Array

  def pick_random
    self[rand(self.length)]
  end

end
```

Finally, we should remember that any time we are using rand, we can generate a predictable sequence (for example, in unit testing) simply by seeding with a known seed using srand (see section 5.28 "Generating Random Numbers").

8.1.11   Using Multidimensional Arrays

If you want to use multidimensional arrays for numerical purposes, there is an excellent library in the Ruby Application Archive called NArray (by Masahiro Tanaka). If you want to use matrices, there is also the matrix.rb standard library as mentioned in section 5.10, "Matrix Manipulation."

The following example presents a way of handling multidimensional arrays by overloading the [] and []= methods to map elements onto a nested array. The class Array3 presented here handles three-dimensional arrays in a rudimentary fashion, but it is far from complete:

```
class Array3

  def initialize
    @store = [[[]]]
  end
```

```
def [](a,b,c)
  if @store[a]==nil ||
     @store[a][b]==nil ||
     @store[a][b][c]==nil
    return nil
  else
    return @store[a][b][c]
  end
end

def []=(a,b,c,x)
  @store[a] = [[]] if @store[a]==nil
  @store[a][b] = [] if @store[a][b]==nil
  @store[a][b][c] = x
end

end


x = Array3.new
x[0,0,0] = 5
x[0,0,1] = 6
x[1,2,3] = 99

puts x[1,2,3]
```

Note that all we really gain here is the convenience of a "comma" notation [x,y,z] instead of the more C-like [x][y][z]. If the C-style notation is acceptable to you, you can just use nested arrays in Ruby. Another minor benefit is the prevention of the situation in which nil is the receiver for the bracket method.

8.1.12 Finding Elements in One Array But Not Another

This is simpler in Ruby than in many languages. It is a simple "set difference" problem:

```
text = %w[the magic words are squeamish ossifrage]
dictionary = %w[an are magic the them these words]
# Find potential misspellings
unknown = text - dictionary   # ["squeamish", "ossifrage"]
```

8.1.13   Transforming or Mapping Arrays

The collect method (part of Enumerable) is a useful tool that proves to be a time
and labor saver in many circumstances. If you are a Smalltalk programmer, this may
be more intuitive than if you come from a C background.

This method simply operates on each element of an array in some arbitrary way
to produce a new array. In other words, it "maps" an array onto another array (hence
the synonym map).

```
x = %w[alpha bravo charlie delta echo foxtrot]
# Get the initial letters
a = x.collect {|w| w[0..0]}        # %w[a b c d e f]
# Get the string lengths
b = x.collect {|w| w.length}       # [5, 5, 7, 5, 4, 7]
# map is just an alias
c = x.map {|w| w.length}           # [5, 5, 7, 5, 4, 7]
```

The in-place variant collect! (or map!) is also defined.

```
x.collect! {|w| w.upcase}
# x is now %w[ALPHA BRAVO CHARLIE DELTA ECHO FOXTROT]
x.map! {|w| w.reverse}
# x is now %w[AHPLA OVARB EILRAHC ATLED OHCE TORTXOF]
```

8.1.14   Removing nil Values from an Array

The compact method (or its in-place version compact!) removes nil values from an
array, leaving the rest untouched:

```
a = [1, 2, nil, 3, nil, 4, 5]
b = a.compact      # [1, 2, 3, 4, 5]
a.compact!         # a is now [1, 2, 3, 4, 5]
```

8.1.15   Removing Specific Array Elements

It is easy to delete elements from a Ruby array, and there are many ways to do it. If
you want to delete one specific element by index, delete_at is a good way:

```
a = [10, 12, 14, 16, 18]
a.delete_at(3)                     # Returns 16
```

```
# a is now [10, 12, 14, 18]
a.delete_at(9)                    # Returns nil (out of range)
```

If you want to delete all instances of a certain piece of data, delete will do the job. It returns the value of the objects deleted or nil if it was not found:

```
b = %w(spam spam bacon spam eggs ham spam)
b.delete("spam")                  # Returns "spam"
# b is now ["bacon", "eggs", "ham"]
b.delete("caviar")                # Returns nil
```

The delete method also accepts a block. This may be a little counterintuitive; all that happens is that the block is evaluated (potentially performing a wide range of operations) if the object is not found, and the value of the block is returned.

```
c = ["alpha", "beta", "gamma", "delta"]
c.delete("delta") { "Nonexistent" }
# Returns "delta" (block is never evaulated)
c.delete("omega") { "Nonexistent" }
# Returns "Nonexistent"
```

The delete_if passes every element into the supplied block and deletes the elements for which the block evaluates to true. It behaves similarly to reject!, except that the latter can return nil when the array remains unchanged.

```
email = ["job offers", "greetings", "spam", "news items"]
# Delete four-letter words
email.delete_if {|x| x.length==4 }
# email is now ["job offers", "greetings", "news items"]
```

The slice! method accesses the same elements as slice but deletes them from the array as it returns their values:

```
x = [0, 2, 4, 6, 8, 10, 12, 14, 16]
a = x.slice!(2)                           # 4
# x is now [0, 2, 6, 8, 10, 12, 14, 16]
b = x.slice!(2,3)                         # [6, 8, 10]
# x is now [0, 2, 12, 14, 16]
c = x.slice!(2..3)                        # [12, 14]
# x is now [0, 2, 16]
```

The `shift` and `pop` methods can be used for deleting array elements. (For more about their intended uses, see section 9.2, "Working with Stacks and Queues.")

```
x = [1, 2, 3, 4, 5]
x.pop                 # Delete the last element
# x is now [1, 2, 3, 4]
x.shift               # Delete the first element
# x is now [2, 3, 4]
```

The `reject` method takes a block and produces a new array *without* the elements for which the block returns true:

```
arr = [1,2,3,4,5,6,7,8]
odd = arr.reject {|x| x % 2 == 0 }      # [1,3,5,7]
```

Finally, the `clear` method deletes all the elements in an array. It is equivalent to assigning an empty array to the variable but is marginally more efficient:

```
x = [1, 2, 3]
x.clear
# x is now []
```

8.1.16   Concatenating and Appending onto Arrays

Frequently we want to append an element or another array onto an array. You can do this in many ways with a Ruby array.

The "append" operator `<<` appends an object onto an array; the return value is the array itself, so that these operations can be "chained."

```
x = [1, 5, 9]
x << 13        # x is now [1, 5, 9, 13]
x << 17 << 21  # x is now [1, 5, 9, 13, 17, 21]
```

Similar to the append operator are the `unshift` and `push` methods, which add to the beginning and end of an array, respectively. See section 8.1.17 "Using an Array As a Stack or Queue" later in this chapter.

Arrays may be concatenated with the `concat` method or by using the `+` and `+=` operators:

```
x = [1,2]
y = [3,4]
z = [5,6]
b = y + z          # [3,4,5,6]
b += x             # [3,4,5,6,1,2]
z.concat y         # z is now [5,6,3,4]
```

Bear in mind that `+=` always creates a new object. Also bear in mind that `<<` appends a new array element (which may itself be an array).

```
a = [1,2]
b = [3,4]
a += b             # [1,2,3,4]


a = [1,2]
b = [3,4]
a << b             # [1,2,[3,4]]


a = [1,2]
b = [3,4]
a = a.concat(b)    # [1,2,3,4]
```

8.1.17   Using an Array As a Stack or Queue

The basic stack operations are `push` and `pop`, which add and remove items at the end of an array. The basic queue operations are `shift` (which removes an item from the beginning of an array) and `unshift` (which adds an element to the beginning). The append operator `<<` can also be used to add an item to the end of an array (basically a synonym for `push`).

Don't get confused. The `shift` and `unshift` methods work on the *beginning* of an array; the `push`, `pop`, and `<<` methods work on the *end*.

For a better discussion of this topic, see section 9.2, "Working with Stacks and Queues."

8.1.18   Iterating Over an Array

The `Array` class has the standard iterator `each` as is to be expected. However, it also has other useful iterators.

The `reverse_each` method iterates in reverse order. It is equivalent to using reverse and then `each`, but it is faster.

```
words = %w(Son I am able she said)
str = ""
words.reverse_each { |w| str += "#{w} "}
# str is now "said she able am I Son "
```

If we only want to iterate over the indices, we can use `each_index`. Saying `x.each_index` is equivalent to saying `(0..(x.size-1)).each` (that is, iterating over the range of indices).

The iterator `each_with_index` (mixed in from `Comparable`) passes both the element and the index into the block.

```
x = ["alpha", "beta", "gamma"]
x.each_with_index do |x,i|
  puts "Element #{i} is #{x}"
end
# Produces three lines of output
```

Suppose that we wanted to iterate over an array in random order. We show here the iterator `random_each` (which simply invokes the `randomize` method from section 8.1.10, "Randomizing an Array."

```
class Array

# Assumes we have defined randomize

  def random_each
    temp = self.randomize
    temp.each {|x| yield x}
  end

end
```

```
dwarves = %w(Sleepy Dopey Happy Sneezy Grumpy Bashful Doc)
list = ""
dwarves.random_each {|x| list += "#{x} "}
# list is now:
# "Bashful Dopey Sleepy Happy Grumpy Doc Sneezy "
# (Your mileage may vary.)
```

8.1.19 Interposing Delimiters to Form a String

Frequently we will want to insert delimiters in between array elements in a "fencepost" fashion; that is, we want to put delimiters between the elements but not before the first one or after the last one. The method join will do this, as will the * operator.

```
been_there = ["Veni", "vidi", "vici."]
journal = been_there.join(", ")        # "Veni, vidi, vici."

letters = ["Phi","Mu","Alpha"]
musicians = letters.join(" ")          # "Phi Mu Alpha"

people = ["Bob","Carol","Ted","Alice"]
movie = people * " and "
# movie is now "Bob and Carol and Ted and Alice"
```

Note that if we really need to treat the last element differently, perhaps by inserting the word *and*, we can do it manually:

```
list = %w[A B C D E F]
with_commas = list[0..-2]*", " + ", and " + list[-1]
# with_commas is now "A, B, C, D, E, and F"
```

8.1.20 Reversing an Array

To reverse the order of an array, use the reverse or reverse! methods:

```
inputs = ["red", "green", "blue"]
outputs = inputs.reverse         # ["green","blue","red"]
priorities = %w(eat sleep code)
priorities.reverse!              # ["code","sleep","eat"]
```

8.1.21   Removing Duplicate Elements from an Array

If you want to remove duplicate elements from an array, the uniq method (or its in-place mutator uniq!) will do the job:

```
breakfast = %w[spam spam eggs ham eggs spam]
lunch = breakfast.uniq    # ["spam","eggs","ham"]
breakfast.uniq!           # breakfast has changed now
```

8.1.22   Interleaving Arrays

Suppose that we wanted to take two arrays and "interleave" them so that the new array contains smaller arrays of paired elements from each of the two original ones. Recent versions of Ruby have the zip method in Enumerable.

```
a = [1, 2, 3, 4]
b = ["a", "b", "c", "d"]
c = a.zip(b)
# c is now [[1,"a"], [2,"b"], [3,"c"], [4,"d"]]
# Use flatten if you want to eliminate the nesting
d = c.flatten
# d is now [1, "a", 2, "b", 3, "c", 4, "d"]
```

8.1.23   Counting Frequency of Values in an Array

There is no count method for arrays as there is for strings (to count the occurrences of each data item). So we create one here:

```
class Array

  def count
    k=Hash.new(0)
    self.each{|x| k[x]+=1 }
    k
  end

end

meal = %w[spam spam eggs ham eggs spam]
```

```
items = meal.count
# items is {"ham" => 1, "spam" => 3, "eggs" => 2}
spams = items["spam"]    # 3
```

Note that a hash is returned. No pun intended.

8.1.24   Inverting an Array to Form a Hash

An array is used to associate an integer index with a piece of data. But what if you want to invert that association—that is, associate the data with the index, producing a hash? The following method will do just that:

```
class Array

  def invert
    h={}
    self.each_with_index{|x,i| h[x]=i}
    h
  end

end

a = ["red","yellow","orange"]
h = a.invert       # {"orange"=>2, "yellow"=>1, "red"=>0}
```

8.1.25   Synchronized Sorting of Multiple Arrays

Suppose we wanted to sort an array, but we had other arrays that corresponded with this one on an element-for-element basis. In other words, we don't want to get them out of sync.

The solution presented here sorts an array and gathers the resulting set of indices. The list of indices (itself an array) can be applied to any other array to put its elements in the same order.

```
class Array

  def sort_index
    d=[]
    self.each_with_index{|x,i| d[i]=[x,i]}
```

```
      if block_given?
        d.sort {|x,y| yield x[0],y[0]}.collect{|x| x[1]}
      else
        d.sort.collect{|x| x[1]}
      end
    end


  def sort_with(ord=[])
    return nil if self.length!=ord.length
    self.values_at(*ord)
  end

end


a = [21, 33, 11, 34, 36, 24, 14]
b = a.sort_index
a2 = a.sort_with(b)
c = a.sort_index {|x,y| x%2 <=> y%2 }
a3 = a.sort_with(c)

p a         # [21, 33, 11, 34, 36, 24, 14]
p b         # [2, 6, 0, 5, 1, 3, 4]
p a2        # [11, 14, 21, 24, 33, 34, 36]
p c         # [6, 5, 4, 3, 2, 1, 0]
p a3        # [14, 24, 36, 34, 11, 33, 21]
```

8.1.26   Establishing a Default Value for New Array Elements

When an array grows and new (unassigned) elements are created, these default to `nil` values:

```
a = Array.new
a[0]="x"
a[3]="y"
# a is now ["x", nil, nil, "y"]
```

What if we want to set those new elements to some other value? As a specific instance of a general principle, we offer the `ZArray` class, which defaults new unassigned elements to 0:

```
class ZArray < Array

  def [](x)
    if x > size
      for i in size+1..x
        self[i]=0
      end
    end
    v = super(x)
  end

  def []=(x,v)
    max = size
    super(x,v)
    if size - max > 1
      (max..size-2).each do |i|
        self[i] = 0
      end
    end
  end

end


num = ZArray.new
num[1] = 1
num[2] = 4
num[5] = 25
# num is now [0, 1, 4, 0, 0, 25]
```

8.2 Working with Hashes

Hashes are known in some circles as associative arrays, dictionaries, and various other names. Perl and Java programmers in particular will be familiar with this data structure.

Think of an array as an entity that creates an association between an index x and a data item y. A hash creates a similar association with at least two exceptions. First, for an array, x is always an integer; for a hash, it need not be. Second, an array is an ordered data structure; a hash typically has no ordering.

A hash key can be of any arbitrary type. As a side effect, this makes a hash a non-sequential data structure. In an array, we know that element 4 follows element 3; but in a hash, the key may be of a type that does not define a real predecessor or successor. For this reason (and others), there is no notion in Ruby of the pairs in a hash being in any particular order.

You may think of a hash as an array with a specialized index, or as a database "synonym table" with two fields stored in memory. Regardless of how you perceive it, a hash is a powerful and useful programming construct.

8.2.1   Creating a New Hash

As with Array, the special class method [] is used to create a hash. The data items listed in the brackets are used to form the mapping of the hash.

Six ways of calling this method are shown here. (Hashes a1 through c2 will all be populated identically.)

```
a1 = Hash.[]("flat",3,"curved",2)
a2 = Hash.[]("flat"=>3,"curved"=>2)
b1 = Hash["flat",3,"curved",2]
b2 = Hash["flat"=>3,"curved"=>2]
c1 = {"flat",3,"curved",2}
c2 = {"flat"=>3,"curved"=>2}
# For a1, b1, and c1: There must be
# an even number of elements.
```

There is also a class method called new that can take a parameter specifying a *default* value. Note that this default value is not actually part of the hash; it is simply a value returned in place of nil.

```
d = Hash.new           # Create an empty hash
e = Hash.new(99)       # Create an empty hash
f = Hash.new("a"=>3)   # Create an empty hash
e["angled"]            # 99
e.inspect              # {}
f["b"]                 # {"a"=>3} (default value is
                       #   actually a hash itself)
f.inspect              # {}
```

8.2.2 Specifying a Default Value for a Hash

The default value of a hash is an object referenced in place of `nil` in the case of a missing key. This is useful if you plan to use methods with the hash value that are not defined for `nil`. It can be assigned upon creation of the hash or at a later time using the `default=` method.

All missing keys point to the same default value object, so changing the default value has a side effect.

```
a = Hash.new("missing")  # default value object is "missing"
a["hello"]                        # "missing"
a.default="nothing"
a["hello"]                        # "nothing"
a["good"] << "bye"                # "nothingbye"
a.default               # "nothingbye"
```

There is also a special instance method `fetch` that raises an `IndexError` exception if the key does not exist in the `Hash` object. It takes a second parameter that serves as a default value. Also `fetch` optionally accepts a block to produce a default value in case the key is not found. This is in contrast to `default` because the block allows each missing key to have its own default.

```
a = {"flat",3,"curved",2,"angled",5}
a.fetch("pointed")                # IndexError
a.fetch("curved","na")            # 2
a.fetch("x","na")                 # "na"
a.fetch("flat") {|x| x.upcase}    # 3
a.fetch("pointed") {|x| x.upcase} # "POINTED"
```

8.2.3 Accessing and Adding Key-Value Pairs

`Hash` has class methods `[]` and `[]=` just as `Array` has; they are used much the same way, except that they accept only one parameter. The parameter can be any object, not just a string (although string objects are commonly used).

```
a = {}
a["flat"] = 3          # {"flat"=>3}
a.[]=("curved",2)      # {"flat"=>3,"curved"=>2}
a.store("angled",5)    # {"flat"=>3,"curved"=>2,"angled"=>5}
```

The method `store` is simply an alias for the `[]=` method, both of which take two arguments as shown in the preceding example.

The method `fetch` is similar to the `[]` method, except that it raises an `IndexError` for missing keys. It also has an optional second argument (or alternatively a code block) for dealing with default values (see section 8.2.2, "Specifying a Default Value for a Hash" earlier in this chapter).

```
a["flat"]         # 3
a.[]("flat")      # 3
a.fetch("flat")   # 3
a["bent"]         # nil
```

Suppose that we are not sure whether the `Hash` object exists, and we want to avoid clearing an existing hash. The obvious way is to check whether the hash is defined:

```
unless defined? a
   a={}
end
a["flat"] = 3
```

Another way to do this is as follows:

```
a ||= {}
a["flat"] = 3
# Or even:
(a ||= {})["flat"] = 3
```

The same problem can be applied to individual keys, where you want to assign a value only if the key does not exist:

```
a=Hash.new(99)
a[2]              # 99
a                 # {}
a[2] ||= 5        # 99
a                 # {}
b=Hash.new
b                 # {}
b[2]              # nil
b[2] ||= 5        # 5
b                 # {2=>5}
```

Note that `nil` may be used as either a key or an associated value:

```
b={}
b[2]        # nil
b[3]=nil
b           # {3=>nil}
b[2].nil? # true
b[3].nil? # true
b[nil]=5
b           # {3=>nil,nil=>5}
b[nil]      # 5
b[b[3]]     # 5
```

8.2.4   Deleting Key-Value Pairs

Key-value pairs of a `Hash` object can be deleted using `clear`, `delete`, `delete_if`, `reject`, `reject!`, and `shift`.

Use `clear` to remove all key-value pairs. This is essentially the same as assigning a new empty hash but marginally faster.

Use `shift` to remove an unspecified key-value pair. This method returns the pair as a two-element array, or `nil` if no keys are left.

```
a = {1=>2, 3=>4}
b = a.shift        # [1,2]
# a is now {3=>4}
```

Use `delete` to remove a specific key-value pair. It accepts a key and returns the value associated with the key removed (if found). If not found, the default value is returned. It also accepts a block to produce a unique default value rather than just a reused object reference.

```
a = {1=>1, 2=>4, 3=>9, 4=>16}
a.delete(3)                      # 9
# a is now {1=>1, 2=>4, 4=>16}
a.delete(5)                      # nil in this case
a.delete(6) { "not found" }      # "not found"
```

Use delete_if, reject, or reject! in conjunction with the required block to delete all keys for which the block evaluates to true. The method reject uses a copy of the hash, and reject! returns nil if no changes were made.

8.2.5 Iterating Over a Hash

The Hash class has the standard iterator each as is to be expected. It also has each_key, each_pair, and each_value. (each_pair is an alias for each.)

```ruby
{"a"=>3,"b"=>2}.each do |key, val|
  print val, " from ", key, "; "    # 3 from a; 2 from b;
end
```

The other two provide only one or the other of key or value to the block:

```ruby
{"a"=>3,"b"=>2}.each_key do |key|
  print "key = #{key};"        # Prints: key = a; key = b;
end
```

```ruby
{"a"=>3,"b"=>2}.each_value do |value|
  print "val = #{value};"      # Prints: val = 3; val = 2;
end
```

8.2.6 Inverting a Hash

Inverting a hash in Ruby is trivial with the invert method:

```ruby
a = {"fred"=>"555-1122","jane"=>"555-7779"}
b = a.invert
b["555-7779"]     # "jane"
```

Since hashes have unique keys, there is potential for data loss when doing this: Duplicate associated values will be converted to a unique key using only one of the associated keys as its value. There is no predictable way to tell which one will be used.

8.2.7 Detecting Keys and Values in a Hash

Determining whether a key has been assigned can be done with has_key? or any one of its aliases include?, key?, and member?:

```
a = {"a"=>1,"b"=>2}
a.has_key? "c"        # false
a.include? "a"        # true
a.key? 2              # false
a.member? "b"         # true
```

You can also use empty? to see whether any keys at all are left in the hash. Likewise length or its alias size can be used to determine how many there are:

```
a.empty?        # false
a.length        # 2
```

Alternatively, you can test for the existence of an associated value using has_value? or value? :

```
a.has_value? 2        # true
a.value? 99           # false
```

8.2.8 Extracting Hashes into Arrays

To convert the entire hash into an array, use the to_a method. In the resulting array, keys will be even-numbered elements (starting with 0), and values will be odd-numbered elements of the array:

```
h = {"a"=>1,"b"=>2}
h.to_a        # ["a",1,"b",2]
```

It is also possible to convert only the keys or only the values of the hash into an array:

```
h.keys        # ["a","b"]
h.values      # [1,2]
```

Finally, you can extract an array of values selectively based on a list of keys, using the method. This works for hashes much as the method of the same name works for arrays. (Also, as for arrays, values_at replaces the obsolete methods indices and indexes.)

```
h = {1=>"one",2=>"two",3=>"three",4=>"four","cinco"=>"five"}
h.values_at(3,"cinco",4)        # ["three","five","four"]
h.values_at(1,3)                # ["one","three"]
```

8.2.9 Selecting Key-Value Pairs by Criteria

The Hash class mixes in the Enumerable module, so you can use detect (find), select, (find_all), grep, min, max, and reject as with arrays.

The detect method (alias find) finds a single key-value pair. It takes a block (into which the pairs are passed one at a time) and returns the first pair for which the block evaluates to true.

```
names = {"fred"=>"jones","jane"=>"tucker",
          "joe"=>"tucker","mary"=>"SMITH"}
# Find a tucker
names.detect {|k,v| v=="tucker" }     # ["joe","tucker"]
# Find a capitalized surname
names.find {|k,v| v==v.upcase }     # ["mary", "SMITH"]
```

Of course, the objects in the hash can be of arbitrary complexity, as can the test in the block, but comparisons between differing types can cause problems.

The select method (alias find_all) returns multiple matches as opposed to a single match:

```
names.select {|k,v| v=="tucker" }
# [["joe", "tucker"], ["jane", "tucker"]]
names.find_all {|k,v| k.count("r")>0}
# [["mary", "SMITH"], ["fred", "jones"]]
```

8.2.10 Sorting a Hash

Hashes are by their nature not ordered according to the value of their keys or associated values. In performing a sort on a hash, Ruby converts the hash to an array and then sorts that array. The result is naturally an array.

```
names = {"Jack"=>"Ruby","Monty"=>"Python",
         "Blaise"=>"Pascal", "Minnie"=>"Perl"}
list = names.sort
# list is now:
# [["Blaise","Pascal"], ["Jack","Ruby"],
#  ["Minnie","Perl"], ["Monty","Python"]]
```

8.2.11 Merging Two Hashes

Merging hashes may be useful sometimes. Ruby's merge method merges the entries of two hashes, forming a third hash and overwriting any previous duplicates:

```
dict = {"base"=>"foundation", "pedestal"=>"base"}
added = {"base"=>"non-acid", "salt"=>"NaCl"}
new_dict = dict.merge(added)
# {"base"=>"non-acid", "pedestal"=>"base", "salt"=>"NaCl"}
```

An alias for merge is update.

If a block is specified, it can contain logic to deal with collisions. For example, here we assume that if we have two keys colliding, we use the value that is *less* than the other (alphabetically, numerically, or however):

```
dict = {"base"=>"foundation", "pedestal"=>"base"}
added = {"base"=>"non-acid", "salt"=>"NaCl"}
new_dict = dict.merge(added) {|key,old,new| old < new ? old : new }
# {"salt"=>"NaCl", "pedestal"=>"base", "base"=>"foundation"}
```

The second result using the block is thus different from the previous example. Also be aware that there are mutator methods merge! and update!, which will change the receiver in place.

8.2.12   Creating a Hash from an Array

The easiest way to do this is to remember the bracket notation for creating hashes. This works if the array has an even number of elements.

```
array = [2, 3, 4, 5, 6, 7]
hash = Hash[*array]
# hash is now: {2=>3, 4=>5, 6=>7}
```

8.2.13   Finding Difference or Intersection of Hash Keys

Since the keys of a hash can be extracted as a separate array, the extracted arrays of different hashes can be manipulated using the Array class methods & and - to produce the intersection and difference of the keys. The matching values can be generated with the each method performed on a third hash representing the merge of the two hashes (to ensure all keys can be found in one place).

```
a = {"a"=>1,"b"=>2,"z"=>3}
b = {"x"=>99,"y"=>88,"z"=>77}
intersection = a.keys & b.keys
difference = a.keys - b.keys
c = a.dup.update(b)
inter = {}
intersection.each {|k| inter[k]=c[k] }
# inter is {"z"=>77}
diff={}
difference.each {|k| diff[k]=c[k] }
# diff is {"a"=>1, "b"=>2}
```

8.2.14   Using a Hash As a Sparse Matrix

Often we want to use an array or matrix that is nearly empty. We could store it in the conventional way, but this is often wasteful of memory. A hash provides a way to store only the values that actually exist.

In the following example we assume that the nonexistent values should default to zero:

```
values = Hash.new(0)
values[1001] = 5
```

```
values[2010] = 7
values[9237] = 9
x = values[9237]      # 9
y = values[5005]      # 0
```

Obviously, in the preceding example, an array would have created more than 9,000 unused elements. This may not be acceptable.

What if we want to implement a sparse matrix of two or more dimensions? All we need do is use arrays as the hash keys:

```
cube = Hash.new(0)
cube[[2000,2000,2000]] = 2
z = cube[[36,24,36]]        # 0
```

In this case, we see that literally *billions* of array elements would need to be created if this three-dimensional matrix were to be complete.

8.2.15   Implementing a Hash with Duplicate Keys

Purists would likely say that if a hash has duplicate keys, it isn't really a hash. We don't want to argue. Call it what you will; there might be occasions where you want a data structure that offers the flexibility and convenience of a hash but allows duplicate key values.

We offer a partial solution here (Listing 8.1). It is partial for two reasons. First, we have not bothered to implement all the functionality that could be desired but only a good representative subset. Second, the inner workings of Ruby are such that a hash literal is always an instance of the Hash class, and even though we were to inherit from Hash, a literal would not be allowed to contain duplicates. (We're thinking about this one further.)

Listing 8.1   Hash with Duplicate Keys
_____

```
class HashDup

  def initialize(*all)
    raise IndexError if all.size % 2 != 0
    @store = {}
    if all[0]  # not nil
      keyval = all.dup
      while !keyval.empty?
        key = keyval.shift
        if @store.has_key?(key)
```

Continues

```ruby
          @store[key] += [keyval.shift]
        else
          @store[key] = [keyval.shift]
        end
      end
    end
  end

  def store(k,v)
    if @store.has_key?(k)
      @store[k] += [v]
    else
      @store[k] = [v]
    end
  end

  def [](key)
    @store[key]
  end

  def []=(key,value)
    self.store(key,value)
  end

  def to_s
    @store.to_s
  end

  def to_a
    @store.to_a
  end

  def inspect
    @store.inspect
  end

  def keys
    result=[]
    @store.each do |k,v|
      result += ([k]*v.size)
    end
    result
  end

  def values
    @store.values.flatten
  end

  def each
    @store.each {|k,v| v.each {|y| yield k,y}}
  end
```

```
alias each_pair each

def each_key
  self.keys.each {|k| yield k}
end

def each_value
  self.values.each {|v| yield v}
end

def has_key? k
  self.keys.include? k
end

def has_value? v
  self.values.include? v
end

def length
  self.values.size
end

alias size length

def delete k
  val = @store[k]
  @store.delete k
  val
end

def delete k,v
  @store[k] -= [v] if @store[k]
  v
end

  # Other methods omitted here...

end


# This won't work... dup key will ignore
# first occurrence.
h = {1=>1, 2=>4, 3=>9, 4=>16, 2=>0}

# This will work...
h = HashDup.new(1,1, 2,4, 3,9, 4,16, 2,0)

k = h.keys        # [4, 1, 2, 2, 3]
v = h.values      # [16, 1, 4, 0, 9]
```

Continues

```
n = h.size          # 5

h.each {|k,v| puts "#{k} => #{v}"}
# Prints:
# 4 => 16
# 1 => 1
# 2 => 4
# 2 => 0
# 3 => 9
```

But as long as you stay away from the hash-literal notation, this problem is doable. In Listing 8.1 we implement a class that has a "store" (`@store`), which is a simple hash; each value in the hash is an array. We control access to the hash in such a way that when we find ourselves adding a key that already exists, we add the value to the existing array of items associated with that key.

What should `size` return? Obviously the "real" number of key-value pairs *including* duplicates. Likewise the `keys` method returns a value potentially containing duplicates. The iterators behave as expected; as with a normal hash, there is no predicting the order in which the pairs will be visited.

Besides the usual `delete`, we have implemented a `delete_pair` method. The former deletes *all* values associated with a key; the latter deletes only the specified key-value pair. (Note that it would have been difficult to make a single method like `delete(k,v=nil)` because `nil` is a valid value for any hash.

For brevity we have not implemented the entire class, and, frankly, some of the methods such as `invert` would require some design decisions as to what their behavior should be. The interested reader can flesh out the rest as needed.

8.3   Enumerables in General

What makes a collection *enumerable*? Largely it is just the fact of being a collection. The module `Enumerable` has the requirement that the default iterator `each` should be defined. Sequence as such is not an issue since even an unordered collection such as a hash can have an iterator.

Additionally, if the methods `min`, `max`, and `sort` are to be used, the collection must have a comparison method (`<=>`). This is fairly obvious.

So an enumerable is just a collection that can be searched, traversed, and possibly sorted. As a rule of thumb, any user-defined collection that does not subclass an existing core class should probably mix in the `Enumerable` module.

Bear in mind that what we say about one enumerable applies in effect to all of them. The actual data structure could be an array, a hash, or a tree, to name a few.

There are, of course, some nuances of behavior. An array is an ordered collection of individual items, whereas a hash is an unordered collection of paired key-value associations. Naturally there will be differences in their behavior.

Many of the methods we looked at for arrays and/or hashes (such as `map` and `find`) really originate here in the `Enumerable` module. In many cases it was difficult to determine how to cover this material. Any confusion or inaccuracy should be considered my fault.

The array is the most common and representative collection that mixes in this module. Therefore by default I will use it as an example.

8.3.1   The `inject` Method

The `inject` method comes to Ruby via Smalltalk (and was introduced in Ruby 1.8). Its behavior is interesting, if a little difficult to grasp at first sight.

This method relies on the fact that frequently we will iterate through a list and "accumulate" a result that changes as we iterate. The most common example, of course, would be finding the sum of a list of numbers. Whatever the operation, there is usually an "accumulator" of some kind (for which we supply an initial value) and a function or operation we apply (represented in Ruby as a block).

For a trivial example or two, suppose that we have this array of numbers and we want to find the sum of all of them:

```
nums = [3,5,7,9,11,13]
sum = nums.inject(0) {|x,n| x+n }
```

Note how we start with an accumulator of 0 (the "addition identity"). Then the block gets the current accumulated value and the current value from the list passed in. In each case, the block takes the previous sum and adds the current item to it.

Obviously, this is equivalent to the following piece of code:

```
sum = 0
nums.each {|n| sum += n }
```

So the abstraction level is only slightly higher. If `inject` never fits nicely in your brain, don't use it. But if you get over the initial confusion, you might find yourself inventing new and elegant ways to use it.

The accumulator value is optional. If it is omitted, the first item is used as the accumulator and is then omitted from iteration.

```
sum = nums.inject { |x,n| x+n }

# Means the same as:

sum = nums[0]
nums[1..-1].each { |n| sum += n }
```

A similar example is finding the product of the numbers. Note that the accumulator, if given, must be 1 since that is the "multiplication identity."

```
prod = nums.inject(1) { |x,n| x*n }

# or:

prod = nums.inject { |x,n| x*n }
```

The following slightly more complex example takes a list of words and finds the longest words in the list:

```
words = %w[ alpha beta gamma delta epsilon eta theta ]
longest_word = words.inject do |best,w|
  w.length > best.length ? w : best
end
# return value is "epsilon"
```

8.3.2   Using Quantifiers

The quantifiers any? and all? were added in Ruby 1.8 to make it easier to test the nature of a collection. Each of these takes a block (which of course tests true or false).

```
nums = [1,3,5,8,9]

# Are any of these numbers even?
flag1 = nums.any? { |x| x % 2 == 0 }     # true

# Are all of these numbers even?
flag2 = nums.all? { |x| x % 2 == 0 }     # false
```

In the absence of a block, these simply test the truth value of each element. That is, a block `{|x| x }` is added implicitly.

```
flag1 = list.all?    # list contains no falses or nils
flag1 = list.any?    # list contains at least one true value (non-nil
                     #   or non-false)
```

8.3.3 The `partition` Method

As the saying goes, "There are two kinds of people in the world—those who divide people into two kinds, and those who don't." The `partition` doesn't deal with people (unless we can encode them as Ruby objects), but it does divide a collection into two parts.

When `partition` is called and passed a block, the block is evaluated for each element in the collection. The truth value of each result is then evaluated, and a pair of arrays (inside another array) is returned. All the elements resulting in true go in the first array; the others go in the second.

```
nums = [1, 2, 3, 4, 5, 6, 7, 8, 9]

odd_even = nums.partition {|x| x % 2 == 1 }
# [[1,3,5,7,9],[2,3,4,6,8]]

under5 = nums.partition {|x| x < 5 }
# [[1,2,3,4],[5,6,7,8,9]]

squares = nums.partition {|x| Math.sqrt(x).to_i**2 == x }
# [[1,4,9],[2,3,5,6,7,8]]
```

If we wanted to partition into more than two groups, we'd have to write our own simple method for that. I will call this `classify` after the method in the `Set` class.

```
module Enumerable
  def classify(&block)
    hash = {}
    self.each do |x|
      result = block.call(x)
      (hash[result] ||= []) << x
    end
    hash
```

```
    end
  end

nums = [1,2,3,4,5,6,7,8,9]
mod3 = nums.classify {|x| x % 3 }
# { 0=>[3,6,9], 1=>[1,4,7], 2=>[2,5,8] }

words = %w[ area arboreal brick estrous clear donor ether filial
patina ]
vowels = words.classify {|x| x.count("aeiou") }
# {1=>["brick"], 2=>["clear", "donor", "ether"],
#  3=>["area", "estrous", "filial", "patina"], 4=>["arboreal"]}

initials = words.classify {|x| x[0..0] }
# {"a"=>["area", "arboreal"], "b"=>["brick"], "c"=>["clear"],
#  "d"=>["donor"], "p"=>["patina"], "e"=>["estrous", "ether"],
#  "f"=>["filial"]}
```

8.3.4   Iterating by Groups

In every case we've seen so far, we iterate over a list a single item at a time. However, there might be times we want to grab these in pairs or triples or some other quantity.

The iterator each_slice takes a parameter n and iterates over that many elements at a time. (To use this, we need the enumerator library.) If there are not enough items left to form a slice, that slice will be smaller in size.

```
require 'enumerator'

arr = [1,2,3,4,5,6,7,8,9,10]
arr.each_slice(3) do |triple|
  puts triple.join(",")
end

# Output:
# 1,2,3
# 4,5,6
# 7,8,9
# 10
```

There is also the possibility of iterating with a "sliding window" of the given size with the each_cons iterator. (If this name seems unintuitive, it is part of the heritage of Lisp.) In this case, the slices will always be the same size.

```
require 'enumerator'

arr = [1,2,3,4,5,6,7,8,9,10]
arr.each_cons(3) do |triple|
  puts triple.join(",")
end

# Output:
# 1,2,3
# 2,3,4
# 3,4,5
# 4,5,6
# 5,6,7
# 6,7,8
# 7,8,9
# 8,9,10
```

8.3.5   Converting to Arrays or Sets

Every enumerable can in theory be converted trivially to an array (by using to_a). For example, a hash results in a nested array of pairs:

```
hash = {1=>2, 3=>4, 5=>6}
arr  = hash.to_a        #  [[5, 6], [1, 2], [3, 4]]
```

The method entries is an alias for the to_a method.

If the set library has been required, there will also be a to_set method that works as expected. See section 9.1, "Working with Sets," for a discussion of sets.

```
require 'set'
hash = {1=>2, 3=>4, 5=>6}
set = hash.to_set         # #<Set: {[1, 2], [3, 4], [5, 6]}>
```

8.3.6   Using Enumerator Objects

An Enumerator object is basically a wrapper that turns an iterator method into a full-fledged Enumerable. After being wrapped in this way, it naturally has all the usual methods and features available to it.

In this contrived example, class Foo has an iterator but nothing else. In fact, the iterator itself does nothing but four yield operations. To further clarify how this works, the iterator is named every rather than each:

```
require 'enumerator'

class Foo
  def every
    yield 3
    yield 2
    yield 1
    yield 4
  end
end


foo = Foo.new

# Pass in the object and the iterator name...
enum = Enumerable::Enumerator.new(foo,:every)

enum.each {|x| p x }      # Print out the items
array = enum.to_a         # [3,2,1,4]
sorted = enum.sort        # [1,2,3,4]
```

If this conversion seems puzzling to you, it is essentially the same as this:

```
enum = []
foo.every {|x| enum << x }
```

In the previous example, enum is a real array, not just an Enumerator object. So although there are subtle differences, this is another way to convert an object to an Enumerable.

If enumerator is required, Object will have an enum_for method. So the object instantiation in the first example could also be written more compactly:

```
enum = foo.enum_for(:every)
```

We've already seen that we can iterate over groups with each_slice and each_cons. As it turns out, there are special methods enum_slice and enum_cons that will create enumerator objects using these iterators (in effect transforming the iterator name to each). Bear in mind that Enumerable::Enumerator.new and enum_for can both take an optional list of arguments at the end. Here we use that fact to pass in the "window size" to the iterator:

```
array = [5,3,1,2]

discrete = array.enum_slice(2)
# Same as: Enumerable::Enumerator.new(array,:each_slice,2)

overlap  = array.enum_cons(2)
# Same as: Enumerable::Enumerator.new(array,:each_cons,2)

discrete.each {|x| puts x.join(",") }
# Output:
# 5,3
# 1,2

overlap.each {|x| puts x.join(",") }
# Output:
# 5,3
# 3,1
# 1,2
```

8.3.7 Using Generator Objects

The idea of a *generator* is interesting. The normal Ruby iterator is an *internal* iterator; the iterator drives the logic by repeatedly calling the code block.

There is also an *external* iterator, where the code drives the logic, and the iterator provides data items "on demand" rather than on its own precise schedule.

By analogy, think of getline as providing an external iterator onto an IO object. You call it at will, and it provides you data. Contrast that with the internal iterator each_line, which simply passes each line in succession into the code block.

Sometimes internal iterators are not appropriate to the problem at hand. There is always a valid solution, but it may not always be convenient. Sometimes an external iterator is more convenient.

The generator library simply enables the conversion from an internal iterator to an external one. It provides an IO-like interface with methods such as next, rewind, and end?. Here's an example:

```ruby
require 'generator'

array = [7,8,9,10,11,12]

gen = Generator.new(array)

what  = gen.current     # 7
where = gen.index       # 0   (same as pos)

while gen.end? and gen.current < 11
  gen.next
end

puts gen.current        # 11
puts gen.next           # 11
puts gen.index          # 4       (index same as pos)
puts gen.next?          # true    (next? same as end?)
puts gen.next           # 12
puts gen.next?          # false
```

Note how we can "read" through the collection an item at a time at will, using one loop or multiple loops. The end? method detects an end of collection; the generator literally throws an EOFError if you ignore this. An alias for end? is next?.

The index method (alias pos) tells us our index or position in the collection. Naturally it is indexed from zero just like an array or file offset.

The current and next methods *may* be a little unintuitive. Imagine an implicit "get" done at the beginning so that the current item is the same as the next item. Obviously, next advances the pointer, whereas current does not.

Because many collections can only move forward by their nature, the generator behaves the same way. There is no prev method; in theory there could be, but it would not always apply. The rewind method will reset to the beginning if needed.

The real drawback to the generator library is that it is implemented with continuations. In all current versions of Ruby, these are computationally expensive, so large numbers of repetitions might expose the slowness.

8.4 Conclusion

We've taken a good look here at arrays, hashes, and enumerables in general. We've seen some similarities between arrays and hashes—most of which are due to the fact that both mix in `Enumerable`—as well as some differences. We've looked at converting between arrays and hashes, and we've seen some interesting ways of extending their standard behavior.

We've examined common methods of iteration such as `each_slice` and `each_cons`. We've also seen how enumerator and generator objects work.

In Chapter 9, we again look at high-level data structures. But these will be slightly higher level and may not necessarily be provided as part of the Ruby core or standard libraries. These include sets, stacks, queues, trees, and graphs.

CHAPTER 9

More Advanced Data Structures

A graphic representation of data abstracted from the banks of every computer in the human system. Unthinkable complexity. Lines of light ranged in the nonspace of the mind, clusters and constellations of data. Like city lights, receding.

—*William Gibson*

There are, of course, more complex and interesting data structures than arrays, hashes, and their cousins. Some of the ones we'll look at here have direct or indirect support in Ruby; others are "roll-your-own" for the most part. Fortunately, Ruby simplifies the construction of custom data structures.

The mathematical set can be dealt with by means of arrays, as we've already seen. But recent versions of Ruby have a Set class that serves this purpose well.

Stacks and queues are two common data structures in computer science. The first edition of this book paid rather too much attention to them; if you want to know about their uses in general, I have outlined a few of those here. For the rest, there are numerous first-year computer science books.

Trees are useful from the perspective of sorting, searching, and simply representing hierarchical data. We cover binary trees here, with a few notes about multiway trees.

The generalization of a tree is a *graph*. A graph is simply a collection of nodes joined by edges that may have weights or directions associated with them. These are useful in many different areas of problem-solving such as networking and knowledge engineering.

But sets are the easiest topic. We'll look at sets first.

9.1   Working with Sets

We've already seen how certain methods of the Array class let it serve as an acceptable representation of a mathematical set. But for a little more rigor and a little tighter coding, Ruby has a Set class that hides more of the detail from the programmer.

A simple require makes the Set class available:

```
require 'set'
```

This also adds a to_set method to Enumerable so that any enumerable object can be converted to a set.

Creating a new set is easy. The [] method works much as for hashes. The new method takes an optional enumerable object and an optional block. If the block is specified, it is used as a kind of "preprocessor" for the list (like a map operation).

```
s1 = Set[3,4,5]                   # {3,4,5} in math notation
arr = [3,4,5]
s2 = Set.new(arr)                 # same
s3 = Set.new(arr) {|x| x.to_s }   # set of strings, not numbers
```

9.1.1   Simple Set Operations

Union is accomplished by the union method (aliases are | and +):

```
x = Set[1,2,3]
y = Set[3,4,5]

a = x.union(y)    # Set[1,2,3,4,5]
b = x | y         # same
c = x + y         # same
```

Intersection is done by `intersection` or `&`, which is an alias:

```
x = Set[1,2,3]
y = Set[3,4,5]

a = x.intersection(y)    # Set[3]
b = x & y                # same
```

The unary minus is set difference, as we saw in the array discussion (section 8.1.9, "Using Arrays As Mathematical Sets").

```
diff = Set[1,2,3] - Set[3,4,5]    # Set[1,2]
```

Membership is tested with `member?` or `include?` as with arrays. Remember the operands are "backwards" from mathematics.

```
Set[1,2,3].include?(2)    # true
Set[1,2,3].include?(4)    # false
Set[1,2,3].member?(4)     # false
```

We can test for the null or empty set with `empty?` as we would an array. The `clear` method will empty a set regardless of its current contents.

```
s = Set[1,2,3,4,5,6]
s.empty?           # false
s.clear
s.empty?           # true
```

We can test the relationship of two sets: Is the receiver a subset of the other set? Is it a proper subset? Is it a superset?

```
x = Set[3,4,5]
y = Set[3,4]

x.subset?(y)            # false
y.subset?(x)            # true
y.proper_subset?(x)     # true
x.subset?(x)            # true
x.proper_subset?(x)     # false
x.superset?(y)          # true
```

The add method (alias <<) adds a single item to a set, normally returning its own value; add? returns nil if the item was already there. The merge method is useful for adding several items at once. All these potentially modify the receiver, of course. The replace method acts as it does for a string or array.

Finally, two sets can be tested for equality in an intuitive way:

```
Set[3,4,5] == Set[5,4,3]    # true
```

9.1.2   More Advanced Set Operations

It's possible of course to iterate over a set, but (as with hashes) do not expect a sensible ordering because sets are inherently unordered, and Ruby does not guarantee a sequence. (You may even get consistent, unsurprising results at times, but it is unwise to depend on that fact.)

```
s = Set[1,2,3,4,5]
s.each {|x| puts x; break }    # Output: 5
```

The classify is like a multiway partition method; it was the inspiration for our classify method in section 8.3.3, "The partition Method."

```
files = Set.new(Dir["*"])
hash = files.classify do |f|
  if File.size(f) <= 10_000
    :small
  elsif File.size(f) <= 10_000_000
    :medium
  else
    :large
  end
end

big_files = hash[:large]    # big_files is a Set
```

The divide method is similar, but it calls the block to determine "commonality" of items, and it results in a set of sets.

If the arity of the block is 1, it will perform calls of the form block.call(a) == block.call(b) to determine whether a and b belong together in a subset. If the arity is 2, it will perform calls of the form `block.call(a,b)` to determine whether these two items belong together.

For example, the following block (with arity 1) divides the set into two sets, one containing the even numbers and one containing the odd ones:

```
require 'set'
numbers = Set[1,2,3,4,5,6,7,8,9,0]
set = numbers.divide{|i| i % 2}
p set #  #<Set: {#<Set: {5, 1, 7, 3, 9}>,  #<Set: {0, 6, 2, 8, 4}>}>
```

Here's another contrived example. Twin primes are prime numbers that differ by 2 (such as 11 and 13); singleton primes are the others (such as 23). The following example separates these two groups, putting pairs of twin primes in the same set with each other. This example uses a block with arity 2:

```
primes = Set[2, 3, 5, 7, 11, 13, 17, 19, 23, 29, 31]
set = primes.divide{|i,j| (i-j).abs == 2}
# set is: #<Set: {#<Set: {23}>, #<Set: {11, 13}>,
#             #<Set: {17, 19}>,    #<Set: {5, 7, 3}>,
#             #<Set: {2}>, #<Set: {29, 31}>}>
# More compactly: {{23},{11,13},{17,19},{5,7,3},{2},{29,31}}
```

This method is difficult and confusing, in my opinion. I recommend the use of `classify` instead, which I find simple and intuitive.

It's important to realize that the `Set` class doesn't always insist that a parameter or operand has to be another set. (Refer to the discussion of *duck typing* in Chapter 1 if this confuses you.) In fact, most of these methods will take *any enumerable object* as an operand. Consider this a feature.

Other incidental methods can be applied to sets (including all methods in `Enumerable`). I don't choose to cover things here such as `flatten`; for more information, consult http://ruby-doc.org/ or any other reference.

9.2   Working with Stacks and Queues

Stacks and queues are the first entities we have discussed that are not strictly built into Ruby. By this we mean that Ruby does not have `Stack` and `Queue` classes as it does `Array` and `Hash` classes (except for the `Queue` class in `thread.rb`, which we'll mention later).

And yet, in a way, they are built into Ruby after all. In fact, the `Array` class implements all the functionality we need to treat an array as a stack or a queue. We'll see this in detail shortly.

A *stack* is a last-in first-out (LIFO) data structure. The traditional everyday example is a stack of cafeteria trays on its spring-loaded platform; trays are added at the top and also taken away from the top.

A limited set of operations can be performed on a stack. These include *push* and *pop* (to add and remove items) at the very least; usually there is a way to test for an empty stack, and there may be a way to examine the top element without removing it. A stack implementation never provides a way to examine an item in the middle of the stack.

You might ask how an array can implement a stack since array elements may be accessed randomly, and stack elements may not. The answer is simple. A stack sits at a higher level of abstraction than an array; it is a stack only so long as you treat it as one. The moment you access an element illegally, it ceases to be a stack.

Of course, you can easily define a `Stack` class so that elements can only be accessed legally. We will show how this is done.

It is worth noting that many algorithms that use a stack also have elegant recursive solutions. The reason for this becomes clear with a moment's reflection. Function or method calls result in data being pushed onto the system stack, and these data are popped upon return. Thus a recursive algorithm simply trades an explicit user-defined stack for the implicit system-level stack. Which is better? That depends on how you value readability, efficiency, and other considerations.

A *queue* is a first-in first out (FIFO) data structure. It is analogous to a group of people standing in line at (for example) a movie theater. Newcomers go to the end of the line, while those who have waited the longest are the next served. In most areas of programming, queues are probably used less often than stacks.

Queues are useful in more real-time environments where entities are processed as they are presented to the system. They are useful in producer-consumer situations (especially where threads or multitasking are involved). A printer queue is a good example; print jobs are added to one end of the queue, and they "stand in line" until they are removed at the other end.

The two basic queue operations are usually called *enqueue* and *dequeue* in the literature. The corresponding instance methods in the `Array` class are called `unpush` and `shift`, respectively.

Note that `unshift` could serve as a companion for `shift` in implementing a stack, not a queue, because `unshift` adds to the same end from which `shift` removes.

Various combinations of these methods could implement stacks and queues, but we will not concern ourselves with all the variations.

That ends our introductory discussion of stacks and queues. Now let's look at some examples.

9.2.1   Implementing a Stricter Stack

We promised earlier to show how a stack could be made "idiot-proof" against illegal access. We may as well do that now. Here is a simple class that has an internal array and manages access to that array. (There are other ways of doing this—by delegating, for example—but what we show here is simple and works fine.)

```
class Stack

  def initialize
    @store = []
  end

  def push(x)
    @store.push x
  end

  def pop
    @store.pop
  end

  def peek
    @store.last
  end

  def empty?
    @store.empty?
  end

end
```

We have added one more operation that is not defined for arrays; peek simply examines the top of the stack and returns a result without disturbing the stack.

Some of the rest of our examples assume this class definition.

9.2.2   Detecting Unbalanced Punctuation in Expressions

Because of the nature of grouped expressions such as parentheses and brackets, their validity can be checked using a stack. For every level of nesting in the expression, the stack will grow one level higher; when we find closing symbols, we can pop the corresponding symbol off the stack. If the symbol does not correspond as expected, or if there are symbols left on the stack at the end, we know the expression is not well-formed.

```ruby
def paren_match(str)
  stack = Stack.new
  lsym = "{[(<"
  rsym = "}])>"
  str.each_byte do |byte|
    sym = byte.chr
    if lsym.include? sym
      stack.push(sym)
    elsif rsym.include? sym
      top = stack.peek
      if lsym.index(top) != rsym.index(sym)
        return false
      else
        stack.pop
      end
      # Ignore non-grouped characters...
    end
  end
  # Ensure stack is empty...
  return stack.empty?
end

str1 = "(((a+b))*((c-d)-(e*f))"
str2 = "[[(a-(b-c))], [[x,y]]]"

paren_match str1          # false
paren_match str2          # true
```

The nested nature of this problem makes it natural for a stack-oriented solution. A slightly more complex example would be the detection of unbalanced tags in HTML and XML. The tokens are multiple characters rather than single characters, but the structure and logic of the problem remain exactly the same. Some other common stack-oriented problems are conversion of infix expressions to postfix form (or vice versa), evaluation of a postfix expression (as is done in a Java VM or many other interpreters), and in general any problem that has a recursive solution. In the next section, we'll take a short look at the relationship between stacks and recursion.

9.2.3 Understanding Stacks and Recursion

As an example of the isomorphism between stack-oriented algorithms and recursive algorithms, we will take a look at the classic "Tower of Hanoi" problem.

According to legend, there is an ancient temple somewhere in the far east, where monks have the sole task of moving disks from one pole to another while obeying certain rules about the moves they can make. There were originally 64 disks on the first pole; when they finished, the world would come to an end.

As an aside, we like to dispel myths when we can. It seems that in reality, this puzzle originated with the French mathematician Edouard Lucas in 1883 and has no actual basis in eastern culture. What's more, Lucas himself named the puzzle the "Tower of Hanoi" (in the singular).

So if you were worried about the world ending . . . don't worry on that account. And anyway, 64 disks would take $2^{64}-1$ moves. A few minutes with a calculator reveals that those monks would be busy for millions of years.

But on to the rules of the game. (We'll explain this even though every first-year computer science student in the world has already seen the puzzle.) We have a pole with a certain number of disks stacked on it; call this the *source pole*. We want to move all of these to the *destination pole*, using a third (*auxiliary*) pole as an intermediate resting place. The catch is that you can only move one disk at a time, and you cannot ever place a larger disk onto a smaller one.

The following example uses a stack to solve the problem. We use only 3 disks because 64 would occupy a computer for centuries.

```
def towers(list)
  while !list.empty?
    n, src, dst, aux = list.pop
    if n == 1
      puts "Move disk from #{src} to #{dst}"
    else
      list.push [n-1, aux, dst, src]
```

```
        list.push [1, src, dst, aux]
        list.push [n-1, src, aux, dst]
      end
    end
  end
end


list = []
list.push([3, "a", "c", "b"])

towers(list)
```

The output produced here is:

```
Move disk from a to c
Move disk from a to b
Move disk from c to b
Move disk from a to c
Move disk from b to a
Move disk from b to c
Move disk from a to c
```

Of course, the classic solution to this problem is recursive. And as we already pointed out, the close relationship between the two algorithms is no surprise because recursion implies the use of an invisible system-level stack.

```
def towers(n, src, dst, aux)
  if n==1
    puts "Move disk from #{src} to #{dst}"
  else
    towers(n-1, src, aux, dst)
    towers(1, src, dst, aux)
    towers(n-1, aux, dst, src)
  end
end

towers(3, "a", "c", "b")
```

The output produced here is the same. And it may interest you to know that we tried commenting out the output statements and comparing the runtimes of these two methods. Don't tell anyone, but the recursive version is twice as fast.

9.2.4 Implementing a Stricter Queue

We define a queue here in much the same way we defined a stack earlier. If you want to protect yourself from accessing such a data structure in an illegal way, we recommend this practice.

```ruby
class Queue

  def initialize
    @store = []
  end

  def enqueue(x)
    @store << x
  end

  def dequeue
    @store.shift
  end

  def peek
    @store.first
  end

  def length
    @store.length
  end

  def empty?
    @store.empty?
  end

end
```

We should mention that there is a Queue class in the thread library that works very well in threaded code. There is even a SizedQueue variant.

These queues use the method names enq and deq rather than the longer names shown in the preceding example. They also allow the names *push* and *pop*, which seems misleading to me. The data structure is FIFO, not LIFO; that is, it is a true queue and not a stack.

Of course, the `Queue` class in `thread.rb` is thread-safe, which is a good enough reason for it to exist. If you need a thread-safe `Stack` class, I recommend you take the `Queue` class as a starting point. This should be a quick and easy fix.

The first edition of this book had a lengthy example of queue usage here. Like some of the stack examples, it has been omitted from this edition to save space.

9.3   Working with Trees

I think that I shall never see
A poem as lovely as a tree...

— *"Trees,"* [Alfred] Joyce Kilmer

Trees in computer science are a relatively intuitive concept (except that they are usually drawn with the "root" at the top and the "leaves" at the bottom). This is because we are familiar with so many kinds of hierarchical data in everyday life, from the family tree to the corporate organization chart to the directory structures on our hard drives.

The terminology of trees is rich but easy to understand. Any item in a tree is a *node*; the first or topmost node is the *root*. A node may have *descendants* that are below it, and the immediate descendants are called *children*. Conversely, a node may also have a *parent* (only one) and *ancestors*. A node with no child nodes is called a *leaf*. A *subtree* consists of a node and all its descendants. To travel through a tree (for example, to print it out) is called *traversing* the tree.

We will look mostly at binary trees, though in practice a node can have any number of children. We will see how to create a tree, populate it, and traverse it; and we will look at a few real-life tasks that use trees.

We will mention here that in many languages such as C or Pascal, trees would be implemented using true address pointers. But in Ruby (as in Java, for instance), we don't use pointers; object references work just as well or better.

9.3.1   Implementing a Binary Tree

There is more than one way to implement a binary tree in Ruby. For example, we could use an array to store the values. Here we use a more traditional approach, coding much as we would in C, except that pointers are replaced with object references.

What is required to describe a binary tree? Well, each node needs an attribute of some kind for storing a piece of data. Each node also needs a pair of attributes for referring to the left and right subtrees under that node.

We also need a way to insert into the tree and a way of getting information out of the tree. A pair of methods will serve these purposes.

The first tree we'll look at implements these methods in a slightly unorthodox way. Then we will expand on the Tree class in later examples.

A tree is in a sense defined by its insertion algorithm and by how it is traversed. In this first example (see Listing 9.1), we define an insert method that inserts in a *breadth-first* fashion—that is, top to bottom and left to right. This guarantees that the tree grows in depth relatively slowly and that the tree is always balanced. Corresponding to the *insert* method, the traverse iterator will iterate over the tree in the same breadth-first order.

Listing 9.1   Breadth-First Insertion and Traversal in a Tree

```
class Tree

attr_accessor :left
attr_accessor :right
attr_accessor :data

def initialize(x=nil)
  @left = nil
  @right = nil
  @data = x
end

def insert(x)
  list = []
  if @data == nil
    @data = x
  elsif @left == nil
    @left = Tree.new(x)
  elsif @right == nil
    @right = Tree.new(x)
  else
    list << @left
    list << @right
    loop do
      node = list.shift
      if node.left == nil
        node.insert(x)
        break
```

Continues

```
      else
        list << node.left
      end
      if node.right == nil
        node.insert(x)
        break
      else
        list << node.right
      end
    end
  end
end

def traverse()
  list = []
  yield @data
  list << @left if @left != nil
  list << @right if @right != nil
  loop do
    break if list.empty?
    node = list.shift
    yield node.data
    list << node.left if node.left != nil
    list << node.right if node.right != nil
  enä
end

end


items = [1, 2, 3, 4, 5, 6, 7]

tree = Tree.new

items.each {|x| tree.insert(x)}

tree.traverse {|x| print "#{x} "}
print "\n"

# Prints "1 2 3 4 5 6 7 "
```

This kind of tree, as defined by its insertion and traversal algorithms, is not especially interesting. It does serve as an introduction and something on which we can build.

9.3.2   Sorting Using a Binary Tree

For random data, a binary tree is a good way to sort. (Although in the case of already sorted data, it degenerates into a simple linked list.) The reason, of course, is that with each comparison, we are eliminating half the remaining alternatives as to where we should place a new node.

Although it might be fairly rare to do this nowadays, it can't hurt to know how to do it. The code in Listing 9.2 builds on the previous example.

Listing 9.2 Sorting with a Binary Tree

```
class Tree

  # Assumes definitions from
  # previous example...

  def insert(x)
    if @data == nil
      @data = x
    elsif x <= @data
      if @left == nil
        @left = Tree.new x
      else
        @left.insert x
      end
    else
      if @right == nil
        @right = Tree.new x
      else
        @right.insert x
      end
    end
  end

  def inorder()
    @left.inorder {|y| yield y} if @left != nil
    yield @data
    @right.inorder {|y| yield y} if @right != nil
  end

  def preorder()
    yield @data
    @left.preorder {|y| yield y} if @left != nil
    @right.preorder {|y| yield y} if @right != nil
  end

  def postorder()
    @left.postorder {|y| yield y} if @left != nil
    @right.postorder {|y| yield y} if @right != nil
    yield @data
  end
```

Continues

```
end

items = [50, 20, 80, 10, 30, 70, 90, 5, 14,
         28, 41, 66, 75, 88, 96]

tree = Tree.new

items.each {|x| tree.insert(x)}

tree.inorder {|x| print x, " "}
print "\n"
tree.preorder {|x| print x, " "}
print "\n"
tree.postorder {|x| print x, " "}
print "\n"

# Output:
# 5 10 14 20 28 30 41 50 66 70 75 80 88 90 96
# 50 20 10 5 14 30 28 41 80 70 66 75 90 88 96
# 5 14 10 28 41 30 20 66 75 70 88 96 90 80 50          print "\n"
```

9.3.3   Using a Binary Tree As a Lookup Table

Suppose we have a tree already sorted. Traditionally this has made a good lookup table; for example, a balanced tree of a million items would take no more than 20 comparisons (the depth of the tree or log base 2 of the number of nodes) to find a specific node. For this to be useful, we assume that the data for each node is not just a single value but has a key value and other information associated with it.

In most, if not all situations, a hash or even an external database table will be preferable. But we present this code to you anyhow:

```
class Tree

  # Assumes definitions
  # from previous example...

  def search(x)
    if self.data == x
      return self
    elsif x < self.data
      return left ? left.search(x) : nil
    else
      return right ? right.search(x) : nil
```

```
      end
    end

  end

  keys = [50, 20, 80, 10, 30, 70, 90, 5, 14,
          28, 41, 66, 75, 88, 96]

  tree = Tree.new

  keys.each {|x| tree.insert(x)}

  s1 = tree.search(75)    # Returns a reference to the node
                          # containing 75...

  s2 = tree.search(100)   # Returns nil (not found)
```

9.3.4 Converting a Tree to a String or Array

The same old tricks that allow us to traverse a tree will allow us to convert it to a string
or array if we want. Here we assume an *inorder* traversal, though any other kind could
be used:

```
  class Tree

    # Assumes definitions from
    # previous example...

    def to_s
      "[" +
      if left then left.to_s + "," else "" end +
      data.inspect +
      if right then "," + right.to_s else "" end + "]"
    end

    def to_a
      temp = []
      temp += left.to_a if left
      temp << data
      temp += right.to_a if right
      temp
```

```
    end

  end

  items = %w[bongo grimace monoid jewel plover nexus synergy]

  tree = Tree.new
  items.each {|x| tree.insert x}

  str = tree.to_a * ","
  # str is now "bongo,grimace,jewel,monoid,nexus,plover,synergy"
  arr = tree.to_a
  # arr is now:
  # ["bongo",["grimace",[["jewel"],"monoid",[["nexus"],"plover",
  #   ["synergy"]]]]]
```

Note that the resulting array is as deeply nested as the depth of the tree from which it came. You can, of course, use flatten to produce a non-nested array.

9.4   Working with Graphs

A *graph* is a collection of nodes that interconnect with each other arbitrarily. (A tree is a special case of a graph.) We will not delve deeply into the subject of graphs because the theory and terminology can have a steep learning curve. Before long, we would find ourselves wandering out of the field of computer science entirely and into the province of mathematicians.

Yet graphs do have many practical applications. Consider any ordinary highway map with highways connecting cities, or consider a circuit diagram. These are both best represented as graphs. A computer network can be thought of in terms of graph theory, whether it is a LAN of a dozen systems or the Internet itself with its countless millions of nodes.

When we say *graph*, we usually mean an *undirected graph*. In naive terms, this is a graph in which the connecting lines don't have arrows; two nodes are either connected or they are not. By contrast, a *directed graph* or *digraph* can have "one-way streets"; just because node *x* is connected to node *y* doesn't mean that the reverse is true. (A node is also commonly called a *vertex*.) Finally, a *weighted graph* has connections (or edges) that have weights associated with them; these weights may express, for instance, the "distance" between two nodes. We won't go beyond these basic kinds of graphs; the interested reader can refer to numerous references in computer science and mathematics.

In Ruby, as in most languages, a graph can be represented in multiple ways; for example, a true network of interconnected objects or a matrix storing the set of edges in the graph. We will look at both of these as we show a few practical examples of manipulating graphs.

9.4.1 Implementing a Graph as an Adjacency Matrix

The example here builds on two previous examples. In Listing 9.3 we implement an undirected graph as an adjacency matrix, using the ZArray class (see section 8.1.26, "Establishing a Default Value for New Array Elements") to make sure that new elements are zero and inheriting from the TriMatrix (see section 8.1.7, "Using Specialized Indexing Functions") to get a *lower triangular matrix* form.

Listing 9.3 Adjacency Matrix

```ruby
class LowerMatrix < TriMatrix

  def initialize
    @store = ZArray.new
  end

end


class Graph

  def initialize(*edges)
    @store = LowerMatrix.new
    @max = 0
    for e in edges
      e[0], e[1] = e[1], e[0] if e[1] > e[0]
      @store[e[0],e[1]] = 1
      @max = [@max, e[0], e[1]].max
    end
  end

  def [](x,y)
    if x > y
      @store[x,y]
    elsif x < y
      @store[y,x]
    else
```

Continues

```
      0
    end
  end

  def []=(x,y,v)
    if x > y
      @store[x,y]=v
    elsif x < y
      @store[y,x]=v
    else
      0
    end
  end

  def edge? x,y
    x,y = y,x if x < y
    @store[x,y]==1
  end

  def add x,y
    @store[x,y] = 1
  end

  def remove x,y
    x,y = y,x if x < y
    @store[x,y] = 0
    if (degree @max) == 0
      @max -= 1
    end
  end

  def vmax
    @max
  end

  def degree x
    sum = 0
    0.upto @max do |i|
      sum += self[x,i]
    end
    sum
  end

  def each_vertex
    (0..@max).each {|v| yield v}
  end

  def each_edge
    for v0 in 0..@max
      for v1 in 0..v0-1
```

```
        yield v0,v1 if self[v0,v1]==1
      end
    end
  end

end


mygraph = Graph.new([1,0],[0,3],[2,1],[3,1],[3,2])

# Print the degrees of all the vertices: 2 3 2 3
mygraph.each_vertex {|v| puts mygraph.degree(v)}

# Print the list of edges
mygraph.each_edge do |a,b|
  puts "(#{a},#{b})"
end

# Remove a single edge
mygraph.remove 1,3

# Print the degrees of all the vertices: 2 2 2 2
mygraph.each_vertex {|v| p mygraph.degree v}
```

Note that in the kind of graph we are implementing here, a node cannot be connected to itself, and two nodes can be connected by only one edge.

We provide a way to specify edges initially by passing pairs into the constructor. We also provide a way to add and remove edges and detect the presence of edges. The vmax method returns the highest-numbered vertex in the graph. The degree method finds the *degree* of the specified vertex—that is, the number of edges that connect to it.

Finally, we provide two iterators, each_vertex and each_edge. These iterate over edges and vertices, respectively.

9.4.2 Determining Whether a Graph Is Fully Connected

Not all graphs are fully connected. That is, sometimes "you can't get there from here"; there may be vertices that are unreachable from other vertices no matter what path you try. Connectivity is an important property of a graph to be able to assess, telling whether the graph is "of one piece." If it is, every node is ultimately reachable from every other node.

We won't explain the algorithm; the interested reader can refer to any discrete math book. But we offer the Ruby method in Listing 9.4.

Listing 9.4   Determining Whether a Graph is Fully Connected

```ruby
class Graph

  def connected?
    x = vmax
    k = [x]
    l = [x]
    for i in 0..@max
      l << i if self[x,i]==1
    end
    while !k.empty?
      y = k.shift
      # Now find all edges (y,z)
      self.each_edge do |a,b|
        if a==y || b==y
          z = a==y ? b : a
          if !l.include? z
            l << z
            k << z
          end
        end
      end
    end
    if l.size < @max
      false
    else
      true
    end
  end

end


mygraph = Graph.new([0,1], [1,2], [2,3], [3,0], [1,3])

puts mygraph.connected?      # true

puts mygraph.euler_path?     # true

mygraph.remove 1,2
mygraph.remove 0,3
mygraph.remove 1,3

puts mygraph.connected?      # false

puts mygraph.euler_path?     # false
```

I've referenced a method here (euler_path?) that you haven't seen yet. It is defined in section 9.4.4, "Determining Whether a Graph Has an Euler Path."

A refinement of this algorithm could be used to determine the set of all connected components (or *cliques*) in a graph that is not overall fully connected. I won't cover this here.

9.4.3   Determining Whether a Graph Has an Euler Circuit

There is no branch of mathematics, however abstract, which may not some day be applied to phenomena of the real world.

— *Nikolai Lobachevsky*

Sometimes we want to know whether a graph has an *Euler circuit*. This term comes from the mathematician Leonhard Euler who essentially founded the field of topology by dealing with a particular instance of this question. (A graph of this nature is sometimes called a *unicursive* graph since it can be drawn without lifting the pen from the paper or retracing.)

In the German town of Königsberg, there was an island in the middle of the river (near where the river split into two parts). Seven bridges crisscrossed at various places between opposite shores and the island. The townspeople wondered whether it was possible to make a walking tour of the city in such a way that you would cross each bridge exactly once and return to your starting place. In 1735, Euler proved that it was impossible. This, then, is not just a classic problem, but the *original* graph theory problem.

And, as with many things in life, when you discover the answer, it is easy. It turns out that for a graph to have an Euler circuit, it must possess only vertices with *even degree*. Here we add a little method to check that property:

```
class Graph

  def euler_circuit?
    return false if !connected?
    for i in 0..@max
      return false if degree(i) % 2 != 0
    end
    true
  end
```

```
  end


mygraph = Graph.new([1,0],[0,3],[2,1],[3,1],[3,2])

flag1 =  mygraph.euler_circuit?      # false

mygraph.remove 1,3

flag2 =  mygraph.euler_circuit?      # true
```

9.4.4   Determining Whether a Graph Has an Euler Path

An *Euler path* is not quite the same as an Euler circuit. The word *circuit* implies that you must return to your starting point; with a *path*, we are really only concerned with visiting each edge exactly once. The following code fragment illustrates the difference:

```
class Graph

  def euler_path?
    return false if !connected?
    odd=0
    each_vertex do |x|
      if degree(x) % 2 == 1
        odd += 1
      end
    end
    odd <= 2
  end

end


mygraph = Graph.new([0,1],[1,2],[1,3],[2,3],[3,0])

flag1 =  mygraph.euler_circuit?      # false
flag2 =  mygraph.euler_path?         # true
```

9.4.5 Graph Tools in Ruby

There are a few tools known to exist in the Ruby community. Most of these have some limited functionality for dealing with directed and undirected graphs. They can be found with a search of RAA (http://raa.ruby-lang.org) and Rubyforge (http://rubyforge.org). Most of them have names such as RubyGraph, RGraph, and GraphR, and they are fairly immature.

If you are interested in the excellent GraphViz package, which renders complex graphs both as images and as printable Postscript, there are at least two workable interfaces to this software. There is even a `GnomeGraphwidget`, which according to the documentation "can be used by a Ruby Gnome application to generate, visualize and interact with graphs." We haven't looked at it, however; be warned it is pre-alpha.

In short, there may be a need for tools of this sort. If so, I urge you to write your own, or better, to join an existing project. If working with graphs becomes easy enough, it may be one of those techniques we wonder how we did without.

9.5 Conclusion

We've taken a look here at the `Set` class in Ruby as well as a few examples of "home-grown" data structures. Where more advanced data structures are concerned, we've seen examples of inheriting from an existing class and examples of limited delegation by encapsulating an instance of another class. We've seen ways to store data creatively, ways to use various data structures, and how to create iterators for these classes.

We've looked at stacks and queues in general, and how they might be used in problem solving. We've taken a cursory look at trees and graphs.

In the next chapter, we are again looking at the manipulation of data. But where we have so far been concerned with objects stored in memory, we will now be looking at secondary storage—working with files (and I/O in general), databases, and persistent objects.

CHAPTER 10

I/O and Data Storage

On a clean disk you can seek forever.

—Thomas B. Steel, Jr.

Computers are good at computing. This tautology is more profound than it appears. If we only had to sit and chew up the CPU cycles and reference RAM as needed, life would be easy.

A computer that only sits and thinks to itself is of little use, however. Sooner or later we have to get information into it and out of it, and that is where life becomes more difficult.

Several things make I/O complicated. First, input and output are rather different things, but we naturally lump them together. Second, the varieties of I/O operations (and their usages) are as diverse as species of insects.

History has seen such devices as drums, paper tapes, magnetic tapes, punched cards, and teletypes. Some operated with a mechanical component; others were purely electromagnetic. Some were read-only; others were write-only or read-write. Some writable media were erasable, and others were not. Some devices were inherently sequential; others were random access. Some media were permanent; others were transient or volatile. Some devices depended on human intervention; others did not. Some were character oriented; others were block oriented. Some block devices were fixed length; others were variable length. Some devices were polled; others were interrupt-driven. Interrupts could be implemented in hardware or software or both. We have both buffered and non-buffered I/O. We have seen memory-mapped I/O and channel-oriented I/O, and with the advent of operating systems such as UNIX, we have seen I/O devices mapped to files in a filesystem. We have done I/O in machine language, in assembly language, and in high-level languages. Some languages have the I/O capabilities firmly hard-wired in place; others leave it out of the language specification completely. We have done I/O with and without suitable device drivers or layers of abstraction.

If this seems like a confusing mess, that is because it is. Part of the complexity is inherent in the concept of input/output, part of it is the result of design trade-offs, and part of it is the result of legacies or traditions in computer science and the quirks of various languages and operating systems.

Ruby's I/O is complex because I/O in general is complex. But we have tried here to make it understandable and present a good overview of how and when to use various techniques.

The core of all Ruby I/O is the IO class, which defines behavior for every kind of input/output operation. Closely allied to IO (and inheriting from it) is the File class. There is a nested class within File called Stat, which encapsulates various details about a file that we might want to examine (such as its permissions and time stamps). The methods stat and lstat return objects of type File::Stat.

The module FileTest also has methods that allow us to test much the same set of properties. This is mixed into the File class and can also be used on its own.

Finally, there are I/O methods in the Kernel module, which is mixed into Object (the ancestor of all objects, including classes). These are the simple I/O routines that we have used all along without worrying about what their receiver was. These naturally default to standard input and standard output.

The beginner may find these classes to be a confused jumble of overlapping functionality. The good news is that you need only use small pieces of this framework at any given time.

On a higher level, Ruby offers features to make object persistence possible. The Marshal enables simple serialization of objects, and the more sophisticated PStore library is based on Marshal. We include the DBM library in the same section with these, although it is only string-based.

On the highest level of all, data access can be performed by interfacing to a separate database management system such as MySQL or Oracle. This issue is complex enough that one or more books could be devoted to these. We will provide only a brief overview to get the programmer started. In some cases, we provide only a pointer to an online archive.

10.1   Working with Files and Directories

When we say *file*, we usually mean a disk file, though not always. We do use the concept of a file as a meaningful abstraction in Ruby as in other programming languages. When we say *directory*, we mean a directory in the normal Windows or UNIX sense.

The File class is closely related to the IO class from which it inherits. The Dir class is not so closely related, but we chose to discuss files and directories together because they are still conceptually related.

10.1.1   Opening and Closing Files

The class method File.new, which instantiates a File object also opens that file. The first parameter is naturally the filename.

The optional second parameter is called the *mode string*, telling how to open the file (whether for reading, writing, and so on). (The mode string has nothing to do with the mode as in permissions.) This defaults to "r" for reading. The following code demonstrates opening files for reading and writing.

```
file1 = File.new("one")        # Open for reading
file2 = File.new("two", "w")   # Open for writing
```

Another form for new takes three parameters. In this case, the second parameter specifies the original permissions for the file (usually as an octal constant), and the third is a set of flags ORed together. The flags are constants such as File::CREAT (create the file when it is opened if it doesn't already exist) and File::RDONLY (open for reading only). This form will rarely be used.

```
file = File.new("three", 0755, File::CREAT|File::WRONLY)
```

As a courtesy to the operating system and the runtime environment, always close a file that you open. In the case of a file open for writing, this is more than mere politeness and can actually prevent lost data. Not surprisingly, the `close` method serves this purpose:

```
out = File.new("captains.log", "w")
# Process as needed...
out.close
```

There is also an open method. In its simplest form, it is merely a synonym for new as we see here:

```
trans = File.open("transactions","w")
```

But open can also take a block; this is the form that is more interesting. When a block is specified, the open file is passed in as a parameter to the block. The file remains open throughout the scope of the block and is closed automatically at the end. For example:

```
File.open("somefile","w") do |file|
   file.puts "Line 1"
   file.puts "Line 2"
   file.puts "Third and final line"
end
# The file is now closed
```

This is obviously an elegant way of ensuring that a file is closed when we've finished with it. In addition, the code that handles the file is grouped visually into a unit.

10.1.2   Updating a File

Suppose that we want to open a file for reading and writing. This is done simply by adding a plus sign (+) in the file mode when we open the file (see section 10.1.1, "Opening and Closing Files"):

```
f1 = File.new("file1", "r+")
# Read/write, starting at beginning of file.

f2 = File.new("file2", "w+")
# Read/write; truncate existing file or create a new one.

f3 = File.new("file3", "a+")
```

```
# Read/write; start at end of existing file or create a
# new one.
```

10.1.3 Appending to a File

Suppose that we want to append information onto an existing file. This is done simply by using "a" in the file mode when we open the file (see section 10.1.1, "Opening and Closing Files"):

```
logfile = File.open("captains_log", "a")
# Add a line at the end, then close.
logfile.puts "Stardate 47824.1: Our show has been canceled."
logfile.close
```

10.1.4 Random Access to Files

If you want to read a file randomly rather than sequentially, you can use the method seek, which File inherits from IO. The simplest usage is to seek to a specific byte position. The position is relative to the beginning of the file, where the first byte is numbered 0.

```
# myfile contains only: abcdefghi
file = File.new("myfile")
file.seek(5)
str = file.gets              # "fghi"
```

If you took care to ensure that each line was a fixed length, you could seek to a specific line, as in the following example:

```
# Assume 20 bytes per line.
# Line N starts at byte (N-1)*20
file = File.new("fixedlines")
file.seek(5*20)              # Sixth line!
# Elegance is left as an exercise.
```

If you want to do a relative seek, you can use a second parameter. The constant IO::SEEK_CUR assumes that the offset is relative to the current position (which may be negative).

```
file = File.new("somefile")
file.seek(55)                   # Position is 55
file.seek(-22, IO::SEEK_CUR)    # Position is 33
file.seek(47, IO::SEEK_CUR)     # Position is 80
```

You can also seek relative to the end of the file. Only a negative offset makes sense here:

```
file.seek(-20, IO::SEEK_END)   # twenty bytes from eof
```

There is also a third constant IO::SEEK_SET, but it is the default value (seek relative to beginning of file).

The method tell reports the file position; pos is an alias:

```
file.seek(20)
pos1 = file.tell            # 20
file.seek(50, IO::SEEK_CUR)
pos2 = file.pos             # 70
```

The rewind method can also be used to reposition the file pointer at the beginning. This terminology comes from the use of magnetic tapes.

If you are performing random access on a file, you may want to open it for update (reading and writing). Updating a file is done by specifying a plus sign (+) in the mode string. See section 10.1.2, "Updating a File."

10.1.5 Working with Binary Files

In days gone by, C programmers used the "b" character appended to the mode string to open a file as a binary. (Contrary to popular belief, this *was* true of UNIX in earlier versions.) This character is still allowed for compatibility in most cases; but nowadays binary files are not so tricky as they used to be. A Ruby string can easily hold binary data, and a file need not be read in any special way.

The exception is the Windows family of operating systems, where this distinction still survives. The chief difference between binary and text files on these platforms is that in binary mode, the end-of-line is not translated into a single linefeed but is kept as a carriage-return/linefeed pair.

The other important difference is that control-Z is treated as end-of-file if the file is not opened in binary mode, as shown here:

```
# Create a file (in binary mode)
File.open("myfile","wb") {|f| f.syswrite("12345\0326789\r") }
# Above note the embedded octal 032 (^Z)

# Read it as binary
str = nil
File.open("myfile","rb") {|f| str = f.sysread(15) }
puts str.size             # 11

# Read it as text
str = nil
File.open("myfile","r") {|f| str = f.sysread(15) }
puts str.size             # 5
```

The following code fragment shows that carriage returns remain untranslated in binary mode on Windows:

```
# Input file contains a single line: Line 1.
file = File.open("data")
line = file.readline               # "Line 1.\n"
puts "#{line.size} characters."    # 8 characters
file.close

file = File.open("data","rb")
line = file.readline               # "Line 1.\r\n"
puts "#{line.size} characters."    # 9 characters
file.close
```

Note that the binmode method, shown in the following code example, can switch a stream to binary mode. Once switched, it cannot be switched back.

```
file = File.open("data")
file.binmode
line = file.readline               # "Line 1.\r\n"
puts "#{line.size} characters."    # 9 characters
file.close
```

If you really want to do low-level input/output, you can use the sysread and syswrite methods. The former takes a number of bytes as a parameter; the latter takes a string and returns the actual number of bytes written. (You should *not* use other methods to read from the same stream; the results may be unpredictable.)

```
input = File.new("infile")
output = File.new("outfile")
instr = input.sysread(10);
bytes = output.syswrite("This is a test.")
```

Note that `sysread` raises `EOFError` if it is invoked at end of file (though not if it encounters end of file during a successful read). Either of these methods will raise `SystemCallError` when an error occurs.

Note that the `Array` method `pack` and the `String` method `unpack` can be useful in dealing with binary data.

10.1.6 Locking Files

On operating systems where it is supported, the `flock` method of `File` will lock or unlock a file. The second parameter is one of these constants: `File::LOCK_EX`, `File::LOCK_NB`, `File::LOCK_SH`, `File::LOCK_UN`, or a logical-OR of two or more of these. Note, of course, that many of these combinations will be nonsensical; the non-blocking flag is the one most frequently used.

```
file = File.new("somefile")

file.flock(File::LOCK_EX)   # Lock exclusively; no other process
                            # may use this file.
file.flock(File::LOCK_UN)   # Now unlock it.

file.flock(File::LOCK_SH)   # Lock file with a shared lock (other
                            # processes may do the same).
file.flock(File::LOCK_UN)   # Now unlock it.

locked = file.flock(File::LOCK_EX | File::LOCK_NB)
# Try to lock the file, but don't block if we can't; in that case,
# locked will be false.
```

This function is not available on the Windows family of operating systems.

10.1.7 Performing Simple I/O

You are already familiar with some of the I/O routines in the `Kernel` module; these are the ones we have called all along without specifying a receiver for the methods. Calls such as `gets` and `puts` originate here; others are `print`, `printf`, and `p` (which calls the object's `inspect` method to display it in some way readable to humans).

There are some others that we should mention for completeness, though. The `putc` method outputs a single character. (The corresponding method `getc` is *not* implemented in `Kernel` for technical reasons; it can be found in any `IO` object, however.) If a `String` is specified, the first character of the string will be taken.

```
putc(?\n)    # Output a newline
putc("X")    # Output the letter X
```

A reasonable question is where does output go when we use these methods without a receiver. Well, to begin with, three constants are defined in the Ruby environment corresponding to the three standard I/O streams we are accustomed to on UNIX. These are `STDIN`, `STDOUT`, and `STDERR`. All are global constants of the type `IO`.

There is also a global variable called `$stdout`, which is the destination of all the output coming from `Kernel` methods. This is initialized (indirectly) to the value of `STDOUT` so that this output all gets written to standard output as we expect. The variable `$stdout` can be reassigned to refer to some other `IO` object at any time.

```
diskfile = File.new("foofile","w")
puts "Hello..."      # prints to stdout
$stdout = diskfile
puts "Goodbye!"      # prints to "foofile"
diskfile.close
$stdout = STDOUT     # reassign to default
puts "That's all."   # prints to stdout
```

Beside `gets`, `Kernel` also has methods `readline` and `readlines` for input. The former is equivalent to `gets` except that it raises `EOFError` at the end of a file instead of just returning a `nil` value. The latter is equivalent to the `IO.readlines` method (that is, it reads an entire file into memory).

Where does input come from? Well, there is also the standard input stream `$stdin`, which defaults to `STDIN`. In the same way, there is a standard error stream (`$stderr` defaulting to `STDERR`).

There is also an interesting global object called `ARGF`, which represents the concatenation of all the files named on the command line. It is not really a `File` object, though it resembles one. Default input is connected to this object in the event files are named on the command line.

```
# Read all files, then output again
puts ARGF.read
# Or more memory-efficient:
while ! ARGF.eof?
  puts ARGF.readline
end
# Example:  ruby cat.rb file1 file2 file3
```

Reading from standard input (`STDIN`) will bypass the Kernel methods. That way you can bypass ARGF (or not), as shown here:

```
# Read a line from standard input
str1 =  STDIN.gets
# Read a line from ARGF
str2 = ARGF.gets
# Now read again from standard input
str3 =  STDIN.gets
```

10.1.8   Performing Buffered and Unbuffered I/O

Ruby does its own internal buffering in some cases. Consider this fragment:

```
print "Hello... "
sleep 10
print "Goodbye!\n"
```

If you run this, you will notice that the hello and goodbye messages both appear at the same time, *after* the sleep. The first output is not terminated by a newline.

This can be fixed by calling `flush` to flush the output buffer. In this case we use the stream `$defout` (the default stream for all `Kernel` method output) as the receiver. It then behaves as we probably wanted, with the first message appearing earlier than the second one.

```
print "Hello... "
STDOUT.flush
sleep 10
print "Goodbye!\n"
```

This buffering can be turned off (or on) with the `sync=` method; the `sync` method lets us know the status.

```
buf_flag = $defout.sync      # true
STDOUT.sync = false
buf_flag = STDOUT.sync       # false
```

There is also at least one lower level of buffering going on behind the scenes. Just as the `getc` method returns a character and moves the file or stream pointer, so `ungetc` will push a character back onto the stream.

```
ch = mystream.getc      # ?A
mystream.ungetc(?C)
ch = mystream.getc      # ?C
```

You should be aware of three things. First, the buffering we speak of here is unrelated to the buffering mentioned earlier in this section; in other words, `sync=false` won't turn it off. Second, only one character can be pushed back; if you attempt more than one, only the last one will actually be pushed back onto the input stream. Finally, the `ungetc` method will not work for inherently unbuffered read operations (such as `sysread`).

10.1.9   Manipulating File Ownership and Permissions

The issue of file ownership and permissions is highly platform dependent. Typically UNIX provides a superset of the functionality; for other platforms many features may be unimplemented.

To determine the owner and group of a file (which are integers), `File::Stat` has a pair of instance methods `uid` and `gid` as shown here:

```
data = File.stat("somefile")
owner_id = data.uid
group_id = data.gid
```

Class `File::Stat` has an instance method `mode`, which will return the mode (or permissions) of the file.

```
perms = File.stat("somefile").mode
```

`File` has class and instance methods named `chown` to change the owner and group IDs of a file. The class method accepts an arbitrary number of filenames. Where an ID is not to be changed, `nil` or `-1` can be used.

```
uid = 201
gid = 10
File.chown(uid, gid, "alpha", "beta")
f1 = File.new("delta")
f1.chown(uid, gid)
f2 = File.new("gamma")
f2.chown(nil, gid)        # Keep original owner id
```

Likewise, the permissions can be changed by `chmod` (also implemented both as class and instance methods). The permissions are traditionally represented in octal, though they need not be.

```
File.chmod(0644, "epsilon", "theta")
f = File.new("eta")
f.chmod(0444)
```

A process always runs under the identity of some user (possibly root); as such, there is a user id associated with it. (Here we are talking about the *effective* user ID.) We frequently need to know whether that user has permission to read, write, or execute a given file. There are instance methods in `File::Stat` to make this determination.

```
info = File.stat("/tmp/secrets")
rflag = info.readable?
wflag = info.writable?
xflag = info.executable?
```

Sometimes we need to distinguish between the effective user ID and the real user ID. The appropriate instance methods are `readable_real?`, `writable_real?`, and `executable_real?`, respectively.

```
info = File.stat("/tmp/secrets")
rflag2 = info.readable_real?
wflag2 = info.writable_real?
xflag2 = info.executable_real?
```

We can test the ownership of the file as compared with the effective user ID (and group ID) of the current process. The class File::Stat has instance methods owned? and grpowned? to accomplish this.

Note that many of these methods can also be found in the module FileTest:

```
rflag = FileTest::readable?("pentagon_files")
# Other methods are: writable? executable? readable_real?
writable_real?
# executable_real? owned? grpowned?
# Not found here: uid gid mode
```

The umask associated with a process determines the initial permissions of new files created. The standard mode 0777 is logically ANDed with the negation of the umask so that the bits set in the umask are "masked" or cleared. If you prefer, you can think of this as a simple subtraction (without borrow). Thus a umask of 022 results in files being created with a mode of 0755.

The umask can be retrieved or set with the class method umask of class File. If a parameter is specified, the umask will be set to that value (and the previous value will be returned).

```
File.umask(0237)             # Set the umask
current_umask = File.umask   # 0237
```

Some file mode bits (such as the *sticky bit*) are not strictly related to permissions. For a discussion of these, see section 10.1.12, "Checking Special File Characteristics."

10.1.10 Retrieving and Setting Time Stamp Information

Each disk file has multiple time stamps associated with it (though there are some variations between operating systems). The three time stamps that Ruby understands are the modification time (the last time the file contents were changed), the access time (the last time the file was read), and the change time (the last time the file's directory information was changed).

These three pieces of information can be accessed in three different ways. Each of these fortunately gives the same results.

The `File` class methods `mtime`, `atime`, and `ctime` return the times without the file being opened or any `File` object being instantiated.

```
t1 = File.mtime("somefile")
# Thu Jan 04 09:03:10 GMT-6:00 2001
t2 = File.atime("somefile")
# Tue Jan 09 10:03:34 GMT-6:00 2001
t3 = File.ctime("somefile")
# Sun Nov 26 23:48:32 GMT-6:00 2000
```

If there happens to be a `File` instance already created, the instance method can be used.

```
myfile = File.new("somefile")
t1 = myfile.mtime
t2 = myfile.atime
t3 = myfile.ctime
```

And if there happens to be a `File::Stat` instance already created, it has instance methods to do the same thing.

```
myfile = File.new("somefile")
info = myfile.stat
t1 = info.mtime
t2 = info.atime
t3 = info.ctime
```

Note that a `File::Stat` is returned by `File`'s class (or instance) method `stat`. The class method `lstat` (or the instance method of the same name) is identical except that it reports on the status of the link itself instead of following the link to the actual file. In the case of links to links, all links are followed but the last one.

File access and modification times may be changed using the `utime` method. It will change the times on one or more files specified. The times may be given either as `Time` objects or a number of seconds since the epoch.

```
today = Time.now
yesterday = today - 86400
File.utime(today, today, "alpha")
File.utime(today, yesterday, "beta", "gamma")
```

Because both times are changed together, if you want to leave one of them unchanged, you have to save it off first.

```
mtime = File.mtime("delta")
File.utime(Time.now, mtime, "delta")
```

10.1.11   Checking File Existence and Size

One fundamental question we sometimes want to know is whether a file of a given name exists. The exist? method in the FileTest module provides a way to find out:

```
flag = FileTest::exist?("LochNessMonster")
flag = FileTest::exists?("UFO")
# exists? is a synonym for exist?
```

Intuitively, such a method could not be a class instance of File because by the time the object is instantiated the file has been opened; File conceivably could have a class method exist?, but in fact it does not.

Related to the question of a file's existence is the question of whether it has any contents. After all, a file may exist but have zero length (which is the next best thing to not existing).

If we are only interested in this yes/no question, File::Stat has two instance methods that are useful. The method zero? returns true if the file is zero length and false otherwise:

```
flag = File.new("somefile").stat.zero?
```

Conversely, the method size? returns either the size of the file in bytes if it is nonzero length, or the value nil if it is zero length. It may not be immediately obvious why nil is returned rather than 0. The answer is that the method is primarily intended for use as a predicate, and 0 is true in Ruby, whereas nil tests as false.

```
if File.new("myfile").stat.size?
  puts "The file has contents."
else
  puts "The file is empty."
end
```

Methods zero? and size? also appear in the FileTest module:

```
flag1 = FileTest::zero?("file1")
flag2 = FileTest::size?("file2")
```

This leads naturally to the question "How big is this file?" We've already seen that in the case of a nonempty file, size? returns the length; but if we're not using it as a predicate, the nil value would confuse us.

The File class has a class method (but *not* an instance method) to give us this answer. The instance method of the same name is inherited from the IO class, and File::Stat has a corresponding instance method.

```
size1 = File.size("file1")
size2 = File.stat("file2").size
```

If we want the file size in blocks rather than bytes, we can use the instance method blocks in File::Stat. This is certainly dependent on the operating system. (The method blksize also reports on the operating system's idea of how big a block is.)

```
info = File.stat("somefile")
total_bytes = info.blocks * info.blksize
```

10.1.12   Checking Special File Characteristics

There are numerous aspects of a file that we can test. We summarize here the relevant built-in methods that we don't discuss elsewhere. Most, though not all, are predicates.

Bear in mind two facts throughout this section (and most of this chapter). First, because File mixes in FileTest, any test that can be done by invoking the method qualified with the module name may also be called as an instance method of any file object. Second, remember that there is a high degree of overlap between the FileTest module and the File::Stat object returned by stat (or lstat). In some cases, there will be three different ways to call what is essentially the same method. We won't necessarily show this every time.

Some operating systems have the concept of block-oriented devices as opposed to character-oriented devices. A file may refer to either but not both. The methods blockdev? and chardev? in the FileTest module tests for this:

```
flag1 = FileTest::chardev?("/dev/hdisk0")   # false
flag2 = FileTest::blockdev?("/dev/hdisk0")  # true
```

Sometimes we want to know whether the stream is associated with a terminal. The IO class method tty? tests for this (as does the synonym isatty):

```
flag1 = STDIN.tty?                       # true
flag2 = File.new("diskfile").isatty      # false
```

A stream can be a pipe or a socket. There are corresponding FileTest methods to test for these cases:

```
flag1 = FileTest::pipe?(myfile)
flag2 = FileTest::socket?(myfile)
```

Recall that a directory is really just a special case of a file. So we need to be able to distinguish between directories and ordinary files, which a pair of FileTest methods enable us to do.

```
file1 = File.new("/tmp")
file2 = File.new("/tmp/myfile")
test1 = file1.directory?     # true
test2 = file1.file?          # false
test3 = file2.directory?     # false
test4 = file2.file?          # true
```

There is also a File class method named ftype, which tells us what kind of thing a stream is; it can also be found as an instance method in the File::Stat class. This method returns a string that has one of the following values: file, directory, blockSpecial, characterSpecial, fifo, link, or socket. (The string fifo refers to a pipe.)

```
this_kind = File.ftype("/dev/hdisk0")        # "blockSpecial"
that_kind = File.new("/tmp").stat.ftype      # "directory"
```

Certain special bits may be set or cleared in the permissions of a file. These are not strictly related to the other bits that we discuss in section 10.1.9, "Manipulating

File Ownership and Permissions." These are the *set-group-id bit*, the *set-user-id bit*, and the *sticky bit*. There are methods in `FileTest` for each of these.

```
file = File.new("somefile")
info = file.stat
sticky_flag = info.sticky?
setgid_flag = info.setgid?
setuid_flag = info.setuid?
```

A disk file may have symbolic or hard links that refer to it (on operating systems supporting these features). To test whether a file is actually a symbolic link to some other file, use the `symlink?` method of `FileTest`. To count the number of hard links associated with a file, use the `nlink` method (found only in `File::Stat`). A hard link is virtually indistinguishable from an ordinary file; in fact, it *is* an ordinary file that happens to have multiple names and directory entries.

```
File.symlink("yourfile","myfile")         # Make a link
is_sym = FileTest::symlink?("myfile")     # true
hard_count = File.new("myfile").stat.nlink  # 0
```

Incidentally, note that in the previous example we used the `File` class method `symlink` to create a symbolic link.

In rare cases, you may want even lower-level information about a file. The `File::Stat` class has three more instance methods that give you the gory details. The method `dev` gives you an integer identifying the device on which the file resides, `rdev` returns an integer specifying the kind of device, and for disk files, `ino` gives you the starting *inode* number for the file.

```
file = File.new("diskfile")
info = file.stat
device = info.dev
devtype = info.rdev
inode = info.ino
```

10.1.13 Working with Pipes

There are various ways of reading and writing pipes in Ruby. The class method `IO.popen` opens a pipe and hooks the process's standard input and standard output into the IO object returned. Frequently we will have different threads handling each end of the pipe; here we just show a single thread writing and then reading:

```
check = IO.popen("spell","r+")
check.puts("'T was brillig, and the slithy toves")
check.puts("Did gyre and gimble in the wabe.")
check.close_write
list = check.readlines
list.collect! { |x| x.chomp }
# list is now %w[brillig gimble gyre slithy toves wabe]
```

Note that the close_write call is necessary. If it were not issued, we would not be able to reach the end of file when we read the pipe.

There is a block form that works as follows:

```
File.popen("/usr/games/fortune") do |pipe|
  quote = pipe.gets
  puts quote
  # On a clean disk, you can seek forever. - Thomas Steel
end
```

If the string "-" is specified, a new Ruby instance is started. If a block is specified with this, the block is run as two separate processes rather like a fork; the child gets nil passed into the block, and the parent gets an IO object with the child's standard input and/or output connected to it.

```
IO.popen("-") do |mypipe|
  if mypipe
    puts "I'm the parent: pid = #{Process.pid}"
    listen = mypipe.gets
    puts listen
  else
    puts "I'm the child: pid = #{Process.pid}"
  end
end

# Prints:
#    I'm the parent: pid = 10580
#    I'm the child: pid = 10582
```

A pipe method also returns a pair of pipe ends connected to each other. In the following code example, we create a pair of threads and let one pass a message to the other (the first message that Samuel Morse sent over the telegraph). Refer to Chapter 13, "Threads in Ruby" if this aspect confuses you.

```ruby
pipe = IO.pipe
reader = pipe[0]
writer = pipe[1]

str = nil
thread1 = Thread.new(reader,writer) do |reader,writer|
  # writer.close_write
  str = reader.gets
  reader.close
end

thread2 = Thread.new(reader,writer) do |reader,writer|
  # reader.close_read
  writer.puts("What hath God wrought?")
  writer.close
end

thread1.join
thread2.join

puts str          # What hath God wrought?
```

10.1.14   Performing Special I/O Operations

It is possible to do lower-level I/O in Ruby. We will only mention the existence of these methods; if you need to use them, some of them will be highly machine-specific anyway (varying even between different versions of UNIX).

The ioctl method ("I/O control") accepts two arguments. The first is an integer specifying the operation to be done. The second is either an integer or a string representing a binary number.

The fcntl method is also for low-level control of file-oriented streams in a system-dependent manner. It takes the same kinds of parameters as ioctl.

The select method (in the Kernel module) accepts up to four parameters; the first is the *read-array*, and the last three are optional (*write-array*, *error-array*, and the *timeout* value). When input is available from one or more devices in the read-array, or when one or more devices in the write-array are ready, the call returns an array of three elements representing the respective arrays of devices that are ready for I/O.

The `Kernel` method `syscall` takes at least one integer parameter (and up to nine string or integer parameters in all). The first parameter specifies the I/O operation to be done.

The `fileno` method returns an old-fashioned file descriptor associated with an I/O stream. This is the least system-dependent of all the methods mentioned here.

```
desc = $stderr.fileno      # 2
```

10.1.15 Using Nonblocking I/O

Ruby makes a concerted effort "behind the scenes" to ensure that I/O does not block. For this reason, it is possible in most cases to use Ruby threads to manage I/O—a single thread may block on an I/O operation while another thread goes on processing.

This is a little counterintuitive. Ruby's threads are all in the same process because they are not native threads. Your expectation then might be that a blocking I/O operation would block the entire process and all the threads associated with it. The reason it doesn't work this way is that Ruby manages its I/O carefully in a way transparent to the programmer.

However, those who want to turn off nonblocking I/O can do so. The small library `io/nonblock` provides a simple setter, a query method, and a block-oriented setter for an `IO` object.

```
require 'io/nonblock'

# ...

test = mysock.nonblock?         # false

mysock.nonblock = true          # turn off blocking
# ...
mysock.nonblock = false         # turn on again

mysock.nonblock { some_operation(mysock) }
# Perform some_operation with nonblocking set to true

mysock.nonblock(false) { other_operation(mysock) }
# Perform other_operation with non-blocking set to false
```

10.1.16 Using `readpartial`

The `readpartial` method is a relatively new method designed to make I/O easier in certain circumstances. It is designed to be used on a stream such as a socket.

The "max length" parameter is required. If the buffer parameter is specified, it should refer to a string where the data will be stored.

```
data = sock.readpartial(128)   # Read at most 128 bytes
```

The `readpartial` method doesn't honor the nonblocking flag. It will sometimes block, but only when three conditions are true: The IO object's buffer is empty; the stream content is empty; and the stream has not yet reached an end-of-file condition.

So in effect, if there is data in the stream, `readpartial` will *not* block. It will read up to the maximum number of bytes specified, but if there are fewer bytes available, it will grab those and continue.

If the stream has no data, but it is at end of file, `readpartial` will immediately raise an `EOFError`.

If the call blocks, it waits until either it receives data or it detects an EOF condition. If it receives data, it simply returns it. If it detects EOF, it raises an `EOFError`.

When `sysread` is called in blocking mode, its behavior is similar to the way `readpartial` works. If the buffer is empty, their behavior is identical.

10.1.17 Manipulating Pathnames

In manipulating pathnames, the first things to be aware of are the class methods `File.dirname` and `File.basename`; these work like the UNIX commands of the same name and return the directory name and the filename, respectively. If an extension is specified as a second parameter to basename, that extension will be removed.

```
str = "/home/dave/podbay.rb"
dir = File.dirname(str)          # "/home/dave"
file1 = File.basename(str)       # "podbay.rb"
file2 = File.basename(str,".rb") # "podbay"
```

Note that although these are methods of `File`, they are really simply doing string manipulation.

A comparable method is `File.split`, which returns these two components (directory and filename) in a two-element array.

```
info = File.split(str)          # ["/home/dave","podbay.rb"]
```

The `expand_path` class method expands a relative pathname, converting to an absolute path. If the operating system understands such idioms as ~ and ~user, these will be expanded also.

```
Dir.chdir("/home/poole/personal/docs")
abs = File.expand_path("../../misc")    # "/home/poole/misc"
```

Given an open file, the `path` instance method returns the pathname used to open the file.

```
file = File.new("../../foobar")
name = file.path                 # "../../foobar"
```

The constant `File::Separator` gives the character used to separate pathname components (typically backslash for Windows, slash for UNIX). An alias is `File::SEPARATOR`.

The class method `join` uses this separator to produce a path from a list of directory components:

```
path = File.join("usr","local","bin","someprog")
# path is "usr/local/bin/someprog"
# Note that it doesn't put a separator on the front!
```

Don't fall into the trap of thinking that `File.join` and `File.split` are somehow inverses. They're not.

10.1.18   Using the `Pathname` Class

You should also be aware of the standard library `pathname`, which gives us the `Pathname` class. This is essentially a wrapper for `Dir`, `File`, `FileTest`, and `FileUtils`; as such, it has much of the functionality of these, unified in a way that is supposed to be logical and intuitive.

```
path = Pathname.new("/home/hal")
file = Pathname.new("file.txt")
p2 = path + file
```

```
path.directory?            # true
path.file?                 # false
p2.directory?              # false
p2.file?                   # true

parts = path2.split        # [Pathname:/home/hal, Pathname:file.txt]
ext = path2.extname        # .txt
```

There are also a number of convenience methods as you would expect. The root? method attempts to detect whether a path refers to the root directory; it can be "fooled" because it merely analyzes the string and does not access the filesystem. The parent? method returns the pathname of this path's parent. The children method returns a list of the next-level children below this path; it includes both files and directories but is not recursive.

```
p1 = Pathname.new("//")    # odd but legal
p1.root?                   # true
p2 = Pathname.new("/home/poole")
p3 = p2.parent             # Pathname:/home
items = p2.children        # array of Pathnames (all files and
                           # dirs immediately under poole)
```

As you would expect, relative and absolute try to determine whether a path is relative (by looking for a leading slash):

```
p1 = Pathname.new("/home/dave")
p1.absolute?               # true
p1.relative?               # false
```

Many methods such as size, unlink, and others are actually delegated to File, FileTest, and FileUtils; the functionality is not reimplemented.

For more details on Pathname, consult ruby-doc.org or any good reference.

10.1.19 Command-Level File Manipulation

Often we need to manipulate files in a manner similar to the way we would at a command line. That is, we need to copy, delete, rename, and so on.

Many of these capabilities are built-in methods; a few are in the `FileUtils` module in the `fileutils` library. Be aware that `FileUtils` used to mix functionality directly into the `File` class by reopening it; now these methods stay in their own module.

To delete a file, we can use `File.delete` or its synonym `File.unlink`:

```
File.delete("history")
File.unlink("toast")
```

To rename a file, we can use `File.rename` as follows

```
File.rename("Ceylon","SriLanka")
```

File links (hard and symbolic) can be created using `File.link` and `File.symlink`, respectively:

```
File.link("/etc/hosts","/etc/hostfile")    # hard link
File.symlink("/etc/hosts","/tmp/hosts")    # symbolic link
```

We can truncate a file to zero bytes (or any other specified number) by using the truncate instance method:

```
File.truncate("myfile",1000)     # Now at most 1000 bytes
```

Two files may be compared by means of the `compare_file` method. There is an alias named `cmp` (and there is also `compare_stream`).

```
require "fileutils"

same = FileUtils.compare_file("alpha","beta")  # true
```

The copy method will copy a file to a new name or location. It has an optional flag parameter to write error messages to standard error. The UNIX-like name `cp` is an alias.

```
require "fileutils"

# Copy epsilon to theta and log any errors.
FileUtils.copy("epsilon","theta", true)
```

A file may be moved with the move method (alias mv). Like copy, it also has an optional verbose flag.

```
require "fileutils"

FileUtils.move("/tmp/names","/etc")      # Move to new directory
FileUtils.move("colours","colors")       # Just a rename
```

The safe_unlink method deletes the specified file or files, first trying to make the files writable so as to avoid errors. If the last parameter is true or false, that value will be taken as the verbose flag.

```
require "fileutils"

FileUtils.safe_unlink("alpha","beta","gamma")
# Log errors on the next two files
FileUtils.safe_unlink("delta","epsilon",true)
```

Finally, the install method basically does a syscopy, except that it first checks that the file either does not exist or has different content.

```
require "fileutils"

FileUtils.install("foo.so","/usr/lib")
# Existing foo.so will not be overwritten
# if it is the same as the new one.
```

For more on FileUtils, consult ruby-doc.org or any other reference.

10.1.20 Grabbing Characters from the Keyboard

Here we use the term *grabbing* because we sometimes want to process a character as soon as it is pressed rather than buffer it and wait for a newline to be entered.

This can be done in both UNIX variants and Windows variants. Unfortunately, the two methods are completely unrelated to each other.

The UNIX version is straightforward. We use the well-known technique of putting the terminal in raw mode (and we usually turn off echoing at the same time).

```
def getchar
  system("stty raw -echo")  # Raw mode, no echo
```

```
    char = STDIN.getc
    system("stty -raw echo")  # Reset terminal mode
    char
  end
```

In the Windows world, we would need to write a C extension for this. An alternative for now is to use a small feature of the Win32API library.

```
require 'Win32API'

def getchar
  char = Win32API.new("crtdll", "_getch", [], 'L').Call
end
```

In either case the behavior is effectively the same.

10.1.21   Reading an Entire File into Memory

To read an entire file into an array, you need not even open the file. The method IO.readlines will do this, opening and closing the file on its own.

```
arr = IO.readlines("myfile")
lines = arr.size
puts "myfile has #{lines} lines in it."

longest = arr.collect {|x| x.length}.max
puts "The longest line in it has #{longest} characters."
```

We can also use IO.read (which returns a single large string rather than an array of lines).

```
str = IO.read("myfile")
bytes = arr.size
puts "myfile has #{bytes} bytes in it."

longest = str.collect {|x| x.length}.max     # strings are enumerable!
puts "The longest line in it has #{longest} characters."
```

Obviously because IO is an ancestor of File, we can say File.readlines and File.read just as easily.

10.1.22   Iterating Over a File by Lines

To iterate over a file a line at a time, we can use the class method IO.foreach or the instance method each. In the former case, the file need not be opened in our code.

```
# Print all lines containing the word "target"
IO.foreach("somefile") do |line|
  puts line if line =~ /target/
end


# Another way...
file = File.new("somefile")
file.each do |line|
  puts line if line =~ /target/
end
```

Note that each_line is an alias for each.

10.1.23   Iterating Over a File by Byte

To iterate a byte at a time, use the each_byte instance method. Remember that it feeds a character (that is, an integer) into the block; use the chr method if you need to convert to a "real" character.

```
file = File.new("myfile")
e_count = 0
file.each_byte do |byte|
  e_count += 1 if byte == ?e
end
```

10.1.24   Treating a String As a File

Sometimes people want to know how to treat a string as though it were a file. The answer depends on the exact meaning of the question.

An object is defined mostly in terms of its methods. The following code shows an iterator applied to an object called source; with each iteration, a line of output is produced. Can you tell the type of source by reading this fragment?

```
source.each do |line|
  puts line
end
```

Actually, source could be a file, or it could be a string containing embedded new-lines. So in cases like these, a string can trivially be treated as a file.

In newer versions of Ruby, the stringio standard library makes this possible.

This StringIO implementation has an interface virtually identical to the implementation shown in the first edition of this book. It also has a string accessor that refers to the contents of the string itself.

```ruby
require 'stringio'

ios = StringIO.new("abcdefghijkl\nABC\n123")

ios.seek(5)
ios.puts("xyz")

puts ios.tell              # 8

puts ios.string.dump       # "abcdexyzijkl\nABC\n123"

c = ios.getc
puts "c = #{c}"            # c = 105

ios.ungetc(?w)

puts ios.string.dump       # "abcdexyzwjkl\nABC\n123"

puts "Ptr = #{ios.tell}"

s1 = ios.gets              # "wjkl"
s2 = ios.gets              # "ABC"
```

10.1.25   Reading Data Embedded in a Program

When you were twelve years old and you learned BASIC by copying programs out of magazines, you may have used a DATA statement for convenience. The information was embedded in the program, but it could be read as if it originated outside.

Should you ever want to, you can do much the same thing in Ruby. The directive __END__ at the end of a Ruby program signals that embedded data follow. This can be read using the global constant DATA, which is an IO object like any other. (Note that the __END__ marker must be at the beginning of the line on which it appears.)

```
# Print each line backwards...
DATA.each_line do |line|
  puts line.reverse
end
__END__
A man, a plan, a canal... Panama!
Madam, I'm Adam.
,siht daer nac uoy fI
.drah oot gnikrow neeb ev'uoy
```

10.1.26 Reading Program Source

Suppose you wanted to access the source of your own program. This can be done using a variation on a trick we used elsewhere (see section 10.1.25 "Reading Data Embedded in a Program").

The global constant DATA is an IO object that refers to the data following the __END__ directive. But if you do a rewind operation, it resets the file pointer to the beginning of the program source.

The following program produces a listing of itself with line numbers. It is not particularly useful, but maybe you can find some other good use for this capability.

```
DATA.rewind
num = 1
DATA.each_line do |line|
  puts "#{'%03d' % num}  #{line}"
  num += 1
end
__END__
```

Note that the __END__ directive *is* necessary; without it, DATA cannot be accessed at all.

10.1.27 Working with Temporary Files

There are many circumstances in which we need to work with files that are all but anonymous. We don't want to trouble with naming them or making sure there is no name conflict, and we don't want to bother with deleting them.

All these issues are addressed in the Tempfile library. The new method (alias open) takes a basename as a *seed string* and concatenates onto it the process id and a unique sequence number. The optional second parameter is the directory to be used; it defaults to the value of environment variables TMPDIR, TMP, or TEMP, and finally the value "/tmp".

The resulting IO object may be opened and closed many times during the execution of the program. Upon termination of the program, the temporary file will be deleted.

The close method has an optional flag; if set to true, the file will be deleted immediately after it is closed (instead of waiting until program termination). The path method returns the actual pathname of the file, should you need it.

```ruby
require "tempfile"

temp = Tempfile.new("stuff")
name = temp.path                # "/tmp/stuff17060.0"
temp.puts "Kilroy was here"
temp.close

# Later...
temp.open
str = temp.gets                 # "Kilroy was here"
temp.close(true)                # Delete it NOW
```

10.1.28 Changing and Setting the Current Directory

The current directory may be determined by the use of Dir.pwd or its alias Dir.getwd; these abbreviations historically stand for *print working directory* and *get working directory*, respectively. In a Windows environment, the backslashes probably show up as normal (forward) slashes.

The method Dir.chdir may be used to change the current directory. On Windows, the logged drive may appear at the front of the string.

```ruby
Dir.chdir("/var/tmp")
puts Dir.pwd        # "/var/tmp"
puts Dir.getwd      # "/var/tmp"
```

This method also takes a block parameter. If a block is specified, the current directory is changed only while the block is executed (and restored afterward):

```
Dir.chdir("/home")
Dir.chdir("/tmp") do
  puts Dir.pwd          # /tmp
  # other code...
end
puts Dir.pwd            # /home
```

10.1.29 Changing the Current Root

On most UNIX variants, it is possible to change the current process's idea of where root or "slash" is. This is typically done for security reasons—for example, when running unsafe or untested code. The chroot method sets the new root to the specified directory.

```
Dir.chdir("/home/guy/sandbox/tmp")
Dir.chroot("/home/guy/sandbox")
puts Dir.pwd                        # "/tmp"
```

10.1.30 Iterating Over Directory Entries

The class method foreach is an iterator that successively passes each directory entry into the block. The instance method each behaves the same way.

```
Dir.foreach("/tmp") { |entry| puts entry }

dir = Dir.new("/tmp")
dir.each  { |entry| puts entry }
```

Both of the preceding code fragments print the same output (the names of all files and subdirectories in /tmp).

10.1.31   Getting a List of Directory Entries

The class method `Dir.entries` returns an array of all the entries in the specified directory.

```
list = Dir.entries("/tmp")  # %w[. .. alpha.txt beta.doc]
```

As shown in the preceding code, the current and parent directories are included. If you don't want these, you'll have to remove them manually.

10.1.32   Creating a Chain of Directories

Sometimes we want to create a chain of directories where the intermediate directories themselves don't necessarily exist yet. At the UNIX command line, we would use `mkdir -p` for this.

In Ruby code, we can do this by using the `FileUtils.makedirs` method (from the `fileutils` library):

```
require "fileutils"

FileUtils.makedirs("/tmp/these/dirs/need/not/exist")
```

10.1.33   Deleting a Directory Recursively

In the UNIX world, we can type `rm -rf dir` at the command line, and the entire subtree starting with `dir` will be deleted. Obviously, we should exercise caution in doing this.

In recent versions of Ruby, `Pathname` has a method `rmtree` that will accomplish this. There is also a method `rm_r` in `FileUtils` that will do the same.

```
require 'pathname'
dir = Pathname.new("/home/poole/")
dir.rmtree

# or:

require 'fileutils'
FileUtils.rm_r("/home/poole")
```

10.1.34   Finding Files and Directories

Here we use the standard library `find.rb` to create a method that finds one or more files and returns the list of files as an array. The first parameter is the starting directory; the second is either a filename (that is, a string) or a regular expression.

```ruby
require "find"

def findfiles(dir, name)
  list = []
  Find.find(dir) do |path|
    Find.prune if [".",".."].include? path
    case name
      when String
        list << path if File.basename(path) == name
      when Regexp
        list << path if File.basename(path) =~ name
      else
        raise ArgumentError
    end
  end
  list
end

findfiles "/home/hal", "toc.txt"
# ["/home/hal/docs/toc.txt", "/home/hal/misc/toc.txt"]

findfiles "/home", /^[a-z]+.doc/
# ["/home/hal/docs/alpha.doc", "/home/guy/guide.doc",
#   "/home/bill/help/readme.doc"]
```

10.2   Performing Higher-Level Data Access

Frequently we want to store and retrieve data in a more transparent manner. The `Marshal` module offers simple object persistence, and the `PStore` library builds on that functionality. Finally, the `dbm` library is used like a hash stored permanently on disk. It does not truly belong in this section, but it is too simple to put in the database section.

10.2.1   Simple Marshaling

In many cases we want to create an object and simply save it for use later. Ruby provides rudimentary support for such object persistence or *marshaling*. The `Marshal` module enables programs to *serialize* and *unserialize* Ruby objects in this way.

```
# array of elements [composer, work, minutes]
  works = [["Leonard Bernstein","Overture to Candide",11],
          ["Aaron Copland","Symphony No. 3",45],
          ["Jean Sibelius","Finlandia",20]]
# We want to keep this for later...
File.open("store","w") do |file|
  Marshal.dump(works,file)
end

# Much later...
File.open("store") do |file|
  works = Marshal.load(file)
end
```

This technique does have the shortcoming that not all objects can be dumped. If an object includes an object of a fairly low-level class, it cannot be marshaled; these include `IO`, `Proc`, and `Binding`. Singleton objects, anonymous classes, and modules also cannot be serialized.

`Marshal.dump` takes two other forms of parameter passing. When called with just one parameter, it returns the data as a string along with a major and minor version number in the first two bytes of the marshaled string.

```
s = Marshal.dump(works)
p s[0]  #  4
p s[1]  #  8
```

Normally, if you try to load such data, it will load only if the major version number is the same and minor version number is less than or equal. However, if the verbose flag for the Ruby interpreter is set (using –verbose or –v) then the versions must match exactly. These version numbers are independent of the Ruby's version numbers.

The third `limit` parameter makes sense only if the object being marshaled contains nested objects. If it is specified (as an integer) to `Marshal.dump`, then it uses that as the limit to traverse the depth of the object being marshaled. If the nesting is less than the mentioned limit, then the object is marshaled without an error; otherwise an `ArgumentError` is thrown. An example will make it clearer:

```
File.open("store","w") do |file|
  arr = [ ]
Marshal.dump(arr,file,0)        #   in `dump': exceed depth limit
                                #   (ArgumentError)
  Marshal.dump(arr,file,1)

  arr = [1, 2, 3]
Marshal.dump(arr,file,1)        # in `dump': exceed depth limit
                                # (ArgumentError)
  Marshal.dump(arr,file,2)

  arr = [1, [2], 3]
Marshal.dump(arr,file,2)        # in `dump': exceed depth limit
                                # (ArgumentError)
  Marshal.dump(arr,file,3)
end

File.open("store") do |file|
  p Marshal.load(file)          #   [ ]
  p Marshal.load(file)          #   [1, 2, 3]
  p Marshal.load(file)          #   arr = [1, [2], 3]
end
```

The default value of the third parameter is –1. A negative depth implies no depth checking.

10.2.2   More Complex Marshaling

Sometimes we want to customize our marshaling to some extent. Creating _load and _dump methods enable you to do this. These hooks are called when marshaling is done so that you are handling your own conversion to and from a string.

In the following example, a person has been earning 5% interest on his beginning balance since he was born. We don't store the age and the current balance because they are a function of time.

```
class Person

    attr_reader :name
```

```ruby
  attr_reader :age
  attr_reader :balance

  def initialize(name,birthdate,beginning)
    @name = name
    @birthdate = birthdate
    @beginning = beginning
    @age = (Time.now - @birthdate)/(365*86400)
    @balance = @beginning*(1.05**@age)
  end

  def marshal_dump
    Struct.new("Human",:name,:birthdate,:beginning)
    str = Struct::Human.new(@name,@birthdate,@beginning)
    str
  end

  def marshal_load(str)
    self.instance_eval do
      initialize(str.name, str.birthdate, str.beginning)
    end
  end

  # Other methods...

end

p1 = Person.new("Rudy",Time.now - (14 * 365 * 86400), 100)
p [p1.name, p1.age, p1.balance]  # ["Rudy", 14.0, 197.99315994394]

str = Marshal.dump(p1)
p2  = Marshal.load(str)

p [p2.name, p2.age, p2.balance]  # ["Rudy", 14.0, 197.99315994394]
```

When an object of this type is saved, the age and current balance will not be stored; when the object is "reconstituted," they will be computed. Notice how the marshal_load method assumes an existing object; this is one of the few times you might want to call initialize explicitly (just as new calls it).

10.2.3   Performing Limited "Deep Copying" Using Marshal

Ruby has no "deep copy" operation. The methods dup and clone may not always work as you would initially expect. An object may contain nested object references that turn a copy operation into a game of Pick-Up-Sticks.

We offer here a way to handle a restricted deep copy. It is restricted because it is still based on Marshal and has the same inherent limitations:

```ruby
def deep_copy(obj)
  Marshal.load(Marshal.dump(obj))
end


a = deep_copy(b)
```

10.2.4   Better Object Persistence with PStore

The PStore library provides file-based persistent storage of Ruby objects. A PStore object can hold a number of Ruby object hierarchies. Each hierarchy has a *root* identified by a key. Hierarchies are read from a disk file at the start of a transaction and written back at the end.

```ruby
require "pstore"

# save
db = PStore.new("employee.dat")
db.transaction do
    db["params"] = {"name" => "Fred", "age" => 32,
                    "salary" => 48000 }
end


# retrieve
require "pstore"
db = PStore.new("employee.dat")
emp = nil
db.transaction { emp = db["params"] }
```

Typically, within a transaction block we use the PStore object passed in. We can also use the receiver directly, however, as shown in the previous code.

This technique is transaction oriented; at the start of the block, data are retrieved from the disk file to be manipulated. Afterward, they are transparently written back out to disk.

In the middle of a transaction, we can interrupt with either commit or abort; the former keep the changes we have made, while the latter will throw them away. Refer to this longer example:

```ruby
require "pstore"

# Assume existing file with two objects stored
store = PStore.new("objects")
store.transaction do |s|

  a = s["my_array"]
  h = s["my_hash"]

  # Imaginary code omitted, manipulating
  # a, h, etc.

  # Assume a variable named "condition" having
  # the value 1, 2, or 3...

  case condition
    when 1
      puts "Oops... aborting."
      s.abort   # Changes will be lost.
    when 2
      puts "Committing and jumping out."
      s.commit  # Changes will be saved.
    when 3
      # Do nothing...
  end

  puts "We finished the transaction to the end."
  # Changes will be saved.

end
```

Within a transaction, you can also use the method roots to return an array of roots (or root? to test membership). There is also a delete method to remove a root.

```
store.transaction do |s|
  list = s.roots          # ["my_array","my_hash"]
  if s.root?("my_tree")
    puts "Found my_tree."
  else
    puts "Didn't find # my_tree."
  end
  s.delete("my_hash")
  list2 = s.roots         # ["my_array"]
end
```

10.2.5   Working with CSV Data

CSV (comma-separated values) format is something you may have had to deal with if you have ever worked with spreadsheets or databases. Fortunately, Hiroshi Nakamura has created a module for Ruby and made it available in the Ruby Application Archive.

There is also a FasterCSV library created by James Edward Gray III. As the name implies, it runs faster, but it also has some changes and enhancements in the interface (though with a "compatibility mode" for users of the other library). At the time of this writing, there is some discussion that FasterCSV may become standard and replace the older library (likely taking over its name as well).

This is obviously not a true database system. However, a discussion of it fits better in this chapter than anywhere else.

The CSV module (csv.rb) will parse or generate data in CSV format. There is no universal agreement on the exact format of CSV data; the library author defines this format as follows:

- Record separator: CR + LF

- Field separator: comma (,)

- Quote data with double quotes if it contains CR, LF, or comma

- Quote double quote by prefixing it with another double quote (" -> "")

- Empty field with quotes means null string (data,"",data)

- Empty field without quotes means NULL (data,,data)

This section covers only a portion of the functionality of this library. It will be enough to get you started, but as always, the newest docs are to be found online (starting with ruby-doc.org).

Let's start by creating a file. To write out comma-separated data, we can simply open a file for writing; the open method will pass a writer object into the attached block. We then use the append operator to append arrays of data (which are converted to comma-separated format upon writing). The first line will be a header.

```
require 'csv'

CSV.open("data.csv","w") do |wr|
  wr << ["name", "age", "salary"]
  wr << ["mark", "29", "34500"]
  wr << ["joe", "42", "32000"]
  wr << ["fred", "22", "22000"]
  wr << ["jake", "25", "24000"]
  wr << ["don", "32", "52000"]
end
```

The preceding code gives us a data file data.csv:

```
"name","age","salary"
"mark",29,34500
"joe",42,32000
"fred",22,22000
"jake",25,24000
"don",32,52000
```

Another program can read this file as follows:

```
require 'csv'

CSV.open('data.csv', 'r') do |row|
  p row
end

# Output:
# ["name", "age", "salary"]
# ["mark", "29", "34500"]
# ["joe", "42", "32000"]
# ["fred", "22", "22000"]
# ["jake", "25", "24000"]
# ["don", "32", "52000"]
```

The preceding code could also be written *without* a block; then the open call would return a reader object. We could then invoke shift on the reader (as though it were an array) to retrieve the next row. But the block-oriented way seems more straightforward.

There are a few more advanced features and convenience methods in this library. For more information, see ruby-doc.org or the Ruby Application Archive.

10.2.6   Marshaling with YAML

YAML reportedly stands for *YAML Ain't Markup Language*. It is nothing but a flexible, human-readable data storage format. As such, it is similar to XML but arguably "prettier."

When we require the yaml library, we add a to_yaml method to every object. It is instructive to dump a few simple objects and a few more complex ones to see how YAML deals with them.

```ruby
require 'yaml'

str = "Hello, world"
num = 237
arr = %w[ Jan Feb Mar Apr ]
hsh = {"This" => "is", "just a"=>"hash."}

puts str.to_yaml
puts num.to_yaml
puts arr.to_yaml
puts hsh.to_yaml

# Output:
# --- "Hello, world"
# --- 237
# ---
# - Jan
# - Feb
# - Mar
# - Apr
# ---
# just a: hash.
# This: is
```

The inverse of the to_yaml method is the YAML.load method, which can take a string or a stream as a parameter.

Assume that we had a file such as data.yaml here:

```
---
- "Hello, world"
- 237
-
  - Jan
  - Feb
  - Mar
  - Apr
-
  just a: hash.
  This: is
```

This is the same as the four data items we just looked at, except they are collected into a single array. If we now load this stream, we get this array back:

```
require 'yaml'
file = File.new("data.yaml")
array = YAML.load(file)
file.close
p array
# Output:
# ["Hello, world", 237, ["Jan", "Feb", "Mar", "Apr"],
#  {"just a"=>"hash.", "This"=>"is"}]
```

In general, YAML is just a way to marshal objects. At a higher level, it can be used for many purposes. For example, the fact that it is human-readable also makes it human-editable, and it becomes a natural format for configuration files and such things.

There is more to YAML than we have shown here. For further information, consult ruby-doc.org or any written reference.

10.2.7   Object Prevalence with Madeleine

In some circles, *object prevalence* is popular. The idea is that memory is cheap and getting cheaper, and most databases are fairly small, so we'll forget the database and keep all our objects in memory.

The classic implementation was Prevayler, implemented in Java. The Ruby version is called *Madeleine*.

Madeleine isn't for everyone or every application. Object prevalence comes with its own set of rules and constraints. First, all objects must fit in memory—all at once. Second, all objects must be marshalable.

All objects must be *deterministic*—they must behave in exactly the same way based on their inputs. (This means that using the system clock or using random numbers is problematic.)

The objects should be isolated from all I/O (file and network) as much as possible. The general technique is to make calls outside the prevalence system to do such I/O.

Finally, every command that alters the state of the prevalence system must be issued in the form of a command object (so that these objects themselves can be marshaled and stored).

Madeleine provides two basic methods for accessing the object system. The `execute_query` method provides query capability or read-only access. The `execute_command` method encapsulates any operation that changes the state of any object in the object system.

Both these methods take a `Command` object as a parameter. A `Command` object by definition has an `execute` method.

The system works by taking snapshots of the object system at periodic points in the application's execution. The commands are serialized along with the other objects. Currently there is no way to "roll back" a set of transactions.

It's difficult to create a good meaningful example of the usage of this library. If you are familiar with the Java version, I suggest you study the Ruby API and learn it that way. In the absence of any really good tutorials, perhaps you can write one.

10.2.8 Using the DBM Library

DBM is a simple platform-independent string-based hash file-storage mechanism. It stores a key and some associated data, both of which must be strings. Ruby's `dbm` interface is built into the standard installation.

To use this class, create a DBM object associated with a filename and work with the string-based hash however you want. When you have finished, you should close the file.

```
require 'dbm'

d = DBM.new("data")
d["123"] = "toodle-oo!"
puts d["123"]          # "toodle-oo!"
d.close

puts d["123"]          # RuntimeError: closed DBM file

e = DBM.open("data")
e["123"]                  # "toodle-oo!"
w=e.to_hash               # {"123"=>"toodle-oo!"}
e.close

e["123"]                  # RuntimeError: closed DBM file
w["123"]                  # "toodle-oo!
```

DBM is implemented as a single class that mixes in Enumerable. The two
(aliased) class methods new and open are singletons, which means you may only have
one DBM object per data file open at any given time.

```
q=DBM.new("data.dbm")   #
f=DBM.open("data.dbm")  # Errno::EWOULDBLOCK:
                        #    Try again - "data.dbm"
```

There are 34 instance methods, many of them aliases or similar to the hash methods. Basically, if you are used to manipulating a real hash in a certain way, there is a
good chance you can apply the same operation to a dbm object.

The method to_hash makes a copy of the hash file object in memory, and close
permanently closes the link to the hash file. Most of the rest of the methods are analogous to hash methods, but there are no rehash, sort, default, or default= methods.
The to_s method just returns a string representation of the object id.

10.3   Using KirbyBase

KirbyBase is one of those little libraries that everyone should learn to use. At present
it is not a standard library packaged with Ruby; if it were, its usefulness might increase
even more.

KirbyBase is the work of Jamey Cribbs (apparently named after his dog). Although it is in many ways a full-fledged database, it is mentioned here rather than along with MySQL and Oracle for a few reasons.

First, it is not a separate application. It is a pure-Ruby library and is not usable without Ruby. Second, it doesn't know SQL at all; so if you are dependent on SQL for some reason, it isn't for you. Third, if your application is sophisticated enough, you may have issues with KirbyBase's functionality or its speed.

Having said all that, there are numerous reasons to like KirbyBase. It is a single-file pure-Ruby library with zero installation/configuration overhead. It works across platforms, and its data files are interchangeable across those platforms. It is a "true" database in the sense that the data are not all held in memory at once.

It is easy to use and has a Rubyesque interface with a little DBI flavor. In general, a database corresponds to a directory and each table to a file. It produces tables that are human-readable (and editable), or optionally these can be encrypted (only enough to discourage editing). It is aware of Ruby objects and can store and retrieve objects intelligently.

Finally, it can operate in distributed mode thanks to a dRuby interface. It is as simple to access KirbyBase data from a remote machine as from a local one.

To open a database, you specify first whether it is local; the next two parameters are typically `nil`, and the fourth specifies the directory in which database files will be kept (defaulting to the current directory).

To create a table, call `create_table` on the database, passing in a table name (as a Symbol); the name on disk will be based on this name. Then pass in a series of pairs of symbols, indicating the field names and types.

```
require 'kirbybase'

db = KirbyBase.new(:local, nil, nil, "mydata")

books = db.create_table(:books,            # name of table
                        :title, :String,   # field, type, ...
                        :author, :String)
```

The field types currently recognized by KirbyBase are `String`, `Integer`, `Float`, `Boolean`, `Time`, `Date`, `DateTime`, `Memo`, `Blob`, and `YAML`. By the time you read this, there may be others.

To insert into a table, call its `insert` method. You may pass in a list of values, a hash, or any object that responds to the given field names.

```
books.insert("The Case for Mars","Robert Zubrin")
books.insert(:title => "Democracy in America",
             :author => "Alexis de Tocqueville")
Book = Struct.new(:title, :author)
book = Book.new("The Ruby Way","Hal Fulton")
books.insert(book)
```

In every case, the `insert` method returns the row id of the new record (which you may use or ignore). This is a "hidden" autoincrement field that is present in every record of every table.

Records are selected with the `select` method. With no parameters at all, it simply selects every field of every record in the table. The fields may be limited to certain ones by specifying symbols as parameters. If a block is specified, it is used to determine which records to select (much as the `find_all` method works for an array).

```
list1 = people.select            # All people, all fields
list2 = people.select(:name,:age)   # All people, name/age only

list3 = people.select(:name) {|x| x.age >= 18 && x.age < 30 }
# Names of all people 18 to 30
```

Any operation can be performed in the code block. This means that, for example, you can query using Ruby regular expressions (unlike the typical SQL-oriented database).

A KirbyBase resultset can be sorted by multiple keys, ascending or descending. To sort descending, specify a minus before the key name. (This works because `Symbol` has a unary minus method added to it.)

```
sorted = people.select.sort(:name,-:age)
# sort ascending by name, descending by age
```

A resultset also has the interesting feature that it can provide arrays that "cross-cut" the results. This is slightly tricky to understand at first.

Suppose that we have a resultset composed of people, where each element stores the name, age, height, and weight. Naturally the resultset can be indexed like an array, but it also has methods named the same as the field names, which store arrays of values for *just those field names*. For example:

```
list = people.select(:name,:age,:height,:weight)
p list[0]         # All info for person 0
p list[1].age     # Age for person 1
p list[2].height  # Height for person 2

ages  = list.age  # Array: Ages for all people
names = list.name # Array: Names for all people
```

KirbyBase has some limited report-printing features; just call `to_report` on any resultset. Here is an example:

```
rpt = books.select.sort(:title).to_report
puts rpt

# Output:
# recno | title                | author
# ----------------------------------------------------
#     2 | Democracy in America | Alexis de Tocqueville
#     1 | The Case for Mars    | Robert Zubrin
#     3 | The Ruby Way         | Hal Fulton
```

The `encrypt` accessor on a table can be set to `true` to prevent the table from being readable/editable as plain text. Be aware that it is based on a Vigenere cipher—not exactly a "toy" but not cryptographically secure. Therefore use this feature only as a way to discourage editing; don't use it as a way to hide sensitive data. You would typically set this using a block when the table is created:

```
db.create_table(:mytable, f1, :String, f2, :Date) {|t| t.encrypt = true }
```

Because remote access is an interesting feature, we'll mention briefly how it works. A sample server looks like this:

```
require 'kirbybase'
require 'drb'
```

```
host = 'localhost'
port = 44444
db = KirbyBase.new(:server)    # Create an instance of the database.

DRb.start_service("druby://#{host}:#{port}", db)
DRb.thread.join
```

This is a straightforward application of dRuby (refer to Chapter 20, "Distributed Ruby"). On the client side, you would specify :client rather than the usual :local when you connect to the database.

```
db = KirbyBase.new(:client,'localhost',44444)
# All other code remains the same.
```

It's also possible to perform the usual operations you would expect: Update or delete a record, drop a table, and so on. In addition there are more sophisticated features I don't mention here, such as one-to-many links, calculated fields, and custom record classes. Consult the KirbyBase documentation on RubyForge for more details.

10.4   Connecting to External Databases

Ruby can interface to various databases, thanks to the development work of many different people. These range from monolithic systems such as Oracle down to the more petite MySQL. We have included CSV here for some measure of completeness.

The level of functionality provided by these packages will change continually. Be sure to refer to an online reference for the latest information. The Ruby Application Archive is always a good starting point.

10.4.1   Interfacing to SQLite

SQLite is a popular database for those who appreciate *zero configuration* software. It is a small self-contained executable, written in C, which can handle a complete database in a single file. Although it is usually used for small databases, it can deal with data up into the terabyte range.

The Ruby bindings for SQLite are relatively straightforward. The C API is wrapped within the SQLite::API class; because the wrapping is basically one-to-one and not particularly object-oriented, you should use this API directly only when absolutely necessary.

In most situations, the SQLite::Database class will meet all your needs. Here is a brief piece of sample code:

```
require 'sqlite'

db = SQLite::Database.new("library.db")

db.execute("select title,author from books") do |row|
  p row
end

db.close

# Output:
# ["The Case for Mars", "Robert Zubrin"]
# ["Democracy in America", "Alexis de Tocqueville"]
# ...
```

If a block is not specified, execute returns an instance of ResultSet (in essence a cursor that can be iterated over).

```
rs = db.execute("select title,author from books")
rs.each {|row| p row }    # Same results as before
rs.close
```

If a ResultSet is returned, the user's code is responsible for closing it (as shown in the preceding code example). If you need to traverse the list of records more than once, you can do a reset to start over. (This feature is experimental and may change.) Additionally, you can do generator-style iteration (external iteration) with next and eof? if you want.

```
rs = db.execute("select title,author from books")
while ! rs.eof?
  rec = rs.next
  p rec                   # Same results as before
end
rs.close
```

An extensive set of exceptions may be raised by this library's methods. All are subclasses of SQLite::Exception so that it is easy to catch any or all of them.

It should be noted briefly that this library is written to interoperate well with Ara Howard's `ArrayFields` library (which we don't cover here). This is essentially a way to let array elements be indexed or accessed by name as well as by an integer value. If the `arrayfields` library is required before the `sqlite` library, a `ResultSet` object can be indexed by name as well as by number. (However, this is configurable to return a `Hash` instead.)

Although the `sqlite` library is fairly full-featured, it does not cover all the functionality you might want, simply because SQLite itself does not *completely* implement the SQL92 standard. For more information on SQLite or its Ruby binding, do a web search.

10.4.2 Interfacing to MySQL

Ruby's MySQL interface is among the most stable and fully functional of its database interfaces. It is an extension and must be installed after both Ruby and MySQL are installed and running.

There are three steps to using this module after you have it installed. First load the module in your script; then connect to the database; and finally work with your tables. Connecting requires the usual parameters for host, username, password, database, and so on.

```
require 'mysql'

m = Mysql.new("localhost","ruby","secret","maillist")
r = m.query("SELECT * FROM people ORDER BY name")
r.each_hash do |f|
  print "#{f['name']} - #{f['email']}"
end

# Output looks like:

# John Doe - jdoe@rubynewbie.com
# Fred Smith - smithf@rubyexpert.com
```

The class methods `Mysql.new` and `MysqlRes.each_hash` are useful, along with the instance method `query`.

The module is composed of four classes (`Mysql`, `MysqlRes`, `MysqlField`, and `MysqlError`), as described in the README. We summarize some useful methods here, but you can always find more information in the actual documentation.

The class method `Mysql.new` takes several string parameters, all defaulting to `nil`, and returns a connection object. The parameters are `host`, `user`, `passwd`, `db`, `port`, `sock`, and `flag`. Aliases for `new` are `real_connect` and `connect`.

The methods `create_db`, `select_db`, and `drop_db` all take a database name as a parameter; they are used as shown here. The method `close` closes the connection to the server.

```
m=Mysql.new("localhost","ruby","secret")
m.create_db("rtest")     # Create a new database
m.select_db("rtest2")    # Select a different database
m.drop_db("rtest")       # Delete a database
m.close                  # Close the connection
```

In recent versions, `create_db` and `drop_db` are considered obsolete. But you can make them work by defining them in this way:

```
class Mysql
  def create_db(db)
    query("CREATE DATABASE #{db}")
  end

  def drop_db(db)
    query("DROP DATABASE #{db}")
  end
end
```

Method `list_dbs` returns a list of available database names in an array.

```
dbs = m.list_dbs       # ["people","places","things"]
```

The `query` takes a string parameter and returns a `MysqlRes` object by default. Depending on how `query_with_result` is set, it may return a `Mysql` object.

In the event of an error, the error number can be retrieved by `errno`; `error`, on the other hand, returns the actual error message.

```
begin
  r=m.query("create table rtable
    (
      id int not null auto_increment,
      name varchar(35) not null,
      desc varchar(128) not null,
```

```
      unique id(id)
    )")

  # exception happens...

  rescue
    puts m.error
    # Prints: You have an error in your SQL syntax
    # near 'desc varchar(128) not null ,
    #   unique id(id)
    # )' at line 5"

    puts m.errno
    # Prints 1064
    # ('desc' is reserved for descending order)
  end
```

A few useful instance methods of `MysqlRes` are summarized here:

- `fetch_fields`—Returns an array of MysqlField objects from the next row

- `fetch_row`—Returns an array of field values from the next row

- `fetch_hash(with_table=false)`—Returns a hash containing the next row's field names and values

- `num_rows`—Returns number of rows in the resultset

- `each`—Iterator that sequentially returns array of field values

- `each_hash(with_table=false)`—Iterator that sequentially returns hash of `{fieldname => fieldvalue}` (Use `x['field name']` to get the field value.)

These are some instance methods of `MysqlField`:

- `name`—Returns name of designated field

- `table`—Returns name of table to which designated field belongs

- `length`—Returns defined length of field

- `max_length`—Returns length of longest field from resultset

- `hash`—Returns hash with name and values for `name`, `table`, `def`, `type`, `length`, `max_length`, `flags`, and `decimals`

Any material here is always superseded by online documentation. For more information, see the MySQL website (http://www.mysql.com) and the Ruby Application Archive.

10.4.3   Interfacing to PostgreSQL

There is an extension available from the RAA that provides access to PostgreSQL also (it works with PostgreSQL 6.5/7.0).

Assuming you already have PostgreSQL installed and set up (and you have a table named testdb), you merely need to follow essentially the same steps as used with other database interfaces in Ruby: Load the module, connect to the database, and then do your work with the tables. You'll probably want a way of executing queries, getting the results of a select back, and working with transactions.

```
require 'postgres'
conn = PGconn.connect("",5432, "", "", "testdb")

conn.exec("create table rtest ( number integer default 0 );")
conn.exec("insert into rtest values ( 99 )")
res = conn.query("select * from rtest")
# res id [["99"]]
```

The PGconn class contains the connect method, which takes the typical database connection parameters such as host, port, database, username, and login; but it also takes options and tty parameters in positions three and four. We have connected in our example to the UNIX socket via a privileged user, so we did not need a username or password, and the host, options, and tty were left empty. The port must be an integer, whereas the others are strings. An alias for this is the new method.

The next thing of interest is working with our tables; this requires some means to do queries. The instance methods PGconn#exec and PGconn#query are just what we need.

The exec method sends its string parameter as an SQL query request to PostgreSQL and returns a PGresult instance on success. On failure, it raises a PGError exception.

The query method also sends its string parameter as an SQL query request to PostgreSQL. However, it returns an array on success. The returned array is actually an array of *tuples*. On failure, it returns nil, and error details can be obtained by the error method call.

There is a special method for inserting values into a specific table, called
insert_table. Despite the name, it actually means "insert into table." This method
returns a PGconn object.

```
conn.insert_table("rtest",[[34]])
res = conn.query("select * from rtest")
# res is [["99"], ["34"]]
```

This inserts one row of values into the table rtest. For our simple example, there
is only one column to begin with. Notice that the PGresult object res shows updated
results with two tuples. We will discuss PGresult methods shortly.

Other potentially useful methods from the PGconn class include the following:

- db—Returns the connected database name.

- host—Returns the connected server name.

- user—Returns the authenticated username.

- error—Returns the error message about connection.

- finish, close—Closes the backend connection.

- loimport(file)—Imports a file to a large object; returns the PGlarge instance
  on success. On failure, raise the PGError exception.

- loexport(oid, file)—Saves a large object of oid to a file.

- locreate([mode])—Returns the PGlarge instance on success. On failure, raise
  the PGError exception.

- loopen(oid, [mode])—Opens a large object of oid; returns the PGlarge
  instance on success. The mode argument specifies the mode for the opened large
  object, which is either "INV_READ" or "INV_WRITE" (if the mode is omitted, the
  default is "INV_READ").

- lounlink(oid)—Unlinks (deletes) the Postgres large object of oid.

Notice that the last five methods in the preceding list (loimport, loexport,
locreate, loopen, and lounlink) involve objects of the PGlarge class. The PGlarge
class has specific methods for accessing and changing its own objects. (The objects are
created as a result of the PGconn instance methods loimport, locreate, and loopen,
discussed in the preceding list.)

The following is a list of PGlarge methods:

- open([mode])—Opens a large object. The mode argument specifies its mode as with the preceding PGconn#loopen).

- close—Closes a large object (also closed when they are garbage-collected).

- read([length])—Attempts to read "length" bytes from large object. If no length is given, all data is read.

- write(str)—Writes the string to the large object and returns the number of bytes written.

- tell—Returns the current position of the pointer.

- seek(offset, whence)—Moves the pointer to offset. The possible values for whence are SEEK_SET, SEEK_CUR, and SEEK_END (or 0,1,2).

- unlink—Deletes large object.

- oid—Returns the large object oid.

- size—Returns the size of large object.

- export(file)—Saves a large object of oid to a file.

Of more interest to us are the instance methods (shown in the list below) of the PGresult class, which are created as the result of queries. (Use PGresult#clear when finished with these objects to improve memory performance.)

- result—Returns the query result tuple in the array.

- each—Iterator

- []—Accessor

- fields—Returns the array of the fields of the query result.

- num_tuples—Returns the number of tuples of the query result.

- fieldnum(name)—Returns the index of the named field.

- type(index)—Returns an integer corresponding the type of the field.

- size(index)—Returns the size of the field in bytes. −1 indicates the field is variable length.

- getvalue(tup_num, field_num)—Returns the field value for the given parameters. tup_num is the same as row number.

- getlength(tup_num, field_num)—Returns the length of the field in bytes.

- cmdstatus—Returns the status string of the last query command.

- clear—Clears the PGresult object.

10.4.4   Interfacing to LDAP

There are at least three usable LDAP libraries for Ruby. The Ruby/LDAP library by Takaaki Tateishi is a fairly "thin" wrapper. If you are an LDAP expert, this might be sufficient for your needs; if not, you may find it a little complex. Here is an example:

```
conn = LDAP::Conn.new("rsads02.foo.com")

conn.bind("CN=username,CN=Users,DC=foo,DC=com","password") do |bound|
   bound.search("DC=foo,DC=com", LDAP::LDAP_SCOPE_SUBTREE,
              "(&(name=*)(objectCategory=person))", ['name','ipPhone']) do |user|
      puts "#{user['name']} #{user['ipPhone']}"
   end
end
```

ActiveLDAP is patterned, not surprisingly, after ActiveRecord. Here is a sample usage of it, taken from its home page:

```
require 'activeldap'
require 'examples/objects/user'
require 'password'


# Instantiate Ruby/ActiveLDAP connection, etc
ActiveLDAP::Base.connect(:password_block => Proc.new { Password.get('Password: ') },
                         :allow_anonymous => false)

# Load a user record (Class defined in the examples)
wad = User.new('wad')
```

```
# Print the common name
p wad.cn

# Change the common name
wad.cn = "Will"

# Save it back to LDAP
wad.write
```

There is also a newer library by Francis Cianfrocca, which is preferred by some. Here is a sample of its usage:

```
require 'net/ldap'

ldap = Net::LDAP.new :host => server_ip_address,
      :port => 389,
      :auth => {
            :method => :simple,
            :username => "cn=manager,dc=example,dc=com",
            :password => "opensesame"
      }

filter = Net::LDAP::Filter.eq( "cn", "George*" )
treebase = "dc=example,dc=com"

ldap.search( :base => treebase, :filter => filter ) do |entry|
  puts "DN: #{entry.dn}"
  entry.each do |attribute, values|
    puts "   #{attribute}:"
    values.each do |value|
      puts "      --->#{value}"
    end
  end
end

p ldap.get_operation_result
```

It is a matter of opinion which of these libraries is better. I urge you to investigate all of them and form your own opinion.

10.4.5   Interfacing to Oracle

Oracle is one of the most powerful and popular database systems in the world. Naturally there have been multiple attempts to interface this database with Ruby. Currently the best library out there is OCI8, the work of Kubo Takehiro.

Despite the name, OCI8 works well with versions of Oracle later than 8. However, because it is not completely mature, it may not offer access to all the newest features of later versions.

The API is split into a "thin" wrapper (the low-level API that closely follows the Oracle Call Interface API) and a higher-level API. In most cases, the higher-level API is the only one you need concern yourself with. In the future, the low-level API may be undocumented.

The OCI8 module encompasses the Cursor and Blob classes. The OCIException class is the superclass of the three classes of exceptions that may be thrown during a database operation: OCIError, OCIBreak, and OCIInvalidHandle.

Connect with the database with OCI8.new, at minimum passing in a username and password. A handle is returned that you can then use to perform queries. Here is an example:

```ruby
require 'oci8'

session = OCI8.new('user', 'password')

query = "SELECT TO_CHAR(SYSDATE, 'YYYY/MM/DD') FROM DUAL"
cursor = session.exec(query)
result = cursor.fetch          # Only one iteration in this case
cursor.close
session.logoff
```

The preceding example shows a cursor being manipulated, although we only do a single fetch against it before we close it. Of course, we can retrieve multiple rows also:

```ruby
query = 'select * from some_table'
cursor = session.exec(query)
while row = cursor.fetch
  puts row.join(",")
end
cursor.close
```

```
# Or with a block:

nrows = session.exec(query) do |row|
  puts row.join(",")
end
```

Bind variables "look like" symbols in the query. There are multiple ways to associate these bind variables with actual values.

```
session = OCI8.new("user","password")
query = "select * from people where name = :name"

# One way...
session.exec(query,'John Smith')

# Another...
cursor = session.parse(query)
cursor.exec('John Smith')

# And another...
cursor = session.parse(query)
cursor.bind_param(':name','John Smith')   # bind by name
cursor.exec

# And another.
cursor = session.parse(query)
cursor.bind_param(1,'John Smith')             # bind by position
cursor.exec
```

There is also a DBI adapter for those who prefer DBI. For more information, consult the OCI8 documentation.

10.4.6   Using the DBI Wrapper

In theory, DBI allows database-independent access to your database. That is, the code should work the same whether the underlying database is Oracle, MySQL, PostgreSQL, or something else. Normally only a single line of code should change, specifying which adapter to use. Sometimes DBI breaks down in the face of complex or database-specific operations, but for most day-to-day work, it is a convenient tool.

Let's assume we have an Oracle database, and we are using the driver or adapter that comes with OCI8. The `connect` method is given enough information to connect successfully with the database. After that, all is mostly intuitive.

```
require "dbi"

db = DBI.connect("dbi:OCI8:mydb", "user", "password")
query = "select * from people"

stmt = db.prepare(query)
stmt.execute

while row = stmt.fetch do
  puts row.join(",")
end

stmt.finish
db.disconnect
```

In the preceding example, the `prepare` can be thought of as compiling or parsing the query, which is then executed. The `fetch` method retrieves a single row from the resultset, returning `nil` when there are no more rows (hence the `while` loop in the preceding code). The `finish` can be thought of as a close or deallocate operation.

For a full treatment of all the features of DBI, consult any reference. For a list of all database drivers, refer to sources such as RubyForge and the RAA.

10.4.7   Object-Relational Mappers (ORMs)

The traditional relational database is good at what it does. It handles queries in an efficient way without foreknowledge of the nature of those *ad hoc* queries. But this model is not very object-oriented.

The ubiquity of both these models (RDBMS and OOP) and the "impedance mismatch" between them has led many people to try to bridge this gap. The software bridge that accomplishes this is called an *Object-Relational Mapper* (*ORM*).

There are many ways of approaching this problem. All have their advantages and disadvantages. Here we'll take a short look at two popular ORMs, `ActiveRecord` and `Og` (the latter of which stands for *object graph*).

The `ActiveRecord` library for Ruby is named after Martin Fowler's "Active Record" design pattern. In essence, it ties database tables to classes so that the data can be manipulated intuitively without SQL. To be more specific, it "wraps a row in a database table or view, encapsulates the database access, and adds domain logic on that data" (see *Patterns of Enterprise Application Architecture* by Martin Fowler, Addison Wesley, 2003 [ISBN: 0-321-12742-0*e*]).

Each table is described by inheriting from `ActiveRecord::Base` and then customizing the class. As with DBI, we have to connect giving it enough information to identify and reach the database. Here is a short example of how it all works:

```
require 'active_record'

ActiveRecord::Base.establish_connection(:adapter => "oci8",
                                        :username => "username",
                                        :password => "password",
                                        :database => "mydb",
                                        :host => "myhost")

class SomeTable < ActiveRecord::Base
  set_table_name "test_table"
  set_primary_key "some_id"
end

SomeTable.find(:all).each do |rec|
  # process rec as needed...
end

item = SomeTable.new
item.id = 1001
item.some_column = "test"
item.save
```

The API is rich and complex. I recommend that you study whatever tutorials you can find on the Web or in books. Because this library is an integral part of "Ruby on Rails," it will be covered in materials on that topic.

Og is different from `ActiveRecord` in the sense that the latter is more database-centric, and the former is more object-centric. Og can generate a database schema from Ruby class definitions (rather than vice versa).

Og is a different way of thinking, and it is less common than `ActiveRecord`. But I believe it has interesting qualities and should be considered a powerful, usable ORM, especially if you design your database *after* your objects.

When we define a class to be stored, we use the property method, which is like attr_accessor except that it has a type (class) associated with it.

```
class SomeClass
  property :alpha, String
  property :beta, String
  property :gamma, String
end
```

Other data types are Integer, Float, Time, Date, and others. It is also potentially possible to have a property that is an arbitrary Ruby object.

Connect to the database much as you would with ActiveRecord or DBI.

```
db = Og::Database.new(:destroy  => false,
                       :name => 'mydb',
                       :store  => :mysql,
                       :user      => 'hal9000',
                       :password => 'chandra')
```

Every object has a save method that does an actual insert of the object into the database:

```
obj = SomeClass.new
obj.alpha  = "Poole"
obj.beta   = "Whitehead"
obj.gamma  = "Kaminski"
obj.save
```

There are also methods that describe object relationships in classical database terms:

```
class Dog
  has_one :house
  belongs_to :owner
  has_many :fleas
end
```

These methods, along with others such as many_to_many and refers_to, can assist in creating complex object and table relationships.

Og is also too large to document here. Refer to other resources online (such as those at http://oxyliquit.de) for more information.

10.5 Conclusion

This chapter provided an overview of I/O in Ruby. We've looked at the IO class itself and its descendant File, along with other related classes such as Dir and Pathname. We've seen some useful tricks for manipulating IO objects and files.

We've also looked at data storage at a slightly higher level—storing data externally as marshaled objects. Finally, we've had a short overview of the true database solutions available in Ruby, along with some OOP techniques for interacting with them in easier ways.

Later, we will look at I/O again from the perspective of sockets and network programming. But before getting too deep into that, let's examine some other topics.

CHAPTER 11

OOP and Dynamic Features in Ruby

Just as the introduction of the irrational numbers... is a convenient myth [which] simplifies the laws of arithmetic... so physical objects are postulated entities which round out and simplify our account of the flux of existence... The conceptional scheme of physical objects is [likewise] a convenient myth, simpler than the literal truth and yet containing that literal truth as a scattered part.

—*Willard Van Orman Quine*

This is an unusual chapter. Whereas many of the chapters in this book deal with a specific problem subdomain such as strings or files, this one doesn't. If the "problem space" is viewed as stretching out on one axis of a graph, this chapter extends out on the other axis, encompassing a slice of each of the other areas. This is because object-oriented programming and dynamicity aren't problem domains themselves but are paradigms that can be applied to any problem whether it be system administration, low-level networking, or Web development.

For this reason, much of this chapter's information should already be familiar to a programmer who knows Ruby. In fact, the rest of the book wouldn't make sense without some of the fundamental knowledge here. Any Ruby programmer knows how to create a subclass, for instance.

This raises the question of what to include and what to exclude. Does every Ruby programmer know about the extend method? What about the instance_eval method? What is obvious to one person might be big news to another.

We have decided to err on the side of completeness. We include in this chapter some of the more esoteric tasks you might want to do with dynamic OOP in Ruby, but we also include the more routine tasks in case anyone is unfamiliar with them. We go right down to the simplest level because people won't agree on where the "middle" level ends. And we have tried to offer a little extra information even on the most basic of topics to justify their inclusion here. On the other hand, topics that are fully covered elsewhere in the book are omitted here.

We'll also make two other comments. First, there is nothing magical about dynamic OOP. Ruby's object orientation and its dynamic nature do interact with each other, but they aren't inherently interrelated; we put them in a single chapter largely for convenience. Second, some language features might be mentioned here that aren't strictly related to either topic. Consider this to be cheating, if you will. We wanted to put them *somewhere*.

11.1 Everyday OOP Tasks

Of his quick objects hath the mind no part,
Nor his own vision holds what it doth catch . . .

— *William Shakespeare, "Sonnet 113"*

If you don't already understand OOP, you won't learn it here. And if you don't already understand OOP *in Ruby*, you probably won't learn it here either. If you're rusty on those concepts, you can scan Chapter 1, "Ruby in Review," where we cover it rapidly (or you can go to another book).

On the other hand, much of this current chapter is tutorial oriented and fairly elementary. So it will be of some value to the beginner and perhaps less value to the intermediate Ruby programmer. We maintain that a book is a random access storage device so that you can easily skip the parts that don't interest you.

11.1.1 Using Multiple Constructors

There is no real "constructor" in Ruby as there is in C++ or Java. The concept is certainly there because objects have to be instantiated and initialized, but the behavior is somewhat different.

In Ruby, a class has a class method new, which is used to instantiate new objects. The new method calls the user-defined special method initialize, which then initializes the attributes of the object appropriately, and new returns a reference to the new object.

But what if we want to have multiple constructors for an object? How should we handle that?

There is nothing to prevent creation of additional class methods that return new objects. Listing 11.1 shows a contrived example in which a rectangle can have two side lengths and three color values. We create additional class methods that assume certain defaults for some of the parameters. (For example, a square is a rectangle with all sides the same length.)

Listing 11.1 Multiple Constructors

```ruby
class ColoredRectangle

  def initialize(r, g, b, s1, s2)
    @r, @g, @b, @s1, @s2 = r, g, b, s1, s2
  end

  def ColoredRectangle.white_rect(s1, s2)
    new(0xff, 0xff, 0xff, s1, s2)
  end

  def ColoredRectangle.gray_rect(s1, s2)
    new(0x88, 0x88, 0x88, s1, s2)
  end

  def ColoredRectangle.colored_square(r, g, b, s)
    new(r, g, b, s, s)
  end

  def ColoredRectangle.red_square(s)
    new(0xff, 0, 0, s, s)
  end

  def inspect
    "#@r #@g #@b #@s1 #@s2"
```

Continues

```
    end
  end

a = ColoredRectangle.new(0x88, 0xaa, 0xff, 20, 30)
b = ColoredRectangle.white_rect(15,25)
c = ColoredRectangle.red_square(40)
```

So we can define any number of methods that create objects according to various specifications. Whether the term *constructor* is appropriate here is a question that we will leave to the language lawyers.

11.1.2   Creating Instance Attributes

An instance attribute in Ruby is always prefixed by an @ sign. It is like an ordinary variable in that it springs into existence when it is first assigned.

In OO languages, we frequently create methods that access attributes to avoid issues of data hiding. We want to have control over how the internals of an object are accessed from the outside. Typically we use *setter* and *getter* methods for this purpose (although in Ruby we don't typically use these terms). These are simply methods used to assign (set) a value or retrieve (get) a value, respectively.

Of course, it is possible to create these functions "by hand," as shown here:

```
class Person

  def name
    @name
  end

  def name=(x)
    @name = x
  end

  def age
    @age
  end

  # ...

end
```

However, Ruby gives us a shorthand for creating these methods. The `attr` method takes a symbol as a parameter and creates the associated attribute. It also creates a getter of the same name, and if the optional second parameter is `true`, it creates a setter also.

```
class Person
   attr :name, true  # Create @name, name, name=
   attr :age         # Create @age, age
end
```

The related methods `attr_reader`, `attr_writer`, and `attr_accessor` take any number of symbols as parameters. The first creates only "read" methods (to get the value of an attribute); the second creates only write methods (to set values); and the third creates both. For example:

```
class SomeClass
   attr_reader :a1, :a2    # Creates @a1, a1, @a2, a2
   attr_writer :b1, :b2    # Creates @b1, b1=, @b2, b2=
   attr_accessor :c1, :c2  # Creates @c1, c1, c1=, @c2, c2, c2=
   # ...
end
```

Recall that assignment to a writer of this form can only be done with a receiver, so within a method the receiver `self` must be used.

11.1.3 Using More Elaborate Constructors

As objects grow more complex, they accumulate more attributes that must be initialized when an object is created. The corresponding constructor can be long and cumbersome, forcing us to count parameters and wrap the line past the margin.

One good way to deal with this complexity is to pass in a *block* to the `initialize` method (see Listing 11.2). We can then evaluate the block to initialize the object. The trick is to use `instance_eval` instead of `eval` to evaluate the block *in the context of the object* rather than that of the caller.

Listing 11.2   A "Fancy" Constructor

```ruby
class PersonalComputer
  attr_accessor :manufacturer,
                :model, :processor, :clock,
                :ram, :disk, :monitor,
                :colors, :vres, :hres, :net

  def initialize(&block)
    instance_eval &block
  end

  # Other methods...
end

desktop = PersonalComputer.new do
  self.manufacturer = "Acme"
  self.model = "THX-1138"
  self.processor = "986"
  self.clock = 9.6        # GHz
  self.ram = 16           # Gb
  self.disk = 20          # Tb
  self.monitor = 25       # inches
  self.colors = 16777216
  self.vres = 1280
  self.hres = 1600
  self.net = "T3"
end

p desktop
```

Several things should be noted here. First, we're using accessors for our attributes so that we can assign values to them intuitively. Second, the reference to self is necessary because a setter method always takes an explicit receiver to distinguish the method call from an ordinary assignment to a local variable. Of course, rather than define accessors, we could use setter functions.

Obviously, we could perform any arbitrary logic we wanted inside the body of this block. For example, we could derive certain fields from others by computation.

Also, what if you didn't really want an object to have accessors for each of the attributes? If you prefer, you can use undef (at the bottom of the constructor block) to get rid of any or all of these. At the least, this could prevent "accidental" assignment of an attribute from outside the object.

11.1.4 Creating Class-level Attributes and Methods

A method or attribute isn't always associated with a specific instance of a class; it can be associated with the class itself. The typical example of a *class method* is the new method; it is always invoked in this way because it is called to create a new instance (and thus can't belong to any particular instance).

We can define class methods of our own. We have already seen this in section 11.1.1, "Using Multiple Constructors." But their functionality certainly isn't limited to constructors; they can be used for any general-purpose task that makes sense at the class level.

In this next highly incomplete fragment, we assume that we are creating a class to play sound files. The `play` method can reasonably be implemented as an instance method; we can instantiate many objects referring to many different sound files. But the `detect_hardware` method has a larger context; depending on our implementation, it might not even make sense to create new objects if this method fails. Its context is that of the whole sound-playing environment rather than any particular sound file.

```
class SoundPlayer

  MAX_SAMPLE = 192

  def SoundPlayer.detect_hardware
    # ...
  end

  def play
    # ...
  end

end
```

Notice that there is another way to declare this class method. The following fragment is essentially the same:

```
class SoundPlayer

  MAX_SAMPLE = 192

  def play
    # ...
```

```
    end

  end

  def SoundPlayer.detect_hardware
    # ...
  end
```

The only difference relates to constants declared in the class. When the class method is declared *outside* its class declaration, these constants aren't in scope. For example, detect_hardware in the first fragment can refer directly to MAX_SAMPLE if it needs to; in the second fragment, the notation SoundPlayer::MAX_SAMPLE would have to be used instead.

Not surprisingly, there are class variables as well as class methods. These begin with a double @ sign, and their scope is the class rather than any instance of the class.

The traditional example of using class variables is counting instances of the class as they are created. But they can actually be used for any purpose in which the information is meaningful in the context of the class rather than the object. For a different example, see Listing 11.3.

Listing 11.3   Class Variables and Methods

```
class Metal

  @@current_temp = 70

  attr_accessor :atomic_number

  def Metal.current_temp=(x)
    @@current_temp = x
  end

  def Metal.current_temp
    @@current_temp
  end

  def liquid?
    @@current_temp >= @melting
  end

  def initialize(atnum, melt)
    @atomic_number = atnum
    @melting = melt
  end
```

```
end


aluminum = Metal.new(13, 1236)
copper = Metal.new(29, 1982)
gold = Metal.new(79, 1948)

Metal.current_temp = 1600

puts aluminum.liquid?        # true
puts copper.liquid?          # false
puts gold.liquid?            # false

Metal.current_temp = 2100

puts aluminum.liquid?        # true
puts copper.liquid?          # true
puts gold.liquid?            # true
```

Note here that the class variable is initialized at the class level before it is used in a class method. Note also that we can access a class variable from an instance method, but we can't access an instance variable from a class method. After a moment of thought, this makes sense.

But what happens if you try? What if we try to print the attribute @atomic_number from within the Metal.current_temp method? We find that it seems to exist—it doesn't cause an error—but it has the value nil. What is happening here?

The answer is that we're not actually accessing the instance variable of class Metal at all. We're accessing an instance variable of class Class instead. (Remember that in Ruby, Class is a class!)

Such a thing is called a *class instance variable* (a term that comes from Smalltalk). For more comments on this, see section 11.2.4, "Creating Parametric Classes."

Listing 11.4 summarizes the situation.

Listing 11.4 Class and Instance Data

```
class MyClass

  SOME_CONST = "alpha"       # A class-level constant

  @@var = "beta"             # A class variable
  @var = "gamma"             # A class instance variable

  def initialize
    @var = "delta"           # An instance variable
```

Continues

```
    end

    def mymethod
      puts SOME_CONST          # (the class constant)
      puts @@var               # (the class variable)
      puts @var                # (the instance variable)
    end

    def MyClass.classmeth1
      puts SOME_CONST          # (the class constant)
      puts @@var               # (the class variable)
      puts @var                # (the class instance variable)
    end

  end

  def MyClass.classmeth2
    puts MyClass::SOME_CONST   # (the class constant)
    # puts @@var               # error - out of scope
    puts @var                  # (the class instance variable)
  end


  myobj = MyClass.new
  MyClass.classmeth1           # alpha, beta, gamma
  MyClass.classmeth2           # alpha, gamma
  myobj.mymethod               # alpha, beta, delta
```

We should mention that a class method can be made private with the method
private_class_method. This works the same way private works at the instance level.
See also section 11.2.10, "Automatically Defining Class-level Readers and Writers."

11.1.5   Inheriting from a Superclass

We can inherit from a class by using the < symbol:

```
class Boojum < Snark
  # ...
end
```

Given this declaration, we can say that the class Boojum is a *subclass* of the class
Snark, or in the same way, Snark is a *superclass* of Boojum. As we all know, every boojum is a snark, but not every snark is a boojum.

The purpose of inheritance, of course, is to add or enhance functionality. We are going from the more general to the more specific.

As an aside, many languages such as C++ implement *multiple inheritance (MI)*. Ruby (like Java and some others) doesn't allow MI, but the mixin facility can compensate for this; see section 11.1.12, "Working with Modules."

Let's look at a (slightly) more realistic example. Suppose that we have a Person class and want to create a Student class that derives from it.

We'll define Person this way:

```ruby
class Person

  attr_accessor :name, :age, :sex

  def initialize(name, age, sex)
    @name, @age, @sex = name, age, sex
  end

  # ...

end
```

And we'll then define Student this way:

```ruby
class Student < Person

  attr_accessor :idnum, :hours

  def initialize(name, age, sex, idnum, hours)
    super(name, age, sex)
    @idnum = idnum
    @hours = hours
  end

  # ...

end
```

```ruby
# Create two objects
a = Person.new("Dave Bowman", 37, "m")
b = Student.new("Franklin Poole", 36, "m", "000-13-5031", 24)
```

Now let's look at what we've done here. What is this super that we see called from Student's initialize method? It is simply *a call to the corresponding method in the parent class*. As such, we give it three parameters (whereas our own initialize method takes five).

It's not always necessary to use super in such a way, but it is often convenient. After all, the attributes of a class form a superset of the attributes of the parent class, so why not use the parent's constructor to initialize them?

Concerning what inheritance really means, it definitely represents the "is-a" relationship. A Student *is-a* Person, just as we expect. We'll make three other observations:

- Every attribute (and method) of the parent is reflected in the child. If Person had a height attribute, Student would inherit it, and if the parent had a method named say_hello, the child would inherit that, too.

- The child can have additional attributes and methods, as you have already seen. That is why the creation of a subclass is often referred to as *extending* a superclass.

- The child can *override* or redefine any of the attributes and methods of its parent.

This last point brings up the question of how a method call is resolved. How do I know whether I'm calling the method of this particular class or its superclass?

The short answer is you don't know, and you don't care. If we invoke a method on a Student object, the method for that class will be called *if it exists*. If it doesn't, the method in the superclass will be called, and so on. We say "and so on" because every class (except Object) has a superclass.

What if we specifically want to call a superclass method, but we don't happen to be in the corresponding method? We can always create an alias in the subclass before we do anything with it.

```
class Student    # reopening class

  # Assuming Person has a say_hello method...

  alias :say_hi :say_hello

  def say_hello
    puts "Hi, there."
  end
```

```
def formal_greeting
  # Say hello the way my superclass would.
  say_hi
end

end
```

There are various subtleties relating to inheritance that we don't discuss here, but this is essentially how it works. Be sure to refer to the next section.

11.1.6 Testing Classes of Objects

Frequently we will want to know: What kind of object is this, or how does it relate to this class? There are many ways of making a determination such as this.

First, the `class` method (that is, the instance method named `class`) always returns the class of an object. The former synonym `type` is obsolete.

```
s = "Hello"
n = 237
sc = s.class     # String
nc = n.class     # Fixnum
```

Don't be misled into thinking that the thing returned by `class` or `type` is a string representing the class. It is an actual instance of the class `Class`! Thus if we wanted, we could call a class method of the target type as though it were an instance method of `Class` (which it is).

```
s2 = "some string"
var = s2.class              # String
my_str = var.new("Hi...")   # A new string
```

We could compare such a variable with a constant class name to see whether they were equal; we could even use a variable as the superclass from which to define a subclass! Confused? Just remember that in Ruby, `Class` is an object, and `Object` is a class.

Sometimes we want to compare an object with a class to see whether the object belongs to that class. The method `instance_of?` will accomplish this. For example:

```
puts (5.instance_of? Fixnum)         # true
puts ("XYZZY".instance_of? Fixnum)   # false
puts ("PLUGH".instance_of? String)   # true
```

But what if we want to take inheritance relationships into account? The kind_of? method (similar to instance_of?) takes this issue into account. A synonym is is_a?, naturally enough because what we are describing is the classic *is-a* relationship.

```
n = 9876543210
flag1 = n.instance_of? Bignum      # true
flag2 = n.kind_of? Bignum          # true
flag3 = n.is_a? Bignum             # true
flag3 = n.is_a? Integer            # true
flag4 = n.is_a? Numeric            # true
flag5 = n.is_a? Object             # true
flag6 = n.is_a? String             # false
flag7 = n.is_a? Array              # false
```

Obviously kind_of or is_a? is more generalized than the instance_of? relationship. For an example from everyday life, every dog is a mammal, but not every mammal is a dog.

There is one surprise here for the Ruby neophyte. Any module that is mixed in by a class maintains the *is-a* relationship with the instances. For example, the Array class mixes in Enumerable; this means that any array is a kind of enumerable entity.

```
x = [1, 2, 3]
flag8 = x.kind_of? Enumerable      # true
flag9 = x.is_a? Enumerable         # true
```

We can also use the numeric relational operators in a fairly intuitive way to compare one class to another. We say "intuitive" because the less-than operator is used to denote inheritance from a superclass.

```
flag1 = Integer < Numeric          # true
flag2 = Integer < Object           # true
flag3 = Object == Array            # false
flag4 = IO >= File                 # true
flag5 = Float < Integer            # nil
```

Every class typically has a "threequal" operator === defined. The expression class === instance will be true if the instance belongs to the class. The relationship operator is usually known as the *case equality* operator because it is used implicitly in a case statement. This is therefore a way to act on the class of an expression.

For more information on this operator, see section 11.1.7, "Testing Equality of Objects."

We should also mention the `respond_to` method. This is used when we don't really care what the class is but just want to know whether it implements a certain method. This, of course, is a rudimentary kind of type information. (In fact, we might say this is the most important type information of all.) The method is passed a symbol and an optional flag (indicating whether to include private methods in the search).

```
# Search public methods
if wumpus.respond_to?(:bite)
  puts "It's got teeth!"
else
  puts "Go ahead and taunt it."
end

# Optional second parameter will search
# private methods also.

if woozle.respond_to?(:bite,true)
  puts "Woozles bite!"
else
  puts "Ah, the non-biting woozle."
end
```

Sometimes we want to know what class is the immediate parent of an object or class. The instance method `superclass` of class `Class` can be used for this.

```
array_parent = Array.superclass     # Object
fn_parent = 237.class.superclass     # Integer
obj_parent = Object.superclass       # nil
```

Every class except `Object` will have a superclass.

11.1.7   Testing Equality of Objects

All animals are equal, but some are more equal than others.

— *George Orwell,* Animal Farm

When you write classes, it's convenient if the semantics for common operations are the same as for Ruby's built-in classes. For example, if your classes implement objects that may be ranked, it makes sense to implement the method <=> and mix in the Comparable module. Doing so means that all the normal comparison operators work with objects of your class.

However, the picture is less clear when it comes to dealing with object equality. Ruby objects implement five different methods that test for equality. Your classes might well end up implementing some of these, so let's look at each in turn.

The most basic comparison is the equal? method (which comes from Object), which returns true if its receiver and parameter have the same object ID. This is a fundamental part of the semantics of objects and shouldn't be overridden in your classes.

The most common test for equality uses our old friend ==, which tests the values of its receiver with its argument. This is probably the most intuitive test for equality.

Next on the scale of abstraction is the method eql?, which is part of Object. (Actually, eql? is implemented in the Kernel module, which is mixed in to Object.) Like ==, eql? compares its receiver and its argument but is slightly stricter. For example, different numeric objects will be coerced into a common type when compared using ==, but numbers of different types will never test equal using eql?.

```
flag1 = (1 == 1.0)      # true
flag2 = (1.eql?(1.0))   # false
```

The eql? method exists for one reason: It is used to compare the values of hash keys. If you want to override Ruby's default behavior when using your objects as hash keys, you'll need to override the methods eql? and hash for those objects.

Two more equality tests are implemented by every object. The === method is used to compare the target in a case statement against each of the selectors, using selector===target. Although apparently complex, this rule allows Ruby case statements to be intuitive in practice. For example, you can switch based on the class of an object:

```
case an_object
  when String
    puts "It's a string."
  when Numeric
    puts "It's a number."
  else
    puts "It's something else entirely."
end
```

This works because class Module implements === to test whether its parameter is an instance of its receiver (or the receiver's parents). So, if an_object is the string "cat", the expression String === an_object would be true, and the first clause in the case statement would fire.

Finally, Ruby implements the match operator =~. Conventionally this is used by strings and regular expressions to implement pattern matching. However, if you find a use for it in some unrelated classes, you're free to overload it.

The equality tests == and =~ also have negated forms, != and !~, respectively. These are implemented internally by reversing the sense of the non-negated form. This means that you implement (say) the method ==; you also get the method != for free.

11.1.8 Controlling Access to Methods

In Ruby, an object is pretty much defined by the interface it provides: the methods it makes available to others. However, when writing a class, you often need to write other helper methods, used within your class but dangerous if available externally. That is where the private method of class Module comes in handy.

You can use private in two different ways. If in the body of a class or method definition you call private with no parameters, subsequent methods will be made private to that class or module. Alternatively, you can pass a list of method names (as symbols) to private, and these named methods will be made private. Listing 11.5 shows both forms.

Listing 11.5 Private Methods

```
class Bank
  def open_safe
    # ...
  end

  def close_safe
    # ...
  end

  private :open_safe, :close_safe

  def make_withdrawal(amount)
    if access_allowed
      open_safe
      get_cash(amount)
      close_safe
    end
```

Continues

```
  end

  # make the rest private

  private

  def get_cash
    # ...
  end

  def access_allowed
    # ...
  end
end
```

Because the `attr` family of statements effectively just defines methods, attributes are affected by the access control statements such as `private`.

The implementation of `private` might seem strange but is actually clever. Private methods cannot be called with an explicit receiver: They are always called with an implicit receiver of `self`. This means that you can never invoke a private method in another object: There is no way to specify that other object as the receiver of the method call. It also means that private methods are available to subclasses of the class that defines them but again only in the same object.

The `protected` access modifier is less restrictive. Protected methods can be accessed only by instances of the defining class and its subclasses. You can specify a receiver with protected methods, so you can invoke those in different objects (as long as they are objects of the same class as the sender). A common use for protected methods is defining accessors to allow two objects of the same type to cooperate with each other. In the following example, objects of class `Person` can be compared based on the person's age, but that age is not accessible outside the `Person` class:

```
class Person
  def initialize(name, age)
    @name, @age = name, age
  end

  def <=>(other)
    age <=> other.age
  end

  attr_reader :name, :age
```

```
    protected    :age
end

p1 = Person.new("fred", 31)
p2 = Person.new("agnes", 43)
compare = (p1 <=> p2)        # -1
x = p1.age                   # Error!
```

To complete the picture, the access modifier public is used to make methods public. This shouldn't be a surprise.

As a final twist, normal methods defined outside a class or module definition (that is, the methods defined at the top level) are made private by default. Because they are defined in class Object, they are globally available, but they cannot be called with a receiver.

11.1.9 Copying an Object

The Ruby built-in methods Object#clone and #dup produce copies of their receiver. They differ in the amount of context they copy. The dup method copies just the object's content, whereas clone also preserves things such as singleton classes associated with the object.

```
s1 = "cat"

def s1.upcase
  "CaT"
end

s1_dup   = s1.dup
s1_clone = s1.clone
s1                   #=> "cat"
s1_dup.upcase        #=> "CAT"   (singleton method not copied)
s1_clone.upcase      #=> "CaT"   (uses singleton method)
```

Both dup and clone are *shallow copies*: They copy the immediate contents of their receiver only. If the receiver contains references to other objects, those objects aren't in turn copied; the duplicate simply holds references to them. The following example illustrates this. The object arr2 is a copy of arr1, so changing entire elements, such as arr2[2] has no effect on arr1. However, both the original array and the duplicate contain a reference to the same String object, so changing its contents via arr2 also affects the value referenced by arr1.

```
arr1 = [ 1, "flipper", 3 ]
arr2 = arr1.dup

arr2[2] = 99
arr2[1][2] = 'a'

arr1              # [1, "flapper", 3]
arr2              # [1, "flapper", 99]
```

Sometimes, you want a *deep copy*, where the entire object tree rooted in one object is copied to create the second object. This way, there is guaranteed to be no interaction between the two. Ruby provides no built-in method to perform a deep copy, but there are a couple of techniques you can use to implement one.

The pure way to do it is to have your classes implement a deep_copy method. As part of its processing, this method calls deep_copy recursively on all the objects referenced by the receiver. You then add a deep_copy method to all the Ruby built-in classes that you use.

Fortunately, there's a quicker hack using the Marshal module. If you use marshaling to dump an object into a string and then load it back into a new object, that new object will be a deep copy of the original.

```
arr1 = [ 1, "flipper", 3 ]
arr2 = Marshal.load(Marshal.dump(arr1))

arr2[2] = 99
arr2[1][2] = 'a'

arr1              # [1, "flipper", 3]
arr2              # [1, "flapper", 99]
```

In this case, notice how changing the string via arr2 doesn't affect the string referenced by arr1.

11.1.10   Using `initialize_copy`

When you copy an object with `dup` or `clone`, the constructor is bypassed. All the state information is copied.

But what if you don't want this to happen? Consider this example:

```ruby
class Document
  attr_accessor :title, :text
  attr_reader   :timestamp

  def initialize(title, text)
    @title, @text = title, text
    @timestamp = Time.now
  end
end

doc1 = Document.new("Random Stuff",File.read("somefile"))
sleep 300                         # Wait awhile...
doc2 = doc1.clone

doc1.timestamp == doc2.timestamp  # true
# Oops... the timestamps are the same!
```

When a `Document` is created, it is given a time stamp. If we copy that object, we copy the time stamp also. But what if we wanted instead to capture the time that the *copy* operation happened?

Defining an `initialize_copy` makes this possible. This method is called when an object is copied. It is analogous to `initialize`, giving us complete control over the object's state.

```ruby
class Document      # Reopen the class
  def initialize_copy(other)
    @timestamp = Time.now
  end
end

doc3 = Document.new("More Stuff",File.read("otherfile"))
sleep 300                         # Wait awhile...
doc4 = doc3.clone

doc3.timestamp == doc4.timestamp  # false
# Timestamps are now accurate.
```

Note that the `initialize_copy` is called *after* the information is copied. That is why we omitted this line:

```
@title, @text = other.title, other.text
```

As a matter of fact, an *empty* `initialize_copy` would behave just as if the method were not there at all.

11.1.11   Understanding `allocate`

In rare circumstances you might want to create an object without calling its constructor (bypassing `initialize`). For example, maybe you have an object whose state is determined entirely by its accessors; then it isn't necessary to call mew (which calls `initialize`) unless you really want to. Imagine you are gathering data a piece at a time to fill in the state of an object; you might want to start with an "empty" object rather than gathering all the data up front and calling the constructor.

The `allocate` method was introduced in Ruby 1.8 to make this easier. It returns a "blank" object of the proper class, yet uninitialized.

```
class Person
  attr_accessor :name, :age, :phone

  def initialize(n,a,p)
    @name, @age, @phone = n, a, p
  end
end


p1 = Person.new("John Smith",29,"555-1234")

p2 = Person.allocate

p p1.age    # 29
p p2.age    # nil
```

11.1.12   Working with Modules

There are two basic reasons to use modules in Ruby. The first is simply namespace management; we'll have fewer name collisions if we store constants and methods in modules. A method stored in this way (a module method) is called with the module name; that is, without a real receiver. This is analogous to the way a class method is called. If we see calls such as `File.ctime` and `FileTest.exist?`, we can't tell just from context that `File` is a class and `FileTest` is a module.

The second reason is more interesting: We can use a module as a *mixin*. A mixin is like a specialized implementation of multiple inheritance in which only the interface portion is inherited.

We've talked about module methods, but what about instance methods? A module isn't a class, so it can't have instances, and an instance method can't be called without a receiver.

As it turns out, a module *can* have instance methods. These become part of whatever class does the `include` of the module.

```
module MyMod

  def meth1
    puts "This is method 1"
  end

end


class MyClass

  include MyMod

  # ...
end


x = MyClass.new
x.meth1                 # This is method 1
```

Here `MyMod` is mixed into `MyClass`, and the instance method `meth1` is inherited. You have also seen an `include` done at the top level; in that case, the module is mixed into `Object` as you might expect.

But what happens to our module methods, if there are any? You might think they would be included as class methods, but Ruby doesn't behave that way. The module methods aren't mixed in.

But we have a trick we can use if we want that behavior. There is a hook called append_features that we can override. It is called with a parameter, which is the "destination" class or module (into which this module is being included). For an example of its use, see Listing 11.6.

Listing 11.6   Including a Module with `append_features`

```ruby
module MyMod

  def MyMod.append_features(someClass)
    def someClass.modmeth
      puts "Module (class) method"
    end
    super    # This call is necessary!
  end

  def meth1
    puts "Method 1"
  end

end


class MyClass

  include MyMod

  def MyClass.classmeth
    puts "Class method"
  end

  def meth2
    puts "Method 2"
  end

end


x = MyClass.new

                     # Output:
MyClass.classmeth    #   Class method
x.meth1              #   Method 1
MyClass.modmeth      #   Module (class) method
x.meth2              #   Method 2
```

This example is worth examining in detail. First, we should understand that append_features isn't *just* a hook that is called when an include happens; it actually does the work of the include operation. That's why the call to super is needed; without it, the rest of the module (in this case, meth1) wouldn't be included at all.

Also note that within the append_features call, there is a method definition. This looks unusual, but it works because the inner method definition is a singleton method (class-level or module-level). An attempt to define an instance method in the same way would result in a Nested method error.

Conceivably a module might want to determine the initiator of a mixin. The append_features method can also be used for this because the class is passed in as a parameter.

It is also possible to mix in the instance methods of a module as class methods. Listing 11.7 shows an example.

Listing 11.7   Module Instance Methods Becoming Class Methods

```
module MyMod

  def meth3
    puts "Module instance method meth3"
    puts "can become a class method."
  end

end


class MyClass

  class << self      # Here, self is MyClass
    include MyMod
  end

end


MyClass.meth3

# Output:
#   Module instance method meth3
#   can become a class method.
```

The extend method is useful here. This example simply becomes:

```
class MyClass
    extend MyMod
end
```

We've been talking about methods. What about instance variables? Although it is certainly possible for modules to have their own instance data, it usually isn't done. However, if you find a need for this capability, there is nothing stopping you from using it.

It is possible to mix a module into an object rather than a class (for example, with the extend method). See section 11.2.2, "Specializing an Individual Object."

It's important to understand one more fact about modules. It is possible to define methods in your class that will be called by the mixin. This is a powerful technique that will seem familiar to those who have used Java interfaces.

The classic example (which we've seen elsewhere) is mixing in the Comparable module and defining a <=> method. Because the mixed-in methods can call the comparison method, we now have such operators as <, >, <=, and so on.

Another example is mixing in the Enumerable module and defining <=> and an iterator each. This gives us numerous useful methods such as collect, sort, min, max, and select.

You can also define modules of your own to be used in the same way. The principal limitation is the programmer's imagination.

11.1.13   Transforming or Converting Objects

Sometimes an object comes in exactly the right form at the right time, but sometimes we need to convert it to something else or pretend it's something it isn't. A good example is the well-known to_s method.

Every object can be converted to a string representation in some fashion. But not every object can successfully masquerade as a string. That in essence is the difference between the to_s and to_str methods. Let's elaborate on that.

Methods such as puts and contexts such as #{...} interpolation in strings expect to receive a String as a parameter. If they don't, they ask the object they *did* receive to convert itself to a String by sending it a to_s message. This is where you can specify how your object will appear when displayed; simply implement a to_s method in your class that returns an appropriate String.

```
class Pet

  def initialize(name)
    @name = name
  end

  # ...

  def to_s
    "Pet: #@name"
  end

end
```

Other methods (such as the String concatenation operator +) are more picky; they expect you to pass in something that is really pretty close to a String. In this case, Matz decided not to have the interpreter call to_s to convert non-string arguments because he felt this would lead to too many errors. Instead, the interpreter invokes a stricter method, to_str. Of the built-in classes, only String and Exception implement to_str, and only String, Regexp, and Marshal call it. Typically when you see the runtime error TypeError: Failed to convert xyz into String, you know that the interpreter tried to invoke to_str and failed.

You can implement to_str yourself. For example, you might want to allow numbers to be concatenated to strings:

```
class Numeric

  def to_str
    to_s
  end

end

label = "Number " + 9      # "Number 9"
```

An analogous situation holds for arrays. The method to_a is called to convert an object to an array representation, and to_ary is called when an array is expected.

An example of when `to_ary` is called is with multiple assignment. Suppose we have a statement of this form:

```
a, b, c = x
```

Assuming that x were an array of three elements, this would behave in the expected way. But if it isn't an array, the interpreter will try to call `to_ary` to convert it to one. For what it's worth, the method we define can be a singleton (belonging to a specific object). The conversion can be completely arbitrary; here we show an (unrealistic) example in which a string is converted to an array of strings:

```
class String

  def to_ary
    return self.split("")
  end

end

str = "UFO"
a, b, c = str      # ["U", "F", "O"]
```

The `inspect` method implements another convention. Debuggers, utilities such as `irb`, and the debug print method `p` use the `inspect` method to convert an object to a printable representation. If you want classes to reveal internal details when being debugged, you should override `inspect`.

There is another situation in which we'd like to be able to do conversions of this sort "under the hood." As a language user, you'd expect to be able to add a `Fixnum` to a `Float`, or divide a `Complex` number by a rational number. However, this is a problem for a language designer. If the `Fixnum` method + receives a `Float` as an argument, what can it do? It only knows how to add `Fixnum` values. Ruby implements the `coerce` mechanism to deal with this.

When (for example) + is passed an argument it doesn't understand, it tries to coerce the receiver and the argument to compatible types and then do the addition based on those types. The pattern for using `coerce` in a class you write is straightforward:

```
class MyNumberSystem

  def +(other)
    if other.kind_of?(MyNumberSystem)
```

```
      result = some_calculation_between_self_and_other
      MyNumberSystem.new(result)
    else
      n1, n2 = other.coerce(self)
      n1 + n2
    end
  end

end
```

The value returned by `coerce` is a two-element array containing its argument and its receiver converted to compatible types.

In this previous example, we're relying on the type of our argument to perform some kind of coercion. If we want to be good citizens, we also need to implement coercion in our class, allowing other types of numbers to work with us. To do this, we need to know the specific types that we can work with directly and convert the object to those types when appropriate. When we can't do that, we fall back on asking our parent, as in the following example:

```
def coerce(other)
  if other.kind_of?(Float)
    return other, self.to_f
  elsif other.kind_of?(Integer)
    return other, self.to_i
  else
    super
  end
end
```

Of course, for this to work, our object must implement `to_i` and `to_f`.

You can use `coerce` as part of the solution for implementing a Perl-like auto-conversion of strings to numbers:

```
class String

  def coerce(n)
    if self['.']
      [n, Float(self)]
    else
      [n, Integer(self)]
    end
  end
```

```
end

x = 1 + "23"        # 24
y = 23 * "1.23"     # 29.29
```

We don't necessarily recommend this. But we do recommend that you implement a coerce method whenever you are creating some kind of numeric class.

11.1.14   Creating Data-only Classes (`Structs`)

Sometimes you need to group together a bunch of related data with no other associated processing. You could do this by defining a class:

```
class Address

  attr_accessor :street, :city, :state

  def initialize(street1, city, state)
    @street, @city, @state = street, city, state
  end

end

books = Address.new("411 Elm St", "Dallas", "TX")
```

This works, but it's tedious, and a fair amount of repetition is in there. That's why the built-in class Struct comes in handy. In the same way that convenience methods such as attr_accessor define methods to access attributes, class Struct defines classes that contain just attributes. These classes are *structure templates*.

```
Address = Struct.new("Address", :street, :city, :state)
books = Address.new("411 Elm St", "Dallas", "TX")
```

So, why do we pass the name of the structure to be created in as the first parameter of the constructor and also assign the result to a constant (Address in this case)?

When we create a new structure template by calling Struct.new, a new class is created within class Struct itself. This class is given the name passed in as the first parameter and the attributes given as the rest of the parameters. This means that if we wanted, we could access this newly created class within the namespace of class Struct.

```
Struct.new("Address", :street, :city, :state)
books = Struct::Address.new("411 Elm St", "Dallas", "TX")
```

After you've created a structure template, you call its new method to create new instances of that particular structure. You don't have to assign values to all the attributes in the constructor: Those that you omit will be initialized to nil. Once it is created, you can access the structure's attributes using normal syntax or by indexing the structure object as if it were a Hash. For more information, look up class Struct in any reference (such as ruby-doc.org online).

By the way, we advise against the creation of a Struct named Tms because there is already a predefined Struct::Tms class.

11.1.15 Freezing Objects

Sometimes we want to prevent an object from being changed. The freeze method (in Object) allows us to do this, effectively turning an object into a constant.

After we freeze an object, an attempt to modify it results in a TypeError. Listing 11.8 shows a pair of examples.

Listing 11.8 Freezing an Object

```
str = "This is a test. "
str.freeze

begin
  str << " Don't be alarmed."    # Attempting to modify
rescue => err
  puts "#{err.class} #{err}"
end

arr = [1, 2, 3]
arr.freeze

begin
  arr << 4                       # Attempting to modify
rescue => err
  puts "#{err.class} #{err}"
end

# Output:
#    TypeError: can't modify frozen string
#    TypeError: can't modify frozen array
```

However, bear in mind that `freeze` operates on an object reference, not on a variable! This means that any operation resulting in a new object will work. Sometimes this isn't intuitive. In the example below, we might expect that the += operation would fail; but it acts normally. This is because assignment is not a method call. It acts on variables, not objects; and it creates a new object as needed. The old object is indeed still frozen, but it is no longer referenced by that variable name.

```
str = "counter-"
str.freeze
str += "intuitive"          # "counter-intuitive"

arr = [8, 6, 7]
arr.freeze
arr += [5, 3, 0, 9]         # [8, 6, 7, 5, 3, 0, 9]
```

Why does this happen? A statement a += x is semantically equivalent to a = a + x. The expression a + x is evaluated to a new object, which is then assigned to a! The object isn't changed, but the variable now refers to a new object. All the reflexive assignment operators exhibit this behavior, as do some other methods. Always ask yourself whether you are creating a new object or modifying an existing one; then freeze will not surprise you.

There is a method `frozen?` that will tell you whether an object is frozen.

```
hash = { 1 => 1, 2 => 4, 3 => 9 }
hash.freeze
arr = hash.to_a
puts hash.frozen?                    # true
puts arr.frozen?                     # false
hash2 = hash
puts hash2.frozen?                   # true
```

As we see here (with hash2), the object, not the variable, is frozen.

11.2   More Advanced Techniques

Not everything in Ruby OOP is straightforward. Some techniques are more complex than others, and some are rarely used. The dividing line will be different for each programmer. We've tried to put items in this part of the chapter that were slightly more involved or slightly more rare in terms of usage.

From time to time, you might ask yourself whether it's possible to do some task or other in Ruby. The short answer is that Ruby is a rich dynamic OOP language with a good set of reasonably orthogonal features, and if you want to do something that you're used to in another language, you can *probably* do it in Ruby.

As a matter of fact, all Turing-complete languages are pretty much the same from a theoretical standpoint. The whole field of language design is the search for a meaningful, convenient notation. The reader who doubts the importance of a convenient notation should try writing a LISP interpreter in COBOL or doing long division with Roman numerals.

Of course, we won't say that *every* language task is elegant or natural in Ruby. Someone would quickly prove us wrong if we made that assertion.

This section also touches on the use of Ruby in various advanced programming styles such as functional programming and aspect-oriented programming. We don't claim expertise in these areas; we are only reporting what other people are saying. Take it all with a grain of salt.

11.2.1   Sending an Explicit Message to an Object

In a static language, you take it for granted that when you call a function that function name is hard-coded into the program; it is part of the program source. In a dynamic language, we have more flexibility than that.

Every time you invoke a method, you're sending a message to an object. Most of the time, these messages are hard-coded as in a static language, but they need not always be. We can write code that determines at runtime which method to call. The send method will allow us to use a Symbol to represent a method name.

For an example, suppose that we had an array of objects we wanted to sort, and we wanted to be able to use different fields as sort keys. That's not a problem; we can easily write customized sort blocks. But suppose that we wanted to be a little more elegant and write only a single routine that could sort based on whatever key we specified. Listing 11.9 shows an example.

This example was written for the first edition of this book. The sort_by method is now standard in Ruby, and it is more efficient than this one because it implements a Schwartzian transform (named for Randal Schwartz of Perl fame), saving the transformed values so as to avoid recomputing them. Listing 11.9, however, is still a valid example of using send.

Listing 11.9   Sorting by Any Key

```ruby
class Person
  attr_reader :name, :age, :height

  def initialize(name, age, height)
    @name, @age, @height = name, age, height
  end

  def inspect
    "#@name #@age #@height"
  end
end


class Array
  def sort_by(sym)    # Our own version of sort_by
    self.sort { |x,y| x.send(sym) <=> y.send(sym) }
  end
end


people = []
people << Person.new("Hansel", 35, 69)
people << Person.new("Gretel", 32, 64)
people << Person.new("Ted", 36, 68)
people << Person.new("Alice", 33, 63)

p1 = people.sort_by(:name)
p2 = people.sort_by(:age)
p3 = people.sort_by(:height)

p p1    # [Alice 33 63, Gretel 32 64, Hansel 35 69, Ted 36 68]
p p2    # [Gretel 32 64, Alice 33 63, Hansel 35 69, Ted 36 68]
p p3    # [Alice 33 63, Gretel 32 64, Ted 36 68, Hansel 35 69]
```

We'll also mention the alias __send__, which does exactly the same thing. It is given this peculiar name, of course, because send is a name that might be used (purposely or accidentally) as a user-defined method name.

11.2.2 Specializing an Individual Object

I'm a Solipsist, and I must say I'm surprised there aren't more of us.

— Letter received by Bertrand Russell

In most object-oriented languages, all objects of a particular class share the same behavior. The class acts as a template, producing an object with the same interface each time the constructor is called.

Although Ruby acts the same way, that isn't the end of the story. Once you have a Ruby object, you can change its behavior on-the-fly. Effectively, you're giving that object a private, anonymous subclass: All the methods of the original class are available, but you've added additional behavior for just that object. Because this behavior is private to the associated object, it can only occur once. A thing occurring only once is called a *singleton*, as in *singleton methods* and *singleton classes*.

The word "singleton" can be confusing because it is also used in a different sense, as the name of a well-known design pattern for a class that can only be instantiated once. For this usage, refer to the `singleton.rb` library.

In the following example we see a pair of objects, both of which are strings. For the second one, we will add a method upcase that will override the existing method of that name.

```
a = "hello"
b = "goodbye"

def b.upcase        # create single method
  gsub(/(.)(.)/) { $1.upcase + $2 }
end

puts a.upcase    # HELLO
puts b.upcase    # GoOdBye
```

Adding a singleton method to an object creates a singleton class for that object if one doesn't already exist. This singleton class's parent will be the object's original class. (This could be considered an anonymous subclass of the original class.) If you want to add multiple methods to an object, you can create the singleton class directly.

```
b = "goodbye"

class << b
```

```
def upcase      # create single method
  gsub(/(.)(.)/) { $1.upcase + $2 }
end

def upcase!
  gsub!(/(.)(.)/) { $1.upcase + $2 }
end

end

puts b.upcase  # GoOdBye
puts b         # goodbye
b.upcase!
puts b         # GoOdBye
```

As an aside, note that the more "primitive" objects (such as a Fixnum) cannot have singleton methods added. This is because an object of this nature is stored as an immediate value rather than as an object reference. However, this functionality is planned for a future revision of Ruby (though the values will still be immediate).

If you read some of the library code, you're bound to come across an idiomatic use of singleton classes. Within class definitions, you might see something like this:

```
class SomeClass

  # Stuff...

  class << self
    # more stuff...
  end

  # ... and so on.

end
```

Within the body of a class definition, self is the class you're defining, so creating a singleton based on it modifies the class's class. At the simplest level, this means that instance methods in the singleton class are class methods externally.

```
class TheClass
  class << self
    def hello
      puts "hi"
    end
  end
```

```
end

# invoke a class method
TheClass.hello              # hi
```

Another common use of this technique is to define class-level helper functions, which we can then access in the rest of the class definition. As an example, we want to define several accessor functions that always convert their results to a string. We could do this by coding each individually. A neater way might be to define a class-level function `accessor_string` that generates these functions for us (as shown in Listing 11.10).

Listing 11.10   A Class-Level Method `accessor_string`

```
class MyClass

  class << self

    def accessor_string(*names)
      names.each do |name|
        class_eval <<-EOF
          def #{name}
            @#{name}.to_s
          end
        EOF
      end
    end

  end

  def initialize
    @a = [ 1, 2, 3 ]
    @b = Time.now
  end

  accessor_string :a, :b

end


o = MyClass.new
puts o.a              # 123
puts o.b              # Mon Apr 30 23:12:15 CDT 2001
```

More imaginative examples are left up to you.

The `extend` method will mix a module into an object. The instance methods from the module become instance methods for the object. Let's look at Listing 11.11.

Listing 11.11 Using extend

```
module Quantifier

  def any?
    self.each { |x| return true if yield x }
    false
  end

  def all?
    self.each { |x| return false if not yield x }
    true
  end

end


list = [1, 2, 3, 4, 5]


list.extend(Quantifier)

flag1 = list.any? {|x| x > 5 }          # false
flag2 = list.any? {|x| x >= 5 }         # true
flag3 = list.all? {|x| x <= 10 }        # true
flag4 = list.all? {|x| x % 2 == 0 }     # false
```

In this example, the any? and all? methods are mixed into the list array.

11.2.3 Nesting Classes and Modules

It's possible to nest classes and modules arbitrarily. The programmer new to Ruby might not know this.

Mostly this is for namespace management. Note that the File class has a Stat class embedded inside it. This helps to "encapsulate" the Stat class inside a class of related functionality and also allows for a future class named Stat, which won't conflict with that one (perhaps a statistics class, for instance).

The Struct::Tms class is a similar example. Any new Struct is placed in this namespace so as not to pollute the one above it, and Tms is really just another Struct.

It's also conceivable that you might want to create a nested class simply because the outside world doesn't need that class or shouldn't access it. In other words, you can create classes that are subject to the principle of "data hiding" just as the instance variables and methods are subject to the same principle at a lower level.

```
class BugTrackingSystem

  class Bug
    #...
  end

  #...

end

# Nothing out here knows about Bug.
```

You can nest a class within a module, a module within a class, and so on. If you find interesting and creative uses for this technique, please let us all know about it.

11.2.4   Creating Parametric Classes

Learn the rules; then break them.

— Basho

Suppose that we wanted to create multiple classes that differed only in the initial values of the class-level variables. Recall that a class variable is typically initialized as a part of the class definition.

```
class Terran

  @@home_planet = "Earth"

  def Terran.home_planet
    @@home_planet
  end

  def Terran.home_planet=(x)
    @@home_planet = x
  end

  #...

end
```

That is all fine, but suppose that we had a number of similar classes to define. The novice will think, "Ah, I'll just define a superclass" (see Listing 11.12).

Listing 11.12   Parametric Classes: The Wrong Way

```ruby
class IntelligentLife    # Wrong way to do this!

  @@home_planet = nil

  def IntelligentLife.home_planet
    @@home_planet
  end

  def IntelligentLife.home_planet=(x)
    @@home_planet = x
  end

  #...
end

class Terran < IntelligentLife
  @@home_planet = "Earth"
  #...
end

class Martian < IntelligentLife
  @@home_planet = "Mars"
  #...
end
```

But this won't work. If we call `Terran.home_planet`, we expect a result of `"Earth"`—but we get `"Mars"`!

Why would this happen? The answer is that class variables aren't *truly* class variables; they belong not to the class but to the entire inheritance hierarchy. The class variables aren't copied from the parent class but are shared with the parent (and thus with the "sibling" classes).

We could eliminate the definition of the class variable in the base class, but then the class methods we define no longer work!

We *could* fix this by moving these definitions to the child classes, but now we've defeated our whole purpose. We're declaring separate classes without any "parameterization."

We'll offer a different solution. We'll defer the evaluation of the class variable until runtime by using the `class_eval` method. Listing 11.13 shows a complete solution.

Listing 11.13   Parametric Classes: A Better Way

```
class IntelligentLife

  def IntelligentLife.home_planet
    class_eval("@@home_planet")
  end

  def IntelligentLife.home_planet=(x)
    class_eval("@@home_planet = #{x}")
  end

  #...
end

class Terran < IntelligentLife
  @@home_planet = "Earth"
  #...
end

class Martian < IntelligentLife
  @@home_planet = "Mars"
  #...
end


puts Terran.home_planet          # Earth
puts Martian.home_planet         # Mars
```

It goes without saying that inheritance still operates normally here. Any instance methods or instance variables defined within IntelligentLife will be inherited by Terran and Martian just as you would expect.

Listing 11.14 is perhaps the best solution. Here we don't use class variables at all but class instance variables.

Listing 11.14   Parametric Classes: The Best Way

```
class IntelligentLife
  class << self
    attr_accessor :home_planet
  end

  #...
end

class Terran < IntelligentLife
  self.home_planet = "Earth"
```

Continues

```
  #...
end

class Martian < IntelligentLife
  self.home_planet = "Mars"
  #...
end


puts Terran.home_planet          # Earth
puts Martian.home_planet         # Mars
```

Here we open up the singleton class and define an accessor called home_planet. The two child classes call their own accessors and set the variable. These accessors work strictly on a per-class basis now.

As a small enhancement, let's also add a private call in the singleton class:

```
    private :home_planet=
```

Making the writer private will prevent any code outside the hierarchy from changing this value. As always, using private is an "advisory" protection and is easily bypassed by the programmer who wants to. Making a method private at least tells us we are not *meant* to call that method in this particular context.

I should mention that there are other ways of implementing these techniques. Use your creativity.

11.2.5   Using Continuations to Implement a Generator

One of the more abstruse features of Ruby is the *continuation*. This is a structured way of handling a nonlocal jump and return; a continuation object stores a return address and an execution context. It is somewhat analogous to the setjmp/longjmp feature in C, but it stores more context.

The Kernel method callcc takes a block and returns an object of the Continuation class. The object returned is also passed into the block as a parameter, just to keep things confusing.

The only method of Continuation is call, which causes a nonlocal return to the end of the callcc block. The callcc can be terminated either by falling through the block or by calling the call method.

Think of a continuation as being like the "save game" feature in a classic adventure game. You save the game at a well-known place where all is calm; you go off and do something dangerous and experimental; and when you die, you go back and restore the game so you can try something else.

The best way to understand continuations is to watch the movie *Run, Lola, Run* (or the original German version, *Lola Rennt*).

There are a few good examples of how to use continuations. Some of the best ones we have seen come from Jim Weirich. In this next example, we see how Jim implemented a "generator" as a result of his discussion with another Ruby programmer, Hugh Sasse.

A generator is made possible by the suspend of Icon (also found in Prolog), which allows a function to resume execution just after the last place it returned a value. Hugh describes it as like an "inside-out yield."

A generator library is now a part of Ruby. For more on this topic, refer to section 8.3.7, "Using Generator Objects."

Listing 11.15, then, is Jim's implementation of a generator that generates Fibonacci numbers one after another. Continuations are used to preserve the call state from one invocation to the next.

Listing 11.15   Fibonacci Generator

```ruby
class Generator

  def initialize
    do_generation
  end

  def next
    callcc do |here|
      @main_context = here;
      @generator_context.call
    end
  end

  private

  def do_generation
    callcc do |context|
      @generator_context = context;
      return
    end
    generating_loop
  end
```

Continues

```ruby
    def generate(value)
      callcc do |context|
        @generator_context = context;
        @main_context.call(value)
      end
    end
end

# Subclass this and define a generating_loop

class FibGenerator < Generator
  def generating_loop
    generate(1)
    a, b = 1, 1
    loop do
      generate(b)
      a, b = b, a+b
    end
  end
end


# Now instantiate the class...

fib = FibGenerator.new

puts fib.next            # 1
puts fib.next            # 1
puts fib.next            # 2
puts fib.next            # 3
puts fib.next            # 5
puts fib.next            # 8
puts fib.next            # 13

# And so on...
```

There are certainly practical applications for continuations. One example is the web framework *Borges* (named for the author Jorge Luis Borges), which takes its inspiration from Seaside. In this paradigm, the traditional flow of control of a web application is "re-inverted" so that the logic appears "normal." For example, you display a page, get a result from a form, display the next page, and so on with intuitive logic.

The problem with this approach is that continuations in general are "expensive" operations. They save quite a bit of state and require significant time to switch contexts. Use them with caution if you're concerned about performance.

11.2.6   Storing Code As Objects

Not surprisingly, Ruby gives you several alternatives when it comes to storing a chunk of code in the form of an object. In this section, we'll take a look at Proc objects, Method objects, and UnboundMethod objects.

The built-in class Proc is used to wrap Ruby blocks in an object. Proc objects, like blocks, are closures, and therefore carry around the context in which they were defined.

```ruby
myproc = Proc.new { |a| puts "Param is #{a}" }

myproc.call(99)          # Param is 99
```

Proc objects are also created automatically by Ruby when a method defined with a trailing & parameter is called with a block:

```ruby
def take_block(x, &block)
  puts block.class
  x.times {|i| block[i, i*i] }
end

take_block(3) { |n,s| puts "#{n} squared is #{s}" }
```

This example also shows the use of brackets ([]) as an alias for the call method. The output is shown here:

```
Proc
0 squared is 0
1 squared is 1
2 squared is 4
```

If you have a Proc object, you can pass it to a method that's expecting a block, preceding its name with an &, as shown here:

```ruby
myproc = proc { |n| print n, "... " }
(1..3).each(&myproc)                      # 1... 2... 3...
```

Ruby also lets you turn a method into an object. Historically, this is done using Object#method, which creates a Method object as a closure in a particular object.

```ruby
str = "cat"
meth = str.method(:length)

a = meth.call                      #   3   (length of "cat")

str << "erpillar"

b = meth.call                      #  11   (length of "caterpillar")

str = "dog"

# Note the next call! The variable str refers to a new object
# ("dog") now, but meth is still bound to the old object.

c = meth.call                      #  11   (length of "caterpillar")
```

As of Ruby 1.6.2, you can also use Module#instance_method to create UnboundMethod objects. These represent a method associated with a class rather than one particular object. Before calling an UnboundMethod object, you must first bind it to a particular object. This act of binding produces a Method object, which you call normally.

```ruby
umeth = String.instance_method(:length)

m1 = umeth.bind("cat")
m1.call                            # 3

m2 = umeth.bind("caterpillar")
m2.call                            # 11
```

This explicit binding makes the UnboundMethod object a little more intuitive than Method.

11.2.7   How Module Inclusion Works

When a module is included into a class, Ruby in effect creates a proxy class as the immediate ancestor of that class. You may or may not find this intuitive. Any methods in an included module are "masked" by any methods that appear in the class.

```
module MyMod
  def meth
    "from module"
  end
end

class ParentClass
  def meth
    "from parent"
  end
end

class ChildClass < ParentClass
  include MyMod
  def meth
    "from child"
  end
end

x = ChildClass.new
p x.meth              # from child
```

This is just like a real inheritance relationship: Anything the child redefines is the new current definition. This is true *regardless* of whether the include is done before or after the redefinition.

Here's a similar example, where the child method invokes super instead of returning a simple string. What do you expect it to return?

```
# MyMod and ParentClass unchanged

class ChildClass < ParentClass
  include MyMod
  def meth
    "from child: super = " + super
  end
end

x = ChildClass.new
p x.meth              # from child: super = from module
```

This previous example shows that the module is really the new parent of the class. What if we also let the module invoke super in the same way?

```
module MyMod
  def meth
    "from module: super = " + super
  end
end

# ParentClass is unchanged

class ChildClass < ParentClass
  include MyMod
  def meth
    "from child: super = " + super
  end
end

x = ChildClass.new
p x.meth        # from child: super = from module: super = from parent
```

The meth from MyMod can call super only because there actually is a meth in the superclass (that is, in at least one ancestor). What would happen if we called this in another circumstance?

```
module MyMod
  def meth
    "from module: super = " + super
  end
end

class Foo        include MyMod
end

x = Foo.new
x.meth
```

This code would result in a NoMethodError (or a call to method_missing if one existed).

11.2.8   Detecting Default Parameters

In 2004, Ian Macdonald asked on the mailing list: "How can I detect whether a parameter was specified by the caller, or the default was taken?" It was an interesting question; not something you would use every day, but still interesting.

At least three solutions were suggested. By far the simplest and best was by Nobu Nakada. This trick is shown in the following code:

```
def meth(a, b=(flag=true; 345))
  puts "b is #{b} and flag is #{flag.inspect}"
end


meth(123)          # b is 345 and flag is true
meth(123,345)      # b is 345 and flag is nil
meth(123,456)      # b is 456 and flag is nil
```

As the preceding example shows, this works even if the caller explicitly supplies what happens to be the default value. The trick is obvious when you see it: The parenthesized expression sets a local variable called `flag` but then returns the default value 345. This is a tribute to the power of Ruby.

11.2.9   Delegating or Forwarding

Ruby has two libraries that offer solutions for delegating or forwarding method calls from the receiver to another object. These are `delegate` and `forwardable`; we'll look at them in that order.

The `delegate` library gives you three ways of solving this problem.

The `SimpleDelegator` class can be useful when the object delegated to can change over the lifespan of the receiving object. The `__setobj__` method is used to select the object to which we're delegating.

However, I find the `SimpleDelegator` technique to be a little too simple. Since I am not convinced it offers a significant improvement over doing the same thing by hand, I won't cover it here.

The `DelegateClass` top-level method takes a class (to be delegated to) as a parameter. It then creates a new class from which we can inherit. Here's an example of creating our own `Queue` class that delegates to an `Array` object:

```
require 'delegate'

class MyQueue < DelegateClass(Array)

  def initialize(arg=[])
    super(arg)
  end

  alias_method :enqueue, :push
  alias_method :dequeue, :shift
end

mq = MyQueue.new

mq.enqueue(123)
mq.enqueue(234)

p mq.dequeue        # 123
p mq.dequeue        # 234
```

It's also possible to inherit from `Delegator` and implement a `__getobj__` method; this is the way `SimpleDelegator` is implemented, and it offers more control over the delegation.

But if you want more control, you should probably be doing per-method delegation rather than per-class anyway. The `forwardable` library enables you to do this. Let's revisit the queue example:

```
require 'forwardable'

class MyQueue
  extend Forwardable

  def initialize(obj=[])
    @queue = obj      # delegate to this object
  end

  def_delegator :@queue, :push,   :enqueue
```

```
    def_delegator :@queue, :shift, :dequeue

    def_delegators :@queue, :clear, :empty?, :length, :size, :<<

    # Any additional stuff...
  end
```

This example shows that the `def_delegator` method associates a method call (for example, enqueue) with a delegated object `@queue` and the correct method to call on that object (push). In other words, when we call `enqueue` on a `MyQueue` object, we delegate that by making a `push` call on our object `@queue` (which is usually an array).

Notice how we say `:@queue` rather than `:queue` or `@queue`; this is simply because of the way the `Forwardable` class is written. It could have been done differently.

Sometimes we want to pass methods through to the delegate object by using the same method name. The `def_delegators` method allows us to specify an unlimited number of these. For example, as shown in the preceding code example, invoking `length` on a `MyQueue` object will in turn call `length` on `@queue`.

Unlike the first example in this chapter, the other methods on the delegate object are simply not supported. This can be a good thing. For example, you don't want to invoke `[]` or `[]=` on a queue; if you do, you're not using it as a queue anymore.

Also notice that the previous code allows the caller to pass an object into the constructor (to be used as the delegate object). In the spirit of duck-typing, this means that I can choose the kind of object I want to delegate to; as long as it supports the set of methods that I reference in the code.

For example, these calls are all valid. (The last two assume that we've done a `require 'thread'` previously.)

```
q1 = MyQueue.new                    # use an array
q2 = MyQueue.new(my_array)          # use one specific array
q3 = MyQueue.new(Queue.new)         # use a Queue (thread.rb)
q4 = MyQueue.new(SizedQueue.new)    # use a SizedQueue (thread.rb)
```

So for example, q3 and q4 in the preceding examples are now magically thread-safe because they delegate to an object that is thread-safe. (That's unless any customized code not shown here violates that.)

There is also a `SingleForwardable` class that operates on an instance rather than on an entire class. This is useful if you want *one certain object* of a class to delegate to another object, but the other objects of that class will *not* delegate.

You might ask: Is delegation better than inheritance? But it's the wrong question in a sense. Sometimes the situation calls for delegation rather than inheritance; for example, suppose that a class already has a parent class. We can still use delegation (in some form), but we can't inherit from an additional parent (because Ruby doesn't allow multiple inheritance).

11.2.10   Automatically Defining Class-level Readers and Writers

We have seen the methods `attr_reader`, `attr_writer`, and `attr_accessor`, which make it a little easier to define readers and writers (getters and setters) for instance attributes. But what about class-level attributes?

Ruby has no similar facility for creating these automatically. But we could create something similar on our own.

In the first edition of this book, we showed you an elaborate scheme involving `class_eval`. We created new methods such as `cattr_reader` and `cattr_writer`.

There is an easier, better way. Open the singleton class and just use the ordinary `attr` family of methods. The resulting instance variables in the singleton class will be class instance variables. These are often better for our purposes than class variables because they are strictly per-class and are not shared up and down the hierarchy.

```
class MyClass

  @alpha = 123                # Initialize @alpha

  class << self
    attr_reader :alpha        # MyClass.alpha()
    attr_writer :beta         # MyClass.beta=()
    attr_accessor :gamma      # MyClass.gamma() and
  end                         #   MyClass.gamma=()

  def MyClass.look
    puts "#@alpha, #@beta, #@gamma"
  end

  #...
```

```
end


puts MyClass.alpha              # 123
MyClass.beta = 456
MyClass.gamma = 789
puts MyClass.gamma              # 789


MyClass.look                    # 123, 456, 789
```

Most classes are no good without instance level data. We've only omitted it here for clarity.

11.2.11   Working in Advanced Programming Disciplines

Brother, can you paradigm?

— Grafitti seen at IBM Austin, 1989

Many philosophies of programming are popular in various circles. These are often difficult to characterize in relation to object-oriented or dynamic techniques, and some of these styles can be actually independent of whether a language is dynamic or object-oriented.

Because we are far from experts in these matters, we are relying mostly on hearsay. So take these next paragraphs with a grain of sodium chloride.

Some programmers prefer a flavor of OOP known as *prototype-based* OOP (or *classless* OOP). In this world, an object isn't described as a member of a class; it is built from the ground up, and other objects are created based on the prototype. Ruby has at least rudimentary support for this programming style because it allows singleton methods for individual objects, and the `clone` method will clone these singletons. Interested readers should also look at the simple `OpenStruct` class for building Python-like objects; you should also be aware of how `method_missing` works.

One or two limitations in Ruby hamper classless OOP. Certain objects such as `Fixnums` are stored not as references but as immediate values so that they can't have singleton methods. This is supposed to change in the future, but at the time of this writing, it's impossible to project when it will happen.

In *functional programming (FP)*, emphasis is placed on the evaluation of expressions rather than the execution of commands. An FP language is one that encourages and supports functional programming, and as such, there is a natural gray area. Nearly all would agree that Haskell is a *pure* functional language, whereas Ruby certainly isn't one.

But Ruby has at least some minimal support for FP; it has a fairly rich set of methods for operating on arrays (lists), and it has `Proc` objects so that code can be encapsulated and called over and over. Ruby allows the method chaining that is so common in FP, although it is easy to be bitten by the phenomenon of a bang method (such as `sort!` or `gsub!`) that returns `nil` when the receiver doesn't actually change.

There have been some initial efforts at a library that would serve as a kind of FP "compatibility layer," borrowing certain ideas from Haskell. At the time of this writing, these efforts aren't complete.

The concept of *aspect-oriented programming* (AOP) is an interesting one. In AOP, we try to deal with programming issues that crosscut the modular structure of the program. In other words, some activities or features of a system will be scattered across the system in code fragments here and there, rather than being gathered into one tidy location. In other words, we are attempting to modularize things that in traditional OOP or procedural techniques are difficult to modularize. We are working at right angles to our usual way of thinking.

Ruby certainly wasn't created specifically with AOP in mind. But it was designed to be a flexible and dynamic language, and it is conceivable that these techniques can be facilitated by a library. In fact, a library called `AspectR` is an early effort at implementing AOP; see the Ruby Application Archive for the most recent version.

The concept of *Design by Contract* (DBC) is well known to Eiffel devotees, although it is certainly known outside those circles also. The general idea is that a piece of code (a method or class) implements a contract; certain preconditions must be true if the code is going to do its job, and the code guarantees that certain post-conditions are true afterward. The robustness of a system can be greatly enhanced by the ability to specify this contract explicitly and have it automatically checked at runtime. The usefulness of the technique is expanded by the inheritance of contract information as classes are extended.

The Eiffel language has DBC explicitly built in; Ruby does not. There are at least two usable implementations of DBC libraries, however, and we recommend that you choose one and learn it.

Design patterns have inspired much discussion over the last few years. These, of course, are highly language-independent and can be implemented well in many languages. But again, Ruby's unusual flexibility makes them perhaps more practical than in some other environments. Well-known examples of these are given elsewhere; the

Visitor pattern is essentially implemented in Ruby's default iterator `each`, and other patterns are part of Ruby's standard distribution (the standard libraries `delegator.rb` and `singleton.rb`).

The *Extreme Programming (XP)* discipline is gaining devotees daily. This methodology encourages (among other things) early testing and refactoring on-the-fly.

XP isn't language specific, although it might be easier in some languages than others. Certainly we maintain that Ruby makes refactoring easier than many languages would, although that is a highly subjective claim. But the existence of the `Test::Unit` library (and others) makes for a real blending of Ruby and XP. This library facilitates unit testing; it is powerful, easy to use, and has proven useful in developing other Ruby software in current use. We highly recommend the XP practice of testing early and often, and we recommend `Test::Unit` for those who want to do this in Ruby. (`ZenTest` is another excellent package with several features not found in `Test::Unit`.)

By the time you read this, many of the issues we talk about in this section will have been fleshed out more. As always, your four best resources for the latest information are

The comp.lang.ruby newsgroup

The Ruby Application Archive

rubyforge.org

ruby-doc.org

Other useful resources also are available, especially if you speak Japanese. It's difficult to list online resources in print because they are in constant flux. The search engine is your friend.

11.3 Working with Dynamic Features

Skynet became self-aware at at 2:14am EDT August 29, 1997.

— Terminator 2: Judgment Day

Many of you will come from the background of a static language such as C. To those readers, we will address this rhetorical question: Can you imagine writing a C function that will take a string, treat it as a variable name, and return the value of the variable?

No? Then can you imagine removing or replacing the definition of a function? Can you imagine trapping calls to nonexistent functions? Or determining the name of the calling function? Or automatically obtaining a list of user-defined program elements (such as a list of all your functions)?

Ruby makes this sort of thing possible. This runtime flexibility, the capability to examine and change program elements at runtime, makes many problems easier. A runtime tracing utility, a debugger, and a profiling utility are all easy to write *for* Ruby and *in* Ruby. The well-known programs irb and xmp both use dynamic features of Ruby to perform their magic.

These capabilities take getting used to, and they are easy to abuse. But the concepts have been around for many years (they are at least as old as LISP) and are regarded as "tried and true" in the Scheme and Smalltalk communities as well. Even Java, which owes so much to C and C++, has some dynamic features, so we expect this way of thinking to increase in popularity as time goes by.

11.3.1   Evaluating Code Dynamically

The global function eval compiles and executes a string that contains a fragment of Ruby code. This is a powerful (if slightly dangerous) mechanism because it allows you to build up code to be executed at runtime. For example, the following code reads in lines of the form *name = expression*; it then evaluates each expression and stores the result in a hash indexed by the corresponding variable name.

```
parameters = {}

ARGF.each do |line|
  name, expr = line.split(/\s*=\s*/, 2)
  parameters[name] = eval expr
end
```

Suppose the input contained these lines:

```
a = 1
b = 2 + 3
c = `date`
```

Then the hash parameters would end up with the value {"a"=>1, "b"=>5, "c"=>"Mon Apr 30 21:17:47 CDT 2001\n"}. This example also illustrates the danger of evaling strings when you don't control their contents; a malicious user could put d=`rm *` in the input and ruin your day.

Ruby has three other methods that evaluate code "on the fly": class_eval, module_eval, and instance_eval. The first two are synonyms, and all three do effectively the same thing; they evaluate a string or a block, but while doing so they change the value of self to their own receiver. Perhaps the most common use of class_eval allows you to add methods to a class when all you have is a reference to that class. We use this in the hook_method code in the Trace example in section11.3.13, "Tracking Changes to a Class or Object Definition." You'll find other examples in the more dynamic library modules, such as delegate.rb.

The eval method also makes it possible to evaluate local variables in a context outside their scope. We don't advise doing this lightly, but it's nice to have the capability.

Ruby associates local variables with blocks, with high-level definition constructs (class, module, and method definitions), and with the top-level of your program (the code outside any definition constructs). Associated with each of these scopes is the binding of variables, along with other housekeeping details. Probably the ultimate user of bindings is irb, the interactive Ruby shell, which uses bindings to keep the variables in the program that you type in separate from its own.

You can encapsulate the current binding in an object using the method Kernel#binding. Having done that, you can pass the binding as the second parameter to eval, setting the execution context for the code being evaluated.

```
def some_ethod
  a = "local variable"
  return binding
end

the_binding = some_method
eval "a", the_binding    # "local variable"
```

Interestingly, the presence of a block associated with a method is stored as part of the binding, enabling tricks such as this:

```
def some_method
  return binding
end

the_binding = some_method { puts "hello" }
eval "yield", the_binding              # hello
```

11.3.2   Using `const_get`

The `const_get` method retrieves the value of a constant (by name) from the module or class to which it belongs.

```
str = "PI"
Math.const_get(str)      # Evaluates to Math::PI
```

This is a way of avoiding the use of `eval`, which is sometimes considered inelegant. This type of solution is better code, it's computationally cheaper, and it's safer. Other similar methods are `instance_variable_set`, `instance_variable_get`, and `define_method`.

It's true that `const_get` is faster than `eval`. In informal tests, `const_get` was roughly 350% as fast; your results will vary. But is this really significant? The fact is, the test code ran a loop *10 million times* to get good results and still finished under 30 seconds.

The usefulness of `const_get` is that it is easier to read, more specific, and more self-documenting. This is the real reason to use it. In fact, even if it did not exist, to make it a synonym for `eval` would still be a large step forward.

See also the next section (section 11.3.3, "Dynamically Instantiating a Class by Name") for another trick.

11.3.3   Dynamically Instantiating a Class by Name

We have seen this question more than once. Given a string containing the name of a class, how can we create an instance of that class?

The proper way is with `const_get`, which we just saw. All classes in Ruby are normally named as constants in the "global" namespace—that is, members of `Object`.

```
classname = "Array"

klass = Object.const_get(classname)
x = klass.new(4, 1)         # [1, 1, 1, 1]
```

What if the names are nested? It turns out this doesn't work:

```
class Alpha
  class Beta
    class Gamma
```

```
        FOOBAR = 237
      end
    end
end


str = "Alpha::Beta::Gamma::FOOBAR"
val = Object.const_get(str)              # error!
```

This is because const_get just isn't "smart" enough to recognize nested names of this sort. The following example is an idiom that will work well, however:

```
# Same class structure

str = "Alpha::Beta::Gamma::FOOBAR"
val = str.split("::").inject(Object) {|x,y| x.const_get(y) }   # 237
```

This is a commonly needed piece of code (and a neat use of inject).

11.3.4   Getting and Setting Instance Variables

In accordance with our desire to use eval only when necessary, Ruby now has methods that can retrieve or assign instance variable values, given the variable name as a string.

```
class MyClass
  attr_reader :alpha, :beta

  def initialize(a,b,g)
    @alpha, @beta, @gamma = a, b, g
  end
end


x = MyClass.new(10,11,12)

x.instance_variable_set("@alpha",234)
p x.alpha                                # 234

x.instance_variable_set("@gamma",345)    # 345
v = x.instance_variable_get("@gamma")    # 345
```

Note first of all that we *do* have to use the at-sign on the variable name; not to do so is an error. If this is unintuitive, remember that methods such as `attr_accessor` actually take a symbol used to name the *methods*, which is why they omit the at-sign.

You may wonder whether the existence of these methods is a violation of encapsulation. The answer is *no*.

It's true these methods are powerful and potentially dangerous. They should be used cautiously, not casually. But it's impossible to say whether encapsulation is violated without looking at *how these tools are used*. If they are used intentionally as part of a good design, then all is well. If they are used to violate the design, or to circumvent a bad design, then all is not well. Ruby intentionally grants access to the interiors of objects for people who really need it; the mark of the responsible programmer is not to abuse that freedom.

11.3.5   Using `define_method`

Other than `def`, `define_method` is the only normal way to add a method to a class or object; the latter, however, enables you to do it at runtime.

Of course, essentially *everything* in Ruby happens at runtime. If you surround a method definition with `puts` calls, as in the following example, you can see that.

```
class MyClass
  puts "before"

  def meth
    #...
  end

  puts "after"
end
```

But within a method body or similar place, we can't just reopen a class (unless it's a singleton class). In such a case, we had to use `eval` in older versions of Ruby; now we have `define_method`. It takes a symbol (for the name of the method) and a block (for the body of the method).

A first attempt to use it might look like this (which has an error):

```
# This doesn't work because define_method is private
```

```
if today =~ /Saturday|Sunday/
  define_method(:activity)  { puts "Playing!" }
else
  define_method(:activity)  { puts "Working!" }
end

activity
```

Because `define_method` is private, we have to do this:

```
# Works fine (Object is context at top level)

if today =~ /Saturday|Sunday/
  Object.class_eval { define_method(:activity)  { puts "Playing!" } }
else
  Object.class_eval { define_method(:activity)  { puts "Working!" } }
end

activity
```

We could also do this inside a class definition (with `Object` or any other class). It's rare that this will be justifiable, but if you can do it inside the class definition, privacy is not an issue.

```
class MyClass
  define_method(:mymeth) { puts "This is my method." }
end
```

There is also a trick where you give a class a method that indirectly exposes `define_method`'s functionality.

```
class MyClass
  def self.new_method(name, &block)
    define_method(name, &block)
  end
end

MyClass.new_method(:mymeth) { puts "This is my method." }
x = MyClass.new
x.mymeth                # Prints "This is my method."
```

The same could be done at the instance level rather than the class level:

```
class MyClass
  def new_method(name, &block)
    self.class.send(:define_method,name, &block)
  end
end


x = MyClass.new
x.new_method(:mymeth) { puts "This is my method." }
x.mymeth               # Prints "This is my method."
```

Here we're still defining an instance method dynamically. Only the means of invoking new_method has changed. Note the send trick that we use to circumvent the privacy of define_method. This works because send in current Ruby versions always allows you to call private methods. (This is another "loophole," as some would call it, that has to be used responsibly.)

It's important to realize another fact about define_method: It takes a block, and a block in Ruby is a *closure*. That means that, unlike an ordinary method definition, we are capturing context when we define the method. The following example is useless, but it illustrates the point:

```
class MyClass
  def self.new_method(name, &block)
    define_method(name, &block)
  end
end


a,b = 3,79


MyClass.new_method(:compute) { a*b }
x = MyClass.new
puts x.compute            # 237


a,b = 23,24
puts x.compute            # 552
```

The point is that the new method can access variables in the original scope of the block, even if that scope "goes away" and is otherwise inaccessible. This will be useful at times, perhaps in a metaprogramming situation or with a GUI toolkit that allows defining methods for event callbacks.

Note that the closure is only a closure when the variable name is the same. On rare occasions, this can be tricky. Here we use define to expose a class variable (not really the way we should do it, but it illustrates the point):

```
class SomeClass
  @@var = 999

  define_method(:peek) { @@var }
end

x = SomeClass.new
p x.peek            # 999
```

Now let's try this with a class instance variable:

```
class SomeClass
  @var = 999

  define_method(:peek) { @var }
end

x = SomeClass.new
p x.peek            # prints nil
```

We expect 999 but get nil instead. Why is that? I'll defer the explanation for a moment.

Observe, on the other hand, this works fine:

```
class SomeClass
  @var = 999
  x = @var

  define_method(:peek) { x }
end

x = SomeClass.new
p x.peek      # 999
```

So what is happening? Well, it is true that a closure captures the variables from its context. But even though a closure knows the variables from its scope, the intended context of the new method is the context of the instance of the *object*, not the class itself.

Since @var in that context would refer to an instance variable of the object, not the class, the class instance variable is overridden (hidden) by the object's instance variable even though it has never been used and technically doesn't exist.

In previous versions of Ruby, we often defined methods at runtime by calling eval. In essence, define_method can and should be used in all these circumstances. Minor subtleties like the one above shouldn't deter you.

11.3.6   Using const_missing

The const_missing method is analogous to method_missing. If you try to reference a constant that isn't known, this method will be called if it is found. A symbol referring to the constant is passed in.

To capture a constant globally, define this method within Module itself (Module is the parent of Class).

```
class Module
  def const_missing(x)
    "from Module"
  end
end

class X
end

p X::BAR          # "from Module"
p BAR             # "from Module"
p Array::BAR      # "from Module"
```

You can, of course, do anything you want to give the constant a fake value, compute its value, or whatever. Remember the Roman class we saw in Chapter 6, "Symbols and Ranges"? Here we use it to ensure that arbitrary uppercase Roman numeral constants are treated as such:

```
class Module
  def const_missing(name)
    Roman.decode(name)
```

```
    end
  end
```

```
  year1 = MCMLCCIV        # 1974
  year2 = MMVIII          # 2008
```

If you want something less global, define the method as a class method on a class. That class and all its children will call that version of the method as needed.

```ruby
class Alpha
  def self.const_missing(sym)
    "Alpha has no #{sym}"
  end
end

class Beta
  def self.const_missing(sym)
    "Beta has no #{sym}"
  end
end

class A < Alpha
end

class B < Beta
end

p Alpha::FOO        # "Alpha has no FOO"
p Beta::FOO         # "Beta has no FOO"
p A::FOO            # "Alpha has no FOO"
p B::FOO            # "Beta has no FOO"
```

11.3.7   Removing Definitions

The dynamic nature of Ruby means that pretty much anything that can be defined can also be undefined. One conceivable reason to do this is to decouple pieces of code that are in the same scope by getting rid of variables after they have been used; another reason might be to specifically disallow certain dangerous method calls. Whatever your reason for removing a definition, it should naturally be done with caution because it can conceivably lead to debugging problems.

The radical way to undefine something is with the `undef` keyword (not surprisingly the opposite of `def`). You can `undef` methods, local variables, and constants at the top level. Although a class name is a constant, you *cannot* remove a class definition this way.

```ruby
def asbestos
  puts "Now fireproof"
end

tax = 0.08

PI = 3

asbestos
puts "PI=#{PI}, tax=#{tax}"

undef asbestos
undef tax
undef PI

# Any reference to the above three
# would now give an error.
```

Within a class definition, a method or constant can be undefined in the same context in which it was defined. You can't `undef` within a method definition or `undef` an instance variable.

The `remove_method` and `undef_method` methods also are available (defined in `Module`). The difference is subtle: `remove_method` will remove the current (or nearest) definition of the method; `undef_method` will literally cause the method to be undefined (removing it from superclasses as well). Listing 11.16 is an illustration of this.

Listing 11.16 Removing and Undefining Methods

```ruby
class Parent

  def alpha
    puts "parent alpha"
  end

  def beta
    puts "parent beta"
  end
```

```
end

class Child < Parent

  def alpha
    puts "child alpha"
  end

  def beta
    puts "child beta"
  end

  remove_method :alpha    # Remove "this" alpha
  undef_method :beta      # Remove every beta

end


x = Child.new

x.alpha           # parent alpha
x.beta            # Error!
```

The remove_const method will remove a constant.

```
module Math

  remove_const :PI

end


# No PI anymore!
```

Note that it is possible to remove a class definition in this way (because a class identifier is simply a constant). The following code demonstrates this:

```
class BriefCandle
  #...
end


out_out = BriefCandle.new

class Object
  remove_const :BriefCandle
end
```

```
# Can't instantiate BriefCandle again!
# (Though out_out still exists...)
```

Note that methods such as remove_const and remove_method are (naturally enough) private methods. That is why we show them being called from inside a class or module definition rather than outside.

11.3.8   Obtaining Lists of Defined Entities

The reflection API of Ruby enables us to examine the classes and objects in our environment at runtime. We'll look at methods defined in Module, Class, and Object.

The Module module has a method named constants that returns an array of all the constants in the system (including class and module names). The nesting method returns an array of all the modules nested at the current location in the code.

The instance method Module#ancestors returns an array of all the ancestors of the specified class or module.

```
list = Array.ancestors
# [Array, Enumerable, Object, Kernel]
```

The constants method lists all the constants accessible in the specified module. Any ancestor modules are included.

```
list = Math.constants    # ["E", "PI"]
```

The class_variables method returns a list of all class variables in the given class and its superclasses. The included_modules method lists the modules included in a class.

```
class Parent
  @@var1 = nil
end

class Child < Parent
  @@var2 = nil
end

list1 = Parent.class_variables   # ["@@var1"]
list2 = Array.included_modules   # [Enumerable, Kernel]
```

The `Class` methods `instance_methods` and `public_instance_methods` are synonyms; they return a list of the public instance methods for a class. The methods `private_instance_methods` and `protected_instance_methods` behave as expected. Any of these can take a Boolean parameter, which defaults to `true`; if it is set to `false`, superclasses will not be searched, resulting in a smaller list.

```
n1 = Array.instance_methods.size              # 121
n2 = Array.public_instance_methods.size       # 121
n3 = Array.private_instance_methods.size      # 71
n4 = Array.protected_instance_methods.size    # 0
n5 = Array.public_instance_methods(falsee).size  # 71
```

The `Object` class has a number of similar methods that operate on instances (see Listing 11.17). Calling `methods` will return a list of all methods that can be invoked on that object. Calling `public_methods` will return a list of publicly accessible methods; this takes a parameter, defaulting to `true`, to choose whether methods from superclasses are included. The methods `private_methods`, `protected_methods`, and `singleton_methods` all take a similar parameter.

Listing 11.17 Reflection and Instance Variables

```
class SomeClass

  def initialize
    @a = 1
    @b = 2
  end

  def mymeth
    #...
  end

  protected :mymeth

end


x = SomeClass.new

def x.newmeth
  # ...
end

iv = x.instance_variables        # ["@b", "@a"]
```

Continues

```
p x.methods.size                      # 42

p x.public_methods.size               # 41
p x.public_methods(false).size        # 1

p x.private_methods.size              # 71
p x.private_methods(false).size       # 1

p x.protected_methods.size            # 1
p x.singleton_methods.size            # 1
```

If you have been using Ruby for a few years, you will notice that these methods have changed a little. Default parameters are now true rather than false.

11.3.9   Examining the Call Stack

And you may ask yourself:
Well, how did I get here?

— *Talking Heads, "Once in a Lifetime"*

Sometimes we want to know who our caller was. This could be useful information if, for example, we had a fatal exception. The `caller` method, defined in `Kernel`, makes this possible. It returns an array of strings in which the first element represents the caller, the next element represents the caller's caller, and so on.

```
def func1
  puts caller[0]
end

def func2
  func1
end

func2              # Prints: somefile.rb:6:in `func2'
```

The string is in the form *file;line* or *file:line: in method*, as shown previously.

11.3.10   Monitoring Execution of a Program

A Ruby program can introspect or examine its own execution. There are many applications for such a capability; the interested reader can refer to the sources debug.rb, profile.rb, and tracer.rb. It is even conceivable to use this facility in creating a design-by-contract (DBC) library (although the most popular one at the time of this writing doesn't use this technique).

The interesting thing is that this trick is implemented purely in Ruby. We use the Ruby method set_trace_func, which allows you to invoke a block whenever significant events happen in the execution of a program. A good reference will show the calling sequence for set_trace_func, so we'll just show a simple example here:

```ruby
def meth(n)
  sum = 0
  for i in 1..n
    sum += i
  end
  sum
end

set_trace_func(proc do |event, file, line,
                        id, binding, klass, *rest|
  printf "%8s %s:%d  %s/%s\n", event, file, line,
                              klass, id
end)

meth(2)
```

Notice that this code follows the common convention of using do and end for a multi-line block. Because of the way Ruby is parsed, this makes the parentheses necessary. An alternative, of course, would be to use braces.

The preceding code produces the following output:

```
   line prog.rb:13   false/
   call prog.rb:1    Object/meth
   line prog.rb:2    Object/meth
   line prog.rb:3    Object/meth
 c-call prog.rb:3    Range/each
   line prog.rb:4    Object/meth
 c-call prog.rb:4    Fixnum/+
```

```
c-return prog.rb:4   Fixnum/+
    line prog.rb:4   Object/meth
  c-call prog.rb:4   Fixnum/+
c-return prog.rb:4   Fixnum/+
c-return prog.rb:4   Range/each
    line prog.rb:6   Object/meth
  return prog.rb:6   Object/meth
```

Another related method is `Kernel#trace_var`, which invokes a block whenever a global variable is assigned a value.

Suppose that you want to trace the execution of a program from outside, strictly as an aid in debugging. The simplest way to see what a program is doing is to use the `tracer` library mentioned previously. Given a program `prog.rb`:

```
def meth(n)
  (1..n).each {|i| puts i}
end

meth(3)
```

You can simply load `tracer` from the command line:

```
% ruby -r tracer prog.rb
#0:prog.rb:1::-:      def meth(n)
#0:prog.rb:1:Module:>:    def meth(n)
#0:prog.rb:1:Module:<:    def meth(n)
#0:prog.rb:8::-:      meth(2)
#0:prog.rb:1:Object:>:    def meth(n)
#0:prog.rb:2:Object:-:    sum = 0
#0:prog.rb:3:Object:-:    for i in 1..n
#0:prog.rb:3:Range:>:    for i in 1..n
#0:prog.rb:4:Object:-:     sum += i
#0:prog.rb:4:Fixnum:>:     sum += i
#0:prog.rb:4:Fixnum:<:     sum += i
#0:prog.rb:4:Object:-:     sum += i
#0:prog.rb:4:Fixnum:>:     sum += i
#0:prog.rb:4:Fixnum:<:     sum += i
#0:prog.rb:4:Range:<:     sum += i
#0:prog.rb:6:Object:-:    sum
#0:prog.rb:6:Object:<:    sum
```

The lines output by `tracer` show the thread number, the filename and line number, the class being used, the event type, and the line from the source file being executed. The event types include `'-'` when a source line is executed, `'>'` for a call, `'<'` for a return, `'C'` for a class, and `'E'` for an end. (If you are automatically including a library via `RUBYOPT` or some other way, you may actually get thousands of lines of output instead.)

11.3.11   Traversing the Object Space

The Ruby runtime system needs to keep track of all known objects (if for no other reason than to be able to garbage collect those that are no longer referenced). This information is made accessible via the `ObjectSpace.each_object` method.

```
ObjectSpace.each_object do |obj|
  printf "%20s: %s\n", obj.class, obj.inspect
end
```

If you specify a class or module as a parameter to `each_object`, only objects of that type will be returned.

The `ObjectSpace` module is also useful in defining object finalizers (see section 11.3.14, "Defining Finalizers for Objects").

11.3.12   Handling Calls to Nonexistent Methods

Sometimes it's useful to be able to write classes that respond to arbitrary method calls. For example, you might want to wrap calls to external programs in a class, providing access to each program as a method call. You can't know ahead of time the names of all these programs, so you can't create the methods as you write the class. Here comes `Object#method_missing` to the rescue. Whenever a Ruby object receives a message for a method that isn't implemented in the receiver, it invokes the `method_missing` method instead. You can use that to catch what would otherwise be an error, treating it as a normal method call. Let's implement the operating system command wrapper class:

```
class CommandWrapper

  def method_missing(method, *args)
    system(method.to_s, *args)
```

```
      end

   end


   cw = CommandWrapper.new
   cw.date                   # Sat Apr 28 22:50:11 CDT 2001
   cw.du '-s', '/tmp'        # 166749  /tmp
```

The first parameter to method_missing is the name of the method that was called (and that couldn't be found). Whatever was passed in that method call is then given as the remaining parameters.

If your method_missing handler decides that it doesn't want to handle a particular call, it should call super rather than raising an exception. That allows method_missing handlers in superclasses to have a shot at dealing with the situation. Eventually, the method_missing method defined in class Object will be invoked, and that will raise an exception.

11.3.13   Tracking Changes to a Class or Object Definition

Perhaps we should start this by asking: Who cares? Why are we interested in tracking changes to classes?

One possible reason is that we're trying to keep track of the state of the Ruby program being run. Perhaps we're implementing some kind of GUI-based debugger, and we need to refresh a list of methods if our user adds one on the fly.

Another reason might be that we're doing clever things to other classes. For example, say that we wanted to write a module that could be included in any class definition. From then on, any call to a method in that class will be traced. We might use it something like this:

```
class MyClass
   include Tracing

   def one
   end

   def two(x, y)
   end

end
```

```
m = MyClass.new
m.one                    # one called. Params =
m.two(1, 'cat')          # two called. Params = 1, cat
```

It will also work for any subclasses of the class we're tracing:

```
class Fred < MyClass

  def meth(*a)
  end

end

Fred.new.meth(2,3,4,5)     # meth called. Params = 2, 3, 4, 5
```

We could implement this module as shown in Listing 11.18.

Listing 11.18 Tracing Module

```
module Tracing
  def Tracing.included(into)
    into.instance_methods(false).each { |m|
Tracing.hook_method(into, m) }
    def into.method_added(meth)
      unless @adding
        @adding = true
        Tracing.hook_method(self, meth)
        @adding = false
      end
    end
  end

  def Tracing.hook_method(klass, meth)
    klass.class_eval do
      alias_method "old_#{meth}", "#{meth}"
      define_method(meth) do |*args|
        puts "#{meth} called. Params = #{args.join(', ')}"
        self.send("old_#{meth}",*args)
      end
    end
  end
end

class MyClass
  include Tracing

  def first_meth
```

Continues

```
      end

    def second_meth(x, y)
    end
  end


  m = MyClass.new
  m.first_meth                    # first_meth called. Params =
  m.second_meth(1, 'cat')         # second_meth called. Params = 1, cat
```

This code has two main methods. The first, included, is a callback invoked whenever a module is inserted into a class. Our version does two things. It calls hook_method for every method that's already been defined in the target class, and it inserts a definition for method_added into that class. This means that any subsequently added method will also be detected and hooked.

The hook itself is pretty straightforward: When a method is added, it is immediately aliased to the name old_name. The original method is then replaced by our tracing code, which dumps out the method name and parameters before invoking the original method.

Note the use of alias_method here. This works much like alias, except that it works only on methods (and it itself is a method, not a keyword). It could have been written other ways also:

```
  # Two other ways to write that line...

  # Symbols with interpolation:
  alias_method :"old_#{meth}", :"#{meth}"

  # Strings converted via to_sym:
  alias_method "old_#{meth}".to_sym, meth.to_sym
```

To detect the addition of a new class method to a class or module, we can define a class method singleton_method_added within that class. (Recall that a singleton method in this sense is what we usually refer to as a class method—because Class is an object.) This method comes from Kernel and by default does nothing, but we can make it behave as we want.

```
  class MyClass

    def MyClass.singleton_method_added(sym)
```

```
    puts "Added method #{sym.to_s} to class MyClass."
  end

  def MyClass.meth1
    puts "I'm meth1."
  end

end

def MyClass.meth2
  puts "And I'm meth2."
end
```

The output we get from this is as follows:

```
Added method singleton_method_added to class MyClass.
Added method meth1 to class MyClass.
Added method meth2 to class MyClass.
```

Note that actually three methods are added here. Perhaps contrary to expectation, singleton_method_added can track its own addition to the class.

The inherited method (from Class) is used in much the same way. It is called whenever a class is subclassed by another.

```
class MyClass

  def MyClass.inherited(subclass)
    puts "#{subclass} inherits from MyClass."
  end

  # ...

end


class OtherClass < MyClass

  # ...

end


# Output: OtherClass inherits from MyClass.
```

We can also track the addition of a module's instance methods to an object (done via the extend method). The method extend_object is called whenever an extend is done.

```
module MyMod

  def MyMod.extend_object(obj)
    puts "Extending object id #{obj.object_id}, class #{obj.class}"
    super
  end

  # ...

end


x = [1, 2, 3]
x.extend(MyMod)

# Output:
# Extending object id 36491192, type Array
```

Note that the call to super is needed for the real extend_object method to do its work. This is analogous to the behavior of append_features (see section11.1.12, "Working with Modules"); this method can also be used to track the use of modules.

11.3.14   Defining Finalizers for Objects

Ruby classes have *constructors* (the methods new and initialize) but don't have *destructors* (methods that delete objects). That's because Ruby uses *mark-and-sweep garbage collection* to remove unreferenced objects; a destructor would make no sense.

However, people coming to Ruby from languages such as C++ seem to miss the facility and often ask how they can write code to handle the finalization of objects. The simple answer is that there is no real way to do it reliably. But you *can* arrange to have code called when an object is garbage collected.

```
a = "hello"
puts "The string 'hello' has an object id #{a.id}"
ObjectSpace.define_finalizer(a) { |id| puts "Destroying #{id}" }
puts "Nothing to tidy"
```

```
GC.start
a = nil
puts "The original string is now a candidate for collection"
GC.start
```

This produces the following output:

```
The string 'hello' has an object id 537684890
Nothing to tidy
The original string is now a candidate for collection
Destroying 537684890
```

Note that by the time the finalizer is called, the object has basically been destroyed already. An attempt to convert the ID you receive back into an object reference using ObjectSpace._id2ref will raise a RangeError, complaining that you are attempting to use a recycled object.

Also, be aware that Ruby uses a conservative mark-and-sweep GC mechanism. There is no guarantee that an object will undergo garbage collection before the program terminates.

However, all this might be moot. There's a style of programming in Ruby that uses blocks to encapsulate the use of a resource. At the end of the block, the resource is deleted, and life carries on merrily, all without the use of finalizers. For example, consider the block form of File.open:

```
File.open("myfile.txt") do |file|
  line1 = file.read
  # ...
end
```

Here the File object is passed into the block, and when the block exits, the file is closed, all under control of the open method. If you wanted to write a subset of File.open in Ruby (for efficiency it's currently written in C as part of the runtime system), it might look something like this:

```
def File.open(name, mode = "r")
  f = os_file_open(name, mode)
  if block_given?
    begin
      yield f
    ensure
```

```
        f.close
      end
      return nil
    else
      return f
    end
  end
```

The preceding routine tests for the presence of a block. If found, it invokes that block, passing in the open file. It does this in the context of a `begin-end` block, ensuring that it will close the file after the block terminates, even if an exception is thrown.

11.4   Conclusion

In this chapter we've seen a few of the more esoteric or advanced techniques in OOP, as well as some of the more everyday usages. We've seen some of the design patterns implemented (and some that don't need to be). We've also looked at Ruby's reflection API, some interesting consequences of Ruby's dynamic nature, and various neat tricks that can be done in a dynamic language.

It's time now to rejoin the real world. After all, OOP is not an end in itself but a means to an end; the end is to write applications that are effective, bug-free, and maintainable.

In modern computing, these applications frequently need a graphical interface. In Chapter 12, "Graphical Interfaces for Ruby," we discuss creating graphical interfaces in Ruby.

CHAPTER 12

Graphical Interfaces
for Ruby

There is nothing worse than a sharp image of a fuzzy concept.

—*Ansel Adams*

There is no denying that we are in the age of the graphical user interface (GUI). For as far into the future as we can see, some form of graphical interface is going to be the preferred way to interact with a computer.

I don't see the command line going away in the next decade or so; it definitely has its place in the world. But even the old-time hackers (who would rather use cp -R than a drag-and-drop interface) still enjoy a GUI when it is appropriate.

There are, however, significant difficulties with programming graphically. The first problem, of course, is designing a meaningful, usable "front end" for a program; in interface design, a picture is *not* always worth a thousand words. This book can't address these issues; our topic here is not ergonomics, aesthetics, or psychology.

The second obvious problem is that graphical programming is more complex. We have to worry about the sizes, shapes, locations, and behaviors of all the controls that can be displayed on the screen and manipulated with mouse and/or keyboard.

The third difficulty is that various computing subcultures have differing ideas of what a windowing system is and how it should be implemented. The disparity between these systems has to be experienced to be fully appreciated; many a programmer has attempted to produce a cross-platform tool only to find that the impedance mismatch between the GUIs was the hardest part to deal with.

This chapter can't help much with these problems. The most I can do is give a gentle introduction to a few popular GUI systems (as they relate to Ruby) and offer a few hints and observations.

The bulk of this chapter is devoted to Tk, GTK+, FOX, and Qt. Whatever your background, there is a good chance you are asking, "Why wasn't (*insert name of favorite GUI*) included here?"

There could be several reasons. One reason is limited space, since this book is not primarily about graphical interfaces. Another reason might be that your favorite system doesn't have a mature set of Ruby bindings yet (in which case you are encouraged to create them). Finally, not all GUI systems are created equal. This chapter tries to cover the ones that are most important and most mature and give the rest a passing mention.

12.1   Ruby/Tk

The roots of Tk go back as far as 1988, if you count prerelease versions. It was long thought of as a companion of Tcl, but for several years it has been used with several other languages, including Perl and Ruby.

If Ruby had a native GUI, Tk would probably be it. It is still in widespread use at the time of this writing, and some Ruby download versions include Tk in a more or less turnkey fashion.

The previous reference to Perl is not entirely gratuitous. The Tk bindings for Ruby and Perl are similar, enough so that any reference material for Perl/Tk should be mostly applicable to Ruby/Tk. One such reference is *Learning Perl/Tk*; ISBN: 1565923146 by Nancy Walsh.

12.1.1 Overview

In 2001, Tk was probably the most common GUI in use with Ruby. It was the first one made available and has long been part of the standard Ruby installation. Though it is probably not as popular as it was then, it is still in wide use.

Some say that Tk is showing its age; for those who like clean, object-oriented interfaces, it may be something of a disappointment. But it has the advantages of being well-known, portable, and stable.

Any Ruby/Tk application must use `require` to load the `tk` extension. Following that, the application's interface is built up piecemeal starting with some kind of container and the controls that populate it. Finally, a call to `Tk.mainloop` is made; this method captures all the events such as mouse movements and button presses and acts on them accordingly.

```
require "tk"
# Setting up the app...
Tk.mainloop
```

As with most or all windowing systems, Tk graphical controls are called *widgets*; these widgets are typically grouped together in containers. The top-level container is called the *root*; it is not always necessary to specify an explicit root, but it is a good idea.

Every widget class is named according to its name in the Tk world (by appending `Tk` to the front). Thus the `Frame` widget corresponds to the `TkFrame` class.

Widgets are naturally instantiated using the `new` method. The first parameter specifies the container into which the widget is placed; if it is omitted, the root is assumed.

The options used to instantiate a widget may be specified in two ways. The first (Perl-like) way is to pass in a hash of attributes and values. (Recall that it is a quirk of Ruby syntax that a hash passed in as the last or only parameter may have its braces omitted.)

```
my_widget = TkSomewidget.new( "borderwidth" => 2, "height" => 40 ,
                              "justify" => "center" )
```

The other way is to pass a block to the constructor that will be evaluated with `instance_eval`. Within this block, we can call methods to set the attributes of the widget (using methods that are named the same as the attributes). Bear in mind that the code block is evaluated *in the context of the object, not the caller*. This means, for instance, that the caller's instance variables cannot be referenced inside this block.

```
my_widget = TkSomewidget.new do
              borderwidth 2
              height 40
              justify "center"
            end
```

Three geometry managers are available with Tk; they all serve the purpose of control-ling the relative size and placement of the widgets as they appear onscreen. The first (and most commonly used) is pack; the other two are grid and place. The grid man-ager is sophisticated but somewhat prone to bugs; the place manager is the most sim-pleminded of all because it requires absolute values for the positioning of widgets. We will only use pack in our examples.

12.1.2 A Simple Windowed Application

Here we'll demonstrate the simplest possible application—a simple calendar app that displays the current date.

For good form, we'll begin by explicitly creating a root and placing a Label widget inside it.

```
require "tk"

root = TkRoot.new() { title "Today's Date" }
str = Time.now.strftime("Today is \n%B %d, %Y")
lab = TkLabel.new(root) do
        text str
        pack("padx" => 15, "pady" => 10,
             "side" => "top")
      end
Tk.mainloop
```

In the preceding code we create the root, set the date string, and create a label. In cre-ating the label, we set the text to be the value of str, and we call pack to arrange every-thing neatly. We tell pack to use a padding of 15 pixels horizontally and 10 pixels vertically, and we ask that the text be centered on the label.

Figure 12.1 shows what the application looks like.

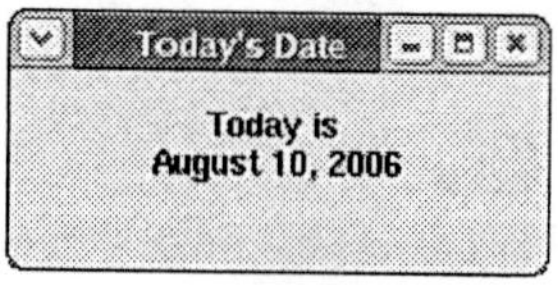

Figure 12.1   A simple Tk application.

As we mentioned, the creation of the label could also be done in this way:

```
lab = TkLabel.new(root) do
       text str
       pack("padx" => 15, "pady" => 10,
            "side" => "top")
     end
```

The units for screen measurement (as used in this example for padx and pady) are in pixels by default. We can also work in another unit by appending a suffix onto the number; the value now becomes a string, of course, but since Ruby/Tk doesn't care about that, we don't care, either. The available units are centimeters (c), millimeters (m), inches (i), and points (p). All of these are valid padx calls:

```
pack("padx" => "80m")
pack("padx" => "8c")
pack("padx" => "3i")
pack("padx" => "12p")
```

The side attribute doesn't actually contribute anything in this case since we have set it to its default. If you resize the application window, you will notice that the text "sticks" to the top part of the area in which it lives. Other possible values are right, left, and bottom, as you might expect.

The pack method has other options that govern the placement of widgets onscreen. We'll look at just a few.

The fill option specifies whether a widget fills its allocation rectangle (in the horizontal and/or vertical directions). Possible values are x, y, both, and none (the default being none).

The anchor option will anchor the widget inside its allocation rectangle using a "compass point" notation; the default is center, and the other possible values are n, s, e, w, ne, nw, se, and sw.

The in option will pack the widget with respect to some container other than its parent. The default, of course, is the parent.

The before and after options can be used to change the packing order of the widgets in any way desired. This is useful because widgets may not be created in any particular order as compared to their locations onscreen.

All in all, Tk is fairly flexible about placing widgets onscreen. Search the documentation and try things out.

12.1.3 Working with Buttons

One of the most common widgets in any GUI is the *pushbutton* (or simply *button*). As you would expect, the TkButton class enables the use of buttons in Ruby/Tk applications.

In any nontrivial application, we usually create frames to contain the various widgets we'll be placing onscreen. Button widgets can be placed in these containers.

A button will ordinarily have at least three attributes set:

- The text of the button

- The command associated with the button (to be executed when it is pressed)

- The packing of the button within its container

Here is a little example of a button:

```
btn_OK = TkButton.new do
  text "OK"
  command (proc { puts "The user says OK." })
  pack("side" => "left")
end
```

Here we create a new button and assign the new object to the btn_OK variable; we pass in a block to the constructor, although we could use a hash if we chose. In this case, we use the multiline form (which we prefer), though in practice you can cram as much code onto a single line as you want. Recall, by the way, that the block is executed using instance_eval, so that it is evaluated in the context of the object (in this case, the new TkButton object).

The text specified as a parameter to the text method will simply be placed on the button. It can be multiple words or even multiple lines.

The pack method we have already seen. It is nothing interesting, though it is essential if the widget is going to be visible at all.

The interesting part here is the command method, which takes a Proc object and associates it with the button. Frequently, as we do here, we will use the Kernel method lambdaproc, which will convert a block to a Proc object.

The action we're performing here is rather silly. When the user presses the button, a (nongraphical) puts will be done; the output will go to the command-line window from which the program was started or perhaps an auxiliary console window.

We now offer a better example. Listing 12.1 is a fake thermostat application that will increment and decrement the displayed temperature (giving us at least the illusion that we are controlling the heating or cooling and making ourselves more comfortable). An explanation follows the code.

Listing 12.1   A Simulated Thermostat

```ruby
require 'tk'

# Common packing options...
Top    = { 'side' => 'top',  'padx'=>5, 'pady'=>5 }
Left   = { 'side' => 'left', 'padx'=>5, 'pady'=>5 }
Bottom = { 'side' => 'bottom', 'padx'=>5, 'pady'=>5 }

temp = 74    # Starting temperature...

root = TkRoot.new { title "Thermostat" }

top = TkFrame.new(root) { background "#606060" }
bottom = TkFrame.new(root)

tlab = TkLabel.new(top) do
  text temp.to_s
  font "{Arial} 54 {bold}"
  foreground "green"
  background "#606060"
  pack Left
end

TkLabel.new(top) do          # the "degree" symbol
  text "o"
  font "{Arial} 14 {bold}"
  foreground "green"
  background "#606060"
  # Add anchor-north to the hash (make a superscript)
  pack Left.update({ 'anchor' => 'n' })
end

TkButton.new(bottom) do
  text " Up "
  command proc { tlab.configure("text"=>(temp+=1).to_s) }
  pack Left
end

TkButton.new(bottom) do
  text "Down"
  command proc { tlab.configure("text"=>(temp-=1).to_s) }
  pack Left
end

top.pack Top
bottom.pack Bottom

Tk.mainloop
```

We create two frames here. The upper one holds only a display. We display the temperature in Fahrenheit in a large font for realism (using a small, strategically placed letter "o" for a degree mark). The bottom frame holds the "up" and "down" buttons.

Notice that we are using some new attributes for the TkLabel object. The font method specifies the typeface and size of the text in the label. The string value is platform-dependent; the one shown here is valid on a Windows system. On a UNIX system, it would typically be a full X-style font name, long and unwieldy, something like -Adobe-Helvetica-Bold-R-Normal-*-120-*-*-*-*-*-*.

The foreground method sets the color of the text itself. Here we pass in the string "green" (which has a predefined meaning in the internals of Tk). If you wonder whether a color is predefined in Tk, an easy way to find out is simply to try it.

Likewise, the background sets the color of the background against which the text appears. In this case, we pass it a different kind of string as a parameter, a color in typical red-green-blue hex format as you would see in HTML or in various other situations. (The string "#606060" represents a nice gray color.)

Notice that we haven't added any kind of "exit" button here (to avoid cluttering a nice simple design). As always, you can close the app by clicking the Close icon at the upper right of the window frame.

Note that the configure method is used in the commands for the buttons; this changes the text of the top label as it increments or decrements the current temperature. As we mentioned earlier, basically any attribute can be changed at runtime in this way, and the change will be reflected onscreen immediately.

We'll mention two other tricks that you can do with text buttons. The justify method will accept a parameter ("left", "right", or "center" to specify how the text will be placed on the button ("center" is the default). We already mentioned that multiple lines could be displayed; the wraplength method will specify the column at which word wrapping should occur.

The button's style may be changed with the relief method, giving it a slight three-dimensional appearance. The parameter to this method must be one of these strings: "flat", "groove", "raised", "ridge" (the default), "sunken", or "solid". The width and height methods will control the size of the button explicitly, and methods such as borderwidth also are available. For other options (which are numerous), consult a reference.

Let's look at an additional example of using a button. This new button will have an image on it rather than just text.

I created a pair of GIF images of an upward-pointing arrow and a downward-pointing one (up.gif and down.gif). We can use the TkPhotoImage class to get references to each of these. Then we can use these references when we instantiate the buttons.

```ruby
up_img = TkPhotoImage.new("file"=>"up.gif")
down_img = TkPhotoImage.new("file"=>"down.gif")

TkButton.new(bottom) do
   image up_img
   command proc { tlab.configure("text"=>(temp+=1).to_s) }
   pack Left
end

TkButton.new(bottom) do
   image down_img
   command proc { tlab.configure("text"=>(temp-=1).to_s) }
   pack Left
end
```

This button code simply replaces the corresponding lines in our first thermostat example. Except for the appearance of the buttons, the behavior is the same. Figure 12.2 shows the thermostat application.

Figure 12.2 Thermostat simulation (with graphical buttons).

12.1.4 Working with Text Fields

A text entry field can be displayed and manipulated using the TkEntry widget. As you would expect, numerous options are available for governing the size, color, and behavior of this widget; we will offer one sizable example that illustrates a few of these.

An entry field is only useful if there is some way to retrieve the value typed into it. Typically the field will be bound to a variable (actually a `TkVariable` as we'll see), though the `get` method can also be used.

For our code fragment, let's assume that we're writing a telnet client that will accept four pieces of information: the host machine, the port number (defaulting to 23), the user ID, and the password. We'll add a couple of buttons just for looks, for the "sign on" and "cancel" operations.

As we've written it, this code fragment also does some little tricks with frames to make things line up and look better. It's not written in a truly portable way, and a real Tk guru would disdain this approach. But just for your information, we've documented this "quick and dirty" approach to screen layout.

The screenshot is shown in Figure 12.3, and the code in Listing 12.2.

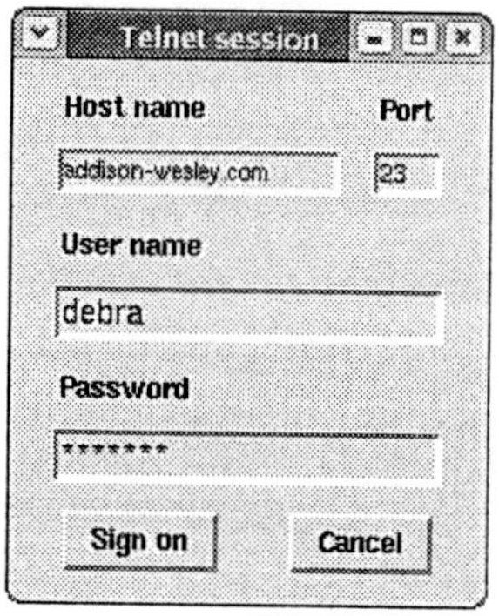

Figure 12.3   A simulated telnet client.

Listing 12.2   A Simulated Telnet Client

```
require "tk"

def packing(padx, pady, side=:left, anchor=:n)
  { "padx" => padx, "pady" => pady,
    "side" => side.to_s, "anchor" => anchor.to_s  }
end

root = TkRoot.new() { title "Telnet session" }
top = TkFrame.new(root)
fr1   = TkFrame.new(top)
fr1a  = TkFrame.new(fr1)
fr1b  = TkFrame.new(fr1)
fr2   = TkFrame.new(top)
```

```ruby
fr3   = TkFrame.new(top)
fr4   = TkFrame.new(top)

LabelPack  = packing(5, 5, :top, :w)
EntryPack  = packing(5, 2, :top)
ButtonPack = packing(15, 5, :left, :center)
FramePack  = packing(2, 2, :top)
Frame1Pack = packing(2, 2, :left)

var_host = TkVariable.new
var_port = TkVariable.new
var_user = TkVariable.new
var_pass = TkVariable.new

lab_host = TkLabel.new(fr1a) do
  text "Host name"
  pack LabelPack
end
ent_host = TkEntry.new(fr1a) do
  textvariable var_host
  font "{Arial} 10"
  pack EntryPack
end

lab_port = TkLabel.new(fr1b) do
  text "Port"
  pack LabelPack
end

ent_port = TkEntry.new(fr1b) do
  width 4
  textvariable var_port
  font "{Arial} 10"
  pack EntryPack
end

lab_user = TkLabel.new(fr2) do
  text "User name"
  pack LabelPack
end

ent_user = TkEntry.new(fr2) do
  width 21
  font "{Arial} 12"
  textvariable var_user
  pack EntryPack
end

lab_pass = TkLabel.new(fr3) do
  text "Password"
  pack LabelPack
```

Continues

```
    end

  ent_pass = TkEntry.new(fr3) do
    width 21
    show "*"
    textvariable var_pass
    font "{Arial} 12"
    pack EntryPack
  end

  btn_signon = TkButton.new(fr4) do
    text "Sign on"
    command proc {}          # Does nothing!
    pack ButtonPack
  end

  btn_cancel = TkButton.new(fr4) do
    text "Cancel"
    command proc { exit }    # Just exits
    pack ButtonPack
  end

  top.pack FramePack
  fr1.pack FramePack
  fr2.pack FramePack
  fr3.pack FramePack
  fr4.pack FramePack
  fr1a.pack Frame1Pack
  fr1b.pack Frame1Pack

  var_host.value = "addison-wesley.com"
  var_user.value = "debra"
  var_port.value = 23

  ent_pass.focus
  foo = ent_user.font

  Tk.mainloop
```

Let's get the layout issues out of the way. Note that we begin by creating some frames that will stack vertically from top to bottom. The topmost frame will have two smaller ones inside it, placed onscreen from left to right.

Listing 12.2 also has a method called packing, which exists only to make the code a tiny bit cleaner. It returns a hash with the specified values set for the padx, pady, side, and anchor options.

We use the TkVariable objects just to associate the entry fields with variables. A TkVariable has a value accessor that will allow these values to be set and retrieved.

When we create a `TkEntry` such as `ent_host`, we use the `textvariable` option to associate it with its corresponding `TkVariable` object. In some cases, we use `width` to set the horizontal width of the field; if it is omitted, a reasonable default will be picked, usually based on the width of the current value stored in the field. Often it's acceptable to pick these widths by trial and error.

Fonts work for entry fields as they do for labels; so do colors, which aren't addressed in this example. If a font is proportional, two fields that are given the same width may not appear equal-sized onscreen.

As always, `pack` must be called. We've simplified these calls a little with constants.

The password field has a call to the `show` method because it is the one field whose value is kept secret from people reading over our shoulders. The character specified as a parameter to `show` (here an asterisk) will be displayed in place of each of the user's keystrokes.

As I said, the buttons are there for show. The Sign on button does nothing at all; the Cancel button does exit the program, however.

There are other options for manipulating entry fields. We can change the value under program control rather than having the user change it; we can specify the font and the foreground/background colors; we can change the characteristics of the insertion cursor and move it where we want; and much more. For all the details, consult a reference.

Because the topic is entering text, it's appropriate to mention the related `Text` widget. It is related to the entry widget rather in the way a two-seater plane is related to the space shuttle. It is specifically designed to handle large pieces of multiline text and in effect forms the basis for a full-fledged editor. It's not covered here because of its complexity.

12.1.5 Working with Other Widgets

Many other widgets are available for Tk. We'll mention a few here.

A check box is commonly used for a toggled value, a simple true/false or on/off field. The Tk terminology is *check button*, and `TkCheckButton` is the class name for the widget.

The example shown in Listing 12.3 is a completely bare-bones code fragment because it does not even have any buttons. It displays check boxes for three areas in which you might take coursework (computer science, music, and literature). It prints a message to the console when you select (or deselect) one of these.

Listing 12.3   Tk Check Boxes

```
require 'tk'

root = TkRoot.new { title "Checkbutton demo" }
top = TkFrame.new(root)

PackOpts  = { "side" => "top", "anchor" => "w" }

cb1var = TkVariable.new
cb2var = TkVariable.new
cb3var = TkVariable.new

cb1 = TkCheckButton.new(top) do
  variable cb1var
  text "Computer science"
  command { puts "Button 1 = #{cb1var.value}" }
  pack PackOpts
end

cb2 = TkCheckButton.new(top) do
  variable cb2var
  text "Music"
  command { puts "Button 2 = #{cb2var.value}" }
  pack PackOpts
end

cb3 = TkCheckButton.new(top) do
  variable cb3var
  text "Literature"
  command { puts "Button 3 = #{cb3var.value}" }
  pack PackOpts
end

top.pack PackOpts

Tk.mainloop
```

Note that the variable associated with a check box receives the value 1 when the box
is selected and 0 when it is deselected. These default values can be changed with the
onvalue and offvalue methods. Furthermore, the variable can be set prior to the creation of the check box to establish its initial on/off status.

   If for some reason we want a check box to be grayed out, we can use the state
method to set its state to disabled. The other states are active and normal; the latter is the default.

Let's alter the example in Listing 12.3. Suppose we are representing not just areas of potential but actual university majors. Ignoring double majors, it's not appropriate for more than one option to be selected at a time. In this case, of course, we need *radio buttons* (implemented by the TkRadioButton class).

The example in Listing 12.4 is nearly the same as the example in Listing 12.3. Obviously the class name is different. Another critical difference is that the radio buttons all share the *same variable*. In fact, this is how Tk knows that these buttons all belong to the same group. It is possible to have more than one group of radio buttons, but each group must share one variable among its buttons.

Listing 12.4 Tk Radio Buttons

```
require 'tk'

root = TkRoot.new() { title "Radiobutton demo" }
top = TkFrame.new(root)

PackOpts = { "side" => "top", "anchor" => "w" }

major = TkVariable.new

b1 = TkRadioButton.new(top) do
  variable major
  text "Computer science"
  value 1
  command { puts "Major = #{major.value}" }
  pack PackOpts
end

b2 = TkRadioButton.new(top) do
  variable major
  text "Music"
  value 2
  command { puts "Major = #{major.value}" }
  pack PackOpts
end

b3 = TkRadioButton.new(top) do
  variable major
  text "Literature"
  value 3
  command { puts "Major = #{major.value}" }
  pack PackOpts
end

top.pack PackOpts

Tk.mainloop
```

The value method is used here to associate a specific value with each of the buttons. It's important to realize that *any* values can be used here (strings, for example). We didn't use strings simply because we wanted to emphasize that there is no direct relationship between the text of the widget and the value that is returned.

Numerous options are available to customize the appearance and behavior of both check boxes and radio button groups. The image method, for example, allows you to display an image rather than a text string. Most of the usual options for formatting and displaying widgets also apply; consult a reference for complete details.

If this book (or even this chapter) were fully devoted to Tk, we would have more to say. But it's not possible to cover these in detail; they are mentioned only to make you aware of their existence.

The list box (TkListBox) widget allows you to specify a list of values in a pull-down format so that the user can select from these. The selection mode (governed by the selectmode method) makes it possible to select these in single, extended, or browse modes. The first two modes simply determine whether the user can select only one or more than one item at a time. Browse mode is like single mode except that the selection can be moved around as the mouse button is held down. List boxes can be made fully scrollable and can hold an arbitrary number of items.

Tk has advanced menuing capabilities, including pull-down menus, tear-off menus, cascade submenus, keyboard shortcut facilities, radio button menu items, and much more. Investigate the classes TkMenu, TkMenubar, and TkMenuButton.

Perhaps the sexiest of the widgets is TkCanvas, which enables the programmer to manipulate images more or less at the pixel level. It has facilities for drawing lines and shapes, manipulating colors, and loading images in various graphics formats. If your application involves advanced graphics or user-controlled drawing, this widget will be of interest to you.

The scrollbar widget handles customized scrolling, both horizontal and vertical (for example, synchronized scrolling of two separate windows). The scale widget is basically a slider that represents a numeric value; it can be placed horizontally or vertically and can be used as input or output. For any others, consult advanced documentation.

12.1.6 Other Notes

The future of Tk is uncertain (as is true of any software system), but it is not going away in the immediate future. Ruby/Tk is based on Tk 8.4 at the time of this writing, though it will likely be updated in the future.

I should also say a few words about operating systems. In theory, Tk is platform-independent, and the practice is close to the theory. Some users, however, have reported that the Windows version is not as stable as the UNIX version. For the record, all the Tk examples in this chapter have been tested on Windows platforms and are known to work as expected.

12.2 Ruby/GTK2

The GTK+ library is a by-product of the GIMP (the *GNU Image Manipulation Program*); the name actually means *the GIMP Toolkit*. Like UNIX and LSD, GTK+ comes to us from the University of California at Berkeley.

For those familiar with X/Motif, GTK+ has a similar look and feel but is more lightweight. GTK+ originates in the UNIX world and forms the underlying basis for GNOME (increasingly familiar to Linux users), but it is relatively cross-platform. Since GTK+ 2.0, it supports not only UNIX-like systems but also the MS Windows family and Mac OS X with the X Window System. There is an ongoing port to the Mac OS X natively, though at the time of this writing it is not stable.

Ruby/GTK2 is a port of GTK+ 2.0. Don't confuse it with Ruby/GTK (based on GTK+ 1.2), which is incompatible and even obsolete. This section deals only with Ruby/GTK2.

12.2.1 Overview

Ruby/GTK2 is a library that allows Ruby applications to use the GTK+ 2.x library. GTK+ is open source and is released under the GNU LGPL license, so it may be used freely in commercial applications.

Like most GUI toolkits, GTK+ has such concepts as frames, windows, dialog boxes, and layout managers. It has a rich set of widgets; it includes all the most basic ones such as labels, buttons, and text edit boxes, as well as advanced widgets such as tree controls and multicolumn lists.

Although GTK+ was written in C, it was designed with a strong object-oriented flavor. Ruby/GTK2 thus presents a clean, object-oriented API, while also staying close to the underlying C. In addition, Ruby/GTK2 is implemented carefully by hand, not by using a code generator such as SWIG. As a result, the API is very Ruby-like, using blocks, omittable arguments, and so on. The API reference is available at http://ruby-gnome2.sourceforge.jp/.

GTK+ is actually built on top of libraries named GLib, Pango, ATK, Cairo, and GDK. It supports nongraphical functions (GLib), layout and rendering of internationalized text using UTF-8 (Pango), accessibility (Atk), Graphic rendering (Cairo), lower-level graphical objects (Gdk), and a lot of widgets and high-level graphic objects (Gtk).

At the time of this writing, Ruby/GTK2 is at version 0.14.1 and is compatible with the current stable versions of Ruby and GTK+ (2.0). Besides Linux, it supports the Windows family of operating systems and Mac OS X (with the X Window System). There is an ongoing port to native Mac OS X, though it is currently not stable.

GTK+ is object-oriented and has a logical widget hierarchy. The concepts of `Gtk::Bin` and `Gtk::Container` are powerful, and the combination of `Gtk::Box` and `Gtk::Table` layout managers is simple yet flexible. The Ruby/GTK2 mechanism for setting up signal handlers is convenient.

Some of the GTK+ widgets include menus, toolbars, tooltips, trees, progress bars, sliders, and calendars. But one current weakness of GTK+ is that it does not yet provide a good selection of standard dialog boxes, and it is difficult to set them up modally. In addition, the standard multiline text editor widget has some weaknesses.

All strings you pass to Ruby/GTK2 methods must be in UTF-8. You cannot just use non-ASCII characters from some Windows single- or multibyte codepage. Take care to edit your Ruby script in UTF-8 mode and add `$KCODE="U"` at the top of your Ruby script.

12.2.2 A Simple Windowed Application

Any program using Ruby/GTK2 must do a `require` of the `gtk2` library. Ruby/GTK2 provides its functionality through the `Gtk` and `Gdk` modules, meaning that GTK+ classes are typically prefixed with `Gtk::` (or `Gdk::`).

Normally we call `Gtk.init` to initialize Ruby/GTK2 and then create a top-level window and a handler for the `destroy` signal (which results when a window is closed by the user). A call to `show_all` makes the window (and its children) visible, and a call to `Gtk.main` initiates the event loop.

We'll expand on this a little after looking at an example. The following code fragment is similar to the one for Tk, which displays the current date:

```
$KCODE = "U"
require "gtk2"
Gtk.init

window = Gtk::Window.new("Today's Date")
```

```
window.signal_connect("destroy") { Gtk.main_quit }
str = Time.now.strftime("Today is \n%B %d, %Y")
window.add(Gtk::Label.new(str))
window.set_default_size(200, 100)
window.show_all
Gtk.main
```

The $KCODE variable was discussed in Chapter 4, "Internationalization in Ruby." The Gtk.init call initializes Ruby/GTK2.

The main window (of type Gtk::Window) is created as a "top level" window with the text that will appear in the title bar. Top-level windows have a standard title bar and generally behave as you would expect the main window of an application to behave.

Next, a handler is created for the destroy signal, which is generated after the main window is closed. This handler (here, a single block) simply exits the main event loop. The Ruby/GTK2 documentation lists all the signals that each widget might receive. (Be sure to look at superclasses, too). These are typically triggered by mouse or keyboard input, timers, changes in window state, and so on.

The next line of code adds a text label widget directly to the main window. The default size of the label will be calculated automatically based on the size of the text.

By default, GTK+ parent widgets are automatically sized according to the sizes of their children. In this case, the size of the string in the default font will determine the size of the label widget, and the main window would become just large enough to hold the label. That's pretty small, so set_default_size is used to indicate that the initial size of the main window is 200 pixels wide and 100 pixels tall.

After that, show_all is used to make the main window and all its children visible. By default, the main window is hidden, so it is necessary to invoke this method for the main window of most applications.

The call to Gtk.main starts the GTK+ event loop. This method will not return until GTK+ is terminated. In this application, the destroy event handler will cause Gtk.main to exit, at which point the app will terminate.

12.2.3 Working with Buttons

To create a pushbutton in Ruby/GTK2, we define it using the Gtk::Button class. In the simple case, we set up a handler for the clicked event that is generated when a user clicks on the button.

Listing 12.5 will accept a simple line of text in a text entry field and (when the All Caps! button is clicked) will convert the string to uppercase. Figure 12.4 shows the text entry field before the button is clicked.

Listing 12.5 Buttons in GTK

```
$KCODE = "U"
require "gtk2"

class SampleWindow < Gtk::Window

  def initialize
    super("Ruby/GTK2 Sample")
    signal_connect("destroy") { Gtk.main_quit }

    entry = Gtk::Entry.new

    button = Gtk::Button.new("All Caps!")
    button.signal_connect("clicked") {
      entry.text = entry.text.upcase
    }

    box = Gtk::HBox.new
    box.add(Gtk::Label.new("Text:"))
    box.add(entry)
    box.add(button)

    add(box)
    show_all
  end
end

Gtk.init
SampleWindow.new
Gtk.main
```

Figure 12.4   A simple GTK pushbutton example.

In Listing 12.5, a SampleWindow class is defined; this is a cleaner approach because it allows the class to control its own look and behavior (rather than requiring the caller to configure the window). This main window is derived from Gtk::Window.

As with the "Today's Date" example, a signal handler for destroy exits the GTK+ event loop when the main window is closed.

This class creates a single-line text entry field using the Gtk::Entry class and a Gtk::Button with the text label All Caps!. The signal handler for the button's clicked event calls the signal handler. (The clicked event is generated after the user *clicks and releases* the button.)

The Gtk::Window class is a Gtk::Bin, so it can only contain a single child widget. To put our two child widgets in the window, we place those widgets in a box and add the box to the main window. As widgets are added to a Gtk::HBox, they are positioned at the right edge of the box (by default). There is a corresponding Gtk::VBox widget that can stack multiple widgets vertically.

As with the earlier example, show_all is necessary to make the main window (and all its children) visible.

The signal handler of clicked is invoked whenever the button is clicked. It gets the current text out of the entry field, converts it to uppercase, and sets it back into the entry field.

The actual application code is below the SampleWindow class definition. It simply creates the main window and runs the GTK+ event loop.

12.2.4 Working with Text Fields

GTK+ provides the Gtk::Entry class for single-line input, as shown in the previous example. It also has a Gtk::TextView class, which is a powerful multiline editor that we will describe here.

Listing 12.6 creates a multiline edit box and inserts some text into it. As the contents change, the current length of the text is reflected in a label at the bottom of the window (see Figure 12.5).

Listing 12.6   A GTK Text Editor

```
$KCODE = "U"
require "gtk2"

class TextWindow < Gtk::Window

  def initialize
    super("Ruby/GTK2 Text Sample")
    signal_connect("destroy") { Gtk.main_quit }
    set_default_size(200, 100)
```

Continues

```ruby
@text = Gtk::TextView.new
@text.wrap_mode = Gtk::TextTag::WRAP_WORD

@buffer = @text.buffer
@buffer.signal_connect("changed") {
  @status.text = "Length: " + @buffer.char_count.to_s
}

@buffer.create_tag('notice',
                   'font' => "Times Bold Italic 18",
                   'foreground' => "red")

@status = Gtk::Label.new

scroller = Gtk::ScrolledWindow.new
scroller.set_policy(Gtk::POLICY_AUTOMATIC, Gtk::POLICY_NEVER)
scroller.add(@text)

box = Gtk::VBox.new
box.add(scroller)
box.add(@status)
add(box)

iter = @buffer.start_iter
@buffer.insert(iter, "This is an editor")
iter.offset = 5
@buffer.insert(iter, "really ", "notice")

show_all
  end
end

Gtk.init
TextWindow.new
Gtk.main
```

Figure 12.5   A small GTK text editor.

The basic structure of the code is similar to the button example: Initialize Ruby/GTK2, define a window class with an event handler to terminate the app cleanly, and set the initial size of the main window. At the end of `initialize`, `show_all` is used to make the window visible. The last two lines actually create the window and run the GTK+ event loop.

We create an editor widget named `@text`. Word wrap is enabled here; the default is to wrap lines regardless of word breaks.

The variable `@buffer` is the text buffer of `@text`. We give it a signal handler for the `changed` event; any time text is inserted, deleted, or modified, this signal will fire, and the signal handler will be called. The signal handler uses `char_count` to determine the length of the current text in the text editor and creates a message string; that message is displayed by setting `@status.text = text`.

Next we want to configure the `@text` widget to display its text in a different style. Create a "notice" tag using `create_tag`. This tag has the font "Times Bold Italic 18" and a foreground color of red. In a similar way, you can define tags with various other properties using `Gtk::TextTag`.

In this case, we attempt to use a font from the Times family, which on a Windows platform is likely to bring up some variant of Times Roman. On a Linux/UNIX platform, the parameter would be a standard X Window System font string. The system will return whatever font is the closest match available.

The `@status` label is initially empty. We will change its text later.

GTK+ provides two ways to add scrollbars to an application. You can directly create `Gtk::ScrollBar` objects and use signals to synchronize them with the content widget(s). However, in most cases, it is simpler to use the `Gtk::ScrolledWindow` widget instead.

The `Gtk::ScrolledWindow` widget is a `Gtk::Bin`, meaning it can only contain a single child widget. Of course, that child widget could be a `Gtk::Box` or other container that allows multiple children. Several GTK+ widgets, including `Gtk::TextView`, automatically interact with a `Gtk::ScrolledWindow`, requiring almost no additional code.

In this sample, we create a `Gtk::ScrolledWindow` named `scroller` and configure it using `set_policy`. We choose never to display a horizontal scrollbar and to automatically display a vertical scrollbar only when the editor has more lines than can be seen at once. We add the text editor directly to `scroller`.

We now set up a `Gtk::Vbox` that will stack our widgets vertically. The scrolling window that contains the text field is added first, so it will appear at the top of the main window. The `@status` text will appear at the bottom. The box is then added to our main window.

The next four lines insert text into the text editor. The first line gets the `Gtk::TextIter` of the beginning of the text (offset = 0) and then inserts a string there. Because there was no text, zero is the only reasonable place to insert. We then insert some additional text at offset five. The result is a text editor containing the string This really is an editor.

Because we already configured the handler for the changed event, it will be triggered by our calls to insert. This means the status will already display correctly, even before the user makes any changes to the text.

12.2.5 Working with Other Widgets

Even a relatively simple GUI may need more than text fields and buttons. Often we find a need for radio buttons, check boxes, and similar widgets. This next example illustrates a few of these.

Listing 12.7 assumes that the user is making an airline reservation. The Gtk::TreeView, Gtk::ListStore, and Gtk::TreeViewColumn classes (representing a multicolumn list) are used for the destination city. A check box (actually called a Gtk::CheckButton) determines whether the ticket is round-trip, and a set of radio buttons (class Gtk::RadioButton) is used for the seating. A Purchase button completes the interface (see Figure 12.6).

Listing 12.7 Airline Ticket Example

```
$KCODE = "U"
require "gtk2"

class TicketWindow < Gtk::Window

  def initialize
    super("Purchase Ticket")
    signal_connect("destroy") { Gtk.main_quit }

    dest_model = Gtk::ListStore.new(String, String)
    dest_view = Gtk::TreeView.new(dest_model)
    dest_column = Gtk::TreeViewColumn.new("Destination",
                      Gtk::CellRendererText.new,
                      :text => 0)
    dest_view.append_column(dest_column)
    country_column = Gtk::TreeViewColumn.new("Country",
                        Gtk::CellRendererText.new,
                        :text => 1)
    dest_view.append_column(country_column)
    dest_view.selection.set_mode(Gtk::SELECTION_SINGLE)

    [["Cairo", "Egypt"], ["New York", "USA"],
     ["Tokyo", "Japan"]].each do |destination, country|
      iter = dest_model.append
      iter[0] = destination
```

```
      iter[1] = country
    end
  dest_view.selection.signal_connect("changed") do
    @city = dest_view.selection.selected[0]
  end

  @round_trip = Gtk::CheckButton.new("Round Trip")

  purchase = Gtk::Button.new("Purchase")
  purchase.signal_connect("clicked") { cmd_purchase }

  @result = Gtk::Label.new

  @coach = Gtk::RadioButton.new("Coach class")
  @business = Gtk::RadioButton.new(@coach, "Business class")
  @first = Gtk::RadioButton.new(@coach, "First class")

  flight_box = Gtk::VBox.new
  flight_box.add(dest_view).add(@round_trip)

  seat_box = Gtk::VBox.new
  seat_box.add(@coach).add(@business).add(@first)

  top_box = Gtk::HBox.new
  top_box.add(flight_box).add(seat_box)

  main_box = Gtk::VBox.new
  main_box.add(top_box).add(purchase).add(@result)

  add(main_box)
  show_all
end

def cmd_purchase
  text = @city
  if @first.active?
    text += ": first class"
  elsif @business.active?
    text += ": business class"
  elsif @coach.active?
    text += ": coach"
  end
  text += ", round trip " if @round_trip.active?
  @result.text = text
end

end

Gtk.init
TicketWindow.new
Gtk.main
```

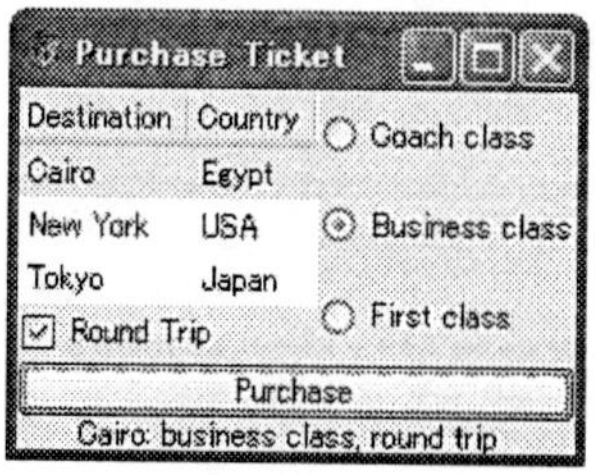

Figure 12.6   Various GTK widgets.

This application creates a main window with a signal handler as before. Next, a multicolumn list box widget is created with two columns. This list box is designed around a Model-View-Controller (MVC) design; Gtk::ListStore (the model class) has two String columns.

Then Gtk::TreeView is created. Gtk::TreeViewColumn configures the column. The title of first column is "Destination", and the cell renderer is Gtk::CellRendererText. The first column (column number zero) of the model (Gtk::ListStore) is used as the text property value. In this way, cell renderers are used to draw the data in the tree model. Several cell renderers come with GTK+ 2.x, including the Gtk::CellRendererText, Gtk::CellRendererPixbuf, and the Gtk::CellRendererToggle. Then three rows of data are added to the list, and a signal handler is created for the "changed" event. This will be invoked whenever the user selects a different row. The handler will update the @city member variable to contain the text from the first column (column number zero) of the newly selected row.

A simple check box (Gtk::CheckButton) and pushbutton (Gtk::Button) are created. The signal handler for the pushbutton will execute the cmd_purchase method whenever the button is clicked. The label named @result is initially blank but later will be set to a string indicating what type of ticket was purchased.

Three radio buttons are created as a group, meaning that only one of them can be selected at a time. When the user clicks on any of these radio buttons, any previously selected button will automatically be deselected. The first parameter to the radio button constructor is the previous radio button within the same group. So the first radio button doesn't have group as an argument, and the rest of the buttons pass the first radio button.

The widgets need to be arranged in a way that will make sense to the user, so a combination of Gtk::HBoxes and Gtk::VBoxes is used. The list box will appear above the check box. The three radio buttons will appear in a vertical stack to the right of the list box. Finally, the purchase pushbutton will appear below all the other widgets.

The cmd_purchase method is straightforward: It builds a string that reflects all the current widget states when the purchase button was pressed. Radio buttons and check boxes have a method named active? that returns true if the button is selected. The text is then placed in the @result label so it will appear on the screen.

Most applications use menus as a key part of their user interface. This next sample demonstrates how to set up menus using Ruby/GTK2. It also shows how easy it is to add tooltips, a nice touch for any program.

Listing 12.8 creates a main window that has a File menu, along with two other dummy items on the menu bar. The File menu contains an Exit item that exits the application. Both the File and Exit items have tooltips.

Listing 12.8   GTK Menu Example

```
$KCODE = "U"
require "gtk2"

class MenuWindow < Gtk::Window

  def initialize
    super("Ruby/GTK2 Menu Sample")
    signal_connect("destroy") { Gtk.main_quit }

    file_exit_item = Gtk::MenuItem.new("_Exit")
    file_exit_item.signal_connect("activate") { Gtk.main_quit }

    file_menu = Gtk::Menu.new
    file_menu.add(file_exit_item)

    file_menu_item = Gtk::MenuItem.new("_File")
    file_menu_item.submenu = file_menu

    menubar = Gtk::MenuBar.new
    menubar.append(file_menu_item)
    menubar.append(Gtk::MenuItem.new("_Nothing"))
    menubar.append(Gtk::MenuItem.new("_Useless"))

    tooltips = Gtk::Tooltips.new
    tooltips.set_tip(file_exit_item, "Exit the app", "")

    box = Gtk::VBox.new
    box.pack_start(menubar, false, false, 0)
    box.add(Gtk::Label.new("Try the menu and tooltips!"))
```

Continues

```
      add(box)
      set_default_size(300, 100)
      show_all
    end
  end

Gtk.init
MenuWindow.new
Gtk.main
```

Again, the basic structure is like the other samples. In this case, we create a Gtk::MenuItem named Exit and create a signal handler so it will actually exit the program. The signal is activate, and it will be generated when a user actually invokes this item on the menu.

The File menu is created, and the Exit item is added to it. This is all that is required to create a pop-up menu. Next, the File menu item is created—this is what will actually appear on the menu bar. We call submenu= to connect the File menu item with the File menu itself.

We create the Gtk::MenuBar and add its three items: File, Nothing, and Useless. Only the first item is actually functional‐ the other two are just for show.

A single Gtk::Tooltips object manages all the actual tooltips. To create a tooltip for any widget, such as a menu item, call set_tip, passing the widget, the tooltip text, and another string that contains additional private text. This private text is not shown as part of the tooltip; it could be used by a help system, for example.

A Gtk::Vbox is used to place the menu bar at the top of the main window, above any other widgets. In this case, instead of using add to place the menu bar in the box, we use pack_start to gain more control over the exact look and placement of the widget.

The first parameter to pack_start is the widget we are placing. The second parameter is a boolean indicating whether this widget should take up all the available space. Note that it won't make the widget actually grow; instead it will typically center the widget. In this case, we want the menu bar at the top of the screen, so we pass false.

The third parameter is a Boolean for whether this widget should grow to fill all the available space. Because we just want a small menu bar, we pass false for this as well. The last parameter to pack_start is for padding. This would be used to create additional space all around the widget. We don't want any, so we pass zero.

A text label will take up most of the main window. Finally, we force the initial size of the window to be 300 pixels wide by 100 pixels tall.

12.2.6 Other Notes

Ruby/GTK2 is a part of the Ruby-GNOME2 project. GNOME is a higher-level package that depends on GTK+, and Ruby-GNOME2 is the set of bindings of GNOME libraries.

Ruby-GNOME2 includes these libraries:

- Core libraries—These libraries are included in ruby-gtk2 packages. Sometimes the term "Ruby/GTK2" is used to mean all of these libraries. All of these work on UNIX-like systems, MS Windows, Mac OS X (under X11), and Cygwin (under X11). These are required from other Ruby-GNOME2 libraries.

- Ruby/GLib2—GLib is the low-level core library that forms the lowest-level infrastructure. It provides data structure handling for C, portability wrappers, Unicode support, and interfaces for such runtime functionality as an event loop, threads, dynamic loading, and an object system. Ruby/GLib2 is a wrapper for the GLib library. Because Ruby already has good string and list classes, some GLib functions are not implemented. On the other hand, it does provide some important functions to convert C and Ruby objects. This library is required from all other Ruby/GTK2 libraries.

- Ruby/ATK—This provides a set of interfaces for accessibility. By supporting the ATK interfaces, an application or toolkit can be used with such tools as screen readers, magnifiers, and alternative input devices.

- Ruby/Pango—A library for layout and rendering of text, with an emphasis on internationalization using UTF-8. It forms the core of text and font handling for GTK+ (2.0).

- Ruby/GdkPixbuf2—An image loading and manipulation library. It supports numerous image formats such as JPEG, PNG, GIF, and others.

- Ruby/GDK2—An intermediate layer that isolates GTK+ from the details of the windowing system.

- Ruby/GTK2—This comprises the main GUI widgets.

- Extra libraries—These libraries are included in ruby-gnome2 packages with the core libraries. All of them work on UNIX-like systems. Some libraries (Ruby/GtkGLExt, Ruby/Libglade2) work on MS Windows, and Mac OS X. Also some libraries should work on Mac OS X (under X11) and Cygwin (under X11), though these are not well tested.

- Ruby/GNOME2—Contains extra widgets for the GNOME environment.

- Ruby/GnomeCanvas2—A widget for creating interactive structured graphics.

- Ruby/GConf2—A process-transparent configuration database (similar to the Windows Registry).

- Ruby/GnomeVFS—Lets applications seamlessly access remote and local files.

- Ruby/Gstreamer—A multimedia framework for audio and video.

- Ruby/GtkHtml2—An HTML widget.

- Ruby/GtkGLExt—Offers 3D rendering using OpenGL.

- Ruby/GtkSourceView—A Text widget with syntax highlighting and other features typical of a source code editor.

- Ruby/GtkMozEmbed—A widget embedding a Mozilla Gecko renderer.

- Ruby/Libart2—Handles the basic drawing capabilities.

- Ruby/Libgda—An interface to the GDA (GNU Data Access) architecture to access data sources such as databases or LDAP.

- Ruby/Libglade2—Gives applications the capability to load user interfaces from XML files at runtime. The XML files are created with GLADE, a powerful user interface builder that eases the creation of internationalized GUIs.

- Ruby/PanelApplet—A panel applet library for the GNOME panel.

- Ruby/GnomePrint and Ruby/GnomePrintUI—Offer widgets for printing.

- Ruby/RSVG—Enables rendering of SVG vector graphics.

- External libraries—These libraries are required from the Ruby-GNOME2 libraries.

- Ruby/Cairo—A 2D graphics library with support for multiple output devices. Currently supported output targets include the X Window System, win32, and image buffers. Experimental backends include OpenGL (through glitz), Quartz, XCB, PostScript, and PDF file output. This library is required from the core libraries. Ruby/Cairo also requires Ruby/GLib2. The official home page is at http://cairographics.org/.

- Ruby/OpenGL is an interface to the OpenGL 3D graphics library. This library is required from Ruby/GtkGLExt2. It also works on many platforms. The official home page is at http://www2.giganet.net/~yoshi/.

- Ruby-GetText-Package provides features to manage translated message catalogs for localization. (Refer to Chapter 4.) Ruby/Libglade2 is localized with this package (though it is optional), and other libraries also can localize with this library. The official home page is at http://gettext.rubyforge.org/.

The official Ruby-GNOME2 home page is at http://ruby-gnome2.sourceforge.jp/. You can find released files, the install guide, API references, tutorials, and sample code. The official GNOME home page is at http://www.gnome.org/, and the GTK+ home page is at http://www.gtk.org/.

12.3 FXRuby (FOX)

The FOX system is also relatively new technology; its emphasis is on speed and consistency between platforms. Its extreme consistency is achieved in part by its self-reliance; it is not a wrapper for a native GUI, as some other systems are implemented.

At its heart, it is based on C++, though of course, bindings can be created for essentially any language (as they have been for Ruby). Because its internals are object-oriented from the start, it interfaces well with Ruby and is fairly naturally extensible.

FOX isn't as widespread as Tk or GTK+, but it is popular among Ruby programmers. Part of the reason for this is the excellent Ruby binding called FXRuby (hosted at http://fxruby.org). FXRuby is the work of Lyle Johnson, who has gone to great lengths to maintain and document this library; he also has provided excellent technical support over the years and offered invaluable assistance in the writing of this FXRuby section.

12.3.1 Overview

FXRuby is a Ruby binding to the FOX C++ library; it has many classes for developing full-featured GUI applications. Although *FOX* stands for *Free Objects for X*, it has been ported to a variety of platforms including MS Windows. Lyle Johnson created the Ruby binding to FOX as well as much of the Windows port of the FOX C++ toolkit itself. FOX was created by Jeroen van der Zijp with the support of CFD Research Corporation.

FOX widgets provide a modern look and feel. The widget choices rival native GUI interfaces, including MS Windows, and the toolkit also has features beyond many other widget libraries.

The FOX class library is clean and powerful, and can be learned easily by programmers familiar with most other GUI toolkits. Platform dependencies are not apparent in the API. Because FOX itself is implemented in C++, some aspects of the FXRuby API are still influenced by the static nature and programming conventions of C++ (for example, the use of enumerations and bit operations).

A central simplifying mechanism in FOX is the message/target paradigm. A FOX object is an instance of FXObject, or one of its subclasses. User-defined FOX objects must inherit from one of these classes. Every instance of FXObject can send and receive messages; a message is associated with a specific target at runtime, when the message is sent.

A message in FOX is represented internally by a message type, a message identifier, and some message data. Many of the FOX classes use a common set of message definitions to allow widgets to interoperate.

A message handler should return 1 to indicate that the message has been handled or 0 to indicate that it has not. FOX does not implicitly forward unhandled messages to other widgets. The return value is used by FOX to determine whether the GUI requires updating. An FXRuby application could use the return value to forward unhandled messages itself and thus implement the *Chain of Responsibility* pattern (as mentioned in the book *Design Patterns;* ISBN:0201633612 by the "Gang of Four"— Gamma, Helm, Johnson, and Vlissides).

Another simplifying mechanism in FOX is the automatic update paradigm. The implicit FOX event loop includes an update phase where instances of FOX objects can handle update messages. An update handler is typically used to change the look and feel of a widget based on the new state of some application data. For example, Listing 12.9 later in this chapter has a button that updates its active/deactive status based on an application variable.

12.3.2 A Simple Windowed Application

Here is a minimal FXRuby application, the equivalent of the others you saw for Tk and GTK+ earlier:

```
require 'fox16'      # Use the FOX 1.6 bindings

include Fox
```

```
application = FXApp.new
main = FXMainWindow.new(application, "Today's Date")
str = Time.now.strftime("&Today is %B %d, %Y")
button = FXButton.new(main, str)
button.connect(SEL_COMMAND) { application.exit }
application.create
main.show(PLACEMENT_SCREEN)
application.run
```

This application is enough to illustrate two fundamental classes of FXRuby: FXApp and FXMainWindow. An application must create and initialize an instance of FXApp before anything can be done with the other FOX classes. FXMainWindow is a subclass of FXTopWindow; every widget in FOX is a kind of "window." An FXTopWindow is a top-level window, or one that appears directly on the screen. A more complex FXRuby application will typically create a subclass of FXMainWindow and create its widgets during initialization.

The FXMainWindow constructor requires an instance of FXApp as its first argument. The second argument is the window title. By default, an instance of FXMainWindow will be placed in the center of the screen with all the standard window decorations of an FXTopWindow. Therefore, it will be resizable, show its title bar, and include minimize, maximize, and close buttons in the title bar.

The decorations attribute for a main window can explicitly name each decoration to be included. For example, it is possible to prevent a window from being resized:

```
main = FXMainWindow.new(application, "Today's Date")
main.decorations = DECOR_TITLE | DECOR_CLOSE
```

The decoration options are bitwise ORed together in true C++ fashion. The result is a window that has a title and just a close button in the title bar.

This simple application has one widget in its main window—an instance of FXButton displaying some text with today's date:

```
str = Time.now.strftime("&Today is %B %d, %Y")
button = FXButton.new(main, str)
```

The first argument to the FXButton constructor is the parent window that contains the widget. In this example, it is the main window. The second argument is the button's text.

The next line shows how to associate the button with a block of code using the connect method:

```
button.connect(SEL_COMMAND) { application.exit }
```

This code says that when the button sends a command message (that is, a message of type SEL_COMMAND), the application's exit method will be called.

The remaining lines of the application illustrate the common "mating ritual" of FXApp and FXMainWindow instances:

```
application.create
main.show(PLACEMENT_SCREEN)
application.run
```

All FXRuby applications should include lines like these to create the application, show the FXMainWindow, and run the FXApp event loop for processing GUI events. The PLACEMENT_SCREEN argument to the show procedure determines where the main window will appear on the screen. Interesting alternative arguments are PLACEMENT_CURSOR to place it under the cursor location, PLACEMENT_OWNER to place it centered on its owner, and PLACEMENT_MAXIMIZED to place it maximized to the screen size.

12.3.3 Working with Buttons

You have already seen simple button handling in FXRuby. Now let's look a little deeper.

A button can display more than a short text string. For example, a button can display multiple lines of text separated by newline characters:

```
text = "&Hello, World!\n" +
       "Do you see multiple lines of text?"
FXButton.new(self, text)
```

Note the ampersand character that appears before the letter "H" in "Hello, World!" An ampersand in a button's label defines a *hot key* equated with a button click.

A button can also display an icon image constructed from any of a large number of file formats. For example:

```
text = "&Hello, World!\n" +
       "Do you see the icon?\n" +
```

```
        "Do you see multiple lines of text?"
icon = File.open("some_icon.gif", "rb") do |file|
        FXGIFIcon.new(app, file.read)
      end
FXButton.new(self, text, icon)
```

Listing 12.9 illustrates the mechanism the FOX toolkit provides for updating GUI state.

Listing 12.9   Updating GUI State in FOX

```
require 'fox16'

include Fox

class TwoButtonUpdateWindow < FXMainWindow

  def initialize(app)
    # Invoke base class initialize first
    super(app, "Update Example", nil, nil,
          DECOR_TITLE | DECOR_CLOSE)

    # First button
    @button_one = FXButton.new(self, "Enable Button 2")
    @button_one_enabled = true

    # Second button
    @button_two = FXButton.new(self, "Enable Button 1")
    @button_two.disable
    @button_two_enabled = false

# Hook up the message handlers
@button_one.connect(SEL_COMMAND, method(:onCommand))
@button_two.connect(SEL_COMMAND, method(:onCommand))
@button_one.connect(SEL_UPDATE,  method(:onUpdate))
@button_two.connect(SEL_UPDATE,  method(:onUpdate))
  end

  def onCommand(sender, sel, ptr)
    # Update the application state
    @button_one_enabled = !@button_one_enabled
    @button_two_enabled = !@button_two_enabled
  end

  def onUpdate(sender, sel, ptr)
    # Update the buttons based on the application state
    @button_one_enabled ?
      @button_one.enable : @button_one.disable
```

Continues

```
         @button_two_enabled ?
            @button_two.enable : @button_two.disable
      end

   end

   application = FXApp.new
   main = TwoButtonUpdateWindow.new(application)
   application.create
   main.show(PLACEMENT_SCREEN)
   application.run
```

In this example, two buttons are added to the main window. We again use the connect method to associate the buttons' SEL_COMMAND messages with a piece of code, but this time the code is found in a method instead of a block:

```
   @button_one.connect(SEL_COMMAND, method(:onCommand))
```

This example also introduces a new message type. The use of the SEL_UPDATE message type allows for the independence of GUI widgets from each other and the application code. This example illustrates that the two buttons are unaware of each other. One updates the state of the other via sending messages to handlers that maintain their state.

12.3.4 Working with Text Fields

FOX has some useful features for text entry. The following example illustrates the use of FXTextField for editing single lines of text. The options are used to constrain the format of the text. TEXTFIELD_PASSWD is used for disguising the text when it is a password, TEXTFIELD_REAL constrains the text to the syntax for numbers in scientific notation, and TEXTFIELD_INTEGER constrains the text to the syntax for integers:

```
   simple = FXTextField.new(main, 20, nil, 0,
                            JUSTIFY_RIGHT|FRAME_SUNKEN|
                            FRAME_THICK|LAYOUT_SIDE_TOP)
   simple.text = "Simple Text Field"
   passwd = FXTextField.new(main, 20, nil, 0,
                            JUSTIFY_RIGHT|TEXTFIELD_PASSWD|
                            FRAME_SUNKEN|FRAME_THICK|
                            LAYOUT_SIDE_TOP)
```

```
passwd.text = "Password"
real = FXTextField.new(main, 20, nil, 0,
                       TEXTFIELD_REAL|FRAME_SUNKEN|
                       FRAME_THICK|LAYOUT_SIDE_TOP|
                       LAYOUT_FIX_HEIGHT, 0, 0, 0, 30)
real.text = "1.0E+3"
int = FXTextField.new(main, 20, nil, 0, TEXTFIELD_INTEGER|
                      FRAME_SUNKEN|FRAME_THICK|
                      LAYOUT_SIDE_TOP|LAYOUT_FIX_HEIGHT,
                      0, 0, 0, 30)
int.text = "1000"
```

The following example illustrates a simple way to enter text using a dialog box. Again the text can be constrained to an integer or scientific number based on the method used.

```
puts FXInputDialog.getString("initial text",
                             self, "Text Entry Dialog",
                             "Enter some text:", nil)
puts FXInputDialog.getInteger(1200, self,
                              "Integer Entry Dialog",
                              "Enter an integer:", nil)
puts FXInputDialog.getReal(1.03e7, self,
                           "Scientific Entry Dialog",
                           "Enter a real number:", nil)
```

To save space, we don't show the full application here. But, of course, the FOX toolkit requires initialization before it can display a dialog window.

12.3.5 Working with Other Widgets

The next example illustrates the use of menus and menu bars in FXRuby applications. Note that instances of FXMenuCommand follow the FOX message/target paradigm that we've already seen demonstrated for buttons:

```
require 'fox16'

include Fox

application = FXApp.new
main = FXMainWindow.new(application, "Simple Menu")
```

```
menubar = FXMenuBar.new(main, LAYOUT_SIDE_TOP |
                             LAYOUT_FILL_X)
filemenu = FXMenuPane.new(main)
quit_cmd = FXMenuCommand.new(filemenu, "&Quit\tCtl-Q")
quit_cmd.connect(SEL_COMMAND) { application.exit }
FXMenuTitle.new(menubar, "&File", nil, filemenu)
application.create
main.show(PLACEMENT_SCREEN)
application.run
```

Both FXMenuBar and FXMenuPane appear directly on the FXMainWindow object in this example. The options LAYOUT_SIDE_TOP and LAYOUT_FILL_X place the menu bar at the top of the parent window and stretch it across the width of the window. The text of the menu command, "&Quit\tCtl-Q", defines the Alt+Q keystroke as a keyboard hot key equivalent and Ctrl+Q as a keyboard shortcut. Typing Alt+F and then Alt+Q is equivalent to clicking on the File menu and then the Quit menu command. Typing Ctrl+Q is a shortcut equivalent for the entire sequence.

The FXTopWindow class provides a method that can be called to minimize the main window. The following three lines add another menu command to the File menu that will cause the main window to be minimized:

```
FXMenuCommand.new(filemenu, "&Icon\tCtl-I") do |cmd|
   cmd.connect(SEL_COMMAND) { main.minimize }
end
```

This example demonstrates another technique that you can use when constructing a menu command. If you don't have any need to keep a reference to a new menu command widget, you can just attach a block to the call to FXMenuCommand.new and do all of your widget initialization inside that block. This technique can of course be used with any of the built-in FOX classes.

The example shown in Listing 12.10 illustrates the use of radio buttons.

Listing 12.10   FOX Radio Buttons

```
require 'fox16'

include Fox

class RadioButtonHandlerWindow < FXMainWindow
```

```
def initialize(app)
   # Invoke base class initialize first
   super(app, "Radio Button Handler", nil, nil,
     DECOR_TITLE | DECOR_CLOSE)

   choices = [ "Good", "Better", "Best" ]

   group = FXGroupBox.new(self, "Radio Test Group",
           LAYOUT_SIDE_TOP |
           FRAME_GROOVE |
           LAYOUT_FILL_X)

   choices.each do |choice|
     FXRadioButton.new(group, choice,
           nil, 0,
           ICON_BEFORE_TEXT |
           LAYOUT_SIDE_TOP)
   end
  end
end

application = FXApp.new
main = RadioButtonHandlerWindow.new(application)
application.create
main.show(PLACEMENT_SCREEN)
application.run
```

Groups of radio buttons are a standard tool used in GUI applications to present a collection of related but mutually exclusive choices. In this example, the choices are defined as an array of strings:

```
choices = [ "Good", "Better", "Best" ]
```

An instance of FXGroupBox is added to the main window to provide a visual cue that the radio buttons belong together and then radio buttons are added to that group box (one for each choice). However, the FXGroupBox container doesn't actually do anything to enforce the "radio behavior" of the radio buttons. If you run this example as is, you'll discover that you can select more than one radio button at a time.

There are a number of ways you could go about enforcing radio behavior of the choices for this example, but the preferred way to do this in FOX applications is through the use of data targets. The FXDataTarget class defines a special kind of FOX object that acts as a placeholder for some data value. Like any other FOX object, an instance of FXDataTarget can send and respond to messages.

Listing 12.11 shows a modified version of Listing 12.10 that demonstrates how to use data targets.

Listing 12.11   FOX Radio Buttons with Data Targets

```ruby
require 'fox16'

include Fox

class RadioButtonHandlerWindow < FXMainWindow

  def initialize(app)
    # Invoke base class initialize first
    super(app, "Radio Button Handler", nil, nil,
      DECOR_TITLE | DECOR_CLOSE)

    choices = [ "Good", "Better", "Best" ]

default_choice = 0
    @choice = FXDataTarget.new(default_choice)

    group = FXGroupBox.new(self, "Radio Test Group",
          LAYOUT_SIDE_TOP |
          FRAME_GROOVE |
          LAYOUT_FILL_X)

    choices.each_with_index do |choice, index|
      FXRadioButton.new(group, choice,
          @choice, FXDataTarget::ID_OPTION+index,
          ICON_BEFORE_TEXT |
          LAYOUT_SIDE_TOP)
    end
  end
end

application = FXApp.new
main = RadioButtonHandlerWindow.new(application)
application.create
main.show(PLACEMENT_SCREEN)
application.run
```

In this example, @choice is an instance of FXDataTarget whose value is the integer index of the currently selected choice. The data target is initialized with its default value of zero, which corresponds to the "Good" element in the choices array.

Each newly constructed radio button has its target set to the data target, and the message identifier for each radio button is equal to FXDataTarget::ID_OPTION plus the desired value. If you rerun this example, you should now see that the radio behavior of the buttons is properly enforced.

A list widget, FXList, can also be added to a window and populated in just a few lines. The LIST_BROWSESELECT option enforces one item being selected at all times. The first item is selected initially. Replacing this option with LIST_SINGLESELECT allows zero or one item to be selected. With this option, zero items are initially selected:

```
@list = FXList.new(self, nil, 0,
                     LIST_BROWSESELECT |
                     LAYOUT_FILL_X)
@names = ["Chuck", "Sally", "Franklin", "Schroeder",
            "Woodstock", "Matz", "Lucy"]
@names.each { |name| @list.appendItem(name) }
```

Note that the insertion operator for arrays can be used as a shortcut for the appendItem method. We could replace the last line of the previous example with this:

```
@names.each { |name| @list << name }
```

The entire example is shown in Listing 12.12. The message is handled in the main window by displaying the item that was clicked. If the LIST_SINGLESELECT option were used as discussed previously, it would be important to distinguish a click that selects an item from a click that deselects an item.

Listing 12.12   The FXList Widget

```
require 'fox16'

include Fox

class ListHandlerWindow < FXMainWindow

  def initialize(app)
    # Invoke base class initialize first
    super(app, "List Handler", nil, nil,
          DECOR_TITLE | DECOR_CLOSE)

    @list = FXList.new(self, nil, 0,
                         LIST_BROWSESELECT |
                         LAYOUT_FILL_X)
```

Continues

```
      @list.connect(SEL_COMMAND) do |sender, sel, pos|
        puts pos.to_s + " => " + @names[pos]
    end

      @names = ["Chuck", "Sally", "Franklin",
                "Schroeder", "Woodstock",
                "Matz", "Lucy"]
      @names.each { |name| @list << name }
    end
  end

  application = FXApp.new
  main = ListHandlerWindow.new(application)
  application.create
  main.show(PLACEMENT_SCREEN)
  application.run
```

Changing the LIST_BROWSESELECT option to LIST_EXTENDEDSELECT allows the list to
have more than one item selected at once:

```
@list = FXList.new(self, nil, 0, LIST_EXTENDEDSELECT | LAYOUT_FILL_X)
```

The message handler can be redefined to display all the selected items. All items in the
list have to be enumerated to find those that are selected:

```
@list.connect(SEL_COMMAND) do |sender, sel, pos|
  puts "Clicked on " + pos.to_s + " => " +
      @names[pos]
  puts "Currently selected:"
  @list.each do |item|
    if item.selected?
      puts "     " + item.text
    end
  end
end
```

The numVisible attribute for an FXList instance can be modified to change the number of list items visible in the list. Another widget, FXListBox, can be used to display
just the current selection. The FXListBox interface is similar to FXList, with a few
exceptions. The arguments to the constructor are the same, as shown in the following
code. Note that FXListBox can only be used to select a single item, so options such as
LIST_EXTENDEDSELECT are ignored:

```
@list_box = FXListBox.new(self, nil, 0, LIST_BROWSESELECT | LAYOUT_FILL_X)
@names = ["Chuck", "Sally", "Franklin", "Schroeder",
          "Woodstock", "Matz", "Lucy"]
@names.each { |name| @list_box << name }
```

A dialog box can be defined once as a subclass of FXDialogBox. That class can then be used to create modal or nonmodal dialog boxes. However modal dialogs interact with their owners differently from their nonmodal counterparts.

By *modal*, we mean that a window or dialog box prevents access to other parts of the application until it is serviced; that is, the software is in a mode that requires this dialog to be given attention. A nonmodal entity, on the other hand, will allow focus to change from itself to other entities.

The following example defines a modal and a nonmodal dialog class. The modal class uses the predefined messages ID_CANCEL and ID_ACCEPT. The nonmodal class uses the predefined message ID_HIDE.

The nonmodal dialog is displayed using the familiar FXTopWindow.show method. The modal dialog is displayed in its own event loop, which preempts the application's event loop. This is accomplished with the FXDialogBox.execute method. As you will see in the full program listing, the return value of the execute method depends on what value is passed to the application's stopModal method to terminate the modal dialog's event loop. For this example program, a return value of 1 indicates that the user clicked the Accept button in the dialog box:

```
modal_btn.connect do
  dialog = ModalDialogBox.new(self)
  if dialog.execute(PLACEMENT_OWNER) == 1
    puts dialog.text
  end
end
```

The nonmodal dialog box runs continuously alongside the other windows of an application. The application should query the dialog for interesting values as they are needed. One mechanism to announce the availability of new values would be an Apply button on the dialog box sending an application-specific message to the main window. The following example uses a *timer*, which is another interesting feature of FXRuby. When the timer goes off, a message is sent to the main window. The handler for that message (shown in the following code) queries the dialog box for a new value and then reestablishes the timer for another second:

```
def onTimer(sender, sel, ptr)
  text = @non_modal_dialog.text
  unless text == @previous
    @previous = text
    puts @previous
  end
  getApp().addTimeout(1000, method(:onTimer))
end
```

Listing 12.13 shows the complete example for the modal and nonmodal dialog boxes.

Listing 12.13   Modal and Nonmodal Dialog Boxes

```
require 'fox16'

include Fox

class NonModalDialogBox < FXDialogBox

  def initialize(owner)
    # Invoke base class initialize function first
    super(owner, "Test of Dialog Box",
          DECOR_TITLE|DECOR_BORDER)

    text_options = JUSTIFY_RIGHT | FRAME_SUNKEN |
                   FRAME_THICK | LAYOUT_SIDE_TOP
    @text_field = FXTextField.new(self, 20, nil, 0,
                   text_options)
    @text_field.text = ""

    layout_options = LAYOUT_SIDE_TOP | FRAME_NONE |
                     LAYOUT_FILL_X | LAYOUT_FILL_Y |
                     PACK_UNIFORM_WIDTH
    layout = FXHorizontalFrame.new(self, layout_options)

    options = FRAME_RAISED | FRAME_THICK |
              LAYOUT_RIGHT | LAYOUT_CENTER_Y
    hide_btn = FXButton.new(layout, "&Hide", nil, nil, 0,
                   options)
    hide_btn.connect(SEL_COMMAND) { hide }
  end

  def text
    @text_field.text
  end
```

```ruby
end

class ModalDialogBox < FXDialogBox

  def initialize(owner)
    # Invoke base class initialize function first
    super(owner, "Test of Dialog Box",
          DECOR_TITLE|DECOR_BORDER)

    text_options = JUSTIFY_RIGHT | FRAME_SUNKEN |
                   FRAME_THICK | LAYOUT_SIDE_TOP
    @text_field = FXTextField.new(self, 20, nil, 0,
                  text_options)
    @text_field.text = ""

    layout_options = LAYOUT_SIDE_TOP | FRAME_NONE |
                     LAYOUT_FILL_X | LAYOUT_FILL_Y |
                     PACK_UNIFORM_WIDTH
    layout = FXHorizontalFrame.new(self, layout_options)

    options = FRAME_RAISED | FRAME_THICK |
              LAYOUT_RIGHT | LAYOUT_CENTER_Y

    cancel_btn = FXButton.new(layout, "&Cancel", nil,
                 self, 0, options)
    cancel_btn.connect(SEL_COMMAND) do
        app.stopModal(self, 0)
        hide
    end

    accept_btn = FXButton.new(layout, "&Accept", nil,
                 self, 0, options)
    accept_btn.connect(SEL_COMMAND) do
        app.stopModal(self, 1)
        hide
    end
  end

  def text
    @text_field.text
  end
end

class DialogTestWindow < FXMainWindow

  def initialize(app)
    # Invoke base class initialize first
    super(app, "Dialog Test", nil, nil,
          DECOR_ALL, 0, 0, 400, 200)
```

Continues

```ruby
      layout_options = LAYOUT_SIDE_TOP | FRAME_NONE |
                       LAYOUT_FILL_X | LAYOUT_FILL_Y |
                       PACK_UNIFORM_WIDTH
      layout = FXHorizontalFrame.new(self, layout_options)

      button_options = FRAME_RAISED | FRAME_THICK |
                       LAYOUT_CENTER_X | LAYOUT_CENTER_Y

  nonmodal_btn = FXButton.new(layout, "&Non-Modal Dialog...", nil,
                  nil, 0, button_options)
  nonmodal_btn.connect(SEL_COMMAND) do
    @non_modal_dialog.show(PLACEMENT_OWNER)
  end

      modal_btn = FXButton.new(layout, "&Modal Dialog...",     nil,
                  nil, 0, button_options)
  modal_btn.connect(SEL_COMMAND) do
      dialog = ModalDialogBox.new(self)
      if dialog.execute(PLACEMENT_OWNER) == 1
        puts dialog.text
      end
  end

      getApp.addTimeout(1000, method(:onTimer))
      @non_modal_dialog = NonModalDialogBox.new(self)
    end

    def onTimer(sender, sel, ptr)
      text = @non_modal_dialog.text
      unless text == @previous
        @previous = text
        puts @previous
      end
      getApp.addTimeout(1000, method(:onTimer))
    end

    def create
      super
      show(PLACEMENT_SCREEN)
    end
  end

  application = FXApp.new
  DialogTestWindow.new(application)
  application.create
  application.run
```

Long computations in FXRuby should change the current cursor to a wait cursor and then restore the original cursor afterward. The FXApp application class has two convenient methods for making the change without having to remember the original cursor. These methods are `beginWaitCursor` and `endWaitCursor`. When `beginWaitCursor` is called with a block, it ensures that `endWaitCursor` is called when the block exits:

```
getApp.beginWaitCursor do
  # Perform time-consuming operation here...
end
```

12.3.6 Other Notes

Many other widgets and features are available using the FOX toolkit. Examples include tree widgets, dockable toolbars, tooltips, status lines, and tabbed pages. More advanced GUI features include drag-and-drop operations between applications and data targets for ease of connecting application data to widgets. FOX also includes nongraphical features that support cross-platform programming, such as the `FXRegistry` class.

Messages can be used to connect an application with its environment using signal and input-based messages. Operating system signals, as well as input and output, will cause messages to be sent to FOX objects.

The FOX toolkit has widgets that support most common image formats as well as the OpenGL 3D API. This appears not to be just lip service to 3D capability. The FOX C++ toolkit has been used in a number of engineering applications.

All things considered, the FXRuby toolkit is a powerful and flexible environment. It has become popular in the Ruby community in the last few years, and its popularity is expected to increase. The capabilities of this toolkit are rapidly changing and expanding; go to http://fxruby.org for the latest information on the Ruby bindings.

12.4   QtRuby

Qt is a GUI toolkit created and distributed by Trolltech. The main focus of Qt is to be a multiplatform toolkit that provides the same programmatic interface for Windows, Mac, and UNIX operating systems. Developers need only write the code once; it compiles on each of the three platforms without modification.

Qt is distributed via dual license—either the GPL or a purchased commercial license for proprietary work. This dual license scenario is also used by other companies such as MySQL. It allows the toolkit to be used by open-source projects that may benefit from many of the offered features. It also allows Trolltech a revenue stream from the sale of commercial licenses for customers who may want to use a less restrictive license than the GPL.

12.4.1 Overview

The QtRuby bindings are the result of the work of many people, most notably Richard Dale. Ashley Winters, Germain Garand, and David Faure were responsible for much of the work involved in writing the backend used to generate the binding code (called SMOKE). Many others have contributed bug reports and fixes.

The QtRuby bindings have not only a large set of GUI-related classes but also a whole suite of application add-ons that are often needed by programmers (such as XML and SQL libraries). The entire Qt toolkit is supported.

For the past few years, the QtRuby bindings were centered around the version 3 major release of the Qt toolkit. In late 2005, version 4 became available. There are QtRuby bindings for both Qt3 and Qt4, but note that they are two different packages. Because Qt3 was not available as an open-source package on the Windows platform, this book only looks at the QtRuby bindings for Qt4. However, the code and example presented here are generally applicable to the Qt3 version as well. All code presented here runs equally well on Windows, Linux, and Mac platforms using the Qt4 QtRuby bindings.

A key aspect of Qt, and thus QtRuby, is the concept of signals and slots. Signals are asynchronous events that occur when something spontaneous happens, such as a mouse button press or a user entering some text into a field. A slot is simply a reacting method that will be called when a certain signal happens. We take advantage of them by using the `connect` method to associate signals with slots.

To take advantage of signals and slots, as well as many other QtRuby features, all of our classes use the `Qt::Object` class. Furthermore, any GUI classes we may create will inherit from the base class `Qt::Widget`, which itself inherits from `Qt::Object`.

12.4.2 A Simple Windowed Application

A QtRuby program must first do a `require` of the Qt library. QtRuby provides its functionality through the `Qt` module (meaning that Qt classes are prefixed with `Qt::`). Because all Qt classes start with the letter Q, this Q is dropped during the conversion from Qt to QtRuby. So for example, the Qt-based `QWidget` class becomes `Qt::Widget` in QtRuby.

```
require 'Qt'

app = Qt::Application.new(ARGV)
str = Time.now.strftime("Today is %B %d, %Y")
label = Qt::Label.new(str)
label.show
app.exec
```

Let's look at the preceding code in detail. The initial call to `Qt::Application.new` is performed to start up a Qt-based application; it initializes the window system and gets it ready for us to create the widgets we will be using.

Then we create a `Qt::Label`, which is a simple way of presenting text to the user. In this case, the text is initialized to the string created in the previous line. The next line tells the label to display itself on the screen.

Finally, the application event loop is started with a call to `app.exec`. This method does not return until the application is told to terminate, generally by the user clicking the close button on the window.

12.4.3 Working with Buttons

Creating a pushbutton with QtRuby is as easy as creating a new instance of `Qt::PushButton` (see Listing 12.14 and Figure 12.7). Most likely, we will want to perform some event when the button is clicked. This is handled via QtRuby's signal and slots.

Listing 12.14   Buttons in Qt

```
require 'Qt'

class MyWidget < Qt::Widget
  slots 'buttonClickedSlot()'

  def initialize(parent = nil)
    super(parent)

    setWindowTitle("QtRuby example");
```

Continues

```
    @lineedit = Qt::LineEdit.new(self)
    @button = Qt::PushButton.new("All Caps!",self)

    connect(@button, SIGNAL('clicked()'),
            self, SLOT('buttonClickedSlot()'))

    box = Qt::HBoxLayout.new
    box.addWidget(Qt::Label.new("Text:"))
    box.addWidget(@lineedit)
    box.addWidget(@button)

    setLayout(box)
  end

  def buttonClickedSlot
    @lineedit.setText(@lineedit.text.upcase)
  end

end

app = Qt::Application.new(ARGV)
widget = MyWidget.new
widget.show
app.exec
```

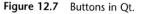

Figure 12.7   Buttons in Qt.

In this example, we create our own widget class named MyWidget; this inherits from
the generic Qt::Widget class that we use for all custom widget classes.

Before the initializer, we establish a list of the slots that we will be defining in this
class. Slots are ordinary Ruby class methods, but we must specify them by name so
that the QtRuby runtime is aware that we want to be able to use them as slots. The
call to the class method slots takes a list of strings, as shown here:

```
slots 'slot1()', 'slot2()'
```

The initializer for this class takes an argument named parent; almost all widget classes
in the Qt world take such an argument. The parent argument simply specifies a widget

that will take ownership of the widget being created. Passing `nil` as the parent means that it is a "top level widget" and that no other widget owns it. The "ownership" concept probably makes more sense in the C++ world; parents take ownership of their child widgets, so that when parents are destroyed or removed, their children are removed as well.

The class creates a `Qt::LineEdit` to allow a user to enter text and a `Qt::PushButton` with the text `All Caps!` on it. Note that we pass `self` as the parent argument to each of these widgets. This means that when a `MyWidget` instance is created, it "adopts" these widgets.

Next we use a key part of the Qt toolkit—the capability to connect signals and slots together. The `Qt::PushButton` class defines a `clicked` signal that is *emitted* whenever the button is clicked. We can connect that to a slot, which in this case is the ordinary method `buttonClickedSlot`. The name of the slot we connect to is not important; we sometimes use the suffix `Slot` for emphasis.

Finally, we create an instance of the `Qt::HBoxLayout` class. This class provides a nice way to have an automatically resizing layout by simply adding widgets to it. It handles the rest for us.

12.4.4 Working with Text Fields

As shown in Listing 12.14, QtRuby provides the `Qt::LineEdit` class for simple single-line input. The `Qt::TextEdit` class is for multiline editing.

In Listing 12.15, we see a multiline edit box. As the contents change, the current length of the text is reflected in a label at the bottom of the window, as shown in Figure 12.8.

Listing 12.15 A Simple Qt Editor

```
require 'Qt'

class MyTextWindow < Qt::Widget
  slots 'theTextChanged()'

  def initialize(parent = nil)
    super(parent)

    @textedit = Qt::TextEdit.new(self)
    @textedit.setWordWrapMode(Qt::TextOption::WordWrap)
```

Continues

```ruby
    @textedit.setFont( Qt::Font.new("Times", 24) )

    @status = Qt::Label.new(self)

    box = Qt::VBoxLayout.new
    box.addWidget(@textedit)
    box.addWidget(@status)
    setLayout(box)

    @textedit.insertPlainText("This really is an editor")

    connect(@textedit, SIGNAL('textChanged()'),
            self, SLOT('theTextChanged()'))
  end

  def theTextChanged
    text = "Length: " + @textedit.toPlainText.length.to_s
    @status.setText(text)
  end

end

app = Qt::Application.new(ARGV)
widget = MyTextWindow.new
widget.setWindowTitle("QtRuby Text Editor")
widget.show
app.exec
```

Figure 12.8   A simple Qt editor.

We create our own custom widget much like the earlier button example. In this case, we create an instance of Qt::TextEdit and a Qt::Label used for status updates.

The first interesting thing of note is that we set the font of the @textedit to an instance of a 24-point Times font. Each class inheriting from Qt:Widget (including Qt::TextEdit) has a font property that we can both retrieve and set.

Next we create a vertical box layout (Qt::VBoxLayout) that holds the child widgets, inserts some text into the @textedit widget, and then performs the connection of the editor widget's textChanged signal to our custom theTextChanged slot.

Within the slot theTextChanged, we grab the text from the editor and query its length. Then we update the @status label to reflect this length.

Note that all the signal and slot action happens asynchronously. After the application enters into the event loop (app.exec), the GUI event loop takes over. This is why signals and slots are so important. We define the actions that can happen (signals) and the actions we want to take when they do (slots).

12.4.5 Working with Other Widgets

Qt provides many more GUI widgets for general consumption such as radio buttons, check boxes, and other display widgets. Listing 12.16 shows some more of these, and Figure 12.9 provides a screenshot.

Listing 12.16 Other Qt Widgets

```
require 'Qt'

class MyWindow < Qt::Widget
  slots 'somethingClicked(QAbstractButton *)'

  def initialize(parent = nil)
    super(parent)

    groupbox = Qt::GroupBox.new("Some Radio Button",self)

    radio1 = Qt::RadioButton.new("Radio Button 1", groupbox)
    radio2 = Qt::RadioButton.new("Radio Button 2", groupbox)
    check1 = Qt::CheckBox.new("Check Box 1", groupbox)

    vbox = Qt::VBoxLayout.new
    vbox.addWidget(radio1)
    vbox.addWidget(radio2)
    vbox.addWidget(check1)
    groupbox.setLayout(vbox)

    bg = Qt::ButtonGroup.new(self)
    bg.addButton(radio1)
```

Continues

```ruby
    bg.addButton(radio2)
    bg.addButton(check1)

    connect(bg, SIGNAL('buttonClicked(QAbstractButton *)'),
            self, SLOT('somethingClicked(QAbstractButton *)') )

    @label = Qt::Label.new(self)

    vbox = Qt::VBoxLayout.new
    vbox.addWidget(groupbox)
    vbox.addWidget(@label)
    setLayout(vbox)
  end

  def somethingClicked(who)
    @label.setText("You clicked on a " + who.className)
  end

end

app = Qt::Application.new(ARGV)
widget = MyWindow.new
widget.show
app.exec
```

Figure 12.9 Other Qt widgets.

In this new class we first create a Qt::GroupBox, which is a box with a frame and an optional title that can hold other widgets. We then create two Qt::RadioButtons and a Qt::CheckBox, setting the group box as their parent.

Next we create a Qt::VBoxLayout that holds the radio buttons and check box. Then we set that layout on the group box.

The next important thing is to create a Qt::ButtonGroup and add our check box and radio buttons to it. A Qt::ButtonGroup is a logical grouping of buttons, check boxes, and radio buttons. It has no impact on the visual layout of these widgets; instead, it allows us to group them together logically to provide things such as *exclusion* (unclicking certain widgets when certain others are clicked). In this case, we use the button group as a source of the `buttonClicked` signal, which is emitted when one of the buttons in that group becomes clicked.

The emission of this signal is a bit different from what we've previously seen, because this signal also emits an argument. In this case, it emits the object that was clicked. Note the C++ style syntax, namely in the use of the `QAbstractButton *` argument. Remember that Qt is a C++ toolkit, so some use of the C++ notation for certain parameter types is currently unavoidable (though it perhaps may be fixed in future versions).

The final result of the `connect` statement is that any time a button is clicked, that button is passed into the `somethingClicked` slot. Finally, we create a `Qt::Label` and a `Qt::VBoxLayout` and bring the whole thing together.

In the `somethingClicked` slot definition, we modify the text of the label every time a button is clicked. In this case, we display the class name of the object that caused the signal to be emitted and the slot to be invoked.

When using built-in widgets is not enough, Qt provides a powerful painting system for creation of your own custom widgets. Listing 12.17 shows a small example to highlight some of those features.

Listing 12.17   A Custom `TimerClock` Widget

```ruby
require 'Qt'

class TimerClock < Qt::Widget

    def initialize(parent = nil)
        super(parent)

        @timer = Qt::Timer.new(self)
        connect(@timer, SIGNAL('timeout()'), self, SLOT('update()'))
        @timer.start(25)

        setWindowTitle('Stop Watch')
        resize(200, 200)
    end

    def paintEvent(e)
        fastHand = Qt::Polygon.new([Qt::Point.new(7, 8),
                                    Qt::Point.new(-7, 8),
                                    Qt::Point.new(0, -80)])

        secondHand = Qt::Polygon.new([Qt::Point.new(7, 8),
                                      Qt::Point.new(-7, 8),
                                      Qt::Point.new(0, -65)])
```

Continues

```ruby
        secondColor = Qt::Color.new(100, 0, 100)
        fastColor = Qt::Color.new(0, 150, 150, 150)

        side = [width, height].min
        time = Qt::Time.currentTime

        painter = Qt::Painter.new(self)
        painter.renderHint = Qt::Painter::Antialiasing
        painter.translate(width() / 2, height() / 2)
        painter.scale(side / 200.0, side / 200.0)

        painter.pen = Qt::NoPen
        painter.brush = Qt::Brush.new(secondColor)

        painter.save
        painter.rotate(6.0 * time.second)
        painter.drawConvexPolygon(secondHand)
        painter.restore

        painter.pen = secondColor
        (0...12).each do |i|
            painter.drawLine(88, 0, 96, 0)
            painter.rotate(30.0)
        end

        painter.pen = Qt::NoPen
        painter.brush = Qt::Brush.new(fastColor)

        painter.save
        painter.rotate(36.0 * (time.msec / 100.0) )
        painter.drawConvexPolygon(fastHand)
        painter.restore

        painter.pen = fastColor
        (0...60).each do |j|
            if (j % 5) != 0
                painter.drawLine(92, 0, 96, 0)
            end
            painter.rotate(6.0)
        end

        painter.end
      end
  end

app = Qt::Application.new(ARGV)
wid = TimerClock.new
wid.show
app.exec
```

In this example we again create a custom widget, this time called `TimerClock`. In its initializer we create an instance of `Qt::Timer`, which we can set up to emit a signal periodically. In this case, we connect its `timeout` signal to the `update` slot of the `TimerClock`. The `update` slot is built-in; it causes the widget to repaint itself.

The timer is started through a call to the `start` method. Its argument specifies that it is to timeout every 25 milliseconds (and emit a `timeout` signal). This means that the widget's `update` slot will also get executed every 25 milliseconds.

Next we create the `paintEvent` method. This method is an override of the method provided by `Qt::Widget`. When a widget wants to repaint itself (as this one will every time the `Qt::Timer` expires), this method gets called. Overriding this method allows us to customize how the widget draws itself on the screen. Within this method, the code is responsible for handling the primitive drawing routines for the widget.

From here, it's all about geometry. We create some `Qt::Polygons` that represent the hands on the clock we are about to draw. Note that the orientation of the polygons doesn't matter, as we will be able to manipulate them later.

We set up a few properties we will want to use. We define two `Qt::Colors` for the two hands that will be on the timer. The arguments to the `Qt::Color` initializer are "RGB" values followed by an optional alpha transparency value.

Because the timer we're drawing is laid out in a square, it is possible that the window could be rectangular making our widget an odd shape. We use the `side` variable to store whichever is smaller between the width and the height of the widget as it will be drawn on the screen. We also grab the current time using `Qt::Time.currentTime`.

Next we create a `Qt::Painter` and use it to begin executing drawing routines. We set up antialiasing during drawing to make edges look smooth. We also move the painter's starting coordinate to the middle of the drawing area by the call to `painter.translate(width/2, height/2)`. The painter is also rescaled to a 200:200 frame of reference. This means that all of our drawing commands can rely on the fact that the drawing will be 200:200 units. If it gets resized bigger or smaller, the scaling automatically adjusts for us.

From here we perform a series of drawing operations. In some places where there are transformations such as rotations, they are enveloped inside a call to `painter.save` and `painter.restore`. The `save` operation stores the current painter properties on a stack so that they can easily be restored.

The code draws the two hands after rotating them to the proper angle to represent the time. Also we tell the painter to draw some tick marks at certain intervals along the outer edge of the clock face.

Finally we tell the painter we've finished (with a call to `painter.end`). We tie up our final loose ends with the four lines of code that create the `Qt::Application` and our timer clock widget and then start the event loop. Figure 12.10 shows the final result.

Figure 12.10   The `TimerClock` widget.

12.4.6 Other Notes

Because Qt is a C++ toolkit, some idioms are used in the toolkit that are necessary due to constraints in the language. Sometimes the translation to Ruby isn't 100% natural because the Ruby way of doing the same thing may be slightly different. So, in some places there are overrides that let you do some things in QtRuby in a Rubyish way.

For example, the camelCase naming of Qt methods can also be written as underscored names. The following two are equivalent:

```
Qt::Widget::minimumSizeHint
Qt::Widget::minimum_size_hint
```

All Qt setters begin with the word `set`, such as `Qt::Widget::setMinimumSize`. This can be overridden in Ruby by dropping the set and using assignment. This means the following three statements are equivalent:

```
widget.setMinimumSize(50)
widget.minimumSize = 50      # same
widget.minimum_size = 50     # same
```

Similarly, some Boolean methods in Qt begin with is or has, such as Qt::Widget::isVisible. Again, QtRuby gives us a more Rubyish way of calling this method:

```
a.isVisible
a.visible?    # same
```

12.5 Other GUI Toolkits

As already mentioned, your favorite GUI may not be covered here. We'll use the remaining space in this chapter just to mention some other alternatives.

Some of these alternatives are not fully mature and may be buggy or incomplete. However, we expect this list to grow and the supported bindings to become more stable as time goes on.

12.5.1 Ruby and X

The *X Window System* is colloquially (though not correctly) referred to as X Windows. It is perhaps not the grandfather of all GUI systems, but it is certainly the ancestor of many of them.

UNIX users of all breeds have long been familiar with X (as users, even if not as developers). Frequently the Motif window manager is run on top of X.

The advantages of X are that it is widely known, portable, and has a rich feature set. The disadvantages are that it is complex and difficult to use.

Not surprisingly, there are libraries for using X with Ruby. They aren't documented here because of their complexity.

We refer you instead to the Ruby Application Archive, where you can find Xlib by Kazuhiro Yoshida (also known as moriq) and Ruby/X11 by Mathieu Bouchard (also known as matju). Either can be used to create X client applications.

12.5.2 Ruby and wxWidgets

The wxWidgets system (formerly wxWindows) is full-featured and stable; it is widely used in the Python world, virtually the native GUI for that language. The philosophy behind the toolkit in general is to use the native OS widgets as much as possible. It is somewhat more mature on the UNIX platforms than in its Windows version, but this is changing daily, of course.

At this time, there is a reasonably mature wxRuby library. If this is your toolkit of choice, go to http://wxruby.rubyforge.org/ for documentation and downloads.

12.5.3 Apollo (Ruby and Delphi)

The true hacker knows that standard Pascal is all but useless. However, there have been many attempts over the years to improve it so that it could be a language worth the effort of using. One of the most successful of these is Borland's Object Pascal, used in its RAD tool called Delphi.

The popularity of Delphi is not due to the Pascal language extensions, though these are a contributing factor, but to the development environment itself and the richness of the graphical interface. Delphi has a rich set of widgets for creating stable, attractive GUI applications on MS Windows.

The Apollo library is a marriage of Ruby and Delphi; it is the brainchild of Kazuhiro Yoshida, although others are also working on it. The advantage of Apollo, of course, is that it makes a giant set of stable, usable widgets available; the biggest disadvantage is that it currently requires a slightly "tweaked" version of Ruby. It should interoperate with Borland's "classic" software Kylix, which is essentially a Linux-based Delphi. See the Ruby Application Archive for more details.

12.5.4 Ruby and the Windows API

In Chapter 8, "Arrays, Hashes, and Other Enumerables," we describe a sort of "poor man's GUI" in which we use the WIN32OLE library to get access to the features of Internet Explorer and other such things. Refer to those examples for more details. If you need something quick and dirty, this might be acceptable.

If you are a real glutton for punishment, you could access the Windows API directly. The WIN32API library (also discussed in Chapter 14, "Scripting and System Administration") makes this kind of coding possible. I don't necessarily recommend the practice, but you should be aware of the possibility.

12.6   Conclusion

In this chapter, we've seen a good overview of the GUI toolkits available for Ruby. We've looked at general concepts such as event loops, messages or signals, and more. We've looked at widgets of various kinds, including pushbuttons, check boxes, radio buttons, text fields, and more.

We've looked at the implementations of these concepts in Tk, GTK, FOX, and Qt. We've also seen some of the special terminology and minor changes in paradigm from one toolkit to another and looked at some of the special features and benefits that each toolkit offers.

Now let's move on to a different topic entirely. Chapter 13 will discuss how to manipulate threads in Ruby.

CHAPTER 13

Threads in Ruby

He draweth out the thread of his argument
finer than the staple of his verbosity

—*William Shakespeare,*
Love's Labours Lost, *Act V, Sc. 1*

Threads are sometimes called *lightweight processes*. They are nothing more than a way to achieve concurrency without all the overhead of switching tasks at the operating system level. (Of course, the computing community is not in perfect agreement about the definition of threads, but we won't go into that.)

Ruby threads are *user-level* threads and are operating system independent. They work on DOS as well as on UNIX. There will definitely be a performance hit, however, which also varies by operating system.

Threads are useful in circumstances where, for instance, separate pieces of code naturally function independently of each other. They are also used when an application spends much of its time waiting for an event. Often while one thread is waiting, another can be doing useful processing.

On the other hand, there are some potential disadvantages in the use of threads. The decrease in speed has to be weighed against the benefits. Also, in some cases access to a resource is inherently serialized, so that threading doesn't help. Finally, sometimes the overhead of synchronizing access to global resources exceeds the saving due to multithreading.

For these and other reasons, some authorities claim that threaded programming is to be avoided. Indeed, concurrent code can be complex, error-prone, and difficult to debug. But we will leave it to the reader to decide when it is appropriate to use these techniques.

The difficulties associated with unsynchronized threads are well-known. Global data may be corrupted by threads attempting simultaneous access to those data. Race conditions may occur wherein one thread makes some assumption about what another has done already; these commonly result in "nondeterministic" code that may run differently with each execution. Finally, there is the danger of deadlock, wherein no thread can continue because it is waiting for a resource held by some other thread, which is also blocked. Code written to avoid these problems is referred to as *thread-safe* code.

Not all of Ruby is thread-safe, but synchronization methods are available that enable you to control access to variables and resources, protect critical sections of code, and avoid deadlock. We will deal with these techniques in this chapter and give code fragments to illustrate them.

13.1   Creating and Manipulating Threads

The most basic operations on threads include creating a thread, passing information in and out, stopping a thread, and so on. We can also obtain lists of threads, check the state of a thread, and check various other information.

We present an overview of these basic operations here.

13.1.1   Creating Threads

Creating a thread is easy. Simply call the new method and attach a block that will be the body of the thread.

```
thread = Thread.new do
  # Statements comprising
  #   the thread...
end
```

The value returned is obviously an object of type Thread. This is usable by the main thread to control the thread it has created.

What if we want to pass parameters into a thread? We can do this by passing parameters into `Thread.new`, which in turn will pass them into the block.

```
a = 4
b = 5
c = 6
thread2 = Thread.new(a,b,c) do |a, x, y|
  # Manipulate a, x, and y as needed.
end

# Note that if a is changed in the new thread, it will
#    change suddenly and without warning in the main
#    thread.
```

Like any other block parameters, any of these that correspond to existing variables will be effectively identical to those variables. The variable a in the preceding code fragment is a "dangerous" variable in this sense, as the comment points out.

Threads may also access variables from the scope in which they were created. Obviously without synchronization this can be problematic. The main thread and one or more other threads may modify the variable independently of each other, and the results may be unpredictable.

```
x = 1
y = 2
thread3 = Thread.new do
  # This thread can manipulate x and y from the outer scope,
  #    but this is not always safe.
  sleep(rand(0))  # Sleep a random fraction of a second.
  x = 3
end

sleep(rand(0))
puts x
# Running this code repeatedly, x may be 1 or 3 when it
#    is printed here!
```

The method `fork` is an alias for `new`; this name is derived from the well-known UNIX system call of the same name.

13.1.2   Accessing Thread-local Variables

We know that it can be dangerous for a thread to use variables from outside its scope; we know also that a thread can have local data of its own. But what if a thread wants to "make public" some of the data that it owns?

There is a special mechanism for this purpose. If a thread object is treated as a hash, thread-local data can be accessed from anywhere within the scope of that thread object. We don't mean that actual local variables can be accessed in this way, but only that we have access to named data on a per-thread basis.

There is also a method called key? that will tell us whether a given name is in use for this thread.

Within the thread, we must refer to the data in the same hashlike way. Using Thread.current will make this a little less unwieldy.

```
thread = Thread.new do
  t = Thread.current
  t[:var1] = "This is a string"
  t[:var2] = 365
end


# Access the thread-local data from outside...

x = thread[:var1]                 # "This is a string"
y = thread[:var2]                 # 365

has_var2 = thread.key?("var2")  # true
has_var3 = thread.key?("var3")  # false
```

Note that these data are accessible from other threads even after the thread that owned them is dead (as in this case).

Besides a symbol (as we just saw) we can also use a string to identify the thread-local variable.

```
thread = Thread.new do
  t = Thread.current
  t["var3"] = 25
  t[:var4] = "foobar"
end


a = thread[:var3] = 25
b = thread["var4"] = "foobar"
```

Don't confuse these special names with actual local variables. The following code fragment illustrates the difference a little more clearly:

```
thread = Thread.new do
  t = Thread.current
  t["var3"] = 25
  t[:var4] = "foobar"
  var3 = 99              # True local variables (not
  var4 = "zorch"         # accessible from outside)
end

a = thread[:var3]      # 25
b = thread["var4"]     # "foobar"
```

Finally, note that an object reference (to a true local variable) can be used as a sort of shorthand within the thread. This is true as long as you are careful to preserve the same object reference rather than create a new one.

```
thread = Thread.new do
  t = Thread.current
  x = "nXxeQPdMdxiBAxh"
  t[:my_message] = x
  x.reverse!
  x.delete! "x"
  x.gsub!(/[A-Z]/,"")
  # On the other hand, assignment would create a new
  # object and make this shorthand useless...
end

a = thread[:my_message]   # "hidden"
```

Also, this shortcut will obviously not work when you are dealing with values such as Fixnums, which are stored as immediate values rather than object references.

13.1.3 Querying and Changing Thread Status

The Thread class has several class methods that serve various purposes. The list method returns an array of all living threads; the main method returns a reference to the main thread, which spawns the others; and the current method allows a thread to find its own identity.

```
t1 = Thread.new { sleep 100 }
t2 = Thread.new do
  if Thread.current == Thread.main
    puts "This is the main thread."    # Does NOT print
  end
  1.upto(1000) { sleep 0.1 }
end

count = Thread.list.size               # 3
if Thread.list.include?(Thread.main)
  puts "Main thread is alive."         # Always prints!
end
if Thread.current == Thread.main
  puts "I'm the main thread."          # Prints here...
end
```

The exit, pass, start, stop, and kill methods are used to control the execution of threads (often from inside or outside):

```
# In the main thread...
Thread.kill(t1)          # Kill this thread now
Thread.pass              # Pass execution to t2 now
t3 = Thread.new do
  sleep 20
  Thread.exit            # Exit the thread
  puts "Can't happen!"   # Never reached
end
Thread.kill(t2)          # Now kill t2
# Now exit the main thread (killing any others)
Thread.exit
```

Note that there is no instance method stop, so a thread can stop itself but not another thread.

There are various methods for checking the state of a thread. The instance method alive? will tell whether the thread is still "living" (not exited), and stop? will tell whether the thread is in a stopped state.

```
count = 0
t1 = Thread.new { loop { count += 1 } }
t2 = Thread.new { Thread.stop }
sleep 1
flags = [t1.alive?,     # true
         t1.stop?,      # false
         t2.alive?,     # true
         t2.stop?]      # true
```

The status of a thread may be determined using the status method. The value returned will be "run" if the thread is currently running; sleep if it is stopped, sleeping, or waiting on I/O; false if it terminated normally; and nil if it terminated with an exception.

```
t1 = Thread.new { loop {} }
t2 = Thread.new { sleep 5 }
t3 = Thread.new { Thread.stop }
t4 = Thread.new { Thread.exit }
t5 = Thread.new { raise "exception" }
s1 = t1.status     # "run"
s2 = t2.status     # "sleep"
s3 = t3.status     # "sleep"
s4 = t4.status     # false
s5 = t5.status     # nil
```

The global variable $SAFE may be set differently in different threads. In this sense, it is not truly a global variable at all, but we should not complain because this allows us to have threads run with different levels of safety. The safe_level method will tell us at what level a thread is running.

```
t1 = Thread.new { $SAFE = 1; sleep 5 }
t2 = Thread.new { $SAFE = 3; sleep 5 }
sleep 1
lev0 = Thread.main.safe_level     # 0
lev1 = t1.safe_level              # 1
lev2 = t2.safe_level              # 3
```

The priority of a thread may be examined and changed using the `priority` accessor:

```
t1 = Thread.new { loop { sleep 1 } }
t2 = Thread.new { loop { sleep 1 } }
t2.priority = 3    # Set t2 at priority 3
p1 = t1.priority   # 0
p2 = t2.priority   # 3
```

A thread with higher (numerically greater) priority will be scheduled more often.

The special method `pass` is used when a thread wants to yield control to the scheduler. The thread merely yields its current timeslice; it doesn't actually stop or go to sleep.

```
t1 = Thread.new do
  puts "alpha"
  Thread.pass
  puts "beta"
end
t2 = Thread.new do
  puts "gamma"
  puts "delta"
end

t1.join
t2.join
```

In this contrived example, we get output in the order `alpha gamma delta beta` when `Thread.pass` is called as shown. Without it we get `alpha beta gamma delta` as the order. Of course, this feature should not be used for synchronization but only for the thrifty allocation of timeslices.

A thread that is stopped may be awakened by use of the `run` or `wakeup` methods:

```
t1 = Thread.new do
  Thread.stop
  puts "There is an emerald here."
end
t2 = Thread.new do
  Thread.stop
  puts "You're at Y2."
end
```

```
sleep 1
t1.wakeup
t2.run
```

The difference in these is subtle. The wakeup call will change the state of the thread so that it is runnable but will not schedule it to be run; on the other hand, run will wake up the thread and schedule it for immediate running.

In this particular case, the result is that t1 wakes up *before* t2, but t2 gets scheduled first, producing the following output:

```
You're at Y2.
There is an emerald here.
```

Of course, it would be unwise to attempt true synchronization by depending on this subtlety.

The raise instance method will raise an exception in the thread specified as the receiver. (The call does not have to originate within the thread.)

```
factorial1000 = Thread.new do
  begin
    prod = 1
    1.upto(1000) {|n| prod *= n }
    puts "1000! = #{prod}"
  rescue
    # Do nothing...
  end
end

sleep 0.01                    # Your mileage may vary.
if factorial1000.alive?
  factorial1000.raise("Stop!")
  puts "Calculation was interrupted!"
else
  puts "Calculation was successful."
end
```

The thread spawned in the preceding example tries to calculate the factorial of 1,000; if it doesn't succeed within a hundredth of a second, the main thread will kill it. Thus on a relatively slow machine, this code fragment will print the message Calculation was interrupted! As for the rescue clause inside the thread, obviously we could have put any code there that we wanted, as with any other such clause.

13.1.4   Achieving a Rendezvous (and Capturing a Return Value)

Sometimes the main thread wants to wait for another thread to finish. The instance method join will accomplish this.

```
t1 = Thread.new { do_something_long() }

do_something_brief()
t1.join                 # Wait for t1
```

Note that a join is necessary if the main thread is to wait on another thread. When the main thread exits, a thread is killed otherwise. For example, the following code fragment would never give us its final answer without the join at the end:

```
meaning_of_life = Thread.new do
  puts "The answer is..."
  sleep 10
  puts 42
end

sleep 9
meaning_of_life.join
```

Here is a useful little idiom. It will call join on every living thread except the main one. (It is an error for any thread, even the main thread, to call join on itself.)

```
Thread.list.each { |t| t.join if t != Thread.main }
```

It is, of course, possible for one thread to do a join on another when neither is the main thread. If the main thread and another attempt to join each other, a deadlock results; the interpreter will detect this case and exit the program.

```
thr = Thread.new { sleep 1; Thread.main.join }

thr.join        # Deadlock results!
```

A thread has an associated block, and a block can have a return value. This implies that a thread can return a value. The value method will implicitly do a join operation and wait for the thread to complete; then it will return the value of the last evaluated expression in the thread.

```
max = 10000
thr = Thread.new do
  sum = 0
  1.upto(max) { |i| sum += i }
  sum
end

guess = (max*(max+1))/2
print "Formula is "
if guess == thr.value
  puts "right."
else
  puts "wrong."
end
```

13.1.5   Dealing with Exceptions

What happens if an exception occurs within a thread? As it turns out, the behavior is configurable.

There is a flag called `abort_on_exception` that operates both at the class and instance levels. This is implemented as an accessor at both levels (that is, it is readable and writable).

In short, if `abort_on_exception` is true for a thread, an exception in that thread will terminate all the other threads also.

```
Thread.abort_on_exception = true

t1 = Thread.new do
  puts "Hello"
  sleep 2
  raise "some exception"
  puts "Goodbye"
end

t2 = Thread.new { sleep 100 }

sleep 2
puts "The End"
```

In the preceding code, the systemwide `abort_on_exception` is set to `true` (overriding the default). Thus when `t1` gets an exception, `t1` and the main thread are also killed. The word `Hello` is the only output generated.

In this next example, the effect is the same:

```
t1 = Thread.new do
  puts "Hello"
  sleep 2
  raise "some exception"
  puts "Goodbye"
end

t1.abort_on_exception = true

t2 = Thread.new { sleep 100 }

sleep 2
puts "The End"
```

In the following example, the default of `false` is assumed, and we finally get to see the output The End from the main thread. (We never see Goodbye because `t1` is always terminated when the exception is raised.)

```
t1 = Thread.new do
  puts "Hello"
  sleep 2
  raise "some exception"
  puts "Goodbye"
end

t2 = Thread.new { sleep 100 }

sleep 2
puts "The End"

# Output:

Hello
The End
```

13.1.6   Using a Thread Group

A *thread group* is a way of managing threads that are logically related to each other. Normally all threads belong to the Default thread group (which is a class constant). But if a new thread group is created, new threads may be added to it.

A thread may be in only one thread group at a time. When a thread is added to a thread group, it is automatically removed from whatever group it was in previously.

The ThreadGroup.new class method will create a new thread group, and the add instance method will add a thread to the group.

```
f1 = Thread.new("file1") { |file| waitfor(file) }
f2 = Thread.new("file2") { |file| waitfor(file) }

file_threads = ThreadGroup.new
file_threads.add f1
file_threads.add f2
```

The instance method list will return an array of all the threads in the thread group.

```
# Count living threads in this_group
count = 0
this_group.list.each {|x| count += 1 if x.alive? }
if count < this_group.list.size
  puts "Some threads in this_group are not living."
else
  puts "All threads in this_group are alive."
end
```

There is plenty of room for useful methods to be added to ThreadGroup. The following example shows methods to wake up every thread in a group, to wait for all threads to catch up (via join), and to kill all threads in a group:

```
class ThreadGroup

  def wakeup
    list.each { |t| t.wakeup }
  end
```

```
def join
  list.each { |t| t.join if t != Thread.current }
end

def kill
  list.each { |t| t.kill }
end

end
```

13.2   Synchronizing Threads

Why is synchronization necessary? It is because the "interleaving" of operations causes variables and other entities to be accessed in ways that are not obvious from reading the code of the individual threads. Two or more threads accessing the same variable may interact with each other in ways that are unforeseen and difficult to debug.

Let's take this simple piece of code as an example:

```
x = 0
t1 = Thread.new do
  1.upto(1000) do
    x = x + 1
  end
end

t2 = Thread.new do
  1.upto(1000) do
    x = x + 1
  end
end

t1.join
t2.join
puts x
```

The variable x starts at zero. Each thread increments it a thousand times. Logic tells us that x must be 2000 when it is printed out.

But you may find that the actual results contradict this logic. On one particular system, it prints 1044 as the result. What has gone wrong?

Our code assumes that the incrementing of an integer is an *atomic* (or indivisible) operation. But it isn't. Consider the logic flow in the following code example. We put thread t1 on the left side and t2 on the right. We put each separate timeslice on a separate line and assume that when we enter this piece of logic, x has the value 123.

```
t1                              t2


Retrieve value of x (123)
                                Retrieve value of x (123)

Add one to value (124)
                                Add one to value (124)

Store result back in x
                                Store result back in x
```

It's obvious that each thread is doing a simple increment from its own point of view. But it's also obvious that, in this case, x is only 124 after having been incremented by both threads.

This is only the simplest of synchronization problems. The worst ones become truly difficult to manage and become genuine objects of study by computer scientists and mathematicians.

13.2.1 Performing Simple Synchronization with Critical Sections

The simplest form of synchronization is to use a *critical section*. When a thread enters a critical section of code, this technique guarantees that no other thread will run until the first thread has left its critical section.

The Thread.critical accessor, when set to true, will prevent other threads from being scheduled. In the following code, we revisit the previous example and use the critical accessor to define the critical section and protect the sensitive parts of the code.

```
x = 0
t1 = Thread.new do
  1.upto(1000) do
    Thread.critical = true
    x = x + 1
    Thread.critical = false
```

```
      end
  end

  t2 = Thread.new do
    1.upto(1000) do
      Thread.critical = true
      x = x + 1
      Thread.critical = false
    end
  end

  t1.join
  t2.join
  puts x
```

Now the logic flow is different; refer to the following description of how t1 and t2 now act. (Of course, outside the incrementing part, the threads are free to interleave operations more or less randomly.)

```
t1                                    t2
_____               _____


Retrieve value of x (123)
Add one to value (124)
Store result back in x
                                      Retrieve value of x (124)
                                      Add one to value (125)
                                      Store result back in x
```

It is possible to perform combinations of thread manipulation operations that will cause a thread to be scheduled even if another thread is in a critical section. In the simplest case, a *newly created* thread will be run immediately regardless of whether another thread is in a critical section. For this reason, this technique should be used only in the simplest of circumstances.

13.2.2   Synchronizing Access to Resources (`mutex.rb`)

Let's take a web-indexing application as an example. We retrieve words from multiple sources over the Net and store them in a hash. The word itself will be the key, and the value will be a string that identifies the document and the line number within the document.

This is a crude example. But we will make it even more crude with these simplifying assumptions:

- We will represent the remote documents as simple strings.

- We will limit it to three such strings (simple hard-coded data).

- We will simulate the variability of Net access with random sleeps.

Let's look at the example in Listing 13.1. It doesn't even print out the data it collects but only a (non-unique) count of the number of words found. Note that every time the hash is examined or changed, we call the `hesitate` method to sleep for a random interval. This will cause the program to run in a less deterministic and more realistic way.

Listing 13.1 Flawed Indexing Example (with a Race Condition)

```
@list = []
@list[0]="shoes ships\nsealing-wax"
@list[1]="cabbages kings"
@list[2]="quarks\nships\ncabbages"

def hesitate
  sleep rand(0)
end

@hash = {}

def process_list(listnum)
  lnum = 0
  @list[listnum].each do |line|
    words = line.chomp.split
    words.each do |w|
      hesitate
      if @hash[w]
        hesitate
        @hash[w] += ["#{listnum}:#{lnum}"]
      else
        hesitate
        @hash[w] = ["#{listnum}:#{lnum}"]
      end
    end
    lnum += 1
  end
end

t1 = Thread.new(0) {|num| process_list(num) }
```

Continues

```
t2 = Thread.new(1) {|num| process_list(num) }
t3 = Thread.new(2) {|num| process_list(num) }

t1.join
t2.join
t3.join

count = 0
@hash.values.each {|v| count += v.size }

puts "Total: #{count} words"        # May print 7 or 8!
```

But there is a problem. If your system behaves as ours have, there are two possible numbers this program can output! In our tests, it prints the answers 7 and 8 with approximately equal likelihood. In a situation with more words and more lists, there would be even more variation.

Let's try to fix this with a *mutex*, which controls access to a shared resource. (The term is derived, of course, from the words *mutual exclusion*.) See Listing 13.2.

The Mutex library allows us to create and manipulate a mutex. We can lock it when we are about to access the hash and unlock it when we have finished with it.

Listing 13.2   Mutex-Protected Indexing Example

```
require 'thread.rb'

@list = []
@list[0]="shoes ships\nsealing-wax"
@list[1]="cabbages kings"
@list[2]="quarks\nships\ncabbages"

def hesitate
  sleep rand(0)
end

@hash = {}

@mutex = Mutex.new

def process_list(listnum)
  lnum = 0
  @list[listnum].each do |line|
    words = line.chomp.split
    words.each do |w|
      hesitate
      @mutex.lock
        if @hash[w]
```

```
          hesitate
          @hash[w] += ["#{listnum}:#{lnum}"]
        else
          hesitate
          @hash[w] = ["#{listnum}:#{lnum}"]
        end
        @mutex.unlock
      end
      lnum += 1
    end
  end
end

t1 = Thread.new(0) {|num| process_list(num) }
t2 = Thread.new(1) {|num| process_list(num) }
t3 = Thread.new(2) {|num| process_list(num) }

t1.join
t2.join
t3.join

count = 0
@hash.values.each {|v| count += v.size }

puts "Total: #{count} words"        # Always prints 8!
```

We should mention that in addition to `lock`, the `Mutex` class also has a `try_lock` method. It behaves the same as `lock` except that if another thread already has the lock, it will return `false` immediately rather than waiting.

```
require 'thread'

mutex = Mutex.new
t1 = Thread.new { mutex.lock; sleep 30 }

sleep 1

t2 = Thread.new do
  if mutex.try_lock
    puts "Locked it"
  else
    puts "Could not lock"   # Prints immediately
  end
end

sleep 2
```

This feature is useful any time a thread doesn't want to be blocked. There is a synchronize method that takes a block.

```
mutex = Mutex.new

mutex.synchronize do
  # Whatever code needs to be
  #   protected...
end
```

There is also a mutex_m library defining a Mutex_m module, which can be mixed into a class (or used to extend an object). Any such extended object has mutex methods so that the object itself can be treated as a mutex.

```
require 'mutex_m'

class MyClass
  include Mutex_m

  # Now any MyClass object can call
  # lock, unlock, synchronize, ...
  # or external objects can invoke
  # these methods on a MyClass object.
end
```

13.2.3   Using the Predefined Synchronized Queue Classes

The thread library thread.rb has a couple of classes that will be useful from time to time. The class Queue is a thread-aware queue that synchronizes access to the ends of the queue; that is, different threads may use the same queue without fear of problems. The class SizedQueue is essentially the same, except that it allows a limit to be placed on the size of the queue (the number of elements it can contain).

These have much the same set of methods available because SizedQueue actually inherits from Queue. The descendant also has the accessor max, used to get or set the maximum size of the queue.

```
buff = SizedQueue.new(25)
upper1 = buff.max              # 25
```

```
# Now raise it...
buff.max = 50
upper2 = buff.max          # 50
```

Listing 13.3 is a simple producer/consumer illustration. The consumer is delayed slightly longer on average (through a longer sleep) so that the items will "pile up" a little.

Listing 13.3 The Producer-Consumer Problem

```
require 'thread'

buffer = SizedQueue.new(2)

producer = Thread.new do
  item = 0
  loop do
    sleep rand 0
    puts "Producer makes #{item}"
    buffer.enq item
    item += 1
  end
end

consumer = Thread.new do
  loop do
    sleep (rand 0)+0.9
    item = buffer.deq
    puts "Consumer retrieves #{item}"
    puts "  waiting = #{buffer.num_waiting}"
  end
end

sleep 60    # Run a minute, then die and kill threads
```

The methods `enq` and `deq` are the recommended way to get items into and out of the queue. We can also use `push` to add to the queue and `pop` or `shift` to remove items, but these names have somewhat less mnemonic value when we are explicitly using a queue.

The method `empty?` will test for an empty queue, and `clear` will cause a queue to be empty. The method `size` (or its alias `length`) will return the actual number of items in the queue.

```
# Assume no other threads interfering...

buff = Queue.new
buff.enq "one"
buff.enq "two"
buff.enq "three"
n1 = buff.size        # 3
flag1 = buff.empty?   # false
buff.clear
n2 = buff.size        # 0
flag2 = buff.empty?   # true
```

The `num_waiting` method is the number of threads waiting to access the queue. In the nonsized queue, this is the number of threads waiting to remove elements; in the sized queue, this also the threads waiting to add elements to the queue.

An optional parameter `non_block` defaults to `false` for the `deq` method in the `Queue` class. If it is `true`, an empty queue will give a `ThreadError` rather than block the thread.

13.2.4   Using Condition Variables

And he called for his fiddlers three.

—*"Old King Cole" (traditional folk tune)*

A *condition variable* is really just a queue of threads. It is used in conjunction with a mutex to provide a higher level of control when synchronizing threads.

A condition variable is always associated with a specific mutex; it is used to relinquish control of the mutex *until a certain condition has been met.* Imagine a situation in which a thread has a mutex locked but cannot continue because the circumstances aren't right. It can sleep on the condition variable and wait to be awakened when the condition is met.

It is important to understand that while a thread is waiting on a condition variable, the mutex is released so that other threads can gain access. It is also important to realize that when another thread does a signal operation (to awaken the waiting thread), the waiting thread *reacquires* the lock on the mutex.

Let's look at a contrived example in the tradition of the Dining Philosophers. Imagine a table where three violinists are seated, all of whom want to take turns playing. However, there are only two violins and only one bow. Obviously a violinist can play only if she has one of the violins *and* the lone bow at the same time.

We keep a count of the violins and bows available. When a player wants a violin or a bow, she must wait for it. In our code, we protect the test with a mutex and do separate waits for the violin and the bow, both associated with that mutex. If a violin or a bow is not available, the thread sleeps. It loses the mutex until it is awakened by another thread signaling that the resource is available, whereupon the original thread wakes up and once again owns the lock on the mutex.

Listing 13.4 shows the code.

Listing 13.4 The Three Violinists

```
require 'thread'

@music  = Mutex.new
@violin = ConditionVariable.new
@bow    = ConditionVariable.new

@violins_free = 2
@bows_free    = 1

def musician(n)
  loop do
    sleep rand(0)
    @music.synchronize do
      @violin.wait(@music) while @violins_free == 0
      @violins_free -= 1
      puts "#{n} has a violin"
      puts "violins #@violins_free, bows #@bows_free"

      @bow.wait(@music) while @bows_free == 0
      @bows_free -= 1
      puts "#{n} has a bow"
      puts "violins #@violins_free, bows #@bows_free"
    end

    sleep rand(0)
    puts "#{n}:  (...playing...)"
    sleep rand(0)
    puts "#{n}: Now I've finished."
```

Continues

```
    @music.synchronize do
      @violins_free += 1
      @violin.signal if @violins_free == 1
      @bows_free += 1
      @bow.signal if @bows_free == 1
    end
  end
end

threads = []
3.times {|i| threads << Thread.new { musician(i) } }

threads.each {|t| t.join }
```

We believe that this solution will never deadlock, though we've found it difficult to prove. But it is interesting to note that this algorithm is not a *fair* one. In our tests, the first player always got to play more often than the other two, and the second more often than the third. The cause and cure for this behavior are left as an interesting exercise.

13.2.5   Using Other Synchronization Techniques

Yet another synchronization mechanism is the *monitor*, implemented in Ruby in the form of the monitor.rb library. This technique is somewhat more advanced than the mutex; notably, a mutex lock cannot be nested, but a monitor lock can.

The trivial case of this would never occur. That is, no one would ever write the following:

```
@mutex = Mutex.new

@mutex.synchronize do
  @mutex.synchronize do
    #...
  end
end
```

But it might happen this way (or through a recursive method call). The result is deadlock in any of these situations. Avoiding deadlock in this circumstance is one of the advantages of the Monitor mixin.

```
@mutex = Mutex.new

def some_method
  @mutex.synchronize do
    #...
    some_other_method     # Deadlock!
  end
end

def some_other_method
  @mutex.synchronize do
    #...
  end
end
```

The Monitor mixin is typically used to extend any object. The new_cond method can then be used to instantiate a condition variable.

The class ConditionVariable in monitor.rb), is enhanced from the definition in the thread library. It has methods wait_until and wait_while, which will block a thread based on a condition. It also allows a timeout while waiting because the wait method has a timeout parameter, which is a number of seconds (defaulting to nil).

Because we are rapidly running out of thread examples, Listing 13.5 presents to you a rewrite of the Queue and SizedQueue classes using the monitor technique. The code is by Shugo Maeda, used with permission.

Listing 13.5   Implementing a Queue with a Monitor

```
# Author:  Shugo Maeda

require 'monitor'

class Queue
  def initialize
    @que = []
    @monitor = Monitor.new
    @empty_cond = @monitor.new_cond
  end

  def enq(obj)
    @monitor.synchronize do
      @que.push(obj)
      @empty_cond.signal
    end
  end
```

Continues

```ruby
    def deq
      @monitor.synchronize do
        while @que.empty?
          @empty_cond.wait
        end
        return @que.shift
      end
    end
  end

  class SizedQueue < Queue
    attr :max

    def initialize(max)
      super()
      @max = max
      @full_cond = @monitor.new_cond
    end

    def enq(obj)
      @monitor.synchronize do
        while @que.length >= @max
          @full_cond.wait
        end
        super(obj)
      end
    end

    def deq
      @monitor.synchronize do
        obj = super
        if @que.length < @max
          @full_cond.signal
        end
        return obj
      end
    end

    def max=(max)
      @monitor.synchronize do
        @max = max
        @full_cond.broadcast
      end
    end
  end
```

The sync.rb library is one more way of performing thread synchronization (using a two-phase lock with a counter). It defines a Sync_m module used in an include or an extend (much like Mutex_m). This module makes available methods such as locked?, shared?, exclusive?, lock, unlock, and try_lock.

13.2.6 Allowing Timeout of an Operation

There are many situations in which we want to allow a maximum length of time for an action to be performed. This avoids infinite loops and allows an additional level of control over processing. A feature like this is useful in the environment of the Net, where we may or may not get a response from a distant server, and in other circumstances.

The timeout.rb library is a thread-based solution to this problem (see Listing 13.6). The timeout method executes the block associated with the method call; when the specified number of seconds has elapsed, it throws a TimeoutError, which can be caught with a rescue clause.

Listing 13.6 A Timeout Example

```ruby
require 'timeout.rb'

flag = false
answer = nil

begin
  timeout(5) do
    puts "I want a cookie!"
    answer = gets.chomp
    flag = true
  end
rescue TimeoutError
  flag = false
end

if flag
  if answer == "cookie"
    puts "Thank you! Chomp, chomp, ..."
  else
    puts "That's not a cookie!"
    exit
  end
else
  puts "Hey, too slow!"
  exit
end

puts "Bye now..."
```

13.2.7   Waiting for an Event

In many situations we might want to have one or more threads monitoring the "outside world" while other threads are doing other things. The examples here are all rather contrived, but they do illustrate the general principle.

In the following example we see three threads doing the "work" of an application. Another thread simply wakes up every five seconds, checks the global variable $flag, and wakes up two other threads when it sees the flag set. This saves the three worker threads from interacting directly with the two other threads and possibly making multiple attempts to awaken them.

```ruby
$flag = false
work1 = Thread.new { job1() }
work2 = Thread.new { job2() }
work3 = Thread.new { job3() }

thread4 = Thread.new { Thread.stop; job4() }
thread5 = Thread.new { Thread.stop; job5() }

watcher = Thread.new do
  loop do
    sleep 5
    if $flag
      thread4.wakeup
      thread5.wakeup
      Thread.exit
    end
  end
end
```

If at any point during the execution of the job methods the variable $flag becomes true, thread4 and thread5 are guaranteed to start within five seconds. After that, the watcher thread terminates.

In this next example we are waiting for a file to be created. We check every 30 seconds for it, and start another thread if we see it; meanwhile, other threads can be doing anything at all. Actually, we are watching for three separate files here.

```ruby
def waitfor(filename)
  loop do
    if File.exist? filename
```

```
            file_processor = Thread.new { process_file(filename) }
            Thread.exit
         else
            sleep 30
         end
      end
   end

waiter1 = Thread.new { waitfor("Godot") }
sleep 10
waiter2 = Thread.new { waitfor("Guffman") }
sleep 10
headwaiter = Thread.new { waitfor("head") }

# Main thread goes off to do other things...
```

There are many other situations in which a thread might wait for an outside event, such as a networked application where the server at the other end of a socket is slow or unreliable.

13.2.8   Continuing Processing During I/O

Frequently an application may have one or more I/O operations that are lengthy or time-consuming. This is especially true in the case of user input because a user typing at a keyboard is slower even than any disk operation. We can make use of this time by using threads.

Consider the case of a chess program that must wait for the human player to make his or her move. Of course, we present here only the barest outline of this concept.

We assume that the iterator predict_move will repeatedly generate likely moves that the person might make (and then determine the program's own responses to those moves). Then when the person moves, it is possible that the move has already been anticipated.

```
scenario = {}      # move-response hash
humans_turn = true
thinking_ahead = Thread.new(board) do
   predict_move do |m|
      scenario[m] = my_response(board,m)
      Thread.exit if humans_turn == false
   end
```

```
    end

    human_move = get_human_move(board)
    humans_turn = false    # Stop the thread gracefully

    # Now we can access scenario which may contain the
    # move the person just made...
```

Of course, real chess programs don't usually work this way.

13.2.9   Implementing Parallel Iterators

Imagine that you wanted to iterate in parallel over more than one object. That is, for each of *n* objects, you want the first item of each of them, then the second item of each, then the third, and so on.

To make this a little more concrete, look at the following example. Here we assume that compose is the name of the magic method that provides a composition of iterators. We also assume that every object specified has a default iterator each that will be used and that each object contributes one item at a time.

```
    arr1 = [1, 2, 3, 4]
    arr2 = [5, 10, 15, 20]
    compose(arr1, arr2) {|a,b| puts "#{a} and #{b}" }

    # Should output:
    # 1 and 5
    # 2 and 10
    # 3 and 15
    # 4 and 20
```

We could use zip for this, of course. But if we want a more elegant solution, one that does not actually store all the items, threads are the only easy way.

We offer our solution in Listing 13.7.

Listing 13.7   Iterating in Parallel

```
    def compose(*objects)
      threads = []
      for obj in objects do
        threads << Thread.new(obj) do |myobj|
```

```
        me = Thread.current
        me[:queue] = []
        myobj.each {|x| me[:queue].push(x) }
      end
    end

    list = [0]                          # Dummy non-nil value
    while list.nitems > 0 do            # Still some non-nils
      list = []
      for thr in threads
        list << thr[:queue].shift       # Remove one from each
      end
      yield list if list.nitems > 0     # Don't yield all nils
    end
  end

x = [1, 2, 3, 4, 5, 6, 7, 8]
y = " first\n second\n  third\n fourth\n  fifth\n"
z = %w[a b c d e f]

compose(x, y, z) {|a,b,c| p [a, b, c] }

# Output:
#
# [1, " first\n", "a"]
# [2, " second\n", "b"]
# [3, "  third\n", "c"]
# [4, " fourth\n", "d"]
# [5, "  fifth\n", "e"]
# [6, nil, "f"]
# [7, nil, nil]
# [8, nil, nil]
```

Notice that we do *not* assume that the objects all have the same number of items over which to iterate. If an iterator "runs out" before the others, it will generate nil values until the longest-running iterator has exhausted itself.

Of course, it is possible to write a more general method that will grab more than one value from each iteration. (After all, not all iterators return just one value at a time.) We could let the first parameter specify the number of values per iterator.

It would also be possible to use arbitrary iterators (rather than the default each). We might pass in their names as strings and use send to invoke them. Other tricks also could be performed.

However, we think that the example given here is adequate for most circumstances. The other variations we will leave as an exercise for the reader.

13.2.10   Recursive Deletion in Parallel

Just for fun, let's write some code to delete an entire directory tree, and let's make it concurrent. The recursive deletion routine appears here in a threaded form. When we find that a directory entry is itself a directory, we start a new thread to traverse that directory and delete its contents.

As we go along, we keep track of the threads we've created in an array called threads; because this is a local variable, each thread will have its own copy of the array. It can be accessed by only one thread at a time, and there is no need to synchronize access to it.

Note also that we pass fullname into the thread block so that we don't have to worry about the thread accessing a variable that is changing. The thread uses fn as a local copy of the same variable.

When we have traversed an entire directory, we want to wait on the threads we have created before deleting the directory we've just finished working on.

```
def delete_all(dir)
  threads = []
  Dir.foreach(dir) do |e|
    next if [".",".."].include? e          # Skip . and ..
    fullname = dir + "/" + e
    if FileTest.directory?(fullname)
      threads << Thread.new(fullname) {|fn| delete_all(fn) }
    else
      File.delete(fullname)
    end
  end
  threads.each { |t| t.join }
  Dir.delete(dir)
end

delete_all("/tmp/stuff")
```

Is this actually faster than the nonthreaded version? We've found that the answer is not consistent. It probably depends on your operating system as well as on the actual directory structure being deleted—that is, its depth, size of files, and so on.

13.3 Conclusion

As we've seen here, Ruby has so-called *green threads* (not native threads). These do not benefit from having multiple processors in a machine, but they can still be used for some level of concurrency. Threads can be a useful technique in many circumstances, but they can be somewhat problematic to code and debug. This is particularly true when we use sophisticated synchronization methods to achieve correct results.

Ruby provides classes such as `Mutex`, `Monitor`, and `ConditionVariable` to aid in synchronization. It also provides the built-in `Queue` and `SizedQueue` classes, which are thread-safe.

In Chapter 14, "Scripting and System Administration," we move away from a discussion of programming technique in itself to a more task-oriented topic. We'll be discussing the use of Ruby for everyday scripting and system administration tasks.

CHAPTER 14

Scripting and System Administration

Thus spake the master programmer: "Though a program be but three lines long, someday it will have to be maintained."

—*Geoffrey James*, The Tao of Programming

Programmers often need to "glue" programs together with little scripts that talk to the operating system at a fairly high level and run external programs. This is especially true in the UNIX world, which daily relies on shell scripts for countless tasks.

Ruby is not always a convenient glue language because it is more general-purpose than that. But in the long run, anything that can be done in bash (or the others) can also be done in Ruby.

In many cases, you might just as well use one of the more traditional languages for this purpose. The advantage that Ruby has, of course, is that it really is a general-purpose language, full-featured, and truly object-oriented. On the theory that people might want to use Ruby to talk to the OS at this level, we present here a few tricks that might prove useful.

This chapter was difficult to organize. Much of the functionality could logically be grouped in different ways. If you don't find what you are looking for in the expected place, scan the rest of the chapter also.

In addition, much of what *could* be covered here is actually dealt with in other chapters entirely. Refer in particular to Chapter 10, "I/O and Data Storage," which covers file I/O and attributes of files; these features are frequently used in scripts of the kind discussed in the present chapter.

14.1   Running External Programs

A language can't be a glue language unless it can run external programs. Ruby offers more than one way to do this.

I can't resist mentioning here that if you are going to run an external program, make sure that you know what that program does. I'm thinking about viruses and other potentially destructive programs. Don't just run any old command string, especially if it came from a source outside the program. This is true regardless of whether the application is web-based.

14.1.1   Using `system` and `exec`

The `system` method (in `Kernel`) is equivalent to the C call of the same name. It will execute the given command in a subshell.

```
system("/usr/games/fortune")
# Output goes to stdout as usual...
```

Note that the second parameter, if present, will be used as list of arguments; in most cases, the arguments can also be specified as part of the command string with the same effect. The only difference is that filename expansion is done on the first string but not on the others.

```
system("rm", "/tmp/file1")
system("rm /tmp/file2")
# Both the above work fine.

# However, below, there's a difference...
system("echo *")      # Print list of all files
system("echo","*")    # Print an asterisk (no filename
                      # expansion done)

# More complex command lines also work.
system("ls -l | head -n 1")
```

Let's look at how this works on the Windows family of operating systems. For a simple executable, the behavior should be the same. Depending on your exact variant of Ruby, invoking a shell builtin might require a reference to cmd.exe, the Windows command processor (which may be command.com on some versions). Both cases, executable and builtin, are shown here.

```ruby
system("notepad.exe","myfile.txt")  # No problem...
system("cmd /c dir","somefile")     # 'dir' is a builtin!
```

Another solution to this is to use the Win32API library and define your own version of the system method.

```ruby
require "Win32API"

def system(cmd)
  sys = Win32API.new("crtdll", "system", ['P'], 'L')
  sys.Call(cmd)
end

system("dir")  # cmd /c not needed!
```

So the behavior of system can be made relatively OS-independent. But, getting back to the big picture, if you want to capture the output (for example, in a variable), system of course isn't the right way—see the next section.

I'll also mention exec here. The exec method behaves much the same as system except that the new process actually overlays or replaces the current one. Thus any code following the exec won't be executed.

```ruby
puts "Here's a directory listing:"
exec("ls", "-l")

puts "This line is never reached!"
```

14.1.2   Command Output Substitution

The simplest way to capture command output is to use the *backtick* (also called *backquote* or *grave accent*) to delimit the command. Here are a couple of examples:

```ruby
listing = `ls -l`   # Multiple lines in one string
now = `date`        # "Mon Mar 12 16:50:11 CST 2001"
```

The generalized delimiter %x calls the backquote operator (which is really a kernel method). It works essentially the same way:

```
listing = %x(ls -l)
now = %x(date)
```

The %x form is often useful when the string to be executed contains characters such as single and double quotes.

Because the backquote method really is (in some sense) a method, it is possible to override it. Here we change the functionality so that we return an array of lines rather than a single string. Of course, we have to save an alias to the old method so that we can call it.

```
alias old_execute `

def `(cmd)
  out = old_execute(cmd)    # Call the old backtick method
  out.split("\n")           # Return an array of strings!
end

entries = `ls -l /tmp`
num = entries.size                    # 95

first3lines = %x(ls -l | head -n 3)
how_many = first3lines.size           # 3
```

Note that, as shown here, the functionality of %x is affected when we perform this redefinition.

In the following example we append a "shellism" to the end of the command to ensure that standard error is mixed with standard output:

```
alias old_execute `

def `(cmd)
  old_execute(cmd + " 2>&1")
end

entries = `ls -l /tmp/foobar`
# "/tmp/foobar: No such file or directory\n"
```

There are, of course, many other ways to change the default behavior of the backquote.

14.1.3 Manipulating Processes

We discuss process manipulation in this section even though a new process might not involve calling an external program. The principal way to create a new process is the `fork` method, which takes its name from UNIX tradition from the idea of a fork in the path of execution, like a fork in the road. (Note that the Ruby core does not support the `fork` method on Windows platforms.)

The `fork` method in `Kernel` (also found in the `Process` module) shouldn't, of course, be confused with the `Thread` instance method of the same name.

There are two ways to invoke the `fork` method. The first is the more UNIX-like way: Simply call it and test its return value. If that value is `nil`, we are in the child process; otherwise, we execute the parent code. The value returned to the parent is actually the process ID (or *pid*) of the child.

```
pid = fork
if (pid == nil)
   puts "Ah, I must be the child."
   puts "I guess I'll speak as a child."
else
   puts "I'm the parent."
   puts "Time to put away childish things."
end
```

In this unrealistic example, the output might be interleaved, or the parent's output might appear first. For purposes of this example, it's irrelevant.

We should also note that the child process might outlive the parent. We've seen that this isn't the case with Ruby threads, but system-level processes are entirely different.

The second form of `fork` takes a block. The code in the block comprises the child process. The previous example could thus be rewritten in this simpler way:

```
fork do
   puts "Ah, I must be the child."
   puts "I guess I'll speak as a child."
end

puts "I'm the parent."
puts "Time to put away childish things."
```

The pid is still returned, of course. We just don't show it in the previous example.

When we want to wait for a process to finish, we can call the `wait` method in the `Process` module. It waits for any child to exit and returns the process ID of that child. The `wait2` method behaves similarly except that it returns a two-value array consisting of the pid and a left-shifted exit status.

```
pid1 = fork { sleep 5; exit 3 }
pid2 = fork { sleep 2; exit 3 }

Process.wait    # Returns pid2
Process.wait2   # Returns [pid1,768]
```

To wait for a specific child, use `waitpid` and `waitpid2`, respectively.

```
pid3 = fork { sleep 5; exit 3 }
pid4 = fork { sleep 2; exit 3 }

Process.waitpid(pid4,Process::WNOHANG)      # Returns pid4
Process.waitpid2(pid3,Process:WNOHANG)      # Returns [pid3,768]
```

If the second parameter is unspecified, the call might block (if no such child exists). It might be ORed logically with `Process::WUNTRACED` to catch child processes that have been stopped. This second parameter is rather OS-sensitive; experiment before relying on its behavior.

The `exit!` method exits immediately from a process (bypassing any exit handlers). The integer value, if specified, will be returned as a return code; -1 (not 0) is the default.

```
pid1 = fork { exit! }      # Return -1 exit code
pid2 = fork { exit! 0 }    # Return 0 exit code
```

The `pid` and `ppid` methods will return the process ID of the current process and the parent process, respectively.

```
proc1 = Process.pid
fork do
  if Process.ppid == proc1
    puts "proc1 is my parent"  # Prints this message
  else
    puts "What's going on?"
  end
end
```

The `kill` method can be used to send a UNIX-style signal to a process. The first parameter can be an integer, a POSIX signal name including the `SIG` prefix, or a non-prefixed signal name. The second parameter represents a pid; if it is zero, it refers to the current process.

```
Process.kill(1,pid1)          # Send signal 1 to process pid1
Process.kill("HUP",pid2)      # Send SIGHUP to pid2
Process.kill("SIGHUP",pid2)   # Send SIGHUP to pid3
Process.kill("SIGHUP",0)      # Send SIGHUP to self
```

The `Kernel.trap` method can be used to handle such signals. It typically takes a signal number or name and a block to be executed.

```
trap(1) { puts "Caught signal 1" }
sleep 2
Process.kill(1,0)   # Send to self
```

For advanced uses of `trap`, consult Ruby and UNIX references.

The `Process` module also has methods for examining and setting such attributes as userid, effective userid, priority, and others. Consult any Ruby reference for details.

14.1.4 Manipulating Standard Input/Output

We've seen how `IO.popen` and `IO.pipe` work in Chapter 10, but there is a little library we haven't looked at that can prove handy at times.

The `Open3.rb` library contains a method `popen3`, which will return an array of three `IO` objects. These objects correspond to the standard input, standard output, and standard error for the process kicked off by the `popen3` call. Here's an example:

```
require "open3"

filenames = %w[ file1 file2 this that another one_more ]

inp, out, err = Open3.popen3("xargs", "ls", "-l")

filenames.each { |f| inp.puts f }   # Write to the process's stdin
inp.close                           # Close is necessary!

output = out.readlines              # Read from its stdout
errout = err.readlines              # Also read from its stderr
```

```
puts "Sent #{filenames.size} lines of input."
puts "Got back #{output.size} lines from stdout"
puts "and #{errout.size} lines from stderr."
```

This contrived example does an `ls -l` on each of the specified filenames and captures the standard output and standard error separately. Note that the `close` is needed so that the subprocess will be aware that end of file has been reached. Also note that Open3 uses `fork`, which doesn't exist on Windows; on that platform, you will have to use the `win32-open3` library (written and maintained by Daniel Berger and Park Heesob).

See also section 14.3, "The Shell Library."

14.2   Command-Line Options and Arguments

Rumors of the death of the command line are greatly exaggerated. Although we live in the age of the GUI, every day thousands of us retreat to the older text-based interfaces for one reason or another.

Ruby has many of its roots in UNIX, as we've said. Yet even in the Windows world, there is such a thing as a command line, and, frankly, we don't see it going away any time soon.

When operating at this level, parameters and switches are used to communicate with the program at the time of its invocation. This section shows how to deal with these parameters (or arguments) and switches (or options).

14.2.1   Parsing Command-Line Options

The `getoptlong` library is probably the most commonly used command-line parser. (The `getopts.rb` library is considered obsolete because it has more limited functionality.) It can accept both single-letter and longer option names, and it recognizes the double hyphen (--) as meaning the end of all the options. Its behavior is essentially the same as its GNU counterpart.

The `GetoptLong` class must be instantiated, giving a parser object. This object can then be set up with the allowed command-line options and used to retrieve them one at a time.

The parser object has a `set_options` method that takes a list of arrays. Each array contains one or more options (as strings) and one "argument flag," which tells whether an argument is allowed for that option. The options in each array are considered synonyms; the first one mentioned is the "canonical name" of the option, as returned by a get operation.

As an example, suppose that we have a tool with these options: -h or --help will print help information; -f or --file will specify a filename argument; and -l or --lines will truncate the output after the specified number of lines (defaulting to 100).

We could begin in this way:

```
require "getoptlong"

parser = GetoptLong.new
parser.set_options(
        ["-h", "--help", GetoptLong::NO_ARGUMENT],
        ["-f", "--file", GetoptLong::REQUIRED_ARGUMENT],
        ["-l", "--lines", GetoptLong::OPTIONAL_ARGUMENT])
```

Now we can use a loop to call get repeatedly (see Listing 14.1); we can fake a post-test loop because we are using begin and end anyway.) A synonym for get is get_option; there are also iterators named each and each_option, which are identical.

Listing 14.1   Getting Command-Line Options

```
filename = nil
lines = 0                 # Default means no truncating

loop do
  begin
    opt, arg = parser.get
    break if not opt
    # Only for debugging purposes...
    puts (opt + " => " + arg)

    case opt
      when "-h"
        puts "Usage: ..."
        break             # Stop processing if -h
      when "-f"
        filename = arg    # Save the file argument
      when "-l"
        if arg != ""
          lines = arg     # Save lines arg (if given)
        else
          lines = 100     # Default for truncating
```

Continues

```
        end
      end

    rescue => err
      puts err
      break
    end
  end

  puts "filename = #{filename}"
  puts "lines    = #{lines}"
```

Note that get returns nil for a nonexistent option but a null string for a nonexistent argument. This may be a bug.

Note also that we are catching errors here. Four possible exceptions could be raised, as summarized here:

- AmbiguousOption—A long option name seems to have been abbreviated, but it isn't unique.

- InvalidOption—The option is unknown.

- MissingArgument—The option is missing its argument.

- NeedlessArgument—The option has an argument when it isn't expected to take an argument.

Errors are normally reported to stderr when they occur, but the quiet= accessor can be set to true to override this.

There are other features of getoptlong, which we haven't discussed here. See the documentation for further details.

There are also other possibilities, such as OptionParser, that offer somewhat different functionality and usage. Refer to the Ruby Application Archive for more information.

14.2.2   Working with ARGF

The special global constant ARGF represents the pseudo-file, resulting from a concatenation of every file named on the command line. It behaves like an IO object in most ways.

When you have a "bare" input method (without a receiver), you are typically using a method mixed in from the `Kernel` module. (Examples are `gets` and `readlines`.) The actual source of input will default to `STDIN` if no files are on the command line. If there are files, however, input will be taken from them. End of file will of course be reached only at the end of the last file.

If you prefer, you can access `ARGF` explicitly using the following fragment:

```
# Copy all files to stdout
puts ARGF.readlines
```

Perhaps contrary to most people's expectations, end of file is set after each file. The previous code fragment will output all the files. This one will output only the first:

```
until ARGF.eof?
  puts ARGF.gets
end
```

Whether this is a bug or a feature, we will leave to you to decide. Of course, other unexpected surprises might actually be pleasant. The input isn't simply a stream of bytes flowing through our program; we can actually perform operations such as `seek` and `rewind` on `ARGF` as though it were a "real file."

There is a `file` method associated with `ARGF`; it returns an `IO` object corresponding to the file currently being processed. As such, the value it returns will change as the files on the command line are processed in sequence.

What if we don't want command-line arguments to be interpreted as files? The solution is to not use the "bare" (receiverless) call of the input methods. If you want to read standard input, you can use `STDIN` as the receiver, and all will work as expected.

14.2.3 Working with ARGV

The global constant `ARGV` represents the list of arguments passed to the Ruby program via the command line. This is essentially an array.

```
n = ARGV.size
argstr = '"' + ARGV*"," + '"'
puts "I was given #{n} arguments..."
puts "They are: #{argstr}"
puts "Note that ARGV[0] = #{ARGV[0]}"
```

Assume that we invoke this little program with the arguments red green blue on the command line. It then produces this output:

```
I was given 3 arguments.
They are: "red,green,blue"
Note that ARGV[0] = red
```

Obviously there is no need for an argument count as in the old days; that information is part of the array.

Another thing that might trip up oldtimers is the assignment of the zeroth argument to an actual argument (rather than, for example, the script name). The arguments themselves are zero-based rather than one-based as in C and the various shell languages.

14.3   The Shell Library

Ruby isn't necessarily convenient to use as a scripting language in every situation. For example, a bash script can execute external programs simply by naming them, with no extraneous syntax.

The power and flexibility of Ruby has given it a more complex syntax than the average shell language. Additionally its functionality is segmented into different classes, modules, and libraries.

This situation motivated the creation of the Shell library. This library makes it easier to do things such as connecting commands with pipes and redirecting output to files. It also consolidates functionality from several different sources so that they are transparently accessible from a Shell object. (It doesn't always work well on Windows.)

14.3.1   Using Shell for I/O Redirection

The Shell class has two methods—new and cd—for instantiating a new object. The former creates a shell object associated with the current directory; the latter creates a shell object whose working directory will be the one specified.

```
require "shell"

sh1 = Shell.new              # Work in the current directory
sh2 = Shell.cd("/tmp/hal")   # Work in /tmp/hal
```

The Shell library defines a few built-in commands as methods, such as echo, cat, and tee. These always return objects of class Filter (as do the user-defined commands that we'll look at shortly).

The nice thing about a Filter is that it understands I/O redirection. The methods (or operators) <, >, and | are defined so that they behave more or less as we expect from long experience with shell scripts.

If a redirection method has a string as a parameter, that string is taken to be the name of a file. If it has an IO object as a parameter, that object is used for the input or output operation. Here are some small examples:

```
sh = Shell.new

# Print the motd file to stdout
sh.cat("/etc/motd") > STDOUT

# Print it again
(sh.cat < "/etc/motd") > STDOUT
(sh.echo "This is a test") > "myfile.txt"

# Append a line to /etc/motd
sh.echo("Hello, world!") >> "/etc/motd"

# Cat two files to stdout, tee-ing to a third
(sh.cat "file1" "file2") | (tee "file3") > STDOUT
```

Note that the > binds tightly. The parentheses that you see in the preceding code are necessary in most cases. Here are two correct usages and one incorrect one:

```
# Ruby parser understands this...
sh.cat("myfile.txt") > STDOUT

# ...and this also.
(sh.cat "myfile.txt") > STDOUT

# TypeError! (a precedence problem)
sh.cat "myfile.txt" > STDOUT
```

Note that it's also possible to "install" system commands of your own choosing. The method def_system_command will accomplish this. For example, here we define two methods—ls and ll—which will list files in the current directory (short and long listings, respectively).

```
# Method name is identical to command...
# only one parameter necessary
Shell.def_system_command "ls"

# Two parameters needed here
Shell.def_system_command "ll", "ls -l"

sh = Shell.new
sh.ls > STDOUT    # Short listing
sh.ll > STDOUT    # Long listing
```

You will notice that in many cases we explicitly send output to STDOUT. This is because output from a Shell command doesn't automatically go anywhere. It's simply associated with the Filter object until that object is connected to a file or an IO object.

14.3.2   Other Notes on `shell.rb`

The transact method will execute a block using the receiver for its context. Thus we can use this shorthand:

```
sh = Shell.new
sh.transact do
  echo("A line of data") > "somefile.txt"
  cat("somefile.txt","otherfile.txt") > "thirdfile"
  cat("thirdfile") | tee("file4") > STDOUT
end
```

The iterator foreach will take either a file or a directory as a parameter. If it is a file, it will iterate over the lines of that file; if it is a directory, it will iterate over the filenames in that directory.

```
sh = Shell.new

# List all lines in /tmp/foo
sh.foreach("/tmp/foo") {|l| puts l }

# List all files in /tmp
sh.foreach("/tmp") {|f| puts f }
```

The `pushdir` and `popdir` methods will save and restore the current directory, respectively. Aliases are `pushd` and `popd`. The method `pwd` will determine the current working directory; aliases are `getwd`, `cwd`, and `dir`.

```
sh = Shell.cd "/home"

puts sh.pwd       # /home
sh.pushd "/tmp"
puts sh.pwd       # /tmp

sh.popd
puts sh.pwd       # /home
```

For convenience, numerous methods are imported into `Shell` from various sources, including the `File` class, the `FileTest` module, and the `ftools.rb` library. This saves the trouble of doing requires, includes, creating objects, qualifying method calls, and so on.

```
sh = Shell.new
flag1 = sh.exist? "myfile"        # Test file existence
sh.delete "somefile"              # Delete a file
sh.move "/tmp/foo", "/tmp/bar"    # Move a file
```

There are other features of the `Shell` library that we don't cover here. See the associated documentation for more details.

14.4 Accessing Environment Variables

Occasionally we need to access *environment variables* as a link between our program and the outer world. An environment variable is essentially a label referring to a piece of text (typically a small piece); environment variables can be used to store configuration information such as paths, usernames, and so on.

The notion of an environment variable is common in the UNIX world. The Windows world has borrowed it from UNIX (by way of MS-DOS), so the code we show here should run on variants of both Windows and UNIX.

14.4.1   Getting and Setting Environment Variables

The global constant ENV can be used as a hash both for purposes of retrieving and assigning values. In the following code, we retrieve the value of an environment variable. (You would use a semicolon rather than a colon on Windows.)

```
mypath = ENV["PATH"]
# Let's get an array now...
dirs = mypath.split(":")
```

Here's an example of setting a variable. We take the trouble to fork another process to illustrate two facts. First, a child process inherits the environment variables that its parent knows. Second, an environment variable set by a child is *not* propagated back up to the parent.

```
ENV["alpha"] = "123"
ENV["beta"]  = "456"
puts "Parent: alpha = #{ENV['alpha']}"
puts "Parent: beta  = #{ENV['beta']}"
fork do   # Child code...
  x = ENV["alpha"]
  ENV["beta"] = "789"
  y = ENV["beta"]
  puts " Child: alpha = #{x}"
  puts " Child: beta  = #{y}"
end
Process.wait
a = ENV["alpha"]
b = ENV["beta"]
puts "Parent: alpha = #{a}"
puts "Parent: beta  = #{b}"
```

The output here would be the following:

```
Parent: alpha = 123
Parent: beta  = 456
 Child: alpha = 123
 Child: beta  = 789
Parent: alpha = 123
Parent: beta  = 456
```

There is a consequence of the fact that parent processes don't know about their children's variables. Because a Ruby program is typically run in a subshell, any variables changed during execution will *not* be reflected in the current shell after execution has terminated.

14.4.2   Storing Environment Variables As an Array or Hash

It's important to realize that ENV isn't really a hash; it just looks like one. For example, we can't call the invert method on it; it gives us a NameError because there is no such method. The reason for this implementation is the close tie between the ENV object and the underlying operating system; setting a value has an actual impact on the OS, a behavior that a mere hash can't mimic.

However, we can call the to_hash method to give us a real live hash:

```
envhash = ENV.to_hash
val2var = envhash.invert
```

Of course, after we have a hash, we can convert it to any other form we prefer (for example, an array):

```
envarr = ENV.to_hash.to_a
```

It's not possible to directly reassign a hash to ENV; but we can fake it easily if we need to:

```
envhash = ENV.to_hash
# Manipulate as needed... then assign back.
envhash.each {|k,v| ENV[k] = v }
```

14.4.3   Importing Environment Variables As Globals

There is a small library called importenv.rb, which will run through all the environment variables and import them into the program as global variables. It is used in this way:

```
require "importenv"

# Now our environment variables are all globals...
# E.g., $PWD and $LOGNAME
```

```
where = $PWD
who = $LOGNAME
puts "In directory #{where}, logged in as #{who}"
```

Note that because the importenv uses trace_var, the reflection is actually two-way:
We can set one of these global variables in our program, and the real environment variable will be set in the same way.

```
require "importenv"

puts "My path is #$PATH"
# Prints: /usr/local/bin:/usr/bin:/usr/ucb:/etc:.
$PATH = "/ruby-1.8.0:" + $PATH

puts "My actual $PATH variable is now #{ENV['PATH']}"
# Prints: /ruby-1.8.0:/usr/local/bin:/usr/bin:/usr/ucb:/etc:.
```

Again we point out that a change in an environment variable within a Ruby program doesn't affect the environment external to the program.

14.5   Scripting in Microsoft Windows

Like the ski resort full of girls hunting for husbands and husbands hunting for girls, the situation is not as symmetrical as it might seem.

— *Alan Lindsay Mackay*

It has been said that Ruby has a UNIX bias. In a sense, this is true; it was conceived in a UNIX environment and works best there. Yet there are other ports out there at the time of this writing, including Macintosh, and there are other ports in progress, such as Palm OS. But if UNIX is the primary platform for Ruby, the secondary platform is Windows.

Windows users certainly aren't left out in the cold. Windows-based tools and libraries are in existence, and more are being created. Much of Ruby is platform-independent anyhow, even the threading capabilities; most of the platform difficulties occur in the areas of I/O, process management, and other similar low-level operations.

In the past, one problem for Windows users was that there were different *variants* of Ruby for the Windows platforms. The interpreter might have been built with gcc or Visual C, it might or might not depend on the Cygwin DLL, and so on. In recent years, we have had the luxury of using the "one-click" installer for Windows (see section 14.6, "The Windows One-Click Installer.")

The environment is changing too rapidly to document at this point, but this section discusses a few of the high points in Windows scripting and automation. These techniques and utilities should work for anyone, and if there are problems, the online support community is helpful with such things.

14.5.1 Using Win32API

The `Win32API` is exceptionally powerful if you want to code at a fairly low level. Essentially it allows access to any Windows API function in any DLL, making it callable from Ruby code.

The specified function is instantiated as an object, with relevant parameters precisely describing the function being passed into the new method. The first parameter, a string, identifies the DLL containing the function (such as `crtdll`). The second parameter is the name of the function itself. The third parameter is an array of strings identifying the types of the function parameters (the import array), and the fourth parameter is a string specifying the function's return type.

The import array can contain these (not case-sensitive) values:

```
I    Integer
L    Number
N    Number
P    Pointer to a string
```

The export string can also contain any one of these. Additionally it can take the value `"V"`, meaning "void."

After we have created this object, we can invoke its `call` method to call the Windows function. Note that `Call` is an alias.

Here we call the Windows function `GetCursorPos`, which returns a pointer to a `POINT` structure. This structure consists of two `long` fields; we can use `unpack` to examine these fields and retrieve their values.

```
require 'Win32API'
result = "0"*8    # Eight bytes (enough for two longs)
getCursorXY = Win32API.new("user32","GetCursorPos",["P"],"V")
getCursorXY.call(result)
x, y = result.unpack("LL")   # Two longs
```

Sometimes we need to pass in complex binary data, whereas in this case it was passed back to us. In that case, we could obviously use pack to pack the data into a string.

Obviously this technique has many possible applications. Two other code fragments can be seen in section 10.1.20, "Grabbing Characters from the Keyboard," and 14.1.1, "Using system and exec."

14.5.2   Using Win32OLE

The Win32OLE extension library (actually spelled in lowercase, win32ole) provides an interface to Windows OLE automation. Your Ruby code can act as a client for any OLE automation server such as Microsoft Word, Outlook, and Internet Explorer, and many third-party software products.

To interact with an external application, we first create a new object of the WIN32OLE class. This object is used to access all the exposed properties and methods of the specified application.

In this example, we associate an object with the Microsoft Word application. We set the visible attribute to true, and eventually we quit, exiting the application.

```
require "win32ole"

word = WIN32OLE.new "Word.Application"

word.visible = true

# ...

word.quit
```

Every property of the automation server is reflected as an attribute of the object. These can be set or examined at will.

An alternate notation uses a hashlike construct to access these properties.

```
player["FileName"] = "file.wav"
name = player["FileName"]
# Equivalent to these statements:
# player.FileName = "file.wav"
# name = player.FileName
```

One advantage of this is that it can easily handle the more "programmatic" situations as shown in this contrived example:

```
puts "Enter the property name"
prop = gets
puts "Enter the new value"
val = gets
old = obj[prop]
obj[prop] = val
puts "#{prop} was #{old}... now is #{obj[prop]}"
```

But let's look at some more concrete examples. Here is a code fragment that takes a filename from the command line, passes it into Microsoft Word, and prints the file:

```
require "win32ole"

print "Enter the filename to print: "
docfile = gets

word = WIN32OLE.new "Word.Application"
word.visible = true
word.documents.open docfile
word.options.printBackground = false

# We could also set printBackground to true, but we
# would have to sleep until the file all got sent to
# the printer buffer before we quit...

word.activeDocument.printOut
word.quit
```

The following is an example of playing a WAV file. It has the disadvantage of an arbitrary sleep at the end rather than waiting for the output to finish. Fixing this is left as an exercise.

```
require "win32ole"

sound = WIN32OLE.new("MCI.MMcontrol")
```

```
wav = "c:\\windows\\media\\tada.wav"
sound.fileName = wav

sound.autoEnable = true

sound.command = "Open"
sound.command = "Play"

sleep 7
```

Listing 14.2 uses Internet Explorer to generate a text input box.

Listing 14.2   Browser Text Input Box

```
require "win32ole"

def ieInputBox( msg, default )
  ie = WIN32OLE.new("InternetExplorer.Application");
  ie.visible = false
  ie.navigate "about:blank"
  sleep 0.01 while (ie.busy)

  script = ie.Document.Script;
  result = script.prompt(msg,default);
  ie.quit

  result
end


# Main...

result = ieInputBox( "Please enter your name",
                     "Dave Bowman")

if result
  puts result
else
  puts "User pressed Cancel"
end
```

In Listing 14.3, we open a small IE window and write HTML to it.

Listing 14.3   Writing to a Browser Window Requires "win32ole"

```
html = <<EOF
<html>
<body>
<h3>And now for something</h3>
<h2>completely</h2>
<h1>different...</h1>
</body>
</html>
EOF

ie = WIN32OLE.new("InternetExplorer.Application");

ie.left      = 150
ie.top       = 150
ie.height    = 200
ie.width     = 300
ie.menubar   = 0
ie.toolbar   = 0
ie.navigate "about:blank"
ie.visible=TRUE;

ie.document.open
ie.document.write html
ie.document.close
sleep 5
ie.quit
```

In the following example we open a file dialog box and allow the user to select a file from a list:

```
require "win32ole"

cd = WIN32OLE.new("MSComDlg.CommonDialog")

# Set file filter
cd.filter = "All Files(*.*)|*.*" +
            "|Ruby Files(*.rb)|*.rb"
cd.filterIndex = 2

cd.maxFileSize = 128     # Set MaxFileSize

cd.showOpen()

file = cd.fileName       # Retrieve file, path
```

```
if not file or file==""
   puts "No filename entered."
else
   puts "The user selected: #{file}\n"
end
```

And finally, the following fragment will discover the IP address of the local machine:

```
require "win32ole"

ws = WIN32OLE.new "MSWinsock.Winsock"

# Retrieve LocalIP property
ipAddress = ws.localIP

puts "The local IP is : #{ipAddress}"
```

As you can see, the possibilities are limitless. Have fun, and don't forget to share your code with others.

14.5.3   Using `ActiveScriptRuby`

You have probably used Internet Explorer at some point to view a web page that contained embedded JavaScript or VBScript code. (We'll ignore the differences between JScript and JavaScript here.)

You can do the same thing with `ActiveScriptRuby`, which is like a bridge between COM and Ruby. For example, we can embed Ruby in an HTML page (as seen in Listing 14.4).

Listing 14.4   Ruby Embedded in HTML

```
<html>

<script language="RubyScript">
  # This is Ruby code...
  def helloMethod
    @window.alert "Running Ruby Inside!"
  end
</script>

<body>
```

```
Here is an input button...
<input id=Hello type=button onclick="helloMethod"
       language="RubyScript">

</body>
</html>
```

Using this technique of embedding Ruby, we can call Ruby code from any native Windows application that supports the IActiveScript interface, such as Internet Explorer or WScript (the WSH executable). You can visit arton's site (http://www.geocities.co.jp/SiliconValley-PaolAlto/9251/rubymain.html) for more information.

14.6   The Windows One-Click Installer

For users of Microsoft Windows, one of the greatest advances in Ruby in recent years is the so-called "one-click installer." The primary developer for this project (officially called *Ruby Installer*) is Curt Hibbs. This offers a very Windows-like installation process with a native look and feel.

The installer is good because it works as Windows users would expect it to. It is graphical and follows a step-by-step, well-defined sequence. It is of course a pure binary distribution, making a compiler unnecessary. But these aren't its only attractions.

The distribution that it gives you is more or less "batteries included." It includes not only the Ruby interpreter with all the core classes and all the standard libraries but also a number of extra libraries and applications. Many of these are unique to the win32 platforms.

The installer includes these pieces (some of which are optional):

- The Ruby interpreter itself (the ruby-mswin32 package and the RubySrc package for those who want to examine the C source)

- Two commonly needed applications, RubyGems and rake

- An open-sourced copy of *Programming Ruby*, first edition, by Dave Thomas and Andy Hunt (in Windows Help format)

- The fxruby library (usually more than one version), which is a binding to the FOX GUI toolkit

- The OpenGL and GLUT tools for 3D graphics

- The fxirb and fxri utilities, graphical versions of irb and ri based on the FXRuby toolkit

- FreeRIDE, the Ruby IDE with an integrated editor, source browser, and debugger (always a work in progress)

- SciTE, the Scintilla-based text editor

- SWin and VRuby, for handling Windows messaging and GUI development (both parts of the VisualuRuby project of Yasuhira Nishikawa)

- Two XML parsers (XMLParser and Expat), along with HTMLParser

- Database-related libraries, RubyDBI and DBD/ODBC

- Miscellaneous other libraries and tools, such as log4r, zlib, OpenSSL, Iconv, readline, and more

Versions of the installer for other platforms are planned but not yet usable.

14.7   Libraries You Need to Know About

If you're a Ruby programmer on Windows, the first package you absolutely need is by Daniel Berger, one of the foremost Ruby developers on those platforms. The win32-utils library is really a whole suite of small libraries. We can't look in detail at all these, but we list them all here:

- win32-changenotify—For monitoring events related to files and directories

- win32-clipboard—For interacting with the Windows Clipboard

- win32-etc—Provides UNIX-like Etc functions for the Windows platform (such as getpwnam and getpwuid)

- win32-event—Interface to Windows Event objects

- win32-eventlog—Interface to the Windows Event Log

- win32-ipc—A base class for Windows synchronization objects (used by win32-event and others)

- `win32-mmap`—Interface to the Windows Memory Mapped File

- `win32-open3`—An open3 library for Windows (run a command and return three file handles)

- `win32-pipe`—Named pipes on Windows

- `win32-process`—UNIX-like fork, wait and kill for Windows

- `win32-sapi`—Interface to the Microsoft Speech API

- `win32-service`—Interface for Windows Services

- `win32-shortcut`—Interface for creating and modifying Windows shortcuts

- `win32-sound`—Interface for playing with sound on Windows systems

Some other libraries that are "nice to have" are as follows:

- `Win32::Console` is a full port of Perl's Win32::Console and Win32::Console:: ANSI libraries. It allows working with Windows consoles much more easily (changing colors, positioning cursor, querying info, and emulating ANSI control characters).

- `ActiveDirectory` enables effortless interaction with Active Directory instances running on Microsoft Windows servers and networks.

- `ruby-inifile` helps you maipulate .ini files (reading, parsing, writing and updating them).

Many other libraries are available online that may fit your individual needs. Search http://raa-ruby-lang.org and http://rubyforge.org to find these.

14.8 Working with Files, Directories, and Trees

A broad area of everyday scripting is to work with files and directories, including entire subtrees of files. Much of the relevant material has already been covered in Chapter 4, "Internationalization in Ruby," but we will hit a few high points here.

Because I/O is a fairly system-dependent thing, many tricks will vary from one operating system to another. If you are in doubt, you should resort to experimentation.

14.8.1   A Few Words on Text Filters

Many tools that we use every day (both vendor-supplied and home-grown) are simply *text filters*; that is, they accept textual input, process or transform it in some way, and output it again. Classic examples of text filters in the UNIX world are `sed` and `tr`, among others.

Sometimes a file is small enough to be read into memory. This allows processing that might otherwise be difficult.

```
file = File.open(filename)
lines = file.readlines
# Manipulate as needed...
lines.each { |x| puts x }
```

Sometimes we'll need to process it a line at a time.

```
IO.foreach(filename) do |line|
  # Manipulate as needed...
  puts line
end
```

Finally, don't forget that any filenames on the command line are automatically gathered into `ARGF`, representing a concatenation of all input. (See section 14.2.2, "Working with `ARGF`.") In this case, we can use calls such as `ARGF.readlines` just as if `ARGF` were an `IO` object. All output would go to standard output as usual.

14.8.2   Copying a Directory Tree (with symlinks)

Suppose that you want to copy an entire directory structure to a new location. There are various ways of doing this operation, but if the tree has internal symbolic links this becomes more difficult.

Listing 14.5 shows a recursive solution with a little added user-friendliness. It is smart enough to check the most basic error conditions and also print a usage message.

Listing 14.5   Copying a Directory Tree

```
require "fileutils"

def recurse(src, dst)
  Dir.mkdir(dst)
  Dir.foreach(src) do |e|
    # Don't bother with . and ..
```

```
    next if [".",".."].include? e
    fullname = src + "/" + e
    newname = fullname.sub(Regexp.new(Regexp.escape(src)),dst)
    if FileTest::directory?(fullname)
      recurse(fullname,newname)
    elsif FileTest::symlink?(fullname)
      linkname = `ls -l #{fullname}`.sub(/.* -> /,"").chomp
      newlink = linkname.dup
      n = newlink.index($oldname)
      next if n == nil
      n2 = n + $oldname.length - 1
      newlink[n..n2] = $newname
      newlink.sub!(/\/\//,"/")
      # newlink = linkname.sub(Regexp.new(Regexp.escape(src)),dst)
        File.symlink(newlink, newname)
    elsif FileTest::file?(fullname)
      FileUtils.copy(fullname, newname)
    else
      puts "??? :  #{fullname}"
    end
  end
end


# "Main"

if ARGV.size != 2
  puts "Usage: copytree oldname newname"
  exit
end

oldname = ARGV[0]
newname = ARGV[1]

if ! FileTest::directory?(oldname)
  puts "Error: First parameter must be an existing directory."
  exit
end

if FileTest::exist?(newname)
  puts "Error: #{newname} already exists."
  exit
end

oldname = File.expand_path(oldname)
newname = File.expand_path(newname)

$oldname=oldname
$newname=newname

recurse(oldname, newname)
```

Probably there are UNIX variants in which there is a cp -R option that will preserve symlinks, but not any that we're using. Listing 14.5 was actually written to address that need in a real-life situation.

14.8.3   Deleting Files by Age or Other Criteria

Imagine that you want to scan through a directory and delete the oldest files. This directory might be some kind of repository for temporary files, log files, browser cache files, or similar data.

Here we present a little code fragment that will remove all the files older than a certain time stamp (passed in as a Time object):

```ruby
def delete_older(dir, time)
  Dir.chdir(dir) do
    Dir.foreach(".") do |entry|
      # We're not handling directories here
      next if File.stat(entry).directory?
      # Use the modification time
      if File.mtime(entry) < time
        File.unlink(entry)
      end
    end
  end
end

delete_older("/tmp",Time.local(2001,3,29,18,38,0))
```

This is nice, but let's generalize it. Let's make a similar method called delete_if that takes a block that will evaluate to true or false. Let's then delete the file only if it fits the given criteria.

```ruby
def delete_if(dir)
  Dir.chdir(dir) do
    Dir.foreach(".") do |entry|
      # We're not handling directories here
      next if File.stat(entry).directory?
      if yield entry
        File.unlink(entry)
      end
    end
  end
end
```

```ruby
# Delete all files over 3000 bytes
delete_if("/tmp") { |f| File.size(f) > 3000 }

# Delete all LOG and BAK files
delete_if("/tmp") { |f| f =~ /(log|bak)$/i }
```

14.8.4 Determining Free Space on a Disk

Suppose that you want to know how many bytes are free on a certain device. The following code example is a crude way of doing this, by running a system utility:

```ruby
def freespace(device=".")
  lines = %x(df -k #{device}).split("\n")
  n = lines.last.split[1].to_i * 1024
end


puts freespace("/tmp")     # 16772204544
```

A better way of doing this would be to wrap statfs in a Ruby extension. This has been done in the past, but the project seems to be a dead one.

On Windows, there is a somewhat more elegant solution (supplied by Daniel Berger):

```ruby
require 'Win32API'

GetDiskFreeSpaceEx = Win32API.new('kernel32', 'GetDiskFreeSpaceEx',
                                   'PPPP', 'I')

def freespace(dir=".")
  total_bytes = [0].pack('Q')
  total_free  = [0].pack('Q')
  GetDiskFreeSpaceEx.call(dir, 0, total_bytes, total_free)

  total_bytes = total_bytes.unpack('Q').first
  total_free  = total_free.unpack('Q').first
end

puts freespace("C:")       # 5340389376
```

This code fragment should work on all variants of Windows.

14.9   Miscellaneous Scripting Tasks

There are a few tidbits left over. These are uncreatively classified as "miscellaneous."

14.9.1   Single-File Ruby Solutions

There are occasions where you may want a quick or temporary Ruby installation. You might even want to distribute Ruby along with your program as a single executable.

We've already looked at Ruby Installer, the "one-click installer" for Windows platforms. There are plans (immature at the time of this writing) to make Linux and Mac OSX versions of the installer.

Erik Veenstra has also made significant progress in packaging Ruby itself as well as Ruby applications. He is the author of AllInOneRuby, Tar2RubyScript, and RubyScript2Exe (all of which can be found on his site at http://www.erikveen.dds.nl).

AllInOneRuby is a single-file Ruby installation. It packages all of the Ruby interpreter, core, and standard libraries in a single archive that is easy to move or copy—it can be stored on a USB drive, for example, so that you can carry an entire Ruby installation in your pocket and "install" it on a new machine in a fraction of a second. It runs on Windows or Linux and has experimental support for Mac OSX.

Tar2RubyScript is exactly what the name implies. It takes a directory structure containing your application and creates a self-extracting program (consisting of a Ruby program with a tar archive appended). This is similar to Java's concept of a JAR file. The script to be run should be named `init.rb`; if the stored item is a library rather than a standalone application, this file can be omitted.

RubyScript2Exe is perhaps slightly misnamed. It does indeed transform an entire Ruby application into a single binary file, but it is cross-platform, running on Windows, Linux, or Mac OSX. You can think of it as a "compiler," but of course it isn't a real one. It collects files from your Ruby installation to produce the package, so there is no need (or possibility) of cross-compiling. Be aware that the executable you get is "stripped" in the sense that any unneeded Ruby libaries are left out.

If you use Tar2RubyScript, the archive created is runnable on any system that has Ruby (and the application's dependencies) installed. RubyScript2Exe doesn't have this limitation because it includes (along with your application) the entire Ruby interpreter and runtime environment and all dependencies. You can use these two tools together or separately.

14.9.2 Piping into the Ruby Interpreter

Because the Ruby interpreter is a single-pass translator, it is possible to pipe code into it and have it executed. One conceivable purpose for this is to use Ruby for more complex tasks when you are required by circumstance to work in a traditional scripting language such as bash.

Listing 14.6, for example, is a bash script that uses Ruby (via a here-document) to calculate the elapsed time in seconds between two dates. The Ruby program prints a single value to standard output, which is then captured by the ksh script.

Listing 14.6 bash Script Invoking Ruby

```
#!/usr/bin/bash

# Let bash find the difference in seconds
# between two dates using Ruby...

export time1="2007-04-02 15:56:12"
export time2="2007-12-08 12:03:19"

cat <<EOF | ruby | read elapsed
require "parsedate"

time1 = ENV["time1"]
time2 = ENV["time2"]

args1 = ParseDate.parsedate(time1)
args2 = ParseDate.parsedate(time2)

args1 = args1[0..5]
args2 = args2[0..5]

t1 = Time.local(*args1)
t2 = Time.local(*args2)

diff = t2 - t1
puts diff
EOF

echo "Elapsed seconds = " $elapsed
```

Note that the two input values in this case are passed as environment variables (which must be exported). The two lines that retrieve these values could also be coded in this way:

```
time1="$time1"  # Embed the shell variable directly
time2="$time2"  #   into a string...
```

However, the difficulties are obvious. It could get very confusing whether a certain string represents a ksh variable or a Ruby global variable, and there could be a host of problems with quoting and escaping.

It's also possible to use a Ruby "one-liner" with the -e option. Here's a little script that reverses a string using Ruby:

```
#!/usr/bin/bash

string="Francis Bacon"

ruby -e "puts '$string'.reverse" | read reversed

#  $reversed now has value "nocaB sicnarF"
```

UNIX geeks will note that awk has been used in a similar way since time immemorial.

14.9.3 Getting and Setting Exit Codes

The exit method will raise a SystemExit exception and ultimately return the specified exit code to the operating system (or to the calling entity). This is a Kernel method. There is also a method exit! that differs in two ways: It doesn't run the exit handlers before quitting, and the default return value is -1.

```
# ...
if (all_OK)
  exit      # Normally (0)
else
  exit!     # In a hurry (-1)
end
```

When a Ruby return code is retrieved by the operating system (for example, by doing echo $?), it is seen as the same integer specified in the code. When a subprocess exits and we use `wait2` (or `waitpid2`) to examine the return code, we will find it left-shifted by eight bits. This is a POSIX quirk that Ruby has inherited.

```ruby
child = fork { sleep 1; exit 3 }

pid, code = Process.wait2        # [12554,768]
status = code << 8              # 3
```

14.9.4 Testing Whether a Program Is Running Interactively

A good way to determine whether a program is interactive is to test its standard input. The method `isatty?` (historically, "is a teletype") will tell us whether the device is an interactive one as opposed to a disk file or socket. (This is not available on Windows.)

```ruby
if STDIN.isatty?
  puts "Hi! I see you're typing at"
  puts "the keyboard."
else
  puts "Input is not from a keyboard."
End
```

14.9.5 Determining the Current Platform or Operating System

If a program wants to know what operating system it's running on, it can access the global constant `RUBY_PLATFORM`. This will return a cryptic string (usually something like `i386-cygwin` or `sparc-solaris2.7`), telling the platform on which the Ruby interpreter was built.

Because we primarily use UNIX variants (Solaris, AIX, Linux) and Windows variants (98, NT, 2000, XP), we've found the following crude piece of code to be useful. It will distinguish between the UNIX family and the Windows family of operating systems (unceremoniously lumping all others into "other").

```ruby
def os_family
  case RUBY_PLATFORM
    when /ix/i, /ux/i, /gnu/i,
         /sysv/i, /solaris/i,
         /sunos/i, /bsd/i
```

```
        "unix"
    when /win/i, /ming/i
        "windows"
    else
        "other"
    end
end
```

This little set of regular expressions will correctly classify the vast majority of platforms. Of course, this is only a clumsy way of determining how to handle OS dependencies. Even if you correctly determine the OS family, that might not always imply the availability (or absence) of any specific feature.

14.9.6   Using the Etc Module

The Etc module retrieves useful information from the /etc/passwd and /etc/group files. Obviously this is only useful in a UNIX environment.

The getlogin method will return the login name of the user. If it fails, getpwuid might work (taking an optional parameter, which is the uid).

```
myself = getlogin              # hal9000
myname = getpwuid(2001).name   # hal9000

# Without a parameter, getpwuid calls
# getuid internally...
me2 = getpwuid.name            # hal9000
```

The getpwnam method returns a passwd struct, which contains relevant entries such as name, dir (home directory), shell (login shell), and others.

```
rootshell = getpwnam("root").shell   # /sbin/sh
```

At the group level, getgrgid or getgrnam behave similarly. They will return a group struct consisting of group name, group passwd, and so on.

The iterator passwd will iterate over all entries in the /etc/passwd file. Each entry passed into the block is a passwd struct.

```
all_users = []
passwd { |entry| all_users << entry.name }
```

There is an analogous iterator group for group entries.

14.10   Conclusion

That ends our discussion of Ruby scripting for everyday automation tasks. We've seen how to get information in and out of a program by way of environment variables and standard I/O. We've seen how to perform many common "glue" operations to get other pieces of software to talk to each other. We've also looked at how to interact with the operating system at various levels.

Because much of this material is operating-system dependent, I urge you to experiment on your own. There are differences between Windows and UNIX, and there are even differences in behavior within those families.

Our next topic is a similarly broad one. We'll look at using Ruby to process various kinds of data formats, from image files to XML.

CHAPTER 15

Ruby and Data Formats

"Your information, sir," the Librarian says.
"Are you smart enough to tie that information into YOU ARE HERE?"
Hiro says.
"I'll see what I can do, sir. The formats appear to be reconcilable."

—Snow Crash *by Neal Stephenson*

This is something of a "catch-all" chapter. Much of this material *could* have been placed elsewhere. The material is not all of equal importance or difficulty, but it is all important and needs to be covered somewhere.

It is a fact of life in computing that when information becomes complex enough, it always evolves its own "minilanguage" in which that information is best expressed. More often, it evolves *multiple* such minilanguages. We call these *file formats* or *data formats*.

Any of us could name hundreds of examples of file formats. There are image formats such as JPG, GIF, and PNG; document formats such as RTF and PDF; "universal" formats such as comma-separated, XML, or YAML; and countless thousands of proprietary data formats, many of which are variations on the fixed-column data storage so common in ancient times (meaning the 1960s).

One of the simplest, most common of data formats is plain text. Even if a file is simple text, however, it may have a structure imposed on it (hence the current popularity of XML). Other formats may be pure binary or some mixture of text and binary. So there are potentially "hierarchies" of formats just as the ISO networking model viewed information differently at different levels of networking.

No matter what format data is stored in, sooner or later we want to read it, parse it, and write it again. This chapter covers a few common file formats; there is no way to cover all of the common ones in a single book, however. If you want to parse such formats as vCard, iCal, or hundreds of others, you will have to do a search for the appropriate libraries (or you may have to write your own).

15.1 Parsing XML with REXML

XML (which "looks like" HTML or SGML) has been popular since the 1990s. It does, in fact, have some good qualities that make it preferable to fixed-column data storage. For example, the fields are given specific names, the overall design makes a hierarchical structure possible, and most of all, it allows variable length data.

Four decades ago, of course, memory constraints would have rendered XML largely impractical. But imagine it had been introduced then. The infamous "Y2K" problem gained much press in 1999 (though it turned out to be more of a nuisance than a problem), but with XML, it would not have shown up on anyone's radar. There was a Y2K issue solely because most of our legacy data was stored and manipulated in a fixed-length format. So, for all its shortcomings, XML has its uses. In Ruby, the most common way to manipulate XML is with the REXML library by Sean Russell. Since 2002, REXML (usually pronounced as three syllables, "rex-m-l") has been part of the standard Ruby distribution.

I should point out here that REXML is relatively slow. Whether it is fast enough for your application, only you can say. You may find, however, that as you scale up, you need to use the libxml2 binding (not covered in this book). This binding is of course very fast (being written in C) but is arguably not quite as Ruby-like.

REXML is a pure-Ruby XML processor conforming to the XML 1.0 standard. It is a *nonvalidating* processor, passing all of the OASIS nonvalidating conformance tests.

REXML has multiple APIs. This, of course, is intended for flexibility not confusion. The two classic APIs may be classified as *DOM-like* and *SAX-like* (or tree-based and stream-based). The first of these is a technique wherein the entire file is read into memory and stored in a hierarchical (tree-based) form. Let's look at these before mentioning the other APIs. The second is a "parse as you go" technique, useful when your documents are large or you have memory limitations; it parses the file as it reads it from disk, and the entire file is never stored in memory.

For all our XML code examples, let's use the same simple XML file (shown in Listing 15.1). It represents part of a private library of books.

Listing 15.1   The books.xml File

```
<library shelf="Recent Acquisitions">
  <section name="Ruby">
    <book isbn="0672328844">
      <title>The Ruby Way</title>
      <author>Hal Fulton</author>
      <description>Second edition. The book you are now reading.
                   Ain't recursion grand?
      </description>
  </section>
  <section name="Space">
    <book isbn="0684835509">
      <title>The Case for Mars</title>
      <author>Robert Zubrin</author>
      <description>Pushing toward a second home for the human
                  race.
      </description>
    </book>
    <book isbn="074325631X">
      <title>First Man: The Life of Neil A. Armstrong</title>
      <author>James R. Hansen</author>
      <description>Definitive biography of the first man on
                  the moon.
      </description>
    </book>
  </section>
</library>
```

15.1.1   Tree Parsing

Let's first parse our XML data in tree fashion. We begin by requiring the `rexml/document` library; often we do an `include REXML` to import into the top-level namespace for convenience. Listing 15.2 illustrates a few simple techniques.

Listing 15.2 DOM-like Parsing

```
require 'rexml/document'
include REXML

input = File.new("books.xml")
doc = Document.new(input)

root = doc.root
puts root.attributes["shelf"]        # Recent Acquisitions

doc.elements.each("library/section") { |e| puts e.attributes["name"] }
# Output:
#    Ruby
#    Space

doc.elements.each("*/section/book") { |e| puts e.attributes["isbn"] }
# Output:
#    0672328844
#    0321445619
#    0684835509
#    074325631X

sec2 = root.elements[2]
author = sec2.elements[1].elements["author"].text     # Robert Zubrin
```

Notice in Listing 15.2 how attributes are represented as a hash. Elements can be accessed via a pathlike notation or by an integer. If you index by integer, remember that XML (by specification) is 1-based, not 0-based as Ruby is.

15.1.2   Stream Parsing

Suppose that we want to process this same data file in a stream-oriented way. (We probably wouldn't do that in reality because this file is small.) There are variations on this concept, but Listing 15.3 shows one way. The trick is to define a *listener* class whose methods will be the target of callbacks from the parser.

Listing 15.3 SAX-like Parsing

```
require 'rexml/document'
require 'rexml/streamlistener'
include REXML

class MyListener
  include REXML::StreamListener
```

```
  def tag_start(*args)
    puts "tag_start: #{args.map {|x| x.inspect}.join(', ')}"
  end

  def text(data)
    return if data =~ /^\w*$/      # whitespace only
    abbrev = data[0..40] + (data.length > 40 ? "..." : "")
    puts "  text    :   #{abbrev.inspect}"
  end
end

list = MyListener.new
source = File.new "books.xml"
Document.parse_stream(source, list)
```

The module StreamListener assists in this; basically it provides stubbed or empty callback methods. Any methods you define will override these. When the parser encounters an opening tag, it calls the tag_open method. You can think of this as behaving something like method_missing, with the tag name passed in as a parameter (and all the attributes in a hash). The text method acts similarly; for others, refer to detailed documentation at http://ruby-doc.org or elsewhere.

In Listing 15.3, which is somewhat contrived, every tag is logged when it is opened, and the enclosed text is logged in the same way. (For simplicity, the text is abbreviated.) The output looks like Listing 15.4.

Listing 15.4 Output from Stream Parsing Example

```
tag_start: "library", {"shelf"=>"Recent Acquisitions"}
tag_start: "section", {"name"=>"Ruby"}
tag_start: "book", {"isbn"=>"0672328844"}
tag_start: "title", {}
  text    :   "The Ruby Way"
tag_start: "author", {}
  text    :   "Hal Fulton"
tag_start: "description", {}
  text    :   "Second edition. The book you are now read..."
tag_start: "section", {"name"=>"Space"}
tag_start: "book", {"isbn"=>"0684835509"}
tag_start: "title", {}
  text    :   "The Case for Mars"
tag_start: "author", {}
  text    :   "Robert Zubrin"
tag_start: "description", {}
  text    :   "Pushing toward a second home for the huma..."
```

Continues

```
tag_start: "book", {"isbn"=>"074325631X"}
tag_start: "title", {}
   text    :    "First Man: The Life of Neil A. Armstrong"
tag_start: "author", {}
   text    :    "James R. Hansen"
tag_start: "description", {}
   text    :    "Definitive biography of the first man on ..."
```

15.1.3   XPath and More

An alternative way to view XML is *XPath*. This is a kind of pseudo-language that describes how to locate specific elements and attributes in an XML document, treating that document as a logical ordered tree.

REXML has XPath support via the XPath class. It assumes tree-based parsing (document object model) as we saw in Listing 15.2. Refer to the following code:

```
# (setup omitted)
book1 = XPath.first(doc, "//book")      # Info for first book found
p book1

# Print out all titles
XPath.each(doc, "//title") { |e| puts e.text }

# Get an array of all of the "author" elements in the document.
names = XPath.match(doc, "//author").map {|x| x.text }
p names
```

The output from the preceding code looks like this:

```
<book isbn='0672328844'> ... </>
The Ruby Way
The Case for Mars
First Man: The Life of Neil A. Armstrong
["Hal Fulton", "Robert Zubrin", "James R. Hansen"]
```

REXML also has an enhanced SAX2 style API (a superset with some Ruby-like additions of its own) and an experimental pull-parser. These are not covered in this book; refer to http://ruby-doc.org or any comparable resource.

15.2   Working with RSS and Atom

Time-sensitive content on the Internet is spread through what we call *web feeds* or *syndication feeds* or simply *feeds*. These are usually in a format that is some dialect of XML.

Probably the most common of these formats is *RSS*. This is an abbreviation for *Rich Site Summary* (or *RDF Site Summary*, according to some, where RDF itself means *Resource Description Format*).

So many things on the Web are temporary or transient. Blog entries, zine articles, and many more things are recognized as being short-term in nature. A web feed is a natural way to distribute or syndicate such things.

The *Atom* format is another popular format that many people say is superior. The trend now is not to think in terms of "an RSS feed" or "an Atom feed"—let everything be simply "a feed."

Let's look briefly at processing both RSS and Atom. The former can be done with a Ruby standard library, but the latter requires another library not included with Ruby.

15.2.1   The rss Standard Library

RSS is XML-based, so you *could* simply parse it as XML. However, the fact that it is slightly higher-level makes it appropriate to have a dedicated parser for the format. Furthermore, the messiness of the RSS standard is legendary, and it is not unusual at all for broken software to produce RSS that a parser may have great difficulty parsing.

This inconvenience is even more true across incompatible versions of the standard; the common ones are 0.9, 1.0, and 2.0. The RSS versions, like the manufacturing of hotdogs, are something whose details you don't want to know unless you must.

Ruby has a standard RSS library that handles versions 0.9, 1.0, and 2.0 of the standard. The different versions, in fact, are handled seamlessly wherever possible; the library will detect the version of the input document if you don't specify it.

Let's look at an example. Here we take the feed from http://marsdrive.com and print the titles of the first few items in the feed:

```
require 'rss'
require 'open-uri'

URL = "http://www.marstoday.com/rss/mars.xml"
```

```
open(URL) do |h|
  resp = h.read
  result = RSS::Parser.parse(resp,false)
  puts "Channel: #{result.channel.title}"
  result.items.each_with_index do |item,i|
    i += 1
    puts "#{i}  #{item.title}"
  end
end
```

Before going any further, let me talk about courtesy to feed providers. A program like the preceding one should be run with caution because it uses the provider's bandwidth. In any real application, such as an actual feed aggregator, caching should always be done. But that is beyond the scope of these simple examples.

In the preceding code, we are using the open-uri library for convenience. This is explained in greater detail in Chapter 18, "Network Programming"; for now, just be aware that it enables us to use the open method on a URI much as if it were a simple file.

Note how the RSS parser retrieves the *channel* for the RSS feed; our code then prints the title associated with that channel. There is also a list of items (retrieved by the items accessor), which can be thought of as a list of articles. Our code retrieves the entire list and prints the title of each one.

Of course, the output from this is highly time-sensitive; at the time I ran it, this was the partial output:

```
Title: Mars Today Top Stories
1  NASA Mars Picture of the Day: Lava Levees
2  NASA Mars Global Surveyor TES Dust And Temperature Maps 25 June -
2 July 2006
3  Mars Institute Core Team Arrives at the HMP Research Station on
Devon Island
4  Assessment of NASA's Mars Architecture 2007-2016
5  NASA Mars Picture of the Day: Rush Hour
```

It's also possible to generate RSS (see Listing 15.5). This procedure is basically the reverse of the process in the previous code fragment.

Listing 15.5 Creating an RSS Feed

```
require 'rss'

feed = RSS::Rss.new("2.0")

chan = RSS::Rss::Channel.new
chan.description = "Feed Your Head"
chan.link = "http://nosuchplace.org/home/"

img = RSS::Rss::Channel::Image.new
img.url = "http://nosuchplace.org/images/headshot.jpg"
img.title = "Y.T."
img.link = chan.link

chan.image = img
feed.channel = chan

i1 = RSS::Rss::Channel::Item.new
i1.title = "Once again, here we are"
i1.link = "http://nosuchplace.org/articles/once_again/"
i1.description = "Don't you feel more like you do now than usual?"

i2 = RSS::Rss::Channel::Item.new
i2.title = "So long, and thanks for all the fiche"
i2.link = "http://nosuchplace.org/articles/so_long_and_thanks/"
i2.description = "I really miss the days of microfilm..."

i3 = RSS::Rss::Channel::Item.new
i3.title = "One hand clapping"
i3.link = "http://nosuchplace.org/articles/one_hand_clapping/"
i3.description = "Yesterday I went to an amputee convention..."

feed.channel.items << i1 << i2 << i3

puts feed
```

Most of the code in Listing 15.5 is intuitive. We create an empty RSS 2.0 feed (along with an empty channel and an empty image) and add data to these objects by means of accessors. The image is assigned to the channel, and the channel is assigned to the feed.

Finally we create a series of items and assign these to the feed. It is worth mentioning that the series of appends onto `feed.channel.items` is actually necessary. It's tempting to try the simple approach:

```
feed.channel.items = [i1,i2,i3]
```

However, this doesn't work; the `Channel` class, for whatever reason, does not have an `items=` accessor. We *could* say `items[0] = i1` and so on, which would work well in a loop, the way we would do it in real life. There might be still other ways to accomplish this, but the technique used here works fine.

The `rss` library has many other features, most of which are not yet well documented. If you can't find the features you're looking for, a last resort is to scan the source code to see how it works.

Many people prefer Atom to RSS. The `rss` library doesn't handle Atom, but the excellent (nonstandard) library `feedtools` does. We'll look at it in the upcoming section.

15.2.2 The `feedtools` Library

The `feedtools` library (available as a gem) is the work of Bob Aman. It works with RSS and Atom in a more or less seamless way, storing all feeds in a common internal format (based primarily on Atom). It also has its own URI-handling code, so you don't have to use `net/http` or `open-uri` explicitly.

Here is a simple example corresponding to the first example in the previous section:

```
require 'feed_tools'

URL = "http://www.marstoday.com/rss/mars.xml"
feed = FeedTools::Feed.open(URL)
puts "Description: #{feed.title}\n"

feed.entries.each_with_index {|x,i| puts "#{i+1}  #{x.title}" }
```

This is arguably a little more concise and clear than the other example. Some things might be less than clear; for example, there is no explicit `channel` method for a feed object. However, you can call methods such as title and description directly on the feed object because a feed is a single channel.

Here's an example that retrieves an Atom feed instead:

```
require 'feedtools'

URL = "http://www.atomenabled.org/atom.xml"
feed = FeedTools::Feed.open(URL)
puts "Description: #{feed.title}\n"

feed.entries.each_with_index {|x,i| puts "#{i+1}  #{x.title}" }
```

Notice how the only line that changed is the URL itself! This is a good thing, in case you were wondering; it means that we can process feeds more or less independently of the format in which they are stored. The output, of course, looks similar to what we saw previously:

```
Description: AtomEnabled.org
1  AtomEnabled's Atom Feed
2  Introduction to Atom
3  Moving from Atom 0.3 to 1.0
4  Atom 1.0 is Almost Final
5  Socialtext Supports Atom
```

Once again, let me stress that you shouldn't waste any feed provider's bandwidth. If you are doing a real application, it should handle caching appropriately; and if you are only doing testing, it's best to use a feed of your own. The feedtools library supports fairly sophisticated database-driven caching which should be adequate in most cases.

Now let's take the previous example and add two lines to it:

```
str = feed.build_xml("rss",2.0)
puts str
```

What we've done here is "translate" the Atom feed to an RSS 2.0 feed. The same could be done for RSS 0.9 or RSS 1.0, of course; in fact, conversion can go the other direction also: We can read an RSS feed and produce an Atom feed. This is one of the strengths of this library.

At the time of this writing, `feedtools` was only at version 0.2.25; it will likely continue to change its API and feature set.

15.3 Manipulating Image Data with RMagick

In the last fifteen years, we have been bombarded with more and more graphical information. Computers have now surpassed television sets as the primary supplier of "eye candy" in all its forms. This means that programmers need ways of manipulating all kinds of image data in multiple conflicting formats. In Ruby, the best way to do this is with RMagick, a library created by Tim Hunter.

RMagick is a Ruby binding for the ImageMagick library (or its branch, GraphicsMagick). RMagick is installable as a gem, but to use RMagick, you must have one of these libraries (IM or GM) installed first. If you are on Linux, you probably already have one or the other; if not, you can go to http://imagemagick.org (or http://graphicsmagick.org).

RMagick is just a binding, of course; asking what image formats it supports is the same as asking what image formats are supported by the underlying library. Those, by the way, are all the common ones such as JPG, GIF, PNG, and TIFF, but also dozens of others.

The same is true for the operations RMagick can do. It is essentially limited only by the capabilities of the library it uses; the full API is implemented in RMagick. The API, by the way, is not only rich and complete but overall is a good example of a "Ruby-like" API; it uses symbols, blocks, and method prefixes in a normal way, and most Ruby programmers will find it has an intuitive feel.

The API is really huge, by the way. This chapter would not be enough to cover it in detail, nor would this book. The upcoming sections will give you a good background in RMagick, however, and you can find out anything else you may need from the project website (http://rmagick.rubyforge.org).

15.3.1 Common Graphics Tasks

One of the easiest and most common tasks you might want to perform on an image file is simply to determine its characteristics (width and height in pixels, and so on). Let's look at retrieving a few of these pieces of metadata.

Figure 15.1 shows a pair of simple images that we'll use for this code example (and later examples in the next section). The first one (smallpic.jpg) is a simple abstract picture created with a drawing program; it features a few different shades of gray, a few straight lines, and a few curves. The second is a photograph I took in 2002 of a battered automobile in rural Mexico. Both images were converted to grayscale for printing purposes. Listing 15.6 shows how to read these images and extract a few pieces of information.

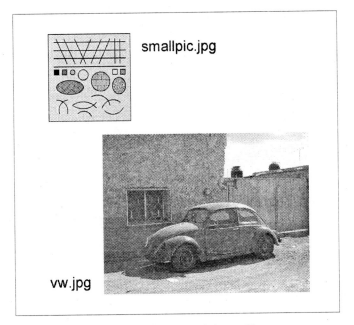

Figure 15.1 Two sample image files.

Listing 15.6 Retrieving Information from an Image

```
require 'RMagick'

def show_info(fname)
  img = Magick::Image::read(fname).first
  fmt = img.format
  w,h = img.columns, img.rows
  dep = img.depth
  nc  = img.number_colors
  nb  = img.filesize
  xr  = img.x_resolution
  yr  = img.y_resolution
  res = Magick::PixelsPerInchResolution ? "inch" : "cm"
```

Continues

```
    puts <<-EOF
    File:       #{fname}
    Format:     #{fmt}
    Dimensions: #{w}x#{h} pixels
    Colors:     #{nc}
    Image size: #{nb} bytes
    Resolution: #{xr}/#{yr} pixels per #{res}
    EOF
    puts
  end

show_info("smallpic.jpg")
show_info("vw.jpg")
```

Here is the output of the Listing 15.6 code:

```
File:       smallpic.jpg
Format:     JPEG
Dimensions: 257x264 pixels
Colors:     248
Image size: 19116 bytes
Resolution: 72.0/72.0 pixels per inch

File:       vw.jpg
Format:     JPEG
Dimensions: 640x480 pixels
Colors:     256
Image size: 55892 bytes
Resolution: 72.0/72.0 pixels per inch
```

Now let's examine the details of how the code in Listing 15.6 gave us that output. Notice how we retrieve all the contents of a file with `Magick::Image::read`; because a file (such as an animated GIF) can contain more than one image, this operation actually returns an array of images (and we look at the first one by calling `first`). We can also use `Magick::ImageList.new` to read an image file.

The image object has a number of readers such as `format` (the name of the image format), `filesize`, `depth`, and others that are intuitive. It may be less intuitive that the width and height of the object are retrieved by `columns` and `rows`, respectively (because we are supposed to think of an image as a grid of pixels). It may not be intuitive to you that the resolution is actually stored as two numbers, but it is (because apparently it can differ horizontally and vertically).

There are other properties and pieces of metadata you can retrieve from an image. Refer to the online documentation for RMagick for more details.

One common task we often perform is to convert an image from one format to another. The easy way to do this in RMagick is to read an image in any supported format and then write it to another file. The file extension is used to determine the new format. Needless to say, it does a lot of conversion behind the scenes. Here is a simple example:

```
img = Magick::Image.read("smallpic.jpg")
img.write("smallpic.gif")                        # Convert to a GIF
```

Frequently we want to change the size of an image (smaller or larger). The four most common methods for this are thumbnail, resize, sample, and scale. All four of these can take either a floating point number (representing a scaling factor) or a pair of numbers (representing the actual new dimensions in pixels). Other differences are summarized in Listing 15.7 and its comments. Where speed is an issue, I urge you to do your own tests on your own machine with your own data.

Listing 15.7   Four Ways to Resize an Image

```
require 'RMagick'

img = Magick::ImageList.new("vw.jpg")

# Each of these methods can take a single "factor" parameter
# or a width,height pair

# thumbnail is fastest, especially when reducing to a very small size

pic1 = img.thumbnail(0.2)       # Reduce to 20%
pic2 = img.thumbnail(64,48)     # Reduce to 64x48 pixels

# resize is of medium speed. If a 3rd and/or 4th parameter are
# specified, they are the filter and blur, respectively. The
# filter defaults to LanczosFilter and blur to 1.0

pic3 = img.resize(0.40)         # Reduce to 40%
pic4 = img.resize(320,240)      # Reduce to 320x240
pic5 = img.resize(300,200,Magick::LanczosFilter,0.92)

# sample is also of medium speed (and doesn't do color interpolation)

pic6 = img.sample(0.35)         # Reduce to 35%
pic7 = img.sample(320,240)      # Reduce to 320x240

# scale is slowest in my tests

pic8 = img.scale(0.60)          # Reduce to 60%
pic9 = img.scale(400,300)       # Reduce to 400x300
```

Many other transformations can be performed on an image. Some of these are simple and easy to understand, whereas others are complex. We'll explore a few interesting transformations and special effects in the next section.

15.3.2   Special Effects and Transformations

Some operations we might want to do on an image are to flip it, reverse it, rotate it, distort it, alter its colors, and so on. RMagick provides literally dozens of methods to perform such operations, and many of these are highly "tunable" by their parameters.

Listing 15.8 demonstrates 12 different effects. To make the code a little more concise, the method `example` simply takes a filename, a symbol corresponding to a method, and a new filename; it basically does a read, a method call, and a write. The individual methods (such as `do_rotate`) are simple for the most part; these are where the image passed in gets an actual instance method called (and then the resulting image is the return value).

Listing 15.8   Twelve Special Effects and Transformations

```
require 'RMagick'

def do_flip(img)
  img.flip
end

def do_rotate(img)
  img.rotate(45)
end

def do_implode(img)
  img = img.implode(0.65)
end

def do_resize(img)
  img.resize(120,240)
end

def do_text(img)
  text = Magick::Draw.new
  text.annotate(img, 0, 0, 0, 100, "HELLO") do
    self.gravity = Magick::SouthGravity
    self.pointsize = 72
    self.stroke = 'black'
    self.fill = '#FAFAFA'
    self.font_weight = Magick::BoldWeight
    self.font_stretch = Magick::UltraCondensedStretch
  end
  img
```

```ruby
end

def do_emboss(img)
  img.emboss
end


def do_spread(img)
  img.spread(10)
end

def do_motion(img)
  img.motion_blur(0,30,170)
end

def do_oil(img)
  img.oil_paint(10)
end

def do_charcoal(img)
  img.charcoal
end

def do_vignette(img)
  img.vignette
end

def do_affine(img)
  spin_xform = Magick::AffineMatrix.new(1, Math::PI/6, Math::PI/6, 1, 0, 0)
  img.affine_transform(spin_xform)          # Apply the transform
end

###

def example(old_file, meth, new_file)
  img = Magick::ImageList.new(old_file)
  new_img = send(meth,img)
  new_img.write(new_file)
end

example("smallpic.jpg", :do_flip,     "flipped.jpg")
example("smallpic.jpg", :do_rotate,   "rotated.jpg")
example("smallpic.jpg", :do_resize,   "resized.jpg")
example("smallpic.jpg", :do_implode,  "imploded.jpg")
example("smallpic.jpg", :do_text,     "withtext.jpg")
example("smallpic.jpg", :do_emboss,   "embossed.jpg")

example("vw.jpg", :do_spread,   "vw_spread.jpg")
example("vw.jpg", :do_motion,   "vw_motion.jpg")
example("vw.jpg", :do_oil,      "vw_oil.jpg")
example("vw.jpg", :do_charcoal, "vw_char.jpg")
example("vw.jpg", :do_vignette, "vw_vig.jpg")
example("vw.jpg", :do_affine,   "vw_spin.jpg")
```

The methods used here are flip, rotate, implode, resize, annotate, and others. The results are shown in Figure 15.2 in a montage.

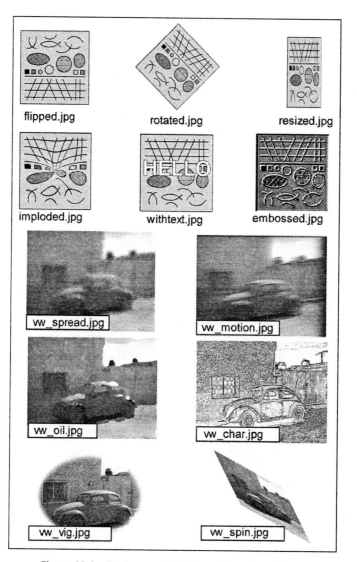

Figure 15.2 Twelve special effects and transformations.

Many other transformations can be performed on an image. Consult the online documentation at http://rmagick.rubyforge.org.

15.3.3   The Drawing API

RMagick has an extensive drawing API for drawing lines, polygons, and curves of various kinds. It deals with filling, opacity, colors, text fonts, rotating/skewing, and other issues.

A full treatment of the API is beyond the scope of this book. Let's look at a simple example, however, to understand a few concepts.

Listing 15.9 shows a program that draws a simple grid on the background and draws a few filled shapes on that grid. The image is converted to grayscale, resulting in the image shown in Figure 15.3.

Listing 15.9   A Simple Drawing

```
require 'RMagick'

img = Magick::ImageList.new
img.new_image(500, 500)

purplish = "#ff55ff"
yuck = "#5fff62"
bleah = "#3333ff"

line = Magick::Draw.new
50.step(450,50) do |n|
  line.line(n,50, n,450)   # vert line
  line.draw(img)
  line.line(50,n, 450,n)   # horiz line
  line.draw(img)
end

# Draw a circle
cir = Magick::Draw.new
cir.fill(purplish)
cir.stroke('black').stroke_width(1)
cir.circle(250,200, 250,310)
cir.draw(img)

rect = Magick::Draw.new
rect.stroke('black').stroke_width(1)
```

Continues

```
rect.fill(yuck)
rect.rectangle(340,380,237,110)
rect.draw(img)

tri = Magick::Draw.new
tri.stroke('black').stroke_width(1)
tri.fill(bleah)
tri.polygon(90,320,160,370,390,120)
tri.draw(img)

img = img.quantize(256,Magick::GRAYColorspace)

img.write("drawing.gif")
```

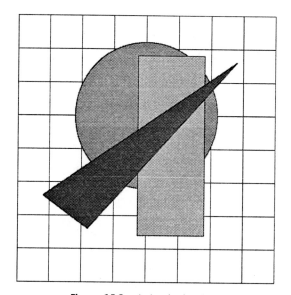

Figure 15.3   A simple drawing.

Let's examine Listing 15.9 in detail. We start by creating an "empty" image with `ImageList.new` and then calling `new_image` on the result. Think of this as giving us a "blank canvas" of the specified size (500 by 500 pixels).

For convenience, let's define a few colors (with creative names such as purplish and yuck). These are strings that specify colors just as we would in HTML. The underlying xMagick library is also capable of understanding many color names such as "red" and "black"; when in doubt, experiment or specify the color in hex.

We then create a drawing object called line; this is the Ruby object corresponding to the graphical object that we will see on the screen. The variable is sometimes named gc or something similar (probably standing for *graphics context*), but a more descriptive name seems natural here.

We then call the method line on our drawing object (which admittedly gets a little confusing). In fact, we call it repeatedly, twice in each iteration of a loop. If you spend a moment studying the coordinates, you'll see that each iteration of the loop draws a horizontal line and a vertical one.

After each line call, we call draw on the same drawing object and pass in the image reference. This is an essential step because it is when the graphical object actually gets added to the canvas.

If you are like me, a call such as shape.draw(image) may be a little confusing. In general, my method calls look like:

```
big_thing.operation(little_thing)
# For example: dog.wag(tail)
```

But this call feels to me more like:

```
little_thing.operation(big_thing)
# Continuing the analogy: tail.wag(dog)
```

But this idiom is actually common, especially in the realm of drawing programs and GUI frameworks. And it makes perfect sense in a classic OOP way: A shape should know how to draw itself, implying it should have a draw method. It needs to know where to draw itself, so it needs the canvas (or whatever) passed in.

But if you're not like me, you were never bothered by the question of which object should be the receiver. That puts you at a tiny advantage.

So after we draw the grid of lines, we then draw a few shapes. The circle method takes the center of the circle and *a point* on the circle as parameters. (Notice we don't draw by specifying the radius!) The rectangle method is even simpler; we draw it by specifying the upper left-hand corner (lower-numbered coordinates) and the lower right-hand corner (higher-numbered coordinates). Finally, we draw a triangle, which is just a special case of a polygon; we specify each point in order, and the final line (from end point to start point) is added automatically.

Each of these graphical objects has a few methods called that we haven't looked at yet. Look at this "chained" call:

```
shape.stroke('black').stroke_width(1)
```

This gives us a "pen" of sorts; it draws in black ink with a width of 1 pixel. The color of the stroke actually does matter in many cases, especially when we are trying to fill a shape with a color.

That of course is the other method we call on our three shapes. We call `fill` to specify what color it should have. (There are other more complex kinds of filling involving hatching, shading, and so on.) The `fill` method replaces the interior color of the shape with the specified color, knowing that the stroke color serves as a boundary between "inside" and "outside" the shape.

Numerous other methods in the drawing API deal with opacity, spatial transformations, and many more things. There are methods that analyze, draw, and manipulate graphical text strings. There is even a special RVG API (Ruby Vector Graphics) that is conformant to the W3C recommendation on SVG (Scalable Vector Graphics).

There is no room here to document these many features. For more information, go to http://rmagick.rubyforge.org as usual.

15.4   Creating PDF Documents with PDF::Writer

PDF::Writer is a library to create PDF documents in Ruby. It can be installed as a RubyGem or downloaded from RubyForge. Basic document creation is pretty simple:

```
require 'rubygems'
require 'pdf/writer'

pdf = PDF::Writer.new
```

15.4.1   Basic Concepts and Techniques

One of the primary issues facing any document designer is that of text fonts (or type-faces). PDF::Writer supports five basic fonts; the first three have bold and italic (or oblique) variants.

- Times-Roman

- Helvetica

- Courier

- ZapfDingbats

- Symbol

If no font is selected, Helvetica will be used by default. When selecting a font, a character substitution table can be created, allowing normally nonprintable characters or code pages to be simulated. There are 315 printable characters in Times-Roman, Helvetica, and Courier (149 have preassigned byte values); 190 printable characters in Symbol (189 have preassigned byte values); and 202 printable (and assigned) characters in ZapfDingbats. The fonts are encoded with an Adobe encoding, but individual characters may be reassigned during font selection.

It is not currently possible to print all 315 characters that are defined in a font file because after a font is selected, a new character substitution table cannot be provided. This should be fixed in a future version of PDF::Writer.

Here, we set the font for the PDF document we are creating to Times-Roman. The PDF reader will translate our text, which is assumed to be in WinAnsiEncoding, but it will substitute character 0x01 with the glyph called *lozenge*. We will see this character used later (in Listing 15.11).

```
pdf.select_font "Times-Roman",
                { :encoding => "WinAnsiEncoding",
                  :differences  => {0x01 => "lozenge"}
                }
```

PDF::Writer sports facilities to automatically format text and create tables that are well documented. What may not be as clear is that, as long as none of the automatic pagination is triggered, PDF::Writer can be used to manually format pages in interesting ways. With judicious axis translation and scaling, we can draw four pages of content on a single page.

Under the current version of PDF::Writer (1.1.3), each of these "pages" must *exactly* fit one page. If the library's automatic pagination kicks in, a new *physical* page will be created. An enhanced version of this technique will be added to a future version PDF::Writer to work similarly to multicolumn support.

To demonstrate this technique, we'll create a method quadrant (shown in Listing 15.10). This will be incorporated into the lengthy example in the upcoming section. (The purpose is twofold: It shows how to produce a 4-up document, and it allows us to display four PDF pages on a single page of this book, as a space-saving measure.)

Listing 15.10 The quadrant Method

```ruby
def quadrant(pdf, quad)
  raise unless block_given?

  mx = pdf.absolute_x_middle
  my = pdf.absolute_y_middle

  pdf.save_state

  case quad
  when :ul
    pdf.translate_axis(0, my)
  when :ur
    pdf.translate_axis(mx, my)
  when :ll
    nil # pdf.translate_axis(0, 0)
  when :lr
    pdf.translate_axis(mx, 0)
  end

  pdf.scale_axis(0.5, 0.5)
  pdf.y = pdf.page_height
  yield
  pdf.restore_state
end
```

In this method, we force each page's construction to be completely contained within a block; in this way, we can transparently manage the drawing scale and axis without the wrapped page construction code knowing anything about it. The *very* first thing we do, though, is save the current state. This will save us from having to manually reset the axis scale and origin when we've finished. To prepare, we must move the origin point of the quadrant to the appropriate location on the drawing page (this is `pdf.translate_axis x, y`).

Suppose I move the origin point from (0, 0) to (50, 50). A line from (15, 20) to (35, 40) will be *effectively* drawn from (65, 70) to (85, 90). But the code that draws the line does not need to know this.

After translating the axis (moving the origin), the axis will be resized, effectively changing the *size* of the ruler that will be used. To achieve a quadrant effect, the axis is being scaled by half on the X scale and half on the Y scale (`pdf.scale_axis 0.5, 0.5`). This means that if I were now to draw my line from (0, 0) to (90, 90), it would *effectively* draw only from (0, 0) to (45, 45) without a translated axis, and from (90, 90) to (135, 135) with the translated axis. The code that drew the line still drew a 90-unit diagonal line. It just happens because of the rescaling that the units are half as big as they used to be.

We then yield to the block; after the block has finished, we restore the state using a built-in feature. If we did not do this, we would need code similar to the following to restore the axis scale and origin. The scale would need to be doubled, and the origin would need to be moved by the negative value of the original amount that it had been moved.

15.4.2   An Example Document

To demonstrate the techniques we just discussed, four different pages will be created and drawn within individual `quadrant` blocks. Three of these are minor variants of demonstration programs provided with PDF::Writer:

- `demo.rb`, quadrant 1
- `individual-i.rb`, quadrant 3
- `gettysburg.rb`, quadrant 4

The fourth (quadrant 2) is also a variant but does not have a direct analogue to any demonstration program; its closest variant is the program `chunkybacon.rb`.

The entire code is in Listing 15.11, and the resulting output (a 4-up document page) is shown in Figure 15.4. This is a long listing; we will examine it in detail in the upcoming discussion.

Listing 15.11   Code for the Example Document

```
require 'rubygems'
require 'pdf/writer'

def quadrant(pdf, quad)
  raise unless block_given?

  mx = pdf.absolute_x_middle
  my = pdf.absolute_y_middle
  pdf.save_state

  case quad
  when :ul
    pdf.translate_axis 0, my
  when :ur
    pdf.translate_axis mx, my
  when :ll
    nil    # no translation needed
  when :lr
    pdf.translate_axis mx, 0
  end

  pdf.scale_axis(0.5, 0.5)
  pdf.y = pdf.page_height
  yield
  pdf.restore_state
end

pdf = PDF::Writer.new
pdf.select_font("Times-Roman",
                :encoding    => "WinAnsiEncoding",
                :differences => { 0x01 => "lozenge" })

mx = pdf.absolute_x_middle
my = pdf.absolute_y_middle

pdf.line(0, my, pdf.page_width, my).stroke
pdf.line(mx, 0, mx, pdf.page_height).stroke

# Top-Left: Demo (UL)

quadrant(pdf, :ul) do
  x  = pdf.absolute_right_margin
  r1 = 25

  40.step(1, -3) do |xw|
    tone = 1.0 - (xw / 40.0) * 0.2
    pdf.stroke_style(PDF::Writer::StrokeStyle.new(xw))
    pdf.stroke_color(Color::RGB.from_fraction(1, tone, tone))
    pdf.line(x, pdf.bottom_margin, x,
             pdf.absolute_top_margin).stroke
```

```ruby
  x -= xw+2
end

40.step(1, -3) do |xw|
  tone = 1.0 - (xw / 40.0) * 0.2
  pdf.stroke_style(PDF::Writer::StrokeStyle.new(xw))
  pdf.stroke_color(Color::RGB.from_fraction(1, tone, tone))
  pdf.circle_at(pdf.left_margin + 10, pdf.margin_height - 15,
                r1).stroke
  r1 += xw
end

pdf.stroke_color(Color::RGB::Black)

x = pdf.absolute_left_margin
y = pdf.absolute_bottom_margin
w = pdf.margin_width
h = pdf.margin_height
pdf.rectangle(x, y, w, h).stroke

text = "The Ruby Way"

y = pdf.absolute_top_margin
50.step(5, -5) do |size|
  height = pdf.font_height(size)
  y -= height
  pdf.add_text(pdf.left_margin + 10, y, text, size)
end

(0...360).step(20) do |angle|
  pdf.fill_color(Color::RGB.from_fraction(rand, rand, rand))

  pdf.add_text(300 + Math.cos(PDF::Math.deg2rad(angle)) * 40,
               300 + Math.sin(PDF::Math.deg2rad(angle)) * 40,
               text, 20, angle)
  end
end

pdf.fill_color Color::RGB::Black

# Top-Right: Grampian Highlands (UR)

quadrant(pdf, :ur) do
  pdf.image("grampian-highlands.jpg",
            :height => pdf.margin_height,
            :resize => :width)
  pdf.text("The Grampian Highlands, Scotland",
           :justification => :center,
           :font_size => 36)
  pdf.text("\001August 2001\001", :justification => :center,
                                  :font_size => 24)
```

Continues

```
  pdf.move_pointer(24)
  info = <<-'EOS'.split($/).join(" ").squeeze(" ")
This picture was taken during a driving vacation through the
Scottish highlands in August 2001 by Austin Ziegler.
  EOS
  pdf.text(info, :justification => :full, :font_size => 16,
                 :left => 100, :right => 100)
end

pdf.fill_color Color::RGB::Black

# Bottom-Left: Individual-I (LL)

quadrant(pdf, :ll) do
  require 'color/palette/monocontrast'

  class IndividualI
    def initialize(size = 100)
      @size = size
    end

    # The size of the "i" in points.
    attr_accessor :size

    def half_i(pdf)
      pdf.move_to(0, 82)
      pdf.line_to(0, 78)
      pdf.line_to(9, 78)
      pdf.line_to(9, 28)
      pdf.line_to(0, 28)
      pdf.line_to(0, 23)
      pdf.line_to(18, 23)
      pdf.line_to(18, 82)
      pdf.fill
    end
    private :half_i

    def draw(pdf, x, y)
      pdf.save_state
      pdf.translate_axis(x, y)
      pdf.scale_axis(1 * (@size / 100.0), -1 * (@size / 100.0))

      pdf.circle_at(20, 10, 7.5)
      pdf.fill

      half_i(pdf)

      pdf.translate_axis(40, 0)
      pdf.scale_axis(-1, 1)

      half_i(pdf)
```

```
      pdf.restore_state
    end
  end

  ii  = IndividualI.new(24)

  x   = pdf.absolute_left_margin
  y   = pdf.absolute_top_margin

  bg  = Color::RGB.from_fraction(rand, rand, rand)
  fg  = Color::RGB.from_fraction(rand, rand, rand)
  pal = Color::Palette::MonoContrast.new(bg, fg)

  sz  = 24

  (-5..5).each do |col|
    pdf.fill_color pal.background[col]
    ii.draw(pdf, x, y)
    ii.size += sz
    x += sz / 2.0
    y -= sz / 2.0
    pdf.fill_color pal.foreground[col]
    ii.draw(pdf, x, y)
    x += sz / 2.0
    y -= sz / 2.0
    ii.size += sz
  end
end

pdf.fill_color Color::RGB::Black

# Bottom-Right: Gettysburg Address (LR)

quadrant(pdf, :lr) do
  pdf.text("The Gettysburg Address\n\n",
           :font_size => 36, :justification => :center)
  y0 = pdf.y + 18

  speech = <<-'EOS'.split($/).join(" ").squeeze(" ")
Four score and seven years ago our fathers brought forth on
this continent a new nation, conceived in liberty and
dedicated to the proposition that all men are created equal.
Now we are engaged in a great civil war, testing whether
that nation or any nation so conceived and so dedicated can
long endure. We are met on a great battlefield of that war.
We have come to dedicate a portion of that field as a final
resting-place for those who here gave their lives that that
nation might live. It is altogether fitting and proper that
we should do this. But in a larger sense, we cannot
dedicate, we cannot consecrate, we cannot hallow this
ground. The brave men, living and dead who struggled here
```

Continues

```
have consecrated it far above our poor power to add or
detract. The world will little note nor long remember what
we say here, but it can never forget what they did here. It
is for us the living rather to be dedicated here to the
unfinished work which they who fought here have thus far so
nobly advanced. It is rather for us to be here dedicated to
the great task remaining before us— that from these honored
dead we take increased devotion to that cause for which they
gave the last full measure of devotion— that we here highly
resolve that these dead shall not have died in vain, that
this nation under God shall have a new birth of freedom, and
that government of the people, by the people, for the people
shall not perish from the earth.
EOS

  pdf.text(speech, :justification => :full, :font_size => 14,
                   :left => 50, :right => 50)
  pdf.move_pointer(36)
  pdf.text("U.S. President Abraham Lincoln, 19 November 1863",
           :justification => :right, :right => 100)
  pdf.text("Gettysburg, Pennsylvania", :justification => :right,
           :right => 100)
  pdf.rounded_rectangle(pdf.left_margin + 25, y0, pdf.margin_width - 50,
     y0 - pdf.y + 18, 10).stroke
end

pdf.save_as("4page.pdf")
```

To summarize, the four quadrants are as follows:

- Upper-left quadrant, demo.rb

- Upper-right quadrant, the Grampian Highlands photo

- Lower-left quadrant, Individual I (individual-i.rb)

- Lower-right quadrant: The Gettysburg Address

Let's refer to the four pieces of the final page by abbreviating the quadrant name as UL, UR, LL, and LR. The code uses the corresponding symbol names (:ul and so on).

The first quadrant (UL) is filled with vertical lines that progressively shrink from 40 units wide in progressively lighter shades. This is followed by circles that increase in radius as they reduce in line thickness, and the shades lighten. Finally, two sets of text are drawn: one in decreasing font sizes down the circles, and one with the text rotating around a central axis just off the edge of the vertical lines.

Figure 15.4   Example document output (4-up).

In the second quadrant (UR), we insert an image into the page and describe it. Of particular interest, note the date line. We are inserting byte 0x01 into the output stream here; when rendered, a lozenge character (diamond) will be substituted, as defined in our substitution table when we selected our font.

In the third quadrant (LL), the *Individual-I* demonstration program further demonstrates axis translation and scaling. The most interesting feature demonstrated here is axis inversion. When an axis is scaled by a negative value, the writing and drawing commands are inverted from the original direction. That means that in drawing the body of the "I", it's only necessary to define the drawing rules for *half* of the body; we can invert the X axis with pdf.scale_axis(-1, 1).

This final quadrant (LR) is relatively simple. The text of President Lincoln's speech at Gettysburg is formatted and enclosed in a box with rounded corners.

Saving the PDF at this point is simplicity itself. If we want to save it to disk, we simply use the save_as method on the PDF object:

```
pdf.save_as("4page.pdf")
```

It's also easy to send the PDF to a web browser from a CGI program:

```
require 'cgi'

cgi = CGI.new
out = pdf.render

puts <<-EOS
Content-Type: application/pdf
Content-Disposition: inline; filename="4page.pdf"
Size: #{out.size}

EOS
```

Of course, this section has touched on only a fraction of the functionality of PDF::Writer. For more information, consult the online documentation. If you are familiar with the PDF format, be aware that PDF::Writer is not yet fully mature and does not support all features of the PDF specification.

15.5 Conclusion

In this chapter, we have looked at how to use REXML to parse XML in both stream-oriented and tree-oriented styles; we've also seen how to use REXML's XPath interface.

We've looked at parsing feeds in XML-based formats. The rss library handles RSS, and the feedtools library handles both RSS and Atom (and interconverts between them).

We've looked at reading and manipulating graphic images in many formats with RMagick; We've also seen its drawing API, which enables us to add arbitrary text and shapes to an image. Finally, we've seen how PDF::Writer can produce complex, high-quality PDF documents in a programmatic fashion.

In the next chapter, we will look at a different topic entirely. The next chapter deals with effective testing and debugging in Ruby.

CHAPTER 16

Testing and Debugging

I've just picked up a fault in the AE35 unit. It's going to go 100% failure in 72 hours.

—*HAL 9000, in* 2001: A Space Odyssey

Testing is important. All competent programmers know this fact even if it isn't always at the forefront of their minds.

Of course, true exhaustive testing is usually impossible. A program or system of any significant size is always going to hold a few surprises as it goes through its life cycle. The best we can do is to test carefully and selectively and get as wide a coverage as we can.

Historically, programmers don't always test as adequately as they should. The typical reasons for this are tests that are difficult to set up and run, require manual intervention, or take too long to run.

In the 1990s, a "culture of testing" began springing up in the computing community. The ideas of *extreme programming* and *test-driven development* started to gain mind-share among developers everywhere.

Whether you are a hard-core "test first" person is not the point. The point is that *everyone* can benefit from tests that are automated, easy to write, and easy to run.

Tools such as `Test::Unit` and the ZenTest tools were easier to write in Ruby because Ruby is dynamic and flexible. In the same way, they are easy to use and (dare I say it?) even *fun* to use. There is something satisfying about making a software change and then watching every test run to completion and pass.

Besides these testing tools, Ruby also has various other tools and libraries for debugging, profiling, and code coverage. This chapter gives an overview of what is available.

16.1   Testing with `Test::Unit`

The "standard" way to do unit testing in Ruby is with Nathaniel Talbott's `Test::Unit`. This has been distributed with Ruby since 2001.

The `Test::Unit` library uses reflection to analyze your test code. When you subclass the `Test::Unit::TestCase` class, any methods named starting with `test` are executed as test code.

```
require 'test/unit'

class TC_MyTest < Test::Unit::TestCase
  def test_001
    # ...
  end
  def test_002
    # ...
  end
  # ...
end
```

The methods do *not* have to be numbered as shown. That tends to be my personal convention, but there are certainly others.

It is inadvisable, arguably *incorrect*, for the behavior of the tests to rely on the order in which they are run. However, `Test::Unit` does in fact run them in alphabetical (or lexicographic) order; I tend to number the methods so that as I watch them being executed I will have some "feel" as to where the test process is in its sequence.

Another convention I have used is to put a "title" on the method name (describing the scope or purpose of the test):

```
def test_053_default_to_current_directory
  # ...
end
def test_054_use_specified_directory
  # ...
end
```

It's also not a bad idea to put at least a one-line comment describing the purpose and meaning of the test. In general, each test should have *one* purpose.

What if we need to do some kind of setup that takes a long time? It's not practical to do it for every single test, and we can't put it inside a test method (since tests should not be order-dependent).

If we need to do special setup for each test, we can create `setup` and `teardown` methods for the class. It might seem counterintuitive, but these methods are called for *every* test. If you want to do some kind of setup only once, before any/all of the tests, you could put that in the body of the class, before the test methods (or even before the class itself).

But what if we want to do a corresponding teardown after all the tests? For technical reasons (because of the way Test::Unit works internally), this is difficult. The "best" way is to override the suite's `run` method (not the class's `run` method) so as to "wrap" its functionality. Look at the example in Listing 16.1.

Listing 16.1 Setup and Teardown

```
require 'test/unit'

class MyTest < Test::Unit::TestCase

  def self.major_setup
    # ...
  end

  def self.major_teardown
    # ...
  end

  def self.suite
    mysuite = super               # call the higher-level suite

    def mysuite.run(*args)        # Now add a singleton method
      MyTest.major_setup
      super
```

Continues

```
    MyTest.major_teardown
  end

  mysuite                          # and return the new value.
end

def setup
  # ...
end

def teardown
  # ...
end

def test_001
  # ...
end

def test_002
  # ...
end

# ...
end
```

You probably won't find yourself doing this kind of thing often. We'll look at the suite method and its real purpose shortly, but first let's look more at the details of the tests.

What goes inside a test? We need to have some way of deciding whether a test passed or failed. We use *assertions* for that purpose.

The simplest assertion is just the assert method. It takes a parameter to be tested and an optional second parameter (which is a message); if the parameter tests true (that is, anything but false or nil), all is well. If it doesn't test true, the test fails and the message (if any) is printed out.

Some other assertion methods are as follows (with comments indicating the meaning). Notice how the "expected" value always comes before the "actual" value; this is significant if you use the default error messages and don't want the results to be stated backwards.

```
assert_equal(expected, actual)      # assert(expected==actual)
assert_not_equal(expected, actual)  # assert(expected!=actual)
assert_match(regex, string)         # assert(regex =~ string)
assert_no_match(regex, string)      # assert(regex !~ string)
assert_nil(object)                  # assert(object.nil?)
assert_not_nil(object)              # assert(!object.nil?)
```

Some assertions have a more object-oriented flavor:

```
assert_instance_of(klass, obj)     # assert(obj.instance_of? klass)
assert_kind_of(klass, obj)         # assert(obj.kind_of? klass)
assert_respond_to(obj, meth)       # assert(obj.respond_to? meth)
```

Some deal specifically with exceptions and thrown symbols. Naturally these will have to take a block:

```
assert_nothing_thrown { ... }      # no throws
assert_nothing_raised { ... }      # no exceptions raised
assert_throws(symbol) { ... }      # throws symbol
assert_raises(exception) { ... }   # throws exception
```

There are several others, but these form a basic complement that will cover most of what you will ever need. For others, consult the online documentation at http://ruby-doc.org.

There is also a `flunk` method, which always fails. This is more or less a placeholder.

When you run a test file and do nothing special, the console test runner is invoked by default. This gives us feedback using good old-fashioned 1970s technology. There are other test runners also, such as the graphical `Test::Unit::UI::GTK::TestRunner`. Any test runner may be run by invoking its `run` method and passing in a special parameter representing the set of tests:

```
class MyTests < Test::Unit::TestCase
  # ...
end

# Making it explicit...
runner = Test::Unit::UI::Console::TestRunner
runner.run(MyTests)
```

The parameter is actually any object that has a `suite` method that returns an object that is a suite of tests. What does this mean?

Let's look more at the concept of a *suite* of tests. As it happens, a suite of tests can consist of a set of tests or a set of subsuites. Therefore it's possible to group tests together so that only a single set of tests may be run, or all the tests may be run.

For example, suppose you have three sets of test cases and you want to run them as a suite. You *could* do it this way:

```ruby
require 'test/unit/testsuite'

require 'tc_set1'
require 'tc_set2'
require 'ts_set3'

class TS_MyTests
  def self.suite
    mysuite = Test::Unit::TestSuite.new
    mysuite << TC_Set1.suite
    mysuite << TC_Set2.suite
    mysuite << TS_Set3.suite
    return mysuite
  end
end

Test::Unit::UI::Console::TestRunner.run(TS_MyTests)
```

However, this is unnecessarily difficult. Given the separate test cases, Test::Unit is smart enough to traverse the object space and combine all the test suites it finds into one. So this following code works just as well (even invoking the default test runner as usual):

```ruby
require 'test/unit'

require 'tc_set1'
require 'tc_set2'
require 'ts_set3'
```

There is more to Test::Unit than we've seen here; it's also likely to have some improvements made in the future. Always do an online search for the latest information.

16.2   The ZenTest Tools

Ryan Davis is the author of this excellent suite of tools. The main tool itself (zentest) is an executable that actually reads your code and produces a file of tests.

The *class under test* (CUT) is used as the basis for the *test class* (TC). The string `Test` is appended to the front of the class name at each scope level; the methods are named by appending `test_` to the front of each name. Method names may also need to be "mangled" if they are methods such as == (which can't have anything prefixed) or if they end in ?, !, or =.

Listing 16.2 shows a sample piece of code to be tested:

Listing 16.2   Class to Be Tested

```
class Alpha

  class Beta

    attr_accessor :foo, :bar

    def initialize
    end

    def foo?
      @foo
    end

  end

  def initialize
  end

  def process
  end

  def process!
  end

  def ==(other)
  end

  def ===(other)
  end

end
```

Run the command `zentest file.rb >tfile.rb` and you will get the code shown in Listing 16.3 as output.

Listing 16.3   Output from ZenTest

```
# Code Generated by ZenTest v. 3.2.0
#                   classname: asrt / meth =  ratio%
#                   Alpha::Beta:    0 /    7 =   0.00%

require 'test/unit' unless defined? $ZENTEST and $ZENTEST

class TestAlpha < Test::Unit::TestCase
  def test_process
    raise NotImplementedError, 'Need to write test_process'
  end

  def test_process_bang
    raise NotImplementedError, 'Need to write test_process_bang'
  end
end

module TestAlpha
  class TestBeta < Test::Unit::TestCase
    def test_bar
      raise NotImplementedError, 'Need to write test_bar'
    end

    def test_bar_equals
      raise NotImplementedError, 'Need to write test_bar_equals'
    end

    def test_foo
      raise NotImplementedError, 'Need to write test_foo'
    end

    def test_foo_eh
      raise NotImplementedError, 'Need to write test_foo_eh'
    end

    def test_foo_equals
      raise NotImplementedError, 'Need to write test_foo_equals'
    end
  end
end

# Number of errors detected: 9
```

Notice how each test method is given a `raise` call so that it will fail. The concept is that all tests fail by default until you write code to make them pass.

For whatever reason, the original file is not pulled into the test file. You can add require 'file' or the equivalent to the top of your test file (after requiring test/unit). Then all of your class definitions will be available to your test code.

Note that it's possible to put a second parameter on the command line. If you add code to your classes under test, your test classes are out of date. Rather than update them by hand, you can generate only the "new" material in this way:

```
zentest file.rb tfile.rb >tfile2.rb
```

The unit_diff program is another useful tool that is part of this suite. Consider the simple assertion assert_equal("foo","bar"). This will produce output such as the following:

```
  1) Failure:
testme(Foo) [(irb):7]:
<"foo"> expected but was
<"bar">.
```

That is simple and clear. But suppose the strings passed in were each multiple lines in length, and the difference was only on the seventh line. The unit_diff tool is the solution to an unreadable mess of that kind. It does a UNIX-like "diff" operation and displays the output. Invoke it as a filter on your usual test program:

```
ruby testfile.rb | unit_diff
```

It knows a few command-line switches:

```
-h   Help (usage)
-v   Version
-b   Ignore whitespace differences
-c   Do a contextual diff
-k   Keep temp diff files around
-l   Prefix line numbers on the diffs
-u   Do a unified diff
```

The autotest tool hovers over your test suites in daemonlike fashion and runs those that have changed recently. This is for the person who is too lazy even to type a filename to run the tests.

To use this tool, you have to obey its naming conventions. The rules are simple:

- All tests live under a `test` directory.
- Test filenames start with `test_`.
- Test class names start with `Test`.
- Your code to be tested lives under the `lib` directory.
- Files under `lib` must have corresponding `test` files (prefixed with `test_`, of course).

When you start `autotest`, it will cycle through your tests as they are updated. When it finds one that fails, it is smart enough to run it repeatedly until you fix it. It will start over "from the top" when you press Ctrl+C and will quit when you press Ctrl+C a second time.

The tool called `multiruby` enables you to test your code against multiple versions of Ruby. It is part of the ZenTest suite, but at the time of this writing it is not completely stable nor well documented.

16.3   Using the Ruby Debugger

Truthfully, the Ruby debugger does not seem to get much use. I do not use it, and I have talked to very few who do. But it's nice to know that it's there. Here's a brief description of how it works.

Invoke the debugger simply by requiring the `debug` library. This can be done on the command line:

```
ruby -rdebug myfile.rb
```

At the prompt (which looks like `(rdb:1)`), you can type such commands as `list` to list any or all of the program, `step` to step into a method call, and so on. A few of these commands are listed in Table 16.1 (with the abbreviation in boldface).

Table 16.1   Common Debugger Commands

Command	Description
break	List or set a breakpoint.
delete	Delete some or all breakpoints.
catch	List or set a catchpoint.
step	Step into a method.
next	Next line (step over a method).
help	Help (list all commands).
quit	Quit the debugger.

Listing 16.4 presents the code of a simple program (too simple to need debugging, really).

Listing 16.4   A Simple Program for Debugging

```ruby
STDOUT.sync = true

def palindrome?(word)
  word == word.reverse
end

def signature(w)
  w.split("").sort.join
end

def anagrams?(w1,w2)
  signature(w1) == signature(w2)
end

print "Give me a word: "
w1 = gets.chomp

print "Give me another word: "
w2 = gets.chomp

verb = palindrome?(w1) ? "is" : "is not"
puts "'#{w1}' #{verb} a palindrome."

verb = palindrome?(w2) ? "is" : "is not"
puts "'#{w2}' #{verb} a palindrome."

verb = anagrams?(w1,w2) ? "are" : "are not"
puts "'#{w1}' and '#{w2}' #{verb} anagrams."
```

Listing 16.5 shows an entire debugging session. Parts of it may be confusing because the console is used for standard I/O as well as for debugging.

Listing 16.5 A Simple Debugging Session

```
$ ruby -rdebug db.rb
Debug.rb
Emacs support available.

db.rb:1:STDOUT.sync = true
(rdb:1) b palindrome?
Set breakpoint 1 at db.rb:palindrome?
(rdb:1) b anagrams?
Set breakpoint 2 at db.rb:anagrams?
(rdb:1) b
Breakpoints:
  1 db.rb:palindrome?
  2 db.rb:anagrams?

(rdb:1) n
db.rb:3:def palindrome?(word)
(rdb:1) n
db.rb:7:def signature(w)
(rdb:1) n
db.rb:11:def anagrams?(w1,w2)
(rdb:1) n
db.rb:15:print "Give me a word: "
(rdb:1) n
Give me a word: db.rb:16:w1 = gets.chomp
(rdb:1) live
db.rb:16:undefined local variable or method `live' for main:Object
(rdb:1) n
live
db.rb:18:print "Give me another word: "
(rdb:1) n
Give me another word: db.rb:19:w2 = gets.chomp
(rdb:1) n
evil
db.rb:21:verb = palindrome?(w1) ? "is" : "is not"
(rdb:1) c
Breakpoint 1, palindrome? at db.rb:palindrome?
db.rb:3:def palindrome?(word)
(rdb:1) n
db.rb:4:  word == word.reverse
(rdb:1) word
"live"
(rdb:1) n
db.rb:22:puts "'#{w1}' #{verb} a palindrome."
(rdb:1) verb
"is not"
```

```
(rdb:1) n
'live' is not a palindrome.
db.rb:24:verb = palindrome?(w2) ? "is" : "is not"
(rdb:1) n
db.rb:24:verb = palindrome?(w2) ? "is" : "is not"
(rdb:1) n
Breakpoint 1, palindrome? at db.rb:palindrome?
db.rb:3:def palindrome?(word)
(rdb:1) n
db.rb:4:  word == word.reverse
(rdb:1) c
'evil' is not a palindrome.
Breakpoint 2, anagrams? at db.rb:anagrams?
db.rb:11:def anagrams?(w1,w2)
(rdb:1) n
db.rb:12:  signature(w1) == signature(w2)
(rdb:1) n
db.rb:28:puts "'#{w1}' and '#{w2}' #{verb} anagrams."
(rdb:1) verb
"are"
(rdb:1) c
'live' and 'evil' are anagrams.
```

Be aware that if you require other libraries, you may find yourself stepping over quite a few things at the beginning. I suggest you first set a breakpoint early in your actual code and then use continue to execute up to that point.

The debugger recognizes many other commands. You can examine the call stack and move up and down in it. You can "watch" expressions and break automatically when they change. You can add expressions to a "display" list. You can handle multiple threads and switch between them.

All these features are probably not well documented anywhere. If you use the debugger, I suggest you use its online help command and proceed by trial and error.

More modern debuggers are graphical, of course. See Chapter 21, "Ruby Development Tools," for a discussion of Ruby IDEs (Integrated Development Environments) if you want this kind of tool.

16.4   Using irb As a Debugger

The ruby-breakpoint library is the creation of Florian Gross. This wonderful little tool enables you to set breakpoints in your code with the breakpoint method. When a breakpoint is encountered, you are thrown into an irb session. (The irb tool, interactive Ruby, is covered in more detail in Chapter 21.)

This is not part of the standard library. Install it by doing a `gem install ruby-breakpoint` or by any other method.

Let's take Listing 16.4 and make a couple of changes. We'll add `require 'breakpoint'` at the beginning and then add a call to the `breakpoint` method sometime after both the `gets` calls:

```
require 'breakpoint'

# ...
w2 = gets.chomp

breakpoint

# ...
```

Now let's run this. The following session shows how we enter `irb` and then we can do *anything* we want, including calling methods that have been previously defined or changing the values of variables.

```
$ ruby myprog.rb
Give me a word: parental
Give me another word: prenatal
Executing break point at myprog.rb:23
irb(main):001:0> w1
=> "parental"
irb(main):002:0> w2
=> "prenatal"
irb(main):003:0> palindrome?(w1)
=> false
irb(main):004:0> palindrome?("detartrated")
=> true
irb(main):005:0> signature(w1)
=> "aaelnprt"
irb(main):006:0> quit
'parental' is not a palindrome.
'prenatal' is not a palindrome.
'parental' and 'prenatal' are anagrams.
```

What is especially useful about this tool is that the code being debugged doesn't have to be command-line oriented or text based. There is a drb (distributed Ruby) client that allows remote debugging of a Ruby program running in another process.

To use this feature, you will have to issue a method call in the code to be tested (naturally *before* any calls to the breakpoint method):

```
Breakpoint.activate_drb("druby://127.0.0.1:2001", "localhost")
# Start server on localhost at port 2001
```

Start the client with the breakpoint_client command. It will try every three seconds to contact the server until it either makes contact or you kill it.

```
$ breakpoint_client druby://localhost:2001
No connection to breakpoint service at druby://localhost:2001
(DRb::DRbConnError)
Tries to connect will be made every 3 seconds...
```

After you connect, you still may not get an irb prompt. Execution will proceed until a breakpoint, at which time you will get a prompt.

There are more details to this library. Consult the documentation that comes with the package.

16.5 Measuring Code Coverage

It is *incredibly* useful to know what parts of your code are not getting exercised. This helps you to know when you have areas that are lacking in unit tests. In some cases, the coverage tool itself can show you bugs. For example, suppose you have an if statement that "should be" executed about half the time. If you find that it is *never* executed, that is an easily pinpointed bug.

The rcov command-line utility (and its corresponding library) are the work of Mauricio Fernandez. Install it as a gem.

To run it in the simplest case, simply invoke it with your program as a parameter:

```
rcov myfile.rb
```

Your program will run, but at the same time, rcov will be gathering statistics. By default, it will create a directory called coverage, where you will find HTML files. The index.html has an overview of the results, and it links to all the sources with the lines highlighted according to whether they were executed.

Because of the color coding, it's difficult to show a screenshot of this in grayscale. But the tool is simple to install and run, so you can see your own results in a matter of two minutes.

The rcov command, although it is useful with its defaults, does have quite a few command-line parameters (around 30, in fact). You can specify the output directory, patterns for filenames to include or exclude, sorting for the filenames, and more. You can do text mode output of the statistics or even colorized output of the coverage information. I suggest you read the documentation that comes with rcov, do an rcov -h to list all the options, and just have fun.

It's also possible to use rcov as a library to write similar analysis tools. Three main classes are exposed in the API:

- Rcov::FileStatistics is used to distinguish between executable statements and comments (and refine the coverage statistics).

- Rcov::CodeCoverageAnalyzer is used to trace execution and return coverage and execution count information.

- Rcov::CallSiteAnalyzer is used to determine where methods are defined and where they are called.

A discussion of this API is far beyond the scope of this section. Consult the included documentation and start experimenting.

16.6   Measuring Performance

I don't like to place too much emphasis on optimizing for speed. The best way to do this in general is to select a reasonable algorithm and use common sense.

Certainly speed matters. In some cases it matters greatly. But it is usually a mistake to worry about speed *too soon* in the development cycle. The saying goes, "Premature optimization is the root of all evil." (This originated with Hoare and was restated by Knuth.) Or as someone else put it: "Make it right, then make it fast." At the application level, this is generally a good heuristic (though at the level of large systems, it may be of less value).

I would add to this precept: *Don't optimize until you measure.*

That isn't so much to ask. Refrain from refactoring for speed until you actually know two things: First, is it really too slow? And second, exactly which parts are causing the speed problem?

The second question is more important than it appears. Programmers tend to think they have a pretty good idea of where the execution time is going, but in reality, studies have shown conclusively that on the average they are extraordinarily *bad* at making these determinations. "Seat of the pants" optimization is not a viable option for most of us.

We need objective measurements. We need a profiler.

Ruby comes with a profiler called `profile`. Invoking it is as easy as requiring the library:

```
ruby -rprofile myprog.rb
```

Consider the program Listing 16.6. Its purpose is to open the /usr/share/dict/ words file and look for anagrams. It then looks for which words have the most anagrams and prints them out.

Listing 16.6 Finding Anagrams in the Dictionary

```
words = File.readlines("/usr/share/dict/words")
words.map! {|x| x.chomp }

hash = {}
words.each do |word|
  key = word.split("").sort.join
  hash[key] ||= []
  hash[key] << word
end

sizes = hash.values.map {|v| v.size }
most = sizes.max
list = hash.find_all {|k,v| v.size == most }

puts "No word has more than #{most-1} anagrams."
list.each do |key,val|
  anagrams = val.sort
  first = anagrams.shift
  puts "The word #{first} has #{most-1} anagrams:"
  anagrams.each {|a| puts "   #{a}" }
end

num = 0
hash.keys.each do |key|
  n = hash[key].size
  num += n if n > 1
end

puts
puts "The dictionary has #{words.size} words,"
puts "of which #{num} have anagrams."
```

I know you are curious about the output. Here it is:

```
No word has more than 14 anagrams.
The word alerts has 14 anagrams:
    alters
    artels
    estral
    laster
    lastre
    rastle
    ratels
    relast
    resalt
    salter
    slater
    staler
    stelar
    talers

The dictionary has 483523 words,
of which 79537 have anagrams.
```

On my system, that file has more than 483,000 words, and the program runs in a little more than 18 seconds. Where do you think the time is going? Let's find out. The output from the profiler is more than 100 lines long, sorted by decreasing time. We'll look at the first 20 lines:

```
  %   cumulative    self              self     total
 time   seconds    seconds    calls  ms/call  ms/call   name
42.78   190.93     190.93        15 12728.67 23647.33   Array#each
10.78   239.04      48.11   1404333     0.03     0.04   Hash#[]
 7.04   270.48      31.44         2 15720.00 25575.00   Hash#each
 5.66   295.73      25.25    483523     0.05     0.05   String#split
 5.55   320.51      24.78   1311730     0.02     0.02   Array#size
 3.64   336.76      16.25         1 16250.00 25710.00   Array#map
 3.24   351.23      14.47    483524     0.03     0.03   Array#sort
 3.12   365.14      13.91    437243     0.03     0.03   Fixnum#==
 3.04   378.72      13.58    483526     0.03     0.03   Array#join
 2.97   391.98      13.26    437244     0.03     0.03   Hash#default
 2.59   403.53      11.55    437626     0.03     0.03   Hash#[]=
 2.43   414.38      10.85    483568     0.02     0.02   Array#<<
```

2.29	424.59	10.21	1	10210.00	13430.00	Array#map!
1.94	433.23	8.64	437242	0.02	0.02	Fixnum#<=>
1.86	441.54	8.31	437244	0.02	0.02	Fixnum#>
0.72	444.76	3.22	483524	0.01	0.01	String#chomp!
0.11	445.26	0.50	4	125.00	125.00	Hash#keys
0.11	445.73	0.47	1	470.00	470.00	Hash#values
0.06	446.00	0.27	1	270.00	270.00	IO#readlines
0.05	446.22	0.22	33257	0.01	0.01	Fixnum#+

Here we see that the Array#each method is taking more time than anything else. That makes sense; we have a loop that runs for each word and does significant work with each iteration. The average is misleading because the first call of each takes almost all the time; the other 14 calls (see anagrams.each) take a short time.

We also notice that Hash#[] is an expensive operation (largely because we do it so often); 1.4 million of these calls take not quite 11 seconds.

Notice where the readlines call fell—almost off our list of the top twenty. This program is not I/O bound at all; it is compute-bound. The read of the entire file took hardly more than a fourth of a second.

The real value of profiling is not seen in this example, however. This program doesn't have any methods or any class structure. In real life, you would see your own methods listed among the core methods. You would then be able to tell which of your methods was among the top 20 "time wasters."

One thing to realize about the Ruby profiler is that (perhaps ironically) the profiler itself is slow. It hooks into the program in many places and monitors execution at a low level (in pure Ruby). So don't be surprised if your program runs an order of magnitude slower. This program when profiled took 7 minutes 40 seconds (or 460 seconds), slowed down by a factor of 25 or more.

Besides the profiler, there is a lower-level tool you should be aware of. The benchmark standard library is also useful in measuring performance.

One way to use this little tool is to invoke the Benchmark.measure method and pass it a block:

```
require 'benchmark'

file = "/usr/share/dict/words"
result = Benchmark.measure { File.readlines(file) }
puts result

# Output:      0.350000   0.070000   0.420000 (  0.418825)
```

The output from this method is as follows:

- User CPU time (in seconds)
- System CPU time
- Sum of user and system times
- Elapsed real time

For comparing several different items, the `Benchmark.bm` method is convenient. Give it a block, and it will pass in a reporting object. Invoke that object with a label and a block, and it will output the label and time the block. Look at the following code:

```
require 'benchmark'

n = 200_000
s1 = ""
s2 = ""
s3 = ""

Benchmark.bm do |rep|
  rep.report("str <<      ") { n.times { s1 << "x" } }
  rep.report("str.insert ") { n.times { s3.insert(-1,"x") } }
  rep.report("str +=      ") { n.times { s2 += "x" } }
end
```

Here we compare three ways of getting a character into the end of a string; the result is the same in each case. We do each operation 200,000 times so as to measure the effect better. Here is the output:

```
            user       system      total        real
str <<      0.180000   0.000000    0.180000  (  0.174697)
str.insert  0.200000   0.000000    0.200000  (  0.200479)
str +=      15.250000  13.120000   28.370000 ( 28.375998)
```

Notice how time-consuming the third case is—a full two orders of magnitude slower. Why is this? What lesson can we learn?

You might conclude that the + operator is slow for some reason, but that isn't the case. This is the only one of the three methods that doesn't operate on the same object every time but creates a new object.

The lesson is that object creation is an expensive operation. There may be many such small lessons to be learned by using Benchmark, but I still recommend profiling at a higher level first.

16.7 Prettyprinting Objects

The purpose of the inspect method (and the p method that invokes it) is to show objects in human-readable form. In that sense, there is a connection with testing and debugging that justifies covering this here.

The only problem with p is that the object it prints out can be difficult to read. That is why we have the standard library pp, which adds a method of the same name.

Consider the following contrived object called my_obj:

```ruby
class MyClass

  attr_accessor :alpha, :beta, :gamma

  def initialize(a,b,c)
    @alpha, @beta, @gamma = a, b, c
  end

end

x = MyClass.new(2, 3, 4)
y = MyClass.new(5, 6, 7)
z = MyClass.new(7, 8, 9)

my_obj = { x => y, z => [:p, :q] }

p my_obj
```

When we do the p, we get this output:

```
{#<MyClass:0xb7eed86c @beta=3, @alpha=2,
  @gamma=4>=>#<MyClass:0xb7eed72c @beta=6, @alpha=5, @gamma=7>,
  #<MyClass:0xb7eed704 @beta=8, @alpha=7, @gamma=9>=>[:p, :q]}
```

It's accurate, and it's technically readable. But it isn't pretty. Now let's require the pp library and use pp instead:

```
require 'pp'

# ...

pp my_obj
```

In this case, we get the following output:

```
{#<MyClass:0xb7f7a050 @alpha=7, @beta=8, @gamma=9>=>[:p, :q],
 #<MyClass:0xb7f7a1b8 @alpha=2, @beta=3, @gamma=4>=>
  #<MyClass:0xb7f7a078 @alpha=5, @beta=6, @gamma=7>}
```

At least it adds some spacing and line breaks. It's an improvement. But we can do better. Suppose we add the special pretty_print method to MyClass:

```
class MyClass

  def pretty_print(printer)
    printer.text "MyClass(#@alpha, #@beta, #@gamma)"
  end

end
```

The printer argument is passed in by the caller (or ultimately by pp). It is a text accumulator of class PP; we call its text method and give it a textual representation of self. The result we get follows:

```
{MyClass(7, 8, 9)=>[:p, :q], MyClass(2, 3, 4)=>MyClass(5, 6, 7)}
```

Of course, we can customize this as much as we want. We could put the instance variables on separate lines and indent them, for instance.

In fact, the pp library does have a number of facilities for "pp-enabling" your own classes. Methods such as object_group, seplist, breakable, and others are available for controlling comma separation, line breaks, and similar formatting tasks. For more details, consult the documentation on http://ruby-doc.org.

16.8   Conclusion

In this chapter, we've looked at some of the mechanics of testing (especially unit testing). We've looked specifically at `Test::Unit` and the ZenTest tool suite.

We've looked briefly at the Ruby debugger. We also saw how the `ruby-breakpoint` library can be used to "jump" into an `irb` debugging session.

We've looked at the `rcov` code coverage tool and discussed a tiny bit of the rationale for such measurements. Finally, we've looked at profiling and benchmarking to measure the speed of our Ruby code.

If you're working on software for public consumption, what do you do after testing is complete? It's time then to worry about packaging and distributing the software. This is the topic of the next chapter.

CHAPTER 17

Packaging and Distributing Code

With aspirin leading the way, more and more products are coming out in fiercely protective packaging designed to prevent consumers from consuming them.

—Dave Barry

This chapter is all about being nice to your end user. If you don't have an end user, or don't want to be nice, you may skip this material.

Two things the typical programmer doesn't want to think about are *user documentation* and *installation procedures*. Here I'll try to present enough information to encourage you to do these things. Others have gone to great lengths writing Ruby tools and libraries to try to make these things easier.

This will, however, be a short chapter. You can learn more about these topics by looking at what others have done.

One of the greatest tools available is RDoc, originally created by Dave Thomas. We'll start there.

17.1   Using RDoc

RDoc isn't the only doc tool around for Ruby; RDTOOL is older. But in many ways, RDoc is superior; it's also more commonly used, at least in the United States.

One great thing about RDoc is that it tries to produce useful output *even if there are no comments in the source.* It does this by parsing the code and organizing information on all the classes, module, constants, methods, and so on.

Therefore you can get reasonably useful HTML out of a program source that doesn't even have any real internal documentation. If you haven't tried this before, I suggest you try it.

But it gets better. RDoc also tries to associate the comments it finds with specific parts of the program. The general rule is: A block comment preceding a definition (such as a class or method) will be taken as the description of that definition.

If you simply invoke RDoc on a Ruby source, it will create a doc directory with all the files under it. (The default template looks good, but there are others.) Browse to index.html and take a look.

Listing 17.1 shows a simple (nearly empty) source file. All the methods are empty, and none of it really does anything. But RDoc will still take it and produce a pretty doc page (see Figure 17.1).

Listing 17.1   A Simple Source File

```
require 'foo'

# The outer class, MyClass

class MyClass
  CONST = 237

  # The inner MyClass::Alpha class...

  class Alpha

    # The MyClass::Alpha::Beta class...

    class Beta
      # Beta's mymeth1 method
      def mymeth1
      end
    end

    # Alpha's mymeth2 method
```

```
      def mymeth2
      end
  end

  # Initialize the object

  def initialize(a,b,c)
  end

  # Create an object with default values

  def self.create
  end

  # An instance method

  def do_something
  end

end
```

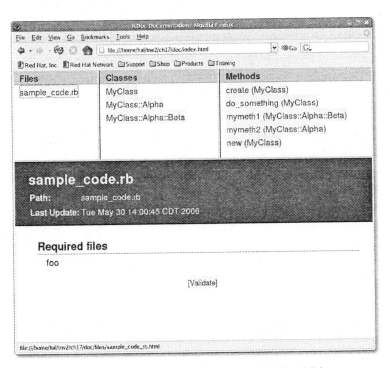

Figure 17.1   RDoc output from source in Listing 17.1.

We'll discuss two other useful features in this section. Every method name is linked to a pop-up that displays the source code of that method. This is an absolutely invaluable tool in learning a library; the API documentation is linked directly back to the code itself.

Also be aware that when RDoc recognizes a URL, it places a hyperlink in the output. The text of the link defaults to be the same as the URL, but you can change this. If you put descriptive text in braces followed by a URL in brackets ({descriptive text}[myurl]), your descriptive text will be used in the link. If the text is a single word, the braces may be omitted.

17.1.1   Simple Markup

If you want to "decorate" your output more, you don't have to edit the HTML files. In fact, that's a bad idea since it's so easy to regenerate the output (and overwrite your changes).

RDoc has a simple markup facility of its own so that you can embed your own formatting information into your source code. The markup rules are chosen so that the text looks "natural" in an editor, but it can be translated into HTML in a straight-forward way.

Listing 17.2 shows a few examples of markup capability; for more examples, consult *Programming Ruby* or any other source of RDoc documentation. The output (bottom frame only) from Listing 17.2 is shown in Figure 17.2.

Listing 17.2   Examples of RDoc Markup

```
# This block comment will be detected and
# included in the rdoc output.
#
=begin rdoc
So will this one. Note the presence of the "rdoc"
tag on the begin-line. This is to distinguish the
block comment as belonging to rdoc as opposed to
being read by some other tool.
=end
=begin rdoc
Here are some formatting tricks.

Boldface, italics, and "code" (without spaces):
This is *bold*, this is _italic_, and this is +code+.

With spaces:
```

```
This is a bold phrase. Have you read Intruder
in the Dust? Don't forget to require thread
at the top.

= First level heading
== Second level heading
=== Third level heading

Here's a horizontal rule:
---

Here's a list:
- item one
- item two
- item three

=end
=begin
This block comment is untagged and will not show up in
rdoc output. Also, I'm not putting blank lines between
the comments, as this will terminate the comments until
some real program source is seen. If this comment had
been before the previous one, processing would have
stopped here until program text appeared.
=end
```

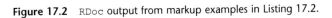

Figure 17.2   RDoc output from markup examples in Listing 17.2.

Listing 17.2 outlines some of the rules RDoc uses to parse comments. Not all of these are necessarily intuitive. There is a strong tendency for blank lines to terminate a section of comments, even if the blank line is immediately followed by another block comment.

Note that inside a block comment starting with #, we can "turn off" the copying of text into the output with a #-- line (and turn it back on again the same way). Not all comments are intended to go into the user docs, after all.

Note also that if =begin and =end are used, they must have an rdoc tag after the =begin, or RDoc will ignore the block. This is to avoid conflict with older tools that make heavy use of such blocks.

17.1.2   More Advanced Formatting

RDoc gives you relatively fine control over what parts of your source are documented and how they are treated. Special tags in the comments (documentation modifiers) accomplish this.

One of the most important of these is :nodoc: (to turn off documentation for something you don't want to appear in output). Typically this is used on the same line when a class or method is introduced.

```
class Alpha      # :nodoc:
  class Beta
    # ...
  end
  # ...
end
```

In the preceding example, Alpha would not be documented. However, :nodoc: is not recursive; Beta would still be documented. To make it recursive, use :nodoc: all instead. In the following example, both Gamma and Delta will be ignored:

```
class Alpha      # :nodoc: all
  class Beta
    # ...
  end
  # ...
end
```

There's also a `:doc:` modifier, which is the opposite. It forces documentation for things that ordinarily would not appear in output.

The `:notnew:` modifier is special; it prevents the documenting of a `new` method (based on an existing `initialize` method).

If you want to give meaningful names to your `yield` parameters, you can use the `yields` keyword. For example, your code may use boring parameter names such as `x` and `i`; you can change these in the documentation.

```
def iterate      # :yields: element, index
  # ...
  yield x, i
end
```

Some tags are used only inside block comments. Here are most of them:

- `:include:`—Include the contents of the specified file in the documentation. Indentation will be adjusted for consistency.

- `:title:`—Set the title of the document.

- `:main:`—Set the initial page displayed in the output.

For more information, consult *Programming Ruby* or any reference you can find online.

17.2   Installation and Packaging

Your end user's "out-of-the-box experience" should be as painless as possible. As users, we agree fervently with this; as developers, we'd sometimes prefer not to be bothered with packaging and installation issues.

Fortunately, these matters are less painful than in some other languages and environments. The two things you most need to know about are the `setup` library and *RubyGems*, Ruby's "native" packaging and deployment system.

17.2.1   `setup.rb`

The `setup.rb` library is the work of Minero Aoki (who also created `install.rb`, used less often now).

Some would say this is becoming obsolete as RubyGems improves. Others would say they have issues with gems (technical, political, or otherwise). Some would say a "good citizen" should include a setup.rb even in a gem (making it easier for people to repackage in other forms, such as a Linux distro-specific packager). We'll leave that for you to decide.

Half the magic of using this library is just putting things in the right places. It requires that you structure your archive in a simple, sensible way (with well-named directories).

Let's assume you are distributing a single package in an archive (the most common case). You would arrange your directories something like this (dropping a copy of setup.rb in at the top level).

```
top_level/
    setup.rb
    metaconfig (optional)
    lib/
    ext/
        myext/
    bin/
    data/
    conf/
    man/
    test/
```

Empty directories may be omitted. These directories are used as follows:

- lib—Ruby programs

- ext—Ruby extensions (in C)

- myext—The name of the extension (others may follow at same level); every extension directory must contain either extconf.rb or MANIFEST

- bin—commands

- data—any accompanying data files

- conf—any configuration files

- man—man (manual) pages

- test—unit tests and other test programs

In general, files that don't require any processing are simply copied to their proper locations. For customized operations you may want to perform, there are hooks into every aspect of the process.

Typically the three main phases are config, setup, and install, invoked by the user in that order. (The last step may require sudo access or actual root access.)

You create a hook simply by placing a Ruby program with the appropriate name in the appropriate directory. For example, if I want to do something special with lib/foobar before it is processed, I could create a file lib/foobar/pre-setup.rb with arbitrary code in it.

These filenames are formed by either pre or post, followed by a hyphen, followed by a task name. The valid task names are config, setup, install, test, clean, and dist-clean.

The setup.rb library has the concept of a source directory and an object directory. In general, you should read from the source directory and write to the current directory as needed.

There is a "hook API" to make some of these programming tasks easier. Some of the methods in the API are as follows:

- get_config_key(key)—Take a key as parameter and return the value associated with it (for example, get_config('prefix') returns the path specified with --prefix.

- set_config_key(key,val)—Set a config value.

- config_key(key)—Same as get_config_key.

- curr_srcdir—The current source directory.

- curr_objdir—The current object directory.

- srcfiles(rel_path=".")—A list of all files under rel_path (relative to the current source dir).

The file metaconfig is optional at the top level. If it exists, it will be used to specify certain global configuration options. For this, there is the "metaconfig API," a small set of convenience methods. Some of these are

- add_path_config(confname,default,description)—Defines a config option that is a path; its name and its default value are specified. The description will be printed if --help is invoked.

- `add_bool_config(confname,default,description)` —Like `add_path_config`, but storing a Boolean value.

For more exhaustive coverage of both these APIs, refer to the latest documentation online.

17.2.2   RubyGems

The initial idea and name for RubyGems came from Ryan Leavengood, but the current implementation has its origins in a late-night hackfest after hours at the 2003 International Ruby Conference in Austin, Texas. That original code base was created by Chad Fowler, Jim Weirich, David Alan Black, Rich Kilmer, and Paul Brannan. Since then, several other individuals have contributed to this effort (notably Eric Hodel and Ryan Davis).

At the time of this writing, RubyGems is probably the best most commonly used packaging scheme. However, it has not yet made it into the distribution. With the ironing out of a few more issues, I think that it will be truly standard in Ruby.

As with the rest of this chapter, we're talking here from the developer's perspective. You will learn here how to *package* your own code as gems, not to manipulate gems from the outside world. That is a later topic.

A natural question is: Why use gems? The following are some of the benefits:

- Easy installation and uninstallation

- Multiple version support

- Dependency management

- Package querying and searching

A gem file typically is named with a short, descriptive unique name followed by a hyphen, followed by a standard version number. The version number is in the form "major dot minor dot tiny" that is nearly universal nowadays (obviously, each number may be more than one digit). The use of rational versioning is encouraged; if you're not familiar with that term, use a search engine to find all the details.

To build a gem, start with a logical directory structure (essentially the same as what `setup` expects). It's good to put a README file at the top level; this should contain such information as author's name and contact information, copyright, license information, known bugs, and so on. If you write this in RDoc format, it can be included as part of the project's HTML documentation.

One critically important step in building a gem is to create a *gem specification* (or *gemspec*) file. This is one of those cases where the line between code and data happily blurs. A gemspec is simply executable Ruby code (as shown here):

```ruby
require 'rubygems'
SPEC = Gem::Specification.new do |s|
    s.name      = "Drummer"
    s.version   = "1.0.2"
    s.author    = "H. Thoreau"
    s.email     = "cabin@waldenpond.com"
    s.homepage  = "http://waldenpond.com/Drummer"
    s.platform  = Gem::Platform::RUBY
    s.summary   = "A Ruby app for those who march to a different drummer"
    s.files     = Dir["./*"] + Dir["*/**"]
    s.test_file = "test/ts_drum.rb"
    s.has_rdoc  = true
    s.require_path = "lib"
    s.extra_rdoc_files = ["README", "ChangeLog"]
    s.add_dependency "KirbyBase", ">=2.5.0"
end
```

Many of these attributes are self-explanatory given the preceding example. There are a few others, mostly less important or less frequently used. Refer to the latest RubyGems documentation online.

Given a gemspec file, you can create a gem in two ways. First, you may simply run the gemspec (after all, it is Ruby code). It will create the gem of the given name in the current directory. Alternatively, you can use the `gem build` command and pass it the gemspec name. There is no difference in the result.

Now that you've packaged a gem, make it available however you want on the Web or elsewhere. I strongly recommend using RubyForge to manage your project; if your uploaded archive contains a gemspec, your gem will be created automatically. In the next section, we'll look at Rubyforge and the Ruby Application Archive (RAA).

17.3 RubyForge and the RAA

There are two important sources any Rubyist should go to when looking for a Ruby library or app (anything outside the standard distribution). The first (and older) of these is the *Ruby Application Archive*, or RAA, hosted on the main Ruby site at http://raa.ruby-lang.org.

The name is a slight misnomer, as most of its entries are libraries, not applications. Furthermore, you should be aware that it is principally a repository for metadata, not for the files themselves. Therefore dead links are a perennial problem for users of the RAA. Nevertheless, this is an important resource because many Rubyists will search the RAA for a solution before trying a generalized search engine on the Web.

Metadata, of course, means things such as the project title and description, the author's name and email, and the URL for the project home page and/or download link. (Obviously it's in everyone's interest to provide as much information as possible and keep it updated.)

At the time of this writing, the RAA contains more than 1,400 items in four major categories and 243 subcategories. The four top-level categories are Application, Documentation, Library, and Ports. The last of these, Ports, is the smallest, because an actual port of Ruby is a nontrivial task; Documentation is not much larger. More than 90% of the RAA falls under Library or Application. Chances are anything you create will fit under one of these also.

The Application category has 94 subcategories comprising 449 projects. Some of the major subcategories are Language, Database, Editor, Cryptography, Wiki, GUI, and HTML. The Library category has 952 entries in 127 subcategories, Some of these subcategories are Audio, Calendar, Chemistry, Filesystems, Numerical, and Telephony. Proper categorizing can help people find your project. There is a search feature, of course, but it's nice to allow people to browse a hierarchy.

Having said that, these subcategories are not always partitioned with complete logic or orthogonality. Make compromises when you need to, or create a new subcategory (with caution).

It goes without saying you should avoid contributing to the problem of dead links. Try to have your project in a stable place when you upload your information. Revisit all your RAA projects from time to time and make sure that you haven't changed hosts or URLs or your email address since then.

The Rubyist's other best friend is RubyForge (http://rubyforge.org), which is a large project repository modeled loosely after SourceForge. RubyForge, of course, is different in philosophy from the RAA. It doesn't just store metadata; it stores the program files themselves, the documentation, and so on. At present, it hosts more than 1,600 projects (more than the RAA) and more than 6,800 users.

RubyForge also has support for mailing lists and such. If your project has many people interested in it, whether users or developers, they can stay in touch through these built-in facilities.

Every project has a download page that is handled pretty much automatically. When you upload files and create a new release, that release is then available to the users who browse RubyForge.

One cool thing about RubyForge is that if your uploaded package contains a gemspec, the gem will be built automatically and served from RubyForge. This is the way the world ought always to work.

Besides the download page, every project can have its own page. Many projects don't take advantage of this; you will often go to a page and it will say "Coming soon!" (which is the default). This might lead you to think that the project is dead or stalled, but in many cases it just means the owner never put up a page there. In case you haven't figured it out, I strongly recommend you *do* put up a page for your project, even if you have another one somewhere else. They're easy to keep in sync.

Typically the UNIX name, or short name, of the project will be used at the far left of the URL. For an example of a project that actually has a page at such a link, go to http://rmagick.rubyforge.org (Tim Hunter's RMagick library).

Access to your RubyForge project is usually accomplished by using scp and simply dropping files into well-known locations. Many operations such as mailing list management are accomplished through the web interface, of course.

There are command-line tools (and perhaps even GUI tools) for better interfacing with your RubyForge projects. These are not "official" or universally used. I suggest you do a web search to find whether they are still maintained.

17.4 Conclusion

In this chapter we learned the basics of how to document a project with RDoc. We also looked at setup.rb and at RubyGems, the two most common ways of packaging files for the end user.

Finally, we took a brief look at Rubyforge and the Ruby Application Archive, which permit us to advertise and/or distribute our software. In the next chapter, we shift gears again and talk about an interesting and complex problem domain: network and web programming.

CHAPTER 18

Network Programming

Never underestimate the bandwidth of a station wagon full of tapes hurtling down the highway.

—Andrew S. Tanenbaum

When a marketing type says *networking*, he probably means he wants to give you his business card. But when a programmer says it, he's talking about electronic communication between physically separated machines—whether across the room, across the city, or across the world.

In the programmer's world, networking usually implies TCP/IP, the native tongue in which millions of machines whisper back and forth across the Internet. I'll say a few words about this before diving into some concrete examples.

Network communication is conceptualized at different levels (or layers) of abstraction. The lowest level is the *data link layer*, or actual hardware-level communication, which we won't discuss here. Immediately above this is the *network layer*, which is concerned with the actual moving around of packets; this is the realm of IP (Internet Protocol). At a still higher level of abstraction is the *transport layer*, where we find TCP (Transmission Control Protocol) and UDP (User Datagram Protocol). At the level above this, we find the *application layer*; at this point we finally enter the world of telnet, FTP, email protocols, and much more.

It's possible to communicate directly in IP, but normally you wouldn't do such a thing. Most of the time we are concerned with TCP or UDP.

TCP provides reliable communication between two hosts; it is concerned with blocking and deblocking of packet data, acknowledgement of receipt, handling time-outs, and so on. Because it is a reliable protocol, the application using it need not worry about whether the remote host receives the data.

UDP is much simpler, merely sending packets (datagrams) to the remote host, like binary postcards. There is no guarantee that these will be received, so the protocol is unreliable (and thus the application has some extra details to worry about).

Ruby supports low-level networking (chiefly in TCP and UDP) as well as coding at higher levels. These higher levels include telnet, FTP, SMTP, and so on.

Figure 18.1 is a class hierarchy showing the highlights of Ruby's networking support. HTTP and certain other high-level items are shown here; some others are omitted for clarity.

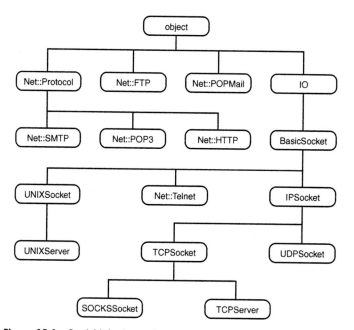

Figure 18.1   Partial inheritance hierarchy for networking support in Ruby.

Note that the bulk of these classes derive from the IO class. This means that we can use the methods of IO that are so familiar to us.

Documenting all the features of all these classes would far exceed the space requirements of this book. I'll only present a task-oriented approach to all of this and offer a little explanation. For a comprehensive list of available methods, consult a reference such as ruby-doc.org.

A few significant areas are not covered here at all, so we'll mention these up front. The Net::Telnet class is mentioned only in connection with NTP servers in section 18.2.2, "Contacting an Official Timeserver"; this class is not just for implementing your own telnet client but is potentially useful for automating anything that has a telnet interface.

The Net::FTP library is also not covered here. In general, FTP is easy to automate in its everyday form, so there is less motivation to use this class than there might be for some others.

The Net::Protocol class, which is the parent of HTTP, POP3, and SMTP, is also not covered in this chapter. It would probably prove useful in the development of other customized networking protocols, but this book does not discuss it.

That ends our broad overview. Let's look at low-level networking in more detail.

18.1 Network Servers

A *server* spends its lifetime waiting for messages and answering them. It may have to do some serious processing to construct those answers, such as accessing a database, but from a networking point of view it simply receives requests and sends responses.

Having said that, there is still more than one way to accomplish this. A server may respond to only one request at a time, or it may thread its responses. The former is easier to code, but the latter is better if many clients are trying to connect simultaneously.

It's also conceivable that a server may be used to facilitate communication in some way between the clients. The classic examples are chat servers, game servers, and peer-to-peer file sharing.

18.1.1 A Simple Server: Time of Day

Let's look at the simplest server we can think of, which may require a little suspension of disbelief. Let's suppose that we have a server whose clock is so accurate that we use it as a standard. There are such servers, of course, but they don't communicate with the simple protocol we show here. (Actually, you can refer to section 18.2.2, "Contacting an Official Timeserver," for an example of contacting such a server via the Telnet interface).

In our example, a single-threaded server handles requests inline. When the client makes a request of us, we return a string with the time of day. Here's the server code:

```
require "socket"

PORT = 12321
HOST = ARGV[0] || 'localhost'

server = UDPSocket.open        # Using UDP here...
server.bind nil, PORT

loop do
  text, sender = server.recvfrom(1)
  server.send(Time.new.to_s + "\n", 0, sender[3], sender[1])
end
```

And here is the client code:

```
require "socket"
require "timeout"

PORT = 12321

HOST = ARGV[0] || 'localhost'

socket = UDPSocket.new
socket.connect(HOST, PORT)

socket.send("", 0)
timeout(10) do
  time = socket.gets
  puts time
end
```

Note that the client makes its request simply by sending a null packet. Because UDP is unreliable, we time out after a reasonable length of time.

The following is a similar server implemented with TCP. It listens on port 12321 and can actually be used by telnetting into that port (or by using the client code we show afterward).

```
require "socket"
```

```
PORT = 12321

server = TCPServer.new(PORT)

while (session = server.accept)
  session.puts Time.new
  session.close
end
```

Note the straightforward use of the TCPServer class. Here is the TCP version of the client code:

```
require "socket"

PORT = 12321
HOST = ARGV[0] || "localhost"

session = TCPSocket.new(HOST, PORT)
time = session.gets
session.close
puts time
```

18.1.2 Implementing a Threaded Server

Some servers get heavy traffic. It can be efficient to handle each request in a separate thread.

Here is a reimplementation of the time-of-day server in the previous example. It uses TCP and threads all the client requests.

```
require "socket"

PORT = 12321

server = TCPServer.new(PORT)

while (session = server.accept)
  Thread.new(session) do |my_session|
    my_session.puts Time.new
    my_session.close
  end
end
```

Because it uses threads and spawns a new one with every client request, greater parallelism is achieved. No `join` is done because the loop is essentially infinite, running until the server is interrupted manually.

The client code is, of course, unchanged. From the point of view of the client, the server's behavior is unchanged (except that it may appear more reliable).

18.1.3   Case Study: A Peer-to-Peer Chess Server

It isn't always the server that we're ultimately concerned about communicating with. Sometimes the server is more of a directory service to put clients in touch with each other. One example is a peer-to-peer file sharing service such as those so popular in 2001; other examples are chat servers such as ICQ or any number of game servers.

Let's create a skeletal implementation of a chess server. Here we don't mean a server that will play chess with a client, but simply one that will point clients to each other so that they can then play without the server's involvement.

I'll warn you that for the sake of simplicity, the code really knows nothing about chess. All of the game logic is simulated (stubbed out) so that we can focus on the networking issues.

First, let's use TCP for the initial communication between each client and the server. We could use UDP, but it isn't reliable; we would have to use timeouts as we saw in an earlier example.

We'll let each client provide two pieces of information: His own name (like a username) and the name of the desired opponent. We'll introduce a notation `user:hostname` to fully identify the opponent; we use a colon instead of the more intuitive @ so that it won't resemble an email address, which it isn't.

When a client contacts the server, the server stores the client's information in a list. When *both* clients have contacted the server, a message is sent back to each of them; each client is given enough information to contact his opponent.

There's the small issue of white and black. Somehow the roles have to be assigned in such a way that both players agree on what color they are playing. For simplicity, we're letting the server assign it. The first client contacting the server will get to play white (and thus move first); the other player will play the black pieces.

Don't get confused here. The initial clients talk to each other so that effectively one of them is really a server by this point. This is a semantic distinction that I won't bother with.

Because the clients will be talking to each other in alternation and there is more than just a single brief exchange, we'll use TCP for their communication. This means that the client that is "really" a server will instantiate a `TCPServer`, and the other will instantiate a `TCPSocket` at the other end. We're assuming a well-known port for peer-to-peer communication as we did with the initial client-server handshaking. (The two ports are different, of course.)

What we're really describing here is a simple application-level protocol. It could be made more sophisticated, of course.

Let's look first at the server (see Listing 18.1). For the convenience of running it at a command line, we start a thread that terminates the server when a carriage return is pressed. The main server logic is threaded; we can handle multiple clients connecting at once. For safety's sake, we use a mutex to protect access to the user data; in theory multiple threads could be trying to add users to the list at one time.

Listing 18.1 The Chess Server

```ruby
require "thread"
require "socket"

PORT = 12000
HOST = "96.97.98.99"  # Replace this IP address

# Exit if user presses Enter at server end
waiter = Thread.new do
  puts "Press Enter to exit the server."
  gets
  exit
end

$mutex = Mutex.new
$list = {}

def match?(p1, p2)
  return false if !$list[p1] or !$list[p2]

  if ($list[p1][0] == p2 and $list[p2][0] == p1)
    true
  else
    false
  end
end

def handle_client(sess, msg, addr, port, ipname)
  $mutex.synchronize do
    cmd, player1, player2 = msg.split
    # Note: We get user:hostname on the command line,
    # but we store it in the form user:address
    p1short = player1.dup                 # Short names (i.e.,
    p2short = player2.split(":")[0]       # no ":address"
    player1 << ":#{addr}"                 # Append user's IP addr
```

Continues

```
      user2, host2 = player2.split(":")
      host2 = ipname if host2 == nil
      player2 = user2 + ":" + IPSocket.getaddress(host2)

      if cmd != "login"
        puts "Protocol error: client msg was #{msg}"
      end

      $list[player1] = [player2, addr, port, ipname, sess]

      if match?(player1, player2)
        # Note these names are "backwards" now: player2
        # logged in first, if we got here.
        p1 = $list[player1]
        p2 = $list[player2]
        # Player ID = name:ipname:color
        # Color: 0=white, 1=black
        p1id = "#{p1short}:#{p1[3]}:1"
        p2id = "#{p2short}:#{p2[3]}:0"
        sess1 = p1[4]
        sess2 = p2[4]
        sess1.puts "#{p2id}"
        sess2.puts "#{p1id}"
        sess1.close
        sess2.close
      end
    end
  end

  text = nil

  $server = TCPServer.new(HOST, PORT)
  while session = $server.accept do
    Thread.new(session) do |sess|
      text = sess.gets
      puts "Received: #{text}"  # So we know server gets it
      domain, port, ipname, ipaddr = sess.peeraddr
      handle_client sess, text, ipaddr, port, ipname
      sleep 1
    end
  end

  waiter.join    # Exit only if user presses Enter
```

The handle_client method stores information for the client. If the corresponding client is already stored, each client is sent a message telling the whereabouts of the other client. As we've defined this simple problem, the server's responsibility ends at this point.

The client code (see Listing 18.2) is naturally written so that there is only a single program; the first invocation will become the TCP server, and the second will become the TCP client. To be fair, we should point out that our choice to make the server white and the client black is arbitrary. There's no particular reason we couldn't implement the application so that the color issue was independent of such considerations.

Listing 18.2   The Chess Client

```ruby
require "socket"
require "timeout"

ChessServer     = '96.97.98.99'  # Replace this IP address
ChessServerPort = 12000
PeerPort        = 12001

WHITE, BLACK = 0, 1
Colors = %w[White Black]

def draw_board(board)
  puts <<-EOF
+----------------------------------+
| Stub! Drawing the board here...  |
+----------------------------------+
  EOF
end

def analyze_move(who, move, num, board)
  # Stub - black always wins on 4th move
  if who == BLACK and num == 4
    move << "  Checkmate!"
  end
  true  # Stub again - always say it's legal.
end

def my_move(who, lastmove, num, board, sock)
  ok = false
  until ok do
    print "\nYour move: "
    move = STDIN.gets.chomp
    ok = analyze_move(who, move, num, board)
    puts "Illegal move" if not ok
  end
  sock.puts move
  move
end

def other_move(who, move, num, board, sock)
  move = sock.gets.chomp
  puts "\nOpponent: #{move}"
```

Continues

```
    move
end

if ARGV[0]
  myself = ARGV[0]
else
  print "Your name? "
  myself = STDIN.gets.chomp
end

if ARGV[1]
  opponent_id = ARGV[1]
else
  print "Your opponent? "
  opponent_id = STDIN.gets.chomp
end

opponent = opponent_id.split(":")[0]    # Remove hostname

# Contact the server

socket = TCPSocket.new(ChessServer, ChessServerPort)

response = nil

socket.puts "login #{myself} #{opponent_id}"
socket.flush
response = socket.gets.chomp

name, ipname, color = response.split ":"
color = color.to_i

if color == BLACK              # Other player's color
  puts "\nConnecting..."

  server = TCPServer.new(PeerPort)
  session = server.accept

  str = nil
  begin
    timeout(30) do
      str = session.gets.chomp
      if str != "ready"
        raise "Protocol error: ready-message was #{str}"
      end
    end
  rescue TimeoutError
    raise "Did not get ready-message from opponent."
  end

  puts "Playing #{opponent}... you are white.\n"
```

```ruby
who = WHITE
move = nil
board = nil        # Not really used in this dummy example
num = 0
draw_board(board) # Draw the board initially for white

loop do
  num += 1
  move = my_move(who, move, num, board, session)
  draw_board(board)
  case move
    when "resign"
      puts "\nYou've resigned. #{opponent} wins."
      break
    when /Checkmate/
      puts "\nYou have checkmated #{opponent}!"
      draw_board(board)
      break
  end
  move = other_move(who, move, num, board, session)
  draw_board(board)
  case move
    when "resign"
      puts "\n#{opponent} has resigned... you win!"
      break
    when /Checkmate/
      puts "\n#{opponent} has checkmated you."
      break
  end
end
else                              # We're black
  puts "\nConnecting..."

  socket = TCPSocket.new(ipname, PeerPort)
  socket.puts "ready"

  puts "Playing #{opponent}... you are black.\n"

  who = BLACK
  move = nil
  board = nil        # Not really used in this dummy example
  num = 0
  draw_board(board)  # Draw board initially

  loop do
    num += 1
    move = other_move(who, move, num, board, socket)
    draw_board(board)  # Draw board after white move
    case move
      when "resign"
        puts "\n#{opponent} has resigned... you win!"
```

Continues

```
        break
      when /Checkmate/
        puts "\n#{opponent} has checkmated you."
        break
    end
    move = my_move(who, move, num, board, socket)
    draw_board(board)
    case move
      when "resign"
        puts "\nYou've resigned. #{opponent} wins."
        break
      when /Checkmate/
        puts "\nYou have checkmated #{opponent}!"
        break
    end
  end
  socket.close
end
```

I've defined this little protocol so that the black client sends a "ready" message to the white client to let it know it's prepared to begin the game. The white player then moves first. The move is sent to the black client so that it can draw its own board in sync with the other player's board.

Again, there's no real knowledge of chess built into this application. There's a stub in place to check the validity of each player's move; this check is done on the local side in each case. But this is only a stub that always says that the move is legal. At the same time, it does a bit of hocus-pocus; we want this simulated game to end after only a few moves, so we fix the game so that black always wins on the fourth move. This win is indicated by appending the string "Checkmate!" to the move; this prints on the opponent's screen and also serves to terminate the loop.

Besides the "traditional" notation (for example, "P-K4"), there is also an "algebraic" notation preferred by most people. However, the code is stubbed so heavily that it doesn't even know which notation we're using.

Because it's easy to do, we allow a player to resign at any time. This is simply a win for the opponent. The drawing of the board is also a stub. Those wanting to do so can easily design some bad ASCII art to output here.

The my_move method always refers to the local side; likewise, other_move refers to the remote side.

Listing 18.3 shows some sample output. The client executions are displayed side by side in this listing.

Listing 18.3   Sample Chess Client Execution

```
% ruby chess.rb Hal                   % ruby chess.rb
  Capablanca:deepthought.org            Hal:deepdoodoo.org

Connecting...                         Connecting...
Playing Capablanca... you are white.  Playing Hal... you are black.
+-----------------------------+      +------------------------------+
| Stub! Drawing the board here... |   | Stub! Drawing the board here... |
+-----------------------------+      +------------------------------+

Your move: N-QB3                      Opponent: N-QB3
+-----------------------------+      +------------------------------+
| Stub! Drawing the board here... |   | Stub! Drawing the board here... |
+-----------------------------+      +------------------------------+

Opponent: P-K4                        Your move: P-K4
+-----------------------------+      +------------------------------+
| Stub! Drawing the board here... |   | Stub! Drawing the board here... |
+-----------------------------+      +------------------------------+

Your move: P-K4                       Opponent: P-K4
+-----------------------------+      +------------------------------+
| Stub! Drawing the board here... |   | Stub! Drawing the board here... |
+-----------------------------+      +------------------------------+

Opponent: B-QB4                       Your move: B-QB4
+-----------------------------+      +------------------------------+
| Stub! Drawing the board here... |   | Stub! Drawing the board here... |
+-----------------------------+      +------------------------------+

Your move: B-QB4                      Opponent: B-QB4
+-----------------------------+      +------------------------------+
| Stub! Drawing the board here... |   | Stub! Drawing the board here... |
+-----------------------------+      +------------------------------+

Opponent: Q-KR5                       Your move: Q-KR5
+-----------------------------+      +------------------------------+
| Stub! Drawing the board here... |   | Stub! Drawing the board here... |
+-----------------------------+      +------------------------------+

Your move: N-KB3                      Opponent: N-KB3
+-----------------------------+      +------------------------------+
| Stub! Drawing the board here... |   | Stub! Drawing the board here... |
+-----------------------------+      +------------------------------+

Opponent: QxP  Checkmate!             Your move: QxP
+-----------------------------+      +------------------------------+
| Stub! Drawing the board here... |   | Stub! Drawing the board here... |
+-----------------------------+      +------------------------------+

Capablanca has checkmated you.        You have checkmated Hal!
```

18.2   Network Clients

Sometimes the server is a well-known entity or is using a well-established protocol. In this case, we need simply to design a client that will talk to this server in the way it expects.

This can be done with TCP or UDP, as we saw in section 18.1. But it is common to use other higher-level protocols such as HTTP or SNMP. We'll look at a few examples here.

18.2.1   Retrieving Truly Random Numbers from the Web

Anyone who attempts to generate random numbers by deterministic means is, of course, living in a state of sin.

— John von Neumann

There is a rand function in Kernel to return a random number; but there is a fundamental problem with it. It isn't really random. If you are a mathematician, cryptographer, or other nitpicker, you will refer to this as a *pseudorandom* number generator because it uses algebraic methods to generate numbers in a deterministic fashion. These numbers "look" random to the casual observer, and may even have the correct statistical properties, but the sequences *do* repeat eventually, and we can even repeat a sequence purposely (or accidentally) by using the same seed.

But processes in nature are considered to be truly random. That is why in state lotteries, winners of millions of dollars are picked based on the chaotic motions of little white balls. Other sources of randomness are radioactive emissions or atmospheric noise.

There are sources of random numbers on the Web. One of these is www.random.org, which we use in this example.

The sample code in Listing 18.4 simulates the throwing of five ordinary (six-sided) dice. Of course, gaming fans could extend it to 10-sided or 20-sided, but the ASCII art would get tedious.

Listing 18.4   Casting Dice at Random

```
require 'net/http'

HOST = "www.random.org"
RAND_URL = "/cgi-bin/randnum?col=5&"

def get_random_numbers(count=1, min=0, max=99)
```

```
    path = RAND_URL + "num=#{count}&min=#{min}&max=#{max}"
    connection = Net::HTTP.new(HOST)
    response, data = connection.get(path)
    if response.code == "200"
      data.split.collect { |num| num.to_i }
    else
      []
    end
  end

  DICE_LINES = [
    "+-----+ +-----+ +-----+ +-----+ +-----+ +-----+ ",
    "|     | |  *  | |  *  | | * * | | * * | | * * | ",
    "|  *  | |     | |  *  | |     | |  *  | | * * | ",
    "|     | |  *  | |  *  | | * * | | * * | | * * | ",
    "+-----+ +-----+ +-----+ +-----+ +-----+ +-----+ "
  ]

  DIE_WIDTH = DICE_LINES[0].length/6

  def draw_dice(values)
    DICE_LINES.each do |line|
      for v in values
        print line[(v-1)*DIE_WIDTH, DIE_WIDTH]
        print " "
      end
      puts
    end
  end

  draw_dice(get_random_numbers(5, 1, 6))
```

In the previous code, we're using the Net::HTTP class to communicate directly with a web server. Think of it as a highly special-purpose web browser. We form the URL and try to connect; when we make a connection, we get a response and a piece of data; if the response indicates that all is well, we can parse the data that we got back. Exceptions are assumed to be handled by the caller.

Let's look at a variation on the same basic idea. What if we really wanted to use these random numbers in an application? Because the CGI at the server end allows us to specify how many numbers we want returned, it's logical to buffer them. It's a fact of life that a delay is usually involved when accessing a remote site. We want to fill a buffer so that we are not making frequent web accesses and incurring delays.

In Listing 18.5, we implement this variation. The buffer is filled by a separate thread, and it is shared among all the instances of the class. The buffer size and the "low water mark" (@slack) are both tunable; appropriate real-world values for them

would be dependent on the reachability (ping-time) of the server and on how often
the application requested a random number from the buffer.

Listing 18.5   A Buffered Random Number Generator

```ruby
require "net/http"
require "thread"

class TrueRandom

  def initialize(min=nil,max=nil,buff=nil,slack=nil)
    @buffer = []
    @site = "www.random.org"
    if ! defined? @init_flag
      # Set real defaults if not specified AND the class
      #   is being instantiated for the first time...
      @min = min || 0
      @max = max || 1
      @bufsize = buff || 1000
      @slacksize = slack || 300
      @mutex = Mutex.new
      @thread = Thread.new { fillbuffer }
      @init_flag = TRUE  # Could really be any value
    else
      @min = min || @min
      @max = max || @max
      @bufsize = buff || @bufsize
      @slacksize = slack || @slacksize
    end
    @url  = "/cgi-bin/randnum" +
            "?num=#@bufsize&min=#@min&max=#@max&col=1"
  end

  def fillbuffer
    h = Net::HTTP.new(@site, 80)
    resp, data = h.get(@url, nil)
    @buffer += data.split
  end

  def rand
    num = nil
    @mutex.synchronize { num = @buffer.shift }
    if @buffer.size < @slacksize
      if ! @thread.alive?
        @thread = Thread.new { fillbuffer }
      end
    end
    if num == nil
      if @thread.alive?
        @thread.join
```

```
      else
        @thread = Thread.new { fillbuffer }
        @thread.join
      end
      @mutex.synchronize { num = @buffer.shift }
    end
    num.to_i
  end

end

t = TrueRandom.new(1,6,1000,300)

count = {1=>0, 2=>0, 3=>0, 4=>0, 5=>0, 6=>0}

10000.times do |n|
  x = t.rand
  count[x] += 1
end

p count

# In one run:
# {4=>1692, 5=>1677, 1=>1678, 6=>1635, 2=>1626, 3=>1692}
```

18.2.2 Contacting an Official Timeserver

As we promised, here's a bit of code to contact an NTP (Network Time Protocol) server on the Net. We do this by means of a telnet client. The following code is adapted from a piece of code by Dave Thomas.

```
require "net/telnet"
timeserver = "www.fakedomain.org"

local = Time.now.strftime("%H:%M:%S")
tn = Net::Telnet.new("Host"       => timeserver,
                     "Port"       => "time",
                     "Timeout"    => 60,
                     "Telnetmode" => false)
msg = tn.recv(4).unpack('N')[0]
# Convert to epoch
remote = Time.at(msg - 2208988800).strftime("%H:%M:%S")

puts "Local : #{local}"
puts "Remote: #{remote}"
```

We establish a connection and grab four bytes. These represent a 32-bit quantity in network byte order (big endian); we convert this number to something we can digest and then convert from the epoch to a `Time` object.

Note that we didn't use a real timeserver name. This is because the usefulness of such a server frequently depends on your geographic location. Furthermore, many of these have access restrictions and may require permission or at least notification before they are used. A web search should turn up an open-access NTP server less than 1,000 miles from you.

18.2.3   Interacting with a POP Server

The *Post Office Protocol* (POP) is commonly used by mail servers. Ruby's POP3 class enables you to examine the headers and bodies of all messages waiting on a server and process them as you see fit. After processing, you can easily delete one or all of them.

The `Net::POP3` class must be instantiated with the name or IP address of the server; the port number defaults to 110. No connection is established until the method `start` is invoked (with the appropriate username and password).

Invoking the method `mails` on this object will return an array of objects of class POPMail. (There is also an iterator `each` that will run through these one at a time.)

A POPMail object corresponds to a single email message. The `header` method will retrieve the message's headers; the method `all` will retrieve the header and the body. (There are also other usages of `all` as we'll see shortly.)

A code fragment is worth a thousand words. Here's a little example that will log on to the server and print the subject line for each email:

```
require "net/pop"

pop = Net::POP3.new("pop.fakedomain.org")
pop.start("gandalf", "mellon")      # user, password
pop.mails.each do |msg|
  puts msg.header.grep /^Subject: /
end
```

The `delete` method will delete a message from the server. (Some servers require that `finish` be called to close the POP connection before such an operation becomes final.) Here is the world's most trivial spam filter:

```
require "net/pop"

pop = Net::POP3.new("pop.fakedomain.org")
pop.start("gandalf", "mellon")      # user, password
pop.mails.each do |msg|
  if msg.all =~ /.*make money fast.*/
    msg.delete
  end
end
pop.finish
```

We'll mention that `start` can be called with a block. By analogy with `File.open`, it opens the connection, executes the block, and closes the connection.

The `all` method can also be called with a block. This will simply iterate over the lines in the email message; it is equivalent to calling `each` on the string resulting from `all`.

```
# Print each line backwards... how useful!
msg.all { |line| print line.reverse }
# Same thing...
msg.all.each { |line| print line.reverse }
```

We can also pass an object into the `all` method. In this case, it will call the append operator (`<<`) repeatedly for each line in the string. Because this operator is defined differently for different objects, the behavior may be radically different, as shown here:

```
arr = []          # Empty array
str = "Mail: "    # String
out = $stdout      # IO object

msg.all(arr)      # Build an array of lines
msg.all(str)      # Concatenate onto str
msg.all(out)      # Write to standard output
```

Finally, we'll give you a way to return only the body of the message, ignoring all headers.

```
module Net

  class POPMail

    def body
      # Skip header bytes
      self.all[self.header.size..-1]
    end

  end

end
```

This doesn't have all the properties that all has, but it could be extended. We'll leave that to you.

For those who prefer IMAP to POP3, see section 18.2.5, "Interacting with an IMAP Server."

18.2.4   Sending Mail with SMTP

A child of five could understand this. Fetch me a child of five.

— Groucho Marx

The Simple Mail Transfer Protocol (SMTP) may seem like a misnomer. If it is "simple," it is only by comparison with more complex protocols.

Of course, the smtp.rb library shields the programmer from most of the details of the protocol. However, we have found that the design of this library is not entirely intuitive and perhaps overly complex (and we hope it will change in the future). In this section, we try to present a few examples to you in easily digested pieces.

The Net::SMTP class has two class methods, new and start. The new method takes two parameters—the name of the server (defaulting to localhost) and the port number (defaulting to the well-known port 25).

The `start` method takes these parameters:

- *server* is the IP name of the SMTP server, defaulting to `"localhost"`.
- *port* is the port number, defaulting to `25`.
- *domain* is the domain of the mail sender, defaulting to `ENV["HOSTNAME"]`.
- *account* is the username, default is `nil`.
- *password* is the user password, defaulting to `nil`.
- *authtype* is the authorization type, defaulting to `:cram_md5`.

Many or most of these parameters may be omitted under normal circumstances.

If `start` is called "normally" (without a block), it returns an object of class `SMTP`. If it is called with a block, that object is passed into the block as a convenience.

An `SMTP` object has an instance method called `sendmail`, which will typically be used to do the work of mailing a message. It takes three parameters:

- *source* is a string or array (or anything with an `each` iterator returning one string at a time).
- *sender* is a string that will appear in the "from" field of the email.
- *recipients* is a string or an array of strings representing the addressee(s).

Here is an example of using the `class` methods to send an email:

```
require 'net/smtp'

msg = <<EOF
Subject: Many things
"The time has come," the Walrus said,
"To talk of many things --
Of shoes, and ships, and sealing wax,
Of cabbages and kings;
And why the sea is boiling hot,
And whether pigs have wings."
EOF

Net::SMTP.start("smtp-server.fake.com") do |smtp|
  smtp.sendmail msg, 'walrus@fake1.com', 'alice@fake2.com'
end
```

Because the string Subject: was specified at the beginning of the string, Many things will appear as the subject line when the message is received.

There is also an instance method named start, which behaves much the same as the class method. Because new specifies the server, start doesn't have to specify it. This parameter is omitted, and the others are the same as for the class method. This gives us a similar example using an SMTP object.

```
require 'net/smtp'

msg = <<EOF
Subject: Logic
"Contrariwise," continued Tweedledee,
"if it was so, it might be, and if it
were so, it would be; but as it isn't,
it ain't. That's logic."
EOF

smtp = Net::SMTP.new("smtp-server.fake.com")
smtp.start
smtp.sendmail msg, 'tweedledee@fake1.com', 'alice@fake2.com'
```

In case you are not confused yet, the instance method can also take a block.

```
require 'net/smtp'

msg = <<EOF
Subject: Moby-Dick
Call me Ishmael.
EOF

addressees = ['reader1@fake2.com', 'reader2@fake3.com']

smtp = Net::SMTP.new("smtp-server.fake.com")
smtp.start do |obj|
  obj.sendmail msg, 'narrator@fake1.com', addressees
end
```

As the example shows, the object passed into the block (obj) certainly need not be named the same as the receiver (smtp). I'll also take this opportunity to emphasize that the recipient can be an array of strings.

There is also an oddly named instance method called ready. This is much the same as sendmail, with some crucial differences. Only the sender and recipients are specified; the body of the message is constructed using an adapter—an object of class Net::NetPrivate::WriteAdapter, which has a write method as well as an append method. This adapter is passed into the block and can be written to in an arbitrary way.

```
require "net/smtp"

smtp = Net::SMTP.new("smtp-server.fake1.com")

smtp.start

smtp.ready("t.s.eliot@fake1.com", "reader@fake2.com") do |obj|
  obj.write "Let us go then, you and I,\r\n"
  obj.write "When the evening is spread out against the sky\r\n"
  obj.write "Like a patient etherised upon a table...\r\n"
end
```

Note here that the carriage-return linefeed pairs are necessary (if we actually want line breaks in the message). Those who are familiar with the actual details of the protocol should note that the message is "finalized" (with "dot" and "QUIT") without any action on our part.

We can append instead of calling write if we want:

```
smtp.ready("t.s.eliot@fake1.com", "reader@fake2.com") do |obj|
  obj << "In the room the women come and go\r\n"
  obj << "Talking of Michelangelo.\r\n"
end
```

Finally, we offer a minor improvement; we add a puts method that will tack on the newline for us.

```
class Net::NetPrivate::WriteAdapter
  def puts(args)
    args << "\r\n"
    self.write(*args)
  end
end
```

This new method enables us to write this way:

```
smtp.ready("t.s.eliot@fake1.com", "reader@fake2.com") do |obj|
  obj.puts "We have lingered in the chambers of the sea"
  obj.puts "By sea-girls wreathed with seaweed red and brown"
  obj.puts "Till human voices wake us, and we drown."
end
```

If your needs are more specific than what we've detailed here, we suggest you do your own experimentation. And if you decide to write a new interface for SMTP, please feel free.

18.2.5   Interacting with an IMAP Server

The IMAP protocol is not the prettiest in the world, but it is superior to POP3 in many ways. Messages may be stored on the server indefinitely (individually marked as read or unread). Messages may be stored in hierarchical folders. These two facts alone are enough to establish IMAP as more powerful than POP3.

The standard library net/imap enables us to interact with an IMAP server. As you would expect, you connect to the server and then log in to an account with a user-name and password, as shown in the following code:

```
require 'net/imap'

host = "imap.hogwarts.edu"
user, pass = "lupin", "riddikulus"

imap = Net::IMAP.new(host)
begin
  imap.login(user, pass)
  # Or alternately:
  # imap.authenticate("LOGIN", user, pass)
rescue Net::IMAP::NoResponseError
  abort "Could not login as #{user}"
end

# Process as needed...

imap.logout    # break the connection
```

After you have a connection, you can do an `examine` on a mailbox; the default mailbox in IMAP is called INBOX. The `responses` method retrieves information about the mailbox, returning a hash of arrays (with the interesting data in the last element of each array). The following code finds the total number of messages in the mailbox (`"EXISTS"`) and the number of unread messages (`"RECENT"`):

```
imap.examine("INBOX")
total = imap.responses["EXISTS"].last      # total messages
recent = imap.responses["RECENT"].last     # unread messages
imap.close                                 # close the mailbox
```

Note that `examine` gives you read-only access to the mailbox. If, for example, you want to delete messages or make other changes, you should use `select` instead.

IMAP mailboxes are hierarchical and look similar to UNIX pathnames. You can use the `create`, `delete`, and `rename` methods to manipulate mailboxes:

```
imap.create("lists")
imap.create("lists/ruby")
imap.create("lists/rails")
imap.create("lists/foobar")

# Oops, kill that last one:
imap.delete("lists/foobar")
```

There are also methods named `list` (to list all the available mailboxes) and `lsub` (to list all the "active" or "subscribed" mailboxes). The `status` method will return information about the mailbox.

The `search` method will find messages according to specified criteria, and `fetch` will fetch a given message. Here is an example:

```
msgs = imap.search("TO","lupin")
msgs.each do |mid|
  env = imap.fetch(mid, "ENVELOPE")[0].attr["ENVELOPE"]
  puts "From #{env.from[0].name}      #{env.subject}"
end
```

The `fetch` command in the preceding code appears convoluted because it returns an array of hashes. The envelope itself is similarly complex; some of its accessors are arrays of complex objects, and some are simply strings.

IMAP has the concept of UID (unique IDs) and sequence numbers for messages. Typically, methods such as fetch deal with sequence numbers and have counterparts such as uid_fetch that deal with UIDs. There is no room here to explain why both numbering systems are appropriate; if you are doing any significant programming with IMAP, however, you will need to know the difference (and never get them mixed up).

The net/imap library has extensive support for handling mailboxes, messages, attachments, and so on. For more details, refer to the online documentation at ruby-doc.org.

18.2.6   Encoding/Decoding Attachments

Files are usually attached to email or news messages in a special encoded form. More often than not, the encoding is base64, which can be encoded or decoded with the pack directive m:

```
bin = File.read("new.gif")
str = [bin].pack("m")        # str is now encoded


orig = str.unpack("m")[0]    # orig == bin
```

Older mail clients may prefer to work with uuencode and uudecode; in a case like this, an attachment is more a state of mind than anything else. The attachment is simply appended to the end of the email text, bracketed inside begin and end lines, with the begin line also specifying file permissions (which may be ignored) and filename. The pack directive u serves to encode a uuencoded string. The following code shows an example:

```
# Assume mailtext holds the text of the email

filename = "new.gif"
bin = File.read(filename)
encoded = [bin].pack("u")

mailtext << "begin 644 #{filename}"
mailtext << encoded
mailtext << "end"
# ...
```

On the receiving end, we would extract the encoded information and use unpack to
decode it:

```
# ...
# Assume 'attached' has the encoded data (including the
# begin and end lines)

lines = attached.split("\n")
filename = /begin \d\d\d (.*)/.scan(lines[0]).first.first
encoded = lines[1..-2].join("\n")
decoded = encoded.unpack("u")        # Ready to write to filename
```

More modern mail readers usually use MIME format for email; even the text part of
the email is wrapped (although the client strips all the header information before the
user sees it).

A complete treatment of MIME would be lengthy and off-topic here. However,
the following code shows a simple example of encoding and sending an email with a
text portion and a binary attachment. The encoding for binaries is usually base64 as
shown here.

```
require 'net/smtp'

def text_plus_attachment(subject,body,filename)
  marker = "MIME_boundary"
  middle = "--#{marker}\n"
  ending = "--#{middle}--\n"
  content = "Content-Type: Multipart/Related; " +
            "boundary=#{marker}; " +
            "typw=text/plain"
  head1 = <<-EOF
MIME-Version: 1.0
#{content}
Subject: #{subject}
  EOF
  binary = File.read(filename)
  encoded = [binary].pack("m")   # base64
  head2 = <<EOF
Content-Description: "#{filename}"
Content-Type: image/gif; name="#{filename}"
Content-Transfer-Encoding: Base64
Content-Disposition: attachment; filename="#{filename}"
```

```
EOF

    # Return...
    head1 + middle + body + middle + head2 + encoded + ending
  end


  domain   = "someserver.com"
  smtp     = "smtp.#{domain}"
  user, pass = "elgar","enigma"


  body = <<EOF
  This is my email. There isn't
  much to say. I attached a
  very small GIF file here.


         -- Bob
  EOF


  mailtext = text_plus_attachment("Hi, there...",body,"new.gif")

  Net::SMTP.start(smtp, 25, domain, user, pass, :plain) do |mailer|
    mailer.sendmail(mailtext, 'fromthisguy@wherever.com',
                    ['destination@elsewhere.com'])
  end
```

18.2.7   Case Study: A Mail-News Gateway

Online communities keep in touch with each other in many ways. Two of the most traditional of these are mailing lists and newsgroups.

Not everyone wants to be on a mailing list that may generate dozens of messages per day; some would rather read a newsgroup and pick through the information at random intervals. On the other hand, some people are impatient with Usenet and want to get the messages before the electrons have time to cool off.

So we get situations in which a fairly small, private mailing list deals with the same subject matter as an unmoderated newsgroup open to the whole world. Eventually someone gets the idea for a mirror—a gateway between the two.

Such a gateway isn't appropriate in every situation, but in the case of the Ruby mailing list, it was and is. The newsgroup messages needed to be copied to the list, and the list emails needed to be posted on the newsgroup.

This need was addressed by Dave Thomas (in Ruby, of course), and we present the code with his kind permission in Listings 18.6 and 18.7.

But let's look at a little background first. We've taken a quick look at how email is sent and received, but how do we handle Usenet? As it turns out, we can access the newsgroups via a protocol called *NNTP* (Network News Transfer Protocol). This creation, incidentally, was the work of Larry Wall, who later on gave us Perl.

Ruby doesn't have a "standard" library to handle NNTP. However, a Japanese developer (known to us only as *greentea*) has written a nice library for this purpose.

The nntp.rb library defines a module NNTP containing a class called NNTPIO; it has instance methods connect, get_head, get_body, and post (among others). To retrieve messages, you connect to the server and call get_head and get_body, repetitively. (We're oversimplifying this.) Likewise, to post a message, you basically construct the headers, connect to the server, and call the post method.

These programs use the smtp library, which we've looked at previously. The original code also does some logging to track progress and record errors; we've removed this logging for greater simplicity.

The file params.rb is used by both programs. This file contains the parameters that drive the whole mirroring process—the names of the servers, account names, and so on. The following is a sample file that you will need to reconfigure for your own purposes. (The domain names used in the code, which all contain the word *fake*, are obviously intended to be fictitious.)

```
# These are various parameters used by the mail-news gateway

module Params
    NEWS_SERVER = "usenet.fake1.org"      # name of the news server
    NEWSGROUP   = "comp.lang.ruby"        # mirrored newsgroup
    LOOP_FLAG   = "X-rubymirror: yes"     #  avoid loops
    LAST_NEWS_FILE = "/tmp/m2n/last_news" # last msg num read
    SMTP_SERVER = "localhost"             # host for outgoing mail

    MAIL_SENDER = "myself@fake2.org"      # Name used to send mail
    # (On a subscription-based list, this
    # name must be a list member.)

    MAILING_LIST = "list@fake3.org"       # Mailing list address
end
```

The module Params merely contains constants that are accessed by the two programs. Most are self-explanatory; we'll only point out a couple of items here. First, the LAST_NEWS_FILE constant identifies a file where the most recent newsgroup message ID is stored; this is "state information," so that work is not duplicated or lost.

Perhaps even more important, the LOOP_FLAG constant defines a string that marks a message as having already passed through the gateway. This avoids infinite recursion and prevents the programmer from being mobbed by hordes of angry netizens who have received thousands of copies of the same message.

You might be wondering: How do we actually get the mail into the mail2news program? After all, it appears to read standard input. Well, the author recommends a setup like this: The sendmail program's .forward file first forwards all incoming mail to procmail. The .procmail file is set up to scan for messages from the mailing list and pipe them into the mail2news program. For the exact details of this, see the documentation associated with RubyMirror (found in the Ruby Application Archive). Of course, if you are on a non-UNIX system, you will likely have to come up with your own scheme for handling this situation.

Aside from what we've already said, we'll let the code stand on its own, as shown in Listings 18.6 and 18.7.

Listing 18.6   Mail-to-News

```
# mail2news: Take a mail message and post it
# as a news article

require "nntp"
include NNTP

require "params"

# Read in the message, splitting it into a
# heading and a body. Only allow certain
# headers through in the heading

HEADERS = %w{From Subject References Message-ID
             Content-Type Content-Transfer-Encoding Date}

allowed_headers = Regexp.new(%{^(#{HEADERS.join("|")}):})

# Read in the header. Only allow certain
# ones. Add a newsgroups line and an
# X-rubymirror line.

head = "Newsgroups: #{Params::NEWSGROUP}\n"
subject = "unknown"
```

```
while line = gets
  exit if line =~ /^#{Params::LOOP_FLAG}/o # shouldn't happen
  break if line =~ /^\s*$/
  next if line =~ /^\s/
  next unless line =~ allowed_headers

  # strip off the [ruby-talk:nnnn] prefix on the subject before
  # posting back to the news group
  if line =~ /^Subject:\s*(.*)/
    subject = $1

    # The following strips off the special ruby-talk number
    # from the front of mailing list messages before
    # forwarding them on to the news server.

    line.sub!(/\[ruby-talk:(\d+)\]\s*/, '')
    subject = "[#$1] #{line}"
    head << "X-ruby-talk: #$1\n"
  end
  head << line
end

head << "#{Params::LOOP_FLAG}\n"


body = ""
while line = gets
  body << line
end

msg = head + "\n" + body
msg.gsub!(/\r?\n/, "\r\n")

nntp = NNTPIO.new(Params::NEWS_SERVER)
raise "Failed to connect" unless nntp.connect
nntp.post(msg)
```

Listing 18.7   News-to-Mail

```
##
# Simple script to help mirror the comp.lang.ruby
# traffic on to the ruby-talk mailing list.
#
# We are called periodically (say once every 20 minutes).
# We look on the news server for any articles that have a
# higher message ID than the last message we'd sent
# previously. If we find any, we read those articles,
# send them on to the mailing list, and record the
# new hightest message id.
```

Continues

```
require 'nntp'
require 'net/smtp'
require 'params'

include NNTP

##
# Send mail to the mailing-list. The mail must be
# from a list participant, although the From: line
# can contain any valid address
#

def send_mail(head, body)
  smtp = Net::SMTP.new
  smtp.start(Params::SMTP_SERVER)
  smtp.ready(Params::MAIL_SENDER, Params::MAILING_LIST) do |a|
    a.write head
    a.write "#{Params::LOOP_FLAG}\r\n"
    a.write "\r\n"
    a.write body
  end
end

##
# We store the message ID of the last news we received.

begin
  last_news = File.open(Params::LAST_NEWS_FILE) {|f| f.read} .to_i
rescue
  last_news = nil
end

##
# Connect to the news server, and get the current
# message numbers for the comp.lang.ruby group
#
nntp = NNTPIO.new(Params::NEWS_SERVER)
raise "Failed to connect" unless nntp.connect
count, first, last = nntp.set_group(Params::NEWSGROUP)

##
# If we didn't previously have a number for the highest
# message number, we do now

if not last_news
  last_news = last
end
```

```
##
# Go to the last one read last time, and then try to get more.
# This may raise an exception if the number is for a
# nonexistent article, but we don't care.

begin
  nntp.set_stat(last_news)
rescue
end

##
# Finally read articles until there aren't any more,
# sending each to the mailing list.

new_last = last_news

begin
  loop do
    nntp.set_next
    head = ""
    body = ""
    new_last, = nntp.get_head do |line|
      head << line
    end

    # Don't sent on articles that the mail2news program has
    # previously forwarded to the newsgroup (or we'd loop)
    next if head =~ %r{^X-rubymirror:}

    nntp.get_body do |line|
      body << line
    end

    send_mail(head, body)
  end
rescue
end

##
# And record the new high water mark

File.open(Params::LAST_NEWS_FILE, "w") do |f|
  f.puts  new_last
end unless new_last == last_news
```

18.2.8   Retrieving a Web Page from a URL

Suppose that, for whatever reason, we want to retrieve an HTML document from where it lives on the Web. Maybe our intent is to do a checksum and find whether it has changed so that our software can inform us of this automatically. Maybe our intent is to write our own web browser; this would be the proverbial first step on a journey of a thousand miles.

Here's the code:

```
require "net/http"

begin
  h = Net::HTTP.new("www.marsdrive.com", 80)    # MarsDrive Consortium
  resp, data = h.get("/index.html", nil)
rescue => err
  puts "Error: #{err}"
  exit
end

puts "Retrieved #{data.split.size} lines, #{data.size} bytes"
# Process as desired...
```

We begin by instantiating an HTTP object with the appropriate domain name and port. (The port, of course, is usually 80.) We then do a get operation, which returns an HTTP response and a string full of data. Here we don't actually test the response, but if there is any kind of error, we'll catch it and exit.

If we skip the rescue clause as we normally would, we can expect to have an entire web page stored in the data string. We can then process it however we want.

What could go wrong here—what kind of errors do we catch? Actually, there are several. The domain name could be nonexistent or unreachable; there could be a redirect to another page (which we don't handle here); or we might get the dreaded 404 error (meaning that the document was not found). We'll leave this kind of error handling to you.

The next section (18.2.9 "Using the Open-URI Library") will also be useful to you. It shows a slightly simpler way of handling this kind of task.

18.2.9   Using the Open-URI Library

The Open-URI library is the work of Tanaka Akira. Its purpose is to "unify" the programmatic treatment of Net resources so that they are all intuitive and easy to handle.

This code is essentially a wrapper for the `net/http`, `net/https`, and `net/ftp` libraries, making available an `open` method that will handle an arbitrary URI. The example from the preceding section can be written this way:

```
require 'open-uri'

data = nil
open("http://www.marsdrive.com/") {|f| data = f.read }

puts "Retrieved #{data.split.size} lines, #{data.size} bytes"
```

The file returned by `open` (`f` in the previous case) is not just a file. This object also has the methods of the `OpenURI::Meta` module so that we can access metadata:

```
# ...
uri = f.base_uri          # a URI object with its own readers
ct  = f.content_type      # "text/html"
cs  = f.charset           # "utf-8"
ce  = f.content_encoding  # []
```

The library allows the specifying of additional header fields by using a hash with the `open` command. It also handles proxy servers and has several other useful features. There are cases where this library may be insufficient; for example, you may need to parse HTTP headers, buffer extremely large downloads, send cookies, and other such tasks. For more information on this library, see the online documentation at http://ruby-doc.org.

18.3 Conclusion

In this chapter, we've had a good introduction to lower-level networking, including simple servers and clients. We've seen how to write a client for an existing server that we didn't create.

We've looked at higher level protocols such as POP and IMAP for receiving mail. Likewise we've looked at SMTP for sending mail. In connection with these, we've seen how to encode and decode file attachments. We've had an exposure to NNTP through the mail-news gateway code.

Now it's time to look more closely at a subset of this topic. One of the most important types of network programming today is web development, which is the topic of the next chapter.

CHAPTER 19

Ruby and Web Applications

O, what a tangled web we weave...!

—Sir Walter Scott, The Lay of the Last Minstrel

Ruby is a general-purpose language; it can't properly be called a "web language" at all. Even so, web applications (and web tools in general) are among the most common uses of Ruby.

There are many ways to do web development in Ruby, from toolkits and libraries that are small and low-level to frameworks that virtually dictate your style of coding and thinking.

Let's begin at the low end. We'll look first at the `cgi.rb` library that is standard in Ruby.

19.1 CGI Programming with Ruby

Anyone familiar with web programming has at least heard of *CGI* ("*Common Gateway Interface*"). CGI was created in the early days of the Web to enable programmatically implemented sites and to allow for more interaction between the end user and the web server. Although countless replacement technologies have been introduced since its inception, CGI is still alive and well in the world of web programming. Much of CGI's success and longevity can be attributed to its simplicity. Because of this simplicity, it is easy to implement CGI programs in any language. The CGI standard specifies how a web server process will pass data between itself and its children. Most of this interaction occurs through standard environment variables and streams in the implementation operating system.

CGI programming, and HTTP for that matter, are based around a "stateless" request and response mechanism. Generally, a single TCP connection is made, and the client (usually a web browser) initiates conversation with a single HTTP command. The two most commonly used commands in the protocol are GET and POST (we'll get to the meaning of these shortly). After issuing the command, the web server responds and closes its output stream.

The following code sample, only slightly more advanced than the standard "Hello, world," shows how to do input and output via CGI.

```
def parse_query_string
  inputs = Hash.new
  raw = ENV['QUERY_STRING']
  raw.split("&").each do |pair|
    name,value = pair.split("=")
    inputs[name] = value
  end
  inputs
end


inputs = parse_query_string
print "Content-type: text/html\n\n"
print "<HTML><BODY>"
print "<B><I>Hello</I>, #{inputs['name']}!</B>"
print "</BODY></HTML>"
```

Accessing the URL (for example) http://mywebserver/cgi-bin/hello.cgi? name=Dali would produce the output "*Hello*, Dali!" in your web browser.

As we previously mentioned, there are two main ways to access a URL: the HTTP GET and POST methods. For the sake of brevity, we offer simple explanations of these rather than rigorous definitions. The GET method is usually called when clicking a link or directly referencing a URL (as in the preceding example). Any parameters are passed via the URL query string, which is made accessible to CGI programs via the QUERY_STRING environment variable. The POST is usually used in HTML form processing. The parameters sent in a POST are included in the message body and are not visible via the URL. They are delivered to CGI programs via the standard input stream.

Though the preceding example was simple, anything less trivial could quickly become messy. Programs needing to deal with multiple HTTP methods, file uploads, cookies, "stateful" sessions, and other complexities are best suited by a general-purpose library for working with the CGI environment. Thankfully, Ruby provides a full-featured set of classes that automate much of the mundane work one would otherwise have to do manually.

Many other toolkits and libraries attempt to make CGI development easier. Among the best of these is Patrick May's ruby-web (formerly Narf). If you want a great deal of low-level control but the standard CGI library isn't to your liking, you might try this library instead (http://ruby-web.org).

If you want a templating solution, Amrita (http://amrita.sourceforge.jp) might be good for you. Also look at Cerise, the web application server based on Amrita (http://cerise.rubyforge.org).

There are probably still other libraries out there. As usual, if you don't find what you're looking for listed here, do an online search or ask on the newsgroup.

19.1.1   Introduction to the `cgi.rb` Library

The CGI library is in the file `cgi.rb` in the standard Ruby distribution. Most of its functionality is implemented around a central class aptly named `CGI`. One of the first things you'll want to do when using the library, then, is to create an instance of `CGI`.

```
require "cgi"
cgi = CGI.new("html4")
```

The initializer for the `CGI` class takes a single parameter, which specifies the level of HTML that should be supported by the HTML generation methods in the CGI package. These methods keep the programmer from having to embed a truckload of escaped HTML in otherwise pristine Ruby code:

```
cgi.out do
  cgi.html do
    cgi.body do
      cgi.h1 { "Hello Again, "} +
      cgi.b { cgi['name']}
    end
  end
end
```

Here, we've used the CGI libraries to almost exactly reproduce the functionality of the previous program. As you can see, the CGI class takes care of parsing any input and stores the resulting values internally as a hashlike structure. So if you specified the URL as some_program.cgi?age=4, the value could be accessed via cgi['age'].

Note in the preceding code that really only the return value of a block is used; the HTML is built up gradually and stored rather than being output immediately. This means that the string concatenation we see here is absolutely necessary; without it, only the last string evaluated would appear.

The CGI class also provides some convenience mechanisms for dealing with URL encoded strings and escaped HTML or XML. URL encoding is the process of translating strings with unsafe characters to a format that is representable in a URL string. The result is all of those weird-looking "%" strings you see in some URLs while you browse the web. These strings are actually the numeric ASCII codes represented in hexadecimal with "%" prepended.

```
require "cgi"
s = "This| is^(aT$test"
s2 = CGI.escape(s)          # "This%7C+is%5E%28aT%24test"
puts CGI.unescape(s2)       # Prints "This| is^(aT$test"
```

Similarly, the CGI class can be used to escape HTML or XML text that should be displayed verbatim in a browser. For example, the string "<some_stuff>" would not display properly in a browser. If there is a need to display HTML or XML literally in a browser—in an HTML tutorial, for example—the CGI class offers support for translating special characters to their appropriate entities:

```
require "cgi"
some_text = "<B>This is how you make text bold</B>"
translated = CGI.escapeHTML(some_text)
# "<B>This is how you make text bold</B>"
puts CGI.unescapeHTML(translated)
# Prints "<B>This is how you make text bold</B>"
```

19.1.2   Displaying and Processing Forms

The most common way of interacting with CGI programs is through HTML forms. HTML forms are created by using specific tags that will be translated to input widgets in a browser. A full discussion or reference is beyond the scope of this text, but numerous references are available both in books and on the Web.

The CGI class offers generation methods for all of the HTML form elements. The following example shows how to both display and process an HTML form.

```ruby
require "cgi"

def reverse_ramblings(ramblings)
  if ramblings[0] == nil then return " " end
  chunks = ramblings[0].split(/\s+/)
  chunks.reverse.join(" ")
end

cgi = CGI.new("html4")
cgi.out do
  cgi.html do
    cgi.body do
      cgi.h1 { "sdrawkcaB txeT" } +
      cgi.b { reverse_ramblings(cgi['ramblings'])} +
      cgi.form("action" => "/cgi-bin/rb/form.cgi") do
        cgi.textarea("ramblings") { cgi['ramblings'] } + cgi.submit
      end
    end
  end
end
```

This example displays a text area, the contents of which will be tokenized into words and reversed. For example, typing "This is a test" into the text area would yield "test a is This" after processing. The form method of the CGI class can accept a method parameter, which will set the HTTP method (GET, POST, and so on) to be used on form submittal. The default, used in this example, is POST.

This example contains only a small sample of the form elements available in an HTML page. For a complete list, go to any HTML reference.

19.1.3   Working with Cookies

HTTP is, as mentioned previously, a stateless protocol. This means that, after a browser finishes a request to a website, the web server has no way to distinguish its next request from any other arbitrary browser on the Web. This is where HTTP cookies come into the picture. Cookies offer a way, albeit somewhat crude, to maintain state between requests from the same browser.

The cookie mechanism works by way of the web server issuing a command to the browser, via an HTTP response header, asking the browser to store a name/value pair. The data can be stored either in memory or on disk. For every successive request to the cookie's specified domain, the browser will send the cookie data in an HTTP request header.

Of course, you could read and write all of these cookies manually, but you've probably already guessed that you're not going to need to. Ruby's CGI libraries provide a Cookie class that conveniently handles these chores.

```
require "cgi"
lastacc = CGI::Cookie.new("kabhi",
                          "lastaccess=#{Time.now.to_s}")
cgi = CGI.new("html3")
if cgi.cookies.size < 1
  cgi.out("cookie" => lastacc) do
    "Hit refresh for a lovely cookie"
  end
else
  cgi.out("cookie" => lastacc) do
    cgi.html do
      "Hi, you were last here at: "+
      "#{cgi.cookies['kabhi'].join.split('=')[1]}"
    end
  end
end
```

Here, a cookie called "kabhi" is created, with the key "lastaccess" set to the current time. Then, if the browser has a previous value stored for this cookie, it is displayed. The cookies are represented as an instance variable on the CGI class and stored as a Hash. Each cookie can store multiple key/value pairs, so when you access a cookie by name, you will receive an array.

19.1.4   Working with User Sessions

Cookies are fine if you want to store simple data and you don't mind the browser being responsible for persistence. But, in many cases, data persistence needs are a bit more complex. What if you have a lot of data you want to maintain persistently and you don't want to have to send it back and forth from the client and server with each request? What if there is sensitive data you need associated with a session and you don't trust the browser with it?

For more advanced persistence in web applications, use the `CGI::Session` class. Working with this class is similar to working with the `CGI::Cookie` class in that values are stored and retrieved via a hashlike structure.

```ruby
require "cgi"
require "cgi/session"

cgi = CGI.new("html4")

sess = CGI::Session.new( cgi, "session_key" => "a_test",
                              "prefix" => "rubysess.")
lastaccess = sess["lastaccess"].to_s
sess["lastaccess"] = Time.now
if cgi['bgcolor'][0] =~ /[a-z]/
  sess["bgcolor"] = cgi['bgcolor']
end

cgi.out do
  cgi.html do
    cgi.body ("bgcolor" => sess["bgcolor"]) do
      "The background of this page"     +
      "changes based on the 'bgcolor'" +
      "each user has in session."       +
      "Last access time: #{lastaccess}"
    end
  end
end
```

Accessing `"/thatscript.cgi?bgcolor=red"` would turn the page red for a single user for each successive hit until a new `"bgcolor"` was specified via the URL. `CGI::Session` is instantiated with a `CGI` object and a set of options in a `Hash`. The optional `session_key` parameter specifies the key that will be used by the browser to identify itself on each request. Session data is stored in a temporary file for each session, and the `prefix` parameter assigns a string to be prepended to the filename, making your sessions easy to identify on the filesystem of the server.

`CGI::Session` still lacks many features, such as the capability to store objects other than `Strings`, session storage across multiple servers, and other "nice-to-haves."

Fortunately, a pluggable `database_manager` mechanism is already in place and would make some of these features easy to add. If you do anything exciting with `CGI::Session`, be sure to share it.

19.2   Using FastCGI

The most often criticized shortcoming of CGI is that it requires a new process to be created for every invocation. The effect on performance is significant. The lack of the capability to leave objects in memory between requests can also have a negative impact on design. The combination of these difficulties has led to the creation of *FastCGI*.

FastCGI is basically nothing more than a protocol definition and software implementing that protocol. Usually implemented as a web server plugin, such as an Apache module, FastCGI allows an in-process helper to intercept HTTP requests and route them via socket to a long running backend process. This has a positive effect on speed compared to the traditional forking approach. It also gives the programmer the freedom to put things in memory and still find them there on the next request.

Conveniently, servers for FastCGI have been implemented in a number of languages, including Ruby. Eli Green created a module (available via the RAA) entirely in Ruby that implements the FastCGI protocol and eases the development of FastCGI programs.

Without going into every detail of how this works, we present a sample application in Listing 9.1. As you can see, this code fragment mirrors the functionality of the earlier example.

Listing 19.1   A FastCGI Example

```
require "fastcgi"
require "cgi"

last_time = ""

def get_ramblings(instream)
  # Unbeautifully retrieve the value of the first name/value pair
  # CGI would have done this for us.
  data = ""
  if instream != nil
    data = instream.split("&")[0].split("=")[1] || ""
  end
  return CGI.unescape(data)
end
```

```
def reverse_ramblings(ramblings)
  if ramblings == nil then return "" end
  chunks = ramblings.split(/\s+/)
  chunks.reverse.join(" ")
end

server = FastCGI::TCP.new('localhost', 9000)
begin
  server.each_request do |request|
  stuff = request.in.read
  out = request.out

  out << "Content-type: text/html\r\n\r\n"
  out << <<-EOF
  <html>
  <head><title>Text Backwardizer</title></head>
  <h1>sdrawkcaB txeT</h1>
  <i>You previously said: #{last_time}</i><BR>
  <b>#{reverse_ramblings(get_ramblings(stuff))}</b>
  <form method="POST" action="/fast/serv.rb">
  <textarea name="ramblings">
  </textarea>
  <input type="submit" name="submit"
  </form>
  </body></html>
  EOF

  last_time = get_ramblings(stuff)
  request.finish
  end
ensure
  server.close
end
```

The first thing that strikes you about this code (if you read the previous section) is a couple of things that you have to do manually in FastCGI that wouldn't have had to do with the CGI library. One is the messy hard-coding of escaped HTML. The other is the get_ramblings method, which manually parses the input and returns only the relevant value. This code, by the way, works only with the HTTP POST method—another convenience lost when not using the CGI library.

That being said, FastCGI is by no means without its advantages. We didn't run any benchmarks on this example, but—it's in the name—FastCGI is *faster* than normal CGI. The overhead of starting up a new process is avoided in favor of making a local network connection to port 9000 (FastCGI::TCP.new('localhost', 9000)).

Also, the `last_time` variable in this example is used to maintain a piece of state in memory in between requests—something impossible with traditional CGI.

We'll also point out that it's possible to a limited extent to "mix and match" these libraries. The "helper" functions from `cgi.rb` can be used on their own (without actually using this library to drive the application). For example, `CGI.escapeHTML` can be used in isolation from the rest of the library. This would make the previous example a little more readable.

19.3   Ruby on Rails

One of the best known web frameworks in the Ruby realm is called *Ruby on Rails* (or simply *Rails*). This framework is the creation of David Heinemeier Hansson.

Rails makes heavy use of the dynamic features of Ruby. It also has its own design philosophy that "streamlines" web development, enabling rapid development of web-based applications.

Rails is well-known and well-documented. This book will only give it cursory coverage.

19.3.1   Principles and Techniques

Rails is built within the paradigm of the *Model-View-Controller* (*MVC*) design pattern. Every web application built with Rails is partitioned naturally into models (which model the problem domain), views (which present information to the user and allow interaction), and controllers (which arbitrate between the views and the models).

Certain principles drive the behavior of Rails as a framework. One principle is less software; don't write code to tie one thing to another if those things can be tied together automatically.

Another related principle is convention over configuration. By following certain predetermined styles in coding and naming, configuration becomes less important (and we approach the ideal "zero-config" environment).

Rails is good at automating tasks that require limited intelligence. It generates code whenever it's practical, making it unnecessary for the programmer to write those pieces manually.

Web applications are often database-backed, and Rails enables smooth, seamless integration with the database. There is also a strong tendency for a web framework to have a "preferred" object-relational mapper (ORM), and Rails is no exception. The standard ORM for Rails is ActiveRecord, which we saw in Chapter 10, "I/O and Data Storage."

The databases are described in `config/database.yaml`, one of the few configuration files you will ever need. This file (stored of course in YAML format) names three different databases—one for development, one for testing, and one for production. These dedicated databases may seem like overkill at first, but this scheme gives Rails much of its power.

Rails will generate empty models and controllers for you. When you edit the models, you define the relationship between the database tables with methods such as `has_many` and `belongs_to` (to name just two). Because models and tables correspond, this code also defines the relationships between the models themselves. Data validation can be accomplished with methods such as `validates_presence_of` (to ensure that a data item isn't missing) or `validates_uniqueness_of` (to ensure that a data item is unique).

When you create a Rails app with a command like `rails appname`, you get a directory *appname* with this structure:

```
app
  controllers
  helpers
  models
  views
config
db
doc
lib
log
public
script
test
vendor
```

The `app` directory is where the bulk of your own code belongs. The MVC separation is evident from this structure, of course.

The database schemas live under the `db` directory. The incremental migration files will also go here as they are created.

One area where Rails simplifies life is *scaffolding*. If you issue a command such as `script/generate scaffold Product` (where `Product` is a model), you will get "create-update-delete" functionality generated for the `Products` table—plural name.

It's also possible to do scaffolding without actually generating the code. Inside the Product controller, you could use the scaffold method:

```
class ProductController < ActiveRecord::Base
  scaffold :product
end
```

The preceding line of code achieves the same purpose without actually generating code that lives on the disk. Either way is acceptable. Scaffolding, of course, produces entry-update pages that are functional but not very pretty; in nearly every case, the scaffolding will eventually be replaced by something better. But this quick technique of interacting with the database is handy, especially during development.

In older versions of Rails, there was a greater disconnect between ActiveRecord and the database. The concept of *migrations* in more recent Rails releases makes the database easier to manage. The same is true for existing database tables, which formerly were problematic; now we can easily create a schema.rb file from the existing database tables (refer also to the rake tasks db:schema:load and db:schema:dump).

19.3.2   Testing and Debugging Rails Apps

Rails has a great deal of support for testing. Notice that a test directory is created with every new application. This is populated slowly as the pieces of the app come together; you can (and should) start adding tests as you create the app.

By convention in Rails, *unit tests* test the models, and *functional tests* test the controllers. This explains the unit and functional subdirectories under the test directory. (These terms are used somewhat differently outside the context of Ruby on Rails.)

An important concept in Rails testing is the *fixture*. A fixture is simply a "snapshot" of the initial contents of a model; in other words, it is a set of fake data used for testing. We specify all this data in the files under the test/fixtures directory. The standard format for storing the initial data is YAML.

The test/mocks directory is for storing code that acts as *mock objects*. A mock object (or simply *mock*) is essentially an "imitation" of a service or class that is not yet implemented. Think of it as a Hollywood false front, with an interface like the real thing but nothing actually working. The classic example is a credit card payment gateway; by using mocks, we can test the interaction with the gateway without involving the *real* gateway.

You should know about the *console* in Rails. Running script/console will give you an irb-like session in which your model code is accessible. You can play with ActiveRecord queries and do similar kinds of operations.

The *breakpointer* is even more useful. Put a call to the `breakpoint` method anywhere in your code, and run the `script/breakpointer` utility. You will find yourself in an `irb` session in the context of the breakpoint that you hit in your code. This naturally will allow you to examine (and change) the values of instance variables and so on before continuing.

Recent versions of Rails also have support for *integration testing*. This uses a kind of custom DSL to describe the flow of control of the web application at a high level. It is designed to be useful in interacting with customers who have less technical knowledge, but it is useful even when all the users are intimately knowledgeable about the application's details.

19.3.3 Core Extensions

One of the beauties of Rails is the large selection of convenience methods defined in the `ActiveSupport::CoreExtensions` module. These are "harmless" methods added to the core classes for use throughout the application.

Some of these are date/time related. Because times are internally stored in seconds, it's possible to use methods such as `minutes` and `hours` in a meaningful way:

```
elapsed = 3.days + 4.hours + 17.minutes
later = Time.now + elapsed
```

Similarly, we can do things like:

```
time = 3.minutes.from_now     # Same as Time.now + 3.minutes
t2 = 5.days.from_now
```

Time operations are particularly well represented here, in fact. Such methods as `midnight`, `next_month`, and `beginning_of_week` allow us to specify times accurately and concisely.

One of the best-known items in this module is the `Symbol#to_proc` hack. This allows us to pass in a symbol representing a method name rather than passing in a block. For example, these two statements do the same thing:

```
arr = array.map {|x| x.upcase }
arr = array.map(&:upcase)
```

Besides the methods mentioned here, there are dozens of others. Some of these handle interconversions between times or other units, some handle conversion to YAML or XML, some manipulate the spelling and punctuation of strings, and so on.

19.3.4   Related Tools and Libraries

It's inevitable that external tools have started to support Rails. The TextMate editor, for example, has good Rails support (in terms of syntax highlighting, code completion, and more). It is probably the most common editor used on the OS X platform by Rails programmers.

The InstantRails project shows great promise (http://instantrails.rubyforge.org). This is a single package containing Ruby, Rails, MySQL, and Apache, all preconfigured and ready to run. The initial version works only on the Windows platforms, but ports are planned.

On the OS/X platform, the equivalent is called Locomotive. This is a "one-click" Rails enviroment that is already mature and works well.

If you're an Eclipse fan, you should know about RadRails, which is a Rails IDE built on top of Eclipse. According to its website (http://radrails.org), "Features include source control, debugging, WEBrick servers, generator wizards, syntax highlighting, data tools and much, much more." It should run on multiple platforms (wherever Eclipse itself will run).

It's also important to understand the concept of *plugins* in Rails. These are small self-contained pieces of code that modify the behavior of ActiveRecord or Rails; they are simple to write and simple to deploy.

A Rails plugin is installed basically by uncompressing it and dropping it into the vendor/plugins directory. An example of a plugin is the well-known *Annotate models* written by Dave Thomas; it simply adds comments that summarize the current schema to the top of each ActiveRecord model source file (making this functionality available via a rake task). Literally hundreds of small plugins are available; these deal with authentication, GUIDs, I18N, CSS, and many other areas of functionality.

It is impossible to cover Rails in a handful of pages; whole books have been written about Ruby on Rails. In fact, some of the earliest ones are already obsolete as of summer 2006. If you need in-depth knowledge, begin with the website (http://rubyonrails.org) where the Rails community is centered.

19.4   Web Development with Nitro

Nitro is a web application development toolkit. Although Nitro, along with its ORM companion Og, is well-suited for constructing conventional MVC-style applications, its intended design affords a variety of architectures.

The simplest way to install Nitro is to use `rubygems`. The Nitro gem has a small number of dependencies that you will also need to install (`og`, `redcloth`, and a few others).

```
gem install nitro  --include-dependencies
```

At the time of writing, the latest release was Nitro 0.31.0. As you might expect, the API and libraries are still shifting. Also know that the overview given here just scratches the surface of what Nitro can do.

19.4.1 Creating a Basic Nitro Application

Nitro is often used with Og, an ORM library that handles the persistence of Ruby objects. But Og is not required; in fact, one of the nice features of Og/Nitro is that you need not decide in advance whether your application requires a database or object persistence. If your design evolves and such a need arises, modifying plain Ruby objects into persistent objects is mostly a matter of changing a few lines of code in your models. There is talk of modifying the use of the `attr` family of methods, so this may get even simpler in the future.

Og is covered in section 10.4.7, "Object-Relational Mappers (ORMs)." The Nitro examples will not make much use of it.

Although Nitro offers a wide range of features, the simplest Nitro application does not require much. Creating a basic Nitro app is not much different from creating a conventional static HTML site.

First, create an application directory:

```
/home/jbritt/demo
```

Then add a `public` folder with `index.html`:

```
/home/jbritt/demo/public/index.html
```

To start, make `index.html` simple:

```
<html>
  <head>
    <title>Nitro!</title>
  </head>
  <body>
```

```
    <h1>The Ruby Way</h1>
    <h2>Hal Fulton</h2>
  </body>
</html>
```

Now create `run.rb` in your application root directory:

```
require 'nitro'
Nitro.run
```

To see this new application in action, execute the file `run.rb` (found in the root of the demo/ directory). Then launch a web browser and navigate to http://127.0.0.1:9999 (where 9999 is the default Nitro port).

If all goes well, you will be greeted by our simple page. Congratulations; you've written your first Nitro application. Nitro offers much more than this, of course, so let's look at how we can expand the application.

The main file of interest is `run.rb`. Depending on how you deploy your code, the execution of `run.rb` might be handled by a dispatcher script in the `public` folder. For demonstration and testing purposes, though, you can execute `run.rb` directly and use the built-in WEBrick dispatcher. In production, though, you would want to take advantage of Nitro's built-in support for Mongrel, SCGI, or FastCGI.

Nitro supports a variety of application architectures and patterns, and web development typically follows MVC (model-view-controller). But the choice is yours, and Nitro makes it easy to evolve from simple view-only sites to fully refactored, database-backed applications.

By default, Nitro will handle page requests by first looking in the `public` folder for a matching file. Nitro assumes that, absent an explicit page name, the request refers to `index.html`. In this regard it behaves much like any static web environment. We can, if needed, add additional static HTML pages to the `public` folder and use subdirectories of `public` that can hold images and CSS files.

More useful, though, is what Nitro does when it cannot find a direct match for a resource request. Change the file extension on `index.html` to *.xhtml*:

```
public/index.xhtml
```

Then restart `run.rb`. Return to http://127.0.0.1:9999, and you should see the page again. Nitro, not finding `index.html`, looks for `index.xhtml` and loads that.

xhtml is the default Nitro file extension for dynamic content. In general, when given a page request, Nitro first looks for the .html file, then the .xhtml version.

Using a Nitro xhtml file allows you to embed template variables and logic. Change index.xhtml to look like this:

```
<html>
  <head>
    <title>Nitro!</title>
  </head>
  <body>
    <h1>The Ruby Way</h1>
    <h2>Hal Fulton</h2>
    <p>Page last updated:  #{Time.now}</p>
  </body>
</html>
```

Reload the page, and you should see the current date and time displayed. Nitro also supports an XML processing instruction syntax:

```
<?r curr_date = Time.new.strftime( "%a, %b %d, %Y")  ?>
<html>
  <head>
    <title>Nitro!</title>
  </head>
  <body>
    <h1>The Ruby Way</h1>
    <h2>Hal Fulton</h2>
    <p>Page last updated:  #{curr_date}</p>
  </body>
</html>
```

Note that the <?r ... ?> syntax does not require your template to be XML. Nitro provides ways for processing templates as XML, and this syntax allows for templates that are also valid XML.

19.4.2 Nitro and the MVC Pattern

Embedding code directly into templates is handy for trying out ideas and migrating from static pages to dynamic content. However, before long, you may find that testing and maintaining the application is increasingly difficult. The Model-View-Controller pattern will improve things by moving code into Ruby classes.

We'll start by creating a controller class, main.rb. If your application directory has an src folder, Nitro will add it to the load path. Following the Nitro convention, we'll create <app_root>/src/controller/book.rb:

```
class BookController
  def index
    @author = "Hal Fulton"
    @title = "The Ruby Way"
    @last_update = Time.new
  end
end
```

The index.xhtml will have to change to use these instance variables:

```
<html>
  <head>
    <title>Nitro!</title>
  </head>
  <body>
    <h1>#{@title}</h1>
    <h2>#{@author}</h2>
    <p>Page last updated:  #{@last_update}</p>
  </body>
</html>
```

We'll need some adjustments to run.rb as well:

```
require 'nitro'

require 'controller/book'
Nitro.run(BookController)
```

Restart the WEBrick server and reload the page to see the results.

Some things to note: Template files can remain in the public folder; the controller class does not need to extend from any special base class; the class passed to Nitro.run is automatically mapped to the root URL of the application. Each of these is configurable.

By default, Nitro will look for templates in the `template` and `public` directories. If you do not want templates in `public` (perhaps preferring to reserve that for static HTML files), you can create a `template` folder and store them there. Template paths are assumed to follow URL paths, relative to the root template folder. Our `index.xhtml` file may be either `public/index.xhtml` or `template/index.xhtml`. The use of the `public` directory for template files eases the transition of a static site to a dynamic one, but you will do better to organize them separately.

Controller classes may be mapped URL paths using `Server.map`. For example, our demo application may have a static main page with books (well, the one book we have so far) listed under a different path. We can arrange this mapping by changing `run.rb`:

```
require 'nitro'
require 'controller/book'

Nitro::Server.map = { '/books' => BookController }
Nitro.run()
```

We'll need to move the corresponding template to match the new path (`template/ books/index.xhtml`).

Restart the server, but this time browse to the new path:

```
http://127.0.0.1:9999/books
```

At this point we'd want to create a proper main page for the site, but we'll omit that here to save space. A more interesting addition would be the capability to request details for more than one book (however terrific that one book may be). We can add a `Book` model in `src/model/book.rb`:

```
class Book
  @@items = {}
  attr_accessor :title
  attr_accessor :author
  attr_accessor :update_time

  def initialize( values = {} )
    @title, @author = values[:title], values[:author]
    @update_time = Time.now
  end
```

```
    def save
      @@items[author] =  self
    end

    def self.find(author)
      @@items[author]
    end
  end
```

The controller can now fetch data from the Book class. We'll change index to this:

```
def index
  book = Book.find_by_author("Mark Twain")
  @author = book.author
  @title = book.title
  @last_update = book.update_time
end
```

And we'll change run.rb to reference the Book model and load some data by adding these lines:

```
require 'model/book'
Book.new(:title => "Life on the Mississippi",
         :author =>  "Mark Twain" ).save
```

Restarting the application and reloading the page should show us the book details. Now suppose that we have other books we'd like to see. Instead of using a hard-coded reference to one book, we can tell the controller to search by author name. Here's a new controller method, find:

```
def find(author)
  book = Book.find_by_author(author)
  @author = book.author
  @title = book.title
  @last_update = book.update_time
end
```

It's the same code as index (and the matching template can be created by renaming index.xhtml to find.xhtml), but it takes a single argument, which will be used to retrieve an item by the name of the author. Note that, although we are developing a web application, the controller class is not much different from a class in any other

Ruby application. The most notable difference is that the methods are not returning any values, but there is no reliance on special environment values or objects. (Be aware, though, that Nitro *does* supply various niceties for coding for a web app, and they are available to your controller code simply by having the class inherit from `Nitro::Controller`. For example, Nitro provides scaffolding, flash message transfer among requests, and a sophisticated rendering pipeline if and when your application needs them.)

We need to make one additional observation about controller methods. Methods designed for use as page request handlers will typically be paired with like-named templates. Nitro combines the method and template to render the final result. We've seen how a Nitro app can work without controllers by using only views. But the complement is true, too. A controller method can generate its complete output without any template. Nitro page requests are processed as *actions*. An action is the combination of view and controller methods. Under the hood, Nitro dynamically creates action methods that merge the two. But if one or the other is missing, no problem. If an action does not have a template, the return value of its controller method becomes the output.

For example, you could have a URL that responds to a search by returning only the book title with this sparse `BookController` method:

```
def sparse(author)
  @context.content_type =    'text/plain'
  book = Book.find_by_author(author)
  book.title
end
```

If your controller method is not returning HTML, you should change the content-type header sent in the response using `@context.content_type=`. (Incidentally, if a matching template exists, you can override its use by calling `render_text`.)

But where does the argument to `find` or `sparse` come from? By default, Nitro follows the familiar web development pattern of mapping URL path segments to controllers, methods, and arguments. Restart the application, and try the URL http://127.0.0.1:9999/books/find/Hal%20Fulton.

Note the use of `%20` to encode the whitespace in the author name. This is removed by Nitro before reaching our `find` method.

In general, then URL paths map to controllers and methods as `/controller/method/arg1`. Additional arguments can be passed as more URL path segments. Nitro provides a routing mechanism as well so that you are not obligated to couple your URLs to implementation details.

19.4.3   Nitro and Og

Although Og, Nitro's object-relation manager, is covered elsewhere, you would miss the full effect if we didn't show how simple it is to make our application database-backed. First we change run.rb to set up Og:

```
# Just before the call to Book.new :
require 'og'

Og.setup(:store => 'mysql',
         :name => 'demo',
         :user => 'root',
         :destroy => true,
         :port => 3316)
```

We next change our Book model:

```
require 'glue/timestamped'

class Book
  is Timestamped

  property :title, String
  property  :author, String

  def initialize( values = {} )
    @title, @author = values[:title], values[:author]
  end

end
```

The class-variable storage of Book instances is deleted. Calls to attr_accessor are replaced with the Og/Nitro method property, which serves multiple purposes. It too creates variable accessor methods, but it also tells Og that this class is marked for persistence. initialize stays almost the same, but by requiring the timestamped file and indicating that the class is Timestamped, we get the update_time attribute automatically.

The remaining methods can be deleted; they are now implemented by Og. Restarting the application will now have Nitro creating a MySQL database for the application, along with a table for our Book objects. This is "all Ruby, no SQL" database-backed web application development.

19.4.4   Common Web Development Tasks in Nitro

Nitro has a remarkably rich rendering subsystem. A proper description would be beyond the scope of this book. However, there are various tasks that web developers commonly need to do, so let's take a look at how we might perform these tasks in Nitro.

If you are building a website of one or two pages, it may not matter much whether you are repeating the same markup and text. But keeping all your pages up-to-date becomes an error-prone chore when you have to maintain the repeated pieces by hand. Nitro helps you adhere to the *DRY* principle (*Don't Repeat Yourself*) by providing a number of ways to reuse such pieces of text.

The simplest way is to use include files. For example, suppose we decide that all our pages should have a common footer. We can stick that footer markup into a template file and render it into our pages in this way:

```
<?include href='/footer' ?>
```

The template file footer.xinc might look like this:

```
<div id='footer'>Read More Ruby Books</div>
```

If you use a relative path as the href value, Nitro will search the template folders defined for the current controller. If you use an absolute path, only that path under the application's template root is searched.

This preceding method is best for static content. There is also the following syntax for file inclusion, which inserts the specified file into the calling template just prior to template compilation:

```
<include href='/footer' />
```

The results are as if the include text were simply part of the calling template.

A more sophisticated form of content inclusion uses the `render` element:

```
<render href='/controller/action' />
```

where the `href` indicates some application URL path.

The compilation process for including these partial views with `<render />` is essentially the same as when calling a full view. You may have methods in your controller that correspond to the included file and use these methods to set instance variables to be used in the included template.

Nitro blurs the line between template source code and Ruby code. One example is how a controller action may be spread between a method and a template file, or just one or the other. Another example is Nitro *Elements*, which are a way of encapsulating code and markup in a custom markup element available in your views.

Rather than have each view define the HTML for a full page, we can define a common HTML layout and reuse it across actions. We'll create the file `element/layout.xhtml`:

```
<html>
  <head>
    <title>#{@title}</title>
    <style>
      body {
        background-color: white;
        font-family: sans-serif;
      }
    </style>
  </head>
  #{content}
</html>
```

We the change `template/books/find.xhtml` to use this new element:

```
<Layout title='Details for #{@title}'>
  <h1>#{@title}</h1>
  <h2>#{@author}</h2>
  <p>Page last updated: #{@last_update}</p>
</Layout>
```

What's inside the `Layout` element is inserted into the `content` variable in `layout.xhtml`. Elements can accept parameters; the `title` attribute in the `Layout` start tag populates the `@title` instance variable in `layout.xhtml`.

If this seems similar to calling a method and passing arguments, it is. We can also define the layout as a Ruby class (`src/element/layout2.rb`):

```ruby
require 'nitro/element'

class Layout2 < Nitro::Element
  def render
    %^<html>
    <head>
      <title>#{@title}</title>
      <style>
        body {
          background-color: white;
          font-family: sans-serif;
        }
      </style>
    </head>
    #{content}
    </html>^
  end

end
```

We can then change `find.xhtml` to use the `Layout2` element (we'll also have to change `run.rb` to require this new element class). Elements may contain other elements, allowing you to assemble your views from a set of reusable components.

Often you have large chunks for code that embody logic common to multiple applications. For example, many web apps have a notion of user account and authorization. Rather than rewrite the code for each program, the capability to mix in existing code saves time and reduces maintenance.

This form of application reuse is called *parts*. A part is essentially a mini-Nitro site focused on some specific function. (Nitro includes one out of the box, called `Admin`.) The code for this subsite does not need to have a `run.rb`, though it is useful to include one so that the part may be executed on its own to demonstrate its behavior.

Parts go, naturally enough, under a `part` folder. Suppose that we have some user authentication code to reuse. Our application parts directory tree would look something like this:

```
<app_root>/part/users
<app_root>/part/users.rb
<app_root>/part/users/public/
<app_root>/part/users/controller.rb
<app_root>/part/users/model/user.rb
<app_root>/part/users/model/acl.rb
<app_root>/part/users/template/login.xhtml
<app_root>/part/users/template/form.xinc
<app_root>/part/users/run.rb
```

Our main `run.rb` would then include the part by doing a simple `require`:

```
require 'part/users'
```

Nitro then treats all the code in the `part/users` directory as if it were located under the main application source code directory. Template file searches begin with the main application template folders and continue down into parts directories. If you want to override a template included with a part, you just need to put your preferred version in a corresponding folder under the main application template path.

Applications often need to display repeated data; this is typically rendered as an HTML table in a template. If you do not know the number of data rows in advance you'll want a way to loop over a collection.

You can use the syntax to embed Ruby code in your template, but Nitro offers a special compiler pipeline class that simplifies common logic constructs.

The compiler pipeline is a sequence of transformations acting on your templates as they are combined into actions. There are transformation classes for various tasks, such as static file inclusion, XSLT transformation, and localization. The `Morphing` class examines template markup, watching for special attributes in the XHTML indicating assorted transformations.

Our demo application is sparse on data, but if we imagine there being many authors and many books for each author, we might want to show a list of an author's books. Our controller method would populate an `@books` variable with a list of books; the section of a template to loop over this list would look like the following code:

```
<h4>Books by #{@author}</h4>
<ul>
<li each="book in @books" > #{book.title}</li>
</ul>
```

The Morphing compiler spots the `each` attribute on the `li` element and converts this into the following code:

```
<?r for book in @books ?>
<li>#{book.title} </li>
<?r end ?>
```

This new Nitro markup is then passed on down the compiler pipeline.

Similarly, you can use the `times` attribute to repeat an element. Look at this fragment:

```
<img src='/img/ruby.png' alt='*' times='@book.rating' />
```

The preceding code has the following result:

```
<?r 3.times do ?>
<img src='/img/ruby.png' alt='*' />
<?r end ?>
```

19.4.5 Other Important Details

Nitro has numerous niceties, too many to cover here. Some of the more notable goodies are discussed briefly in this section.

Nitro comes with helper code to use a number of JavaScript libraries that support various forms of DHTML and Ajax. Nitro defines a high-level syntax for easy integration. For example, the Nitro distribution includes an example of searching Flickr and rendering thumbnails of images. The text field for entering search tags is Ajax-enabled with this markup:

```
<input type="text" id="tags" name="tags" auto_complete="true" />
```

The controller implements `tags_auto_complete` to return an XML string based on field contents.

Nitro allows for caching of actions (that is, rendered pages), method results, and generated text fragments. For example, to cache the rendered results of the index page, a controller would call

```
cache_output :index
```

Caching may be added in code segments as well:

```
<?r cache(:book_list_cache_key) do ?>
 <ul>
  <li each="book in Books.all">#{book.title}</li>
 </ul>
<?r end ?>
```

Nitro has a built-in transformation class for localization that allows for automatic template content substitution. This class is not part of the default compiler pipeline; you must add it in run.rb:

```
require 'nitro/compiler/localization'
include Nitro

Compiler.transformation_pipeline = [
  StaticInclude,
  Elements,
  Morphing,
  Markup,
  Localization,
  Cleanup
]
```

Note that you can also arrange the pipeline sequence to omit standard transformations or to define your own. You then define the locales:

```
Localization.locales = {
  :en => 'conf/locales/en.yml',
  :de => 'conf/locales/de.yml'
}
```

A locale is just a YAML file that maps strings:

```
---
:author: Autor
:language: Sprache
:book_rank: Buchrank
```

Template files then use a special syntax to denote text from substitution:

```
<div class='detail'>[[:author]]: #{@book.author}</div>
<div class='detail'>[[:language]]: #{@book.language}</div>
<div class='detail'>[[:book_rank]]: #{@book.rank}</div>
```

The selection of locale file is based on the value of `session[:LOCALE]`. The value of the current local hash is also available in controller methods from the special variable `@lc`.

```
@language = @lc[:language]
```

More extensive language changes may also be done by using multiple template directories, one for each language. The application template root would then be derived from the assigned locale.

For more information on Nitro, consult the following resources:

- http://www.nitroproject.org/ (the Nitro home page)

- http://rubyforge.org/forum/forum.php?forum_id=5921 (Nitro project page on RubyForge)

- http://oxyliquit.de/ (Nitro user help and tutorial site)

19.5   An Introduction to Wee

According to announcements from its creator Michael Neumann, Wee is "a framework for very dynamic, component-oriented, stateful web applications, largely inspired by Seaside." The name comes from the claim that Wee makes *Web Engineering Easy*.

The simplest way to install Wee is to use rubygems (`gem install wee`). The version at the time of writing was 0.10.0. The Wee documents explain that although the code is pretty stable, there is a chance of some issues when using continuations, and that, overall, you may not want to use the framework for mission-critical applications.

However, even with those caveats, Wee is well worth exploring for its component model, and because continuations are an interesting but underexplored area in mainstream web development. The creator says that he was influenced by ideas presented in Seaside, a continuations-based web framework written in Smalltalk by Avi Bryant.

The Wee gem installation includes a number of varied examples. One is a web-based browser into ObjectSpace; another shows some basic Ajax using the Prototype JavaScript library. There's also an example showing how to use Wee with Nitro.

At the heart of Wee is the idea of *components*. These are like widgets in a GUI. Wee components are thoroughly reusable, encapsulating state, presentation, and behavior, though you may prefer to have them delegate to external templates or models.

19.5.1   A Simple Example

Installing Wee creates a simple application generator script called, naturally, wee. Running wee create my-demo will create a directory named my-demo off the current path and populate it with a simple WEBrick-based application.

The created app does little more than track the number of times a link has been clicked. The server file, run.rb, sets up the application components and main class and starts the application under WEBrick.

```
require 'wee'
require 'wee/utils'
require 'wee/adaptors/webrick'

# Your components
require 'components/main'

app = Wee::Utils.app_for do
  Main.new.add_decoration(Wee::PageDecoration.new('Wee'))
end
Wee::Utils::autoreload_glob('components/**/*.rb')
Wee::WEBrickAdaptor.register('/app' => app).start
```

The class Main will be called as the main application component. Components need to implement a render method to emit their markup. The call to add_decoration(Wee::PageDecoration.new('Wee')) alters the rendering pipeline such that the results of Main#render will be wrapped in an HTML header and footer.

Next, automatic file reloading is set up, so you can change code and retry the application without restarting WEBrick. Finally, an instance of WEBrick is started to serve the application from the URL path '/app'. The default port is 2000; you can pass a different port number as a parameter to start:

```
Wee::WEBrickAdaptor.register('/app' => app).start(:Port => 8787 )
```

The Main component defines the render method to produce the markup.

```
class Main < Wee::Component

  def initialize
    super()
    # Put your own initialization code below...
  end

  def render
    r.anchor.callback(:click).with { r.h1("Welcome to Wee!") }
    r.text "#{ @clicks || 'No' } clicks"
  end

  def click
    @clicks = (@clicks || 0) + 1
  end

end
```

Wee allows you to use Ruby syntax to define the HTML to emit in a manner similar to Jim Weirich's XML Builder library and the XML generator in Nitro. However, in Wee this syntax also allows you to connect a link with an action (in this case, the click method). When a user clicks the link generated by Wee, the application knows that it should invoke click.

19.5.2 Associating State with URLs

This example, as is, tracks the current value of @click but does not tie it to a URL. If you run the program, you'll see that Wee is generating a fairly lengthy URL that is, essentially, a GUID (globally unique identifier). The URL stays the same except for a trailing slash and an integer. Each time you click the *Welcome to Wee* link that integer increases.

If you manually edit the URL in the browser, you'll get the same page; the displayed click count does not change. There is no association between URLs and server state. (Make sure that your browser is not caching pages when you try this.)

We can change this, though, with a simple addition to `main.rb`. Add the following method to `Main`:

```
def backtrack_state(snap)
  super
  snap.add(self)
end
```

Then restart the application. After clicking the link a few times, manually edit the URL in the browser to reload a previous page. The click count should reflect the value of `@click` at the time that URL was rendered.

To try this using Wee's continuation code, add the following after the calls to require in `run.rb`:

```
require 'wee/continuation'
```

There's much more to Wee than can be covered here. For more information, consult these references:

- Wee project page (http://rubyforge.org/projects/wee/)

- Nemo project page (http://rubyforge.org/projects/nemo/)

- Seaside (http://seaside.st/)

One interesting feature is the capability to nest components and chain the behavior, allowing you to assemble websites from reusable UI widgets. You should also take a look at *Nemo*, an implementation of *Mewa* (Meta-level Architecture for Web Applications) in Wee.

19.6 Web Development with IOWA

IOWA (Interpreted Objects for Web Applications) is a web framework written by Kirk Haines. IOWA enables development with reusable, encapsulated web components for site generation.

19.6.1 Basic IOWA Concepts

An IOWA application runs in a persistent Ruby process that listens on a socket for requests. IOWA includes various adapters so that the source of that request may be CGI, Mongrel, WEBrick, and so on.

The IOWA home page includes a good explanation of the underlying architecture plus a tutorial, so here we'll just take a look at some key features.

IOWA is available for downloading from rubyforge.org. A gem version may be ready when version 1.0 is released. The examples here were built with a preview release of version 1.0, available as a zip or tgz file.

The installation includes some examples and test cases demonstrating a variety of uses. Here we'll look at a simple application derived from those examples.

An IOWA application needs some code to start off the persistent server process, and we'll use the built-in WEBrick server as the front end. This script, app.rb, handles both:

```
require 'iowa_webrick'

class HWApplication < Iowa::Application
  self.daemonize = true
  attr_accessor :dbpool

  def initialize(*args)
    super
    Iowa.config[Iowa::Capplication][Iowa::Croot_url] = 'http://127.0.0.1:2000'
  end
end


Iowa.run
```

By default it will try to read a configuration file, app.cnf, in the same directory. Here's our app.cnf:

```
socket:
  hostname: localhost
  path: ..
logging:
  basedir: ../log
  minlevel: 0
```

```
    maxsize: 10000000
    maxage: 86400
application:
  daemonize: false
  sessioncache:
    class: LRUCache
    maxsize: 20
    ttl: 3600
  dispatcher:
    class: StandardDispatcher
  policy:
    class: iowa/Policy
```

The preceding file is a YAML file with assorted information describing how IOWA should behave. One more configuration file is needed as well (`mapfile.cnf`). It tells IOWA how to map page requests to components. Here is a one-line `mapfile.cnf` file:

```
/main.html: Main
```

IOWA requests are typically handled by a combination of HTML template files and IOWA components. Template and component source files share the same base name but use different file extensions. The default template/object is `Main`, so our sample application has `Main.html` and `Main.iwa` files.

Files ending with `.iwa` are just Ruby files; IOWA uses that extension to distinguish them from other Ruby code that may be part of the application. These files act much like controller classes in Nitro or Rails. Methods defined in a component class are available in the corresponding HTML file.

Our demo `Main.html` file is as follows:

```
<html>
    <head><title>The Time Is...</title></head>
    <body>
        <p>The time is @now.</p>
    <p>The count is @count.</p>
        <a oid="reload">RELOAD</a>
    </body>
</html>
```

IOWA templates allow the mixing of plain HTML and component instance variables. Note that those variables do not need to be "interpolated" in the usual way; you just drop them into your markup.

There is also the special oid variable; IOWA uses this to dynamically alter the template during rendering. In our example, it is used to create a link back to the reload method in the component class defined in Main.iwa. If you hover your mouse over that link in the rendered page (or view the generated source), you see something like this:

```
http://127.0.0.1:2000/main.html/6b38f6fb-4f087af7-ab6JaqUM9KyWE.a.1.7
```

IOWA uses such URLs to track session state; if you click that link a few times, you'll see how it changes. If you manually edit it to a prior value, you'll retrieve the session state for that URL.

In this application, that state is in the @count instance variable. Here's Main.iwa:

```
class Main < Iowa::Component
  attr_accessor :count
  def awake
    @count = 0
  end

  def setup
    @count += 1
  end

  def now
    Time.now.asctime
  end
end
```

19.6.2 Templating in IOWA

Although most web applications will benefit from a separation of application code and presentation templates, IOWA, somewhat like Nitro, allows you to skip components entirely and put Ruby code in the view. Here's PureView.html, containing both class and HTML:

```
<%
  class PureView  < Iowa::Component
    def right_now
      Time.now
    end
  end
%>
<html>
    <head><title>A Self-contained View</title></head>
  <body>
        <p>The time is @right_now.</p>
  </body>
</html>
```

Unlike Nitro, though, this only works if there is no corresponding component for the view. When you decide to have both a separate component file and a template, IOWA will not parse the embedded code in the HTML file.

The template file may still contain looping and conditional instructions. Suppose we add a new method to the Main.iwa file:

```
def after_dinner?
  Time.now.hour > 19
end
```

We can then add some conditional rendering to Main.html using IOWA's if element:

```
<if oid='after_dinner?'>
 <p>It's after dinner.  What's for dessert?</p>
</if>
```

Good question! What *is* for dessert? Let's have IOWA tell us. We'll have Main.iwa produce a dessert menu in the form of an array:

```
def desserts
  %w{ Cake
      Brownies
      Fruit
```

```
        Gelato
   }
end
```

We'll then have `Main.html` display it. We update the conditional content to include the list of desserts:

```
<p>It's after dinner.  Here's what we have for dessert:</p>
   <ul oid="dessert_list">
     <li>@dessert_item</li>
   </ul>
  </if>
<p>
```

We also have to tell IOWA how to populate the iteration, so at the end of `Main.iwa` after the class definition we add this binding definition section:

```
<?
dessert_list {
  item = dessert_item
  list = desserts
 }
?>
```

This creates an IOWA binding for the template list `dessert_items`. During the iteration, each list item is available from a variable named `dessert_item`, with list data coming from the `desserts` component method.

19.6.3 Component Control Transfer

It can be useful to partition application logic among multiple component classes. We've seen how URLs may be mapped to components. You may also transfer control without changing the base URL path.

We'll add a new method to `Main.iwa` to handle the link from the dessert selection:

```
def dessert_choice
  new_page = page_named('DessertChoice')
  new_page.choice = @dessert_item
  yield new_page
end
```

We'll also change the dessert choice loop in `Main.html`:

```
<ul oid="dessert_list">
  <li><a oid='dessert_choice'>@dessert_item</a></li>
</ul>
```

There's a fair amount of magic occurring here; the `oid` in the `ul` element guides the loop content, whereas the `oid` in the anchor element will create a special link to our new `dessert_choice` method. To top things off, the text value of the link will be passed (albeit cryptically) in that page request as well. The `dessert_choice` method is short; it uses the IOWA method `page_named` to create an instance of another component class, `DessertChoice`. The `choice=` method is called to pass along the dessert choice. The call to yield then transfers control to this new component.

The new component is defined like any other, using a pair of `.iwa` and `.html` files.

Here's the class code:

```
class DessertChoice < Iowa::Component
  attr_accessor :choice
  def details
      "Details about #{@choice} should really come from a database."
  end
end
```

`DessertChoice.html` renders the details:

```
<html>
 <head><title>Your Dessert Choice</title></head>
  <body>
 <h1>Dessert!</h1>
  <p>@details</p>
  </body>
</html>
```

There is still more to IOWA than can be shown here. To learn more, visit the IOWA home page (http://enigo.com/projects/iowa/) and IOWA's project page on RubyForge (http://rubyforge.org/projects/iowa).

19.7   Ruby and the Web Server

One of the most common servers in use today is Apache. If you use Apache, you need to know about the mod_ruby module, presented in section 19.7.1, "Using mod_ruby."

Another useful concept on the server side is *embedded Ruby*; two tools for this job are *erb* (covered here) and *eruby*. This enables you to embed Ruby code into text (typically HTML or XML) so that it can have data inserted dynamically. This is covered in section 19.7.2, "Using erb."

Some developers in the Ruby community have implemented web servers in Ruby. Of course, you might be wondering why anyone would be concerned with writing a new web server when plenty of good ones—such as Apache—already exist.

There are several situations in which you might actually want your own dedicated web server in Ruby. One is to handle web pages in a specialized way, such as sacrificing functionality for speed, or automatically translating special markup to HTML.

Second, you might also want to experiment with the behavior of the server and its interaction with external code such as CGIs; you might want to play with your own ideas for creating an application server or a server-side development environment. We all know that Ruby is a fun language for software experimentation.

Third, you might want to embed a web server inside another application. This possibility is sometimes exploited by developers who want to expose the functionality of a software system to the outside world; the HTTP protocol is well-defined and simple, and web browsers that serve as clients are everywhere. This trick can even be used as a remote debugging tool, assuming that the system updates its internal state frequently and makes it available to the embedded server.

A final reason is that a small self-contained web server can simplify deployment and configuration. For example, restarting the server in a Rails application is much simpler with WEBrick than if it used Apache by default.

With these ideas in mind, let's look at what is available in the Ruby arena where web servers are concerned. In the past, there have been at least four such servers; as of summer 2006, the two most important ones are WEBrick and Mongrel. These are presented in sections 19.7.3 and 19.7.4, respectively.

19.7.1   Using mod_ruby

Typically when a CGI script is written in an interpreted language, an instance of the interpreter is launched with every invocation of the CGI. This can be expensive in terms of server utilization and execution time.

The Apache server solves this problem by allowing loadable modules that in effect attach themselves to the server and become part of it. These are loaded dynamically as needed and are shared by all the scripts that depend on them. The mod_ruby package (available from the Ruby Application Archive) is such a module.

The mod_ruby package implements several Apache directives. Some of these are

- RubyRequire—Specify one or more libraries needed.
- RubyHandler—Specify a handler for *ruby-object*.
- RubyPassEnv—Specify names of environment variables to pass to scripts.
- RubySetEnv—Set environment variables.
- RubyTimeOut—Specify a timeout value for Ruby scripts.
- RubySafeLevel—Set the $SAFE level.
- RubyKanjiCode—Set the Ruby character encoding.

The software also provides Ruby classes and modules for interacting with Apache. The Apache module (using *module* here in the Ruby sense) has a few module functions as server_version and unescape_url; it also contains the Request and Table classes.

Apache::Request is a wrapper for the request_rec data type, defining methods such as request_method, content_type, readlines, and more. The Apache::Table class is a wrapper for the table data type, defining methods such as get, add, and each.

Extensive instructions are available for compiling and installing the mod_ruby package. Refer to its accompanying documentation (or the equivalent information on the Web).

19.7.2   Using erb

First, let's dispel any confusion over terminology. We're not talking here about embedding a Ruby interpreter in an electronic device such as a TV or a toaster. We're talking about embedding Ruby code inside text.

Second, we'll note that there is more than one scheme for embedding Ruby code in text files. This section discusses only the most common tool, which is erb (created by Shugo Maeda).

Why do we mention such a tool in connection with the Web? Obviously, it's because the most common form of text in which we'll embed Ruby code is HTML (or XML).

Having said that, it's conceivable there might be other uses for it. Perhaps it could be used in an old-fashioned text-based adventure game, or in some kind of mail-merge utility, or as part of a `cron` job to create a customized message-of-the-day file (`/etc/motd`) every night at midnight. Don't let your creativity be constrained by our lack of imagination. Feel free to dig up new and interesting uses for `erb` and share them with the rest of us. Most of the examples we give here are generic (and thus contrived); they don't have much to do with HTML specifically.

The `erb` utility is simply a filter or preprocessor. A special notation is used to delimit Ruby code, expressions, and comments; all other text is simply passed through "as is."

The symbols `<%` and `%>` are used to mark the pieces of text that will be treated specially. There are three forms of this notation, varying in the first character inside the "tag."

If it is an equal sign (`=`), the tag is treated as a Ruby expression that is evaluated; the resulting value is inserted at the current location in the text file. Here is a sample text file:

```
This is <%= "ylno".reverse %> a test.
Do <%= "NOT".downcase %> be alarmed.
```

Assuming the file for this example is called `myfile.txt`, we can filter it in this way:

```
erb myfile.txt
```

The output, by default written to standard output, will look like this:

```
This is only a test.
Do not be alarmed.
```

We can also use the character # to indicate a comment.

```
Life <%# so we've heard %> is but a dream.
```

As you'd expect, the comment is ignored. The line above will produce this line of output.

```
Life is but a dream.
```

Any other character following the percent sign will be taken as a piece of Ruby code, and its *output* (not its evaluated value) will be placed into the text stream. For readability, I recommend using a blank space here, though erb does not demand it.

In this example, the tag in the first line of text does *not* insert any text (because it doesn't produce any output). The second line works as expected.

```
The answer is <% "42" %>.
Or rather, the answer is <% puts "42" %>.
```

So the output would be:

```
The answer is .
Or rather, the answer is 42.
```

The effect of the Ruby code is cumulative. For example, a variable defined in one tag may be used in a subsequent tag.

```
<% x=3; y=4; z=5 %>
Given a triangle of sides <%=x%>, <%=y%>, and <%=z%>,
we know it is a right triangle because
<%= x*x %> + <%= y*y %> = <%= z*z %>.
```

The spaces we used inside the tags in the last line are not necessary, but they do increase readability as we've said. The output will be:

```
Given a triangle of sides 3, 4, and 5,
we know it is a right triangle because
9 + 16 = 25.
```

Try putting a syntax error inside a tag. You'll find that erb has very verbose reporting; it actually prints out the generated Ruby code and tells us as precisely as it can where the error is.

What if we want to include one of the "magic" strings as a literal part of our text? You might be tempted to try a backslash to escape the characters, but this won't work. We recommend a technique like the following.

```
There is a less-than-percent <%="<%"%> on this line
and a percent-greater-than <%="%"+">"%> on this one.
Here we see <%="<%="%> and <%="<%#"%> as well.
```

The output then will be:

```
There is a less-than-percent <% on this line
and a percent-greater-than %> on this one.
Here we see <%= and <%# as well.
```

Note that it's a little easier to embed an opening symbol than a closing one. This is because they can't be nested, and erb is not smart enough to ignore a closing symbol inside a string.

Of course, erb does have certain features that are tailored to HTML. The flag -M can be used to specify a mode of operation; the valid modes are f, c, and n respectively.

The f mode (filter) is the default, which is why all our previous examples worked without the -Mf on the command line. The -Mc option means CGI mode; it prints all errors as HTML. The -Mn option means NPH-CGI mode ("no-parse-headers"); it outputs extra HTML headers automatically. Both CGI and NPH-CGI modes set $SAFE to be 1 for security reasons (assuming that the application is a CGI and thus may be invoked by a hostile user). The -n flag (or the equivalent --noheader) will suppress CGI header output.

It's possible to set up the Apache web server to recognize embedded Ruby pages. You do this by associating the type application/x-httpd-erb with some extension (.rhtml being a logical choice) and defining an action that associates this type with the eruby executable. For more information, consult the Apache documentation.

19.7.3 Using WEBrick

WEBrick is the work of Masayoshi Takahashi and Yuuzou Gotou (with patches from many others). It is a full-featured HTTP server library and is part of the standard Ruby distribution. The name apparently is related to the word *brick*, meaning that it is small, compact, and self-contained.

WEBrick is ignorant of most of the details of web applications. It doesn't know about user sessions or any such thing; it only knows servlets which act independently of each other. If you want higher-level functionality, look for it in another library (possibly layered on top of WEBrick, like IOWA or Tofu), or write it yourself.

The basic usage of WEBrick is as follows: Create a server instance; define any mount handlers; define signal handlers; and start the server. Here is a small example:

```
require 'webrick'

server = WEBrick::HTTPServer.new(:DocumentRoot => '.')
# (No mount handlers in this simple example)
trap('INT')  { server.shutdown}
trap('TERM') { server.shutdown}
server.start
```

If you run the preceding code example, you will get a web server running on port 80 like any other. It serves files from the current directory.

To create a servlet, inherit from the WEBrick::HTTPServlet::AbstractServlet class. Then mount that servlet using a URI prefix. When the server tries to handle a URL, it looks for the longest prefix (that is, the best match). Here is an "empty" example (with handlers that don't do anything):

```
class EventsHandler < HTTPServlet::AbstractServlet
  # ...
end
class RecentHandler < HTTPServlet::AbstractServlet
  # ...
end
class AlphaHandler  < HTTPServlet::AbstractServlet
  # ...
end

# ...

server.mount('/events', EventsHandler)
server.mount('/events/recent', RecentHandler)
server.mount('/events/alpha', AlphaHandler)
```

How does a servlet work? The basic idea is that for every HTTP operation you want to support (such as GET), you define a corresponding method (such as do_GET). If you're used to writing software to contact a web server, you now have to think backwards. Now your code *is* the web server. Rather than getting back a code like 404, you'll be *sending* that code. Here is a very simple example:

```
class TinyHandler < WEBrick::HTTPServlet::AbstractServlet

  def do_GET(request, response)
    # Process request, return response
    status, ctype, body = process_request(request)
    response.status = status
    response['Content-type'] = ctype
    response.body = body
  end

  def process_request(request)
    text = "A very short web page..."
    return 200, "text/html", text
  end

end
```

A more sophisticated servlet would likely have an initialize method. If it did, any parameters you needed to pass to it would go on the end of the server.mount call.

Fortunately, you don't have to write your own servlet for every little task you want WEBrick to perform. It has several predefined handlers of its own (all in the WEBrick::HTTPServlet namespace):

- FileHandler

- ProcHandler

- CGIHandler

- ERBHandler

Since `ProcHandler` is especially interesting, let's look at it briefly. It allows us to be "lazy" and avoid subclassing the `AbstractServlet` class. Instead, we pass in a simple `proc`:

```
# Mount a block directly...

server.mount_proc('/here') do |req, resp|
  resp.body = "This is the output of my block."
end

# Create a Proc and mount it...

some_proc = Proc.new do |req, resp|
  resp.body = 'This is the output from my Proc."
end

server.mount_proc('/there', some_proc)

# Another way to mount a Proc...

my_handler = HTTPServlet::ProcHandler.new(some_proc))
server.mount('/another', my_handler)
```

WEBrick also has many other convenient features such as hooks that you can use to perform extra little tasks as needed (for example, trigger a task at server startup). WEBrick also has extensive logging capabilities, HTTP authentication, and other features. For more details, consult the online documentation at http://ruby-doc.org or elsewhere.

19.7.4   Using Mongrel

Mongrel is the work of Zed Shaw (with contributions by other people). It was created largely to address the performance issues that WEBrick has. As such, it is very successful; it is many times faster than WEBrick (though exact measurements are hard to make, since they depend on so many variables).

Mongrel is commonly used in conjunction with Rails, and the Mongrel documentation tends to be Rails-centric. However, it is *not* "tied" to Rails; it can be used in many other contexts.

It is true that Mongrel is more of an application where WEBrick is more of a library. They do certainly have many features in common, but their usage and their APIs are different.

Very often you will invoke Mongrel as an application without writing any code that specifically supports it. It takes a the three basic commands start, stop, and restart; the start command has a large number of command line parameters that can modify its behavior. Some of these are --port portnum, --log filename, --daemonize, and many others. For a full list, issue this command:

```
mongrel_rails start -h
```

Running with the defaults in place is reasonable, but sooner or later you will want to do something special or uncommon. For these cases, you can use configuration files.

The easy way to write a config file with Mongrel is to use the -G option. This will write a config file containing all the other options you specified on the command line. For example, you could use this command line:

```
mongrel_rails start -G myconfig.yml -p 3000 -r /home/hal/docs -l my.log
```

Then these options would be stored (in YAML form) in the myconfig.yml file. (With -G, the server exits after writing the config file.)

To read a config file, use -C:

```
mongrel_rails start -C myconfig.yml
```

Don't mix -C with other options. This flag assumes that the specified file contains *all* the options you want to use.

Mongrel has its own API for tweaking the server's behavior with fine granularity. The -S option allows you to specify the name of a script written with this API (which is like a small DSL or *Domain-Specific Language*). The documentation gives this example script (which adds a directory handler for another directory):

```
# File: config/mongrel.conf
uri "/newstuff", :handler => DirHandler.new("/var/www/newstuff")

# Invoke this by issuing the command:
# mongrel_rails start -S config/mongrel.conf
```

It's also possible to use Mongrel much in the way we use WEBrick. The following example works fine and is fairly intuitive:

```ruby
require 'mongrel'

class TinyHandler < Mongrel::HttpHandler
   def process(request, response)
      response.start(200) do |head,out|
         head["Content-Type"] = "text/html"
         out.write <<-EOF
           This is only a test...

         EOF
      end
   end
end

server = Mongrel::HttpServer.new("0.0.0.0", "3000")
server.register("/stuff", TinyHandler.new)
server.register("/other", Mongrel::DirHandler.new("./other"))
server.run.join     # Wait on server thread
```

If you are a sophisticated user of Mongrel, you might be interested in its GemPlugin system. These are basically autoloaded gems which become "a part" of the functionality of Mongrel. For example, the "Mongrel cluster" plugin allows easy management of a cluster of Mongrel servers.

There is much more to Mongrel than we've seen here. For a discussion of logging, debugging, the details of the gem plugin system, and more, you can go to the online documentation at http://mongrel.rubyforge.org.

19.8   Conclusion

In this chapter, we've looked at low-level CGI details for implementing Web applications. We've looked at how server-side tools such as mod_ruby can help ease the writing of such applications. There are many tools *not* covered in this book, such as ruby-web, Amrita, Tofu, and Cerise. As always, you should do online research before choosing a tool.

We've also looked briefly at higher-level libraries and frameworks such as Rails, Nitro, IOWA, and Wee. We've examined the small self-contained WEBrick server (and the much faster Mongrel).

Now let's look at network programming in a new way, a much simpler, more abstracted way. The next chapter deals with distributed Ruby.

## CHAPTER 20

Distributed Ruby

Less is more.

—*Robert Browning, "Andrea del Sarto"*

Many technologies that enable distributed computing are available today. These technologies include various flavors of RPC as well as such things as COM, CORBA, DCE, and Java's RMI.

These all vary in complexity, but they do essentially the same thing. They provide relatively transparent communication between objects in a networking context so that remote objects can be used as though they were local.

Why would we want to do something like this in the first place? There might be many reasons. One excellent reason is to share the burden of a computing problem between many processors at once. An example would be the SETI@home program, which uses your PC to process small data sets in the "search for extraterrestrial intelligence." (SETI@home is not a project of the SETI Institute, by the way.) Another example would be the grassroots effort to decode the RSA129 encryption challenge (which succeeded several years ago). There are countless other areas where it is possible to split a problem into individual parts for a distributed solution.

It's also conceivable that you might want to expose an interface to a service without making the code itself available. This is frequently done via a web application, but the inherently stateless nature of the Web makes this a little unwieldy (in addition to other disadvantages). A distributed programming mechanism makes this kind of thing possible in a more direct way.

In the Ruby world, one answer to this challenge is drb or *distributed Ruby* by Masatoshi Seki. (The name is also written DRb.) There are other ways of doing distributed coding with Ruby, but drb is arguably the easiest. It doesn't have such advanced facilities as CORBA's naming service, but it is a simple and usable library with all of the most basic functionality you would need. In this chapter, we'll look at the basics of using distributed Ruby (along with Rinda which is built on top of it).

20.1   An Overview: Using drb

A drb application has two basic components—a server and a client. A rough breakdown of their responsibilities is as follows:

The server:

- Starts a TCPServer and listens on a port

- Binds an object to the drb server instance

- Accepts connections from clients and responds to their messages

- May optionally provide access control (security)

The client:

- Establishes a connection to the server process

- Binds a local object to the remote server object

- Sends messages to the server object and gets responses

The class method start_service takes care of starting a TCP server that listens on a specified port; it takes two parameters. The first is a *URI* (a *Universal Resource Identifier*) specifying a port (if it is nil, a port will be chosen dynamically). The second is an object to which we want to bind. This object will be remotely accessible by the client, invoking its methods as though it were local.

```
require "drb"

myobj = MyServer.new
```

```
DRb.start_service("druby://:1234", myobj)    # Port 1234

# ...
```

If the port is chosen dynamically, the class method uri can be used to retrieve the full URI including the port number.

```
DRb.start_service(nil, myobj)
myURI = DRb.uri                     # "druby://hal9000:2001"
```

Since drb is threaded, any server application will need to do a join on the server thread (to prevent the application from exiting prematurely and killing the thread).

```
# Prevent premature exit
DRb.thread.join
```

On the client side, we can invoke start_service with no parameters and use DRbObject to create a local object that corresponds to the remote one. We typically use nil as the first parameter in creating a new DRbObject.

```
require "drb"

DRb.start_service
obj = DRbObject.new(nil, "druby://hal9000:2001")

# Messages passed to obj will get forwarded to the
# remote object on the server side...
```

We should point out that on the server side, when we bind to an object, we really are binding to a *single object*, which will answer all requests that it receives. If there is more than one client, we will have to make our code *thread-safe* to avoid that object somehow getting into an inconsistent state. (For really simple or specialized applications, this may not be necessary.)

We can't go into great detail here. Just be aware that if a client both reads and writes the internal state of the remote object, then two or more clients have the potential to interfere with each other. To avoid this, we recommend a straightforward solution using an asynchronization mechanism such as a Mutex. (Refer to Chapter 13, "Threads in Ruby," for more on threads and synchronization issues.)

Let's look at security at least a little. After all, you may not want just any old client to connect to your server. You can't prevent clients from trying, but you can prevent their succeeding.

Distributed Ruby has the concept of an *access control list* or *ACL* (often pronounced to rhyme with "crackle"). These are simply lists of clients (or categories of clients) that are specifically allowed (or not allowed) to connect.

Here is an example. We use the ACL class to create a new ACL, passing in one or two parameters.

The second (optional) parameter to ACL.new answers the question, "Do we *deny* all clients except certain ones, or *allow* all clients except certain ones?" The default is DENY_ALLOW, represented by a 0; ALLOW_DENY is represented by a 1.

The first parameter for ACL.new is simply an array of strings; these strings are taken in pairs, where the first in the pair is "deny" or "allow", and the second represents a client or category of clients (by name or address). The following is an example:

```
require "drb/acl"
acl = ACL.new( %w[ deny all
                   allow 192.168.0.*
                   allow 210.251.121.214
                   allow localhost] )
```

The first entry *deny all* is arguably redundant, but it does make the meaning more explicit.

Now how do we use an ACL? The install_acl method will put an ACL into effect for us. Note that this has to be done *before* the call to the start_service method, or it will have no effect.

```
# Continuing the above example...

DRb.install_acl(acl)
DRb.start_service(nil, some_object)
# ...
```

When the service then starts, any unauthorized client connection will result in a RuntimeError being thrown by the server.

There is somewhat more to drb than we cover here. But this is enough for a good overview. In the next section, we'll look at a simple drb server and client that are almost real-world code. We'll also look at Rinda and Ring before we close the chapter.

20.2   Case Study: A Stock Ticker Simulation

In this example, we assume that we have a server application that is making stock prices available to the network. Any client wanting to check the value of his thousand shares of Gizmonic Institute can contact this server.

We've added a twist to this, however. We don't just want to watch every little fluctuation in the stock price. We've implemented an Observer module that will let us subscribe to the stock feed; the client then watches the feed and warns us only when the price goes above or below a certain value.

First let's look at the DrbObservable module. This is a straightforward implementation of the *Observer* pattern from the excellent book *Design Patterns*, published by Addison-Wesley and authored by the so-called "Gang of Four" (Gamma, Helm, Johnson, and Vlissides). This is also known as the *Publish-Subscribe* pattern.

Listing 20.1 defines an *observer* as an object that responds to the update method call. Observers are added (by the server) at their own request and are sent information via the notify_observers call.

Listing 20.1   The drb Observer Module

```ruby
module DRbObservable

  def add_observer(observer)
    @observer_peers ||= []
    unless observer.respond_to? :update
      raise NameError, "observer needs to respond to `update'"
    end
    @observer_peers.push observer
  end

  def delete_observer(observer)
    @observer_peers.delete observer if defined? @observer_peers
  end

  def notify_observers(*arg)
    return unless defined? @observer_peers
    for i in @observer_peers.dup
      begin
        i.update(*arg)
      rescue
        delete_observer(i)
      end
    end
  end

end
```

The server (or feed) in Listing 20.2 simulates the stock price by a sequence of pseudorandom numbers. (This is as good a simulation of the market as I have ever seen, if you will pardon the irony.) The stock symbol identifying the company is used only for cosmetics in the simulation and has no actual purpose in the code. Every time the price changes, the observers are all notified.

Listing 20.2   The drb Stock Price Feed (Server)

```ruby
require "drb"
require "drb_observer"

# Generate random prices
class MockPrice

  MIN = 75
  RANGE = 50

  def initialize(symbol)
    @price = RANGE / 2
  end

  def price
    @price += (rand() - 0.5)*RANGE
    if @price < 0
      @price = -@price
    elsif @price >= RANGE
      @price = 2*RANGE - @price
    end
    MIN + @price
  end
end

class Ticker # Periodically fetch a stock price
  include DRbObservable

  def initialize(price_feed)
    @feed = price_feed
    Thread.new { run }
  end

  def run
    lastPrice = nil
    loop do
      price = @feed.price
      print "Current price: #{price}\n"
      if price != lastPrice
        lastPrice = price
        notify_observers(Time.now, price)
```

```
          end
        sleep 1
      end
    end
  end
end

ticker = Ticker.new(MockPrice.new("MSFT"))

DRb.start_service('druby://localhost:9001', ticker)
puts 'Press [return] to exit.'
gets
```

If you are on a Windows platform, you may have difficulty with the exit idiom used here. The gets on Windows tends to hang the main thread. If you experience this, you should use a DRb.thread.join instead (and use a control-C to kill it).

Not surprisingly, the client (in Listing 20.3) begins by contacting the server. It gets a reference to the stock ticker object and sets its own desired values for the high and low marks. Then the client will print a message for the user every time the stock price goes above the high end or below the low end.

Listing 20.3   The drb Stock Price Watcher (Client)

```
require "drb"

class Warner
  include DRbUndumped

  def initialize(ticker, limit)
    @limit = limit
    ticker.add_observer(self)    # all warners are observers
  end
end

class WarnLow < Warner
  def update(time, price)        # callback for observer
    if price < @limit
      print "--- #{time.to_s}: Price below #@limit: #{price}\n"
    end
  end
end

class WarnHigh < Warner
  def update(time, price)        # callback for observer
    if price > @limit
      print "+++ #{time.to_s}: Price above #@limit: #{price}\n"
    end
```

Continues

```
      end
    end

    DRb.start_service
    ticker = DRbObject.new(nil, "druby://localhost:9001")

    WarnLow.new(ticker, 90)
    WarnHigh.new(ticker, 110)

    puts "Press [return] to exit."
    gets
```

You may wonder about the DRbUndumped module referenced in Listing 20.3. This is included in any object that is not intended to be marshalled. Basically, the mere presence of this module among the ancestors of an object is sufficient to tell drb not to marshal that object. In fact, I recommend you look at the code of this module. Here it is in its entirety:

```
module DRbUndumped
  def _dump(dummy)
    raise TypeError, "can't dump"
  end
end
```

The stock watcher application we saw in this section is long enough to be meaningful but short enough to understand. There are other ways to approach such a problem. But this is a good solution that demonstrates the simplicity and elegance of distributed Ruby.

20.3 Rinda: A Ruby Tuplespace

The term *tuplespace* dates back as far as 1985, and the concept itself is even older than that. A *tuple*, of course, is simply an array or vector of data items (much like a database row); tuplespace is a large object space full of tuples, like a kind of "data soup."

So far, a tuplespace implementation sounds boring. It becomes more interesting when you realize that it is accessible in a synchronized way by multiple clients. In short, it is inherently a distributed entity; any client can read or write the tuplespace, so they can all use it as a large shared storage or even as a way to communicate.

The original tuplespace implementation was the Linda project, an experiment in parallel programming at Yale University in the 1980s. The Ruby implementation (based on drb, of course) is naturally called *Rinda*.

A Rinda tuple can actually be an array or a hash. If it is a hash, it has the additional restriction that all its keys must be strings. Here are some simple tuples:

```
t1 = [:add, 5, 9]
t2 = [:name, :add_service, Adder.new, nil]
t3 = { 'type' => 'add', 'value_1' => 5, 'value_2' => 9 }
```

Each item in a tuple can be an arbitrary object; this works because drb can marshal and unmarshal Ruby objects. (Of course, you may need to use DRbUndumped or make the class definitions available on the server side.)

We create a tuplespace with a simple new call:

```
require 'rinda/tuplespace'

ts = Rinda::TupleSpace.new
# ...
```

So a server would simply look like this:

```
require 'rinda/tuplespace'

ts = Rinda::TupleSpace.new
DRb.start_service("druby://somehost:9000", ts)
gets   # CR to kill server
```

And a client would look like this:

```
require 'rinda/tuplespace'

DRb.start_service
ts = DRbObject.new(nil, "druby://somehost:9000")
# ...
```

We can perform five basic operations on a Rinda tuplespace: *read, read_all, write, take,* and *notify.*

A read operation is exactly what it sounds like: You are retrieving a tuple from tuplespace. However, identifying the tuple to read may be a little unintuitive; we do it by specifying a tuple that will match the one we want to read. A nil value is in effect a wildcard that will match any value.

```
t1 = ts.read [:Sum,nil]        # will retrieve [:Sum, 14] for example
```

Normally a read operation will block (as a way of providing synchronization). If you want to quickly test the existence of a tuple, you can use a nonblocking read by specifying a timeout value of zero:

```
t2 = ts.read [:Result,nil],0   # raises an exception if nonexistent
```

If we know or expect that more than one tuple will match the pattern, we can use read_all and get an array back:

```
tuples = ts.read_all [:Foo, nil, nil]
tuples.each do |t|
  # ...
end
```

The read_all method doesn't take a second parameter. It will always block if no matching tuple is found.

A *take* operation is basically a read followed by an implicit delete. The take actually removes a tuple from the tuplespace and returns it:

```
t = ts.take [:Sum, nil]    # tuple is now removed from tuplespace
```

You might ask why there isn't an explicit method to do a delete. Obviously the take method will serve that purpose.

The write method, of course, stores a tuple in tuplespace. Its second parameter tells how long in seconds the tuple should be kept before it expires. (The default expiration value is nil or never expiring.)

```
ts.write [:Add, 5, 9]        # Keep this "forever"
ts.write [:Foo, "Bar"], 10   # Keep this ten seconds
```

A few words on synchronization are appropriate here. Suppose two clients attempt to take the same tuple at (approximately) the same time. One will succeed, and the other will block. If the first (successful) client then modifies the tuple and writes it back into tuplespace, the second (blocked) client will then retrieve the new modified version of the tuple. So you can think of an "update" operation as being a take followed by a write, and there will be no data loss. Of course, as with all thread programming, you have to watch for deadlocks.

A `notify` method, not surprisingly, enables you to "watch" the tuplespace and be informed when a matching tuple has some operation performed on it. This method (which returns a `NotifyTemplateEntry` object) watches for four kinds of operations:

- `write` operations

- `take` operations

- delete operations (when a tuple has expired)

- close operations (when the `NotifyTemplateEntry` object has expired)

Because read operations are nondestructive, the system does not support notification of reads. Listing 20.4 shows an example of using `notify`.

Listing 20.4   Rinda's Notification Feature

```
require 'rinda/tuplespace'

ts = Rinda::TupleSpace.new

alberts = ts.notify "write", ["Albert", nil]
martins = ts.notify "take",  ["Martin", nil]

thr1 = Thread.new do
  alberts.each {|op,t| puts "#{op}: #{t.join(' ')}" }
end

thr2 = Thread.new do
  martins.each {|op,t| puts "#{op}: #{t.join(' ')}" }
end

sleep 1

ts.write ["Martin", "Luther"]
ts.write ["Albert", "Einstein"]
ts.write ["Martin", "Fowler"]
ts.write ["Albert", "Schweitzer"]
ts.write ["Martin", "Scorsese"]
ts.take  ["Martin", "Luther"]

# Output:
# write: Albert Einstein
# write: Albert Schweitzer
# take: Martin Luther
```

We've seen how read and other operations use *templates* that match tuples (conceptually much as a regular expression works). A nil value can be a wildcard as we've seen, but a class can also be specified to match any instance of that class.

```
tem1 = ["X", Integer]    # matches ["X",5] but not ["X","Files"]
tem2 = ["X", NilClass]   # matches a literal nil in the tuple
```

In addition, you can define your own case equality (===) operator if you want a class to match a value in some special way. Otherwise, of course, the class will match based on the default === operator.

Bear in mind that the lifetime of a tuple can be specified upon writing. This ties in with the timeout values on the various tuple operations, ensuring that it's possible to restrict any simple or complex operation to a finite length of time.

The fact that tuples can expire also means that they can be *renewed* after they expire, often with a custom renewer object. The library comes with a SimpleRenewer that simply contacts the tuple's originating drb server every 180 seconds; if the server is down, the tuple is allowed to expire. But don't bother with renewer objects until you are competent in the tuplespace paradigm.

If you want another tuplespace code fragment, Listing 20.5 shows a simple one. This is based on the producer/consumer example in Chapter 13.

Listing 20.5   The Producer-Consumer Problem Revisited

```
require 'rinda/tuplespace'

ts = Rinda::TupleSpace.new

producer = Thread.new do
  item = 0
  loop do
    sleep rand(0)
    puts "Producer makes item ##{item}"
ts.write ["Item",item]
    item += 1
  end
end

consumer = Thread.new do
  loop do
    sleep rand(0)
    tuple = ts.take ["Item", nil]
word, item = tuple
    puts "Consumer retrieves item ##{item}"
```

```
      end
   end

   sleep 60    # Run a minute, then die and kill threads
```

20.4 Service Discovery with Distributed Ruby

If you have many services running locally, *service discovery* might be a useful concept to you; it allows services to be located by name. But if you have few services at well-known locations, this may not be particularly useful.

Because you are apparently still reading, you must be interested in how service discovery works. The Rinda library provides such a service (naturally based on Rinda) called `Rinda::Ring`. Think of it as providing DNS-like features; it is a central registration service storing information (in a tuplespace) about `drb` processes. The `drb` services can use UDP (datagrams) to find a nearby registration server to advertise themselves and/or to find other services in the neighborhood.

The `Rinda::RingServer` class implements the registration server. It keeps a tuplespace for storing locations of other `drb` services (though actually any service may be advertised). When it comes up, the RingServer listens for UDP broadcast packets requesting the location of the server. It responds to each of these by connecting back (via `drb`) to the requesting service. The following is an example of running a RingServer:

```
require 'rinda/ring'
require 'rinda/tuplespace'

DRb.start_service
Rinda::RingServer.new(Rinda::TupleSpace.new)

DRb.thread.join
```

The `Rinda::RingProvider` class registers (or advertises) a service with a RingServer. A service is identified by a service type, a front-end object providing the service, and a piece of descriptive text. In the following example, we create a simple `Adder` service that adds two numbers; then we advertise it to the world:

```
require 'rinda/ring'

class Adder
```

```
    include DRbUndumped

    def add(val1, val2)
      return val1 + val2
    end
  end

  adder = Adder.new
  DRb.start_service(nil, adder)
  Rinda::RingProvider.new(:adder, adder, 'Simple Adder')

  DRb.thread.join
```

The `Rinda::RingFinger` class (presumably named for the classic UNIX `finger`
command) can be used to locate a RingServer. It sends a UDP broadcast packet and
waits for the RingServer to respond. The RingFinger can then be used to look up
advertised services in the tuplespace.

```
  require 'rinda/ring'

  DRb.start_service
  rs = Rinda::RingFinger.primary
  list = [rs] + Rinda::Ringfinger.to_a
  svc = list.find_all [:name, :adder, nil, nil]
```

20.5 Conclusion

This chapter presented a good introduction to distributed Ruby. We saw the basics of
starting a service and communicating with clients, and we looked at security issues.

In addition, we saw how Rinda can act as a simple object store that is both distributed and synchronized. Finally, we looked at how `Rinda::Ring` can be used for
drb service discovery.

That ends our look at distributed Ruby. Let's move to a new topic: Using development tools associated with Ruby such as Rake, irb, Integrated Development
Environments (IDEs), and more.

CHAPTER 21

Ruby Development Tools

Man is a tool-making animal.

—Benjamin Franklin

A development environment consists of more than just an interpreter. Every good developer is surrounded by a selection of tools that make life easier. Some of these may be language-specific, and others may not.

The most important of these is the editor. Since much of what programmers do day-to-day is manipulate text, the choice of editor (or your proficiency with it) has a significant impact on productivity. The language-specific features or the customization capabilities also have an impact. We'll look very briefly at the most common editors here.

Other tools may assist in documentation, library installation, debugging, and similar tasks. We've already looked at the debugging library (which is not a real standalone application) in Chapter 16, "Testing and Debugging," and we've looked at RDoc in Chapter 17, "Packaging and Distributing Code." These are not covered further here. We looked at RubyGems in Chapter 17 from the standpoint of a developer creating packages; in this chapter, we'll look at it from the viewpoint of a developer using packages created by others.

This chapter also covers irb (interactive Ruby) and ri (the documentation tool). Finally we wrap up with a brief discussion of IDEs (Integrated Development Environments) that work well with Ruby.

21.1   Using RubyGems

RubyGems is not the "official" package management system for Ruby, but it is the one with the most community support. As of July 2006, it is not part of the standard distribution, but it may be in the future. We had a good overview of the mechanics of gem creation in Chapter 17. In this chapter we're concerned with using gems created by others.

The RubyGems concept exists to solve a few basic problems: ease of installation, centralized repositories, library version management, dependency management, and more. Gems give you easy access to your documentation and easy control over what libraries are installed.

You may not have RubyGems installed on your system. If not, go to http://rubyforge.org/projects/rubygems and follow the simple instructions for download and installation. After the first install, RubyGems can of course update itself.

The actual executable is called gem. It has a command structure similar to that of cvs or similar tools; that is, there are subcommands and options that make sense for each subcommand. The usage information is as follows:

```
RubyGems is a sophisticated package manager for Ruby.  This is a
basic help message containing pointers to more information.

  Usage:
    gem -h/--help
    gem -v/--version
    gem command [arguments...] [options...]

  Examples:
    gem install rake
    gem list --local
    gem build package.gemspec
    gem help install

  Further help:
    gem help commands            list all 'gem' commands
    gem help examples            show some examples of usage
```

```
gem help                    show help on COMMAND
                                      (e.g. 'gem help install')
```

```
Further information:
    http://rubygems.rubyforge.org
```

The most basic usage is simple. If (for example) you want to install the `feedtools` library, you can issue this command:

```
gem install feedtools
```

This will first look for a local gem file; if it doesn't find one, it will look on the RubyForge server. By default, it gives you the latest version (though in some cases it may prompt you to clarify which gem you want). You can also specify a version with `-v` or `--version` if necessary. There are several other options for controlling the installation; issue the command `gem help install` for more information.

Sometimes a gem will have dependencies on other gems. In such a case, you will be prompted as to whether you want to install each dependency. Obviously, if you don't install them, the gem you were after can't be installed.

How do you know what to install in the first place? Well, if the item is on RubyForge, it normally has a gem there named with the "UNIX name" of the project. For example, the `rake` tool can be accessed through http://rubyforge.org/projects/rake or simply http://rake.rubyforge.org; therefore `gem install rake` will install it.

If you don't even know that much, the `gem search` command may be useful to you. Specify a fragment of the name of a gem, and it will search for all related gems. By default it will search locally; use the `--remote` flag to search the repository. For example, when I issue `gem search xml --remote` on my system, I get 12 results.

To get information on an installed gem, use the `gem specification` command; it dumps all the available metadata (basically the gemspec itself) to output. There is a `--remote` flag, but at the time of this writing it is not yet implemented.

There is also an `uninstall` subcommand that is convenient, and the `query` and `list` commands seem to overlap with each other a little (and with `search`). Many other commands also are available; consult the built-in documentation or the online documentation for more details.

It's useful to run a *gem server* on your system—not in the sense of a repository from which other people can install but in the sense of a centralized location where you can view all your local gems (and their documentation) via a web browser.

To run the gem server, simply invoke the `gem_server` executable. (Normally you would run it in the background.) When you then open your browser to the URL

`localhost:8808`, you will see a page titled "RubyGems Documentation Index." All
your installed gems are listed alphabetically, with links to the `rdoc` documentation and
to the gem's home page on the Web.

There is more to RubyGems, and the system is still changing. Refer to http://
rubygems.rubyforge.org for the latest information.

21.2 Using Rake

The `rake` utility is like a Rubyesque version of the UNIX `make` utility. Instead of the
bizarre "make" syntax that we know and hate, it uses only pure Ruby code. This utility is the work of Jim Weirich and illustrates (perhaps) the first formal instance of a
DSL (domain-specific language) in Ruby.

You may see the name spelled "Rake" or "rake." The former is the name of the
tool, and the latter is the actual name of the executable itself. It's not worth nitpick-
ing, in my opinion.

The Rake tool is definitely inspired by `make`, so the terminology used is much the
same. We still talk about targets, actions, dependencies, and rules.

The uses of Rake are numerous. If you are working with C, C++, or Java code,
you can use it to build your projects. (It will work for other languages too, of course.)
You can also use it for generating documentation with RDoc, deploying software,
updating a RubyForge project, and many other such tasks.

Not surprisingly, Rake operates on a file of instructions called a *rakefile*. The rakefile will have a literal filename of `Rakefile` or `rakefile` by default. If you want to
name it something else, you can use the `-f` or `--rakefile` option:

```
$ rake             # look for 'rakefile' first, then 'Rakefile'
$ rake -f myfile   # use 'myfile' instead
```

The basic "unit of work" in Rake is the *task*; these are named with Ruby symbols.
Every rakefile is understood to have a default task called `:default`, which will be run
if you don't specify a task name.

```
$ rake             # execute the default task
$ rake mytask      # execute 'mytask'
```

Inside a rakefile, we specify a task by using the `task` method, passing it a symbol and a block:

```
task :mytask do
  # ...
end
```

The contents of the block are omitted in the preceding code. The "stuff" that goes here we refer to as *actions*.

An action can be anything and can involve arbitrary Ruby code. Some convenience methods are available for common operations. The `sh` method (meant to remind us of the UNIX `sh` executable) will run a system command.

The methods `cp`, `mv`, and `rm` are respectively for copying, moving, and deleting files. (Like the `make` utility itself, Rake has an unabashed UNIX flavor about it.) There are other such commands; consult online documentation for more information (http://docs.rubyrake.org).

If you prefer to use braces to delimit a block, you can, but the Ruby parser will typically force you to use parentheses around the parameter in that case:

```
task(:mytask) { do_something }
```

To continue, let's take a more concrete example. Imagine we have a C program named `myprog.c` with two other C files associated with it (each with its own header file). In other words, we have these five source files:

```
myprog.c
sub1.c
sub1.h
sub2.c
sub2.h
```

We want to compile all this together into the executable `myprog`. This is a multi-step process: First we will compile all the `.c` files; then we will link the resulting `.o` files together.

Let's begin by using the `file` method to specify file dependencies:

```
file "myprog.o" => ["myprog.c"]
file "sub1.o" => ["sub1.c", "sub1.h"]
file "sub2.o" => ["sub2.c", "sub2.h"]
file "myprog" => ["sub1.o", "sub2.o"]
```

Notice how the `file` method just takes a hash. It associates a filename with an array of dependent filenames.

Now let's look at building the binary files. We'll take the code we just wrote and extend it a little. If we put a block on the `file` call, we can associate with the file a set of actions that will produce that file:

```
file "myprog.o" => ["myprog.c"] do
  sh "cc -c -o myprog.o myprog.c"
end

file "sub1.o" => ["sub1.c", "sub1.h"] do
  sh "cc -c -o sub1.o sub1.c"
end

file "sub2.o" => ["sub2.c", "sub2.h"] do
  sh "cc -c -o sub2.o sub2.c"
end

file "myprog" => ["sub1.o", "sub2.o"] do
  sh "cc -o myprog myprog.o sub1.o sub2.o"
end
```

There is some duplication here, but we can get rid of it. As it turns out, Rake has a special facility called a `FileList`; it understands wildcards (glob patterns) and allows us to work with multiple files at once. Here we find all the `.c` files and assign the list to a constant `SRC`. This `FileList` constant acts much like an array:

```
SRC = FileList["*.c"]
```

So we *could* use a loop to specify our actions; see the following code fragment. (And note that the dependencies are not specified here; Rake is smart enough to combine this information internally if we specify the dependencies elsewhere.)

```
SRC.each do |src|
  obj = src.sub(/.c$/,".o")
  file(obj) { sh "cc -c -o #{obj} #{src}" }
end
```

However, it's simpler to use *rules*, which are another Rake feature (naturally lifted from make):

```
rule '.o' => '.c' do |target|
  sh "cc -c -o #{target.name} #{target.source}"
end
```

A small bit of magic happens here. The `source` attribute gets set internally, substituting the file extension from the hash key/value information (changing .o to .c in this case).

Now let's do a little more magic. If we require the `rake/clean` library, the constants `CLEAN` and `CLOBBER` (initially empty) and tasks `:clean` and `:clobber` are defined for us. These are traditionally named targets; `clean` will remove the temporary files, and `clobber` will remove all these and the final executable also.

These arraylike constants have an `include` method that takes a file glob. This is like an implicit use of `FileList`.

So our rakefile now looks like this:

```
require 'rake/clean'

CLEAN.include("*.o")
CLOBBER.include("myprog")

SRC = FileList['*.c']
OBJ = SRC.ext('o')

rule '.o' => '.c' do |t|
  sh "cc -c -o #{t.name} #{t.source}"
end

file "hello" => OBJ do
  sh "cc -o hello #{OBJ}"
end

file "myprog.o" => ["myprog.c"]
file "sub1.o" => ["sub1.c", "sub1.h"]
file "sub2.o" => ["sub2.c", "sub2.h"]

task :default => ["myprog"]
```

Notice how we don't have to specify "clean" and "clobber" tasks explicitly. Also note that a "clobber" implicitly includes a "clean" operation. Finally, note that we specified a `default` task for the convenience of the person running the rakefile; it's now unnecessary to specify a task in order to compile.

Rake has several useful command-line options. Sometimes you want to test a rakefile without actually doing any (potentially dangerous) operations; the -n or --dry-run options will allow this. The -T option will list all the targets in a rakefile. There are also options controlling library path searching, tracing and logging, and more.

Rake is more complex than I've hinted at here (especially the rules). It's also still evolving. As always, consult the online documentation for the latest information (http://docs.rubyrake.org).

21.3   Using `irb`

The `irb` utility (interactive Ruby) has been distributed with Ruby for many years. It can be thought of as a "testbed" or "playground" where you try out quick hacks and new ideas.

Basic usage of `irb` is simple. When you start it, you get a prompt where you can type Ruby expressions; each expression is evaluated, and the result is printed for you. Here's a small example of a session:

```
$ irb
irb(main):001:0> "cell" + "o"
=> "cello"
irb(main):002:0> 3*79
=> 237
irb(main):003:0> Dir.entries(".").size
=> 17
irb(main):004:0> rand
=> 0.850757389880155
irb(main):005:0> rand
=> 0.679879756672551
irb(main):006:0> defined? foo
=> nil
irb(main):007:0> defined? Object
=> "constant"
irb(main):008:0> quit
$
```

Of course, it's more than just a calculator. You can type in arbitrary Ruby code if you want:

```
[hal@localhost ch21]$ irb
irb(main):001:0> require 'mathn'
=> true
irb(main):002:0> gen = Prime.new
=> #
```

The -r option will do a require so that you can include code from a file. Suppose this was a source file of yours:

```
# File: foo.rb
class MyClass

  attr_accessor :alpha, :beta

  def initialize(a, b)
    @alpha, @beta = a, b
  end

end

obj1 = MyClass.new(23,34)
obj2 = MyClass.new("abc","xyz")
```

Then we can do this:

```
$ irb -rfoo
irb(main):001:0> obj = MyClass.new(88,99)
=> #
```

But notice that although we can get at the contents of the file (for example, the constant MyClass), that doesn't include the local variables. The local variables for a file are accessible *only* within that file; a require (inside or outside irb) won't allow you to see them.

Newbies are sometimes confused by output printed in irb:

```
$ irb -rfoo
irb(main):001:0> puts "hello"
hello
=> nil
```

What is the `nil` doing there? That, of course, is the return value from the `puts` method.

Another minor source of confusion concerns `eval`. See the behavior in the following session:

```
$ irb
irb(main):001:0> eval("var = 567")
=> 567
irb(main):002:0> eval("var")
=> 567
irb(main):003:0> var
=> 567
```

This may not seem surprising to you. But run the following script and see what happens:

```
p eval("var = 567")
p eval("var")
p var

# Results:
# 567
# 567
# temp.rb:3: undefined local variable or method `var' for main:Object
➥(NameError)
```

It is a quirk of Ruby that when you do an `eval` and then do another, they have in a sense the "same scope." So the variable defined in the first line can be accessed again in the second line (inside or outside `irb`). But the difference comes when we try to access that variable *without* using eval. In `irb` it works, but in the script we get an error. What's going on?

The script's behavior should be considered the more correct one. Bear in mind that `irb` itself is written in Ruby; common sense indicates it probably uses `eval` internally to do its job. But we've seen that `eval` can give us different results from what we see at the top level; therefore, running code in `irb` is *not always exactly the same* as running it in a standalone script. That is the lesson to be remembered here, especially if you are trying some kind of esoteric experiment.

Be aware that irb is highly customizable. When you start it up, it reads whatever initialization data it finds first, looking for them in this order:

- File ~/.irbrc

- File .irbrc

- File irb.rc

- File _irbrc

- Path stored in environment variable $irbrc

The initialization file is pure Ruby. It enables customization of prompts and much more. For a complete discussion of this file, the best source is the so-called "Pickaxe Book," *Programming Ruby*. The remainder of this section will only hit a few highlights.

If your Ruby installation is built with GNU readline support (as is usually the case), you can use the up and down arrow keys to navigate back and forth in the command history. More importantly, you get *tab completion* as a feature. This works as you would expect: When you type a partial identifier and then press the Tab key, irb tries to complete the rest of the identifier name for you.

To enable tab completion, add this fragment to your .irbrc file:

```
IRB.conf[:AUTO_INDENT] = true
IRB.conf[:USE_READLINE] = true
IRB.conf[:LOAD_MODULES] ||= []
IRB.conf[:LOAD_MODULES] |= ['irb/completion']
```

Bear in mind it's possible to put arbitrary code in your .irbrc file. For example, here is a method I find useful sometimes. It is named sm for brevity ("show methods"); its purpose is to list (in alphabetical order) all the methods that can be called on an object, *excluding* the ones it gets from its ancestors:

```
def sm(obj)
  list = obj.methods
  anc = obj.class.ancestors - [obj.class]
  anc.each {|a| list -= a.instance_methods }
  list.sort
end
```

The following is an example of its usage:

```
irb(main):001:0> str = "hello"
=> "hello"
irb(main):002:0> sm str
=> ["%", "*", "+", "<<", "<=>", "[]", "[]=", "capitalize",
"capitalize!", "casecmp", "center", "chomp", "chomp!", "chop", "chop!",
"concat", "count", "crypt", "delete", "delete!", "downcase", "downcase!",
"dump", "each", "each_byte", "each_line", "empty?", "gsub", "gsub!", "hex",
"index", "insert", "intern", "length", "ljust", "lstrip", "lstrip!", "match",
"next", "next!", "oct", "replace", "reverse", "reverse!", "rindex", "rjust",
"rstrip", "rstrip!", "scan", "size", "slice", "slice!", "split", "squeeze",
"squeeze!", "strip", "strip!", "sub", "sub!", "succ", "succ!", "sum",
"swapcase", "swapcase!", "to_f", "to_i", "to_str", "to_sym", "tr", "tr!",
"tr_s", "tr_s!", "unpack", "upcase", "upcase!", "upto"]
irb(main):003:0> sm String
=> ["allocate", "new", "superclass"]
irb(main):004:0> sm 123
=> ["%", "&", "*", "**", "+", "-", "/", "<<", ">>", "[]", "^",
"id2name", "power!", "rdiv", "rpower", "size", "to_f", "to_sym", "|", "~"]
```

It's not seen much, but irb makes it possible to run *subsessions* within a session. It's possible to run multiple sessions and switch back and forth between them; each one maintains a separate binding.

That may not necessarily seem useful, but one trick that makes it more useful is to specify an object along with the irb subcommand. Then the context of the subsession is that object; self is set as you would expect, the scope is that of the object, and so on:

```
$ irb
irb(main):001:0> t0 = Time.now
=> Mon Jul 31 04:51:50 CDT 2006
irb(main):002:0> irb t0
irb#1(Mon Jul 31 04:51:50 CDT 2006):001:0> strftime("%a %b %c")
=> "Mon Jul Mon Jul 31 04:51:50 2006"
irb#1(Mon Jul 31 04:51:50 CDT 2006):002:0> to_i
=> 1154339510
irb#1(Mon Jul 31 04:51:50 CDT 2006):003:0> self + 1000
=> Mon Jul 31 05:08:30 CDT 2006
irb#1(Mon Jul 31 04:51:50 CDT 2006):004:0> wday
=> 1
irb#1(Mon Jul 31 04:51:50 CDT 2006):005:0> class
```

```
SyntaxError: compile error
(irb#1):5: syntax error, unexpected $end
        from (irb#1):5
irb#1(Mon Jul 31 04:51:50 CDT 2006):006:0> self.class
=> Time
irb#1(Mon Jul 31 04:51:50 CDT 2006):007:0> quit
=> #<IRB::Irb: @scanner=#<RubyLex:0xb7ee8394>,
@signal_status=:IN_EVAL, @context=#<IRB::Context:0xb7ee86f0>>
irb(main):003:0> quit
$
```

We've already seen the usefulness of the `ruby-breakpoint` library in Chapter 16. In conjunction with that library, `irb` becomes a more powerful debugging tool because you can set a breakpoint and "jump into" an `irb` session. Of course, it isn't a *real* debugger because you can't step around in the code.

The `xmp` library is sometimes useful. It takes Ruby statements, evaluates them, and places the return value in comments. *Programming Ruby* covers `xmp` and also `rtags` (which generates a TAGS file for emacs or vi).

There is another "goodie" associated with `irb` that you might like to know about. Naturally `irb` is capable of analyzing Ruby code; the lexer is easily used by other applications as well. Here is a simple example of a program that opens its own file to analyze itself; it produces a sorted list of all identifiers and constants used in the program:

```ruby
require 'irb/ruby-lex'

file = File.new(__FILE__)

parse = RubyLex.new # (file)
parse.set_input(file)

idents = []

loop do
  token =  parse.token
  break if token.nil?
  if token.is_a? RubyToken::TkIDENTIFIER or
     token.is_a? RubyToken::TkCONSTANT
    idents << token.name
  end
end
```

```
p idents.uniq.sort

# Output:
# ["File", "RubyLex", "RubyToken", "TkCONSTANT", "TkIDENTIFIER", "file",
#  "idents", "loop", "name", "new", "p", "parse", "require", "set_input",
#  "sort", "token", "uniq"]
```

So far as I am aware, this is not documented anywhere in English. But if you need a Ruby lexer, you can probably read the source and adapt this one for your needs.

21.4   The `ri` Utility

The `ri` is apparently named from "Ruby index" or some such mnemonic. It is a command-line documentation tool, offering information on Ruby classes, methods, modules, and so on. Here is an example:

```
$ ri each_with_index
-----------------------------------------------------------
    enumObj.each_with_index {| obj, i | block }  -> nil
-----------------------------------------------------------

    Calls block with two arguments, the item and its index,
    for each item in enumObj.

        hash = Hash.new
        %w(cat dog wombat).each_with_index {|item, index|
            hash[item] = index
        }
        hash    #=> {"dog"=>1, "wombat"=>2, "cat"=>0}
```

Note that it has a few bugs and quirks. You are encouraged to report these (along with typos and other inaccuracies) if you can find anyone who claims to own it.

Martin Ankerl has a GUI version called `fxri` that works well. It draws its data from the RDoc information just as the command-line `ri` does. It also conveniently has a pane devoted to `irb`.

21.5   Editor Support

Any modern editor should be programmer-friendly. With memories of the 20th century growing dim, we take it for granted that our editors will reconfigure themselves based on the kind of file we are editing. We expect syntax highlighting, auto-indent, and other such features as a matter of course.

The Ruby coder will not be disappointed by the tools and features out there. Many of these are now standard with an editor's distribution; others are not. Let's take a quick look at what's available.

Two excellent editors are SciTe (based on the Scintilla editing widget) and TextMate (which runs on Mac OS X only). Both are good editors with good Ruby support; I have no further information on them, however.

A third is jEdit, the Java-based programmer's editor (www.jedit.com). Its functionality is enhanced by Rob McKinnon's jEdit Ruby Plugin (http://rubyjedit.org/). I can't cover it further in this book.

The two most common editors in the programmers' world are vi (or vim) and emacs. Let's look at these briefly.

Historically three different packages were available for vim users. Fortunately these are now consolidated into a single package called `vim-ruby`. This set of config files offers syntax highlighting, auto-indent, and code completion. It also enables such things as invoking the Ruby interpreter from within the editor (compiler plug-ins).

If you are running vim version 7 (as you should be), you probably already have these features installed. (If you're running 6.x for no good reason, upgrading is recommended.)

However, you may find that these features are disabled (probably for backward compatibility). Turn them on by adding the following to your `.vimrc` file:

```
set nocompatible
syntax on
filetype on
filetype indent on
filetype plugin on
```

There are also at least two implementations of code folding for Ruby. In my opinion, any folding technique that forces you to put special comments or characters in your code is not optimal. A good code-folding mechanism should be smart enough to look at the syntax of your code and recognize classes, modules, methods, and so on. One good implementation of code folding in vim is by Mauricio Fernandez; find it at http://eigenclass.org/hiki.rb?Usable+Ruby+folding+for+Vim.

Arguably there are many reasons to dislike vim; one of the greatest reasons is surely vimscript. The good news is it's possible to script vim's behavior using Ruby. The bad news is this is not well documented. If you want to learn about this, I recommend using

`:help ruby` in vim as a starting point. You can also go to http://wiki.rubygarden.org/ Ruby/page/show/VimRubyInterface for more information. Finally, do a search of http://vim/org to see what recent information you can find.

The other most popular editor in the world is emacs. Actually, to call it an editor is a bit misleading; it is more like a miniature operating system that happens to do text editing on the side. One of the great advantages of emacs is that it is highly extensible; the user can program its behavior in a Lisp variant called *elisp*. The elisp language is more powerful than vimscript; however, it is just as difficult to read (but in a different way).

I am not an `emacs` user, though I have great respect for those who are. I can't comment at great length about Ruby support in emacs; I will only refer you to the wiki at RubyGarden (http://wiki.rubygarden.org/Ruby/page/show/EmacsExtensions).

21.6   Integrated Development Environments

It could be argued that Borland with its Turbo Pascal (in the mid-1980s) was the father of the modern Integrated Development Environment (or IDE); certainly Borland popularized it. Wherever you consider its origin to be, it's clear that the concept is going to be around for a long time to come.

An IDE typically centers on a powerful editor with intimate knowledge of the language syntax. Features such as syntax highlighting and auto-indent are standard. Usually a debugger is included, as is support for project management. Integrated testing and integrated source control are happily becoming more common.

It's difficult to compare IDEs in a meaningful way. They are all alike, and yet they are all different. Choosing one that you like is as personal and subjective as choosing an automobile. I've tried to do a little research to help you decide between the existing solutions:

- One of the most important Ruby IDEs is FreeRIDE. It is tailored specifically for Ruby and is controlled entirely by developers within the Ruby community. Some key developers are Rich Kilmer, Curt Hibbs, and Laurent Juilliard; there are many others. Like any large open-source project, development is proceeding slowly. Refer to http://freeride.rubyforge.org for the latest information and downloads.

- One of the newest solutions is Komodo from ActiveState. It is powerful and full-featured, but be warned it is a commercial product. Find information on it at http://www.activestate.com/Products/Komodo/.

- If you're an Eclipse fan, you need to know about the Ruby Development Tool (RDT). This is a set of Ruby-aware features and plug-ins for the Eclipse platform. Refer to http://sourceforge.net/projects/rubyeclipse for more details.

- ArachnoRuby is another commercial product (written by Lothar Scholz). It is reasonably full-featured, but as of July 2006 may not be quite as robust as other solutions. Refer to http://www.ruby-ide.com/ruby/ruby_ide_and_ruby_editor.php for more details.

- Finally, there is RDE, the Ruby Development Environment. This works well, is reasonably powerful, and is free. However, it runs only on Windows platforms.

Table 21.1 summarizes the features of these IDEs. Naturally this is only a starting place for your research. A true comparison of all these tools would take a hundred pages (and would be outdated by the time it was finished).

Note that only three platforms are considered here: The Linux/UNIX family, the Win32 family, and Mac OS X. Where the table says "all," it means all of these.

Table 21.1 Five Ruby IDEs Compared

Features	FreeRIDE	RDE	RDT	ArachnoRuby	Komodo
Commercial?	no	no	no	yes	yes
Platforms	all	Win32	all	Linux, Win32	all
Syntax highlighting	yes	yes	yes	yes	yes
Auto-indent	yes	yes	yes	yes	yes
Code folding	yes	no	no	yes	yes
Multi-doc editing	yes	yes	yes	yes	yes
Multilanguage support (Perl etc.)	limited	yes	yes	yes	yes
Mappable key bindings	yes	no	no	yes	yes
Editor macros	yes	no	no	yes	yes
Code browsing	yes	yes	yes	yes	yes
Integrated source control	no	no	yes	no	yes
GUI builder	no	no	no	no	yes
Project management	yes	no	yes	yes	yes
Testing integration	yes	no	yes	no	no
Other comments	Pure Ruby	-	-	web tools incl.	Built on Mozilla

21.7   Conclusion

We've seen several tools in this chapter that make life easier for the Ruby developer. Common tools are the interactive Ruby tool `irb`, the RubyGems installer, and the `ri` documentation tool. We've looked at editor add-ons for Ruby. Finally we've looked briefly at some IDEs that support Ruby. But the most important tool of all is not a piece of software. It is "peopleware"—the Ruby community itself. That is the topic of our next (and final) chapter.

CHAPTER 22

The Ruby Community

He who is unable to live in society, or who has no need because he is sufficient for himself, must be either a beast or a god.

—*Aristotle,* Politics

It has been said that one of the best things about Ruby is its community. That's a matter of opinion, of course, and you'll have to judge for yourself. My purpose in this brief chapter is to bring a few of the "watering holes" to your attention—news and learning sources, forums both online and off, and places where Rubyists meet in cyberspace and in real life.

This chapter is intentionally short. Much of the information here is stable, but things will always be in flux. Obviously, when you are in doubt, do a web search.

22.1 Web Resources

The main Ruby site is www.ruby-lang.org, from which all others should be reachable in a few hops. The latest version of Ruby itself can always be obtained here.

Another important site is rubygarden.org, which used to be purely wiki-based. The wiki is still there, but there is also a moderated section with many useful articles and tutorials.

For documentation, don't miss ruby-doc.org, maintained by James Britt. It hosts a wealth of rdoc output for the core and standard libraries as well as other useful items.

RubyCentral is a nonprofit devoted to Ruby advocacy (rubycentral.org). Among other things, this group is in charge of the International Ruby Conference each year. Since it has 501(c)3 status, U.S. citizens may make tax-exempt contributions to this organization.

Don't confuse this site with rubycentral.com, which is unrelated. This is another excellent Ruby site, one of the first in English, created by the Pragmatic Programmers.

22.2   Newsgroup and Mailing Lists

The `ruby-talk` mailing list is probably the oldest English-language forum for Ruby programmers. The Usenet newsgroup `comp.lang.ruby` is somewhat newer, having started late in the twentieth century (May 2000).

Early in the history of the newsgroup, a "mirror" was established (the creation of Dave Thomas) to echo posts back and forth between the newsgroup and the ruby-talk list. Barring occasional technical problems, the two lists should be identical from that point on.

The FAQ for comp.lang.ruby covers basic netiquette and an introduction to the group. It is posted once a month and kept online at rubyhacker.com until further notice.

The ruby-talk list is searchable online at ruby-talk.org (along with some other related lists such as ruby-core and ruby-math).

There are numerous project-related lists out there—in fact, too many to name them all. In nearly every case, a major Ruby project will be listed in the RAA or at rubyforge.org or both. These are the two best starting points in searching for information about a mailing list or a project's main home page.

22.3   Blogs and Online Magazines

I can only assume that the blogging trend is still on the increase. I don't foresee blogging becoming ridiculously *passe* within the life span of this book.

There are many Ruby-related blogs. Search engines will find them all. Here are a few blogs by core Rubyists:

- Dave Thomas: http://blogs.pragprog.com/cgi-bin/pragdave.cgi

- Chad Fowler: http://chadfowler.com/

- Jim Weirich: http://onestepback.org/

- Jamis Buck: http://jamis.jamisbuck.org/

- Nathaniel Talbott: http://blog.talbott.ws/

- *why the lucky stiff*: http://redhanded.hobix.com

A few centralized sites link to or aggregate the content from the individual Ruby blogs. These are new enough that I won't link to them here—the list will be different by the time you read this.

At least two online journals or *zines* are devoted to Ruby. The oldest, *The Rubyist* (http://jp.rubyist.net), is a wiki-based publication in Japanese. It provides good incentive to learn Japanese.

Artima (artima.com) hosts *Ruby Code & Style* (http://www.artima.com/rubycs), a well-done zine that shows great promise. There is talk about new online magazines, but anything printed here would quickly become out of date.

22.4   Ruby Change Requests

Ruby continues to evolve. Part of its beauty is that it changes slowly and deliberately.

But Ruby is definitely not perfect. Therefore a mechanism is in place for users to suggest changes in Ruby's syntax, its core classes, and its standard libraries. This is called the *Ruby Change Request (RCR)* process.

If you go to rcrchive.net ("RCR archive"), you will see a well-defined process (put in place by David Alan Black) allowing individuals to suggest changes, offer peer review or feedback, and even vote for or against those changes.

Before making a new RCR, first make sure that one like it does not exist. An identical RCR might be pending or might even have been rejected already.

Second, make sure you have dotted every *i* and crossed every *t*, metaphorically speaking. If you propose changing the behavior of a method, be sure to address the issue of breaking old code. If you propose a new operator, address the issues of whether it is really a method, what precedence it should have, how much impact there will be on the parser, and so on.

No one can guarantee that your request will be accepted. That is left in Matz's capable hands. But the more homework you do in advance, the better chance you have of being taken seriously. The ruby-core list is also a good place to mention issues like these (but be cautious and don't waste the time of the core developers).

22.5   IRC Channels

At any given time of day, chances are that dozens of Rubyists are talking or lurking in IRC (Internet Relay Chat). The servers are owned by freenode.net—visit them on the Web to find the right one for you. A web search will also find a good IRC client for you, whatever your platform may be.

The `#ruby-lang` channel has fairly heavy traffic. It is an international forum, so you may find people there at all hours. The *de facto* international language is English, but you may find people there who can direct you to channels in your own language.

Observe all normal IRC etiquette. In particular, do not "flood" by pasting sections of code; one or two lines is about the maximum. Instead use a pasting service such as `rafb.net` or the equivalent.

There are other channels, such as one devoted to Rails. As usual, any information I offer here might quickly become obsolete.

22.6   Ruby Conferences

The first International Ruby Conference was held in Florida in 2001, and it has rotated cities every year. Usually Matz himself attends, along with a few other Japanese Rubyists; we have also had attendees from six of the seven continents. (If you work at an Antarctic research station, please feel free to take time off for the next conference.)

This annual conference is coordinated by RubyCentral (rubycentral.com), so you can always go there for current information. Alternatively, you can go directly to http://rubyconf.org to find information, to apply to give a talk, or to register online.

There have also been other conferences in other areas. The European Ruby Conference (EuRuKo) was first held in Karlsruhe, Germany in 2003. It is usually a little smaller in terms of attendance, but if you are in Europe it may be more convenient for you. I am not aware of an official site for this conference; do a search for *EuRuKo* to find out more.

The popularity of Ruby has spawned talks at OOPSLA and OSCON, among others. Expect more of this in the future.

The popularity of the web framework "Ruby on Rails" has led to conferences devoted to Rails. The first International Rails Conference was held in Chicago in June 2006, and others are forthcoming. Go to railsconf.org for current information.

Not long ago I participated in the Silicon Valley Ruby Conference in Santa Clara in late April 2006. This was the first Ruby-specific conference in the United States besides the international conferences sponsored by RubyCentral. I hope that these opportunities continue to proliferate.

22.7   Local Ruby Groups

Numerous users' groups are springing up all over the United States and the rest of the world. These are typically named with a label such as *Cityname.rb*, which resembles a Ruby program's filename (with the .rb also standing for *Ruby Brigade*). Some are informal; others are more structured. Among the larger, more active groups are the ones in Seattle, Washington; Austin, Texas; Portland, Oregon; and New York City. Visit rubygarden.org or search elsewhere to find an active group in your area.

22.8   Conclusion

You have now reached the end of this sizable volume. Contrary to my expectations, readers have told me that they *did* in fact read the first edition cover to cover; some have also told me that they learned Ruby from this book (though I spent very little time teaching the basics).

It doesn't matter to me whether you have read this whole book sequentially or have just stumbled across this paragraph. In any case, you've reached the end, and I congratulate you.

But we don't really *learn* programming from books. We learn it by *applying* what we learn in those books. So I urge you to do what programmers do: Go and program. That's the real learning experience. And when you can't learn from experience or from books, turn to the rest of the community. You will find people there who can help you (and people you can help).

Who is a member of the "Ruby community"? Well, if you are reading this, you probably are a member yourself. On behalf of the others, I welcome you and encourage your participation.

Index

Symbols

& (AND) operator
  mathematical sets, 299
  number bit-level operations, 189
&& operators, 45
< > (angle brackets), 65-66
<< >> append operators, strings, 82
* (asterisk) quantifiers, regex, 109-110
** operators, exponentiation (numbers), 167
@ (at symbol), class instance variables, 56
@@ prefix (variables), 45
{} (braces)
  blocks, 54
  strings, 65
[] brackets
  mathematical sets, creating, 298
  strings, 65
^ (carets)
  ^ (XOR) operator, number bit-level
    operations, 189
  character classes, 115-116
  string parameters, 92
: (colon)
  :include: tags, 665
  :main: tags, 665
  :nodoc: tags, 664-665
  :notnew: tags, 665
  :title: tags, 665
$& variable, string substitutions, 77

$defout stream, buffering/unbuffering I/O, 332
$flag variable, threads waiting for events, 556
$KCODE global variable, 141-142
$MATCH variables, string substitutions, 77
$SAFE variable, threads, 535
$stdout variable, 331
= (equal sign)
  = (equality) operators, 403
  =end markers, embedded documentation, 43
  == (equality operators), 47, 70, 402-403
  === (relationship) operators, 47-48, 59,
    400-402
! (exclamation points), identifiers, 42
` (grave accents), 11, 565
< (greater than) symbol)
  << (left-shift) operators, 189
  <=> comparison operators, 60, 70
- (hyphens), character classes, 115
> (less than) operators
  >>(right-shift) operators, 189
  strings, 65
() (parentheses)
  methods, 60
  strings, 65
% (percent symbol) method
  base number conversions, 191
  formatting numbers for output, 172
  String class, 73
%Q notations, strings, 65
%U specifiers, finding week of the year, 230-231

797

E

I

Q - R

X–Y–Z

RUBYISMS IN RAILS

By JACOB HARRIS • ISBN: 0-321-47407-4

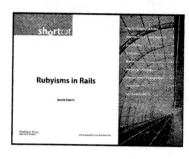

Rubyisms is an examination of how the grace of Ruby informs the design of Rails. In particular, it looks at a few specific examples of how Rails' internal code is implemented in Ruby to instruct about Ruby's design principles. The main goal is simply aesthetic appreciation. But, if you are a beginning programmer in Rails who is stymied in your understanding of Ruby — or an intermediate Rails developer still writing code that looks like Ruby-tinged PHP or Java — this Short Cut will impart enlightenment and inspiration about the Ruby way of programming. It also reveals how the revolutionary design of the Rails framework can only be built upon the beauty of Ruby.

RAILS PLUGINS: Extending Rails Beyond the Core

By JAMES ADAM • ISBN: 0-321-48351-0

One of the most powerful aspects of the Rails framework is the ability to extend and override it within your own applications. This is achieved through the Rails plugin mechanism, which provides an avenue for any Rails developer to add powerful new features to their applications, and share this functionality with the worldwide community.

This Short Cut introduces the Rails plugin mechanism and considers each aspect of their behaviour and development. First, discover how to find and install plugins using the provided plugin script, including the enhanced mechanisms available for developers using version control. Then, find out more on the development of plugins including examples of common plugin idioms. Finally, learn about some of the issues which arise when testing plugins, and how to share your plugin with the rest of the world.

MONGREL: Serving, Deploying and Extending Your Ruby Applications

By MATT PELLETIER and ZED SHAW • ISBN: 0-321-48350-2

Since its initial release in January 2006, Mongrel has quickly gained the attention and support of the Ruby community as a preferred Ruby HTTP Server for development and production. This Short Cut serves as a critical resource for any developer, system/network administrator or business owner interested in understanding Mongrel and using it for development work or in a production environment. It provides background, setup and configuration, and development techniques for extending Mongrel. In addition it details resources for performance tuning and security. This is the only comprehensive documentation on Mongrel detailing the basic how/to, best practices and development instructions from the creator of the software.

SHORT CUTS are succinct, to the point, quick-reads on new and existing technologies. They're digital, delivered in Adobe Reader PDF. They're quick to publish. They're a quick-to knowledge. Short Cuts will show you how to solve a specific problem and introduce you to a new topic. Written by industry experts and bestselling authors, Short Cuts are published with you in mind — getting you the technical information that you need now.